REORGANIZING THE FACTORY

REORGANIZING THE FACTORY

COMPETING THROUGH CELLULAR MANUFACTURING

NANCY HYER
AND
URBAN WEMMERLÖV

PRODUCTIVITY
productivity press

Productivity Press
P.O. Box 13390
Portland, Oregon 97213-0390
United States of America
Telephone: 503-235-0600
Telefax: 503-235-0909
Email: info@productivityinc.com

Production Editor: Michael Ryder, Productivity Press
Design and Composition: William H. Brunson Typography Services
Art Composition: Lorraine Millard, Productivity Press
Cover Design: Stephen Scates, Productivity Press
Proofreader: City Desktop
Indexer: Razorsharp Communications

Printed in the United States of America

ISBN 1-56327-228-8

06 05 04 03 02   5 4 3 2 1

Contents

Preface

This book looks at manufacturing organizations from the perspective of cellular manufacturing. In particular, we consider the many issues you face, and the decisions you must make, in order to create product-focused, process-complete cells. And we provide tools, techniques, and insights you can use for this purpose. Our initial vision for this book was a somewhat shorter monograph on "how to make cells happen." Not far into the project, however, we realized that a truly useful book would need to be more comprehensive in scope, more detailed in content, and more concrete in its prescriptions than what we initially envisioned. So rather than merely referring to well-known but frequently nebulous concepts, or proposing certain practices without full explanation, our book presents detailed and concrete definitions, frameworks, tools, and techniques that can help your firm become more successful. We also note that organization design and implementation is a never-ending process. For this reason, the material in this book is relevant not just for those who are planning to implement their first cell, but also for experienced firms that need to rethink their processes to boost performance.

If you leaf through its pages, you may think this book is about just-in-time, lean manufacturing, quick response manufacturing, process reengineering, teamwork, or some other recent manufacturing management philosophy. To some extent, that is correct. This is because cellular manufacturing, in our view, is the foundation for most of those improvement paradigms.

However, we are not strident supporters and blind advocates of cellular manufacturing and our goal is not to "sell you on cells." In fact, we readily acknowledge that cells may not be the best solution for all situations. But we do believe that the basic principles that underlie cells, i.e., *dedicated and closely located resources assigned responsibility for the completion of families of products, components, or information deliverables*, should be guiding lights for the design of all manufacturing systems (and much office or service work).

More broadly, our mission is to convey a simple but powerful message: to become competitive in manufacturing, and remain so, there are many pieces that must fit together. Some of those pieces are technical in nature, while others are strategic, organizational, and managerial. Cell adoption and cell design should begin with strategy to ensure that the cellular reorganization supports the company's business objectives. In our experience, improving manufacturing systems, including the implementation of cells, is commonly assigned to engineers. They often have very good analytical skills and know the production processes well, but may not always think strategically. Furthermore, effective change hinges on the modification of management systems and the cooperation of people in the organization. But managers and human resource personnel—who know and understand people and systems—often lack detailed knowledge of the technical aspects of effective manufacturing processes. You need both sets of competencies to design, implement, and operate successful cells. Mirroring this required blend of perspectives, our book addresses both the technical and the managerial issues faced in manufacturing change.

Specifically, we present step-by-step methods for making decisions regarding justification, factory analysis, plant focusing, measurement systems, pay, planning and control, employee selection and training, and project planning and implementation. We also discuss basic principles behind lead time reduction. Because all organizations confront these issues, regardless of whether cells are implemented or not, this book goes beyond cellular manufacturing. In fact, we provide useful knowledge and insights on how to efficiently and effectively design, implement, and operate virtually any manufacturing organization.

You will probably not be able to absorb all the concepts, ideas, and techniques in this book in a single reading. For this reason, we have designed *Reorganizing the Factory* to serve as a reference handbook—each chapter is relatively self-contained, but includes extensive cross-references to other chapters. The table of contents or the index can direct you to chapters or sections that will answer any specific question about cellular manufacturing. We have also provided many references should you want to undertake further self-study (references are found both in the endnotes for each chapter and in the alphabetized reference list at the end of the book).

Finally, we have written this book relying not just on our own research and experience, but also on that of others. Drawing from a wide array of credible sources, our aim has been not just to present descriptive "what is" material, but also to go deeper into the "how to" and "why is that" issues. We are convinced that only well-founded insights into organizational and system behavior can help you understand why certain actions are desirable and wise, while others are not (as Deming said: "There is nothing as practical as a good theory"). Furthermore, the material we present is not based on temporary fads but rests on sound ideas and knowledge we are confident will be useful for many years to come. It is our hope that this book will be of great value to you in your efforts to *reorganize the factory* and *compete through cellular manufacturing*.

Should you have any comments or questions on the material in this book, please feel free to contact us directly.

Nancy Hyer
Associate Professor
Owen Graduate School
  of Management
Vanderbilt University
Nashville, Tennessee 37203
nancy.lea.hyer@owen.vanderbilt.edu

Urban Wemmerlöv
Kress Family Wisconsin Distinguished
  Professor
Director, Erdman Center for Manufacturing
  and Technology Management
School of Business, University of
  Wisconsin-Madison
Madison, Wisconsin 53706
uwemmerlov@bus.wisc.edu

Acknowledgments

Writing a book like this is both a lonely undertaking and a collaborative activity. It is lonely since writing, by definition, is a process that requires insulation and solitude, many long hours, and hard work. It is also collaborative since it cannot be done well without the direct or indirect involvement of many people. Hence, we are particularly indebted to those authors who have written about all the topics we cover in this book and on whose research, experiences, and insights we have relied.

A second group of key individuals are our colleagues and friends (and also authors) who have taught us and inspired us, and whose deep knowledge of manufacturing and management systems is rare and unique. Here, we would especially like to mention Stig-Arne Mattsson, Intentia International, and Harold Steudel and Rajan Suri, both professors of Industrial Engineering at the University of Wisconsin-Madison. Rajan Suri, in his capacity as Director for the Manufacturing Systems Engineering Program and the Quick Response Manufacturing Center, has created an especially fertile soil for industrial engagement and learning that benefits faculty and students alike. Many other colleagues have also been very helpful. Professors Barry Gerhart and Ella Mae Matsumura (University of Wisconsin-Madison), Neta Moye (Vanderbilt University), and Greg Stewart (Brigham Young University) were particularly generous in assisting us with the chapters focused on accounting and human resource management. Finally, some of our collaborators on previous research projects also deserve special mention. Our work with Karen Brown (University of Washington), Danny Johnson (Iowa State University), Asoo Vakharia (University of Florida), and Sharon Zimmerman (Agilent Technologies, Inc.) has helped shape our thinking about cells and provided examples and insights on which we have drawn in putting this book together.

A third important group of collaborators are the managers and employees at the firms we have worked with or visited over the years, or encountered at seminars or courses we have given. These individuals are too numerous to mention by name, but sharing in their experiences has been very important to our own education and knowledge of how manufacturing organizations work.

A fourth group of people we need to acknowledge are the graduate students we have worked with. Some have been doctoral students who have engaged us in intellectual inquiries and pursuits that continue to date. Here we would like to especially mention Dr. Shyam Bhaskar who read and commented on drafts of the book. Others have been masters' students doing industry projects and/or participating in our courses on cellular manufacturing. Special thanks for reviewing and critiquing earlier versions of this book go to Wisconsin students Hadrian D'Souza, Wenhui Du, Vivek Dubey, Lori Gagnon, Okan Gürbüz, Dennis Hussey, Patrick Kirsop, Don Lebar, Dennis McRae, Jitesh Metha, Ernest Nicolas, Brook Nienhaus, Leonel Preza, Neil Purisch, Sanjay Rao, Jennifer Romanin, and Rahul Shinde. Vanderbilt students Todd Woodruff and Brent Turner also deserve special thanks for their input to the book.

We also wish to thank our universities for their generous support of this project. In particular, we thank the three Deans at Vanderbilt's Owen Graduate School of Management under whom this book was written: Marty Geisel, Joe Blackburn, and Bill Christie. Also at Vanderbilt, May Woods, Administrative Assistant; Kelly Christie, Director of Academic Programs; and Sylvia Graham, Research Librarian each provided invaluable direct or indirect assistance with the project. At the University of Wisconsin-Madison, Administrative Assistant Kathy McCord deserves special mention. Her dedication to tasks, and her skills in carrying them out, are unparalleled. We would also like to thank the Vilas Associates Fund, the Kress family, and the Erdman family for their financial support.

Taking the step from writing to book production is a process that requires a group of skillful, gifted, and dedicated individuals. We have been very fortunate to work with Maura May, Vice President of Productivity Press, Michael Ryder, Production Editor, Gary Peurasaari, Development Editor, Bill Brunson, compositor, and Stephen Scates, Art Director. Mike Ryder, in particular, has carried the brunt of this heavy load and been very patient with our many requests.

The heaviest burden of a book project—as many have found out before us—falls on the family. During the course of this multi-year project we have pushed our families to the limit by removing ourselves from normal social activities so we could escape into the solitary task of writing. We marvel at their love and endurance, and are deeply grateful for their unending support. *Thank you, Jim and Julianne, and thank you, Mary Beth.*

CELLULAR MANUFACTURING— THE BASICS

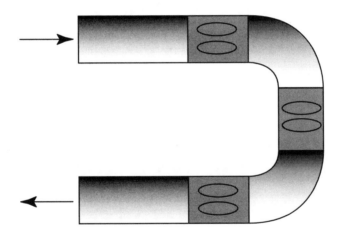

1

Competing through Cellular Manufacturing

> The corporation now demands a great deal more of a production manager. The assignment becomes, "Make an increasing variety of products, on shorter lead times with smaller runs, but with flawless quality. Improve our return on our investment by automating and introducing new technology in processes and materials so that we can cut prices to meet local and foreign competition. Mechanize—but keep your schedules flexible, your inventories low, your capital costs minimal, and your work force contented."
>
> *Wickham Skinner,* Harvard Business Review, *1966*[1]

Skinner's quote from the 1960s provides us with an important lesson: higher quality, lower prices, more product variety, faster delivery, and greater flexibility in meeting customer needs are constant and timeless expectations. There is also the unrelenting pressure to achieve these goals with low levels of investment and satisfied employees. One difference compared to 30 or 40 years ago, however, is the rate of change. Today's production manager must deliver performance improvements at an ever-increasing pace in order to meet the objectives of "better, faster, and cheaper." You will probably agree with us that the demands on manufacturing professionals have actually grown rather than diminished since Professor Skinner's assessment.

No one ever said it was easy to manage operations, but today's manufacturing organizations clearly face a new competitive landscape. Globalization, increasingly diverse and sophisticated customer markets, and the rapid pace of technological change have all contributed to a turbulent business environment. Today, if you are satisfied with the status quo, you are flirting with extinction. For many organizations, this means reconsidering the fundamental ways in which work gets done. Technology, in the form of equipment and information systems, has always been a route to higher efficiency and improvement. However, an equally important—and in some cases more important—avenue for competitiveness is the way we organize and manage production. How to do this, and do it well, is a key issue in an organization's struggle to achieve success. It is also the focus of this book. More specifically, this book will help you design and implement *cellular manufacturing*, a strategy for organizing work to shorten response times, improve quality in production, and drive down inventories and costs.

CELLULAR MANUFACTURING—A PLATFORM FOR IMPROVEMENT

A cell is a small organizational unit within the firm designed to exploit similarities in how you process information, make products, and serve customers. *Manufacturing cells* foster continual performance improvements by closely locating people and equipment required for processing families of like products. Parts may previously have traveled miles to visit all the equipment and labor needed for their fabrication. And parts with different manufacturing requirements and market characteristics may have shared the same equipment and the same workforce. After reorganization, families of similar parts are produced together within the physical confines of cells that house most or all of the required resources. This product-focused arrangement facilitates the rapid flow and efficient processing of material and information (see Figure 1-1). Furthermore, cell operators can be cross-trained on several machines, engage in job rotation, and assume responsibility for tasks that previously belonged to supervisors and support staff. The latter include activities such as planning and scheduling, quality control, troubleshooting, parts ordering, interfacing with customers and suppliers, and record keeping. Such local control creates a natural platform for improvement of the cell's performance.

Gelman Sciences Inc., a Michigan-based manufacturer of membrane filtering products, is one firm that "competes through cellular manufacturing."[2] It faced many typical problems that can drive firms out of business: poor delivery performance despite high inventories, heavy reliance on inspection and testing, high scrap rates, supplier quality problems, and equipment downtime. In response, the company formed employee teams for each work center or department. These made some improvement to factory operations. However, not until these teams were refocused into product teams did significant change occur. The product-oriented teams became the catalyst for introducing cellular manufacturing at Gelman. Cells, in turn, became the real vehicle for employee involvement in performance improvement.

As is common with firms that adopt cell-based manufacturing, many changes besides the introduction of cells took place at Gelman Sciences. For example, employees were trained in matters like improving quality, eliminating waste, planning layouts, reducing setup time, identifying bottlenecks, implementing one piece-flow, balancing lines, establishing process control, and participating in teamwork. They were also cross-trained to perform several different tasks in the cells. Quite importantly, they actively participated in the improvement process by putting this training to work from the very first day. Support personnel were also linked much more closely to the floor activities. But we believe that the greatest impact on performance was made by the reorganization of the workplace into cells and the workforce into cell-based teams. Each team could now focus its improvement efforts on a narrow group of products with similar characteristics.

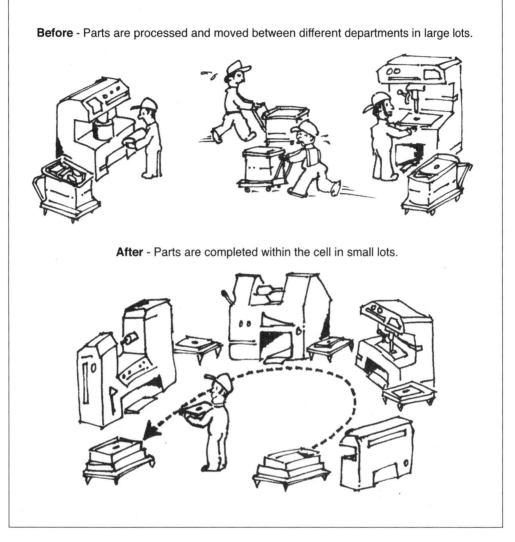

Figure 1-1. Before and after cellular manufacturing

Cellular Concepts for the Office

The cellular concept has broad appeal. In fact, you can apply the powerful ideas of "sameness" and "closeness" not just to the factory floor—as in *manufacturing cells*—but also to administrative work. For example, administrative and/or service-oriented activities, like customer order processing or completing a request for a quote, commonly involve personnel belonging to multiple departments in different locations. An *office cell* groups a small number of broadly trained people in the same location and makes them responsible for the rapid handling of process-complete activities.[3] Thus, both office and manufacturing cells represent the application of the same core ideas: exploiting similarities, dedicating resources, and creating tight connections between successive tasks and the people who perform them. (Chapter 18 explores office cells in greater detail.)

What Can You Expect from Cellular Manufacturing?

Although cell-based manufacturing originated in the early 1900s, its real growth occurred in the 1990s. Some recent studies from Britain and the United States indicate that between 43 and 53 percent of manufacturing firms now have cells.[4] In plants with more than 100 employees, that share increases to 73 percent of all firms. Given that these studies include firms in which you would not expect to see cells (e.g., those in process industries), the usage rates within the mechanical, electronic, and other discrete-part manufacturing sectors are probably even higher.

Many testimonials, from large and small companies in diverse industries, support the ability of cellular manufacturing to increase performance. Gelman Sciences, for example, has been very successful in reducing lead times and inventories while improving quality and delivery performance. At the Falk Corporation in Auburn, Alabama, a maker of coupling devices, the delivery time has fallen from four weeks to one week using cells. Likewise, at the Mine Safety Appliances Corporation in Pittsburgh, Pennsylvania, a producer of gas masks and other safety equipment, cells have reduced paperwork, material-handling efforts, and inspection. Most impressively, the director of operations there, John Heggestad, claims that "by moving to manufacturing cells, we doubled revenues per worker over the past 10 or so years."[5]

Several industry studies back up such anecdotal evidence. In a study of 1,025 U.S. firms, those that considered themselves to be "extremely skilled" users of cells reported the highest sales per employees, and the highest return on investment of all responding firms.[6] Table 1-1 documents two smaller studies of U.S. manufacturing firms that likewise show impressive results in response time, quality, and inventory.[7]

Despite many success stories, our research and consulting experience tells us that the process of designing, implementing, and operating cells is far from straightforward. We have found that although many firms adopt cells, some do it well while others do it less well. The "minimum" and "maximum" improvement columns in Table 1-1 illustrate the fact that companies vary dramatically in the performance improvements they achieve with cells. Interestingly, of the 544 cell users in the large-scale study of U.S. firms, only 18 percent considered themselves "extremely skilled" in using manufacturing cells.[8] Although these respondents may have been overly humble, this means that the other 82 percent viewed themselves as possessing only "some or moderate" skills in practicing cellular manufacturing. This finding is mirrored in a UK study. Here, the percentage of users who claimed they had entirely met their goals with respect to quality, responsiveness, and cost improvement due to cells ranged from 8 to 20 percent.[9] Clearly, in the users' own minds, there is great room for improvement.

As you may already know from experience, seemingly simple ideas are not always easy to implement. Cellular manufacturing is a case in point. At Gelman, for example, "the shift to product-line thinking was a shock to almost the entire plant."[10] Ironically, it is this very different way of thinking about manufacturing—i.e., to focus on completing product families rather than just single operations—that

Table 1-1. Reported performance results from cellular manufacturing implementations

Performance measure	Wemmerlöv and Johnson (1997)—46 Firms			Wemmerlöv and Hyer (1989)—32 Firms		
	Average Improvement	Minimum Improvement	Maximum Improvement	Average Improvement	Minimum Improvement	Maximum Improvement
Reduction of move distances/move times	61.3%	15.0%	99.0%	39.3%	10.0%	83.0%
Reduction in throughput time	61.2	12.5	99.5	45.6	5.0	90.0
Reduction in response time to customer orders	50.1	0.0	93.2	–	–	–
Reduction in WIP inventory	48.2	10.0	99.7	41.4	8.0	80.0
Reduction in setup times	44.2	0.0	96.6	32.0	2.0	95.0
Reduction in finished goods inventory	39.3	0.0	100.0	29.2	10.0	75.0
Improvement in part/product quality	28.4	0.0	62.5	29.6	5.0	90.0
Reduction in unit costs	16.0	0.0	60.0	–	–	–

Note: missing entries in the Wemmerlöv and Hyer (1989) data indicate that responses are not available.

is the source of both the advantages of cells and the problems with implementing them. In our worldview, putting cells to work requires wide-reaching changes to the firm. Therefore, before proceeding further, we want you to understand how we think about cells and what it takes to successfully implement them.

THE HARD AND SOFT SIDES OF CELL IMPLEMENTATION

Companies typically change because they discover performance gaps they want to close (see Figure 1-2). For example, you may have found that sales or revenues are slipping, or that competitors are shipping faster and at lower prices. In searching for remedies, you should conduct an enterprise analysis—taking a hard look at what the firm can do well (strengths) and not so well (weaknesses). You also need to look at your industry and the economy at large. This external perspective helps you identify threats and, hopefully, opportunities such as emerging technologies or markets. Two things should come out of this enterprise analysis:

1. A sense of the *capabilities* the firm needs in order to achieve the desired *outcomes*. For example: "To reach our targeted market share, we must ship products within 36 hours of order receipt."

2. A *plan* for how the firm should go about achieving these capabilities, such as: "What do we need to do differently to be able to ship within 36 hours, and what resources do we need in order to accomplish this?"

We call the latter plan a *strategy*. In a manufacturing strategy you lay out the blueprint for building capabilities that will help the firm gain an advantage relative

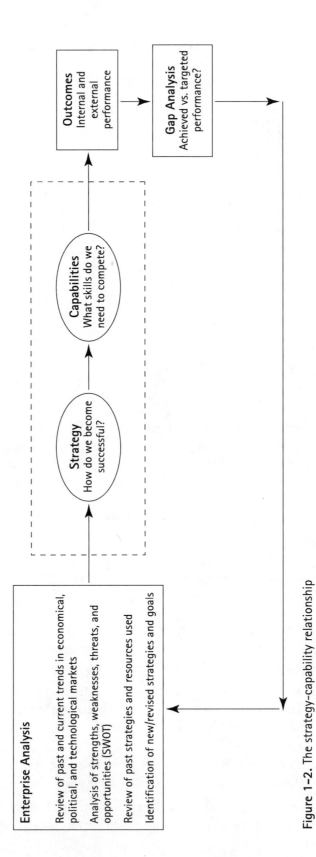

Figure 1-2. The strategy-capability relationship

to its competitors. To build and maintain such an advantage, the strategy should continually push the limits of the firm's existing capabilities.[11] In other words, you can't rest because your competitors are not likely to do so! To succeed, your strategy must be articulated within the organization, pushed by management, and accepted by the employees. Only then will it provide the necessary direction for the firm and guide employees at all levels toward the corporate goals. Without a clear and accepted strategy of how to become successful, the firm is "rudderless" and much less likely to make the tough decisions needed to get things done. It may even drift towards a slow death. Figure 1-2 illustrates the relationship between enterprise analysis, strategy, capabilities, and performance outcomes.

Building Capabilities with Cells

It is never easy to accept that company performance has stalled or declined, or to identify what needs to done to turn this around. However, the most difficult step is to determine how you are going to change course. Understanding what capabilities are required is not the same as knowing how to develop those capabilities. For example, you may realize that your prices must come down 20 percent in order to stay in business, and that you need to reduce manufacturing costs by 20 percent; but you may have no idea how to achieve this.

After a feasibility study conducted along guidelines we will describe in subsequent chapters, you may conclude that manufacturing cells can provide the capabilities your firm requires. You must then analyze how you make your products, find similarities in process steps, group products into families, and assign required resources to produce these families. At a minimum, to pursue a strategy based on cells, you must consider technology and processes (see Figure 1-3).

Finding suitable families and determining appropriate equipment technology are important elements of cell design. However, for the cells to function you must also consider the firm's *infrastructure*, i.e., the numerous subsystems used to plan, manage, and control operations. For example, you must have a system for selecting the operators and the supervisors for the cell, designing their jobs, and providing necessary training. You must also redesign the production planning and control procedures to fit the new operating conditions for the cell, rethink the costing system, devise a new set of performance measures that reflects the new strategy, and change the way you compensate and reward the cell employees. Creating or revising these *management systems*—compensation, planning and control, cost accounting, and so on—represents another critical step in our implementation model.

Implementation also means you have to determine how cells fit in the *organizational structure*. For example, you need to establish each cell as a unit within the organization so that each cell employee "has a home." You also need to determine how employees should be organized inside the cell, how the cell should be supervised, and to whom it should report. Figure 1-4 shows our extended implementation framework (for more details, see Figure 5-24).

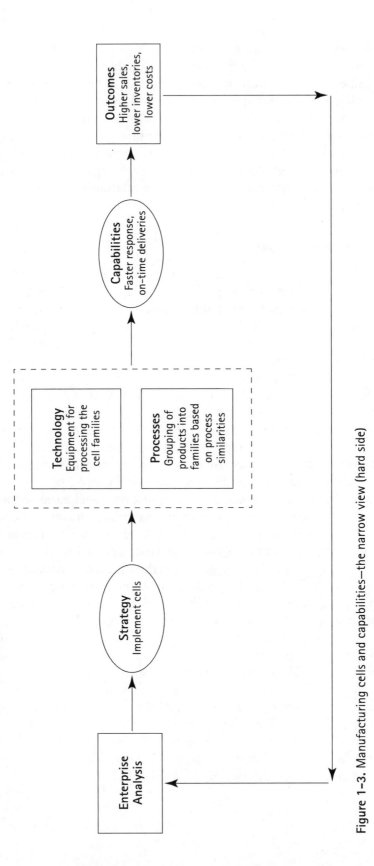

Figure 1-3. Manufacturing cells and capabilities—the narrow view (hard side)

The Matching Game

To develop new capabilities, such as the ability to manufacture with shorter lead times and with less scrap, or to process customer orders more rapidly and with fewer errors, you need to do more than just move people and equipment closer together to follow a new process. Most importantly, you must do a lot of matching and adjusting to ensure that all building blocks fit together and support your vision for the cell system. For example, you must match the new process with appropriate technology or let the technology you select determine the new process. You must also match the skills required in the cell with the existing workforce, providing training where necessary. You further need to match the current way of rewarding employees with the new organizational structure. This may involve changing individual incentives to group-based incentives. You also need to match the current planning and control system with the intended level of self-management in the cell, and adjust accordingly. In subsequent chapters, we discuss many more adjustments made necessary by cellular manufacturing.

Most of this "matching game" is under the direct control of management. However, an important aspect of an organization is informal and intangible, and therefore much harder to manage. Specifically, *people* do the work! Their motivations, attitudes, and behavior ultimately dictate what changes and what does not, and therefore determine how efficient and effective a cell becomes. Perhaps the most powerful aspect of what we call *the informal organization* is the company's culture. By culture we mean the norms, values, and beliefs that the employees *as a group* have adopted and which influence their behavior and actions. Cells represent a fairly radical change to the way work is organized and the way employees are supposed to behave. Resistance to change is natural and expected, at all levels in the organization. Hence, to implement cells effectively, leaders must recognize and understand the current culture and possess strong management skills to influence it.

With the addition of the informal organization to Figure 1-4, our worldview is complete.[12] We believe firmly that if you implement cells simply by rerouting products and assigning people to newly formed groups of equipment, while changing nothing else, you will see only modest improvements. On the other hand, if you decide to adopt cellular manufacturing and understand that all the elements in Figure 1-4 must fit together, you have a much better chance of realizing the full benefits of cells. You could say that technology and processes represent the hard side of cells, while people, management systems, organizational structure, and the informal organization represent the soft side. As you probably can imagine, the soft-side factors are far more difficult to change than are the hard-side factors. Accordingly, you and your firm will spend most of your time struggling with the soft issues. Moreover, achieving the full potential of "better, faster, cheaper" through cells means you must modify and align *all* these key elements of the organization in order to make them work together and support each other.

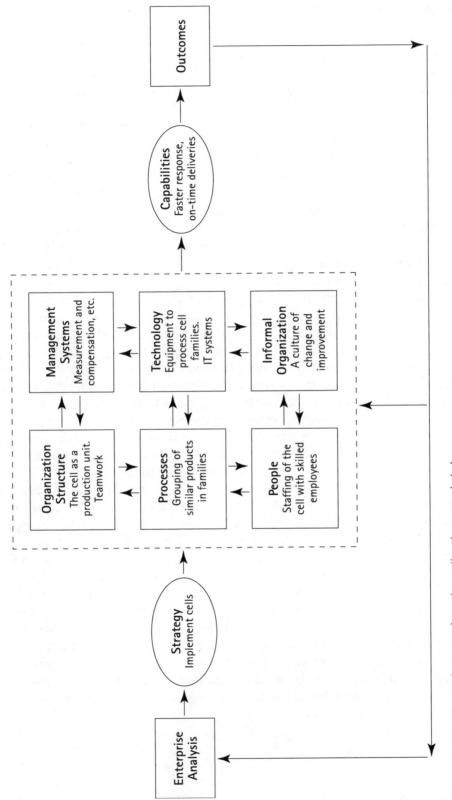

Figure 1-4. Implementing manufacturing cells—the expanded view

CHANGE SEEKS COMPANY

If you already are familiar with cells and their implementation, you know they seldom come alone. As we saw at Gelman Sciences, with the grouping of products, people, and equipment come many other changes to the organization. Typical examples include setup and lot-size reductions, schedule stabilizations, quality systems, pull mechanisms, job design, teamwork, employee empowerment, problem-solving training, pay-for-knowledge compensation systems, and so on. We discuss these and many other related changes in this book, and link them all to the design and implementation of cells. We do this because when we "think cells," we think well beyond just rearranging equipment to include all the things necessary or desirable to successfully build capabilities via cells.

The direct implication of this is that any measured improvement is due to a combination of underlying causes. Table 1-1 shows that implementing cells reduces lead time by an average of 46 to 61 percent. However, we cannot attribute this to cells viewed in a narrow perspective, i.e., cells as merely groups of equipment and products. Because organizations often change many processes and procedures simultaneously, performance improvements can derive from a multitude of sources. Table 1-1 also shows that the reported benefits of cell-based manufacturing vary substantially for each measure. This variation may depend on whether or not the firms provided extensive training, adopted a well thought-out teamwork structure, reduced quality problems through SPC, purchased brand-new equipment technology, reduced lot sizes, and so on. Success also depends on how well firms master the "matching game" we discussed above. The lesson you should take home from this is that *excellence in cellular manufacturing comes from attacking, in a coordinated way, multiple fronts at the same time—not by changing only one thing and hoping for the best.*

THE ORGANIZATION OF THIS BOOK

We have organized this book around our particular vision for a successful transformation to cellular manufacturing. Specifically, we have adopted a *life cycle perspective on cells*, beginning with the concept idea and continuing through the macro- and microdesign, justification, operation, improvement, and evolution of cells. At the end of the book we also discuss how to manage the cell implementation process, and we review typical problems companies face when converting to cells. We also discuss the application of cellular thinking to office environments. In all, the book has six sections.

Section 1: Cellular Manufacturing—The Basics. Chapters 1 through 3 serve as an introduction to the book. We see cells as a way of seeking competitive advantage in manufacturing. To do this successfully, we believe you must look at cells, as we do in these early chapters—and throughout the book—from a strategic, organizational, technical, human, and managerial perspective. And so that you may fully understand the cellular concept and why it can improve performance, we thoroughly define cellular manufacturing and analyze its underlying benefit sources.

Section 2: Adopting and Designing Cells. Chapters 4 through 8 focus on the process of adopting the cellular manufacturing concept, identifying cells, and designing the cell system. We begin by providing an overview of the complete life cycle process from cell adoption through cell evolution. Then, in two separate chapters, we discuss, first, the high-level decisions about products, processes, and layout at the plant level; and second, the detailed decisions regarding design and layout of individual cells. In the following chapter, we look at various design decisions from the perspective of how the cell system behaves in operation. The final chapter in this section illustrates how to determine the economic value of cells.

Section 3: Designing the Cell System Infrastructure. Chapters 9 through 14 address the management systems needed to operate cells. Chapters in this section explore cell performance metrics, cost accounting issues, resource planning and shop floor control, job design, employee selection and training, and compensation systems for cells. The planning of these infrastructural elements typically begins after the cell's technical design process has been initiated.

Section 4: Implementing and Improving Cells. Chapters 15 through 17 provide a systematic approach for putting cells in place and keeping them viable. We look first at how to organize the cell implementation project and manage the change process. We then discuss common pitfalls in cell design, implementation, and operation—and strategies for avoiding them. Finally, we look at the improvement and evolution of cells, and how to continually assure they are adapting to the dynamics of the competitive marketplace.

Section 5: Extending the Concept—Cells in the Office. Chapter 18 looks beyond traditional manufacturing cells and considers how cells can be designed and operated in office settings. It turns out that many of the basic principles for manufacturing cells travel easily into the office arena.

Section 6: What's Next? Chapter 19 briefly reviews everything we have discussed in this book. We then predict what may happen to office and manufacturing cells in the future, especially given advancements in process and information technology.

We do recommend that you read this book from beginning to end. However, because of the integrative nature of work reorganizations, we realize that when you, for example, are reading about product family identification (Chapters 5 and 6), you may also be thinking about how you can motivate employees through appropriately designed measurement (Chapter 9) and pay systems (Chapter 14). If so, feel free to jump to those chapters. In fact, you should be able to read any of the chapters in any order, particularly after having covered the first four. To help you do this, we provide in each chapter cross-references to other relevant chapters in the book. In the end, after you've covered the whole book and the mosaic is complete, you should be in an excellent position to lead your organization's efforts to *compete through cellular manufacturing.*

KEY INSIGHTS

Here are a few key insights from this chapter:

- *Many companies successfully compete through cellular manufacturing.* Cellular manufacturing has proven to be very successful for many firms. Companies that adopt cellular manufacturing have achieved large improvements in lead times, inventories, quality, and cost (see Table 1-1).

- *View cells as a catalyst for change and improvement.* To successfully implement cells, you will need to change your organization's processes and infrastructure. Once in place, you will discover that cells facilitate and stimulate continual improvement through focused production and employee ownership.

- *Begin cell implementation by thinking strategically.* You should design and implement cells so they fit with your firm's strategy regarding quality, cost, and response time improvements. Thus, the cells should provide the capabilities needed to achieve improved business performance.

- *Cells are much more than a "technical" solution.* The hard side (processes and technology) and the soft side (people, organizational structure, management systems, and the informal organization) must work together and *in concert* for fully effective cells. Cells are like small factories: to put them to use successfully requires that you take a broad view of work and management. As this book will show, cells are much more than just grouped equipment.

2

A Closer Look at Cells:
What They Are and the Forms They Take

While the descriptions provided so far should have given you a good sense of what cells are all about, in this chapter we will introduce more formal definitions. In addition, we present four critical perspectives that define the essence of cells. These should help you understand why cells may benefit your plant (an issue we discuss in Chapter 3). Most of the important ideas and principles for manufacturing cells apply to office cells as well. However, as the name implies, cellular manufacturing began in the factory, and we will mainly restrict our discussion to this area.

As you will see in this chapter, the question of what constitutes a cell does not always have a clear and simple answer. This is because many cells possess some, but not all, of the characteristics that we consider necessary for cells. Also, the criteria we use lack precise measures. Therefore, it is easier to determine how you should change a production unit to make it closer to an "ideal cell" than to determine whether it is, already, a cell.

The following key aspects of cells are discussed in this chapter:

- What is the origin and history of cellular manufacturing?
- How do we formally define cells?
- What different forms of cells exist?
- What type of work can be performed in cells?
- What is the relationship between cellular manufacturing and other modern manufacturing management principles and philosophies?

FORMAL DEFINITIONS OF CELLULAR MANUFACTURING

"Family of parts production," and the people and equipment involved with this type of manufacturing, are referred to by a variety of names. In Japan, the terms "group production" and "U-shaped lines" appear to dominate; in Scandinavia, the terms "flow manufacturing" and "flow groups" (or lines) are used; in Germany, the term "production islands" is common; and in Britain, the terms "group technology" and "group technology cells" dominate. While the latter terms have been adopted in America as well, "manufacturing cells," "work cells," "modules,"[1] "JIT cells," or simply "teamwork" are used more frequently (note, however, that teamwork and cell work are not the same; you can have cells without teams, and teamwork without cells).

The word "cell" has troubling associations for some people.[2] For this reason, many companies create their own catchy phrases or acronyms. For example, the Tennant Company uses the term PACE, which is an abbreviation of "Production Activities Combined Economically" but also conveys the image of a steady flow of materials. Likewise, Racine Hydraulics uses the high-technology term CPU, which stands for "Condensed Production Units." The Falk Corporation has adopted the acronym MTOM, short for "More Than One Machine group." Other names we have encountered include PPITS, for "People and Parts In Timed Sequence," OAATS, for "One At A Time System," and "product-focused home teams." In short, there are many alternative ways to refer to cells. However, despite any uneasy feelings the word cell might instill in some readers, we will use it consistently throughout this book.

We define a cell in the following way:

A cell is a group of closely located workstations where multiple, sequential operations are performed on one or more families of similar raw materials, parts, components, products, or information carriers. The cell is a distinctive organizational unit within the firm, staffed by one or more employees, accountable for output performance, and delegated the responsibility of one or more planning, control, support, and improvement tasks.

We have deliberately used the generic term "cell" above to include both manufacturing and office cells. We will use these more narrow terms when we specifically want to consider applications on the factory floor versus in the office. Manufacturing and office cells are defined in more detail as follows:

A *manufacturing cell* is a cell whose main purpose is to physically process, transform, transmit, and add value to materials whose end state are products or components.

An *office cell* is a cell whose main task is to process, transform, transmit, and add value to information.

For completeness, we finally also offer the following broader definition:

A company that operates one or more manufacturing cells is said to have or use cellular manufacturing (CM). Likewise, a company that has one or more office cells in place is said to have or use a cellular office structure (COS).

A HISTORICAL VIEW OF CELLULAR MANUFACTURING

In its basic form, cellular manufacturing has been around for quite some time. In the late 1960s, the Langston Company in Camden, New Jersey, a producer of semi-custom heavy machinery for the paper industry, manufactured a large variety of parts in fairly small quantities.[3] The plant was set up in a traditional job shop mode, where machines and processes were grouped according to function (i.e., separate departments exist for milling operations, grinding, etc.) and where each department was supervised by a foreman. Langston had experienced two major problems: (1) The planning and scheduling of the plant was complex, difficult, and time-consuming, and (2) the progression of parts through the plant was slow, mainly due to excessive waiting and transportation time. In addition, the company was concerned with increasing labor costs and foreign competition. (Do these problems sound familiar?)

To address these problems, Langston adopted a concept it called "family of parts line production." The idea was to create groups of machine tools that allowed the complete manufacture of similar parts in a straight line. One group, for example, consisted of three milling machines, one NC drill press, one sensitive drill press, one contour saw, and a layout table. Each group was manned by multi-skilled operators and supervised by a foreman responsible for making the production schedule. They used standardized toolkits and stored jigs and fixtures next to the line. This arrangement resulted in (1) less time spent on setups due to the processing of similar parts, (2) an ability to make shorter runs due to the reduction in time spent on setups, (3) increased operator productivity due to improved knowledge of the part family, and (4) increased visual control of work-in-process. With this reorganization, throughput times were reduced from 4 to 6 weeks down to 2 to 5 days, the number of shop floor control personnel was lowered from 13 to 6 people, and the need for floor space was reduced from 90,000 to about 77,000 square feet (from 8,360 to 7,153 square meters).

A Brief History of Cells

Although its vice president of manufacturing had experimented with the concept in another firm, Langston believes it was the first U.S. company to pursue "family of parts production" on a large scale. The concept itself, however, is quite old and may have been developed independently by German and American firms.[4] Daimler is reported to have initiated cells in its aircraft manufacturing as early as 1917, and applied it to its automobile production in 1919. In 1922, a book called *Gruppenfabrikation* was published in Germany, a title that literally means "group production." The book describes Daimler's experience with cells at one of its factories.[5]

In 1925, a paper was delivered to the American Society of Mechanical Engineers. The author, R. E. Flanders, described how in the early 1920s a machine tool manufacturer, Jones and Lamson Machine Company, had standardized its products and then organized manufacturing around them. It is interesting to read what a later commentator says about Flanders' views of this approach to manufacturing:[6]

> ... [he] recognized that work organization based on groups of similar machines was disadvantaged by "the constant movement of work from department to department with its consequent slowing up of the work flow, division of responsibility, and difficulty of control." The alternative he suggested was to arrange facilities by product such that any individual piece stay in a single department until it is completely finished. He explained that, "All

long waits … are eliminated, and with them the expensive items of storage space and idle capital for inactive stock. The ideal aimed at has been that of a small, fast-flowing stream of work instead of a large, sluggish one." Flanders also described simplifications to production control, inventory control, and cost accounting procedures that are made possible by changing to product organization.

Although cell manufacturing was practiced in Germany, France, Sweden, and Russia in the 1930s through the 1960s, the modern "wave" of group production was to no small extent caused by—or at least made public by—the Canadian-born consultant and educator John Burbidge. Burbidge, who mostly worked in England, wrote his first paper describing cellular manufacturing in 1961 and continued tirelessly to promote and systematize this concept for more than 30 years.[7]

Apparently, Japanese firms began implementing cellular manufacturing sometime in the 1970s. It is unclear to us how the ideas spread to Japan. However, the Japanese dedication to learning everything they can about a subject and adopting the best ideas they find (an intelligence-gathering practice sometimes referred to as "benchmarking"[8]), is well known. In fact, we can offer a piece of anecdotal evidence in this regard: two write-ups on the Langston experience[9] were sent to us by a former Japanese student who was doing an annual file cleaning at Mitsubishi Heavy Industries. Managers from Mitsubishi had toured Europe and the United States in the late 60s/early 70s to learn more about manufacturing. They had attended a conference presentation in Milwaukee, Wisconsin, on Langston's plant revitalization and heard about its impressive results. In whatever way the cell-based manufacturing philosophy reached Japan, it clearly had a greater impact there than here. Despite Langston's successful experience with cells, which has been quite well publicized, the concept did not take hold in the United States until the just-in-time (JIT) philosophy was imported from Japan in the early 1980s.

The Difference between Job Shops and Cell Systems

The organizational structure used for manufacturing cells is the reverse of the structure on which a job shop (or any typical organization, for that matter) is based. A job shop groups *similar equipment* into functionally specialized units in order to manufacture a variety of *dissimilar parts* that may follow highly variable routings (see Figure 2-1). The focus of this work organization is to maximize the skills of the operators and the efficiency of each functional unit. The flexibility of this arrangement, i.e., the ability to process parts or products regardless of their routing sequence and production needs, is the greatest advantage of the job shop.

A cell, on the other hand, groups *dissimilar equipment* in order to produce *similar parts* using identical or closely related routings (see Figure 2-2). The focus here is on ensuring efficient and uninterrupted materials flow and on completing products, not individual operations, in ways that meet targets set for the cell as a whole. It is difficult to conceive of efficient manufacturing systems, especially those involving mechanized or automated material-handling equipment (robotics

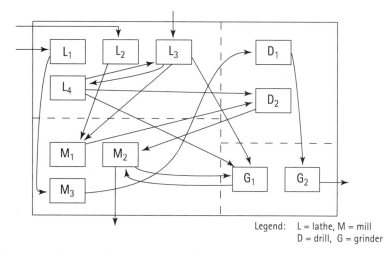

Legend: L = lathe, M = mill
D = drill, G = grinder

Figure 2-1. A schematic view of a functionally organized manufacturing area

or conveyors), that are not based on the idea of processing similar objects in a confined space. On the downside, cells have less flexibility than job shops to adapt to new products. This is primarily due to the selection of specialized equipment and labor, tailored to the cell products, and to the desire to avoid going outside the cell to complete operations.

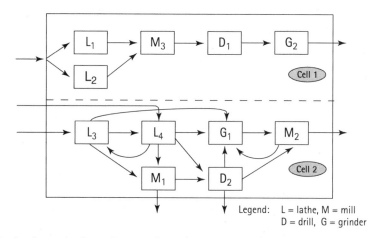

Legend: L = lathe, M = mill
D = drill, G = grinder

Figure 2-2. A schematic view of a manufacturing area organized according to cellular principles

There is a more formalistic way of looking at the difference between job shops and cell systems. Figure 2-3 shows a series of linked process steps that indicate the operations needed to complete each of the parts A, B, C, and D. You could design a system for manufacturing these parts in two fundamentally different ways. The *horizontal* view of work means that all operations of the same type (e.g., milling, drilling, soldering) are performed within separate departments to gain local efficiency. This functional structure is the basis for the job shop. The *vertical view*, on the other hand, argues that the main purpose is to manufacture complete parts. Therefore, a manufacturing system should be built around each of the parts'

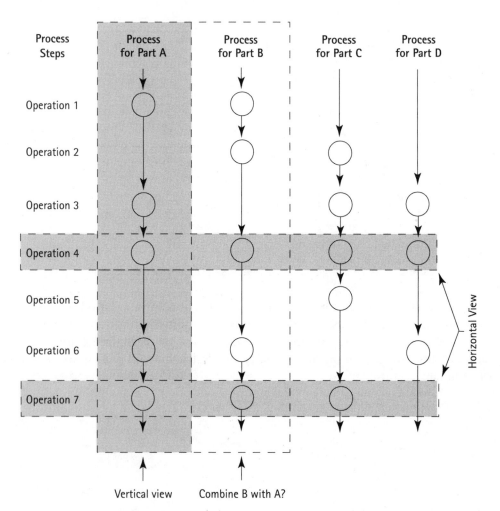

Figure 2–3. The vertical and horizontal views of processes as a basis for organizing work

routings. Each such system should complete "an unbroken sequence of operations," using dedicated equipment located in close physical proximity. In that way, all process steps for part A could form their own production unit, as could those for parts B, C, and D. However, since in most cases a single part has insufficient volume to justify its own manufacturing system, parts with similar processing requirements are grouped to increase the utilization of people and equipment. The result is what we call a cellular structure.

FOUR PERSPECTIVES ON CELLS

As we've mentioned, identifying a group of equipment in a factory as a cell is not always a straightforward process. Table 2-1 shows four perspectives of cells that we have developed to complement our original definition and help reveal the essence of cells. We will periodically return to these four perspectives throughout the book.

Table 2-1. Four critical perspectives on cells

1. From a **resource perspective**, a cell is a small group of resources—human and technical—*dedicated* to the processing of a set of similar objects (products, components, documents, etc.).

2. From a **spatial perspective**, a cell is a group of resources *located in close proximity* within clear physical boundaries.

3. From a **transformation perspective**, a cell is a system designed to perform *multiple and consecutive process steps on a family of objects.* The similarity among the objects, which qualifies them to be referred to as a "family," is based on shared process steps and process flows.

4. From an **organizational perspective**, a cell is an *administrative unit within the firm.* As such, it is allocated resources, supplied with material, used as a planning and control point, and accountable for performance and improvement.

The Resource Perspective

A cell is a small group of human and technical resources (i.e., equipment) dedicated to a group of parts or products. The two key words here are "small" and "dedicated." Small, of course, is a relative and unspecific term. It has frequently been argued, however, that effective work groups should consist of between 4 to 6 people and not exceed 12.[10] Does this mean, then, that a cell with, say, 35 people is really not a cell? Our studies show that the number of operators in a cell can vary between 1 and 40, but that close to three-fourths of all cells have 5 or fewer operators. Cells with a large number of operators tend to be involved with high-volume assembly and packaging operations, while cells with low numbers of employees tend to be dedicated to machining operations.[11]

We would argue that a cell with more than 15 people is too large to create a truly cohesive—and therefore effective—work group. Also, the physical size of such a cell may be too large to have effective visual control of the process flow. This is especially true if the materials flow is jumbled and erratic inside the cell. On the other end, can a cell be too small? As we mentioned, a cell need not have a team of operators working in it. In fact, many successful cells, primarily those performing machining operations, are staffed with a single operator.

The second key word in the resource perspective definition is "dedicated." This implies that the resources are exclusively used for the products allocated to the cell. However, as we discuss later, it is not unusual for cells to share equipment with other cells. In addition, some required equipment does not even belong to the cell but is independently operated so that many products can utilize it. In the same vein, operators are sometimes shared among cells to alleviate temporary workload imbalances. This means that "dedication" is also not an absolute criterion for a cell. In our view, however, employee involvement with process improvement is most pronounced when both human and technical resources are *exclusively* dedicated to the cell products.

The Spatial Perspective

Cells contain resources located in close proximity and with clear physical boundaries. Some companies create obvious boundaries by, for example, painting all equipment blue and hanging signs indicating that this is "Sheet Metal Cell 3." However, some cells do not contain *all* resources within their boundaries. So we must make a distinction between "dedicated equipment" and "cellular manufacturing." In the former case, equipment has been identified and dedicated to a product or part family; however, it has not been grouped *physically* but remains within its original functional area. Thus, there is a spatial separation of the resources used to process the family. This means that the operators are physically as well as visually separated. In addition, the responsibility for the complete process is divided among multiple supervisors.

Although this type of equipment dedication sometimes is referred to as a "virtual cell," it fails to meet both the spatial and the organizational criteria of a "true" cell. *Cells require both physical and organizational grouping of equipment and personnel.* This is what allows them to achieve the benefits that come with the principle of an "unbroken sequence of operations" in close proximity. These benefits include: local responsibility centered on the completion of parts and products rather than on individual operations; better overview and understanding of the process; and reduced move and waiting times due to small lot sizes and closely located workstations.

The closer the resources are located within a cell, the more efficient and effective the cell. But just how close must the resources be? Although we would argue that the closer the better, there are no absolute answers to this question. On the other hand, a physical separation that hinders visual contact among operators and prevents a complete overview of cell processes is "too far." For example, assembly lines and transfer lines both comply with our basic cell definition and do not violate the four perspectives. Whether or not they qualify as true cells depends in part on how closely resources are located on the line. Many assembly/transfer lines are laid out in a linear sequence and can extend for a long distance. An operator stationed at the first station may not be able to see, communicate with, and assist operators located further up the line. Such a line would not be a cell (also see the section "Assembly lines versus assembly cells" in Chapter 5).

The Transformation Perspective

A cell performs *multiple, consecutive process steps on a family of objects* and the *similarity among the objects* is based on shared process steps and flows. But what is meant by "multiple process steps" and "similarity among the objects?" Specifically, how many process steps and how much similarity does a cell require?

Let's first consider the number of steps. Ideally, for any defined family, you want to perform *all* required process steps in the cell. This gives the cell maximum ownership and control over the production process. However, this often is neither practical nor economically feasible. In such cases, a cell should at least perform the majority of the operations required by the majority of the products within its boundaries.

The second key aspect of the transformation perspective is "similarity among objects," a core principle underlying both cell design and cell operation. The notion of similarity originates with the group technology (GT) philosophy. GT argues you can gain efficiencies by grouping similar tasks into families, eliminating redundant tasks, and standardizing (i.e., freezing) the way the remaining tasks are performed. The GT philosophy is broad and powerful and has been applied to many areas besides cellular manufacturing, notably to the problem of growing part populations.

Here's a good example of applying GT thinking to curb part proliferation. When Ferdinand Piëch took over the Volkswagen car manufacturing group as chairman in 1993, the organization was in financial difficulties due to weak sales. Piëch, among other things, focused on identifying potential cost-savings. The following quote illustrates how obvious many such ideas are when product similarity is considered:[12]

> Mr. Piëch used the tiny cigarette lighter as an example of potential cost savings. Volkswagen currently had 12 different lighters among its Audi, SEAT, Skoda, and VW lines, all made by one supplier. But there are only two basic differences: red dashboard lighting for the Audi lighter and green lighting for all other nameplates. The other 10 lighters merely have differently formed tips. Now there are two variations, he said: "I can't tell you the new price, but you can understand what . . . potential cost savings we have around here. They are laying around. You just have to pick them up."

The basic idea is that many *unnecessary* product variations often exist. If you can remove redundant products with only minor variations, and consolidate the remaining family, you can achieve cost benefits. For example, product similarity reduces time-consuming changeovers between tasks, eliminates the need for distinctively different fixtures and tooling, saves on inventories and cost, and increases employee proficiency.[13]

At first glance, it would appear that each department within a job shop is based on the GT principle since similar operations have been grouped within each function. In one sense, that is correct. But GT thinking, and cell creation, strives to push the notion of similarity as far as possible in order to seek gains. This means that, within any group of objects, you should always try to see if establishing smaller groups with greater internal similarity can yield further cost benefits.

For example, consider a job shop with a turning department consisting of 12 different lathes. Assume that this department processes 1,000 part types. Due to their dimensions and tolerances, 100 of these may require the same lathe and the same fixturing. This group of 100 parts then forms a "family" from a GT perspective. This makes it possible to design tools, fixtures, and setup procedures for this machine, thereby eliminating wasteful activities and improving productivity.

However, cells are not just based on similarities among parts for a single operation. More importantly, our definition also requires *similarity of operations along the process flow*. For the purpose of cell design, we therefore identify families of parts based on both *similarity of process steps* (horizontal perspective) and *similarity of process flows* (vertical perspective). Converting a portion of a job shop to a cell therefore means that you should seek reductions in task variety for each workstation in the cell (the horizontal or operations view in Figure 2-3). But you also want process scope expansion by making parts complete (the vertical or process view in Figure 2-3).

A group of machines can be a cell if the equipment is dedicated to a family of similar parts. However, if the family consists of *all* parts produced in the plant, the similarity concept becomes meaningless. Thus, a sheet metal area that produces all sheet metal parts for the facility is not a cell. We have in this regard noted an industry trend in the last decade to label all distinct areas in the factory as "cells," even in cases where the equipment is of the same type and performs identical operations.[14] However, we do not call just any production unit a "cell." To have a cell, a plant must have (1) identified a family of products highly similar in process requirements, (2) physically separated these products from the other products in the plant, and (3) dedicated resources to that family. Other production units should retain their traditional name of "work center" or "department."

Unfortunately, "similarity" is not a well-defined concept and lacks a unified measure. It is in the eye of the beholder. Therefore, there is no minimum level of similarity that qualifies a group of parts as a family for a cell. But one thing is very clear: the higher the similarity, the more efficient the cell processes. This is because there will be less variations in such things as tooling and equipment requirements, setup procedures, operations, process times, and flows.

The Organizational Perspective

A cell should be recognized as *an administrative unit within the firm,* accountable for planning and control, output, measurement, and improvement. This means that a cell is a unit with its own resources, measures of performance, performance targets, and performance achievement responsibilities. The organizational perspective implies that a group of resources within a larger department, even if dedicated and physically clustered, is not considered a cell if the group's performance is not managed and monitored separately from other resources in the department. Note that we do not require that a cell be self-managed for it to satisfy the organizational perspective. However, in the best-performing cells, operators are empowered to solve production and customer problems, and to work on process improvement projects.

RELATED TYPES OF PRODUCTION UNITS

There are many variations of cells that do not qualify as "true" cells. These include concepts like mini-cells, phantom cells, and virtual cells. The lines between cells and "focused factories" are also often blurred. Table 2-2 lists the various types of cell variations we will define and discuss in this and the next section.

Table 2–2. Various types of cells and related production units

• Mini-cells	• Part and product cells
• Phantom cells	• Stand-alone and linked cells
• Virtual cells	• Job shop, hybrid, and flow-shop cells
• Focused factories	• Manual and automated cells

- *Mini-cells*: This refers to a situation where—in an otherwise functional layout—the equipment and operators necessary to perform a couple of consecutive operations along the part routings have been physically moved together.

Though a mini-cell may be the seed or beginning of a cell, it is not a true cell. This is because the "sequence of operations" is broken by performing the required operations in several production units (of which the mini-cell is one). Accordingly, parts are far from being completed in the mini-cell. The Tennant Company and Tektronix, among others, have used mini-cells in their plants.

- *Phantom cells*: These are cells that do not permanently exist. We first learned about this concept from the Owatonna Tool Company, which needed to manufacture a limited number of certain parts per year. Since it could not justify setting up a dedicated cell for this production, the solution was to move the necessary equipment together and create a temporary cell. Once the required production was completed, the phantom cell disappeared, and all pieces of equipment and all employees were returned to their original locations. We've since seen phantom cells in other companies. Both phantom cells and mini-cells fail to fully comply with the resource, spatial, transformation, and organizational perspectives of cells—at least on a permanent basis.

- *Virtual cells*: These are cells that do not exist in the spatial sense.[15] Rather, this concept is similar to that of "dedicated equipment" where a firm formally identifies the part/product families and their required processing equipment, but neither equipment nor employee assignment locations are changed. Thus, each resource required for processing remains in its original position in the plant. Further, compared to real physical cells, companies that use virtual cells dynamically identify families and the equipment needed to produce them. In essence, the "cell configurations" and the families they process change over time depending on available resources and current demand.

  The advantage of virtual cells is that a dynamic allocation of jobs to equipment can overcome the disadvantages of having resources dedicated to products when needs shift over time.[16] However, while a virtual cell is a step in the direction of cellular manufacturing, it is still essentially a job shop. It therefore fails to meet both the spatial and organizational perspectives on a permanent basis. We feel that many of the potential benefits of cells are lost by not creating a permanent cell structure with which employees can identify. This is especially true if you seek continual improvement through cell teams. There is also a problem with operators having to adjust to the tasks demanded by constantly shifting products. As a result, virtual cells may be best suited to the automated factory.

- *Focused factories*: This is a concept that was first introduced in the literature by Wickham Skinner at Harvard Business School in 1974.[17] It has become well known in industry, but is usually not well defined. In particular, the relationship between cells and focused factories is a common area of confusion at seminars we give, and is worthy of a more lengthy discussion.

What Is a Focused Factory?

A growth in the number of products, markets, customers, suppliers, and/or employees ultimately leads to complexity in manufacturing. This means that it becomes difficult to satisfy the increasing internal and external demands using just one manufacturing system. As a result, misfits occur between objectives and measurement systems, the overview of the plant's activities and performance diminishes, the capability to execute tasks rapidly and without errors decreases, and the ability to predict outcomes fades. In short, the ability to manage is lost. These are exactly the same reasons that drive firms to abandon job shops in favor of cells!

The basic idea behind *focus* is to reduce manufacturing complexity so that a plant does fewer things better. In Skinner's own words: "Focused manufacturing is based on the concept that simplicity, repetition, experience, and homogeneity of tasks breed competence."[18] But how do we achieve focus in a factory? Skinner offered the following suggestion: "... focus each plant on a limited, concise, manageable set of products, technologies, volumes, and markets."[19]

There are six dimensions you can consider when creating a focused plant:

1. *Products*. Allocate the same kind of products to one unit; e.g., all 3-horsepower electric motors.

2. *Markets*. Allocate the production of all products sold in a certain geographical market (for instance, Europe) to the same focused factory.

3. *Customers*. Allocate the production of all products sold to one or more customers to the same focused factory.

4. *Processes*. Allocate all products or parts requiring similar processes to the same unit so it can specialize; e.g., the automotive industry's separation of assembly and parts fabrication plants.

5. *Volumes*. Allocate products with similar volumes to same production units; e.g., high-volume manufacturing of motors is done in a separate unit from low-volume manufacturing.

6. *Competitive basis/order winners*. Allocate all products that compete on the same basis to the same production units; e.g., make all standardized motors that mainly compete on cost in one focused factory, and customized motors in another focused factory.

These six dimensions are not independent of each other. Products and processes are related, as are markets and customers. Likewise, order volumes tend to be closely related with the characteristics needed to win orders. Thus, it does not really matter from what perspective you start from when you are trying to focus a plant. However, you may want to apply all the dimensions during the focusing process to see if they can help identify more clearly the products and resources that should belong to each focused factory.

Bergstrom, Inc. is an Illinois-based manufacturer of heating, ventilation, and air-conditioning (HVAC) units for the bus and truck market. It converted from a traditional functional organizational layout to a set of five focused factories, each located in the same building. Gene Berg, Director of Manufacturing at the plant, used this definition of a focused factory: "A focused factory is a small factory within a factory that has all the processes, equipment, tooling, support personnel, inventory, etc., to completely produce a family of products from start to finish."

In the converted Bergstrom plant, two of the focused factories serve two customers each, two serve a single customer, and the fifth is dedicated to service parts and odd customers (see Figure 2-4). Thus, the first four are customer-focused factories while the fifth is a "remainder factory" without clear focus.

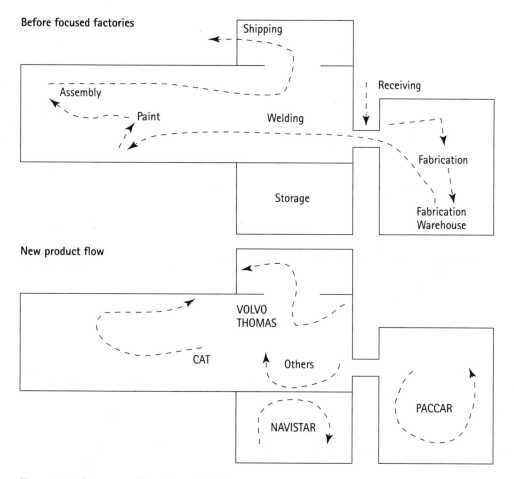

Figure 2-4. Bergstrom Manufacturing's factory organization

Are Cells Focused Factories, and Vice Versa?

Let us now return to the issue of the difference between cells and focused factories (also called "mini-plants"). If you replace *focused factory* in the definition above with *cell*, you can see that they overlap with, or at least do not contradict, our previous cell definitions. What causes the confusion between cells and focused factories is that cells are also based on a product focus (and sometimes a customer focus). There are, however, three major differentiating aspects between a focused factory and cells that you should keep in mind:

    1. *Organizational scope.* Unlike most cells, a focused factory, in addition to operators, encompasses indirect support personnel, such as quality

assurance technicians and materials handlers, and technical support personnel, like maintenance, manufacturing engineers, and, in some cases, design engineers. In other words, a focused factory is typically a sizable, more or less self-governing organizational unit, operating as a profit center and frequently dealing directly with suppliers and customers. The functions most often left out of a focused factory, and thus kept centralized, include design engineering, supply chain management, human resources, marketing, and finance. A cell, on the other hand, is typically a very small administrative unit within a large organization, and cell employees may include only operators.

2. *Product scope.* A focused factory is usually a separate manufacturing facility dedicated to one or more complete product lines and/or to a set of external customers. Cells, on the other hand, are commonly set up to manufacture components or products within product lines and may only supply internal customers, such as other cells or departments.

3. *Internal manufacturing organization.* The definition of a focused factory does not specify its internal organizational structure. Thus, focused factories can use cellular manufacturing but can also operate functionally oriented shops within their boundaries. (This is probably not the most efficient process choice for these plants, but that is another story.) Conversely, the existence of cells does not make a plant into a focused factory. The borderline between the two concepts, however, often gets blurred in companies with cells that make products complete and ship these directly to customers. Some of these firms refer to their work organization as a cell, although it consists of multiple small cells and more appropriately should be called a focused factory. Other firms apply the term "focused factory" to large cells even if these are not assigned support personnel and are not operating as mini business units.

In summary: in comparisons with cells, focused factories (1) are more complete organizations, (2) produce a wider range of products, and (3) are large enough to consist of more than one production unit (such as cells or work centers).

OPERATIONAL CHARACTERISTICS OF CELLS

So far we have identified the major characteristics that define cells and cellular manufacturing. In this section we focus on the detailed operational characteristics that describe the type of work cells typically perform, and on the patterns of material flow that exist inside and outside them. We also briefly discuss manual and automated cells (see Table 2-2).

Work Performed in Manufacturing Cells

You can classify manufacturing cells by considering the type of operations they perform. We recently did a study of 126 cells in 46 American metalworking plants

Table 2-3. Frequency of process usage

Process Types	Number of Cells, Out of 126, with this Process Type	Percentage of Cells with this Process Type
Machining/metal removal (M)	76	60%
Joining/assembly (J)	64	51%
Finishing/washing (W)	44	35%
Testing (T)	32	25%
Packing (P)	32	25%
Forming/metalworking (F)	31	25%
Casting/molding (C)	11	9%
Heat treating (H)	3	2%
Others	14	11%

where we grouped cell processes into nine larger categories. Table 2-3 shows the percentage of the cells in our study that housed each of the nine different process types.[20] The table data indicate that the majority (60 percent) of the cells performed machining or metal-removal processes; over half of the cells performed joining or assembly processes; over one-third performed finishing or washing processes; and one-fourth of the cells carried out testing, packing, and forming/metalworking operations.

Table 2-4 displays the combinations of process categories found in cells and highlights the large diversity of cell types. It turns out that only about 22 percent of the cells were involved with a single process type category. These "pure" cells were either machining/metal-removal cells (13 percent), joining/assembly cells (6 percent), packaging cells (2 percent), or testing cells (2 percent). The remaining cells, called hybrid cells, all performed combinations of process types such as machining/metal removal *and* joining/assembly; e.g., sheet metal parts were welded and grinded in the same cell.

These statistics illustrate that the cell concept is applicable to many different types and combinations of processes. Further, they demonstrate that you can design manufacturing cells to handle not just part manufacturing, as traditionally was the case, but to fully manufacture, test, and package products ready for distribution. For example, PC boards can be assembled, tested, and packaged in the same hybrid cell.

Part versus Product Cells

Manufacturing cells can have either single parts or assemblies as output. We make the distinction between *part cells* and *product cells* to highlight their routing differences. Part cells are involved with single-piece production, and parts follow linear

Table 2-4. Frequency classification of cell types (based on 126 cells)

Combination of Process Types	Number of Cells
M	16*
M, W	13
J, T	8
J, T, P	8
J	7*
M, J, W	7
F, J	5
F, M, W	5
F	4
F, M, J	4
P	3*
J, P	3
F, M	3
M, J	3
F, J, P	3
C, M, W, P	3
M, J, W, T	3
T	2*
J, W	2
M, T	2
M, J, T	2
M, W, P	2
C, M	1
M, P	1
C, M, J	1
C, M, P	1
C, J, P	1
F, W, H	1
J, W, T	1
C, F, T, P	1
C, M, J, W	1
C, W, T, P	1
F, M, J, T	1
F, M, J, P	1
F, M, W, H	1
F, M, W, P	1
M, W, H, T	1
F, M, J, W, P	1
M, J, W, T, P	1
C, M, J, W, T, P	1
Total	**126**

Legend: C=Casting/molding W=Finishing/washing
F=Forming/metalworking H=Heat treating
M=Machining/metal removal T=Testing
J=Joining/assembly P=Packing

Note: cells with processes classified as "Others" in Table 2-3 are not included.
Single-process type cells are marked with *.

routings. Product cells, on the other hand, perform assembly operations. Here, the processes involve the merging of different components fed to the cell at different points along the routing. Therefore, the product routings are in the form of networks or trees of operations (also see Chapter 5).

While part-producing cells can supply many different product lines (and other firms) with components, product cells are typically more narrowly focused and dedicated to subassembly or final assembly of products within the same product line.

Material Flow Patterns Between Cells: Stand-alone versus Linked Cells

The ideal cell contains an "unbroken chain of operations." Specifically, orders for parts or products, once released, should not leave the cell for processing elsewhere, whether in other cells, in other areas of the plant, or at subcontractors. A cell that fully completes orders inside the cell is referred to as a *stand-alone cell*. The reality, however, is that most cells supply, or are supplied by, other production units inside or outside the firm. A special case of such interactions is when cells feed other cells in the system. We refer to this as *linked cells*.[21]

There are three basic types of cell system flow patterns (see Figure 2-5). Pattern 1 represents a stand-alone cell where, say, machining or subassembly operations are fully completed in the cell. Pattern 2 is a situation where products begin their processing in one cell but are then transferred to other units for additional processing.[22] Pattern 3 is the situation where parts/products leave the initial cell, are partially processed by other units (which could be shared resources, like heat treatment), and then return to the original cell for completion.

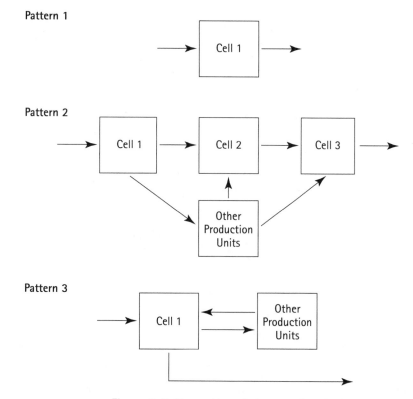

Figure 2–5. Flow patterns between cells

Patterns 2 and 3 are similar in the sense that the operation sequences have been partitioned and allocated to several production units. You may adopt this type of design (1) if you want to separate fabrication and assembly operations and perform them in different cells or shops; (2) if some equipment is toxic and you must isolate it from the rest of the workplace; and (3) if some equipment used by multiple production units cannot practically or economically be placed in all the cells that require it. Paint lines and heat treatment facilities are typical examples. Figure 2-6 shows a six-operator cell system that manufactures five types of shaft and bracket assemblies for pumps. While the layout appears to show a single cell, there are actually three closely linked machining and assembly cells. This cell system fits pattern 2/category (1) above.

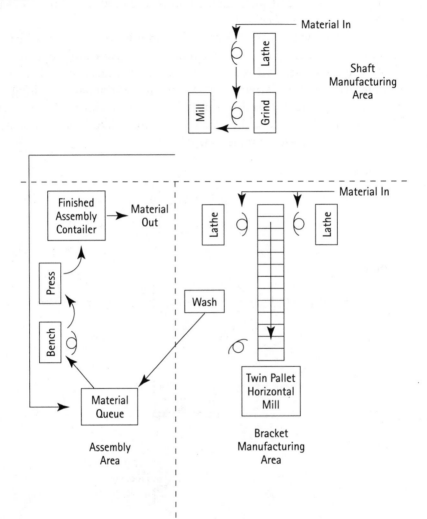

Figure 2-6. Three linked bearing bracket and shaft manufacturing and assembly cells

Material Flow Patterns Inside Cells: Job Shop versus Flow Shop Cells

The pattern of material movements inside a cell depends on the routing similarity among the products assigned to it. As we will discuss in Chapters 5 and 6, the composition of the product families, and the degree to which you can adjust routings to fit a dominant standard routing, both play important roles in determining the flow patterns in cells. These internal patterns determine the ease with which you can schedule the cell, the type of material-handling system you can choose, the ability to visually control production progress, and the required skill level of the operators (also see Chapters 11 and 12).

A variety of distinct flow patterns may exist inside cells.[23] A "pure" *flow-line cell* is one where all parts or products follow the same routings throughout the cell and are processed at each of the workstations (see Cell 1 in Figure 2-2). Several variants of this pattern exist. For example, some cells allow backtracking and forward skipping. This is where parts/products return to previously visited workstations for additional processing and/or bypass stations when they move forward. These represent a "hybrid" type of cells. Finally, at the very opposite end of a flow line cell, is the *job shop cell*. This is a cell where parts can enter and leave at multiple stations and where there is no unidirectional flow pattern (see Cell 2 in Figure 2-2).

Changes to the part or product families over time will affect the internal flow pattern. For example, a cell can begin as a pure flow-line cell, but due to the addition of new parts and the phasing out of old parts, end up as a job shop cell (for other forms of cell evolutions, see Chapter 17). This type of deterioration of the flow pattern affects productivity, scheduling complexity, and ease of control.

Labor Intensity: Degree of Automation in Cells

There are three aspects of the manufacturing process that can be automated, i.e., computer-controlled:

1. *The equipment* (including tooling). This performs machining, fabrication, inspection/gauging, testing, or packaging operations.
2. *The material-handling system.* This connects the workstations in the cell.
3. *The internal scheduling and supervisory system.* This controls which job should be moved and/or processed next.

There are no well-defined measures for "degree of cell automation," so we cannot be very precise with respect to this type of classification. To simplify, we discuss only two extreme types of cells: manual and automated.

Manual cells

A manual cell is a cell with no or only a limited degree of automation. Such cells range from those without any computer support at all to those where computer-controlled equipment or processes are used in a stand-alone mode. These cells depend on the presence of operators most or all of the time. As the name implies, people perform a larger variety of tasks in manual as compared to automated cells. For example, in manual machining cells, cell operators, besides loading and unloading parts, may control tool switching, fixturing, inspection, maintenance, materials handling, scheduling, process improvement, and even parts programming of computer numerically controlled (CNC) equipment.

Most assembly cells are manual due to the difficulties of executing automatic assembly—especially for small products. This is likely to change with a greater emphasis on products designed for easy assembly and the growing capabilities of assembly robots.

Automated cells

A truly automated cell is one where all major functions are under computer control. Accordingly, the cell is capable of operating without manual supervision for a period of time; for example, a second or third shift. This is why an alternative term for automated cells is "cells with limited manning." Cells are often called flexible manufacturing systems (FMS) if a large number of machine tools are connected by a material-handling system. The role of humans is usually limited to the loading and unloading of parts from pallet fixtures, and the ongoing monitoring of the processes. "Smaller" systems are sometimes called flexible manufacturing cells (FMC). For example, a cell with a robot connecting one or two CNC machines can be categorized as an FMC.

FMS/FMCs often contain groups of similar or even identical machine tools. However, the ability of machining centers to perform different types of operations with the purpose of parts completion (the "unbroken sequence of operations" principle) can make each machining center a *mini-cell*. In essence, then, an FMS/FMC can be viewed as an organizational unit composed of several mini-cells. Of course, if the system completes all or the majority of the required operations for a part, it can be seen as a full-fledged cell.

Flexible Process Technology versus Part Similarity

Is the ability to process a wide range of parts a substitute for identifying part families and capitalizing on process similarities? Put another way, do the capabilities of flexible manufacturing systems and machines to process a wide range of parts make group technology obsolete? We were exposed to this issue some years ago at a Wisconsin manufacturing firm. This company had considered acquiring a classification and coding software system to help it identify families of parts.[24] However, the manager decided that investing in a group of CNC machining centers would have a more reliable payback. It would also avoid an ongoing effort of maintaining the coded database.

Although the manager may have made the correct choice between these hard and soft technologies, we believe it is a mistake to think that flexible process technology allows you to ignore part similarities. First, no machine or system is capable of processing all types of parts. Therefore, you must group parts into families before you can specify machine or cell configurations. Second, even if machine tools are capable of machining all part geometries with certain dimensions, such loose specifications can strain the system. In particular, a greater variety of parts require a greater variety of tooling and fixturing. This complicates the planning and scheduling process unless you have large tool magazines and plenty of duplicated tools. It also complicates the development of the CNC programs since there is little overlap between one program and the next.

In other words, flexibility is never free. In fact, flexibility and efficiency are contradictory concepts. Therefore, the identification of product families, within any group of parts that can be manufactured by flexible equipment, can provide additional advantages. In short, it is our contention that GT and cellular manufacturing live—even in the face of flexible technology (however, also see Chapter 19).

THE RELATIONSHIP OF CELLULAR MANUFACTURING TO OTHER ORGANIZATIONAL PRINCIPLES

Cellular manufacturing is closely related to several different types of manufacturing principles and philosophies. Cells have their origin in *group technology* (GT) thinking and were first developed with a single-minded focus on manufacturing efficiencies. However, early industrial experiences quickly discovered that cellular manufacturing is not just about technical issues like rearranging equipment on the factory floor. Equally—or even more—important to the success of these systems is the human side of work. Cellular manufacturing is therefore also closely related to the *socio-technical systems (STS) theory*, which argues for the dual concerns of the technical and human sides of an organization (see Figure 1-4 in Chapter 1). The cell environment can potentially create a positive climate for work. John Burbidge, the "father" of modern cellular manufacturing, said in this regard: "I believe that [cellular manufacturing] holds out the promise of a big improvement in the quality of working life and that in the long run this will be its major contribution."[25]

To think of work as processes or strings of operations is fundamental to the improvement toolkit of *total quality management (TQM)*. The more recent term "reengineering," used to describe radical organizational redesign for greater efficiency and effectiveness, is a concept that puts product-oriented work processes and teams in the center of the analysis. *Business process reengineering (BPR)* projects have mainly been applied to office work and, in our view, many such projects essentially adopt cellular manufacturing concepts and apply them to non-manufacturing settings.

The vertical and horizontal perspective of manufacturing operations has been suggested by the well-known Shiego Shingo, the influential consultant involved with the original Toyota Production System (TPS) (see Figure 2-3). TPS, which relies on GT and cell principles, represents the foundation for what has become known as *just-in-time (JIT)* and *lean manufacturing*.

There is a whole body of research based on the quantitative modeling of systems—what we will summarize as *systems behavior knowledge (SBK)*—that has helped us understand how manufacturing systems behave and what we can do to improve their performance. *Time-based competition (TBC)*, as implied, contends that time is a key competitive variable. Out of the time-based competition paradigm, and resting on cellular manufacturing and SBK, also comes *quick response manufacturing (QRM)*. This is a management philosophy that focuses specifically on lead time reduction in manufacturing firms with mid- to high-variety product mix. Below, we look at the relationships between cellular manufacturing and all these organizational principles and practices in more depth.

Socio-Technical Systems (STS) and Cells

If you have studied industrial engineering or industrial management you are probably familiar with socio-technical systems theory (STS). STS, originating in the early 1950s, holds that organizations are comprised of three interrelated components or subsystems: the technical system, the business system, and the social system.[26] More specifically, business objectives are best met not by the optimization of the technical system and the subsequent adaptation of the social system to fit it, but by the *joint optimization of the technical and the social system*. While all organizations are socio-technical systems, not all organizations have achieved a joint socio-technical optimization. There are nine general STS principles that should govern the design of manufacturing systems. Table 2-5 lists these principles in the left column.[27]

If you look at the right-hand column in Table 2-5, you will find significant similarities between the STS principles and the core elements of cellular manufacturing. The common themes point to team-based design of cells, empowered cell employees, process control at the source, multi-functional operators, closely located resources, immediate feedback on process problems, potential job satisfaction, and cell designs in constant evolution. Although there are large overlaps between STS and cell thinking, an STS-oriented redesign may not necessarily suggest a cellular structure.[28] However, it is reassuring to know that cellular manufacturing actually rests on organizational design principles that are likely to lead to effective performance as well as satisfied employees—outcomes achieved by many organizations using cells.

Total Quality Management (TQM) and Cells

The fundamental assumption behind total quality management (TQM) is that organizational improvements, large and small, are not only possible but also essential for long-term survival. Thus, all organizations must continually improve to remain viable.

TQM can be described as two journeys: a short-term journey of continuous improvement, and a longer journey of cultural change. In the short term, TQM is concerned with making improvements at the process level, i.e., removing waste and realigning processes so that they truly satisfy customers' expectations. An essential building block for these improvement efforts is the recognition that all outcomes are accomplished through work processes. Further, TQM holds that teams of people are best equipped to make process improvements, and that improvement efforts should be grounded in objective data and "the scientific method."

Many TQM principles, such as total employee involvement, the use of teams, and the reliance on data throughout the organization, represent a radical departure from traditional ways of operating. These practices require a redistribution of power in the organization that is often met with significant resistance (from managers). Thus, even though many organizations become enthusiastic about continuous improvement in the short term, the long-term journey of cultural change is more intimidating.

Cellular production is highly consistent with both the short- and long-term aspects of TQM. In fact, cells provide excellent opportunities to put the principles of total quality to work. In many companies, TQM and cells are implemented simultaneously. Often, they become so intimately linked that a separation of the two concepts can be difficult for cell employees to make.

Table 2-5. Cells and the fundamental principles of STS

Socio-Technical Systems Principles	Relationship to Cell-Based Manufacturing
Compatibility: The process of designing the organization should be consistent with the goals of the design. Creating an organization capable of adaptation requires tapping the "creative capacities of the individuals" to create a "constructively participative organization."	Cell work teams may emphasize planning and continuous improvement through joint problem-solving efforts.
Minimal Critical Specification: In the design of jobs, specify no more than is absolutely essential. Too much specification may inhibit creativity or adaptation to circumstances.	Cell work groups may be empowered to decide how to allocate tasks among members.
The Socio-technical Criterion: Work should be designed to control variances (deviations from the ideal state) as close to their source as possible. Design work so that errors can be identified and corrected before they are fed to downstream processes.	The cellular layout facilitates immediate detection and response to variances.
The Multifunctional Criterion: Work design should avoid highly fractionalized tasks and individuals trained to perform only one type of task. Joint optimization is more likely in the presence of multifunctional workers with flexible task assignments.	Job rotation and cross-training characterize many cell environments.
Boundary Location: Departmental boundaries should be drawn to encompass tasks that are temporally (sequentially) related to one another as opposed to technically similar to one another. Organizing work around the product flow facilitates information sharing and encourages ownership and responsibility for within department tasks.	Machines needed to produce a family of parts or products are located close together. This equipment, and those who operate it, are dedicated to the production of these items.
Information Flow: A key category of information is feedback on performance about variances (deviations from the ideal state). The information system should provide workers with the feedback they need to control variances and improve their process.	The close clustering of machines and those who operate them facilitates timely feedback about job performance and variances.
Support Congruence: Social support structures such as reward systems, the selection process, training policies, conflict resolution mechanisms, and the like should be consistent with the objectives that governed the design of the work system.	For their most effective operation, cells require consistent support policies.
Design and Human Values: A key objective of organization design is to provide a high quality of work life for those who work in the system.	It is often assumed that CM leads to higher quality of work life, although there is little empirical evidence to support this contention.
Incompletion: An organization design process is never finished. It is a continuing process.	Changes in product volume, mix, workforce, and technology will require changes to the cells.

Reengineering (BPR) and Cells

Reengineering is "the process of taking a comprehensive, clean slate approach to an organization's work flows in order to achieve dramatic improvements in costs, time, and effectiveness."[29] Although over 70 percent of reengineering efforts are claimed to fail, reengineering has attracted the attention of a large number of organizations and has in some cases led to quantum-leap improvements in operational performance.[30] A number of areas of overlap, as well as subtle differences, exist between cell principles and reengineering. We see BPR mainly as a philosophy that has been applied to office work. In this regard, office cells, as discussed in Chapter 18, can be viewed as outcomes of BPR.

JIT, Lean Manufacturing, and Cells

The Toyota Production System, the foundation of what we call JIT systems, was first communicated to the Western world at a conference in Tokyo in 1976. The text of the presentation, written by four Toyota employees, was published the following year.[31] The rest, one could say, is history. JIT spread worldwide during the 1980s and is now a well-established and practiced philosophy accompanied by a set of principles and techniques.

At its core, JIT is a waste-elimination philosophy, where "waste" refers to the following unnecessary activities:[32]

1. Waste from producing more than what the market demands (overproduction).
2. Waste due to people waiting for materials, equipment, or other employees.
3. Waste due to moving materials long distances.
4. Waste from inefficient processing of material (poor techniques, technologies, fixturing, etc.).
5. Waste from building inventories anywhere in the system (besides the inventories resulting from overproduction).
6. Waste due to unnecessary walking and hand movements by operators.
7. Waste from producing defective parts and products.

You may note that of these seven types of waste, numbers 2, 3, and 6 are directly avoided with cells. Further, numbers 4, 5, and 7 are typically achieved in cells as a result of applying process improvement techniques, using small lots and operator-based quality control (TQM). Only the first type of waste—overproduction—may not seem to be directly associated with cells. However, overproduction is typically also avoided due to two reasons. First, cells are implemented to support a lean operating philosophy, so unnecessary inventory build-up tends to be avoided. Second, because cells can fairly quickly respond to market demands, they facilitate a shift from make-to-stock to make-to-order manufacturing—thereby curbing overproduction.

Table 2-6 shows many other techniques and principles associated with the JIT philosophy.[33] As you can see, the use of cells is only one out of 16 JIT principles.

However, we would argue that these principles are not of equal importance. Rather, we believe there is a necessary sequence by which the principles need to be implemented. *Our admittedly biased view is that cellular manufacturing is a prerequisite for, and one of the core foundations of, JIT.* Thus, we find it difficult to conceive of JIT systems that do not employ the ideas behind cellular manufacturing.

For example, setup reduction, small lots, and efficient layouts are core characteristics of cells, as are multifunctional operators and group problem solving. And the use of level schedules and pull systems, although not suitable for all types of cells, requires cells for their *effective* execution. In other words, the existence of cells is a necessary, although not always sufficient, condition for effective JIT. This means that cellular manufacturing has a broader applicability than do several of the JIT principles in Table 2-6. However, as will become clear from subsequent chapters of this book, the conditions under which cells function the best, and which are the easiest to plan and control for, are also the conditions for which JIT is best suited.

Table 2-6. Core JIT principles

> - Setup time reduction (e.g., continual emphasis on lowering setup time)
> - Small lot sizes (e.g., small lots in the master schedule and elsewhere)
> - JIT delivery from suppliers (e.g., daily shipments)
> - Supplier involvement in quality improvement efforts (e.g., long-term supplier relations)
> - Multifunctional workers (e.g., operators perform several tasks)
> - Small-group problem-solving (e.g., teams are formed to solve problems)
> - Training (e.g., to learn new skills)
> - Daily schedule adherence (e.g., schedule allows for catch-up time)
> - Repetitive master schedule (e.g., product mix is repeated on a regular basis)
> - Preventive maintenance (e.g., time reserved for maintenance activities)
> - Equipment layout (e.g., use of cells)
> - Product design simplicity (e.g., minimization of part count in products)
> - The use of kanban system (inside the plant and for suppliers)
> - Pull system support (e.g., backflushing, efficient layout, authorization to stop production if quality problems occur)
> - MRP adaptation to JIT (e.g., elimination of work orders)
> - Accounting adaptation to JIT (e.g., a switch to process costing)

Lean manufacturing is a more recent name for JIT. As with JIT, lean manufacturing is deeply rooted in the automotive industry and focuses mostly on repetitive manufacturing situations. The literature on lean manufacturing distinguishes itself from work on JIT by its emphasis on paced manufacturing (takt time), the use of cells, and the application of the "value stream" concept as the start of organizational renewal.[34] The value stream concept is strongly related to TQM, BPR, and cellular manufacturing in that it advocates process thinking.

Time-Based Competition (TBC), Quick Response Manufacturing (QRM), and Cells

The important notion of companies "competing on time" (versus price or quality) was first forcefully articulated in the late 1980s and early 1990s.[35] Although time-based competition (TBC) introduced several ideas, such as employee cross-training and reorganization into teams, it has few clear principles for process analysis and implementation. It is, in this regard, similar to BPR in its lack of a systematic framework. Lately, quick response manufacturing (QRM) has emerged as a more developed approach to helping manufacturing firms reduce their lead times in offices and on factory floors. QRM uses cellular manufacturing as a foundation and supports process-improvement efforts with well-founded insights, quantitative modeling, and a systematic approach.[36]

Systems Behavior Knowledge (SBK) and Cells

Although you can find many examples of fairly successful implementations of cells, JIT, TQM, and BPR/TBC projects in the literature, the reasons *why* performance improvements were achieved are noticeably absent from these descriptions. It is, of course, possible to design and operate office and manufacturing systems without such an understanding, but less likely that you will be able to do so successfully. Quantitative modeling, based on simulation and queuing theory, has contributed a great deal to our understanding of how we should set capacity and determine lot sizes, on what equipment we should try to get setup time reductions, what the impact of cross-training will be, and so on. In essence, systems behavior knowledge (SBK) "explains" why and where cells, TQM, BPR, JIT, and QRM can be successful. For more on this topic, see Chapter 7.

Cells Are the Core Foundation for Process Improvement

In summary, this is how we look at the improvement philosophies reviewed above (see Figure 2-7). Socio-technical systems and group technology thinking support cellular manufacturing with basic design principles from both social and technical perspectives. In turn, cellular manufacturing is a core building block for the realization of JIT/lean manufacturing, TQM, BPR, and QRM/TBC. Supporting all of them are the principles and theories about systems dynamics that we call systems behavior knowledge. Thus, in our worldview, as we stressed in Chapter 1, *cells are the core foundation or the core element of all modern improvement frameworks.*

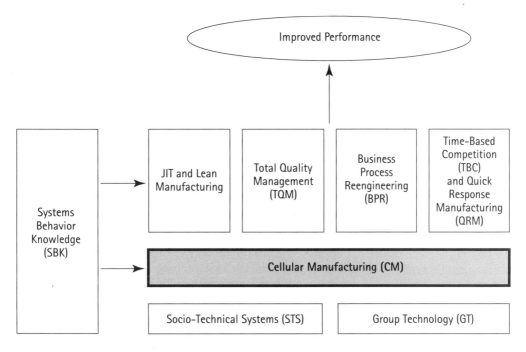

Figure 2-7. The relationship between cellular manufacturing and other principles and philosophies

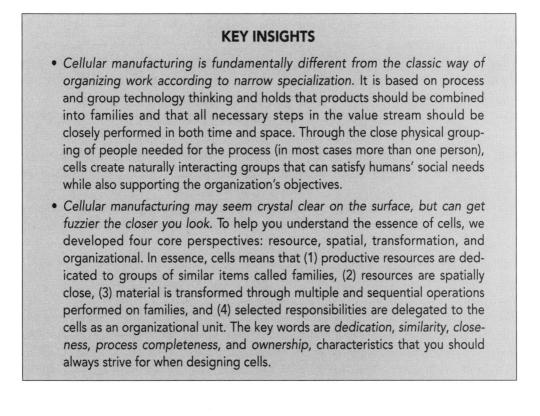

KEY INSIGHTS

- *Cellular manufacturing is fundamentally different from the classic way of organizing work according to narrow specialization.* It is based on process and group technology thinking and holds that products should be combined into families and that all necessary steps in the value stream should be closely performed in both time and space. Through the close physical grouping of people needed for the process (in most cases more than one person), cells create naturally interacting groups that can satisfy humans' social needs while also supporting the organization's objectives.

- *Cellular manufacturing may seem crystal clear on the surface, but can get fuzzier the closer you look.* To help you understand the essence of cells, we developed four core perspectives: resource, spatial, transformation, and organizational. In essence, cells means that (1) productive resources are dedicated to groups of similar items called families, (2) resources are spatially close, (3) material is transformed through multiple and sequential operations performed on families, and (4) selected responsibilities are delegated to the cells as an organizational unit. The key words are *dedication, similarity, closeness, process completeness,* and *ownership,* characteristics that you should always strive for when designing cells.

- *Cells come in many different forms.* Many different process types can be combined and performed in cells. Thus, cells have wide applicability. Cells can also have different sizes, flow patterns, and degrees of automation. Thus, cells don't all look the same.

- *Cellular manufacturing has strong links to other improvement philosophies.* Many organizational processes must be added to cells to make them complete, functioning units. You must, for example, design jobs, determine cell staffing levels, provide training, develop planning and control procedures for cell work, modify performance measurement, institute improvement procedures, and so on. There are strong connections to STS, JIT, TQM, BPR, TBC, QRM, and SBK in these areas when it comes to the design and operation of cellular systems.

3

Why Cells Improve Performance

When it comes right down to it, these are the questions you want to answer: "Will cellular manufacturing work in my company?" and "What kind of benefits can I expect from a cell conversion?" To get to those answers, you need to understand not just the *types* of benefits that can be expected, but also the *sources* of these benefits (why, for example, does conversion to cells result in lead time reductions?). If you understand how and why benefits are created with cells, you are also in a position to analyze your current plant and gauge whether it is likely that you can achieve certain benefits. To get the full picture, however, you must also be aware of the potential disadvantages with cells and the situations for which they may be less suitable.

Here are the main issues we discuss in this chapter:

- How does the starting point for change affect the magnitude of the improvements you can expect with cells?
- Why do cells improve performance?
- Are there any disadvantages with cells?
- What issues should you take into consideration when deciding on whether to adopt cells?

POINT OF DEPARTURE FOR PERFORMANCE IMPROVEMENTS

Some experts imply that cells will yield the same performance improvements in all types of strategic and operating environments. Here are two examples of unqualified endorsements of cellular manufacturing:

> I believe that process [i.e., functional] organization is obsolete, and I see *group technology* [i.e., cellular manufacturing] with *just-in-time production control* as essential for batch and jobbing production companies which want to survive in the future.[1]
>
> J. L. Burbidge

Based on years of benchmarking and observations in organizations around the world, we have developed the following simple *rules of thumb*: converting a classic batch-and-queue production system to continuous flow with effective pull by the customers will *double labor productivity* all the way through the system (for direct, managerial, and technical workers, from raw material to delivered product) while *cutting production throughput times by 90 percent* and reducing inventories in the system by 90 percent as well.[2]

J. P. Womack and D. T. Jones

The situation in the last quote assumes that a conversion from a functional layout to cells has taken place, that lot sizes have been considerably reduced (to one-piece lots), and that a pull system is in place. But the statement ignores the organization's starting point for change. Note that the magnitude of performance improvements depends on your point of departure. The operating conditions your plant faces, and whether your firm has previous experience with reorganizations and improvement activities, makes a difference.

Let's first look at the conditions from which most companies begin their journey towards cellular systems: the functional organization.

Problems with Functional Organizations

In many companies, like the Langston Company described in Chapter 2, plants are organized along functional lines. The shop is here partitioned into departments or work centers, each organized to handle a particular type of operation or process (e.g., grinding, welding, harness assembly, testing). Each process is under the control of a foreman or department head. Operators and supervisors in these departments are typically measured and rewarded for their ability to handle any type of job that comes their way, and to efficiently use the resources available to the department. The timing and quantity of the jobs that flow into a department, and the quality of the incoming work, are typically outside the department's control.

Such "job shops" are highly flexible. They make sense in situations where the advance knowledge of the process requirements of incoming work is low, such as for firms offering low-volume, highly customized products and services to many customers. However, they are not always the most efficient or effective way to organize production.

If you want to get a feeling for the operational inefficiency of a functionally organized facility, simply chart the flow pattern of various parts (and/or employees) as they travel through the plant. Commonly, parts—and often people—move long distances between work centers, departments, and sometimes even between plants. Material also moves in and out of storerooms. Travel times are further extended by inefficient material-handling systems that cause long delays before parts can be moved. These delays occur both before and after parts have been worked on.

Furthermore, large variations in part routings and process requirements, and a focus on departmental efficiency ("keep all resources busy all the time"), often lead to large inventories. A key culprit is large lot sizes, which result in high WIP inventories and long queue times before each workstation. Large lots also create long waiting times after each process step because all parts in a lot must wait for the last part to be completed. The use of large batches also prevents the detection of quality problems and leads to high scrap and rework levels. These and other problems are commonly associated with traditional, functionally organized "batch and queue" (job shop) production systems (see Table 3-1).

Table 3-1. Typical problems in functionally organized manufacturing systems

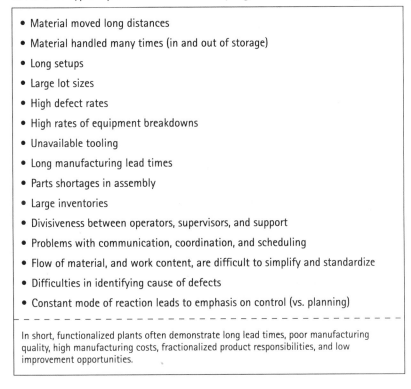

- Material moved long distances
- Material handled many times (in and out of storage)
- Long setups
- Large lot sizes
- High defect rates
- High rates of equipment breakdowns
- Unavailable tooling
- Long manufacturing lead times
- Parts shortages in assembly
- Large inventories
- Divisiveness between operators, supervisors, and support
- Problems with communication, coordination, and scheduling
- Flow of material, and work content, are difficult to simplify and standardize
- Difficulties in identifying cause of defects
- Constant mode of reaction leads to emphasis on control (vs. planning)

In short, functionalized plants often demonstrate long lead times, poor manufacturing quality, high manufacturing costs, fractionalized product responsibilities, and low improvement opportunities.

Although products are manufactured by completing a series of operations, companies are not in the business of performing operations with high efficiency. Rather, the overriding objective is to make complete products to sell and deliver to customers, rapidly and inexpensively, for problem-free use.[3] A major criticism of functionally organized shops, therefore, is that the principle of specialization and "division of labor" has resulted in a production system that has lost its focus on the customer.

Why Firms Implement Cells

When the problems outlined in Table 3-1 persist long enough, and your position in the marketplace is threatened by customer-focused competitors who can deliver higher quality products faster and at lower prices, you inevitably look around for alternative ways to design, manufacture, price, and distribute your products. You may then see cellular manufacturing as a way to achieve competitiveness. The most common reasons firms implement manufacturing cells are to reduce lead and response times, lower WIP inventories, and increase manufacturing quality. Table 2-1 showed the type and magnitude of performance improvements that we have documented in our studies of cell users. If you recall, the largest average improvements due to cells are in the areas of lead/response time and WIP inventories—the very same areas in which companies typically seek improvement.

Now, you may look at the list of problems in Table 3-1 and say to yourself: "We used to have all those problems, but not anymore! We now have some mini-cells and even a real cell or two. And we have several assembly lines. I really don't see the poorly performing functional organization you are talking about. So why should I continue to read?"

These are good points. Most factories are not either job shops or flow shops, but something in between. And some areas perform well while others do not. Our view, however, is that you can often improve your operations by increasing product similarity, moving resources closer, dedicating them to families, and assigning "ownership" to the product-focused units we call cells. Such changes may not always be economically or technically feasible, but the potential is there. However, regardless of where you start, you should first try to understand the causes of performance problems—and the actions you can take to alleviate them. Then you can determine what should be done.

THE SOURCES OF CELL BENEFITS

The two most fundamental benefits associated with cellular manufacturing are reductions in throughput time and inventory. The foundation for these and other advantages can be traced to changes in two areas: (1) the nature of the manufacturing process and how it is organized, and (2) the administrative process that prepares, plans, and controls production. To better structure our discussion of cell benefits, we return to our definition of a cell from Chapter 2:

> A cell is a group of closely located workstations where multiple sequential operations are performed on one or more families of similar raw materials, parts, components, products, or information carriers. The cell is a distinctive organizational unit within a larger firm, staffed by one or more employees, accountable for output performance, and delegated the responsibility of one or more planning, control, support, and improvement tasks.

To reinforce important aspects of this definition, we also provided the four "cell perspectives"—on *resources*, *space*, *transformation*, and *organization* (see Figure 3-1). In the following discussion, we will use these perspectives to demonstrate the benefits that are directly linked to cells, as well as several indirect benefits that occur in cellular organizations.

The Resource Perspective: Benefits Linked to Small Groups of Dedicated Resources

The essence of the resource perspective is that a cell is a *small* group of resources, human and technical, *dedicated* to the processing of a set of similar parts or products. Smallness is important from a social, informational, control, and material-handling perspective; and dedication is important from a psychological as well as an

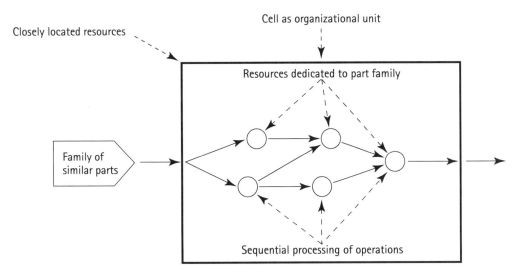

Figure 3-1. The four critical perspectives on cells

improvement standpoint. Resource dedication, directly and indirectly, creates various beneficial outcomes for cells. You may want to use Figure 3-2 to help you navigate through the text below.

Capacity effect

A cell is a production unit that includes a group of people and equipment. Since people and equipment come in increments of one, you may assign more or less capacity to the cell products compared to the situation prior to implementing the cell. If the workload/capacity ratio is lower than before, you will get a direct, immediate impact on lead times and inventories. However, a side effect may be higher production costs due to lower utilized resources. If the ratio has in fact increased in the cell, you can still attain improved performance, but not without also relying on other benefit sources besides capacity (e.g., reduced setup times or increased labor productivity).

Multifunctional employees

How work is shared among the employees in the cell can vary. Adopting the traditional "one worker, one machine" concept is one possibility (we use the term "machine" here to refer to any equipment or process step). Alternatively, you can follow the concept of "one worker, multiple machines."[4] In this latter case, operators move around in the cell and attend to several processes. This requires proficiency in more than one process. Finally, you can use the "multiple workers, multiple machines" concept. This also implies that the operators are trained on two or more processes, and that they move to different workstations during a manufacturing cycle. However, it further implies that at least some of the operators have overlapping responsibilities. This increases the flexibility to assign cell employees to stations where problems occur and capacity is needed (also see Chapter 7).

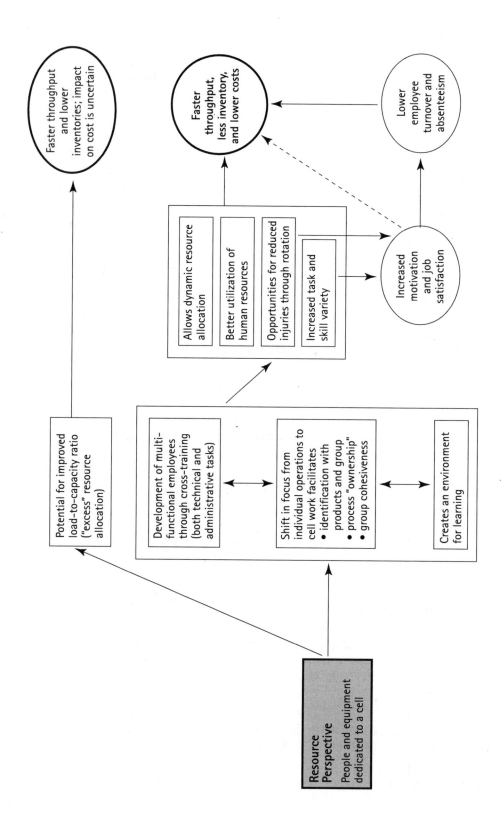

Figure 3-2. Benefits and benefit sources linked to the **Resource Perspective** on cells (dotted arrows indicate somewhat uncertain relationships)

Having cross-trained operators, and more equipment than people in the cell, offers three distinct advantages. First, with an increasing degree of automation, the one worker-one machine concept leads to large amounts of operator idle time. With flexible operators, you can reduce this idle time and increase labor efficiency. This is important since labor cost many times exceeds the equipment cost in the long run. With operators capable of handling several machines, they can also move to where work is backed up and the load is the greatest. This means that the cell is well equipped to adjust to dynamic variations in product mix and volumes.

Second, when operators are trained in multiple processes, the cell can still function even if some operators are absent due to illness, scheduled training periods, etc., or because they are temporarily assigned to other cells.

Third, a very important benefit of cross-trained operators is ergonomic. Through the practice of rotating positions inside a cell, operators are less exposed to injuries such as carpal tunnel syndrome and other repetitive motion injuries.

The social effect of group work

Cell work and teamwork are *not* identical concepts. Although multi-operator cells (cells with more than one employee) dominate in industry, studies show that single-operator cells are quite common.[5] Such cells do not represent as drastic a change in the working environment for the operators as do team-based cells. Because of this, some firms may choose single-operator cells as a way to bypass labor relations problems.

The social environment in cells dramatically changes when operators become members of a group and together run a small cell. (We use "small" as an attribute of a cell to avoid having a whole department, or even a plant, being referred to as a cell.) Identification with the group, and its customers, is a natural outcome due to the shift in focus away from isolated process steps to complete products. Most importantly, it appears that teamwork, for many employees, positively affects motivation and job satisfaction by addressing human needs and feelings such as trust, mutual dependency, social interaction, and peer group identification. Such feelings are reinforced through group-based problem solving, for example in the form of Kaizen blitzes (events of intense, team-based improvement activities, typically lasting no more than 4 to 5 days).

An environment for job expansion and learning

The change from the "one worker, one machine" concept to "one worker, multiple machines" requires a learning process leading to a broadening of operator tasks. Not only is this a form of *job enlargement*, where the operator now must be skilled in several processes, it also implies some form of *job rotation* between workstations in the cell. In addition to simply performing more varied technical tasks, however, cells also lend themselves to the concept of *job enrichment* where operators are responsible for administrative tasks (see "The Organizational Perspective" section below).

Tasks assigned to the cell can be as simple as being in charge of tooling. To reduce unnecessary delays in connection with changeovers, tool inventories are preferably located in the cell rather than in a distant, centralized tool crib. Firms can also train operators to inspect their own output, do data collection (for SPC charts or defect reports), schedule jobs, balance operators among cell equipment, carry out housekeeping and maintenance activities, take part in equipment purchase decisions, receive visitors, visit suppliers and customers, and engage in continuous improvement activities. Shifting these types of tasks—normally done by indirect personnel—to the cell operators can result in lower costs. Support personnel, such as technicians, trainers, and manufacturing engineers, can also become members of the cell team. This dedication of support resources to the cell can lead to faster decisions, better-trained employees, and a greater emphasis on process improvement.

Job enlargement, job rotation, and particularly job enrichment lead to an increased variety of job skills and tasks. Research shows that these changes, in turn, may lead to increased motivation and job satisfaction, and less physical strain.[6] Cells, if carefully designed and coupled with appropriate measurement and reward systems, can improve operator motivation and job satisfaction. This leads to obvious benefits: lower personnel absenteeism and turnover, higher quality cell products, and more productive cell resources.

Yet the link between job satisfaction and increased quality and productivity, often taken for granted, is somewhat uncertain. For example, some studies show increased satisfaction from group work without positive impact on performance. In other cases, enhanced job satisfaction has even been coupled with declining performance. But by most indications, cells tend to lead to operational benefits without a loss in motivation or satisfaction, and thus generate both operational and human benefits.[7]

The Spatial Perspective: Benefits Linked to Physical Closeness

The essence of the spatial perspective is that a cell is a group of people and equipment located in *close proximity* within *clear physical boundaries*. The grouping of resources is the most visual and physical manifestation of cells. As such, it is a very important design feature that supports the elimination of wasteful activities in work processes. Physical closeness in cells can create positive outcomes (see Figure 3-3).

Being close is being able

The most immediate benefit that follows from the close grouping of people and equipment is that operators and parts move only short distances. This reduces both the time and the energy spent moving. The closeness of the workstations also makes it possible for one operator to serve different pieces of equipment in an efficient way. Another very important benefit is the potential for making the material-handling system, whether mechanized or manual, more efficient by reducing delay times. With workstations located closely to one another in the cell, and with the responsibility for the parts movement also allocated to the cell, less time will be spent waiting for transport.

The proximity of the workstations also makes it possible to reduce the lot quantities moved between stations. In fact, the use of small transfer batches is one of the most important advantages with cells over departmentalized work organizations. Taken together, the short distances and small lots (or even single-piece lots) make material "flow like water." The result is faster throughput times and lower inventories.

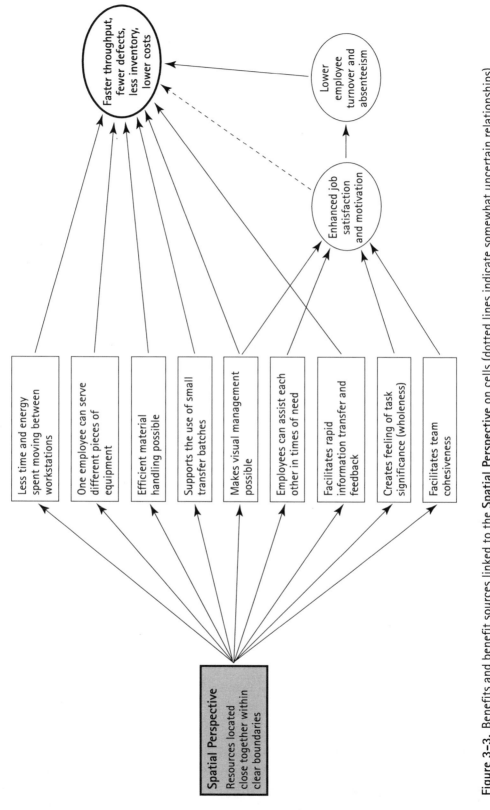

Figure 3-3. Benefits and benefit sources linked to the **Spatial Perspective** on cells (dotted lines indicate somewhat uncertain relationships)

Improved information processing and social climate

Another benefit source is the ability to exercise *visual management and control* of the manufacturing process. Having all equipment and people closely located makes it easy for everyone—operators, support personnel, and managers alike—to get an immediate overview of the status of work in the cell and easily detect problems that need attention. This facilitates a dynamic reallocation of operators and team leaders to those workstations in most need of assistance.

The consolidation of different tasks needed to complete a job within the boundaries of a cell greatly facilitates information processing. By processing jobs at closely located workstations, the feedback between process steps can be almost immediate. If the same person performs two consecutive operations, and there is a quality problem with the first step, this can rapidly be detected and corrected by the operator. If there is a team of operators, they can communicate and solve problems on the spot, thereby improving performance. Teamwork also facilitates both technical and social learning. Operators have the opportunity to learn new tasks from each other, as well as to adjust to each other's work habits.

Seeing, participating in, and understanding the complete process also increases the employees' sense that their work is significant—a contributor to motivation and job satisfaction. Understanding of "the whole process" facilitates the acceptance of decisions and fosters cooperation between people working on different part of the cell process. Further, grouping people with different skills and abilities can improve the outcomes of problem-solving activities. The overall result is greater efficiency and effectiveness, and a commitment to improving the cell's performance.

The Transformation Perspective: Benefits Linked to the Processing of Product Families

From the transformation perspective, a cell is a system designed to perform multiple and consecutive process steps on a family of products. The *similarity among the products*, which classifies them as a family, is based on *shared process steps and process flows*.

Establishing cells automatically shifts the focus, for managers as well as for operators, from single operations to longer chains of operations. The uninterrupted flow of materials through the cell therefore becomes the focal point for process improvement activities. The creation of families of similar parts or products also shifts the focus away from single items to groups of items. With this comes an economy of scale. Any change done to improve a process step, say a setup, now benefits a whole family and not just a single product. The higher the degree of product similarity, and the more of a product's operations you can allocate to the cell, the greater the cell's potential performance. Figure 3-4 illustrates the various benefit sources associated with the transformation perspective.

Shorter setups and smaller lots

Cells are designed to process families of parts or products that require similar operations; each part shares tools and fixtures with other parts in the cell. Thus, the prepa-

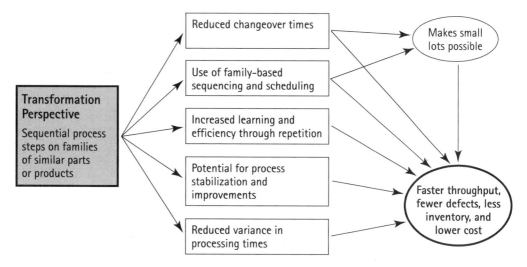

Figure 3-4. Benefits and benefit sources linked to the **Transformation Perspective** on cells

rations and the time spent switching between parts can be shortened for parts belonging to the same *setup families* (i.e., families where the part members require the same or similar changeover activities).[8]

To illustrate: performing a setup on a metalworking machine can involve the changing of tools, fixtures, machine parameters, and instructions. Developing fixtures capable of holding a family of parts eliminates the time needed for changing fixtures. Similarly, the number of tools that are required to process a set of parts is almost automatically reduced following the identification of similar parts. Accordingly, time spent on tool changes can also be minimized. Since fewer tools and fixtures are needed for parts processed in the cell, tooling costs can be reduced.[9] Finally, the more similar the specifications for a family of parts, the less time operators spend reading and interpreting work instructions. The overall result is fewer quality-related problems, greater operator productivity, and higher throughput.

When you reduce setup time, the productive capacity of both equipment and people increases. This, in turn, leads to faster throughput times in the cell. Another benefit of changeover time reduction, and perhaps *the* most important contributor to lead time reduction in cells, is the opportunity to reduce batch sizes. Small lots reduce throughput times and WIP inventories, smooth workload variability, and speed up the detection of defective parts.

Family-based scheduling

Once you identify parts with similar setup requirements and include them in a family, the time to change between these parts can be shortened significantly. However, a cell can process several different families, each of which may use slightly different equipment, tooling, and setup procedures. Recognizing this, there is a second way you can reduce time spent on setups—by prudently sequencing parts at each machine to minimize total setup time. Essentially, if you have established setup families for the cell, the sequential processing of parts belonging to the same families will minimize setup time. This is because the time per setup is now greater when switching between parts from different setup families than between parts from the same families. (We explore family scheduling in Chapter 11.)

Enhanced learning through repetition

Part families have similar flow patterns, setup requirements, geometric shapes, sizes, or weights, and/or are based on the same raw materials. This similarity exposes operators to increased degrees of repetition, which in turn leads to enhanced learning and increased efficiencies. Furthermore, if you work with sets of similar items instead of with individual items, you can make the process improvement tasks inside cells more productive. It is easy to see that activities such as setup time and lot-size reductions, part design, tool and fixture design, programming of robotics and numerically controlled machinery, specification of standard operating procedures, inspection procedures, workplace layout enhancements, operator training, and the like all benefit from dealing with groups of similar parts. The end results are greater quality and productivity improvements than typically seen in traditional shops.

Variance reduction and process stabilization

If you stabilize the time it takes to set up a machine and process a lot (i.e., reduce processing time variance), you will reduce lead time. Keeping lot sizes constant over time is one way to do this. Your ability to stabilize lot sizes for all the members of a part family, which facilitates the use of fixed containers, is easier if the processing time per unit is similar. This is likely to happen when the parts are similar with respect to geometric features and the specific operations they require. *Process stabilization is a prerequisite for process improvement.* The environment in cells, therefore, is highly conducive to the continual improvement of all aspects of cell operations.[10]

The Organizational Perspective: Benefits Linked to the Cell as an Administrative Unit

From the organizational perspective, a cell is an *administrative unit within the firm*. As such, it is allocated resources, supplied with material, used as a planning and control point from the viewpoint of the centralized planning function, and is accountable for performance, problem solving, and improvement. Changing the organizational structure from functional to cellular work changes the way administrative (sometimes called "indirect") work is handled. This is a most significant contributor to the varied and often intertwined benefits linked to cell manufacturing.

To centralize or not centralize—that is the question

When designing and operating cellular systems, you must decide whether to *centralize* or *decentralize* each administrative task that affects cell operation, including materials and capacity planning, scheduling, maintenance, quality inspection, performance tracking, staffing decisions, training, job allocation, tooling, and fixture storage (see Figure 3-5).[11]

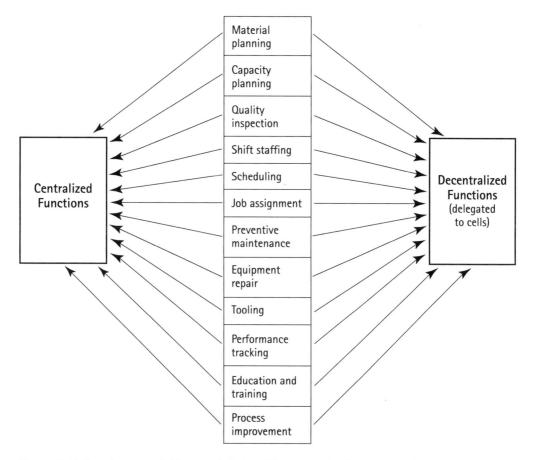

Figure 3-5. Functions can, fully or partially, be either centralized or decentralized

You can limit the centralized tasks to *controlling the boundaries* of the cell, i.e., to ensure that it is supplied with material and capacity, and that targets are set for job completions (unless these tasks also are delegated to the cell). In this way, decisions vital to operating and perfecting the manufacturing process are delegated to the source, permitting immediate actions by the cell operators closest to the process. Decentralization can also mean that support personnel are assigned to cells rather than being part of centralized functions.

There are several benefits traceable to viewing cells as independent administrative units within the firm (see Figure 3-6). These are discussed next.

Cells as responsibility centers

Establishing the cell as an organizational unit means that the responsibility for meeting goals, such as delivery deadlines or quality improvement targets, firmly rests with the cell personnel. Such clear lines of responsibility eliminate the infighting and finger-pointing that frequently occur within functionally organized plants. Another

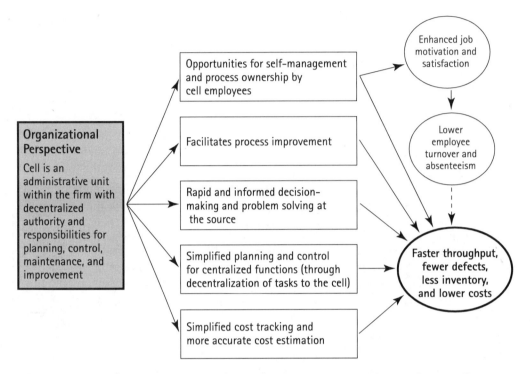

Figure 3-6. Benefits and benefit sources linked to the **Organizational Perspective** on cells (dotted lines indicate somewhat uncertain relationships)

positive effect is greater identification with the workplace and its products, and stronger social bonds among the employees within the cell unit. As previously noted, these "soft benefits" can lead to increased motivation and job satisfaction.

An important source of benefits associated with cells stems from the principle of "unbroken sequences of operations." Process delays frequently occur as a result of breaking operations sequences and distributing the responsibility for job completion to several production units (each with a different supervisor and located in a different area of the plant). Cells, on the other hand, produce parts/products by performing operations that, to the greatest extent possible, are under the control of the cell. The result of controlling the flow of work along a complete process is fewer delays.

In many cases you can trace the source of process inefficiencies to the physical separation of consecutive process steps. Grouping process steps in one area, the cell, creates a small and controllable work environment where self-assigned responsibility for process improvement often develops. The clear lines of responsibility and accountability, and the focus on eliminating inefficiencies related to non-value-added time, also support rapid problem solving and administrative decision making.

Planning and control units

Viewing a cell as a production unit—that is, the smallest unit from a planning and control perspective as seen by the next higher level in the organization—has several implications. First, complexity associated with planning is reduced due to the delegation of tasks down to cell operators and supervisors. In traditional functional shops, the single machine or work center is the planning and control point. In cell shops, however, the cell itself serves as the planning unit. Since each cell houses several pieces of equipment, the total number of planning units is reduced. This greatly simplifies the long-term materials and capacity planning that is performed centrally. In fact, the main task of a central planning office can be restricted to setting output targets for the cell and ensuring uninterrupted material flows and adequate capacity. Inside the cell, operators can sequence and schedule jobs, and handle short-term staffing issues. Cells also can be linked to each other with pull systems, which simplifies the scheduling task for the centralized planning function.[12]

Second, cells also permit you to reduce the effort involved in controlling work. There is little or no need to track individual efficiencies of equipment and labor, nor status and location of jobs. Instead, you can limit the control tasks to keeping track of jobs entering and leaving the cell, and the number of labor hours spent in producing the output.

Third, in most cells, quality control is part of the cell workers' job; there are no inspectors from a centralized quality department inside the cell. You can also delegate material handling, simple maintenance and repair activities, tooling support, materials ordering, and so on to the cell. This often frees up indirect personnel, such as planners and inspectors, to do other jobs in the plant.

Cost systems

For the purpose of cost control, a cell can be both a production unit and a cost center. Indirect employees such as process engineers, materials planners, training technicians, and in some cases even buyers, designers, and sales personnel, can be directly affiliated with one or more cells. If they are permanent cell employees, they spend their time only on activities related to the cells. Their salaries will then be charged to product families in the cell, not to products manufactured in other areas of the plant. Likewise, you can also charge the use of the equipment, unless it is shared with other cells, to the product families in the cell. These opportunities for direct cost allocations, which increase cost accuracy, are possible when the cell is viewed as an organizational unit.

In addition, cells can simplify the costing system if you cease tracking individual operator efficiencies, switch to process rather than job order costing, and apply backflushing (inventory accounting done at the point of product completion or sale). These changes mean you need to spend less time and effort on product costing. (In Chapter 10 we discuss "lean" cost accounting in more depth.)

Benefit Sources Are Many and Varied

As should be clear from the previous discussion, *the benefit sources leading to cell performance are many, varied, and mutually reinforcing.* They include training of operators to handle multiple tasks, the decentralization of planning and control activities, and the assignment of support personnel to cells. They also consist of changes to the physical location of equipment, the reduction in setup time and lot sizes, the development of part family tooling, and the modification to material-handling systems. Finally, benefits also stem from changes to the way individual cell operators perceive their work. Here, the identification with the cell, and the social interaction with a group responsible for its performance, can create social-psychological effects that can be powerful drivers of increased performance and a dedication to improvement.

There are also other aspects of performance enhancements that we have yet to mention. Among them are management's support of the cell strategy, acquisition of new equipment technology, revised quality and maintenance procedures, and modified measurement and compensation systems. Taken together, all these changes, both hard and soft, contribute seamlessly to the improved performance of cell production. As noted in Chapter 1, this makes it difficult to isolate any individual benefit source and determine its particular contribution to performance.

POTENTIAL DISADVANTAGES OF CELLS

The preceding discussion may seem to suggest that a reorganization—from a functional organization to one based on product families processed in cells—only, and *inevitably*, carries with it positive effects. After all, the improvement data available from empirical studies, voluminous anecdotal evidence (perhaps including your own experience), and the fact that the overwhelming number of cell users claim they want to continue to implement cells, are compelling indicators that cellular manufacturing can deliver powerful benefits. However, it is a mistake to believe that cells *automatically* bring performance improvements. In discussing potential negative effects related to cells, we will separate them into those that are technical (related to the product/process) and those that are social (related to the people in the system).

Potential Disadvantages Related to Products and Processes

A significant difference between job shops and cell shops is the difference between production systems designed for *flexibility* and those designed for *product completion*. That is, job shops specialize in individual operations and processes, and the product routings can vary greatly (i.e., new or modified products can be handled without changing the system structure). Job shops, therefore, are built for *economies of scope*.

Cells, on the other hand, are production units dedicated to families of similar parts or products. By design, membership into these families is restricted. Despite this, cells achieve *economies of scale* by capitalizing on similarity so that the product volume of the whole family can be sufficiently high even if the volume of any individual product may be unacceptably low.

The dedication of people and equipment to product families, however, means that these resources are not available for use by other products in the plant. At the same time, the cell is less capable of handling products that require process steps beyond the capabilities of the equipment or outside the operators' skill levels, or that deviate from the ideal routing flows established for the cell. Therefore, there is a loss of both *routing flexibility* and *product flexibility* in cells.

The role of routing flexibility

Routing flexibility refers to the ability to choose among available resources when a job needs processing. Typically, a cell is created by removing equipment and labor from functionally organized work centers and placing them in the new cell area. This reduces the routing flexibility both for the remaining parts still processed by the work centers and for the parts assigned to the cell.

As a result, cells, and the remaining shop, become sensitive to variations in workloads: when demand rises or falls, and when the mix of products fluctuates, cells may become either overloaded or underloaded. In effect, some cells may be starved for work and have forced idle time, while others face growing queues.[13] You can overcome this negative effect through the careful design of the cell and/or by temporarily moving people and/or products between cells or other work centers.

The role of product flexibility

Product flexibility is the ability to manufacture new or redesigned products. Dedicating equipment and people to a cell reduces product flexibility because the equipment and the operators are selected to fit the product family, thereby avoiding unnecessary (and potentially costly) processing capabilities. You should therefore use cells only in situations where there is a "fair degree" of product design stability.

You can prolong the life span of a cell by designing new parts to fit the existing cell equipment and the skills of the operators. It can also be extended through continuous improvement activities, including the upgrading of technology to increase flexibility, quality, and speed.[14] You also can extend the life of a cell by building in redundancy; that is, you choose equipment and operators with a higher degree of flexibility than required at the time the cell is formed. Finally, you can always overcome "the inflexibility disadvantage" by reconfiguring cells to adapt to market and product changes. This option is particularly easy to exercise in the case of assembly cells and/or cells in light industries.

Other potential disadvantages with dedication

There are other potential disadvantages of dedicating process equipment:

- Equipment that previously was shared by many parts may have to be duplicated and put in several cells. This requires an investment that may be unacceptable.

- If equipment is duplicated, utilization will be reduced (unless production volume is stepped up). Low utilization is less important for old, inexpensive, and possibly fully depreciated equipment. But if you have to purchase modern technology and operate at low load levels (say, 5 to 25 percent), the economics may not support cells.

- Since, in most cases, only one unit of each equipment/process type is put in a cell, cells are vulnerable to equipment or tooling breakdown. In addition, because cells operate with low levels of WIP inventory, they have especially low tolerance for disturbances.

- Cells require strict discipline in product design and process planning. You should avoid "polluting" cells with products for which they were not originally designed. This can require costly additions to equipment, tools, and fixtures. You must carefully design and plan new products with an eye towards conformance with existing production capabilities, without sacrificing product features that expand design quality and enhance customer value. If you do not, the performance of the cell may gradually deteriorate over time due to the phasing out of old products and the phasing in of new products that are not well fitted to the cell. Alternatively, if you cannot make newly designed products in the cell, you may have to revert back into job shop-like layouts and reduced operational performance.

A final disadvantage of converting to cells is the expenditure involved with establishing them. Every cell incurs costs for planning, education and training, plant preparation, and possibly lost production in the start-up phase; and for many there will be expenditures for moving equipment and/or buying new technology. (The economic justification of cell systems is discussed in Chapter 8.)

Potential Disadvantages Related to People

A cell operator's perceptions of cell work influence his or her feeling of motivation and job satisfaction. If negative, these can have a destructive effect on the cell's ability to perform as intended. Employees may dislike working in cells with other people for a variety of reasons. For example, they:[15]

- May not enjoy social interaction.
- May not like the physical closeness that inevitably exists in well-designed cells.
- May be unable to cope with the new and increased pace and performance expectations that often come with cell conversions.
- May not like to feel held back by slower employees.
- May not like the loss of control resulting from teamwork.
- May be unable to accept the peer pressure to perform that frequently develops in cells.
- May not cope with the stress of mastering several skills rather than just one.
- May not want to be share difficult-to-acquire skills with others.
- May not want to be trained on new operations or processes by younger colleagues with less seniority and status (for fear of loss of respect).
- May not think that the pay level is commensurate with the variety of tasks and skills required.
- May not want to rotate positions within the cell (due to present comfort level or impact on pay).
- May dislike being rewarded based on group rather than on individual performance (due to the possibility that some "free-riding" individuals may not do their fair share of the work).

These reactions boil down to issues of *skills*, *status*, *pay*, or *stress*. Commonly, psychological reactions against cells and teamwork diminish over time, especially as more and more employees work in cells. Although some cells do get dismantled due to employees' unwillingness to work with others on cell teams, such cases are rare. In fact, few firms report strong resistance to cells from the workforce and, even if they do, they still achieve performance improvements.[16]

In our experience, highly dissatisfied employees tend to leave cells, often even before they are fully implemented. They seek transfers to other production areas or take early retirement. This may be a satisfactory outcome for everyone involved. Another solution, although perhaps less ideal, is to avoid the social conflict and problems with group-pay by creating single-operator cells. In general, you can avoid human resource-related problems by carefully selecting the personnel for the cells. For example, you should choose employees not only on their ability to master the tasks, but also on their compatibility with other employees and their social interaction skills. (Chapter 13 has more on this.)

DETERMINING THE SUITABILITY OF CELLS

When should you use cells and when should you not? Unfortunately, we cannot give precise and definitive answers to these questions. To reason intelligently about the suitability of cells for any particular plant, one must know about the company's competitive strategy, its products or components being considered for cellular manufacturing, its manufacturing processes, and its current operating conditions. However, we can suggest a list of factors to review when deciding whether a cellular work organization is right for your particular situation. (More will be said about this in Chapters 4 through 8.)

In the opening section, "Point of Departure," we argued against unconditional recommendations of cellular manufacturing. We do admit, though, that sweeping endorsements, as exemplified by the quotes at the beginning of this chapter, are valid in one sense. You can design cells to perform a wide variety of tasks, including office work. This gives the cell concept an almost a universal range of potential applications.

Since there are few restrictions on where you can apply cells, the only issue appears to be the performance levels that can be achieved and, of course, the cost of achieving them. The performance data in Table 1-1 indicate quite a bit of variation in reported improvements. For example, not every firm will achieve 90 percent lead-time reductions. Rather, *what* is done will affect the type of benefits shown in Figures 3-2, 3-3, 3-4, and 3-6, and *how much* and *how well* it is done affect the outcomes of these actions and activities.

There are also a few other factors worthy of attention.

Three Categories of Benefits

We group the benefit sources attributable to cellular manufacturing into three categories:

1. *Social.* These are benefit sources linked to employee involvement, self-management of the cell, team cohesiveness, and so on.

2. *Operational*. These are factors such as setup and lot-size reductions, process stability, materials handling efficiencies, and so on.

3. *Managerial/organizational*. This group of benefits sources consists of things such as visual management, delegated control, costing systems, and process improvement activities.

All these benefit sources will impact the performance of a cell. Specifically, you can develop and manage these sources better or worse—and thus achieve better or worse performance. However, the issue of importance here is *how* you decide whether you should adopt cells in a particular situation.

If you look closely, you will find that the effects of the social factors are all related to the cell employees' personal characteristics and how they work in groups. Likewise, the managerial/organizational factors are either directly related to the cell as an administrative unit or to its management. Although critically important to effective cell operation, the social and the managerial factors are not directly linked to the work the cells are created to perform. These factors should therefore not influence a decision to adopt.

Furthermore, these two factors are very much people-based. We believe that you should not make principal decisions regarding organization design based on the present workforce, whether operators or managers.[17] That said, you should not think that "people issues" are unimportant in cellular manufacturing. On the contrary, *we feel very strongly that you cannot achieve well-performing cells unless the human issues continuously receive the highest priority*. In fact, neglecting the human side of cells will guarantee a failed implementation (see Chapters 15 and 16). However, decisions regarding whether or not to adopt cells should preferably be divorced from the specific human resource issues existing at the time of the decision.

This leaves the third category, operational factors, as the most important benefit source to consider in a decision to adopt cells. This makes sense. After all, these factors are intimately related to the work processes that lie at the core of cellular manufacturing. They also are more easily measurable and controllable, and therefore more effective than the other factors in predicting performance improvements from cell implementations. We discuss operational factors in more depth next.

Operational considerations for cell implementations

Firms primarily adopt cells to achieve time and inventory reductions. However, as we discuss in Chapter 7, lead time and WIP inventory are strongly connected in that a reduction in one variable is associated with a reduction in the other. Hence, we focus here on lead time.

Table 3-2 shows the factors you can change to achieve reductions in lead time.[18] Specifically, the more you change a factor in the indicated direction, the greater the impact. For example, the more you can jointly lower lot sizes and setup times, or reduce the variability of the time it takes to process a job, the more lead time will be reduced. This means that if parts already are manufactured using small lots, the potential benefits from cells are smaller than if these parts were made in very large lots. Likewise, the more you can cross-train operators in the cell to perform the productive tasks at the workstations, the shorter the resulting lead time. Similarly, the lower the utilization of the cell, the shorter the lead time.

Table 3-2. Factors with established influence on lead time

Factors that Influence Lead Time	Action Needed to Reduce Lead Time
Machine setup time	Decrease
Machine setup time variability	Decrease
Part processing time	Decrease
Part processing time variability	Decrease
Materials handling time	Decrease
Interarrival time variability	Decrease
Production batch size	Decrease (if coupled with setup time reduction)
Transfer batches	Use (if coupled with family sequencing)
Cross-trained operators	Increase
Labor constraints	Reduce
Interarrival time (time between jobs)	Increase (while keeping lot sizes fixed)
Product mix distribution	Achieve balanced work loads
Equipment capacity	Increase

These relationships indicate that the current operating conditions for products being considered for cell processing will influence the cell's success. In other words, the more you reduce setup and lot sizes, lower utilization (e.g., through additional capacity), reduce variety, stabilize schedules, and cross-train employees when you implement cells, the greater the performance improvement for the products involved.

Strategic and Economic Considerations

Although operational factors shape performance improvement, you should not decide whether to switch to cells unless you have also considered the surrounding strategic and economic factors. Since we devote all of Chapter 8 to the economic justification of cells, we will not discuss that issue here. In regards to strategic perspectives, you should pay close attention to the following four items when determining if you should implement cells:

1. *Your decision to implement cells should be based on strategic reasoning.* The aim of a reorganization is to improve performance—it should not be pursued merely to implement cells. The problems you must deal with are those that prevent your firm from accomplishing its strategy. Products associated with poor performance in terms of response time, quality, inventory, and cost are prime candidates for cells. We have here assumed existing performance problems for existing products in existing plants. But cells are often created in connection with the launching of new product lines, and/or when new plants are built. In such situations the prob-

lem analysis takes place at the design stage, and cells may in fact be the right and obvious solution from the start.

2. *You must look at the level and stability of demand for the products being considered for cell work.* Volume may be the single most important variable affecting cell adoptions. In fact, you may view volume as a surrogate measure for economic value.[19] That is, if a potential product or part family is not supported by sufficient demand volume, you will have insufficiently utilized resources. This would effectively prevent a cell project from getting managerial approval. This does not imply that products with low volume are unsuited for cell work. The combined volume for the whole family may be sufficient to keep resources adequately utilized. However, due to the difficulty in such cases in achieving a stable cell process with low variability, the potential for eliminating waste is lower compared to situations where the products have high and level demand. Also, since lot sizes for low-volume products are small to begin with, the potential reduction in lead time from batch size reduction is small.

3. *You must look at the scope of the conversion.* A single cell devoted to the manufacture of components may have great local impact, but it will play no real role in improving the firm's ability to respond to market demand or schedule changes. So the scope of the conversion, in terms of the number of products or labor hours affected, will influence the strength of the benefits.

4. *You must know how critical the parts or components targeted for cell production are to the rapid delivery of products.* If the components are not on the "critical path" for the supply chain that determines response time, you may get large localized benefits but low impact on the overall response time. In other words, you may reduce lead time and WIP for the cell while customer response time remains essentially unchanged.

KEY INSIGHTS

- *Cells are at the core of a wide array of benefits.* The most obvious benefit achievable in a cell is a reduction in setup and move time. This follows directly from the product similarity and resource closeness characteristics of cellular manufacturing. However, as you have seen, cells are the *foundation* or the *facilitator* for many other "intermediate" benefit sources. This supports the notion we introduced in Chapter 2 that cellular manufacturing is an important basis for the deployment of JIT, BPR, QRM, and other management philosophies (see Figure 2-7).

- *You will get the most from your cells if you understand from where the benefits originate.* Cellular manufacturing has the potential to deliver many types of important benefits to the firm. To design and operate cells successfully you need to know why cells create these benefits.

- *The four cell perspectives—resources, spatial, transformation, and organizational—is one way to understand cell benefits.* We analyzed the sources of benefits according to whether they stem from (1) the dedication of people and equipment to the cell products, (2) the closely located resources, (3) the processing of similar products, or (4) the administrative unit that the cell represents.

- *You can also classify cell benefit sources as social, managerial, and operational.* Another perspective on the cell benefit sources is to classify then according to whether they relate to the (1) social, (2) managerial/organizational, or (3) operational aspects of cell operations.

- *Operational considerations should drive cell adoptions.* The social and organizational benefit sources are crucial to the successful implementation and operation of cells. However, the potential operational benefit sources are *the most important* to consider and if an analysis of these does not indicate that cells will be beneficial, then an adoption should not take place.

- *Cells must fit your business strategy.* In addition to operational benefits, you must also consider the strategic and economic aspects of cells. Be certain that cells fit your business strategy and have the potential to deliver operational benefits before you make a financial assessment.

- *Your point of departure matters.* The performance improvements of cells differ a great deal depending on where you start. A weak improvement potential coupled with a situation with unstable market demand and high conversion cost should probably kill a cell project. On the other hand, if you can greatly change the factors that drive performance, your anticipated improvement can be very large as well.

- *You can avoid the disadvantages of cells through good design, implementation, and operation.* Cells do have some potentially negative features. Most notable among them is their lack of flexibility in dealing with variations in demand and with new product launches. However, if you chose product families and processing equipment carefully, and upgrade both process and cell personnel continually, cells can have long lives.

- *Ask "Why not cells?"* Cells are not right for every situation. As a principle, however, we maintain that cellular manufacturing—and not the functional organization—should be *the base-line case* against which you gauge alternative ways of organizing work. Thus, arguments should not have to be sought as to why cells are viable. Rather, arguments as to why cells are *not* viable should have to be defended.

ADOPTING AND DESIGNING CELLS

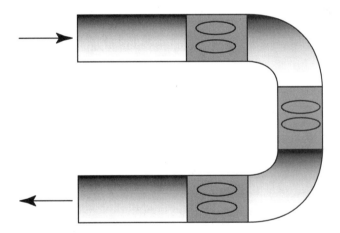

4

The Planning and Implementation of Cellular Manufacturing Systems

The process of planning and implementing cellular systems can vary in scope and complexity. Some processes involve few people and are done quickly, with little advanced planning. Others involve a large portion of the organization and require much time and effort to complete. In either case you may be embarking on a reorganization that may change the company forever. If you are a manager or a member of a team in charge of planning a conversion to a cell system, you need a clear process map for this reorganization. This chapter provides you with the "big picture" of cell system design and implementation. In particular, we address the following important issues:

- What drives a firm to reorganize its manufacturing operations, and what types of analyses are necessary to prepare for a change?
- What process may you follow in order to plan and implement cellular manufacturing?
- Who are involved in the planning and implementation process at various levels, and what roles may they play?

We briefly discuss each phase of a complete planning and implementation process—strategic and operational analysis, adoption, design, implementation, operation, and evolution. Chapters 5 through 18 then provide the details on how to create an effective cellular work system.

THE PLANNING AND IMPLEMENTATION PROCESS AT A GLANCE

It is difficult to outline a complete planning process that spans from strategic considerations and adoption decisions to cell implementation and evolution, and also is applicable to all situations. On the other hand, without an overall process map, presented in a simple and comprehensible format, it is difficult to grasp fully what cell adoption, design, and implementation entail. The planning process we present in this chapter is based on processes observed in several firms. You may not follow it in exactly the same sequence that we have outlined, and may even decide to skip or rush through some of the steps. However, the process we present can hopefully serve

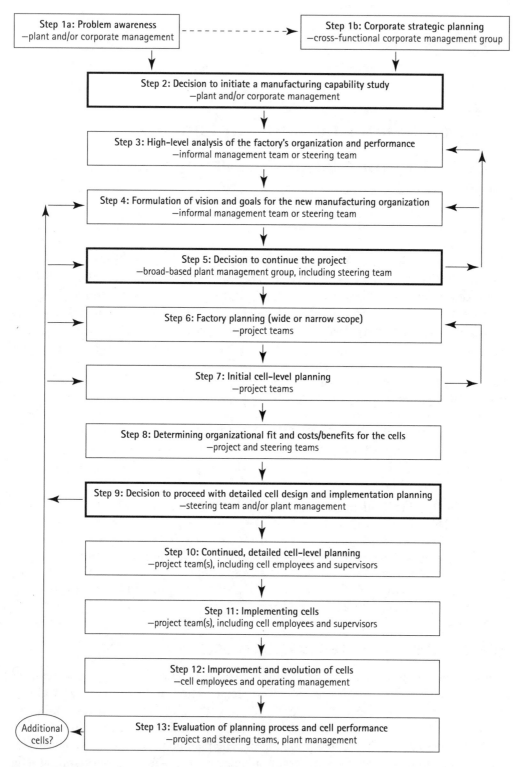

Figure 4-1. The complete planning and implementation process

as a blueprint for your own planning process, and you should modify it according to the situation present at your own firm.

Figure 4-1 shows the steps in the complete planning and implementation process. Before we discuss these steps in detail, we provide a quick overview.

The initiative to launch a project for reviewing and improving a factory's performance typically comes from two sources. The first is the acute awareness by a manager or group of managers that the current capabilities of the firm's operations are deficient (Step 1a). Alternatively, a corporate strategic planning exercise involving a cross-functional group of upper-level managers may conclude that the company needs to recapture (or prevent) losses in customers and markets by improving the performance of its operations (Step 1b). In either case, some event caused one or more managers to overcome the natural inertia of the status quo to initiate a study of the firm's capabilities in manufacturing (Step 2).

As a result, the firm forms a small, often informal, team consisting of a select group of managers and employees and possibly external consultants. The role of this "advance team" or "steering team" is to undertake a broad analysis of the organization. Specifically, it should determine how the manufacturing function may respond to performance problems regarding response time, quality, and cost. Driven mostly by a sense of unacceptable business performance, and because it is still unclear what problems the organization should address or what actions it should take, the steering team may choose to conduct its work without publicly informing the rest of the organization (Step 3).

Through a process of observing, reviewing past performance data, and talking to employees, customers, and suppliers, the steering team crystallizes the information and creates a vision of what the plant must do to compete (Step 4). The vision and goals are very general at this stage since no detailed analysis has been done. For example, the vision could be to create a high-performance plant with a skilled and empowered workforce, and a strong focus on customer service. The steering team should also identify key measures, such as response time and delivered quality, and determine the improvements needed to gain a market advantage.

At this stage, upper management must decide whether the findings and vision of the steering team warrant a more detailed study (Step 5). The managers on the steering team may have the power to decide themselves if the organization should turn their vision into reality. However, it is imperative that a senior group of managers, *representing all major functions of the firm*, provide input into this decision since the firm may be spending a great deal of money and effort if the project continues. In addition, any organizational change is likely to have a long-term and strategic impact on the firm. For these reasons, high-level and broad-based support for continuing the project is crucial.

If the project continues (Step 6)—and assuming that cells are part of the vision—the steering team has one critical decision to make. Should it review all products and manufacturing processes at the plant for a possible restructuring of the manufacturing system (wide scope), or should it directly concentrate on the feasibility of one or a few cells for a group of preselected products or parts (narrow scope)? The latter decision is more focused but less ambitious. A broad analysis of the plant, on the other hand, is less likely to create "suboptimization." Thus, as an open-ended factory review, it may yield greater overall performance gains.

The steering team now appoints project teams to carry out the analysis and design work. If, during the factory planning phase, cellular manufacturing appears appropriate for the plant, the project teams will identify products and resources for the cells. Many of the firm's management systems also need to be reviewed for possible modification, including planning and control, performance measurement, and compensation. This work continues during the initial cell level planning (Step 7). The project teams will also estimate detailed costs and benefits for the cell(s) (Step 8). This permits management to make an economically based decision regarding the cell project (Step 9). If the project teams fail to demonstrate that the cell project can generate sufficient benefits, it may be terminated at this point.

If the project continues, the next step is the final design and layout of each cell (Step 10). This involves the ultimate selection of the products, equipment, and people that will make up the cells. Concurrent with this, the project teams will need to lay the groundwork for implementing the cells, which includes involving and communicating with the workforce at large (Step 11).

Once a cell is physically in place, the process of improvement will begin (Step 12). The people working in the cell can make large contributions by way of concrete suggestions for modifications of equipment layout, procedures, and processes. Finally, the planning and implementation process is not complete until you perform a formal evaluation. This assessment should include not just the performance of the redesigned system, but also the process of planning and implementing the cell system (Step 13).

A 13-STEP BLUEPRINT FOR YOUR PLANNING PROCESS—THE DETAILS

We now return to the process outlined in Figure 4-1 and provide details on each of the 13 steps. Somewhat simplified, the planning process consists of five major sets of issues, most of which are dealt with sequentially: (1) strategic and organizational issues, (2) technical design, (3) infrastructure, (4) change management and implementation, and (5) improvement and performance assessment. These five areas are used to structure the discussion below.

Focus on Strategic and Organizational Issues (Steps 1–5)

Step 1a: Problem awareness

For change to happen, somebody in the organization must become aware that its performance is not meeting expectations. Signs of performance deficiencies tend to first emerge from the market. Examples include customer complaints, new competitors, slower sales, declining profitability, or comments by shareholders and business analysts. But the awareness of movements in the market, or performance gaps, is not always sufficient to overcome the inertia that exists in all organizations.[1]

The "handwriting on the wall"—which is easy to see in retrospect—may go unnoticed for an extended time. Often it takes an event that seriously threatens the company and forces it to rethink its strategy. This could be the loss of a major customer to a competitor, the displacement of the firm's core technology by a radically different way of doing things, or the appointment of a new top manager as part of a merger between two firms.² Events like these often initiate a formal strategic planning process or are used as important inputs to such a process (see Step 1b).

Managers within the manufacturing function, through readings, discussions with colleagues, seminar attendance, plant visits, and the like may realize that their operations fall short. The awareness of performance and capability gaps also can surface through new employees with experience of modernization projects, or by the threat of a loss (or an actual loss) of a key customer.

Based on these insights, the managers may decide to initiate an improvement project study without first going through a corporatewide strategic planning process (see Step 2).³ They may take this approach because they feel other functional managers will resist change, or because of their own lack of clear direction on the proper path to take. The main purpose of the study is to collect evidence useful for a strategic rethinking of the manufacturing function. Although these reasons may be legitimate, failing to involve other functions within the firm in setting overriding goals may lead to less than effective results in the end, a point emphasized in the following quote:

> A decision to install cells, unfortunately, is usually not made as part of answering the "Where do we want to go?" question at the enterprise level; it is usually the result of manufacturing people alone trying to reduce inventory, improve throughput, improve quality, reduce costs, or maybe even respond to customer demands. All could be good reasons for cells, but their connection to anything higher than plant goals is usually obscure. Making ties between market strategy and manufacturing strategy will ensure that cells are applied in the most profitable manner.⁴

We want to reiterate that a reorganization into cells brings strategic change to a firm. That is, it affects the firm's capabilities and associated performance for a long time to come. Hence, designing and implementing cells should involve not just the manufacturing function but rather be based on a companywide perspective that includes corporate and marketing strategies as well.

Step 1b: Corporate strategic planning

Firms with formalized planning processes usually conduct annual strategic planning sessions. These have several purposes: to rethink the organization's purpose and mission, to verify whether its stated goals have been met, to formulate new goals, to clarify its current direction, and to take action to alter this direction if found wanting.

Enterprise analysis. Declining sales or lowered customer satisfaction may not be enough to overcome corporate inertia. A typical reaction to such developments is, "Let's not overreact to what may be a normal variation in the marketplace!" It is therefore important that a firm's enterprise analysis goes beyond its own actual performance (see Figure 1-2). You must also look at the actions being taken by current and potential competitors to improve their internal capabilities. Likewise, you should routinely scan the business environment for events that can affect performance negatively, or that can strengthen it.

Most strategic planning processes, therefore, include some form of SWOT analysis (strength, weaknesses, opportunities, threats). The strengths/weaknesses aspect of the analysis compares the firm's internal capabilities with those of major current competitors. For example, a firm's ability to customize its products can be a strength. Likewise, its tendency to miss delivery due dates could be a serious weakness. The fit between a firm's product and market characteristics, and how market demands are met by the manufacturing system, are also covered in the strength/weakness analysis.

The threats/opportunities analysis, on the other hand, looks toward the future and to events outside the firm. For example, continually rising local labor costs can be a threat if other manufacturers can produce at lower cost. Conversely, lowered trade tariffs or the emergence of new information technologies can represent opportunities for the firm to improve its competitiveness.

A serious SWOT analysis should also include the whole supply chain. How material moves to, through, and from the firm is becoming increasingly important in determining market competitiveness. Designing the supply chain architecture includes deciding what to make and what to buy. These decisions, in turn, influence the product/process design choices.[5]

Closing the performance gaps. A corporate strategic analysis process usually begins with a gap analysis of unmet objectives (again, see Figure 1-2). Here you need to address the following questions:

1. *What* do we need to accomplish to be more competitive?

2. By *how much* must we improve?

3. By *when*?

For example, you may conclude that you cannot compete effectively because of slow response to customer inquiries. You may then decide that you need to (1) respond faster to inquiries, (2) to do so within 24 hours (compared to 72 hours now), and (3) accomplish this within six months. You can make such decisions based on market and competitor analysis, but this will not answer the question of *how* these goals are to be accomplished.

A strategy is the means by which a firm closes competitive gaps and answers the action-oriented question of "how?" The responses to the following three questions describe the strategy:

1. *How* are we going to accomplish the desired outcome?

2. By *how much* must we change to do this?

3. By *when* must we change?

Within the strategic planning process it is especially important to coordinate the marketing, manufacturing, and supply chain functions. These must all base their strategies on a solid understanding of what it takes to succeed in the marketplace. This forces you to identify critical "order winners," such as fast delivery or a wide product range. You also need to understand the obstacles to gaining entry into markets. For example, quality has in recent years been a typical "order qualifier" in that products below a minimum quality level are not competitive.

To develop a complete manufacturing strategy you must analyze the firm's operational capabilities: What do we do well, and what do we do less well? Only after this "soul-searching" can you finalize a strategy. Sometimes this calls for a special manufacturing capability study. In fact, Steps 1 through 4 in Figure 4-1 should be seen as the foundation for the manufacturing strategy formulation that is adopted at Step 5.

In summary, a firm's decisions regarding the products it will make, the technologies it will deploy, the markets it wishes to penetrate, the performance goals it plans to accomplish, and its vision of achieving all this should *precede* any decision to reorganize! In reality, this does not always occur. But if you don't think strategically, and with the whole organization in mind, cells may end up causing just a ripple in a local manufacturing area rather than delivering performance improvement at the business level. Or, as we quote elsewhere: "If manufacturing cells are not part of overall strategy of improvement in each department, they can have great local success but very little overall impact."[6] An example is building a cell to reduce component lead time. You might achieve great lead time and inventory reductions for the components in this cell, but the assembly process may still be held up by other components. Thus, the response time to market can remain unchanged for the product.

Step 2: Decision to initiate a manufacturing capability study

The starting point for change rests on the decision to pursue an analysis of the firm's manufacturing capabilities. As indicated in Figure 4-1 (Step 2), some companies decide to conduct a "manufacturing review" without first performing a formal study of the firm's inner and outer environments. Others reach this point after an initial strategic analysis has been completed.

When and how this decision is made may vary with the size of the company, the formality of its strategy planning process, its culture regarding change and improvement, and the competitiveness of its industry. Also, it is the plant and operations managers who initiate small and continuous changes to the manufacturing systems.[7] Conversely, initiatives to undertake large-scale changes are typically driven by corporate-level decisions involving mergers with other firms, launching of new product lines, or reshuffling of products among plants.

Some firms, particularly those that are small and nimble, proceed directly from the point of becoming aware of a problem (Step 1a) to a decision to study the company's manufacturing and/or business processes (Step 2). This was the case with Steward, Inc., a manufacturer of nickel zinc ferrite parts.[8] The company knew it needed to improve its delivery performance. To facilitate this, it had taken the unusual step of appointing its sales manager to the post of manufacturing director. However, the "catalytic event" that brought about the redesign of the work organization was a missed delivery that shut down the line at a major customer, the Packard Division of General Motors. Packard managers flew down to Steward to look at its operations first-hand. During the visit they suggested that Steward consider cellular manufacturing as a way to improve its operating performance. This convinced Steward's management to initiate an internal study of its manufacturing processes.

Taking a closer look at your company's capabilities in the operations area is a critical step in the adoption of cellular structures in offices and on the plant floor.

Some firms have a preconceived idea at this stage that cells are needed to improve operations. However, we think you are better off undertaking a study with an unbiased mind. The primary purpose should simply be to understand how the firm is operating, what is done well, and what is done poorly. The ideal outcome cannot be known at this point in time.

Step 3: High-level analysis of the factory's organization and performance

Once it is clear that the firm's manufacturing function needs to improve, the next logical step is to map out the current organization. You want to determine how critical business processes and their performance compare with those at other firms. You may already have done some of this gap analysis at Steps 1a or b. However, you now need to develop a better understanding of the firm's operational capabilities and weaknesses. Step 3 is only a first-pass data collection phase. Its main purpose is to let the steering team[9] clarify project goals and determine the future direction of the project. Detailed data collection and analysis are deferred until later.

The team will need to address five major questions during this high-level analysis phase:

1. What are our organization's strategic goals, metrics, and past performance?

2. What type of support will we get, and what type of limitations do we face, from upper management in our efforts to improve manufacturing capabilities?

3. How is our manufacturing function organized and performing? What are current processes and practices? Especially, what are our major competitors doing in the area of manufacturing?

4. What does the ideal factory look like from our point of view?

5. What design and performance goals should we establish for our plant?

We discuss the first three questions immediately below, while the fourth and fifth are covered in connection with our discussion of Step 6.

Strategic goals, metrics, and past performance. Before the steering team starts reviewing the manufacturing organization, it must reach consensus regarding (1) the firm's corporate mission and vision, (2) its current strategy, (3) its most important performance measures, and (4) its past and predicted performance along these metrics. This ensures that later decisions are coherent with the firm's overall strategic intent.

The corporate mission informs all stakeholders (shareholders, employees, customers, suppliers, etc.) of the organization's main purpose, and of its products, markets, competitive emphasis, and values. The vision statement usually provides the corporate goals, although often in vague and rather opaque form. Corporate vision statements are not very useful in guiding manufacturing decisions. The firm's strategy, finally, refers to the plans and actions taken to develop capabilities that the firm must possess in order to compete.

The performance measures at the corporate level tend to be financial or market-oriented in nature. Typical metrics includes annual profit, return on assets, sales per employee, and market shares for key product lines. As discussed under Step 1, market-oriented measures provide the first concrete signals that competitiveness is lagging. However, it is manufacturing as a business function that determines the quality of the products, their cost, and the timing of their deliveries (of course, both cost and quality are strongly dictated by product design). A firm must regularly track its performance along these dimensions to link declining sales to deficient manufacturing performance.

Speed is a measure of strategic importance. Although it has emerged as a key performance measure in recent years, many companies only pay lip service to its importance. In our experience, few firms actually measure customer response times or internal lead times.[10] Accordingly, performance deficiencies in that area tend to be based more on customer or salesperson testimonials, and managers' perceptions, than on actual data.

Managerial support and constraints. Upper management support is an essential element in successful change projects (see Chapters 15 and 16). Although no concrete action plans have been developed at this point in the planning process, you should try to assess the level of support for change and the resources that may be forthcoming. Limited support—and concrete limitations on the scope of the project, such as product lines involved, time limit for the project, and capital spending—will influence the outcome of the project.

Status of current processes and best industry practices. Although the steering team's members probably agree that the firm's manufacturing capabilities are not what they should be, the team needs to collect data to support this view.[11] It should begin by reviewing accessible in-house performance data. At this stage it is not necessary to dig deeply into available data; the purpose here is, simply, to form impressions about the plant's level of performance and whether it is good or poor. You may also observe internal practices, and interview managers and employees. Ask them, for example, about obstacles that prevent them from doing a better job. Employee perceptions of customers', suppliers', and fellow employees' satisfaction with current practices might also prove useful.

During this high-level phase, team members also need to use *benchmarking* to learn about the workings of other organizations. The idea is to learn how excellent organizations operate, and to make their processes the standards for your own firm. Data on other plants' performance also indicate the magnitude of possible improvement for your own plant. You can benchmark:

- *Performance.* For example, how does our ability for on-time delivery compare with our competitors?
- *Products.* For example, what features do our competitors offer that we don't?
- *Processes.* For example, how do industry leaders handle their order promising activities?

Performance data for a direct competitor are available through public documents, market research firms, or customers. However, a firm may be reluctant to let competitors study its internal processes. Therefore, benchmark studies of processes are often prepared by visiting noncompetitors. For example, the first known example of benchmarking involved the Xerox Corporation's study of the mail order firm L. L. Bean's order-picking and warehousing operations.[12]

Members of the steering team also can learn about current practices by reading books and journal articles, or watching training videos. Seminars and workshops focusing on cells, JIT, lean manufacturing, and so on are good complements because they allow for interaction with speakers and fellow attendees. Companies also often learn about other firms' products through reverse engineering (i.e., tearing them apart to study how they are designed and manufactured). For this learning period to be effective, the team members should hold intensive discussions about what they have seen and read in order to determine the practices most useful for their own plant.

A best-practices review may make the team realize that the firm is worse off than originally thought. If so, this can give the team a sense of urgency that helps move the project along. Very effective, in serving as a catalyst for change, are visits to other plants to observe them in action. Bringing in experts to critically analyze your plant can serve the same purpose. Because of the "not invented here"(NIH) syndrome, however, this form of review is effective only if management and employees alike are truly open to change.

Step 4: Formulation of vision and goals for the new manufacturing organization

After a process of review and discussion, the steering team should formulate its vision of the future manufacturing organization. This "picture" could be rather unspecific and flexible, setting boundaries and directions rather than specifying concrete solutions. Up to this point, the team has mostly focused on business/organizational issues and has not done any deeper analysis of the firm's internal operations. While it should have developed a clear understanding of what is wrong, it may not know the best solution. However, during its search for knowledge about modern practices, and by benchmarking other firms, the team may have seen certain elements of organizational design repeat themselves in successful firms. One such element could be the deployment of a cellular organization.

An important part of the vision formulation process is an "analysis of fit," i.e., assessing the pros and cons of various improvement strategies. This assessment could include whether, and how, cellular manufacturing can contribute to corporate goals. If it can, the team can stipulate in its status report (Step 5) that the vision for the new manufacturing system should have cellular manufacturing as one of its foundations. Alternatively, the team may simply consider cells as an alternative solution in future investigations.

The steering team also sets goals and constraints. Formulating goals and constraints is far more difficult when the analysis involves the whole factory than when it is limited to a product line or a group of components. Companies frequently set lead time reduction goals using NRNs—"nice round numbers." In our experience, the most frequently used goal is 50 percent (conveniently located right between 0 and 100). Using the same targets for all products may be unrealistic unless resources are plentiful. Rather, it is better that the steering team outlines a broad vision for the company and suggests numeric goals only for key areas known to be troublesome. In order to set achievable targets, goals for other products should not be formulated pending further analysis.

Step 5: Decision to continue the project

Step 5 is the point in the planning process where a go/no go decision is made. At this stage, upper management may decide whether a manufacturing restructuring is desirable and if more time, and ultimately "real money," should be spent on the project. This step does not always exist, however. In some cases, the steering team continuously assesses the project's potential and can terminate it at any time. In other cases, a formal decision is delayed until more analysis has been done (see Step 9). However, we have inserted Step 5 in the planning and implementation process to highlight the importance of having a formal, high-level review somewhere at this juncture.

A decision to discontinue further analysis of the firm's operations should require strong evidence that the company, in fact, already possesses superior capabilities. This evidence should be based on competitor analysis and customer input, and rest on both quantitative and qualitative data. A "softer" alternative to termination is to return to Steps 3 or 4 for a reformulation of the vision and the strategy. A positive decision, on the other hand, represents a commitment from upper management to support the project. Accordingly, one good reason to have a decision point at this stage in the process is for the project champion to force management to reveal the strength of its commitment. Nobody is well served by a project that continues without solid management support.

Step 5 is also an opportunity for upper management and the steering team to *jointly* refine the scope of the project, select metrics to determine project success, and set quantitative goals. Once the project continues into a more intensive phase, it will require many hours by many people. If the project proceeds without review, upper management loses an early opportunity to influence its direction.

At the review meeting, the steering committee presents its findings to a management group drawn from various functions. The following areas should be covered:

1. The organization's current strengths and weaknesses from an operations perspective.
2. Suggestions on which of the identified gaps should be closed, and by how much.
3. A vision of what the organization needs to look like to be competitive (including performance goals).
4. The scope of the continued study.
5. The project's organization and staffing.
6. The time and resources required to complete the study.
7. Rough cost/benefit projections.
8. Possible obstacles to the successful completion of the project.

We discussed the vision and the goals earlier. Next we cover three other items on the review agenda: scope, project organization, and cost/benefits.

Scope if project continues. The decision at Step 5 places the company at a very important crossroad. It can, on the one hand, select a wide project scope. The aim then is to rethink and revitalize *the whole plant*—its products, processes, layout, technology, organization, and systems. The outcome would be a master plan for upgrading the whole manufacturing system, or at least a large part of it. Another option, if the conditions appear favorable to cells, is to proceed with a feasibility study focused on only *one product or product line.* This more narrow scope may result in a single cell only.

Both the factorywide approach and the narrow scope have pros and cons. The main advantage with analyzing the whole factory is that, due to the need to integrate material and information flows, you will likely get a more efficient and effective solution. Companies disappointed with their cell experience typically have failed to move beyond "islands of improvement" on the factory floor. Such islands, as discovered by Boeing and other firms, tend to emerge when cells are developed independently rather than through a comprehensive factory analysis.[13]

The downside of a factorywide analysis is the time and effort involved. Only a small segment of the company's products may be threatened by competition. Rather than reviewing the whole plant, it could therefore be more expedient to just solve the problem immediately at hand. A firm with a bias for action, especially one without previous experience of cells, is likely to choose the narrow-scope option rather than a full-scale factory study.

Other considerations influence the choice between small- and large-scale projects. One obvious example is when the plant does not yet exist. In such "greenfield" situations the whole factory is designed from scratch, and the narrow-scope option has no meaning. For existing plants, the complexity of the material flow pattern can affect the choice. In plants that have grown slowly over time, and where space has been added as needed, you tend to find highly inefficient layouts. Sooner or later a complete factory review makes sense.

In some plants equipment is large and heavy, requires special floor foundations or ventilation hookups, and may be sensitive to movement. In those cases, a careful analysis of the plant and its future is in order before any equipment is relocated (see Chapter 16 for a discussion of how to deal with such "monuments"). On the other hand, in light industry like electronics or textiles, you can create a pilot assembly cell in the morning and modify it in the afternoon.

Needless to say, available resources also influence the scope of the project. Constraints can take the form of restricted capital available for the project, the time available for the analysis, the number of people that can make up the core team, and so on.

Organizing for change. An important part of the decision to continue concerns project management. You'll need to answer questions such as: "What type of organizational structure should we set up for a project of this kind?" "Who should be involved, and for how long?" And, above all, "Who should be in charge?" Projects that affect multiple business functions should be organized with one cross-functional steering team, and one or more cross-functional project teams.[14] The steering team represents strategic thinking, the companywide integrated perspective, managerial wisdom, and managerial authority. This team is typically composed of 4 to 10 managers from various areas within the firm. It can also include external consultants.

The purpose of the steering team is to guide rather than to act: to provide vision and direction for the project teams, specify project goals and timelines, secure resources for these teams, serve as a sounding board for ideas, evaluate the project teams' analyses and recommendations, and support the implementation of chosen solutions. (As discussed, we are assuming that a steering committee has done the high-level analysis leading up to the decision in Step 5.)

The project teams, on the other hand, are the "doers." They perform the actual investigative work, collect and analyze data, identify alternative solutions, evaluate solutions, present their findings to the steering committee, and, in most cases, make detailed plans for design and implementation of the recommended changes. Future cell operators and supervisors should participate in these activities. Representatives for suppliers, customers, and equipment vendors may also be tied to the project teams and actually serve as members.

The steering committee selects the leader for each project team. These leaders then report to the steering committee. An alternative is to make the team leader for each project group a member of the steering team. The role of the team leader is weighty and includes:

- Being the project champion
- Choosing team members so that an effective team is created
- Delegating responsibilities
- Inspiring the team to accomplish great things in the face of uncertainty
- Being an effective communicator to members both within and outside the team

Team leaders are perhaps the most critical part of the project, so you must choose these individuals carefully. (Chapter 15 covers project management in greater detail.)

Rough cost/benefit projections. Because very little detailed planning has been done up to this point, it is typically not possible to present a credible economic analysis of the project. However, you can determine rough estimates of project costs and associated benefits to get a feeling of the possible economic gains. As noted in Figure 4-1, a detailed estimation of the economic value of cells is deferred to Step 8 in the planning process.

ILLUSTRATING THE FIRST FIVE STEPS

Since we will not discuss the early steps in the planning and implementation process in future chapters, we feel it is valuable to illustrate how some firms have dealt with the first five steps of the process. We will refer to some of these companies later in this chapter.

Capability Studies Driven by Corporate Strategic Mandates

The Beta group. Beta is a large industrial group, a leader in the manufacturing of cooking, refrigeration, and washing appliances.[15] It has more than 20 manufacturing sites in six European countries. Beta had experienced large growth through acquisitions, and in the early 90s required that all companies in the group review their manufacturing and distribution systems. One company in the Beta group, Alfa, produces kitchen appliances using a workforce of approximately 1,000 employees. Alfa felt it was competitive with respect to cost, but deficient with respect to response time and service. Numerous late deliveries had started to erode the company's image. As a consequence, Alfa's management decided to investigate whether a reorganization of the production system would lead to shorter lead times and whether more reliable production planning and control techniques could be implemented.

A plant making washing machines was selected as a test bed for this project, both because of the importance of the products and because of the division's poor delivery performance. The scope of the capability study was broad. All aspects of the production system were to be examined from technical, managerial, and organizational viewpoints. All suggested changes were candidates for implementation. The constraints, however, were that costs were not to increase and current flexibility and agility were not to be lost. Cellular manufacturing was identified early on as a way to achieve the stated goals.

Zanussi. Like Alfa, Zanussi is a member of a large European industrial group, in this case the Electrolux Corporation.[16] When Electrolux took charge of the company in the late 80s, its mission was to become a market leader. It already had improvement programs underway in all its subsidiaries. Electrolux was making large investments in new products and process technologies, and $90 million was allocated to the redesign of one of Zanussi's plants.

This plant was going to make refrigerators for domestic use, utilizing state-of-the-art technology. It was also charged with delivering a product at significantly lower cost than its domestic and foreign competitors, and with significantly reduced delivery times. Plant management discovered at an early stage that to overcome the traditional productivity-flexibility dilemma they needed to capitalize on similarities in design and manufacturing. This pointed to cellular manufacturing. Furthermore, they also realized that cellular structures would allow the efficient use of new technologies, such as robotics and automated material-handling systems.

Ingersoll Cutting Tool Company. Ingersoll is a privately held manufacturer of cutting tools and tool inserts. Faced with new competitors and demands from customers to reduce response times, the owner had decided that all lead times should be reduced by 50 percent.[17] The company's tool insert division had worked for several years with the University of Wisconsin-Madison, and had implemented improvement projects on a regular basis. It had achieved great success with an order-processing cell in the office,[18] and wanted to investigate whether the cellular concept could apply to its manufacturing facility as well. The manufacturing capability study was driven by a combination of management decree and a routine "culture of improvement." Although the subsequent analysis investigated different alternatives that could meet the stated lead-time reduction goal, divisional management saw cellular manufacturing as the solution from the start. This was partly due to the positive experience of the office cell, and the conviction that team-based manufacturing was the way to operate in the future.

Capability Studies Driven by Catalytic Events

Cast Iron Components. This 230-employee plant makes components made of cast iron and steel that are shipped to a sister plant for use in assembled products.[19] A decade ago, the corporation had lost a major customer account, and also failed to win a desired new account. In both cases, the customers went to competitors—allegedly due to Cast Iron's poor product quality, weak delivery performance, and inferior technical support. These events led to the formation of a plant-level steering committee. This committee, by reading and visiting other firms, began studying the management of successful plants. A decision was taken to adopt a long-term improvement program focused on total quality management (TQM). Most of the successful plants studied by the steering committee had employed cells, so Cast Iron Components decided that this strategy should form an integral part of its program as well.

Sheet Metal Products. In the mid-80s, Sheet Metal Products was engaged in the manufacture of both sheet metal products and assembled printed circuit boards.[20] When corporate management decided to focus all plants, circuit board production was transferred to another factory. Taking advantage of this corporate reorganization, plant management at Sheet Metal Products initiated a study to analyze the material flows and the layout in the plant. It had experienced long lead times, large inventories, and low service levels. In addition, it faced large workers' compensation expenses due to injuries related to the loading and unloading of containers at forming and welding operations. The plant chose cellular manufacturing as the best way to overcome these performance problems and reduce the level of repetitive motion injuries.

The Assembly and Test Center (ATC). ATC is a department within a large corporation responsible for the assembly and testing of electronic equipment.[21] ATC annually manufactures about $100 million dollars worth of products, characterized by a high-mix, low-volume pattern. Sales had been flat or declining in recent years. While the existing customer base was eroding, new markets with new customer requirements were opening up. A small, informal team consisting of the department manager and a few of his production managers and engineers recognized the problems. This team spent some time conducting an enterprise analysis during which it interviewed customers and key personnel inside the division and collected data on competitors.

The team concluded that the department needed to be redesigned—a decision approved by upper management. After expanding the core team to include more representatives from engineering, accounting, production planning and control, and the shop floor, the team spent six months developing a new operating vision for the department. The key elements of this vision included:

- Strong external focus
- Work easily with internal and external customers
- On-time delivery
- Control variances at the source (i.e., problems should be solved where they occur by those directly involved)

- Ensure healthy environment
- Produce low-cost products

ATC's manager was newly appointed and, as often is the case, served as the catalyst for change. Due to a less-than-successful reorganization in which he had participated earlier, and which he attributed to a process of "forced change," he stipulated from the start that the analysis and redesign process should be participatory and inclusive. This lead to the involvement of many employees on the project teams. In the continued analysis, cells emerged as a solution that could support the stated vision.

Summary of Steps 1 through 5

In the preceding text box ("Illustrating the First Five Steps"), the companies' decisions to review their manufacturing organization and processes were in most cases triggered by corporate concerns. Thus, corporate dissatisfaction with financial or market-related performance, and a belief that weak performance can be attributed to inferior operations, can lead to mandates to improve at local levels. Likewise, for a multiplant corporation, a consolidation process of focusing (and closing) plants, and shuffling production between facilities, inevitably creates an opportunity—in fact, a mandate—for a review of each individual plant's manufacturing organization. Consolidations of this type can be triggered by merger and acquisition activities or profitability concerns.

Referring back to Figure 4-1, we see that corporate decisions (Step 1b) caused plant management to take a close look at manufacturing operations (Steps 2 through 5). Interestingly, in all of these firms, cellular manufacturing was identified very early on as a model for the reorganization. In some cases this was done by corporate management, in others by plant management.

Focus on Technical and Infrastructural Design Issues (Steps 6-10)

Step 6: Factory planning

The issue of wide versus narrow scope revisited. A firm may undertake an analysis and redesign of the plant as a whole, and then proceed to implement a large-scale plan. Alternatively, it can skip a factorywide analysis and directly study the feasibility of one (or possibly more) cells for chosen product families. We have already discussed why firms may choose one approach or the other. The danger of planning for a single product or product line is that it may lead to a "suboptimization" of the manufacturing system. However, this option, if it turns out to be a positive experience, can later lead to a full-scope analysis of the firm (see the feedback loops leading from Step 13 in Figure 4-1).

Alfa, Zanussi, and ATC (see the earlier textbox) elected to focus their efforts on all of their products and processes. Thus, the goal was to reengineer the production systems in their totality. In contrast, the other three firms followed a simpler approach. They narrowed the scope of the study to an important product line (e.g., one that represented a major portion of revenues) that had either demonstrated or showed the potential for performance degradation with respect to critical variables. As a result, these plants designed and implemented cells one at a time.

Except for green-field plants, most firms do in fact implement cells sequentially rather than all at once, even if a master plan has been laid for the factory. Specifically, about 80 to 85 percent of plants that have cellular manufacturing in place design their cells on an ad-hoc basis and implement them one-by-one (that is, they take the narrow view of factory planning). However, the remaining plants, which do undertake comprehensive factory planning, also phase the cells into the plant facility one at a time.[22] This gradual "cell phasing" allows plants to apply the lessons learned from early cell implementations to subsequent efforts.

The factory planning process. There are several outcomes of factorywide planning:

- One or more product or part families are identified (often based on samples of products and parts rather than on complete populations), each associated with equipment and labor assigned to a cell.

- One or more alternative layout plans are created for the factory. Each layout will show the location of the cells, the support facilities, and the part of the functional organization that remains unchanged (detailed layout planning for the cells occurs at Steps 7 and 11 of the planning process). If the cells are to be implemented sequentially over time, the layout can exist in different versions, each showing the state of the plant after each new cell has been put in place.

- A new organizational structure is proposed for the cell system, and rough plans are developed for how various management systems are to be redesigned to handle the cell system. For example:
  - How does the cost accounting system's need for data fit with the cell operation?
  - How should cell performance be measured, and by whom?
  - How should cell employees be compensated?
  - How should quality inspection be conducted, and by whom?
  - How should preventative maintenance be conducted, and by whom?
  - How should cell scheduling and staffing be conducted, and by whom?
  - How should vendor deliveries be planned, and by whom?

While working on defining cells and creating layouts, project teams will face trade-offs. These typically come down to spending more money on resources to simplify material-flow control and add extra capacity. For example, you can achieve better control by creating fully independent cells, but this may require investment in lowly utilized equipment. On the other hand, you will get faster flow times and lower inventories if more equipment is put in the cell. Similarly, inefficient layouts may be the result of space constraints, and none of the available layout choices may be ideal. Investing in added space is the trade-off.

Faced with such dilemmas, planning teams must decide which products and equipment to include in cells and which should remain unchanged. As part of the process of fitting products, equipment, tooling, and people into workable cellular structures, the teams must consider not just routing changes but also whether out-sourcing and/or product redesign will create better cells and a better overall system.[23]

The factory-planning phase will inevitably involve many people, and it will become evident to everybody, directly or through the rumor mill, that something is going on. If it does not yet exist, this is the time to establish open, multichannel communication. This should involve *frequent messages* directed towards *all employees* regarding the factory reorganization project (see Chapter 15).

Step 7: Initial cell level planning

One or more cells may emerge from the macro-analysis of the plant at Step 6. If so, as indicated in Figure 4-1, each potential cell is then planned in more detail at Step 7 and Step 10. This separation of detailed planning into two phases allows for a second formal project assessment at Step 9, at which point management can decide to proceed with, or terminate, any or all cells planned so far.

The aim at Step 7 is to finalize the cell design to the point where you can do a solid cost/benefit analysis. This calls for the complete selection of parts or products for the cell family. While factorywide planning may have considered samples of parts only, detailed planning looks at all relevant parts. The type of equipment needed to process the family is also chosen so the cell can be "dimensioned," meaning the cell's required output capacity is translated into the need for people and equipment (see Chapter 6). Dimensioning the cell has a direct impact on both its cost and its performance, and therefore on its economic value. Step 7 further involves fine-tuning any management system issues left unresolved.

You should also reconsider the *project organization* at this stage. The teams that did the initial factory analysis may not be the best for finalizing the cell design and planning the implementation. First of all, employees who will work in the cells, or in other ways are directly affected by the switch to cells, should be on the core project teams. Thus, operators and supervisors, at minimum, should take part in implementation planning. Since you must also modify planning and information systems, employees in those areas should be involved in the project as well. Second, you will need new employee skills for the activities that follow. For example, moving equipment on the shop floor, preparing foundations and utilities, and installing equipment in the cell typically require both experienced plant personnel and outside contractors.

The Assembly and Test Center (ATC) discussed earlier represents an interesting example of how project teams can change composition. During the factorywide planning phase the project organization consisted of one steering team and several project teams. The latter were not organized along cells but were focused on a function or a specific task. There were five project teams: a business analysis team, an assembly analysis team, a test analysis team, a social analysis team, and a metrics analysis team.

Each project team was charged with investigating different aspects of the organization and coming up with recommendations. Once an agreement was reached on how the plant should be organized, including both manufacturing and support personnel, and the project continued towards implementation, the previous project teams were dissolved and replaced by teams affiliated with the cells. Their task was to conduct the detailed design and implementation planning for each cell.

Step 8: Determining fit and cost/benefits for the cells

The decision to proceed with the plant analysis, taken at Step 5, is based on general advantages and disadvantages and, possibly, on rough cost/benefit estimations. After having identified products, equipment, and staffing levels, laid out the cells, and analyzed the need to modify the current management systems, it is now possible to determine investment and operating costs in more detail. In addition, you can estimate expected cost savings from planned reductions in inventory, labor, scrap, and other activities, and possibly increased revenues due to improved performance. Based on these cost/benefit data, the cell project can be economically justified.

Besides the economic analysis, you need to consider the issue of the cells' "fit" with the firm's vision for the factory, and with existing processes, systems, and culture. In fact, this analysis should precede the economic analysis (see Chapter 8 for details).

Step 9: Decision to proceed with detailed cell design and implementation planning

This decision point is the last hurdle in the process towards cell implementation. If the economic analysis conducted in Step 8 indicates insufficient net benefits, the project could terminate here. However, if a pilot cell was chosen at Step 5, considerable leeway could exist in determining whether you need to meet economic targets. In other words, management may be willing to pay for the experience gained from the first cell. If several cells are planned at this stage, a go-ahead may be given for some cells while plans for others are held back. As the feedback loops in Figure 4-1 indicate, the project teams then could revisit previous steps to redo the process and economic analyses. A decision to proceed would revisit and refine:

- *Project scope.* For example, which cells should be prioritized for implementation and which should be abandoned or delayed?
- *Project goals.* For example, what metrics should be used to determine success, and what targets should be set?
- *Timeline.* For example, when should we begin and end the remaining project activities?

Step 10: Continued detailed cell level planning

The great American architect Ludwig Mies van der Rohe once said, "God is in the details." This signifies the beauty of a finished piece of work where everything fits together and elegant details accentuate the construction as a whole. Before one reaches such a divine state, however, a more appropriate saying for any large project is that "The Devil is in the details." That is, although you may have put much effort into planning the project, and made many critical choices along the way, numerous detailed design issues remain before you can begin the actual implementation.

At Step 10, the design of each cell will be finalized. This means fine-tuning the part or product families, selecting and documenting process routings, acquiring equipment and tooling, and completing the internal cell layout. The latter specifies the location of processing equipment, material-handling equipment, work areas, materials and tool storage, and visual control boards. You must also consider the material flows into and out of each cell so that the system as a whole, and not just each individual cell, is "optimized." (Chapter 6 describes this part of the detailed cell design process in more depth.)

During the detailed planning phase, you need to firm up many practical details regarding implementation. This means preparing the factory facilities and offices for cells, determining the time for moving equipment and people, making sure the customers get supplied during the start-up phase, and increasing the involvement of the plant's employees.

Finally, this is also the time to start planning a broad and formal education and training process. The members of the previous teams have learned much through visiting other firms, attending seminars, and being engaged in the planning process. You should now begin an education process for the rest of the company's managers, for personnel that may become future cell operators, leaders, supervisors, and support staff, and probably also for the plant as a whole.

Focus on Change Management and Implementation Issues (Step 11)

Step 11: Implementing cells

Unlike what is shown in Figure 4-1, the implementation phase actually proceeds in conjunction with several of the planning activities. In fact, we think of implementation as beginning once any planned change has been put into action. For example, once you have announced job openings in the cells to the employees, and they either bid for the jobs or are selected for them, implementation has begun. This tends to be one of the earliest implementation steps. Before that, though, management and supervisors often go through an education program to help them with the pending changes. If that is the first planned step to be executed, then implementation begins at that time. The ultimate implementation event, naturally, takes place when you have physically created a cell. With operators in place and infrastructural elements working, the start-up may begin.

The goal for an implementation is always to reach full-scale operation as soon as possible, but without "undue" cost to the firm or its employees. Full-scale operation is when a cell operates "according to expectation." This means it meets its stated performance goals, and that the employees are doing all the tasks according to the job design plan (see Chapter 12). Achieving these goals can take time, depending on several factors. Foremost is the issue of scope. If you are implementing multiple cells, bringing them up to speed takes longer than if a single cell is put in place. Likewise, a cell operating with a team of employees takes longer to implement successfully than does a cell that operates with a single employee. Also, the more new tasks you assign to cell employees—along with the requisite education, training, practice, and possibly certification—the longer it takes to reach targeted performance.

It is natural for surprises to occur during the implementation phase, especially if the project involves many individuals, products, and cells. Any good project leader knows and anticipates this, and prepares to deal with the unexpected. However, careless and incomplete planning can lead to inordinate difficulties—something you want to avoid. The very first cell implementation, of course, is likely to go less smoothly than the second, and so on, since the organization learns from the mistakes.

Our research shows that both positive and negative surprises will arise during cell implementation.[24] However, the longer it takes to reach the goals for the cells, the greater the risk for potential opposition among operators, supervisors, and managers alike. Resentment and frustration among the employees can impede or halt implementation all together. Rapid success is critical, especially if cellular manufacturing represents a new and unexplored area for the firm. (Chapters 15 and 16 deal with implementation issues in more detail.)

Focus on Performance and Improvement Issues (Steps 12–13)

Step 12: Improvement and evolution of existing cells

Organizations are typically in a state of constant change. Even the most careful design and implementation process cannot avoid errors or mistakes. Because it is often difficult to visualize a reality you have not seen, you will usually end up making many minor improvements to the cells after implementation. For example, operators may find better locations for tools, materials, and equipment once they actually work in the cell. Small changes can then be made to the layout. Likewise, you may detect that some parts in the family would fit the cell better (i.e., avoid outside operations or revisits to previous process steps) if they were redesigned.

The introduction of new products over time means a cell will be required to manufacture products or components for which it was not originally designed. Such changes often necessitate large, evolutionary modifications to the design of the cell's processes, including its associated management systems. Both small process improvements and evolutionary modifications are critical in order to extend the lives of cells—especially when faced with constant product, market, and technological changes. The cell life cycle is covered more fully in Chapter 17.

Step 13: Evaluation of planning process and cell performance

An assessment of a cell begins immediately after it has been put into operation. With evaluation, however, we refer to *formal* activities that (a) collect and summarize data on a cell's performance and compare it with the goals for the cell, and (b) collect and summarize data on the conduct and execution of the planning and implementation process. The purpose of the latter evaluation is to learn from mistakes in order to do better next time. Here you would review such things as the project's organization, the steps it went through, the duration of each phase, the type of expertise required on the teams, and the need for resources. The purpose of the performance data review, on the other hand, is to ensure that you have met targets or to highlight the need for corrective action.

You also can use an evaluation to decide on future cells. For example, if you have only implemented a single pilot cell at this stage, the experience gathered during the implementation process, together with the cell's achieved performance, can influence a decision on further cells (see the feedback loop from Step 13 in Figure 4-1). Sometimes, companies are reluctant to conduct *post-implementation audits* of this kind for the fear that poor performance will be used against those in charge of the planning process. However, audits are vital to the organization. Without the insights they provide you lose the full learning potential, especially for the project managers and for those approving reorganization projects.

It is important that you don't collect performance data too early after the implementation, or you may draw conclusions that are not valid in the long term. Typically, several months must pass before you can really know how a new cell performs. You should also collect data at several points in time—say after one month, three months, six months, etc.—so you can determine the trend. Many firms are impatient, and if they see clear performance improvements they may not wait for more reliable data before continuing with cell implementations. The Steward Company discussed earlier is an extreme case in point. Rather than waiting for a scheduled six-month review of the prototype cell, management decided after two weeks to implement other cells still at the planning stage.[25]

KEY INSIGHTS

- *It is important that you have a blueprint of the planning process when embarking on a reorganization project.* Knowing the big picture (as outlined in Figure 4-1) makes for a better understanding of how, why, and when various planning steps fit into the process, and what to expect along the way.

- *The planning and implementation process covers many steps.* However, we reiterate that you may not go through all the steps (or you may spend very little time on some of them), and may not execute them in the order we have described. In fact, some firms go directly from Step 1 to Step 7.

- *The planning process is hierarchical in that the level of detail gets finer and finer as you move through the steps.* As you get closer to implementation, the employees involved tend to be at lower and lower organizational levels (see Figure 4-2). Without the participation of employees, you'll miss out on valuable information that would otherwise strengthen and speed up your planning and implementation process. The information you receive from employees also will help you avoid unnecessary improvement adjustments following implementation.

- *You must make four critical decisions during the planning process.* Each decision is based on a different amount of data and problem knowledge (see Figure 4-3). At each decision step, the project can be either terminated or continued. Thus, management is forced to make explicit its support for the project (or lack thereof). If the project continues, its scope can be refined, its goals revised, and the circle of people involved in it expanded.

- *Designing and implementing cells is a process that touches on most aspects of the organization.* As we implied already in Chapter 1, doing it right means you need to consider strategic, economic, technical, managerial, and human issues affecting the organization. Ignoring any one element can have a negative impact on your ultimate success with cellular manufacturing.

- *No cell is forever.* Don't assume that if you go through the planning and implementation process once (Figure 4-1), you do not have to do it again. Rather, *expect* that cells, and the whole manufacturing plant, will be revised and redesigned as products, process, and information technologies change.

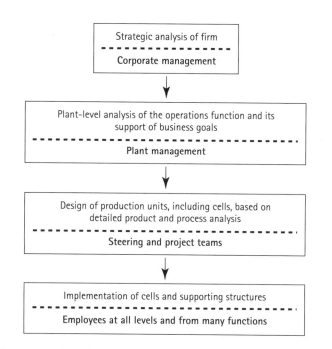

Figure 4-2. Organizational levels involved in the planning process

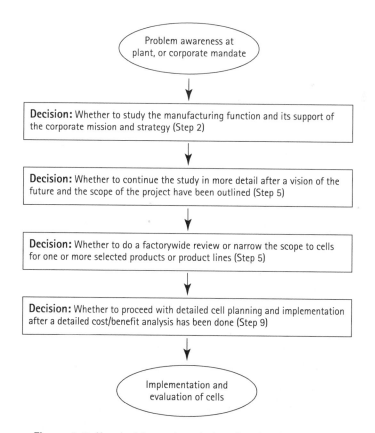

Figure 4-3. Key decision points during the planning process

5

Factory Planning

In Chapter 4 we outlined a complete process for analyzing your manufacturing operations to make them more competitive. This chapter discusses the step we call *factory planning* in more depth (see the shaded area in Figure 5-1). The main purpose of factory planning is to develop a plant organization that can meet the goals and expectations stated by management. Since a factory analysis can be very broad, we narrow the perspective by assuming that the firm has targeted cellular manufacturing as an option to be analyzed. This is in keeping with our view that cells should be adopted unless proven unsuitable for the situation at hand.

Here are the key questions we address in this chapter:

- What is the process by which you map out and come to understand the current AS IS situation at your factory?

- What types of analysis tools and techniques are available to project teams assigned with the task of reviewing and upgrading factory performance?

- Why should you, and how can you, identify opportunities for focused manufacturing (including cells)?

- What techniques are available for designing cells, and what types of goals and constraints should you apply to that process?

- What is the process of rethinking the factory layout after a conversion to cells?

AN OVERVIEW OF FACTORY PLANNING

Factory planning encompasses three related areas: (1) identifying opportunities for restructuring the work organization into cells; (2) designing a new factory layout to accommodate cells; and (3) modifying the firm's management systems[1] to align them with the new work organization and layout. We will concentrate mainly on the first area, especially on how you can make the plant more product-focused and how you can identify cells. We also briefly discuss factory layout. (More detailed cell design and layout issues are covered in Chapter 6). Though management systems usually are not paid much attention until after you have identified cells, they are crucial drivers of performance improvements. Given their importance, we devote several full chapters to management system design (Chapters 9 through 14).

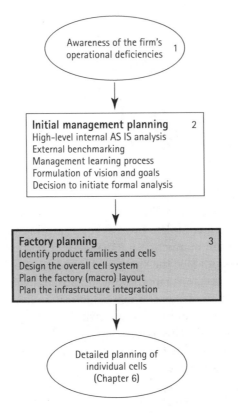

Figure 5-1. The planning and implementation process—a macro perspective

Making Sense of a Mess

Figure 5-2 shows, in bold, the three major phases of factory planning, as well as a preceding phase—*making sense of a mess*. This term requires a brief explanation. If you are given an organizational problem to solve, you initially face a mess. In other words, you may know the areas in which your firm is deficient, and may even suspect what the underlying causes may be, but still not know what the *real* problems are or how to tackle them. Therefore, in the early phases of a project, any team struggles to make sense of the mess. During this period the project team collects much data, and continual data analysis and subjective reasoning help the team to carry out its charge. Obviously, if the steering team decides to take a narrow perspective on factory planning (i.e., by focusing on a single product or product line), the mess is less daunting than would be the case if a wide scope were chosen.

Russell Ackoff, an authority on problem solving, is the originator of what can be called "the mess management theory." According to him, problem messes can be resolved, solved, or dissolved.[2]

These concepts apply very well to problems in manufacturing, which usually are first *resolved* by seat-of-the-pants decision-making. For example, late orders or lack of materials typically are handled one-by-one, without anybody thinking about them in a systematic fashion.

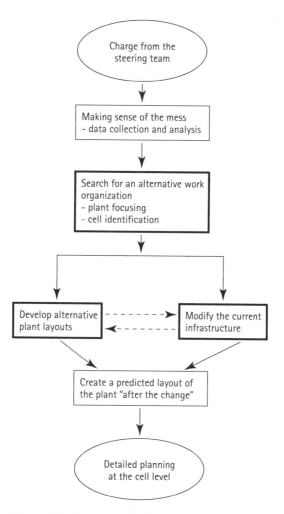

Figure 5-2. Roadmap for factory planning

Sooner or later, however, you may tire of dealing with recurring problems and decide to solve them once and for all. Suppose that late manufacturing orders are a big problem in the factory. In response, you bring in a sophisticated computerized software package to deal with the complex problem of scheduling orders. More likely than not, however, the problems will remain (and new problems may even surface).

Rather than trying to *deal with complex problems through complex solutions*, a better way may be to dissolve the very source of the problem. Performance problems have their roots in the way manufacturing systems are designed and operated. Therefore, your best problem-solving approach may be to restructure work into smaller, more focused units you can manage more easily. *Dissolving the functional organization, and replacing it with a cellular structure, can turn messes into manageable systems.*

The experience at the Gas Equipment Factory of the South African firm Afrox, a manufacturer of gas welding equipment, illustrates mess management.[3] Over a 20-year period the factory had grown from 2,400 to 9,500 square meters (from 25,830 to 102,260 square feet) and was making over 1,000 variations of products on some

300 machine tools. To meet foreign competition, the firm needed to reduce costs and sought to accomplish this by implementing an MRP system. However, this system failed to reduce cost to the necessary degree. Afrox then chose to dissolve organizational complexity as the way to lower manufacturing costs. This led to the adoption of cells.

Data Analysis to Understand the Mess and Support the Redesign

During the making-sense-of-the-mess phase, you need to collect large amounts of both quantitative and qualitative data. Although the steering team already may have assembled some data, most will be new. The data you collect depend on the type of analysis your team is asked to do, and how much detail you want to pursue. These issues ideally should be decided at the outset. In reality, however, the analysis process is often iterative. Analysis of one type of data may make you realize that more detailed data, or data of another type, need to be reviewed as well. We separate the "mess phase" into three steps:

1. Confirming the course.
2. Understanding the current situation.
3. Modifying product and part families.

During the first two steps you reach consensus on project goals and collect background data to get a clear picture of what is going on in the plant (getting a grip on the mess). The third step involves simplifying the product and part base. The last step may precede or be performed simultaneously with the plant focus/cell identification phase (see Figure 5-2).

Table 5-1 lists various types of analyses a project team may undertake. Although you should always do a project clarification, it is not necessary to perform all of the listed analyses. However, the more of them you do, the better you will understand the *as is* situation at the plant. This will better equip you to generate a blueprint for the new organization. We discuss each of the analysis areas in turn in the next three sections. (You may want to refer back to Table 5-1 as we proceed.)

Table 5-1. Possible types of analyses to conduct during factory planning

1. **Confirming the course**
   - Clarification of project scope, metrics, and associated goals

2. **Understanding the current situation**
   - Family grouping analysis
   - Product-volume analysis
   - Performance analysis
   - Resource/technology analysis
   - Capacity-load and bottleneck analysis
   - Space analysis
   - Material-flow analysis
   - Process flow analysis (process mapping)

3. **Modifying product and part families**
   - Product rationalization (standardization) analysis
   - Make/buy (outsourcing) analysis

CONFIRMING THE COURSE

The vision formulated by the steering team should guide the project team as it starts its investigation. It is important that the team fully understands the problems, goals, constraints, and scope of the project. It should thoroughly discuss these issues and not proceed until there is a consensus on where the firm should be heading. You can avoid design solutions that conflict with the overall strategy of the firm, and a lot of "wheel-spinning" for the project team, if the vision and directions are clarified up front.

Vision and Goals

The directions set by management can be open-ended and vague. This is the case for green-field plants or plants that are to be dramatically gutted and upgraded. At Zanussi, for example, the broad charge was to create a state-of-the-art plant focused on domestic refrigerators (see Chapter 4).[4] The goals were to deliver products equivalent to those of the competitors, but considerably faster, with improved quality, and at significantly lower cost. The plant recognized early that new technology, such as robotics and automated material-handling systems, required cellular structures. The need for speed and efficiency also steered the plant toward cellular manufacturing.

Afrox provides an example of more specific directives. Its vision included a product focus in manufacturing. To support this, Afrox formulated a long list of detailed goals:

- Rationalize the number of salable products from over 1,000 to 300 and eventually to 200.
- Standardize the use of purchased and manufactured components.
- Reduce machine set-up time to a maximum of 10 minutes for similar components.
- Shorten manufacturing lead times and improve manufacturing flexibility and customer-service levels.
- Train employees in new concepts, and enrich their jobs by improving their skills and knowledge.
- Create an environment in which workers can identify with the end products.
- Simplify production and inventory control, and create a system with simple visual controls.
- Improve floorspace utilization.
- Reduce material handling and the need for special material-handling equipment.

These goals, in effect, point to the application of group technology and cellular manufacturing in the plant, and also suggest a make/buy analysis.

Performance Measures and Targets

The project should be driven by the plant's performance deficiencies. Specifically, *without measures of performance, along which improvements are sought, the team has no clear direction.* Should you also set targets for improvement? We have found that only about two-thirds of firms that adopt cells actually formulate performance expectations in advance. Of those firms that do, only 60 percent set any quantitative goals.[5] In other words, target setting is fairly rare. This is understandable since the magnitude of improvements can be difficult to know in advance with any specificity. Of course, *absolute* targets can legitimately be derived from the benchmarking of competitors and then serve as carrots for the project team. An example of an absolute target is, "We must be able to respond within 3 days." *Relative* targets, on the other hand, can be based on your own in-house experience of what is possible. An example could be, "We should be able to reduce lead time in order processing by 50 percent." We have noticed, however, that companies often state improvement goals for variables they have *never measured* and, therefore, are unknown.[6] Obviously, if a new performance metric is introduced, you must begin the analysis by establishing the present performance to have a baseline for comparison. You must also consider the possibility that targets can be unrealistic if they were simply "picked out of the air."

Establishing the True Problem

Planning processes are rarely linear. Once the project team starts to collect data and performs an initial analysis, disagreements may arise. These typically concern interpretations of what "the real problem" is, what the project scope should be, and what constitutes realistic goals. Therefore, it is important to revisit these issues after the project team has had an opportunity to reflect on them. For example, suppose a key problem is the inability to respond to customer requests within specified timelines. One of the first things the team needs to understand is the process that determines customer lead time. After you've done process mapping (see this chapter and Chapter 18), the time delays along that process will be better understood. The project team may conclude that 70 percent of the response time is due to administrative processes, such as order entry or product customization, rather than to manufacturing as was first believed. In that case, it should change focus and devote most of its energy to improving office operations (again, see Chapter 18).

UNDERSTANDING THE CURRENT SITUATION

We are moving now into the core area of the data-analysis process, as indicated in Table 5-1. Because every alternative solution is associated with risk and expenditures, and has strategic implications for the firm, choices are not always easy. However, you should beware of the risk of overanalyzing and becoming paralyzed by the data. Rather, you should focus fairly quickly on a few critical analyses that will help the team develop a deep understanding of how to best transform the ailing organization. Assuming that the data can be collected, and the project team consists of "your best people" (some of them working full-time on the project), a first-cut analysis phase should be concluded within a period of ranging from a few weeks to a few months. Of course, having a proposed solution accepted by management and employees, fine-tuning it according to their input, and then actually implementing it may take much longer (see our discussion of change management in Chapter 15).

Family Grouping Analysis

If a plant manufactures more than 25 or 30 products, it may be difficult to get a good grip on what is happening. To simplify the analysis, you should group products into larger families of similar items and also identify products that can serve as representatives for these families. This rule applies to parts and components as well.

In addition to simplifying data analysis, grouping products into families has another purpose. When you seek to organize work, you should always look for a *product focus*. In other words, you should create production units that can manufacture families of similar products (also see our discussion of focused factories in Chapter 2). Only when you cannot find viable product families should you look for other ways of organizing work.[7]

There are many ways to identify families: according to product type, customers, volume, processes, and so on. Ideally, the families you use at this early analysis stage also should be useful for segmenting the production processes. However, that is not always the case. Since your goal is to "get a grip on the mess," you should take advantage of any established families already in use to simplify the analysis, especially in terms of understanding demand volumes and load pictures. (We provide an in-depth discussion of families and their role in segmenting production in the section, "Identifying Opportunities for Product Focus.")

Product-Volume Analysis

Production volume is possibly the single most important factor determining the design of manufacturing systems. The products with the highest volumes usually create the largest load on the manufacturing system and will therefore shape material flow. High-volume products also are prime candidates for automation. On the other hand, products with low volumes may be ignored in your "big-picture" analysis. The parts and products in the middle- to high-volume range typically are the strongest candidates for cellular manufacturing.

Because of the importance of volume, you should identify demand volumes for all products (or parts) within the scope of the project. You can use recent historical data, such as all products produced within the last year or six months, but you *must* look also at the future. Review the projected demand for products that you expect to manufacture in the coming one- to three-year time frame. These forecasted demands can indicate a need for additional capacity.

You can present product-volume data in table form, but they are often best summarized graphically. This can be done either in descending order of volume, in a *product-quantity chart* (P-Q chart), or in cumulative volume form in an ABC graph. If you have created product families in order to simplify the analysis, the demand figures in these charts should be tied to families rather than to individual products. Figure 5-3 shows a P-Q chart for product families as well as the current average lot size for each family. The lot sizes are of particular interest if set by external customers (since they dictate the order stream). Large and infrequent lot sizes often cause load problems for the plant. Each product family, of course, can also have its own P-Q chart indicating the volume and lot size of each product in the respective family.

Product family	Quantity per year	Cumulative %	Current avg. lot size
G467	3,689	24.5%	150
S35	3,005	44.5%	200
L578	2,574	61.6%	150
N744	2,132	75.8%	225
D90	1,304	84.4%	100
R356	983	90.9%	75
S98	672	95.4%	75
Others	690	100.0%	28
	Total = 15,049		

Note: current average lot sizes for each family are shown in the table but are not graphed.

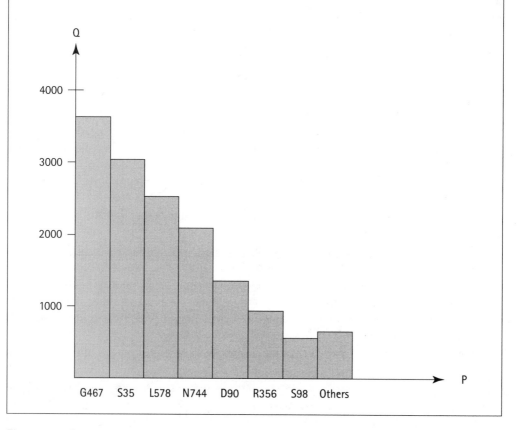

Figure 5–3. Example of a product-quantity chart for product families

Based on these charts, you may decide to concentrate on the families that account for most of the volume. Likewise, you may concentrate on the high-volume products within each family. Often the 80-20 rule applies—about 20 percent of the products create 80 percent of the total volume (or, in general, a small group accounts for the majority of the effect). You may therefore focus on this 20 percent and ignore the rest until a more detailed analysis is required.

At Marathon Electric, a manufacturer of generators and electric motors, the shaft department produces thousands of variants of shafts. However, all shafts belong to one of three families: large motor shafts, medium motor shafts, and generator shafts. A closer analysis showed that 25 model variants in the large shaft family accounted for 64 percent of annual demand, 10 models in the medium shaft family accounted for 96 percent of demand, and 15 model variants of generator shafts made up 96 percent of the volume. Concentrating on these part families greatly simplified the continued analysis.

Since many manufacturing problems tend to stem from volume variations, you should also create time-series charts for key products where you graph order streams over time. Products plagued by late orders and high inventories often demonstrate large swings in demand and/or production schedules.

Performance Analysis

Before a change project begins you should always collect performance data for all measures of interest from the current system. In this way you can assess the gains after you have implemented a change. The measures you review should include metrics of interest to both manufacturing operations and customers. However, you should always collect actual performance data on the following variables, since they are key indicators of manufacturing system performance (Chapter 9 discusses performance measurement for cell systems in great depth):

- *Inventory.* Units or dollars in inventory, or inventory turns, at various stages in the input-output process.
- *Output rates.* The number of units produced per unit of time.
- *Lead times.* The time to complete a job or respond to requests.
- *Lateness.* Number or percentage of orders being late.
- *Quality.* This includes scrap and rework, both of which drive cost and lead times.

Resource and Technology Analysis

A plant's output and lead time performance greatly depend on the capabilities of its resources (what they can do) and their capacity in relation to the imposed workload (their utilization). You therefore need to take an inventory of the plant's resources—at least those considered to be key bottlenecks in the processes. We group these resources into *equipment and critical accessories* and *people.*

Equipment and critical accessories

Here are some data you may want to collect on the plant's equipment and accessories:

- Classification or type
- Number of each type

- Setup or changeover times
- Average unit processing times (or their inverse, maximum average output rates)
- Age and reliability (breakdown) data
- Planned replacements or new acquisitions
- Number of shifts per machine
- Effective number of hours per shift (considering break times, etc.)
- Utilization levels (historical and projected)
- Number and types of key tools and fixtures (and the equipment sharing them)
- Number and types of key gauging and testing equipment (and the equipment sharing them)

You should use the utilization data to screen the equipment population. At this stage you can remove lowly loaded equipment from further analysis. You should also note the number of pieces of equipment of each type, especially when this number is low. If those pieces of equipment cannot be duplicated because of size, restriction on capital investments, or environmental reasons, they must be given special consideration during the cell formation phase.

Three other aspects of the "technology" analysis are of special interest. The first is the age of the existing equipment in the plant. A factory-planning exercise is an opportunity to ask for upgrades to state-of-the-art equipment. This is something that is frequently and appropriately done (unless the charge to the project team states "absolutely no capital expenditures"). The second aspect pertains to process change. If a particular operation is targeted for replacement by a different technology, this will obviously impact routings, equipment, and capacity. Accordingly, you need to take this into consideration from the start. Finally, if the factory analysis was initiated because new products are being launched, the process equipment may not exist yet at the plant. The project team then needs to spend much effort in selecting the best technology and equipment.

People

To plan for the future, you also need to know something about the plant's workforce. Here are some relevant data you may need for the analysis:

- Labor classification system (indicates degree of flexibility)
- Number of employees per skill level
- Number of shifts worked
- Effective number of hours per shift

In almost all applications, cellular manufacturing demands that cell operators be skilled in multiple processes. The existing skill base therefore is of interest to the planning team. This information comes into play when you decide on the size of the cell team and the types of equipment to put in the cell. In some cases the operator skill set, rather than the equipment, is the starting point for cell creation. This is the case in the garment industry, where the equipment may be general-purpose sewing machines. Here, the skill levels of the assigned operators establish the capabilities for the cells.

Capacity-Load and Bottleneck Analysis

When workload (required hours) increases relative to capacity (available hours), the time jobs wait in queue increases as well. The resources (machines or people) with the highest load-to-capacity ratios are called *bottlenecks*. Bottlenecks are important because they "choke the system" by causing delays in the work flow. As a result, they directly determine the levels of inventory and output, and the length of the lead times. You can identify bottlenecks by looking for the most utilized equipment or employees in the plant. Excessive document backlogs in offices or numerous material containers sitting on the factory floor also indicate bottlenecks.

Firms often are oblivious to the relationships between capacity, workloads, and lead times and thus are surprised to learn that jobs may spend only 3 to 10 percent of their time in the shop actually being worked on. The rest of the time is spent just sitting in queue somewhere.[8] The most effective ways to increase output and reduce lead times include lowering load-capacity ratios at the bottlenecks and reducing batch sizes.

The project team will find the following questions useful for identifying the products and resources needing special attention during bottleneck and capacity-load analysis:

- What are the past and projected utilization levels for the machines?
- Where are the bottlenecks located (including external operations performed at subcontractors or sister plants)?
- What products or parts are processed at these bottleneck stations?
- How large are the setup times and lot sizes at these bottlenecks?

Lead times and output always improve if you increase available capacity. However, acquiring capacity, whether from additional resources or from process improvements, costs money. So how much capacity do you need? Although a golden rule in system design is to never operate with utilization levels exceeding 85 percent, more exact answers to this question calls for computer modeling. We discuss that topic in Chapter 7.

Space Analysis

A space analysis entails reviewing the current allocation and utilization of factory space. For example, how much space is devoted to offices, part fabrication, assembly and testing operations, scrap and rework activities, inventory storage, and shipping/receiving (see Figure 5-4)? In connection with the resource/technology and material-flow analyses (discussed below), you may also use more detailed layouts that show the location of all equipment and each process in the plant. Space maps should ideally be color-coded for visual effect and easy interpretation.

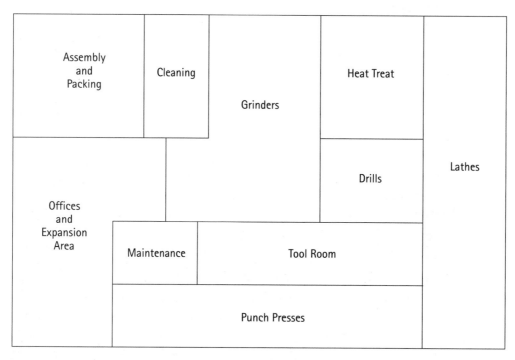

Figure 5-4. Functional factory layout

Material-Flow Analysis

Material handling—specifically, moving material over long distances—contributes to manufacturing inefficiency. The distance problem is especially acute in functionally arranged factory facilities that have grown in a patchwork manner over time. You should do a material-flow analysis early to highlight material-handling inefficiencies, followed by a more detailed analysis during the project's layout phase.

To do a flow analysis, take a sample of high-volume products or parts and trace their movement along the manufacturing processes through the plant (see Figure 5-5). In some cases, you may have to track the materials between floors, to different buildings, and even to/from other plants. Overlaying the transportation path on a factory layout can be visually dramatic, especially if both distance and volume information are included. It can be a compelling part of a presentation to management in support of a factory rearrangement. Cells, of course, solve the distance problems by positioning equipment and people closely together.

Process Flow Analysis/Process Mapping

Process flow analysis, also called "flow charting," "process mapping," or "value stream analysis," is a time-consuming but critical step in the analysis of workflows.[9] Process mapping means documenting the plant's *material and/or information flows* in a flow chart in order to understand how work is performed (i.e., the AS IS situation), and where and how workflow problems originate (see Figure 5-6).

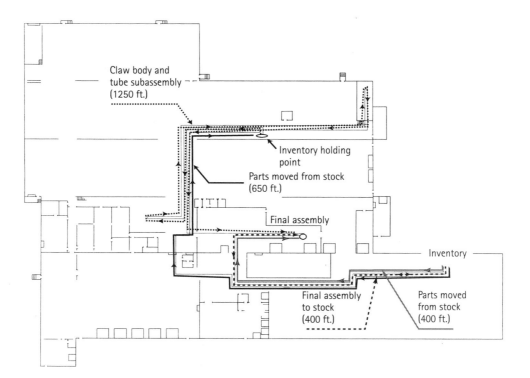

Figure 5-5. Material flow diagram

You may think it unnecessary to begin a process of improvement by documenting a situation known to be poor. However, to be able to improve, you need to understand fully the starting point. Process mapping is an ideal vehicle for documenting current processes. As you may have discovered, the knowledge of what really occurs in organizations frequently is incomplete; bits and pieces of knowledge of what the whole looks like reside with different employees. Using the input of many individuals ensures the accuracy and completeness of your process map.

Although you can start at either end of a process, it is sometimes preferable to start with the completed product and then trace the process steps backwards. This is easier than beginning with components, and it also puts the spotlight on the most important outcome of the manufacturing processes—the final product. Also, you should begin by mapping high-level processes. If you start with too many details you may get bogged down. In fact, many improvement projects get derailed because they spend too much time on process mapping rather than on analysis and finding solutions.[10] If needed, you always can add details later. For example, more detailed process maps may include each step's output capacity, as well as the lot sizes used both for manufacturing and for moving.

You should note the difference between material-flow analysis and process-flow analysis. Although the terms are similar, the first refers to an analysis emphasizing *move distances* and showing the flow pattern—*to scale*—with a facility layout as a background (as in Figure 5-5). A process flow analysis, on the other hand, focuses on the activities required to convert materials and information. As seen from Figure 5-6, a process map is schematic and does not show distances or locations of the resources

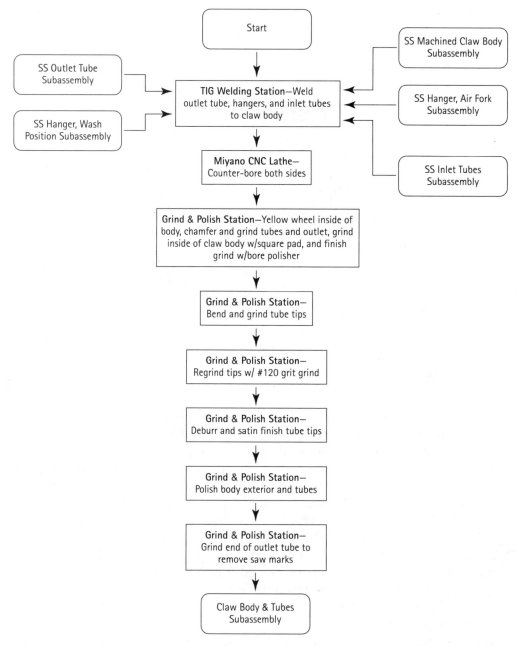

Figure 5-6. Process map

used in the manufacturing process. Rather, its main purpose is to show process steps and their relations, and illustrate overall process complexity.[11]

Modifying Product and Part Families

We now move into the third and last area of the data-analysis process, as indicated in Table 5-1. Here we consider the potential for redesigning parts and products, or removing them from the manufacturing system, in order to gain a performance advantage. This type of analysis, which involves standardization and/or outsourcing, can have a large impact on cell design.

Both standardization and outsourcing are helped by the formation of part/product families. Families make it easier to identify redundant parts (i.e., those that are very similar and can be removed without any loss). Families also help you detect parts that deviate from others and require extra resources and process steps. Since standardization increases the degree of similarity within families, as well as the volumes of manufactured and purchased materials, it should ideally be attempted *before or during* the design of a cell-based organization. The family concept also is very useful for make/buy analyses since you do not want to make such decisions on a product-by-product basis. Both product rationalization and make/buy decisions have strategic impact and should be done with care. The duration of these analyses depends on the scope of the factory-planning project, but they may take several months.

Product Rationalization (Standardization) Analysis

As companies grow over time, they tend to increase the breadth of their product lines. As a result, they expand the number of part and component types used, enlarge the plant, and increase the number of suppliers. In particular, part and product proliferation increase inefficiency and make firms more difficult to manage. *Product proliferation* typically is a result of marketing's desire to broaden the firm's offerings to the market. However, *part proliferation* occurs because there is no procedure in place to prevent it. Commonly, new parts are designed, manufactured, and stored— at high cost—rather than finding ways to reuse old ones. As a consultant friend of ours used to say: "Issuing a new part number is a license to spend money."

As we mentioned in Chapter 2, cellular manufacturing has its origins in the group technology (GT) philosophy. GT is a complexity-reducing approach to work. You apply it by first identifying families of similar parts or products. If you inspect the members of each family, you may discover product or part variants that are unneeded and can be eliminated. You may also redesign parts to make them fit better into the families. Although attempts to eliminate parts or products may meet with resistance from design or marketing, the gains in manufacturing quality, efficiency, and cost can be great.[12] A major problem is to maintain the discipline of standardization in the long run. You can achieve this by creating incentives for design engineers to reuse existing parts rather than creating new ones. Ideally, you should review proliferation on a regular basis to weed out unnecessary product and part variants.

Make/Buy (Outsourcing) Analysis

A tool manufacturer with whom we worked relied heavily on subcontracting for a segment of its products. In essence, the company was buying 30 to 40 percent of the required capacity for certain operations. The main reason was lack of capital to expand. However, in conjunction with a feasibility study of cells, our recommendations included buying more equipment to bring outsourced work back in-house.

Reviewing a plant and its production system is a good opportunity for conducting a make/buy analysis. In fact, sourcing is an almost inevitable part of factory planning. This is clearly the case if the manufacturing capability study was initiated by a corporate decision to reallocate products among plants, or by a decision to launch new products. On the other hand, if the project scope is small, the urgency for such an analysis typically is lower.

The key issue in sourcing is deciding which manufacturing capabilities to possess and which to buy.[13] On the one hand, you can decide to integrate either forward or backward. This means acquiring other firms in the supply chain towards either the customer or the supplier end. You may also decide to break the (internal or external) supply chain. This decision, which represents a buy rather than a make choice, has been a clear trend in recent years.

Companies that outsource materials tend to start at the bottom of the bills of materials. Thus, part production goes first, then subassembly operations. The final assembly process is the last to be outsourced, if ever. This is because firms want to retain the ultimate control over the products' identity and design, their quality, and the link to the customers. Here are some factors that can motivate you to outsource materials:[14]

- *Capability*: You cannot manufacture certain items, or acquire the capability to do so.

- *Competitiveness*: The supplier may be able to produce at lower costs or higher quality, or may deliver faster than you can.

- *Technology*: The supplier's components have better features than your in-house components.

- *Complexity*: By eliminating certain products and processes, your manufacturing focus gets stronger and the managerial tasks get easier.

- *Volume*: By outsourcing either high- or low-volume items, you can streamline (i.e., reduce the variance of) the production process.

- *Capital*: You are short of capacity and capital to expand is limited. Funds may be better used elsewhere in the organization.

There are, however, several important reasons *not* to shed processes and outsource work to other firms:

- *Competitive knowledge*: You may view the component as critical to the performance of your products, and consider the skills required to design and manufacture it as core strategic knowledge (i.e., something you don't want competitors to duplicate).

- *Customer visibility/market differentiation*: Components that differentiate your products in the marketplace should be within control of your firm; others can be outsourced.

- *Barriers to entry*: You may decide to retain production, or even expand vertical integration by acquiring firms up or down the supply chain, in order to raise the financial or managerial barriers to entry into your industry.

- *Assuring supply and demand*: If you are vertically integrated you can secure the supply of materials on the input side, and ensure that the output is purchased by organizations forward in the supply chain (since they belong to the same corporation).

You can make decisions regarding outsourcing at any time, but conducting a factorywide analysis is the perfect time to consider this issue. After all, outsourcing affects manufacturing processes, planning/control systems, and staffing in very direct ways. Make/buy decisions, though, are both *strategic* and *economic* in nature and should be taken at the highest level in the firm.

Comments on Data Collection

Most of the analyses discussed so far are based on quantitative data (see Table 5-1). However, firms often do not record information vital to their own improvement activities. And even if they do capture data, it takes some manipulation to access them. Thus, don't assume that the data you need will be readily available. In fact, *simply finding relevant data is likely to take* at least *50 percent of the time spent on the project*. A good rule, therefore, is to check, early in the project, for data availability and assess how easy it would be to transform the data into useful formats.

Take lead time, for example. To measure this variable you first must define it. A common definition of manufacturing lead time is "the time between manufacturing order release to the floor and completed order arrival at the inventory location." If the information system keeps track of orders releases and completion dates, then lead times can be constructed.

In other cases—and this is a typical situation in office reengineering projects—you will need to put in place a system that can measure current performance. One alternative is to record release and completion dates in the information system and determine lead times from that. Another way is to use a paper trail, such as a tracking or tagging sheet accompanying the job throughout the process. At each stage an employee records start and completion time (or arrival and departure time) at the workstation.[15] Once you have collected information for a number of orders over a reasonable time period, say two to six months, you can determine average lead times.

The project team should not rely on quantitative data alone. An equally important part of data collection and analysis, especially in the "understanding the mess" phase, is to gather the views and opinions of employees who are not members of the project and steering teams. Informal conversations can give you a sense for what is working well in the plant and what is not. Such chats, and small or large meetings arranged to discuss the plant project, can generate rich information for the team. Large meetings, however, are less likely to provide honest and direct input on the relevant issues.

Finally, note that the data analyses listed in Table 5-1 only give you the picture "before the change." Once you have developed a solution to the reorganizatio problem, you need to revisit some of these analyses to produce a picture of the plant as you predict it will appear "after the change" (see Figure 5-2). In particular, you will want to show "to be" performance, space, material-flow, capacity-load, and process-flow analyses.

IDENTIFYING OPPORTUNITIES FOR PRODUCT FOCUS

After having performed some initial data analyses, the project team will have a clearer picture of the plant's current organization and processes. It should also have developed a feel for the plant's strengths and weaknesses. With this preparation in hand, the team is ready to generate solutions to improve plant performance.

We believe factories should adopt a *product focus* unless you can demonstrate that this type of organization has clear disadvantages. The first test is to see if you can partition the plant into product-based minifactories (see Chapter 2). Inside each focused factory, you can then decide whether to arrange work into cells by dividing these broad families into smaller families with greater internal similarities. Alternatively, you may elect to retain the traditional functional mode of operation inside the focused factories. Thus, segmenting the factory serves a dual purpose: it simplifies the search for families and increases the ability to manage each identified subarea efficiently and effectively.

Finding Families

There are many different ways to build families. Whether products are "similar" depends on the *stated purpose* of the improvement project. For example, you may want to achieve efficiencies in manufacturing, or satisfy the needs of marketing and sales. Sometimes these needs can be combined. Table 5-2 shows nine ways in which you can group products (you may already have used one or more of these to simplify the initial data analysis).

The first three categories in the table reflect the way marketing and sales personnel view the products. For example, a firm making motors may categorize them into "large and small horsepower motors" (*product type* and *product characteristics*) and sell them to "commercial and defense industry firms" (*markets*). "Sales families" are often, but not always, meaningful for manufacturing purposes. Likewise, a grouping based on *customers* is not meaningful to manufacturing if you sell to a large customer base. Segmenting production according to customer would in that case require that you put many of the same products in different families. However, if a product or product line is sold only to one or a few large customers, then you can do a product separation. We have seen this approach in several electronics assembly plants where assembly cells were dedicated to one or more dominant customers. We have also seen the customer focus nicely being put in place at Bergstrom, Inc., an HVAC system manufacturer, where the plant was split in five different areas, each with its own customer focus (see Chapter 2). Because very little part fabrication was taking place, this separation did not require any duplication of equipment.

You can classify a plant's manufacturing organization as *make-to-stock (MTS)*, *make-to-order (MTO)*, or *assembly-to-order (ATO)* depending on whether the firm satisfies customer demand from finished goods inventory or stores its inventory further upstream in the process. Products produced in an MTS mode are built on specu-

Table 5-2. Nine different ways to group products

Criteria for Identifying Product Families	Examples
1. **Product type.** Group products of the same type or function into families.	Motors and generators.
2. **Market.** Group all products sold in a certain geographical market in one family.	North America, Europe; market segmentation can also be based on type of user, e.g., commercial vs. residential user.
3. **Customers.** Group all products sold to one or more customers in the same family.	The products for two dominant customers make up two families, the rest of the products a third family; this segmentation does not work if several customers purchase the same products.
4. **Degree of customer contact.** Group products according to the degree of influence the customer has on the final product.	Group all stocked items in one family, all made to order in another, etc.
5. **Volume range.** Group products with similar volume ranges into the same families.	High-volume vs. low-volume products.
6. **Order stream.** Group products with similar customer order patterns in same families.	Large and repetitive orders in one family, small and irregularly placed order in another.
7. **Competitive basis.** Allocate all products that compete on the same basis to the same family.	Those competing on cost and speed to one family, those competing on customized design to another.
8. **Process type.** Group products or parts requiring similar processes in the same families.	All assembled products in one family, all non-assembled products in another, etc.; within each group, products with similar routings form a family.
9. **Product characteristics.** Group products with same physical features or raw material into families.	Large vs. small, light vs. heavy, etc.

lation and sold from inventory. MTO products often are engineered to specifications jointly with the customer. Some materials ordering and prefabrication of parts may take place, while the remaining design and manufacturing work is done after an order has been confirmed. Finally, an ATO manufacturer orders raw materials and produces standard parts to forecast, while assembly is done only after the product has been sold and configured.

A major reason for grouping products according to the *degree of customer contact* is that MTS products tend to exhibit greater design stability than ATO and MTO products. In other words, you lose some control over the manufacturing process as you move from MTS to MTO, and greater flexibility is needed.

The characteristics of MTS, ATO, and MTO manufacturing are strongly related to both *volume* and *order stream*. Volume range is important in system design because it determines capacity needs. If volume is high enough, you can create dedicated production units. It is further important from a sourcing perspective, because volume of raw materials is tied to volume of products. Another very important aspect related to volume is the order stream—the size and the timing of each manufacturing order. The customer, directly or indirectly, determines the order stream. Mixing products or parts with large and small batch sizes can be disruptive to manufacturing efficiency due to varying setup, processing, and material-handling requirements.

You also can separate products into families based on their *competitive basis*, that is, the characteristics on which products compete. Examples include low price (cost), high quality, rapid delivery, or ability to be customized. To manufacture products with different competitive bases requires different manufacturing processes, measurement systems, control systems, labor skills, and so on. A product's competitive basis is usually strongly related to its sales volume.

Basing segmentation on *process type* is meaningful if products use manufacturing processes that differ in radical and exclusive ways. For example, a firm may produce both electric and gas-engine motors. The manufacturing resources are mostly separate due to the different processes used in each case. In the same way, assembled versus nonassembled products can also be segmented by process type.

Finally, the *product characteristics* category covers key aspects of product design and manufacturing features, including:

- Physical size
- Weight
- Key shapes or features
- Major subassemblies
- Key components or raw materials

Typically, you form families based on product characteristics in order to gain efficiencies in manufacturing. For example, by using raw material characteristics you can group products into those based on steel versus those made of aluminum. Product characteristics often have implications for marketing as well. For our motor manufacturer above, the sales department had segmented the market into large and small horsepower motors. However, the product characteristic "size" has clear manufacturing implications as well: large motors require different equipment and assembly arrangements than do small motors.

Identifying Focused Production Areas

You can segment the complete manufacturing process for assembled products into stages based on (1) part production, (2) subassembly, and (3) final assembly and testing operations.[16] In functionally operated plants, as shown in Figure 5-7a, different areas of the factory perform a different segment of the total process. Furthermore, none of the work areas/stations are dedicated to a particular product.

Our goal is to find families of similar products. A natural way of partitioning a production system is to start at the endpoint—the assembly processes for the final products. Let's assume you can group products into families based on one or more similarity criteria (see Table 5-2). As illustrated in Figure 5-7b, you can then separate the final assembly area into smaller areas, each dedicated to the assembly of one product family. Taking this one step further, you can also split the subassembly department so that all subassemblies used by a particular product family are manufactured in their own dedicated areas (see Figure 5-7c). Or you can go all the way and create areas where all parts that are components of a product family are produced separately from all other parts (see Figure 5-7d). This organization is what we call a *focused factory*.

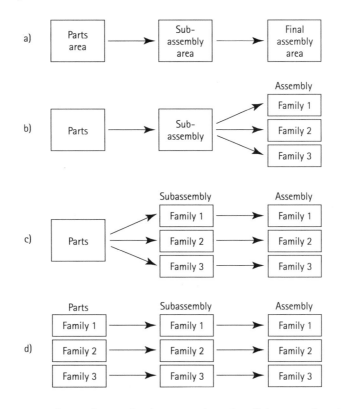

Figure 5-7. Separating production stages based on links to product families

Focus depth

The alternatives in Figure 5-7 each have a different amount of *focus depth*. Thus, a plant where no areas are split, as in Figure 5-7a, has the least depth. Conversely, a plant where all parts, subassemblies, and final product operations are dedicated to the same end products, as in Figure 5-7d, has the largest focus depth.

There are both advantages and disadvantages with focus depth. The advantages are (1) increased control of the product line, (2) less risk for disturbances and delays due to other parts and products, (3) greater employee identification with the product, and (4) a more direct link to the market. These benefits should lead to a stronger customer orientation and service, greater employee involvement and product loyalty, easier process improvement, higher quality, and a more nimble, responsive system.

The most obvious disadvantage with splitting a factory according to product affiliation is the risk of resource and task duplication. That is, *a firm may end up using more people and equipment to perform possibly identical tasks.* This risk gets larger the deeper the focus. Splitting parts production according to end product, as in Figure 5-7d, means that parts common to different products will be made in different work areas, each dedicated to a product family. This leads to duplication of equipment and people, and potentially insufficient or unbalanced resource utilization. Low utilization is of particular concern when capital-intensive equipment is involved.

In brief, the trade-off in achieving product focus is between market orientation, customer satisfaction, employee involvement, and product control on the one hand, and manufacturing efficiency and resource utilization on the other. This conflict is actually quite complex, and you may not be able to easily settle it without deeper analysis. In particular, you should never just consider equipment and people utilization: in order to achieve a full assessment, you must also consider the performance of the system with respect to strategic variables such as quality, total product cost, and response time.

IDENTIFYING OPPORTUNITIES FOR CELLS

In the previous section, we talked about physically separating the manufacturing of products according to families to reduce system complexity. However, we did not specify how manufacturing takes place inside each unit. In the assembly areas, for example, you may use lines, assembly cells, or single-operator workstations. Likewise, in the part production areas you can retain a functional organization or switch to part cells. Therefore, within a focused production area, for any of the three stages (product, subassembly, part production; see Figure 5-7), you now need to search for cell opportunities.

Cell Formation

Cell formation is the process that (1) identifies product or part families, (2) determines their associated work processes, and (3) assigns the required equipment to the families. In cell formation, the first phase of the cell design process, you define only *logical cells* (i.e., simply a collection of parts/products and equipment). In the subsequent phase, layout planning, you determine the space required by the logical cells, as well as their location. This phase turns logical cells into *physical cells*.

The basic principle behind cell formation is to first create a family of parts or products, and then determine the best manufacturing process for this family (see Figure 5-8). Once you have done this, you can plan both equipment and staffing, and evaluate the candidate cell. You can simplify the cell formation problem considerably if you first reduce the populations of parts and equipment from which cells are created. Such reductions can be accomplished at the preceding plant-focusing phase.

As boxes 1 and 2 in Figure 5-8 show, there are two fundamental ways in which to form initial families. One way is to rely on *product type and product characteristics* (such as name, design features, size, and raw material). The other way is to use the *routing information* that specifies the process sequence required for manufacturing. In addition, you can use other data shown in Table 5-2, such as competitive basis, type of customer contact, volume, and order stream information. It is easy to understand

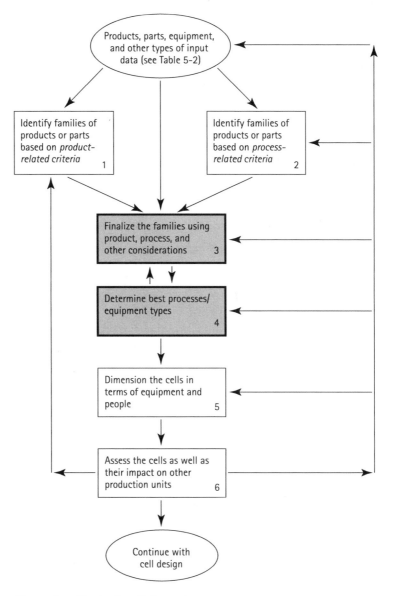

Figure 5-8. The basic cell formation process

that a cell designed to handle MTO production of frequently changing products, in small volumes and where response time is critical, will look different than a cell that serves an MTS market with steady, large orders and where cost is the main competitive variable.[17] These two types of cells require different levels of flexibility and buffer spaces, and different planning and control systems (see Chapter 11). Most companies therefore take advantage of several types of data when forming cells.

Cell formation techniques

There are numerous, quite complex techniques that can help you identify part-producing cells. (There are no formal techniques for identifying product assembly cells.)

However, these techniques are mostly unknown and unused in industry.[18] Cell guru John Burbidge predicted in 1975 that most large software vendors would offer commercially available programs to solve the cell formation problem. This prediction has not materialized.[19] In fact, as far as we know, there are no dedicated commercial software packages for identifying families and the resources to produce them. This may be because cell creation is not a frequent and routine activity. In addition, existing techniques do not consider all the diverse information needed to form cells (again, see Table 5-2). Luckily, companies commonly are able to create cells with fairly little effort and without sophisticated techniques (especially assembly cells). Accordingly, we are not going to discuss advanced cell formation techniques.[20] Instead, we will confine ourselves to describing a few simple but effective methods for identifying cells that most companies can use.

Designing Assembly Cells

An *assembly cell* incorporates a *network routing structure* of operations where, at each connecting branch, some form of joining or assembly operation is performed. Assembly cells, then, produce subassemblies or final products. For simplicity, we refer to all other types of cells as *part cells*. Parts processed in such cells follow *linear routings* (Figure 5-9 contrasts linear and network routing structures).

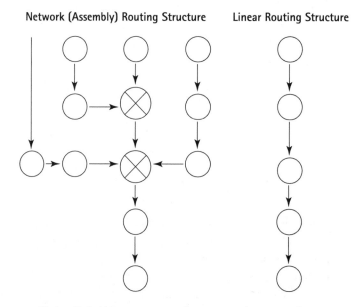

Network (Assembly) Routing Structure   Linear Routing Structure

Figure 5-9. Linear vs. network-structured process charts

As we discuss below, linear part routings lend themselves fairly easily to mathematical manipulation. However, network structures do not, so there are no quantitative procedures available to identify assembly cells. Luckily, assembly cells are much easier to form, and more obvious, than are part cells. For one thing, there are fewer products than there are components. As we discussed in the previous section, dedicating assembly areas to broad product families is an obvious design principle for most companies. By looking for additional manufacturing similarities, you may be able to create "tighter" assembly cells.

An illustration of segmentation—Deltrol Controls

Deltrol Controls is a Milwaukee-based, $15-million manufacturer of electromechanical products. Its product lines include relays, coils, solenoids, valves, and timers. Management was interested in reducing lead times and WIP inventory, and improving manufacturing quality, and saw cellular manufacturing as the vehicle for achieving these results. A study was initiated in cooperation with the Quick Response Manufacturing Center at University of Wisconsin-Madison to see if cells could be applied to the general-purpose relay product line.[21]

This product line included over 200 relay models. In order to reduce the problem size, a P-Q analysis was first performed based on pre-established product families used by the firm. Inside the large family, "general-purpose relays" were smaller families based on relay type (e.g., "166 relays," "265 relays"; these family names identify the capabilities of the relays and are used for sales/marketing purposes). Sorting total sales for one quarter according to relay type showed that four of the families accounted for 93.2 percent of total unit demand. Thus, the continued analysis relied only on these four families.

A process analysis showed that all relays went through the same basic process steps. Detailed process mapping of the four families confirmed that the routings had only very minor variations and that five component/subassembly processes fed the final assembly process (see Figure 5-10). Due to the consistent routing patterns, a cell system composed of one final assembly cell and four part and subassembly fabrication cells was proposed for further analysis (see Figure 5-11).

In summary, this analysis went through the following steps:

- Management chose one broad product family for a feasibility study.
- Based on the product volume criterion, four subfamilies were targeted for detailed evaluation.
- Analysis revealed that all four families displayed essentially the same manufacturing process.
- Because of these great internal similarities, one cell system, consisting of a single assembly cell and four component feeder cells, could effectively manufacture all relays in the overall product family.

This case illustrates that the initial product groupings, based on a sales perspective and used to simplify data analysis, also was useful for achieving product focus in manufacturing. In fact, this focus extends back into subassembly and component fabrication as well. The final solution thus has great focus depth, and corresponds to the situation depicted in Figure 5-7d.

Breaking the links to assembly cells

If you subdivide subassembly and part production according to the end products, as illustrated in the example above and shown in Figures 5-7c and 5-7d, you disregard

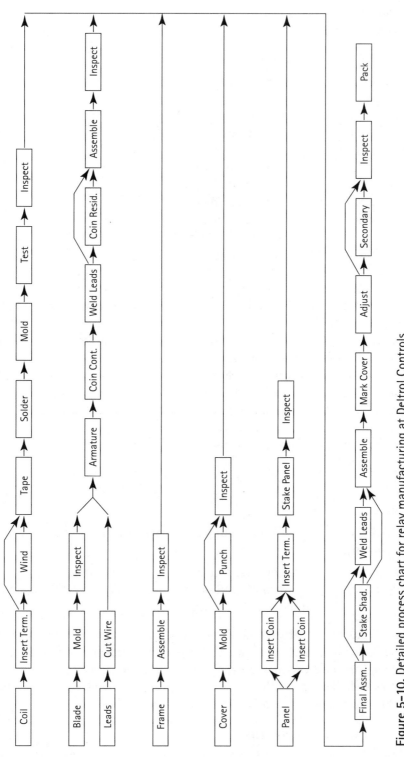

Figure 5-10. Detailed process chart for relay manufacturing at Deltrol Controls

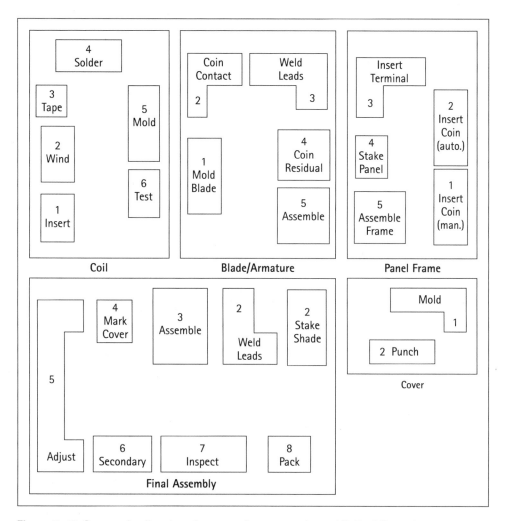

Figure 5–11. Proposed cell system for general-purpose relays at Deltrol Controls

any direct similarity among the subassemblies or parts themselves. On the other hand, if you disregard the products, and rely solely on attributes directly linked to the parts and subassemblies, you can create *families with high internal manufacturing similarity*. The end result may be a segmented manufacturing process of a different nature.

Figure 5-12a, for example, illustrates how the subassembly area has been partitioned into two subsections, each processing a separate family. In this case, the separation is not based on the connection to the end products, but on other criteria listed in Table 5-2 (for example, product characteristics or process similarity). Likewise, Figure 5-12b illustrates the situation where both the subassembly and the part producing areas have been split using, say, raw material and volume characteristics, while the assembly area has been grouped based on product type. Compared to Figure 5-7d, the focus depth has now been lessened, with an accompanying increase in complexity. This happens when the links to the end products are exchanged for local efficiency.

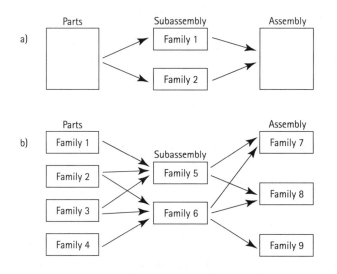

Figure 5-12. Grouping part and subassembly production stages based on product and process characteristics rather than links to product families

Assembly lines versus assembly cells

Assembly work is typically performed either on a *line*, manned by several operators, or at an assembly *station*, manned by a single individual (if a single operator fully completes an assembly, whether at one station or by visiting multiple stations along a line, that is called a "craft operation"). Both cases can fulfill our general definition of a cell. Many people, however, associate cells with teamwork and do not think of single-operator, single-station assembly as being cells. But, as we discussed in Chapter 2, many cells are in fact manned by just one individual. The distinction between assembly lines and assembly cells is more blurred. Although most assembly lines technically also are cells, it is useful to be able to separate the two. The reconfiguration of a "classic" assembly line to an "ideal" assembly cell often involves the following changes:

1. A change from a long, straight line to another physical layout shape—often U-shaped—that allows for an improved social and physical workplace.

2. The removal of paced or unpaced conveyors (if appropriate).

3. A reduction of the space occupied by the assembly unit (workstations are placed more closely together and reduced in number).

4. An increase in the number of tasks assigned to each assembly worker (job enlargement).

5. A reduction in the number of assembly workers.

The last three changes come from having fewer workstations in the cell compared to the line. For example, you may convert a 20-station assembly line to a three-operator cell. This requires that you train each assembler in more tasks. You can also form several cells by splitting a mixed-mode assembly line, i.e., a line currently designed to assemble multiple product variants. The resulting smaller cells can then be dedicated to more narrowly defined product families. Mixed-mode lines may be split to reduce operator learning and forgetting effects or minimize changeover times.

Given that assembly work in many plants already is dedicated to product families, why convert from lines to assembly cells? The major advantages have to do with efficiency, flexibility, output, quality, and the work environment:[22]

1. *Cells can lead to faster changeovers.* It is cumbersome to change over a single, long line between products, with respect to both tooling and materials. By breaking up the line into several smaller and more focused cells, model changes become fewer and easier to handle.

2. *Cells can avoid "line stoppages."* A long line, especially one that relies on mechanized material handling, is vulnerable to breakdowns. Splitting a line into multiple, smaller cells means production can continue even if one cell stops working.

3. *A cell can save space and gain efficiency by not using conveyors.* The use of moving conveyor lines can in some cases be inefficient. Material has to be pulled off and then put back onto the line. Conveyors also take up space.

4. *Cells can have greater output, and operate with less inventory, due to enlarged station times.* Variations in assembly times from operator to operator on an unpaced line (i.e., one not controlled by a moving conveyor) lead to a build-up of inventory and lower output. A cell with fewer stations and enlarged station times avoids that problem because there are fewer opportunities for operators to be blocked (from sending items downstream) or starved (i.e., operators have nothing to work on because previous operator is still busy completing his or her assembly task).

5. *Cells can operate with relatively fewer employees.* Imbalances in task times lead to overstaffing of the traditional line. By enlarging the task times assigned to each operator, you can reduce idle time and thereby the number of operators.

6. *Assembly cells often have fewer quality problems and faster error correction.* In a cell, each operator assembles a larger portion of the product than on a line. Operators also are more closely located. Because cell operators know more about the product and the total process, and each other, they develop a stronger "process ownership" and tend to get more involved with process improvement.

7. *Cells lower the risk for repetitive motion injuries and increase the chances for improved job satisfaction.* This is another outcome of enlarged work assignments for operators in cells (see Chapter 12 for more on this).

Multi-operator assembly cells can be created both by modifying assembly lines and by enlarging single-operator craft cells. The latter may happen when the whole assembly task has proven to be too large for a single operator to master.

Design of Part Cells

You can begin forming part cells using either existing routing information or product/part characteristics (see Figure 5-13).[23] We discuss some alternative methods below.

Simultaneous identification of families and equipment groups

Let us begin with Approach 4, the right-most branch in Figure 5-13. Cell formation techniques that fall into this category identify part families and associated machine groups at the same time, rather than first finding the families and then assigning equipment groups to them (as shown in Figure 5-8). Techniques using Approach 4 have not proven very effective for industrial problems. However, they can be used to illustrate the cell formation problem in a way that helps us understand its nature and complexities.

We'll use an example from Ingersoll Cutting Tool Company. In its insert area, the company makes cutting edges for cutting tools. In its earliest attempt to form cells, 17 families were first created from 78 parts by combining inserts with identical routings. After removing honing and laser marking operations, required by all inserts, the part families and the remaining equipment were entered in a "part/machine matrix" (see Figure 5-14). Each column is a linkage between a part family and a group of machines. In other words, a column is an *unordered* routing (i.e., a routing that does not show the sequence in which the machines are used in the process). Figure 5-14 looks like a matrix of randomly distributed 1's, and it may be difficult to see a pattern. However, by reordering the rows and columns—there are algorithms for doing this—you can create a matrix like the one in Figure 5-15. Formed along the diagonal are clusters of parts and machines that represent *potential* cells.[24]

We refer to the entries that appear outside the blocks in bold in Figure 5-15 as "external operations." They are the ones that prevent independent cells from occurring. An external operation indicates that a part must leave one cell and move to another cell in order to complete all its operations. For example, members of family G7 must leave the third cell to get processed at the Magerle machine. This machine is part of the second cell. In cases like this, you no longer have an "unbroken sequence of operations" inside the cells. So, what can you do? A few alternatives exist.

1. Do nothing and accept cells with intercell moves.
2. Combine two cells so the parts with external operations do not need to leave the enlarged cell.
3. Duplicate the machines needed for the external operations and put them in the cells so that parts do not have to go outside the cell boundaries.
4. Check whether the external operations really are necessary, or if you can eliminate them.
5. Check whether the external operations can be performed on machines already in the cells (i.e., change the process plans by rerouting the parts).
6. Check whether the parts can be redesigned so the external operations are eliminated or moved inside the cells.

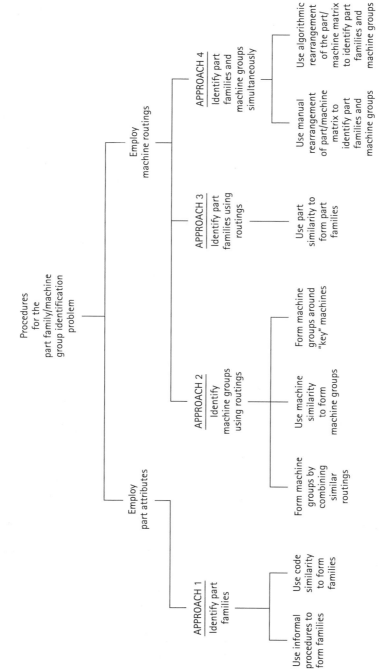

Figure 5-13. Various approaches to cell formation

7. Decide whether the disadvantages of having parts processed in more than one cell are so great that it would be better to remove them from the cell system. In such a case, you could source the parts from the functional areas in the plant or from the outside.

	C1	C2	G1	G2	G3	G4	G5	G6	G7	G8	G9	G10	G11	G12	G13	SC	MM
Aba-Nor	1		1		1	1											
Agathon				1							1						
B & S				1													1
Bes 905				1			1				1	1					
Bes T&B	1	1	1													1	1
Besly	1																
Magerle				1				1	1	1	1	1		1	1		
Matt-Ref																1	1
Mueller					1	1			1	1			1	1	1		
Spitfire					1	1			1	1			1	1	1		
Wendt		1	1		1	1			1	1		1	1	1	1	1	1

Figure 5-14. An unordered part-machine matrix (*top row shows part families, left-most column shows the machine types*)

	C1	C2	G1	G2	G5	G6	G9	G10	SC	MM	G3	G4	G7	G8	G11	G12	G13
Besly	1																
Aba-Nor	1		1		1							1					
B & S				1						1							
Agathon				1			1										
Bes 905				1	1		1	1									
Magerle				1		1	1	1					1	1		1	1
Bes T&B	1	1	1						1	1							
Matt-Ref									1	1							
Spitfire											1	1	1	1	1	1	1
Wendt		1	1					1	1	1	1	1	1	1	1	1	1
Mueller											1	1	1	1	1	1	1

Figure 5-15. Overlapping cells—a typical pattern discovered in rearranged part-machine matrices

Let's say you choose option 3 above and duplicate selected equipment. As shown in Figure 5-16, the three cells now fulfill both the *transformation* and the *resource dedication* perspectives on cells (Chapter 2). That is, the parts are completely processed within each cell, and the cells are independent of each other.

Suppose instead that you rearranged a part/machine matrix *without* adding any new equipment, and directly found independent cell blocks (like the ones in Figure 5-16). For this to be possible, the parts must already be processed on a dedicated group of machines. Thus, to create physical cells, the only thing you would need to do is move the equipment close together and assign operators to each group. Although we have seen examples of cells like this, "waiting to be created," reality typically is not that simple. Rather, job shops are often characterized by a "mess" created by frequent machine sharing and inconsistent routing assignments. By "inconsistent" routings we mean that parts that *should* be manufactured the same way actually follow different routings. For example, one company found that 745 very similar parts were made on 45 different machine tools using 184 different routings. This phenomenon, which may not become apparent until you start to form part families, often lies behind the commonly occurring pattern shown in Figure 5-15.

	C1	C2	G1	G2	G5	G6	G9	G10	SC	MM	G3	G4	G7	G8	G11	G12	G13
Wendt		1															
Besly	1																
Bes T&B	1	1															
Aba-Nor	1																
B & S				1						1							
Agathon				1			1										
Bes 905				1	1		1	1									
Magerle				1		1	1	1									
Bes T&B			1						1	1							
Wendt			1					1	1	1							
Aba-Nor			1		1												
Matt-Ref									1	1							
Spitfire											1	1	1	1	1	1	1
Wendt											1	1	1	1	1	1	1
Mueller											1	1	1	1	1	1	1
Aba-Nor												1					
Magerle													1	1		1	1

Figure 5-16. Rearranged part-machine matrix—after duplication of machines

How to simplify the cell formation problem

The matrix approach does provide one good insight. It shows that the cell formation problem can be simplified by removing troublesome machines or processes. A "troublesome" machine is one that processes many different parts. To create independent cells you must duplicate that machine and put it in multiple cells. Alternatively, you can decide to remove it from all cells and make it a "service center" visited by many parts. Operations that typically fall into this category are heat treat, paint, clean, wash, deburr, degrease, and so on.

There are other ways to facilitate the creation of cells, regardless of the method used. You should always begin the cell formation analysis by grouping parts into larger families based on identical or *contained routings*.[25] (This approach was used for the example shown in Figure 5-14.) Further, although not directly obvious from the part/machine matrix, you can simplify cell formation by removing all machines that are either inexpensive, lowly utilized, or both. Inexpensive machines can, if needed, be duplicated at low cost to create independent cells. And if machines are lowly utilized, they should not drive cell formation. They can therefore be removed from the data set (and reinserted later). A final method, as discussed earlier, is to remove parts or products with low volumes.

Using routings to first find equipment groups

Approaches 2 and 3 in Figure 5-13 also rely on routings during the cell formation process. However, these two approaches differ from Approach 4 just described. In Approaches 2 and 3 we follow the sequence "Find the machine group first, then the part family" and "Find the part family first, then the machine group," respectively. We generally find Approach 2 less appealing because its focus is on machine groups rather than on part families. However, there is one method that begins with a machine focus that is both simple and meaningful: the *key machine approach*.

This method begins by identifying a machine in your plant that is both rare and capital-intensive. You then find the parts processed on this machine and include them in a family. Other equipment needed to complete these parts is then added to the first machine. You now have a small family with its required equipment. If other parts also require the equipment in the group, these are added to the family, and so on. You can stop the process at any time when you feel you have a satisfactory cell (see more below). For example, one company that had two underutilized CNC lathes reviewed the routings for all parts processed on these machines. Based on this analysis, it added a drill press to form a small cell. To create an independent, self-contained cell, some parts that used the drill had their operations rerouted from other machines to the CNC lathes.

Using routings to first find part families

Approach 3 in Figure 5-13 uses routings to find part families. A simple way to find families is by *route sorting*. First, code the actual routes so they can be used for mathematical manipulation. This means assigning a code (like M1, M2, etc., or G1, G2, etc.) to each machine or group of similar machines. Each part's routing can then be written as a string of code symbols. In Figures 5-14 through 5-16, those strings consisted of 0's and 1's. You also can use numbers representing each part's expected workload on a machine, or the number of batches or units it requires in a year. With a spreadsheet or a database program, you can then sort the routings. If you are lucky, the sorted database will show a visible pattern from which you can identify families. If not, you need to use some of the simplifying tips discussed above or rely on additional data (as we illustrate below).

Relying on product type or product characteristics only

The final group of methods, represented by Approach 1 in Figure 5-13, ignores the process by which parts currently are manufactured. In doing so, this approach overcomes an obvious weakness with the other methods. Currently used routings were not designed for cellular manufacturing; rather, they were created with the present (or even past) work organization in mind. In addition, route selection probably depended on the process planners' preferences for certain types of operations or machines, or on the workload in the factory at the time the routings were created. Therefore, if you inspect routings for a group of parts that should be made in similar ways, you may discover that their routings show large differences. Ignoring currently used manufacturing methods in your cell formation allows for an *unbiased* way of creating families of parts. Once you have found a family, you can then create routings designed specifically for the cell (see box 4 in Figure 5-8).

Family formation under Approach 1 relies on either informal procedures or coded information. We have already discussed one informal method wherein parts are grouped based on their use in end products. You may also consider more permanent manufacturing-related characteristics, such as size, weight, shape, special features, raw material, and so on when identifying part families (see Table 5-2). For example, flat, cubic/prismatic, and rotational parts require different equipment and tooling, and you would not make these parts in the same cell. Likewise, raw materials such as brass and steel have different properties that require different machine feeds, speeds, and cutting tools. Again, this puts them in different families for cell formation purposes.

Although it makes sense to create cells using manufacturing-related information, it is easier, faster, and often more effective simply to rely on part types or part names based on function when grouping parts. The reason is that type or function frequently identifies parts that should be produced in a similar fashion. For example, Fisher Controls, a producer of valves, sorted parts into bodies, plugs, rings, and stems, and then created cells for each part type. Likewise, one Tektronix plant in Oregon used component functions to identify cells. Accordingly, it has heat sink cells, tuned cavity cells, and rail cells, among others.

MRP system or CAD databases can store the names or functions of parts. This information is sometimes even imbedded in a part's identification number ("semi-intelligent" part numbers). These codes can be used for family identification through sorting. There is one disadvantage with using names or functions, however. Parts are not always consistently named, or their names cannot be used to identify dissimilarities. Thus, you may find that parts that share similar names have different shapes or are made from different raw materials. Accordingly, they probably should not be manufactured together.

Frequently, codes are associated with (and sometimes considered synonymous with) group technology. Many firms have created databases of classified and coded parts over the years. These databases serve a variety of purposes, including design retrieval, process planning, and cell creation.[26] The emergence of modern relational database technology has facilitated the data capture and use of databases. For example, you no longer need to translate information into alphanumeric strings (e.g., a code of 4 in first position indicates a diameter between 150 and 200 mm) since the actual information can be stored directly (e.g., the exact diameter for a part is 177.65 mm).

However, we don't believe that classifying parts will help most firms in planning their cells. Usually, you can design cells by much easier means. Creating a special part characteristics database for cell formation alone probably is not worth the effort.

An illustration of cell formation—Ingersoll Cutting Tool Company

It is often very effective to use *both* routing information and product type/characteristics to form families (see boxes 1 and 2 in Figure 5-8). In addition, volume and workload should always be taken into account (see top oval in Figure 5-8). This is illustrated by a project carried out at Ingersoll Cutting Tool Company in Rockford, Illinois, jointly with a team from the University of Wisconsin-Madison.[27] Ingersoll, a manufacturer of cutting tools, wanted to explore the use of cells to reduce manufacturing lead times.

The firm grouped the cutting tool bodies, which vary greatly in shape and size, into families by product type such as end mills, face mills, and drills. These cutters were processed in a functionally organized job shop using metal-removing operations like turning, grinding, milling, and broaching. All cutters also went through finishing operations, such as deburring, heat treatment, laser marking, assembly (where cutting tool inserts were mounted on the tool bodies), and inspection. The company had already created a "finishing cell," housing all the processes required for the finishing operations (i.e., not a real cell according to our definition). Thus, the company looked for cell opportunities in the prefinishing operations area only.

The routings for 800 cutting tools that had been released into manufacturing during the previous two months were first coded and entered into a spreadsheet in the form of a part/machine matrix. An early attempt to sort routings in the part/machine matrix did not reveal any clear pattern. It was concluded, therefore, that more information was needed to make sense out of the routing data.

The 11 product families already used by the company served as a basis for the second attempt at cell formation. Simply by counting how many times each machine type had been used by each of these part families in the last two months, it became clear that independent cells could not be established without massive duplication of equipment. Next, the process routes, the majority of which contained six operations or less, were sorted *within* each family. This revealed that the end mills and the drills could be partitioned into two subfamilies each, depending on their routing patterns. These routing groups also exhibited different volume patterns.

Further inspection showed that two families—the high-volume end mills and high-volume drills—shared two machines, a lathe and a milling machine. Furthermore, volume was related to features and size. Thus, high-volume end mills all had straight shanks, and high-volume drills were small and also had straight shanks. The company had intelligent part numbers and these characteristics (size and shank) could be discerned from the part numbers. After rerouting some operations (i.e., from one machine to another), and checking that the workload was feasible, a cell composed of the high-volume end mills and drills was the first cell recommended to management. This cell would handle 70 percent of all drill units and 85 percent of all end mill units.

To summarize, the data used to identify the end mill/drill cell at Ingersoll included *product name/function*, *product routings*, *volume*, *product size*, and *product features*— that is, both product and process characteristics were used. The cells were identified using route sorting, and machine workloads were determined (to check feasibility) using volume, lot sizes, and run and setup time data. As it turned out, our analysis confirmed roughly the same cell structure already identified by the manufacturing engineers at this firm. This shows how important detailed knowledge of the products and processes can be in forming cells. However, even if the cell could have been established on gut feeling, the data analysis reinforced the engineers' intuition. It also helped to fine-tune the solution and provided hard data for management to rely on in its decision-making.

Although they belong to different industries and require very different manufacturing processes, the way cells were identified was quite similar for both Deltrol Controls (discussed earlier) and Ingersoll Cutting Tool Company. Routings, product name/type, and volume data were used in both cases. This parallels what we know about cell formation in general: (1) firms commonly use multiple methods to find families and associated cell equipment, and (2) these cell formation methods are frequently not very sophisticated. In fact, about one-third of companies involved with cell design appear not to rely on computer support at all. For those that do, data are typically stored in MRP and CAD systems. Our research shows that "where-used" information, part routings, and part records are the most frequently used data sources (40 to 45 percent of the studied firms), followed by classified and coded GT data and data stored in CAD systems (12 to 14 percent of the firms).[28]

ISSUES IN CELL DESIGN

The cell design process is not always simple. There are constant conflicts between what you want to achieve and what you actually can do. Specifically, identifying independent cells is not always straightforward, nor is knowing whether you have found a "good" cell. In the following sections, we give you some sense of the key issues and how they shape the nature and outcome of the cell design process.

Goals and Constraints in Cell Formation

A complete cell design process includes family formation, process specification, layout planning, and infrastructure decisions. The first step, formation of families, is the most important and the foundation for all other steps. In the preceding sections we have introduced different characteristics you can use to form families (Table 5-2). We have also discussed different procedures you can apply to identify families and their processing equipment. But how do you come up with not just cells but "good" cells? And how do the specifications set by the steering team or upper management affect the design process?

Cell design goals

The overall goals for the design process are to achieve performance improvements with respect to lead time, inventory, quality, or other measures. However, although you must keep those goals in mind at all times, they cannot guide the design process directly because a cell must be designed *before* you can assess its performance. Accordingly, you have to rely on design considerations to help you identify what you *believe* will become a "good" cell. You then can verify the performance of the cell either through computer modeling (Chapter 7) or through direct observation of the cell once it is in operation.

Table 5-3 provides a ranked list of design considerations used by 46 plants involved with cells.[29] Almost all of the considerations were viewed by many of these firms to be "important" or "very important." The 11 design considerations can be grouped into five categories:

1. Process completeness (rank 1)
2. Resource usage (ranks 2, 3, 4, and 8)
3. Cell size (ranks 5, 7, and 9)
4. Material flow pattern (rank 6)
5. Flexibility (ranks 10 and 11)

We discuss each of them next.

Table 5-3. Importance of design considerations on part/product or equipment selection

Rank	Design Considerations	Avg. Score
1	Part/products to be fully completed in the cell	4.31
2	High operator utilization	3.94
3	Fewer operators than equipment	3.50
4	Balanced equipment utilization in the cell	3.48
5	The number of part/products assigned to the cell	3.38
6	Unidirectional (linear) material flows	3.35
7	The number of cell operators	3.34
8	High utilization on expensive equipment	3.33
9	The number of workstations/machines in the cell	3.13
10	High equipment flexibility to ease new product introductions over time	3.00
11	High flexibility in selecting alternate routes through the cell	2.75

Note: each reason was scored on a scale from 1 to 5, where 1 = "Unimportant" and 5 = "Very important."

Process completeness. This is perhaps the most important consideration during cell formation. "Processing complete" simply means that you want cells wherein products or parts are completed to the greatest degree possible. Process completeness can be pushed far. If you create assembly cells, for example, you should consider whether upstream (i.e., subassembly or part fabrication) or downstream (i.e., testing and packing) processes can be integrated with the assembly operations inside the cell. This is in line with the transformation perspective on cellular manufacturing (see Chapter 2). By closely linking consecutive operations, you can minimize delays that occur when different cell teams are in charge of various parts of the process steps.

Often, though, it is necessary to break a part's or a product's manufacturing process into smaller pieces due to:

- Differences in required operator skills within a cell (e.g., skills required for machining versus assembly operations)

- Differences in output rates for various processes (necessitating buffer inventories between production units)

- Environmental or safety reasons

- Differences in routing similarity along the process (members of a product family can have a high degree of routing similarity for some portion of the process, but low elsewhere—for example, a part family can share one cell for the first portion of the process but then be split into three cells for the remaining operations; see Figure 5-17)

a)

One cell, low internal similarity in processes

b)

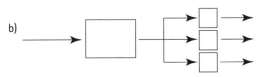

One cell split into three for the latter part of the routings.
Each cell now has higher process similarity among the parts.

Figure 5-17. Splitting one cell into three smaller cells

When completeness is not practical, you may opt to create *mini-cells* by linking only a few consecutive operations for a product family. Figure 5-18 shows a mini-cell created by combining three operations for three products. For contrast, a complete product-focused cell is also shown.[30]

Another term for process completeness is *processing independence*. You want cells to operate independently of other production units in the plant. Specifically, you don't want parts or products to share resources with other units or go outside the cell for partial processing (this is the resource perspective on cells; see Chapter 2). Processing independence, like completeness, means greater control of the process, since both equipment and people are dedicated to the cell family, and less movement of materials and material-handling personnel.

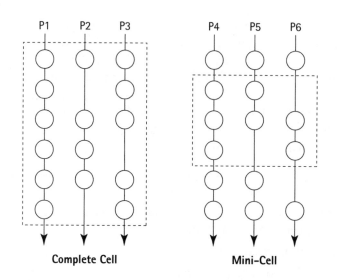

Figure 5-18. A cell that completes all operations vs. a mini-cell

Resource usage. During cell formation you determine first the type and then the number of people and equipment needed to process the cell product families. You would like to fully utilize these resources, because this leads to high output and lowers cost per unit. Although keeping expensive equipment utilized at acceptable levels is important, especially for new equipment acquired for the cell, most firms consider the effective utilization of the people in the cell even more important (see Table 5-3). However, as we will discuss in Chapter 7, high utilizations increase lead times through the cell. Thus, you must balance the goal of low throughput time against that of high output.

In addition to high (but not *too* high) utilization, you also want to achieve an even utilization of the cell's resources. Balanced station utilizations are fair to the operators and will increase output. However, because equipment has different capacities, it is difficult to achieve a fully balanced load. The load balance is also dependent on the product mix assigned to the cell at any point in time. This explains why load imbalance is one of the most common areas of concern to cell users.[31] One way to rectify this problem is to increase the mobility of the operators inside the cell.

Cell size. The size of the cell is determined by the amount of equipment and the number of employees assigned to it. The larger you make a cell, the more product similarity tends to decline. As a result, the flow pattern gets more erratic, the cell becomes unwieldy in terms of visual control, and effective teamwork is hindered. A large cell with many process steps also makes it harder to fully cross-train the operators. This is why the resource perspective on cells calls for a "small" group of resources.

For example, one company created a cell with 27 operators. Management demanded that all should be cross-trained on the close to 50 separate operations performed in the cell. The process engineers thought this would stretch the human limits and proposed less cross-training. This obviously would reduce labor flexibility, but it was the only way such a large cell could be made to operate efficiently.

The cells we have studied display a wide range of team sizes, from 1 up to 40 operators. However, almost three-fourths of all cells (at least in the mechanical industry) have 5 or fewer operators. Parts cells involved with machining tend to have the fewest number of operators, while assembly cells tend to have the largest.[32]

Material flows. You want linear, forward-moving flow in cells. This facilitates material handling as well as visual control of cell production. It is easier to find cell families if you ignore the order in which operations are performed. If you do that, however, you may have to streamline the flow in the cell afterwards. You can do that by (a) resequencing the operations in the routings, (b) redesigning parts to eliminate the need for an operation, (c) duplicating revisited equipment so parts don't have to go backwards in the cell, or (d) eliminating parts with erratic flow patterns from the cell.

Flexibility. Once you have implemented a cell, it runs the risk of being unable to operate as intended. This inability can be due to two reasons. The first is temporary and results from mismatches between capacity and demand. The second stems from the cell's inability to handle new or redesigned parts or products. This is why you must consider the flexibility of the cell during its design, both in terms of handling variations to the original part family and providing alternate routes through the cell. Table 5-3 shows that firms using cells rate equipment flexibility lower than all other design goals. We find this somewhat puzzling. Of course, you can inject flexibility in the cell by cross-training operators. Even so, it is crucial for firms to make sure that cells can deal with product modifications, especially in situations with rapidly changing product designs or if the cells are difficult to reconfigure—as is the case with machining cells (see Chapter 17 for more on this topic).

Constraints in the cell design process

Cell formation is controlled by both managerial and technical constraints. Most common are financial restrictions in the form of hurdle rates (e.g., the investment in cells must meet a specified Internal Rate of Return) or limited capital. A restriction that no new equipment can be purchased for the cell prevents you from upgrading the technology. It also can affect the ability to create independent cells. Other constraints have to do with the cell processes. For example, certain processes must be kept separate from other processes, or from the cell personnel, due to safety reasons (toxicity, fire hazards, etc.). Finally, cell size can be a constraint, whether measured in terms of number of parts or products, amount of equipment, or number of people assigned to the cell. For example, the constraint in one Dutch firm was to create exactly six machine cells out of a job shop. This was due to a very simple reason: the current organization had six foremen, and each was targeted to lead one of the new cells.[33]

How Do You Know When You Have Found a Good Cell?

After you have identified a few product families, determined how they best should be processed within the cells, and made a preliminary assignment of equipment and people to each cell, you still only have a *skeleton* of a cell system. Much work remains before the cells are finalized, such as planning the factory and cell layouts, and modifying the infrastructure. However, as indicated in Figure 5-8 (box 6), you should at this stage evaluate the preliminary cells. Depending on the outcome, you may need to revise the families, the routings, or the equipment/staffing decisions before you continue the planning process. In other words, cell formation is a circular *design-evaluation-redesign* problem.

The evaluation method most commonly used is to verify that a proposed cell can handle the workload. This is done by determining the utilization of each piece of equipment and each operator in the cell (see Chapter 6 for a detailed example). If utilization exceeds 100 percent (or any lower utilization level you have set as the maximum load level), you are forced to make some changes. You can then add equipment and people to meet the demand, or decide not to meet all of the demand. If, on the other hand, utilization levels are too low, you need to revise the cell configuration by expanding the product family, combining two cells, or using other means. Low utilization is a particular concern for capital-intensive equipment.

Of course, verifying that the cell can meet expected demand volumes is just a first step. What you really want to know if whether the cell will improve key performance metrics, such as lead time, quality, cost, and possibly revenues. Those determinations are much more complicated, and we devote much of Chapters 6 through 9 to various aspects of performance assessments. Note, however, that your evaluation should not concentrate exclusively on the new cells. These cells have, most likely, been created by removing products, people, and equipment from existing production units (functional work areas or assembly lines). In that case, you should consider the cells' impact on the rest of the plant as well.

Dynamically Configured Cells

If you do not move equipment into cells, but simply dedicate it to a family, you retain the flexibility to reconfigure the manufacturing system to fit any new products. If this reconfiguration, i.e., the allocation of equipment to families, is done dynamically over time to meet the demand, we have what are called *virtual cells*.

There is another form of dynamic cells where resources are only temporarily close and the composition of product families, equipment, and people may change over time. (Some people call these virtual cells as well; we call them *phantom cells*.) Amadas Industries, which manufactures agricultural machines, had difficulties identifying independent product families due to a wide range of parts and a great degree of resource sharing.[34] However, realizing the benefit of linking consecutive operations, the company now mounts its light equipment on wheels and creates temporary (i.e., phantom) mini-cells around the heavier machine tools. In this way workpieces can be moved easily and quickly between two or more successive operations. As discussed in Chapter 2, however, neither virtual, phantom, nor mini-cells meet our criteria for true cells because the resource dedication, process completeness, and the organizational unit criteria are never or only temporarily met.

DESIGNING A NEW FACTORY LAYOUT

As indicated in Figure 5-2, *layout planning* begins after a new work organization has been designed. As before, we assume that one or more acceptable cells have emerged from the cell formation process.

Facility planning and design is a hierarchical process, where at each successive stage you look at the problem with an increasing level of detail.[35] This process can include planning at the following levels:

- *Global level*. Selecting the location of the plant.
- *Supra level*. Planning the site.
- *Macro level*. Locating cells and other areas and departments within the building. This is part of the factory planning process.
- *Micro level*. Placing work areas, equipment, storage and other areas inside cells/departments. This is part of the detailed cell level planning.
- *Submicro level*. Designing the work place from an ergonomic perspective.

In our factory planning process, we assume that the plant site already exists. To further narrow our scope, we do not address the important issue of workplace ergonomics in this book. Rather, we restrict our discussion of layout planning to the *macro* and *micro* levels because these are the most affected by conversions to cells.[36] The purpose of the layout phase is to fit these cell units into the existing plant and adjust the layout accordingly.

When you adopt the cellular concept you also adopt a new management philosophy. Cellular manufacturing is an integrated system based on cross-trained employees with expanded responsibilities, where operations and support personnel work closely together. This implies that you need to plan space not just for cell equipment, but also for meeting areas (see our discussion of visual control and "green rooms" in Chapter 9) and support personnel offices located nearby the cells.

Basic Considerations in the Factory Layout Process

There are three basic issues you need to consider in factory layout planning: *space*, *relationships*, and *constraints*. The smallest unit that you consider during macro planning is called a "space unit."[37] This could be a cell, a work center, an assembly line, an office, a storage area, or the like. The strength of the relationships among space units depends on the intensity of the flow of material and the amount of information exchanged between the units. Based on relationship mapping you can deduce how important it is to position two space units close to each other, or even if it is desirable to do so. Thus, the strengths of these relationships influence the factory layout. Finally, the layout must meet certain constraints, the foremost of which is the net availability of space (after consideration of aisles, structural support, etc.) into which you can fit the space units. You must also provide room for material-handling systems, external access to the building for deliveries, and so on. Still, within the stated constraints there are usually a large number of alternative layouts.

If you opted for a wide-scoped factory planning phase, and the goal is to recon-figure a large part of the plant, you need a formalized approach to layout planning. This is discussed next. However, unless you are building a new plant from scratch, it is highly unlikely that the whole plant will be affected by the factory planning study. In fact, you may only have identified one or a few viable new cells. In such cases, the layout planning phase may be greatly simplified.

Systematic Layout Planning (SLP)

Several decades ago, Richard Muther developed a very influential framework and methodology for layout planning. Although the planning method originally was totally manual, there now is commercial software that incorporates Muther's Systematic Lay-out Planning (SLP) ideas.[38] We will use a simplified, nine-step SLP framework as a generic way to explain the steps involved with macro layout decisions (see Figure 5-19).

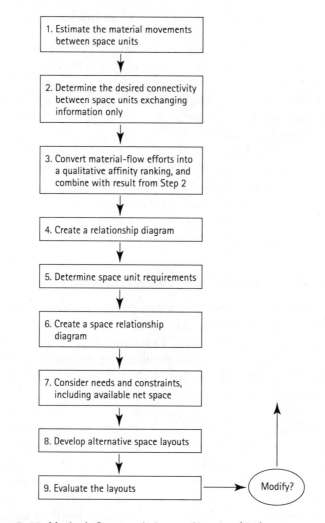

Figure 5-19. Muther's Systematic Layout Planning (SLP) process

Step 1: Estimate material movements between space units

An efficient layout minimizes material flow. To estimate the handling effort, you must *determine the volume moved per unit of time.* To do this you need to know the type of material-handling technology you plan to use (forklift trucks, mechanized conveyors, hand-pushed carts, etc.), and the size of the unit load between each pair of space units. Combined with the information on product volume and routings you can then determine how many units can be moved at a time, as well as the number of units moved between space areas in a day or a month. The end result can be presented in a from-to chart (see Figure 5-20). The data can also be displayed in a table, which may be preferable because it is more compact and also lends itself to data sorting.

	Saw	Grind	NC Mill	Shear	Punch	Deg/deb	Brake	NC drill	Chrom	OUT
Saw	0	0	16	8	47	403	13	16	0	0
Grind	0	0	8	0	0	635	0	0	0	0
NC mill	0	30	0	1	6	146	0	0	2	41
Shear	48	46	59	0	531	2361	1165	191	187	0
Punch	39	524	46	20	0	1596	344	50	62	0
Deg/deb	19	41	75	2163	216	0	2615	62	1486	0
Brake	16	0	20	19	146	573	0	52	1442	1878
NC drill	4	0	2	0	19	232	8	0	15	91
Chrom	0	0	0	0	0	5	1	0	0	3188
IN	377	2	0	2377	1716	726	0	0	0	5198

Figure 5-20. From-to diagram indicating monthly volumes moved between work areas

Step 2: Determine the desired connectivity between space units exchanging information only

At this step you determine the strength of the relationships between space units that do not exchange materials. For example, operators need to visit tool rooms, supervisory offices, restrooms, and the like, while engineers need to consult with quality assurance offices and labs. To express the connectivity between such space units, Muther developed a rating system that expresses the desired strength of connectivity using letters, numbers, or lines (see Figure 5-21).

Step 3: Convert material-flow efforts into a qualitative affinity ranking and combine with result from Step 2

Using the rating system in Figure 5-21 you can consider material-handling efforts together with information closeness and other aspects. This requires that you convert unit load movements into a qualitative rating. In doing that, you should consider the type of material-handling technology (e.g., space units connected by conveyor need to be closer than those connected by forklifts) as well as the need for frequent, face-to-face exchange of information. You can enter the complete ratings of all space units in a table and sort it based on the strengths of the relationships.

Description	Vowel rating	Scalar rating	Manual graphic	CAD graphic	Color
Absolute	A	4			Red
Exceptional	E	3			Yellow
Important	I	2			Green
Ordinary	O	1			Blue
Unimportant	U	0	(none)	(none)	(none)
Apart	X	N/A			Black

Figure 5–21. System for indicating desirability of close location of space units

Step 4: Create a relationship diagram

In this step, you rely on the resulting relationship ratings to produce a "relationship diagram." This is a graphical illustration of the space units' locations relative to each other, with closeness ratings expressed by the thickness of the lines or the number of connecting lines (see Figure 5-22). The relationship diagram is a starting point for the development of to-scale layout drawings. Constructing the diagram is a step-wise process where all units with an A-connection are placed first, then those with E, and I, and so on.[39] You can rearrange the diagram at each step if necessary.

Step 5: Determine space unit requirements

Before scale drawings can be developed, you must determine the size and shape of each space unit. Although you know the space requirements for most existing space units, the new cells may have affected some of them. Included here are the work centers from which you pulled machine tools to place in cells, and the areas allotted to raw materials, WIP, and finished goods. It is difficult to know precisely the size and shape requirements of any new cell at this stage because the detailed cell layouts have not yet been created. Instead, the project team must make a rough estimate of the space needed, including the cells' accessory spaces (meeting places, tool and materials storage, etc.).

Step 6: Create a space relationship diagram

Using scale templates for the space units, you can create a "space relationship diagram." This is essentially the previous relationship diagram merged with each space unit's footprint (see Figure 5-23).[40] With the added space requirements you are one step closer to creating the layout drawing.

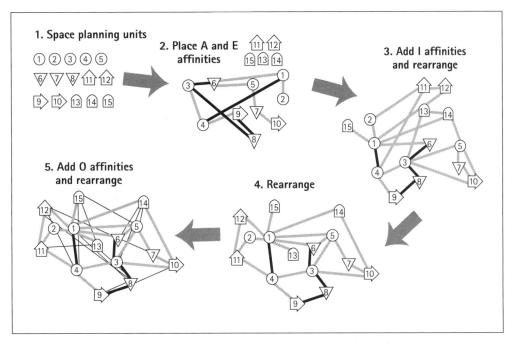

Figure 5-22. Relationship diagram

Step 7: Consider needs and constraints, including available net space

Before you can do the final drawings you need to consider both available space and special constraints imposed on the layout. The expectation with cells, borne out by experience, is that you can achieve considerable space reductions. These reductions should be considered when determining net available space for the layout. Many constraints can affect the placement of space units. One is the need for aisle space. This could require 15 to 35 percent of total factory space and depends on the material-handling system and other factors.[41] You also have to abide by many other restrictions. For example, floor support requirements may limit where you can place heavy equipment, and loading docks limit where you can locate shipping and receiving areas. Health and safety issues may restrict where you can place processes that use hazardous materials, and how you can design workstations or allocate work across cell operators. Constraints such as these need to be considered in the layout design process.

Step 8: Develop alternative space layouts

Mapping the space relationship diagram onto the building layout is a subjective task facilitated by experience and gut feeling. Even though the outer perimeters of a building are fixed, each space relationship diagram can be the seed for alternative layouts. Furthermore, if multiple cells have been proposed you may plan to phase these in successively over time. If so, you should develop several layout alternatives that show the gradual implementation of these cells.

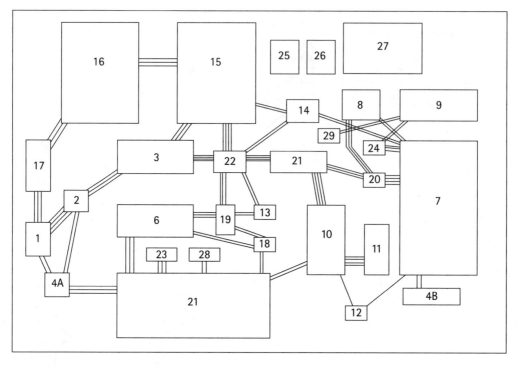

Figure 5-23. Space relationship diagram

Step 9: Evaluate the layouts

In the end, all alternative layout solutions need to be evaluated by the project team and presented to the steering team for final selection. This evaluation, which focuses on the efficient use of space and tight integration of related space units, is preferably done jointly with the choice of final cell configurations and infrastructure modifications. In this way you can assess the upgraded factory from all angles, and not just with respect to the layout issues.

Software for Facility Planning

You can use specialized software to assist you in layout planning. These products are helpful for assessing the current factory before cells have been identified. They can also assist the project team in choosing among alternative cell systems developed in the cell formation phase. Annual software reviews published on the internet or in professional magazines are good sources of information on detailed capabilities, hardware requirements, prices, and vendors.

Layout software possesses one or more of the following main capabilities:

1. Drawing capabilities

2. Evaluation capabilities

3. Construction capabilities

4. Improvement capabilities

Software with *drawing capabilities* helps you illustrate an already designed layout. It uses library icons to help draw walls, windows, machine tools, and the like, and to calculate space needs. It is a sophisticated drawing tool but it does not evaluate the resulting layout. An *evaluative software* package uses a detailed layout as a base. It then relies on product and material-handling data, including paths for the material-handling equipment, to calculate total distance moved, material-handling costs, and the utilization of handling equipment.

Software with drawing and evaluation capabilities requires that you design a layout without the help of the software. *Construction software*, on the other hand, builds layouts. This type of software comes in two forms, depending on whether the layout is automatically created or whether the user is provided with a tool and a methodology for layout construction. For example, some software is essentially a computerized version of the SLP procedure discussed above. As such, it helps you create relationship diagrams and final layouts. More advanced versions of construction software automatically build the space plan based on input data.

Once an initial layout is built, construction software uses improvement algorithms to create better plans by exchanging space unit positions on the layout. Thus, software that can construct layouts typically also incorporates layout *improvement capabilities* (note that evaluation software also can take advantage of improvement algorithms).

Newer software products let employees share facility plans via the web. With drill-down facilities, you can start from the plant outline diagram, drill down to various shops, drill down further to different production lines, and further still down to workstations. The entire layout drawing is broken down into various zones. The ability to only download the relevant zones at any time makes these systems quite fast.

You should view layout software as a complement to rather than a replacement for human planners. Software has limited ability to assess layouts from a multi-objective perspective. However, these packages can no doubt enhance the productivity of the designer, especially for difficult problems: "given two layout planners with comparable experience and skills, the one 'armed' with an appropriate computer-based layout algorithm is far more likely to generate a demonstrably 'better' solution in a shorter time."[42]

MODIFYING THE INFRASTRUCTURE

The process of identifying cells leads naturally into the development of a new plant layout. After all, you cannot create cells without moving equipment and people. However, the issues surrounding infrastructure do not affect the manufacturing process or the materials flow directly. As a consequence, the project teams that were involved with planning families and layouts are not necessarily the best to plan the infrastructure. On the other hand, it is wise to have some overlapping personnel so you can transfer the knowledge gained from the "mess analysis" and subsequent stages between the teams.

As Figure 5-2 shows, you can perform the infrastructure analysis in parallel with layout planning. The issues you need to review are wide-ranging. In Chapter 1 (see

Figure 1-4), we introduced a model of organizational change. Figure 5-24 uses that model to outline the various areas of the company that need to be reviewed in connection with a factory reorganization. Essentially, the infrastructural issues are those listed in the "Organizational structure" and "Management systems" boxes in this figure.

Most infrastructure issues are of concern to the firm as a whole and need to be considered as part of the factorywide analysis. At the same time, many issues have local impact and need to be resolved and fine-tuned at the cell level. Thus, both the layout and the infrastructure analyses have two dimensions: macro and micro, and, in the latter case, before and after final management approval (see Figure 4-1). We devote complete chapters to infrastructural issues: performance measurement in Chapter 9, cost accounting in Chapter 10, production planning and control in Chapter 11, job design and employee selection and training in Chapters 12 and 13, and compensation systems in Chapter 14.

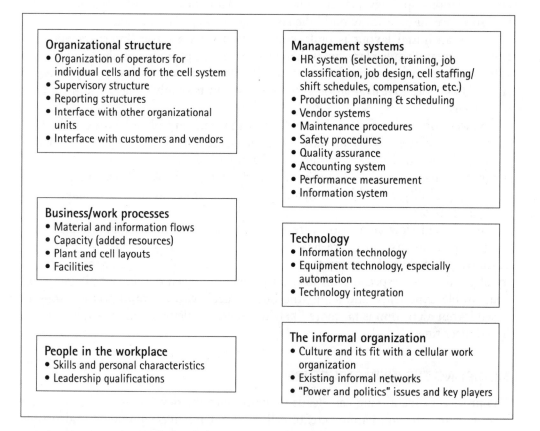

Organizational structure
- Organization of operators for individual cells and for the cell system
- Supervisory structure
- Reporting structures
- Interface with other organizational units
- Interface with customers and vendors

Management systems
- HR system (selection, training, job classification, job design, cell staffing/shift schedules, compensation, etc.)
- Production planning & scheduling
- Vendor systems
- Maintenance procedures
- Safety procedures
- Quality assurance
- Accounting system
- Performance measurement
- Information system

Business/work processes
- Material and information flows
- Capacity (added resources)
- Plant and cell layouts
- Facilities

Technology
- Information technology
- Equipment technology, especially automation
- Technology integration

People in the workplace
- Skills and personal characteristics
- Leadership qualifications

The informal organization
- Culture and its fit with a cellular work organization
- Existing informal networks
- "Power and politics" issues and key players

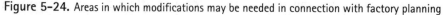

Figure 5-24. Areas in which modifications may be needed in connection with factory planning

KEY INSIGHTS

Factory planning is classic problem solving. The process of formulating problems, collecting/analyzing data, and generating solutions repeats itself for each of its subphases: determining what the work organization should look like, how the various space units should be laid out, and how the infrastructure should be modified (Figure 5-2). A similar problem-solving process is then followed for each individual cell.

In this chapter we focused on the many issues project teams get involved with during factory planning as they analyze the organization and search for cells. Some key points are highlighted below.

- *Expect your initial analysis of the organization to be messy.* Part of this mess comes from vague visions, unclear problem formulations, and a lack of data.

- *To analyze a factory, you need to collect much data and perform a variety of analyses.* We outlined 11 types of activities and analyses in Table 5-1. Be prepared to spend much time locating the data you need before you can begin analyzing current processes, reorganize work into cells, and improve performance.

- *You can reduce the complexity of the factory by partitioning it along product lines.* The two key dimensions of complexity are number of units and relationships. Thus, if you can reduce the number of product families and production units you are working with, and make these groups independent of each other, you will reduce planning and operational complexity. You can start this process by segmenting the plant into focused factories. Within these, you can then continue to search for product and part families with strong internal similarities. These can form cells.

- *To establish cells you must first find logical cells.* This is done during the cell formation phase in which part/product families and associated resources are identified, put together in cell units, and evaluated.

- *You can use a variety of criteria to find part and product families.* These criteria range from customer and market factors to demand volume to innate product characteristics. Most companies rely on multiple criteria to find families. The most difficult part of this process is determining the families that can best meet your performance improvement targets without violating economical or technical constraints.

- *As you plan for cells, focus on making parts complete, keeping resources utilized, limiting the cell size, simplifying the materials flow, and injecting flexibility.* These are some of the most important design considerations and they will all affect cell performance. The extent of the improvement can be verified before implementation with computer modeling.

- *Cells require both a physical and an organizational restructuring of the factory.* This means that you need to re-layout the factory, as well as re-think the plant's infrastructure, when you implement cells. These redesign processes take place first at the macro (factory) level and then at the micro (cell) level. Next chapter deals with cell level issues.

6

Detailed Planning—One Cell at a Time

In this chapter we focus primarily on detailed cell formation, cell dimensioning, and layout planning. As you will see, the tasks required for cell level planning are essentially the same as those we discussed for the factory planning phase, although at a more detailed level. If you identified several potential cells during that phase, you will now concentrate on *one cell at a time*, rather than on a larger cell system. That is, you will finalize the product/part families and their basic processes for each cell, plan the internal cell layouts, and fine-tune the infrastructure. If you took a narrow scope to factory planning, the distinction between that phase and this detailed planning phase could be small. Note, however, that changes to a single cell (for example, in terms of its part family) may force you to revisit the overall factory planning phase to verify the impact on other production units.

Here are the most important issues looked at in this chapter:

- If you have identified several potential cells during the factory planning phase, which do you implement first?
- What are the key steps in the detailed design and layout planning process for cells?
- How do you dimension cells, i.e., determine the required number of people and equipment to meet targeted volumes?
- What are some of the dilemmas that project teams will face during cell design—and how can they be resolved?

PROJECT ORGANIZATION

At this point in the planning process, one or more project teams already exist. You should now reorganize these "factory" teams into cell-based teams. Whether you plan to implement a single cell or several cells at the same time, each team should be responsible for developing and implementing a specific cell. You want to involve personnel that have participated in the "mess analysis" so that insights gleaned from this phase can be shared with the team. You should also make sure that the new teams include the future cell supervisors and some or all of the employees who will work in the cell. This is especially important when it comes to deciding on the cell layout and fine-tuning the processes. Note, however, that having operators on the team from the very beginning is not possible if the cell operators have not yet been selected. In fact, you may want to wait until the steering team has given final approval of the cell project before you engage production workers in the analysis.

In some cases operators are involved in the change process right from the start. The story of Gelman Sciences, discussed in Chapter 1, is interesting in this regard.[1] Gelman, a Michigan-based manufacturer of microporous membrane filtration products, faced high scrap rates, equipment downtime, poor quality and delivery performance, and high WIP and FGI inventories. Management began turning this tide by creating continuous improvement teams, most of them assigned to a machine type (e.g., all operators working on the pleating process were assigned to one team). External consultants were then brought in to train the employees in teamwork. Although the new employee teams reduced setups, and improved manufacturing quality and delivery results, improvement stagnated after 18 months. One problem was that the teams focused only on their own immediate process, neglecting the steps before and after. That is, they took a narrow view, rather than a system's view, of work. Following in-house training on lean manufacturing concepts, management reorganized the workforce from functional to product-based teams.

Although the team structure changed, the equipment remained scattered all over the factory. During a period of cross-training, the operators began to realize the value of closely positioned processes and started to lay out cells for their products. Several cells were identified in this way, and management planned the successive implementation of these over a 12-month period.

In essence, Gelman initially went through a very limited factory planning phase where improvements were localized to each functional area. The company then switched to product-based teams. This marked the beginning of cellular manufacturing at Gelman Sciences. In this change process, the operators were involved with the detailed cell planning from the very beginning. Early education and training of company personnel in process improvement and lean manufacturing increased the value of the employees' contributions to the cell design.

WHICH CELL FIRST?

We break down the detailed cell planning process into two parts—before and after management has approved the project (see Figure 6-1 for an overview of the detailed cell planning phase). You may have done a rough cost justification at the factory planning stage. However, you cannot prepare a solid cost/benefit analysis until you have developed more detailed plans for the cells. As a general rule, the project team should take initial planning to the point where it feels it has sufficient background information to justify the conversion—but no further. This is to minimize the risk of spending unnecessary time and money on a project that is later cancelled.

Figure 6-1 shows that before detailed cell planning can begin you have to choose one or more cells as the starting point for the planning effort. Specifically, if you have identified several cells and laid out a master plan for the factory, you have to decide whether to implement all cells at once or to phase them in over time. The latter approach, as illustrated by Gelman Sciences, is the most common. One benefit of

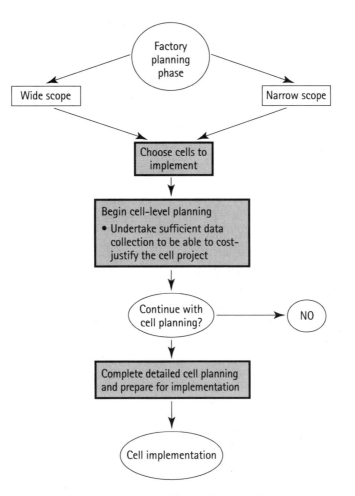

Figure 6-1. Detailed cell planning—overview

sequential implementation is that each preceding cell serves as a learning vehicle for subsequent cells.[2] Accordingly, if your previous analysis identified more than one cell, you must decide which to implement first.

You can use a *problem focus* or an *implementation focus* to help you make this decision. A problem focus ensures that the chosen cell solves a real and substantial problem, while an implementation focus ensures that the selected cell is easy to implement and has a high probability of success. Ideally, you want a cell that meets *both* criteria. Of course, you should also use these considerations when selecting product families for a single cell application.

Problem Focus: What Problems Will the Cell Solve?

Firms implement cells to solve performance problems, such as long lead times, poor quality, or high costs. This is why your initial cell should include the products or components that cause the largest problems in the plant and, therefore, are candidates for the greatest performance improvements.

For example, Kohler Industries had undertaken a complete redesign of its generator factory. Process similarity and the product characteristic size were used to create final assembly cells and stator and rotor winding cells for large and small generators (see Table 5-2). The plan also called for several cells to be shared among product lines, such as a CNC sheet metal cell, a sheet metal welding cell, a coat finishing cell, and a circuit board cell. Kohler concentrated its initial implementation efforts on the winding cells because the largest value-added was created there. In the same vein, Collier Transmission's plant in Richardson, Texas, looked at the dollar value of components going into assembly operations. They selected the parts with the highest dollar value per year for their initial cell effort. In both cases, the part families selected were those for which improvements in quality and lead time would generate the greatest impact on inventory investment and unit cost.

When you apply a problem focus to cell selection, don't confine yourself to material-related problems only. For example, at some plants people-oriented issues drive cell adoption. The purpose can be to eliminate work-related injuries through the assignment of broader sets of tasks, or to create work environments that are more attractive from a social-psychological viewpoint. Table 6-1 shows various considerations for choosing among product or part families. The key question to ask is: "Which problem will this particular cell solve, and how critical is it?"

Table 6-1. Consideration for choosing among potential product/part families

- High scrap rates
- High rework cost
- High value-added
- High dollar volume
- Large WIP inventories
- Long move distances
- High ratio of lead time to processing time
- Large lot sizes
- Large setup times
- Frequent delays for assembly operations
- Core products or components of core products
- Relatively stable demand
- High rates of repetitive motion-based injuries
- Poor social working environment

- -

- Low cost of implementation
- Ease of implementation
- Readiness among employees

Implementation Focus: Will the Implementation Be Successful?

You want to choose a cell that is cost-effective, will be up and running within a fairly short time, and can meet stated goals. In short, you want this cell to be a success so skeptical managers and operators will be convinced that cellular manufacturing can be effective. A high level of "readiness to change" among the employees currently working with the targeted product families will strongly contribute to the cell's performance. *Taking implementation success into account is particularly important if this is the first reorganization project that your firm is undertaking.*

An illustration

In connection with the design of its very first machining cell, the plant manager at one company asked the manufacturing engineers to identify parts that:

1. Were simple to make.
2. Were experiencing delivery problems.
3. Had a lot of WIP inventory.
4. Required machines that were relatively easy to move.
5. Required machines that performed operations that also could be done on other equipment (so that parts not selected for the cell could be reallocated and processed elsewhere).
6. Required machines that could be staffed by operators who would readily accept the change to a cellular concept.

You may note that the plant manager's charge to the engineers consisted of a mixture of problem-focused (items 2 and 3) and implementation-focused (items 1, 4–6) criteria.[3]

DETAILED CELL PLANNING—AN OVERVIEW

Once you have chosen the cells to implement, you can begin detailed cell planning. Figure 6-2 shows the typical steps in this process. Although we have numbered the steps for easy identification, it is not possible to prescribe an exact process sequence that you must follow. Many of the steps are highly interrelated, which means that you will go back and forth between them until you find a satisfactory solution. Despite the strong relationships among the steps, we separate them into three "planning blocks": (1) cell formation and dimensioning, (2) management systems, and (3) employee, layout, and start-up issues. The dotted lines indicate that the boundaries are fluid. The steps in the upper block should be performed first, although the infrastructure planning in the middle block can be performed in parallel with these steps.

After you have completed the planning steps in the two upper blocks, you should be ready to do the detailed cost justification of the cell. And after the project has been approved, you can select cell personnel to participate in the continued planning shown in the bottom block. (Although the teams must also begin planning for cell implementation during this phase, we discuss this and other infrastructure issues in later chapters.)

PLANNING BLOCK 1—CELL FORMATION AND DIMENSIONING

Step 1: Refine Product and Part Families

If the potential cell was "handed down" from a larger factory analysis (i.e., performed by another team), the first task for the cell team is to ensure that the family is complete. This is because the previous analysis may have been based only on a *sample* of representative parts or products, while at the detailed planning stage you need to consider *all* items to be processed in the cell.

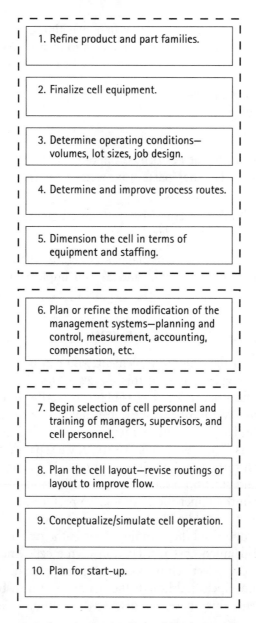

Figure 6-2. Steps in the detailed cell level planning process

Step 2: Finalize Cell Equipment

For the same reasons as above, you also need to finalize selection of the cell equipment. During factory planning, existing plant equipment may tentatively have been allocated to the cell. You now need to make specific equipment choices, possibly including new process technology for the cell. You must also choose a material-handling system, whether manual or mechanized.

Step 3: Determine Operating Conditions

If some time has elapsed between factory planning and detailed planning activities, the cell team should verify that the current and future demand data for the cell are still valid. You should also determine lot sizes for the cell. External lot sizes are those by which material is delivered to and moved from the cell. Likewise, internal lot sizes are those by which material is moved between workstations inside the cell. Internal lot sizes can typically be smaller (preferably, just one unit) than external lots. You also need to think about job design—that is, what will each operator in the cell do? This affects the staffing plans and the cell simulations (Steps 5 and 9 in Figure 6-2, respectively).

Step 4: Finalize and Improve Process Routes

As part of detailed design, you must finalize the manufacturing processes for the cell family. New products, of course, must have their routings developed from scratch. For existing products, you may have used the current routings to create tentative families (see previous chapter). However, those routings are no longer useful if some of the cell equipment will be new. Old routings are often not ideal anyway because they may not lead to the best flow in the cell.

Despite these weaknesses, existing routings represent a convenient way to begin building new routings for the cell family. Routings are also the starting point for developing the sequence in which you position the cell equipment (see Step 8 below).

How to improve process flows

During detailed cell planning, avoid being fixated on the ways products currently are produced. Instead, make a serious effort to *rethink* present manufacturing processes and envision *the best way* to produce the family. The objectives for this effort should be to:

- Minimize the number of process steps or pieces of equipment in order to reduce the number of moves.
- Smooth the material flow in order to minimize the number of backtracks and skips in the cell.
- Reduce the time for changeovers in order to minimize lot sizes and schedule changes.[4]

Table 6-2 lists some specific ways to achieve these goals. Several of these suggestions try to ensure that material always moves forward in the cell—never backward. They also seek to maximize equipment-sharing among products in the family. After all, if products don't share equipment, why are they in the cell family? Note that some of these improvement steps may alter the equipment assignment you made at Step 2, or even the product family itself. Below, we discuss in turn each of the possible actions shown in Table 6-2.

Table 6-2. Ways to improve flows in cells by modifying the routings

> - Group items with identical or highly similar routings
> - Standardize raw materials
> - Change the sequence between operations
> - Reroute the parts or products to different types of equipment
> - Eliminate unnecessary operations
> - Redesign the parts or products to remove process steps
> - Remove parts/products with deviating processes (outliers) from the family

Group identical/similar routings. Often, it is possible to partition a family into smaller subfamilies with greater internal similarities, especially if the original families are based on very coarse criteria. The resulting families can have more consistent flow patterns and more similar setup requirements (see Figure 6-3). You then can decide whether you should create multiple cells, each with smoother flows and lower setup time requirements, or merely use the subfamilies for setup-dependent sequencing (see Chapter 11). The creation of families is also an opportunity to eliminate parts with very similar characteristics. Part and feature standardization is a classic application of group technology to curb unnecessary proliferation. Immediate benefits will be higher volumes for the remaining parts, which can lead to lower material costs and a more efficient manufacturing process.

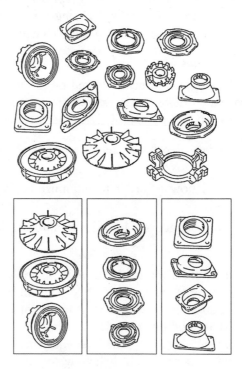

Figure 6-3. A product family and subfamilies with greater internal similarities

Standardize raw materials. You can use the product characteristic "raw material" to form families (see Table 5-2). Standardizing the materials used by products reduces setups and can help consolidate previously separate families. For example, one firm in the electronics industry used material of different thickness, supplied by multiple vendors, for two of its products. This caused unnecessary changeovers in the latter stages of an assembly cell. Since there was no technological reason for using different materials, one of them was eliminated. The result was zero changeover time and lower material cost.

Change the sequence of operations and/or reroute parts or products. The sequence of operations assigned to an item, as shown by the routing, is not always dictated by technical reasons. You may be able to switch the order between operations to make a part or product better fit with the dominant flow in the cell. Another alternative is to "reprocess" the part by changing its basic type of operation. You can do that by rerouting the operation from one type of equipment to another in the cell. For example, some grinding operations can be performed either on a grinder or on a lathe. These changes can improve the flow as well as lead to a better load balance.

Eliminate operations and/or redesign the parts or products. While developing the best process for a family, the team should question each potential operation by asking, "Is it necessary?" For example, by purchasing precut sheet metal, you can avoid cutting operations. Other operations, such as deburring, are due to the quality of the raw materials. You may be able to eliminate some operations, fully or partly, by upgrading material quality.

The very act of identifying a family of parts is the starting point for discovering ideas for process modifications. For example, part features prescribed by design engineers are many times not needed for the part to function properly. Such features, therefore, can be eliminated. At Racine Hydraulics, several parts in a potential cell family had three holes drilled off-center, while the majority of the parts had the holes centered. The body of the parts was identical. Switching between the two types of parts would require the purchase of a new, $35,000 spindle head as well as cause additional setup time. The simple solution was to move all holes to the center, without any impact on the final product or other components, and continue to use the existing multidrill spindle head.

Likewise, when Baker Manufacturing was planning a cell for one of its pumps, one operator suggested redesigning the pump so the housing could be made from two rather than three cast iron parts. This redesign reduced the number of process steps and setups while also improving the quality and performance of the pump.

Remove parts/products from the cell family. The final approach to securing streamlined flows in cells is to remove parts or products with "erratic" routings from the family and have them produced either in other, "noncellularized" areas of the factory, or by outside vendors. This alternative, however, may not be attractive if component manufacturing is to be closely integrated with assembly.

The problem of ill-fitting parts or products can become a constant headache unless newly designed or redesigned parts are made to fit into existing cells. Seemingly innocent design changes otherwise can lead to the need for more sophisticated equipment (e.g., new features requiring a switch from four- to five-axes machines), new tools, fixtures, and gauges—and in all likelihood increase the cost of operating the cell (also see our discussion in Chapter 17).

Consider routing improvements and cell layout together

The ideas we have suggested to improve flows can be applied to the routings in the product family before considering the cell layout. However, as discussed under Step 8 below, the routings for the products will influence the sequence in which the equipment is laid out in the cell. The placement of equipment, in turn, determines the actual flow pattern in the cell. If the material flow is unacceptable, you can go back and modify individual routings using any of the ideas in Table 6-2. Thus, *the routing improvement effort should be revisited when preparing the cell layout in order to fine-tune the flow.*

Step 5: Dimension the Cell in Terms of Equipment and Staffing

After you have determined the best process for the family at Step 4 (remember, you may later find a new "best" process), you can dimension the cell. This means that you determine the minimum number of units of each type of equipment the cell needs to meet the demand, as well as the minimum number of operators needed to run the cell. You should here be guided by the volume, and other operating data, found at Step 3. The number of resources of each type, and their utilization, will very much shape the cost, layout, and performance of the cell. (We discuss cell dimensioning in a separate section later in this chapter.)

PLANNING BLOCK 2—MANAGEMENT SYSTEMS

Step 6: Plan or Refine the Modification of the Management Systems

As we indicate in Figure 6-2, the second planning block contains activities related to the cell's infrastructure. You should already have done some thinking about job design, compensation for cell operators, performance measurement for the cells, planning and control systems, accounting systems, quality and maintenance procedures, and the like as part of factory planning. You will now continue this analysis in more detail and tailor any system to the cell you are currently planning.

The infrastructure analysis is somewhat separate from the more physical and technical aspects of the cell planning. Due to the nature of the management systems, the teams working on these aspects will include a larger portion of managers and support personnel than what you want for teams working on cell design, technology, and layout issues. It also means that the infrastructure planning can take place in parallel with the activities in Planning Block 1. This is one reason why Step 6 is in a planning block of its own. Another reason is that you want to think through these issues before you undertake an economic justification of the cells. For example, you may conclude that new test equipment or a new data-collection system should be part of the cell. Likewise, the supervisory structure for the cells may be such that fewer supervisors are needed in the future, while the operator compensation should be increased. The economic impact of these proposals needs to be included in the cost-benefit analysis. After completing the planning activities in Steps 1 through 6, you should be ready to present the project to management for final approval. (Chapters 8 through 14 cover economic analysis and infrastructural issues in much detail.)

PLANNING BLOCK 3—EMPLOYEE, LAYOUT, AND START-UP ISSUES

You can postpone the final planning activities until the cell project is approved. At that point, however, you definitely want the operators involved. For example, you do not want to finalize the details of the cell's layout without the input from the people who will work there. On the other hand, you do not want operators on a specific cell team earlier than this because it is not yet clear that the cell will be built.

Step 7: Select Cell Personnel and Begin Training Employees

Cell supervisors should be chosen early so they can participate fully in the planning process (you may have done this already during the factory planning phase). Operator selection, as mentioned, is best done after the cells are approved. Education and training should begin as soon as possible and should be hierarchical. That is, managers should be educated before supervisors, and supervisors before the employees who will work for them. You will have to delay part of the operators' training until the cells are in operation because operational procedures and technical skills are best mastered via on-the-job instruction. However, you still can provide classroom education on cellular concepts, interpersonal skills, decision-making and problem-solving, and so on. (Chapter 13 discusses employee selection and also describes the type of training to provide, to whom, and how to best deliver it.)

Step 8: Plan the Detailed Layout

Cell layout focuses on physical placement of equipment and work areas within the cell space. You want the layout to achieve local workplace efficiency, prevent manufacturing quality problems, and satisfy workers' ergonomic requirements and sociopsychological needs. Since the cell is the daily workplace for the operators, you *must* involve them in the layout design.

Determine the equipment sequence

Before you create detailed layout plans, you need to determine the best order between workstations in the cell. This sequence becomes the starting point for the layout. A "best sequence" at this stage is one that: (1) minimizes the percent of volume that must revisit previous workstations (i.e., percent backtrack volume), and (2) maximizes the percentage of the total volume moved between adjacent workstations. These two goals are not necessarily both achievable, so you will have to decide which is most important.

There are a couple of ways to determine the dominant process sequence for the cell family. You could rely on the same relationship-based procedures used to plan the factory layout (see Figures 5-21 through 5-23). A simpler approach, which only considers material flows, is to use a from-to matrix (see Figure 6-4). This shows the volume moved per unit of time between pairs of workstations. A from-to matrix is constructed by combining monthly or annual production volume data with routing information.

	2	3	4	5	OUT
IN		300	20	40	
2	–		100		
3	100	–	200		
4			–	50	360
5			90	–	

Figure 6-4. From-To chart where entries indicate weekly volumes moved between stations

You can create a dominant flow sequence for the cell by first placing the pair of stations with the highest flow volume between them. Then continue with the pair with the next highest flow, and so on, until you have placed all stations in a logical sequence. Figure 6-5 shows the steps you follow to create such a sequence based on the from-to diagram in Figure 6-4.[5] As you can see, the resulting machine sequence shows both "backtracking" and "jumping" moves. Commercial layout software can assess the "move efficiency" of specified layout sequences (see Chapter 5).

In Figure 6-4, we ignored the number of batches moved between stations per unit of time. By looking only at weekly volumes, we effectively assumed that all parts use the same internal transfer batch size. Suppose that one part has a monthly average demand of 1,200 units while another part has a demand of 4,000 units per month. If you plan to build a cell based on the one-piece flow idea (i.e., the transfer batch is a single unit), the number of batches moved per month is 1,200/1 = 1,200 and 4,000/1 = 4,000 units, respectively (you find the number of batches moved by dividing the demand by the batch size). On the other hand, if you set the transfer batch at 50 units for both items, the number of batches moved along the routings are 1,200/50 = 24 and 4,000/50 = 80, respectively. Since 24/80 equals 1,200/4,000, it doesn't matter if you use demand volume or number of batches to express the intensity of movements in the cell.

However, if the batch sizes *differ* for the items, you should use the number of batches moved between workstations per unit of time rather than the raw volume. Consider the case where the first part uses a transfer batch of 1 while the second part's transfer batch size is 50. While the ratio between the total volumes is 1,200/4,000 = 0.3, the ratio between the number of batches moved is 1,200/80 = 15. Thus there are 15 times as many material moves per month between stations in

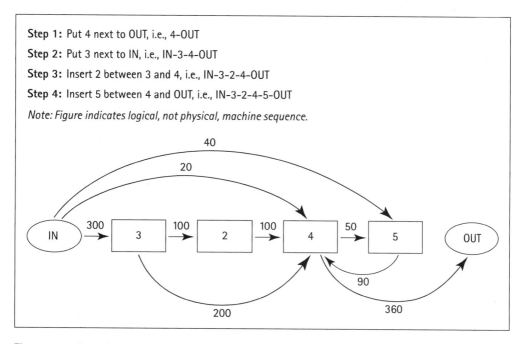

Step 1: Put 4 next to OUT, i.e., 4–OUT

Step 2: Put 3 next to IN, i.e., IN-3-4–OUT

Step 3: Insert 2 between 3 and 4, i.e., IN-3-2-4–OUT

Step 4: Insert 5 between 4 and OUT, i.e., IN-3-2-4-5–OUT

Note: Figure indicates logical, not physical, machine sequence.

Figure 6–5. Steps in creating a sequence of machines based on the From-To chart in Figure 6-4

the cell for the first part compared to the second. Clearly, when transfer batches differ, the number of moves per unit of time is a better indicator of material-handling effort than is production volume and should be considered when laying out the cell.

Should you duplicate equipment to avoid backtracks?

Product families often consist of parts with somewhat different routings. The goal at Step 4 in Figure 6-2 was to modify and standardize these routings to improve flow. Despite these routing modifications, the order in which you place equipment in the cell can force some parts to return to previously visited equipment. You can always eliminate backtracking operations by duplicating equipment. However, whether this is an acceptable solution depends on the cost of the equipment and its utilization, and whether it is physically movable (monuments like heat treatment, painting lines, chroming lines, etc., are often both costly and immovable). Using "obsolete" machinery can deflect cost and utilization issues. Plants often have old equipment just sitting around unused that can be put to good use in a cell (assuming, of course, that its process capabilities are satisfactory). Even if it is permanently set up to do just one operation, it can be cost effective since the equipment was not being used anyway.

Revisit the from-to matrix

If you modify part routings to improve flow, whether using equipment duplication or any of methods shown in Table 6-2, you should reconstruct the from-to matrix to view the revised flow. If the flow pattern is still unsatisfactory, the chart can point to equipment and part routings you should modify further.

Decide the shape of the cell

You can plan the equipment/workstation positions on the floor by using movable paper templates on a board representing the factory, drawing machine templates on a paper layout, or using a CAD drawing system. There are numerous ways to place a set of workstations within a given space. Ideally, you want the material to move forward from station to station. You have provided the basic foundation for such a layout by forming the family, improving the routings, and, as we just described, using a from-to matrix to create the station sequence. Therefore, you could simply place all the equipment in a straight row (see Figure 6-6). But this layout may not be very efficient. It is commonly better to position the workstations in a circle, in the form of a "C," or more openly as a "U" (see Figure 6-7). You can adopt the U-shape for both assembly and part-producing cells. However, the material-handling system and the available space may restrict their use and lead to cell layouts with more irregular forms.

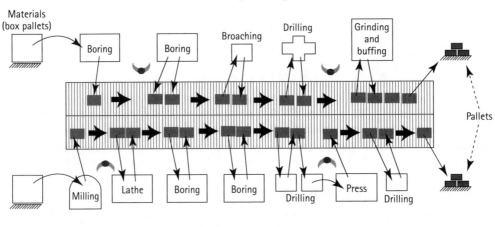

Figure 6-6. Straight station layout

Advantages with U-shaped cell layouts. Among the many advantages with a U-shaped cell (as compared to a straight or linear cell, or any other shape) are that it:

1. Minimizes the walking distance if a single operator runs the cell.

2. Creates more opportunities for assigning operators to workstations because the stations an operator serves need not be adjacent.

3. Minimizes the travel distances for parts that skip workstations or parts that need to backtrack to previously visited stations (since parts can "cross-over" to stations on the other side of the cell rather than passing through each station on their way).

4. Assures a constant WIP and flow rate through the cell if you assign the same operator to the first and the last station. This is because the operator will pull a new part into the cell as soon as one leaves the cell in a finished state. (This outcome can also be achieved using a generic pull system; see Chapter 11.)

5. Places all operators close to each other, making it easy for them to help each other out if need be.

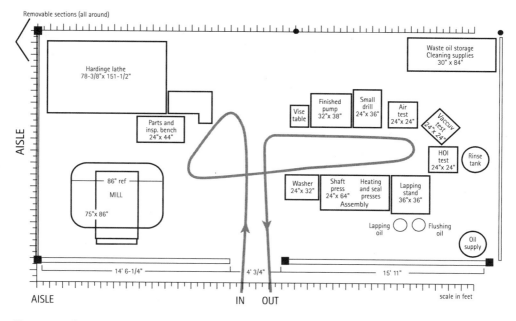

Figure 6-7. U-shaped pump cell at Baker Manufacturing

U-cells appear to have originated in Japan and are strongly advocated by Japanese companies and consultants. A few rules seem to dominate their design, as shown in Table 6-3 and commented upon below.[6]

Table 6-3. Guidelines for designing U-shaped cells

1. Place the workstations as closely as possible to minimize walking distances.
2. Avoid operator walking patterns that cross paths.
3. Position operators so they face outwards.
4. Operators should stand, not sit.
5. Position the workstations so the material moves counterclockwise in the cell.
6. Assign the entry and exit operations to the same operator.
7. Avoid or minimize the use of conveyors in low volume/high variety cells.
8. Rely on one-piece production, one-piece inspection, and one-piece conveyance.

The rationale for locating workstations in close proximity, of course, is to minimize waste in the form of operator movements (Figure 6-8 illustrates walking patterns in a very dense, four-operator U-shaped cell). However, you should note that a common source of initial problems with teamwork in cells stems from the newfound physical closeness that some people find uncomfortable, especially if they are used to greater personal space in the previous layout.

When you place the workstations, avoid—for obvious reasons—having operators cross each other's paths when they move from station to station (i.e., the path in Figure 6-7 is not ideal in this regard). Further, placing workstations in a circle, with the operators inside looking out, facilitates operator movements between stations on the opposite side of the cell. That operators should stand rather than sit is natural in many cells, since they frequently need to move between their assigned workstations, often with a single work piece. Standing operators also are better able to help out other operators, a practice that can be crucial to effective improvement activities in the cell. There is also an ergonomic reason. Some people find it easier and more natural to perform tasks in a standing position. However, others may find it more tiring and prefer to sit.

The counter-clockwise movement of materials in cells (as illustrated in Figure 6-8) probably has its origin in assembly cells where operators remain at their workstations and pull in materials from previous stations. With most people being right-handed, such pulls are facilitated by grabbing the material with the right hand and moving it into the station. With operators facing outwards, this results in counter-clockwise moves.[7] We see this design rule as interesting but not important.

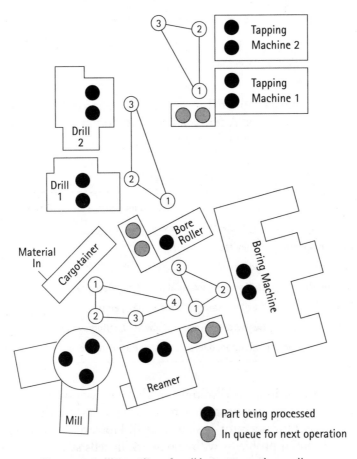

Figure 6-8. Illustration of walking patterns in a cell

Putting the same operator in charge of both entry and exit operations in the cell is an idea advocated by the Japanese consultant Kenichi Sekine.[8] With this design, the operator will be in control of the two most critical quality checks: the state of incoming and outgoing materials. As noted above, it also permits the operator to control the rate of flow through the cell.

Conveyors can move materials, especially heavy workpieces, between workstations efficiently. However, they should be avoided inside low-volume cells. Unpaced conveyors (e.g., roller conveyors) often end up serving as in-process storage places due to variations in task times and can prevent the search for ways to better balance production.

The "one-piece conveyance and one-piece production" concept is an ideal to strive for. However, it is not always practical. If the workpieces are very small (as in the electronics industry) and/or the distance is long, moving one unit at a time is inefficient. Likewise, if setup times are long and there is a changeover between each piece, producing one unit between setups can consume so much capacity that output suffers.

An illustration of conveyor removal. Two part families were originally processed in two "straight" cells where the machines were linked by roller conveyor (see Figure 6-6).[9] The two cells, one making rods and the other crank arms, were laid out facing each other with the conveyor in the middle. Two operators served each cell. Although this layout may seem efficient, it exhibited some of the problems typical of conveyor-based lines. For example, parts were stored on the conveyor. Also, the conveyor prevented the operators from effectively assisting each other. By removing the conveyors and installing auto-clamps, auto-feeds, and improved jigs, the two part families could be processed in two U-cells by single operators. The cells were placed in a mirror position so that further improvements might make it possible for one operator to run both families (see Figure 6-9).

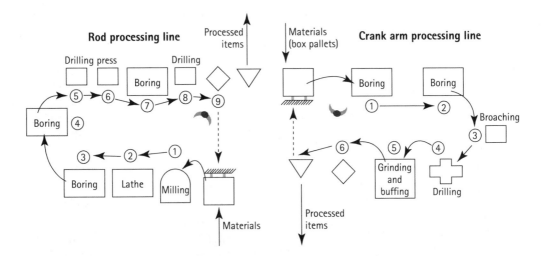

Figure 6-9. U-cells formed from the straight station layout in Figure 6-6

Complete the detailed cell layout

A myriad of questions need to be answered before you are ready to finalize the cell layout and begin implementation. The most important ones include:

1. Where will you place equipment, the material-handling system, buffer spaces, and work areas (assembly area, inspection tables, place to store and review drawings, space for cell computer, etc.)?
2. Where will you place incoming and outgoing materials?
3. How will you design an ergonomically sound workplace?
4. Where will you locate meeting areas and visual management displays?

We discussed the advantages of U-shaped cells earlier. In reality, the shape of the available cell space, and the location of aisles and support pillars, will dictate where you can place cell equipment, material, tools, and so on. The material-handling system also will strongly influence the layout. Conveyors, in particular, restrict the layout of the cell (as shown in Figure 6-6).

The size of the required buffer spaces depends on the size of the transfer batches inside the cell and whether you plan to use WIP limiters like Kanban squares (see more on this in Chapters 7 and 11). In sizing buffer spaces you must also consider the production rates for each connected workstation. If a station with high output rates feeds a slower station, the buffer space between these stations must accommodate this. The choice of a material-handling system is also related to buffer spaces because, in essence, a conveyor serves as a buffer for materials.

You should locate space for incoming and outgoing materials right at the entry/exit point of the cell. If distances are short, operators can move the completed material to the next cell or storage area. In general, however, operators should not have to go to a material location to pick up or deliver materials. Rather, material handlers (or material vendors) should perform such tasks. The space needed for incoming and outgoing materials depends on the external lot sizes by which material is delivered to and moved from the cell. So decisions you made about the cell's material control system (see Steps 3 and 6 in Figure 6-2) will influence decisions regarding the cell's layout.

It is important to design the workplace inside the cell for the people in that cell. That is, supplies, tooling, and gauges should be located to minimize move distances and avoid awkward or uncomfortable positions for the employees. If you expect operators to assist each other, you need a design that permits simultaneous access to the workpieces by multiple operators. The cell layout should also minimize the possibility of accidents or contact with toxic materials and provide adequate lighting and comfortable temperature. It should also supply fresh air, minimize noise, and provide good foot support and correct height of worktables. These all are standard ergonomic considerations and are no different for cells than for any other work area.

Finally, cells, through their compact size, facilitate direct, visual control of production. To support that, you also need to make room for physical displays of various statistics related to the cell, like recent performance, safety instructions, and standard operating instructions. You may also want to display such items as blueprints of the products, pictures of the cell operators, and a matrix indicating their current skills and the skills for which they are being trained. If the cell is to have a pull system for materials control, and you are using physical or electronic cards to trigger production or material movement from internal or external suppliers, you also need to make room for Kanban boards, a fax machine, or a computer next to the cell.

Step 9: Conceptualize/Simulate Cell Operations

Once you have put together a first draft of the cell layout, all cell operators and supervisors should review it. One way to do this is to post enlarged drawings of the cell for everybody to see. The drawings can be combined with a description of how the cell team envisions the process inside the cell. A detailed example follows.

The operation of a combined molding and assembly cell

This molding and assembly cell manufactures oil seals. It is staffed by three operators, one of whom is stationary at the rubber molding press, and two who rotate through the assembly portion of the cell (see Figure 6-10). The cell needs two assemblers to match the cycle time of the molding press. Each assembler takes nine parts at a time through the complete assembly process.

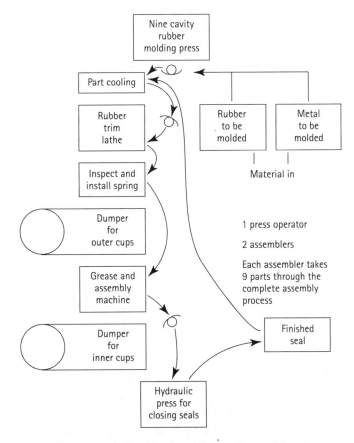

Figure 6-10. Combined molding and assembly cell

The flow through the cell is as follows. The rubber molding press operator removes enough rubber and metal from their respective input queues to form nine seals and loads the nine-cavity molding press. At the completion of the cycle, the operator removes the semicompleted seals from the press and places them on the cooling table. He or she then moves more raw materials from the input queue to the molding machine and repeats the operation.

Once the parts have cooled, one of the two assembly operators takes the nine seals and trims the rubber of each seal on the trim lathe. The operator proceeds to the next station, where he or she installs a spring and inspects the seals. The operator then goes to the grease and assembly machine and joins inner and outer seal cups to the seal. This process is repeated until all nine seals are assembled. The operator then takes the seals to the hydraulic press to be closed. Finally, the operator inspects the completed seals and places them in a finished goods storage container.

The operator then returns to the parts cooling table to begin assembling the next nine seals, and the process repeats itself. A second assembler performs the same sequence of operations, approximately two steps behind the first assembler. This is sometimes referred to as a "rabbit chase" arrangement since one worker always closely follows the other.[10]

Simulate cell operations

With the help of the layout drawings (or even better, a three-dimensional scale model) and the cell process scenario, operators can "walk through" the cell to get a feel for how it will work. Based on this, they can contribute their own ideas on how to refine the cell layout. You might want to use experienced operators from other cells to help out. You can also use board games to familiarize operators (as well as supervisors and managers) with cell operations: employees can run the cell by moving play pieces to simulate their own movements and the movement of material. Understanding operator movements is especially important if you have multiple operators. You can also use the game to demonstrate the impact of changing lot sizes, revising schedules, the effect of buffer spaces, and so on. In short, board games can be very useful in training operators how to act in cells and for eliciting ideas for process and layout improvements. They are most effective for operators and supervisors with no previous cell experience. Besides physical scenario building and board games, you can also develop computer models to simulate how the cell will work. (We discuss this type of evaluation in the next chapter.)

Due to the limits of the human imagination, there is only so much one can do with scenarios and models. As a result, cell layouts are almost always modified once the cell is built (see Step 12 in Figure 4-1). Operators and supervisors will come up with better placements for work areas and equipment, find that the allocated space is too large or too small, or decide that tooling needs to be modifed. Our experience is that once employees start working in cells, process and layout improvements become a way of life. Of course, thorough planning smoothes implementation and saves much improvement effort later on. Thus, while you should still expect incremental improvements, careful planning can prevent radical and expensive redesign of cells at a later stage.

Step 10: Plan for Start-up

The final step in the detailed planning process outlined in Figure 6-2 is implementation planning. This means preparing the facilities for the cells, estimating the time for moving equipment and people, securing the product supply to customers during the changeover (while taking the loss of productivity during start-up into account), intensifying communication, and increasing employee involvement. Some activities, like education and training, should start as early as possible. However, implementation planning should begin in earnest after the final decision has been taken to implement the cell. (We discuss implementation issues in Chapters 15 and 16.)

CELL DIMENSIONING REVISITED

After outlining all the activities that make up detailed cell planning, we now return to the issue of determining the capacity and staffing for the cell (i.e., Step 5 in Figure 6-2). There are essentially two approaches to dimensioning cells. One is frequently used for cells with low volumes and irregular production (typically part-producing cells). The other is used for high-volume, repetitive manufacturing cells (typically assembly cells). In both cases you need to know the expected volume for the product families (determined at Step 3). For parts cells, you translate this volume first into hours of work per resource, and from that into number of resource units required. For assembly cells, demand volume is translated into a cycle time, which is then used to determine both product model sequence and number of workstations in the cell.

Next, we provide a few examples on how these calculations can be performed.

Dimensioning Part-Producing Cells (Irregular Production)

Table 6-4 shows some of the data needed to determine equipment and labor needs for a rod cell. You can find the number of batches produced per year for the five members of the part family by dividing the anticipated production volume (D) by the lot sizes (Q). After extracting the setup and run-time data from the routing of each individual part, you can then determine the expected workload on each type of equipment planned for the cell. By specifying the number of machines of each type, and their available time, the load can be transformed into utilization percentages.

Let:

Unit operation time = r	Time per shift in a year (hours/year) = T
Lot size = Q	Number of shifts per day = s
Annual volume = D	Efficiency (%) = e
Setup time = S	Number of machines of each type = m

Then, for any part processed at a particular machine, the workload per year (in hours) will be:

$$\text{Workload} = (\text{Number of orders/year})*\text{Time per setup} + (\text{Unit operation time})* \text{Demand} = (D/Q)*S + rD$$

Table 6-4. Dimensioning of a machine cell

Part id	Annual volume (D)	Lot size (Q)	Orders/yr (D/Q)	WORKLOAD IN HOURS (SETUP AND RUN TIMES)					
				Drill B1890	Mill A3567	Drill C35721	Mill A9870	Washer C564	Bore B3341
P467808	10000	400	25.0	334.6	1502.9	501.3	838.3	333.8	1336.7
P467809	4500	200	22.5	151.1	677.6	226.1	379.5	150.4	603.0
P469234	9000	100	90.0	304.5	1360.5	454.5	768.0	301.5	1212.0
P469246	8000	250	32.0	268.3	1203.7	401.6	673.1	267.2	1070.9
P470111	6800	300	22.7	227.8	1022.6	341.1	571.2	227.0	909.7
TOTAL HOURS PER YEAR:				1286.3	5767.4	1924.6	3230.1	1279.9	5132.3

	Drill B1890	Mill A3567	Drill C35721	Mill A9870	Washer C564	Bore B3341	
NUMBER OF MACHINES/STATION:	1	1	1	1	1	1	
STATION UTILIZATION/SHIFT (%):	35.7	160.2	53.5	89.7	35.6	142.6	
NUMBER OF MACHINES/STATION:	1	2	1	1	1	2	Ave. util.
STATION UTILIZATION/SHIFT (%):	35.7	80.1	53.5	89.7	35.6	71.3	61.0
OPERATOR ATTENDANCE (%):	50.0	27.0	26.0	18.0	45.0	30.0	
NUMBER OF MACHINES/STATION:	1	1	1	1	1	1	Ave. util.
OPERATOR UTILIZATION/SHIFT (%):	17.9	43.3	13.9	16.2	16.0	42.8	25.0

UTILIZATION OF TWO FULLY CROSS-TRAINED OPERATORS = 75.0%
Note: All efficiencies are assumed to be 90%. Two shifts per day.

To get the total workload on a specific machine, repeat this calculation for each part and then sum the load for all parts. The average utilization for the machine type is then found as:

Utilization = (Total workload from all parts)/(T*e*m*s).

(T*e is the effective number of hours per shift in a year.)

For example, assume the run time and setup time for part P467808 on drill B1890 is 2 and 3 minutes, respectively. The workload on the drill coming from this part, therefore, is (10,000/400)*3 + 2*10,000 = 20,075 minutes, or 334.6 hours per year. The load from all five parts, found in the same way, is 1,286.3 hours per year (see Table 6-4).[11] Assume now there is one drill press, that the cell runs two shifts per day, that the nominal hours per shift in a year is 2,000, and that the efficiency is 90 percent. The utilization for drill B1890 is then 1286.3/(2000*0.9*1*2) = 0.357, or 35.7 percent.

You can easily perform these types of calculations on a spreadsheet. If the part family consists of many members, you may want to simplify the calculations. Rather than considering each individual part in the cell family, it may be possible to group them into subfamilies. You can then determine average demand volume and average batch size for each subfamily, as well as family setup times and run times per machine, and use those parameters in your calculations.[12]

Labor considerations in part-producing cells

The manual labor portion of the operation time is usually much smaller than the equipment-based operation time. This is because a machine, once loaded with a part, typically can run without having the operator watching it and, in case of machining centers, perform multiple operations in sequence without a changeover. To determine the manual workload required for each workstation, you need to know the amount of time an operator spends at the machine during each work cycle. You can estimate that as follows.

Let L1 and L2 be load and unload times per piece, and assume that these times are included in the operation time per piece (i.e., in "r"). We further assume that the manual part of the operation time includes the setup time and load/unload times. Operator attendance—the percentage of the total batch-processing time the operator must be present at the machine—is then found as:

$$\text{Operator attendance} = \frac{S + (L1+L2)*Q}{S + rQ} * 100$$

However, this formula is only for a single part. To get the total operator attendance per machine, you need to consider all parts in the family. You can do that by finding the weighted average of operator attendance, using the number of orders per year as weights.[13] Assume you determined that the average operator attendance is 50 percent; that is, the operator spends half of each machine cycle tending the machine. The operator utilization is then simply half of the machine utilization (in the case of drill B1890 in Table 6-4, 0.50*35.7 = 17.9%).

The equivalent number of operators needed depends on the work processes each can handle. Consider again the data in Table 6-4. If each operator can handle a single operation only, you need six people to run this cell. The average utilization per operator, however, is only 25 percent, while machine utilization is 61 percent. Assume, at the other extreme, that operators are fully cross-trained and can master all processes in the cell. You can then find the number of required operators for the cell by summing the operator utilization row across the machines and dividing by 100. In this case, the sum is (17.9+43.3+ ... + 42.8) = 150.1. Thus, you need at least 150.1/100, or 1.5 operators to run the cell.[14] If you staff the cell with two fully cross-trained operators, their average utilization will be 150.1/2, or 75 percent.

Between having each operator dedicated to a single station, and having operators possess complete mastery of all processes, lie many different alternatives. For example, if there is only one operator qualified to run the two milling machines, you may assign him or her to those machines; another operator can handle the remaining operations. That means, however, you have one operator utilized 43.3 + 16.2 = 59.5%, and the other utilized 17.9 + 13.9 + 16.0 + 42.8 = 90.6%. As you can see, it is difficult to balance workloads among operators with limited skills.

A few comments on dimensioning part-producing cells

If a machine does not require constant attention, it is inefficient to have an operator stationed there at all times. For many firms, achieving high labor utilization in cells is a more important design consideration than achieving high equipment utilization.[15] One of the advantages of cellular manufacturing is the possibility of having operators handle multiple processes. As illustrated by the examples above, this results in a higher and more even utilization of human resources. When operators are skilled in several of the operations, the rod cell can run with anywhere from two to six people. Of course, the number of operators in the cell, and their utilization, determine how long machines have to wait to be loaded and unloaded. Thus, as discussed in the next chapter, staffing decisions influence output rate, lead times, and inventory in the cell.

Using the type of capacity checks shown here, you can determine the minimum number of machines and operators for the cell. Some cell projects come to a halt at this point because the load calculations suggest that you need to purchase a number of new machines—the result of splitting large product families previously produced on the same machine groups. This investment may be unacceptable to management (see Chapter 8 for economic value calculations). Unless you can restructure the families to minimize the new investment, you may have to abandon some candidate cells.

Dimensioning Assembly Cells (Repetitive Manufacturing)

Assume that you plan to assemble one product in a cell, with an annual demand of 2,000 units. If you operate two shifts, each with 2,000 hours per year, and you expect to produce at a steady pace and full efficiency, then how fast do you need to assemble the product? The answer is that you need to have one unit leave the cell every two hours (two shifts*2,000 hours per shift*100 percent efficiency divided by 2,000 units = (2*2,000*1)/2,000 = 2 hours). The time between units produced is called the *cycle time*, C (also referred to as *takt time*). In general, using the symbols introduced earlier, we define cycle time as:

$$\text{Cycle time} = C = \frac{\text{Available time to produce}}{\text{Product demand}} = \frac{T*s*e}{D}$$

The importance of the cycle time lies in the fact that it is the largest time interval that you can allow between completed units. *If you cannot meet average cycle time, you cannot fulfill demand.* If, in our example, the smallest cycle time you can meet is three hours, the annual output will be 4,000/3, or 1,333 units per year, rather than the 2,000 you planned to make.

How to determine the number of stations

Since the cycle time determines the longest time that any station in the cell can be allowed to complete its assigned work, it also determines the smallest number of workstations required to meet demand. Assume again that just one product is produced, with an assembly time of "t." We then have:

$$\text{Minimum number of stations} = n = \frac{\text{Total work content in the product}}{\text{Cycle time}} = \frac{t}{C}$$

For example, if your targeted cycle time is 5 minutes, and the product has an assembly time of 26 minutes, you must have a minimum of 26/5, or 5.2 stations at which work is performed. In other words, you need six workstations.

Determining the number of operators

If some assembly tasks are automated, the human cycle at each station can be smaller than the equipment cycle. You can then determine the minimum number of required operators as:

$$\text{Minimum number of operators} = \frac{\text{Total } \textit{manual} \text{ work content in the product}}{\text{Cycle time}}$$

This calculation assumes that the operators can move between stations and perform multiple tasks. For example, if the product with 26 minutes of work content requires only 14 minutes of human labor, this cell requires at least 14/5, or 2.8 assembly workers to meet demand. In this case, then, you will have three operators working on six stations.

What if multiple products are assembled?

What happens if you want to assemble multiple products in the cell? Our definition of cycle time is essentially the same, except that you now must consider total product demand. For example, if you also want to produce a second product with an annual demand of 3,000 units, the cycle time is now $\{(2*2{,}000*1)/(2{,}000 + 3{,}000)\} = 0.8$ hours. In other words,

$$\text{Cycle time} = C = \frac{\text{Available time to produce}}{\text{Total product demand}} = \frac{T*s*e}{D_1 + D_2}$$

It can be a little more problematic to determine the minimum number of workstations and operators. If all products have the same total assembly time, the formulas above still work. However, if the products have different work content, the number of stations must be determined as follows:

$$\text{Minimum number of stations} = n = \frac{\text{Weighted average work content}}{\text{Cycle time}} = \frac{t_{ave}}{C}$$

Again with two products, using their annual demands as weights and letting D be the sum of all demands, we get:

$$n = \frac{t_1{}^*D_1/D + t_2{}^*D_2/D}{C} = \frac{t_1{}^*D_1/D + t_2{}^*D_2/D}{T*s*e/D} = \frac{t_1{}^*D_1 + t_2{}^*D_2}{T*s*e}$$

The smallest number of operators can be found in a similar way. You should note that these calculations assume that the required demand will be met with an *average* cycle time, C. This is possible for *unpaced* assembly cells (i.e., those without mechanical conveyors) since it is here possible to produce some products faster and others slower. If you run a cell with a paced conveyor, however, the cycle time is fixed and determines the station time for all products. Therefore, if you want to meet demand for all products, you must dimension the cell for the product with the largest work content. This means that the weighted-average assembly time (t_{ave}) must be replaced by the largest assembly time for any product in the cell.

Allocating work to stations

The next problem is to distribute the individual assembly tasks over the workstations so that (1) the cycle time is not violated, and (2) the workload is evenly allocated to stations. The latter objective requires that you consider the production schedule for each product. Since assembly tasks must be assigned to stations *for every product in the cell*, having a product family with highly similar assembly operations facilitates the allocation step. You can manually assign workloads to stations by using process charts. You can also rely on more advanced, and quantitative, assembly-line balancing techniques.[16]

You run into problems if the required cycle time is smaller than an equipment-determined cycle time because you cannot in this case shift work to other stations. For example, if you need to produce a unit every 5 minutes, but one station in the cell has a machine cycle of 10 minutes, you either must duplicate that machine to meet demand or create a second cell.

Small versus large assembly cells

We have assumed for the calculations above that you plan to build just one cell, but firms that convert from lines to assembly cells may decide to split one long line into several smaller cells. For example, if the minimum cycle time to meet demand is 5 minutes (12 units per hour), then you need one cell with a cycle time of 5 minutes. However, you can also use two cells, each with a cycle time of 10 minutes. The result is the same—a *planned* assembly rate of 12 units per hour, with 6 units per hour coming from each cell. The advantage of smaller cells is a larger work content per assembly worker, and therefore better actual performance due to smaller variations in processing time. This is true especially for cells without pacing conveyors. Smaller cells also tend to have fewer quality problems because of fewer hand-offs and greater accountability. Finally, breaking a long line into several smaller cells creates a system that is less vulnerable to down time since each cell can operate independently.

Final comment on dimensioning

Although we have discussed two approaches to determining the number of machines and operators for a cell, one for part-producing cells and another for assembly cells, you can use either method with any type of cell. Of course, establishing and maintaining a fixed cycle or takt time for assembly cells is commonly done only in repetitive manufacturing environments. In those situations, "cycle-time thinking" applies equally well to fabrication and machining cells.

Finally, when dimensioning cells you should try out different future demand scenarios. Each value of the volume D may lead to a different design of the cell in terms of equipment and labor requirements.

DILEMMAS IN CELL DESIGN AND LAYOUT

You will face many difficult choices as you design cells. One particular problem in the dimensioning step is the emphasis on cost versus workflow. On the one hand, you may need to have high equipment investment, high labor cost, and low utilization to achieve a smooth, unbroken flow in the cells. If you choose not to do this, you incur the operational costs of longer lead times, more complex flows, and more managerial headaches. We'll next provide a couple of examples to illustrate typical dilemmas.

Thorny Issue 1: When to Consolidate Cells?

Consider first a simple example where machined parts require turning, drilling, and milling operations. The current layout groups machines according to process, with one operator serving each machine group (see Figure 6-11).[17] A combined analysis of model type and part routings showed that the components could be separated into four families (see Figure 6-12). However, the routings for Model III components can be contained in those of Model II, and the routings for Model I can be contained in those of Model IV, while maintaining their sequences. Thus, we can collapse the original four families into two. This means all Model II and III parts can be processed together in one cell, and all I and IV parts in another. One layout option consists of two U-shaped cells facing each other—one for each enlarged family (see Figure 6-13). Normally, one operator will staff each cell. The advantage of the cell arrangement is that we can now operate with one less operator compared to the previous process layout. Furthermore, if needed, a single operator can run both cells.

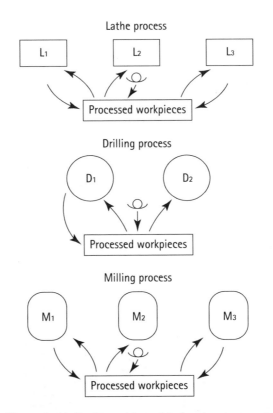

Figure 6-11. Equipment layout before improvement

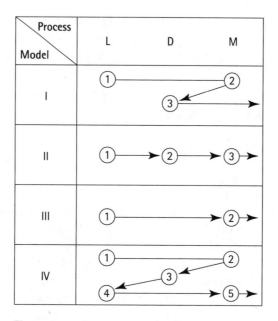

Figure 6-12. Process route families

Material flow is unidirectional in both cells. If you compare the placement of the equipment with the routing chart in Figure 6-12, you see that the machines in both cells are laid out according to the longest routing. This means that parts in the Model I and III families have to skip machines in the sequence. However, there are no backtracking movements in the cell. As we have discussed, forward flows and

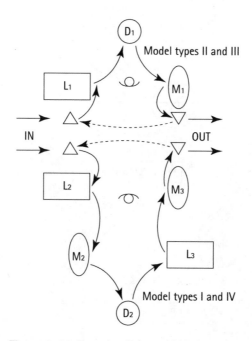

Figure 6-13. Two closely located U-shaped cells

processing independence are ideal characteristics for cells. However, this "ideal" must be balanced against the utilization of the resources. As discussed below, good flow may come at the expense of lead time performance.

If you ignore the parts' operations sequences, you could create several alternative cells, such as bringing together the two lathes and the two mills in the bottom cell in Figure 6-13. This type of equipment "pooling" means that jobs can be processed on either machine (as shown in Figure 6-14; the upper cell is unchanged). You might also decide to have both cells share the entry and exit machines, but keep the remaining operations separate (see Figure 6-15). Finally, you can have a single cell where some of the lathes, mills, and drills have been combined into local machine groups (see Figure 6-16).

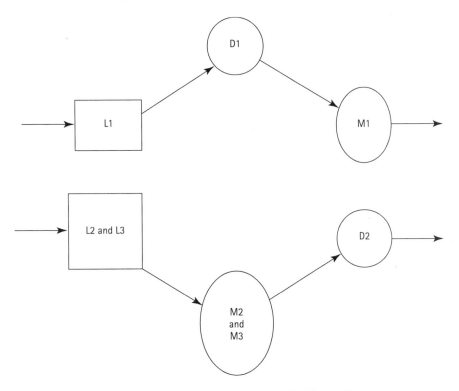

Figure 6-14. Grouping machines inside a cell

What are the advantages and disadvantages of these alternative designs? An immediate disadvantage with the lower cell in Figure 6-14, of course, is that parts (and operators) now have to backtrack, and some parts have to revisit the lathe and mill groups. The arrangements in Figures 6-15 and 6-16 avoid this problem.

The potential advantage of the shared machine solution in Figure 6-15 and the single-cell option in Figure 6-16 is that the lead time through the cells *may* be lower than the lead time for the cells in Figure 6-13. How could that be? Assume that lathe L3 in Figure 6-13 is utilized only 10 percent of the time, while lathe L2 has a utilization of 75 percent. Also assume that L2 is the bottleneck in this cell. By placing the two lathes together, as in Figure 6-14, Model I and Model IV parts can use either lathe. The

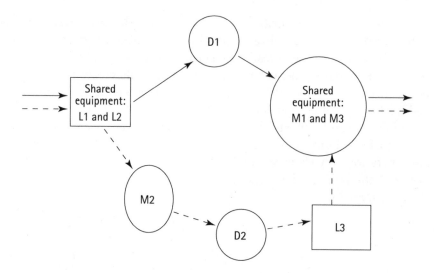

Figure 6-15. Machine sharing among cells at entry and exit points

utilization of the L2/L3 workstation in the cell will now be dramatically reduced compared to L2 alone—42.5 percent versus 75 percent—and cycle time will decrease.

The same type of reasoning applies to the designs in Figures 6-15 and 6-16. In the latter cell you will have more parts skipping stations than before, but neither of these two cell designs have backtracking. On the other hand, by pooling machines you might reduce the cycle times for all part types. Whether this will happen depends on the utilization of each machine group in the cells, which, in turn, depends partly on the setup times the families face on each machine type. Thus, leveling the processing time loads on the machines through pooling

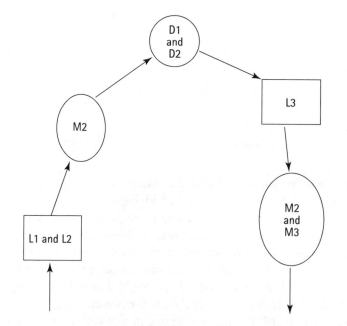

Figure 6-16. Consolidating two cells into a single cell while maintaining flow

machines inside cells may be offset by increased setup times. The lesson of these examples is that cell formation, dimensioning, layout, and performance are all intimately related. Due to the complexity of these relationships, resolution of design dilemmas may require computer modeling.

Thorny Issue 2: Can a Low Cell Machine Utilization Be Justified?

As for the previous example, we assume that the planned cell is to be created by moving machines from the functional areas of the plant into the new cell. Let's say a machine tool needed for a part family shows a current total utilization level of 80 percent, with only 15 percent of the load coming from the future cell parts. Since there is only one such machine in the plant (on which the cell parts now are processed), another must be purchased for the cell at a cost of $350,000. Is it worth it? Since the project team probably finds it hard to justify that investment for a meager 15 percent utilization rate, it may decide to process the parts on the existing machine even if this means that parts have to leave the cell for processing. Thus, achieving process completeness depends on equipment cost and utilization.

Thorny Issue 3: Should You Allow the Cell to Be Diluted with Other Parts?

Now assume the same machine tool shows a utilization of 65 percent coming from the future cell parts, while 15 percent comes from parts not included in the cell family. Although the utilization by the cell parts would motivate the acquisition of a new machine, the utilization level based solely on noncell parts would be very low. So here you have the reversed dilemma: unless a new machine is purchased, the existing machine will be placed in the cell, while noncell parts will be visiting the cell for processing.

Thorny Issue 4: When Should You Allow Machine Sharing Between Cells?

Assume that a machine in the functional part of the plant, if placed in the cell, would be utilized 15 percent of the time. A second team is working on designing a cell that also could use the same machine. In their case, the expected utilization is 25 percent. With both teams strongly encouraged to adhere to a "no new investment" constraint, they may decide to locate the cells adjacent to each other and share the machine between them (for a combined utilization of 40 percent).

Resolving the Dilemmas

Cell design teams constantly face dilemmas like those just described, and they are not always easy to resolve. You must balance the "cost of low utilization" against the "cost of loss of independence" due to equipment sharing between two production units. Equipment and labor utilization can be expressed in monetary terms in the form of hourly rates. However, the "cost" of sharing equipment—and thereby losing some control of production—must be expressed in other terms, such as higher inventories, higher tooling investment, longer lead times, or missed due dates. In some cases you may conclude that the benefit of having more labor and a duplicated machine in the cell, providing a smooth flow and full control over production, is worth a low utilization level. In other cases, that may not be the case. Computer modeling is the best way to evaluate such choices, especially when the critical performance measures are lead time or inventory in the cell.[18]

Finally, in the examples above we assumed, as commonly is the case, that cell parts and cell equipment are pulled from existing machine groups in the plant. This typically means that some parts have to be off-loaded to other equipment, while some machine groups will operate with less equipment than before. Accordingly, building cells with existing equipment will influence the performance of the parts left outside the cells. Thus, for a *complete* evaluation of the impact of a new cell, you must consider not just the cell itself but also the parts and equipment affected by the cell creation in the remainder of the plant.

KEY INSIGHTS

The boundaries between factory-level and cell level planning can be fuzzy, especially if you applied a very narrow scope to the first phase. In extreme cases, only one cell may emerge from the planning effort. In that case, the two stages in the planning process are essentially identical.

This chapter focused mainly on the technical aspects of cell formation, dimensioning, and layout during detailed cell planning. As we mentioned, however, many organizational and systems issues also need to be considered during the planning process. These, and other issues related to the implementation of the cells, are discussed in the remainder of the book. Some key points from this chapter, to keep in mind as we move forward, are highlighted below:

- *Appoint project teams for each cell.* When you move from factory planning to cell planning, the focus must go from broad to specific. Thus, a project team dealing with technical issues should work on one cell only. For the non-technical/infrastructure issues that are common across cells, a separate team with broad representation is the best choice.

- *Involve operators in the cell planning process.* Cells are the future workplaces for operators, so they need to have a say in how equipment, work areas, material-handling systems, and the like are chosen and positioned. You will derive many excellent ideas from employee involvement, and also get a smoother implementation.

- *Look for opportunities to streamline processes.* Before detailed layout planning begins for the cell, you should review the routings for the parts/products in the cell family. The goal is to improve the flow pattern in the cell, reduce or avoid setups, and balance the load.

- *Routing improvement and layout planning are interrelated and iterative.* The actual flow pattern in a cell depends on how you place the equipment. Once you have developed a tentative layout, you may discover that you can smooth the flow even more by making additional changes to individual part routings.

- *Your capacity and staffing plans are only the first step in the cell evaluation process.* The type of cell dimensioning we have discussed here is commonly used in industry.[19] However, you are only establishing the minimum amount of equipment and labor needed to support a target volume. You will not know the resulting throughput times or inventory build-ups in the cell. Unless you wait until the cell is in operation, gaining this knowledge requires advanced modeling (see next chapter).

- *Detailed planning will bring out issues you never considered before.* As the saying goes, "The closer you look at a problem, the fuzzier it gets." As you fine-tune the product family, dimension the cell, and plan the layout, you will unravel difficult trade-off issues. The essence of these boils down to operating cost versus performance. Good decisions require clear business goals and may need to be supported by computer modeling.

- *Detailed planning permits you to determine the economic value of the cells.* At some point during the planning process, you may have to present an economic analysis of the cells to management. Cell level planning provides you with the information you need to determine the cost/benefit picture for the project. Depending on the outcome, cell plans may be accepted or rejected, or will need to be modified.

7

Understanding Cell Performance Using Modeling

As we discussed in the previous chapter, you will face many design dilemmas when planning a cell and determining how it will best operate. Unfortunately, there are few obvious choices when it comes to many of these dilemmas. Systems behavior knowledge (SBK) (see Figure 2-7) can help you find the answers. SBK relies on quantitative modeling to gather insights into the behavior of manufacturing systems. In this chapter we provide an overview of how you can use models and modeling to design and operate cells.

Different types of models can give you information about different types of measures. Because cellular manufacturing implementations primarily are driven by the need to reduce lead times and inventories, we concentrate on these two performance variables. Although we will briefly discuss both *spreadsheet* and *stochastic simulation* models, we focus mostly on queuing models. Queuing models are ideal for demonstrating basic cell system behavior regarding lead time and inventories. They are also available in commercial software and, unlike simulation models, their relative simplicity make modeling a fairly rapid process.

This chapter addresses several important questions:

- Why is lead time so critical in manufacturing?
- What do you need to do to reduce it?
- What are the basics of queuing theory, and how can you use it to gain insights into the design and operation of cellular systems?
- What types of cell design issues are best addressed by simulation models?

This chapter is more theoretical than are the others, and you may skip it at this point without loss of continuity. Of course, you can return to it at any time.

MODELS AND CELL DESIGN

A *model* is a simplified mathematical and logical representation of reality. We use models to answer questions about real or proposed systems without building them, if they don't exist, or without disturbing them, if they already exist. The main advantage of modeling is that you can predict the performance of systems before they are implemented, and can also avoid costly experimentation with them after they are built. Unfortunately, there is no model that solves the following problem: "Given a set of products with associated characteristics (names, routings, demand, etc.), and a set of equipment and operators with associated characteristics (setup and operations times, reliabilities, capabilities, etc.), create cells that will meet performance targets for due dates, lead times, and unit costs."

In other words, existing models do not design cell systems for you; they only *evaluate the impact* of operating a particular cell system. Therefore, to use models effectively, you must formulate "what-if" questions that the model can answer. Examples of such questions include: "Can the cell bottleneck machine handle a demand increase of 30 percent?" and "What is the average lead time through the cell if we staff it with three fully cross-trained operators?" Using *performance evaluation models* is thus an iterative process where you:

- Design the cell.
- Let the model evaluate its performance.
- Compare this performance with your targets.
- Revise the cell design and/or operating parameters if there is a gap in performance.
- Continue this process until you find an acceptable cell (or revise your targets).

There are many measures for which you can set targets and determine cell performance (for a further discussion on measures, see Chapter 9). However, the most common of them track lead time and inventories, the ability to meet due dates, the utilization of equipment and labor, equipment uptimes, product cost, and a variety of quality-related aspects. As mentioned, in this chapter we concentrate on lead time.

WHAT IS MANUFACTURING LEAD TIME?

Lead time has emerged in recent years as a vital measure of strategic competitiveness as well as an indicator of operational efficiency and effectiveness. One obvious reason for this is that lead time reduction yields many benefits:

- You can get to the market faster with new products.
- You can promise faster customer response for existing products.
- There is less opportunity for customers to change their minds once they place an order. This leads to increased manufacturing stability and possibly fewer lost sales.
- Shorter lead times also mean shorter planning horizons and, therefore, smaller forecast errors.
- You will have fewer open manufacturing or purchasing orders to track.
- Shorter manufacturing lead times mean less replanning and "system nervousness."
- Shorter lead times are associated with smaller WIP inventories.

- Shorter lead times mean less need to keep raw material and finished goods inventories. In particular, you can move from make-to stock (MTS) to make-to-order (MTO) manufacturing.
- Shorter lead times typically mean smaller lead time variances, which in turn lead to improved ability to predict order completion times. Smaller variances also lower the risk of holding up assembly processes due to late components.

Two types of lead time are of particular interest:

- *Manufacturing lead time.* This is the time from order start to order completion inside the factory. The terms cycle time and flow time are often used synonymously with manufacturing lead time, although the cycle time concept is best reserved for "time between products" in repetitive manufacturing environments (see previous chapter).
- *Customer lead time.* This is the time from customer order placement to receipt of goods. It is the sum of product development/design lead time, order processing lead time, manufacturing lead time, and shipping/distribution time. In MTS manufacturing, the first and the third components are typically zero; in MTO all of them apply.

The goal should always be to reduce customer lead time first, since this can affect sales directly. In turn, reducing customer lead time may require shortening the manufacturing lead time, but it also often involves reducing administrative lead time. Administrative lead time includes activities such as order entry and promising, processing quotations, product design or customization, inventory and component price checking, credit verifications, and customer order error corrections. In some firms we have studied, over half of the total lead time was due to time spent in office operations.[1] If this is the case in your firm, you may want to tackle administrative lead time reduction first. Although this chapter primarily focuses on manufacturing lead time, the insights we provide apply to administrative lead time as well. (Chapter 18, which discusses office cells, and Chapter 17, which discusses improvement and evolution of cells, provide additional insights in this regard.)

Components that Determine Manufacturing Lead Time

The best way to understand manufacturing lead time, and how to reduce it, is to break it down to its component elements. Imagine yourself following a batch of materials through a process. You would then see that lead time for that batch is composed of four major elements:

1. *Setup time* = the sum of the times spent changing over between parts/products across all workstations along the process.
2. *Operation time* = the sum of the times spent at all workstations working on the parts or products in the batch.
3. *Move time* = the sum of all times spent moving the batch between workstations, from the first to the last.

4. *Waiting time* = the total time the batch spends (1) waiting for equipment, labor, materials, and tools to become available so parts/products can be processed; (2) waiting for inspection personnel or equipment to become available; and (3) waiting for material-handling resources so the batch can be moved to the next station.

In other words,

Lead time for a batch = setup time + operation time + move time + waiting time

The secret to reducing lead time, then, is "simply" to reduce any or all of these four components. Table 7-1 suggests general prescriptions for doing so. While setup, operation, and move times are the result of what you deliberately set out to do, waiting time is an unintended—and unwelcome—outcome! In other words, you deliberately perform setups, transform materials into other shapes or forms through operations, and move the material through the process. But you do not deliberately wait. Rather, you are a victim of waiting.

The waiting time component

You may find it relatively easy to think of ways to reduce the time spent on setting up, processing, or moving a batch. Of course, it takes some creativity and ingenuity to find new, efficient ways to do so, but experience shows that people in the workplace can come up with plenty of valuable ideas.[2] But how do you go about reducing the time the batch spends waiting? This is a much more complicated issue.

Table 7-1. Various ways to reduce manufacturing lead time

Reduce	How?
Time per *setup*	Improve setup procedures by using alternative, low-setup equipment, e.g., family tooling/fixtures and/or modern equipment.
Number of *setups*	Dedicate equipment to the family and/or sequence parts to avoid changeovers.
Time per *operation*	Redesign parts, use new technology and/or more skilled labor for faster processing, reroute operations to faster resources, or use smaller lot sizes.
Planned number of *operations*	Redesign parts to eliminate operations (e.g., using value engineering).
Unplanned number of *operations*	Reduce the amount of rework through quality improvement.
Time per *move*	Improve material-handling procedures and/or use more compressed layouts.
Number of *moves*	Consolidate operations to fewer machines or operators, e.g., through multi-operation machining centers and work enlargement.
Time spent *waiting*	Manipulate the other three components that make up lead time—setup time, operation time, and move time; also provide more capacity.

You may ask, "If there are four basic elements to lead time, and three of them appear fairly easy to reduce, aren't those enough? Why do I have to reduce waiting time as well?" Well, to begin with, you should always concentrate improvement efforts where the payoff is the greatest. To do that, you need to know the relative magnitude of the batch setup, operation, move, and waiting times in the make-up of your average batch lead time. This will help you identify the component most worthy of reduction. It is well known that when batch lead times are measured in functionally organized shops, the time a batch spends waiting makes up the absolute majority of lead time. Common wisdom has it that a 95/5 rule applies: a batch typically spends only 5 percent of its time in the shop being worked on or being moved, and 95 percent of the time just sitting idle. Many managers, when told about this, do not believe it is the reality in their own plants. And, granted, these numbers may actually range from 60/40 to 95/5. But truth remains that *waiting time almost always is the most dominant portion of lead time*. So it deserves your full attention.

In order to understand how to reduce waiting time, you first must understand how and why it occurs. While setup time, operation time, and move time are independent of each other (i.e., a reduction in setup time does not affect move time), all three components affect waiting time. In fact, as we will show, one way to reduce waiting time is by manipulating the three other components that make up lead time. So, for example, if you reduce setup time, you will reduce lead time both directly, through a smaller setup time, and indirectly, through a lowered waiting time.

To demonstrate this, and other influences on lead time, we will rely on a branch of modeling called *analytic queuing theory*. Queuing models represent a very compact and convenient way of illustrating how a manufacturing system, like a cell, behaves when it is in *steady state*. Essentially, steady state exists when a system operates in a stable environment.[3] Although you may argue—and rightfully so, in many cases—that stable conditions really do not exist in manufacturing, you can still apply the general insights that we offer here to more turbulent environments.

ELEMENTARY QUEUING THEORY

On a simplified level, you can view a manufacturing system, such as a cell, as an input/output system to which jobs arrive and depart. For now, think of this system as consisting of a single machine. As mentioned, we assume that this system is in steady state. We also assume that the machine is available at all times, and that labor is so plentiful that it is not affecting the performance of the machine (in other words, for now we ignore labor in our considerations). To model the system we need some notation. Let:

i = product of type i
Q_i = size of the batch
r_i = operation (run) time per unit (incl. any load and unload times)
S_i = time to setup the equipment for a new batch
D_i = demand (in units)
P_i = batch processing time (setup and batch operation time)
Q, r, S, D, P = weighted averages of these parameters across all products
$V(P)$ = the variance of batch processing times
I = average batch interarrival time
$V(I)$ = the variance of batch interarrival times

The *processing time*, P_i, is the time needed to complete all parts in a batch, including setting up for the batch, processing each item in the batch, and loading/unloading all units to/from the machine. For a single part, P is simply $S_1 + r_1Q_1 = S + rQ$. If the system processes multiple parts, the average processing time, P, can be found as the weighted average of all parts' processing times.[4]

The *average batch interarrival time*, I, expresses the average time between any two batch arrivals to the system. For a single part, I = Q/D. If the system processes multiple parts, I = 1/ASUM, where ASUM is the sum of all parts' arrival rates.[5]

The two variances, V(P) and V(I), measure the variations in individual processing and interarrival times. The variance is a classic measure of variations in data.[6] Using these variables we can now formulate some very important relationships.

Machine Utilization

Let us begin with *utilization* (U), one of the most commonly used measures in manufacturing management. Utilization is simply the "long-term" ratio between workload and available capacity. One way to express utilization is as follows:

Utilization = U = (Required capacity)/(Available capacity)

For example, if the schedule calls for 160 standard hours of work next month, and the machine is available 200 hours, the average machine utilization will be 160/200, or 80 percent. Another way of expressing this measure is from the perspective of a batch:

Utilization = U = (Average batch processing time)/(Average batch interarrival time) = P/I

Thus, machine utilization is simply the relation between the time it takes to process an average batch and the time available between successive arrivals of batches. Thus, if batches arrive on average every hour to a machine, and it takes an average of 30 minutes to complete the batch, the machine utilization is 30/60, or 50 percent. Since, as stated above, the machine is available all the time, utilization is a direct measure of productive capacity. It is intuitive that if utilization goes down, so does the volume of output from the system. It is also intuitive that you don't want a utilization exceeding 100 percent, as this would mean that batches would arrive faster than the machine can process them, and inventory would simply grow and grow.

Waiting Time in Queue

Next we introduce a formula that expresses the time a batch sits in queue at a single machine while it waits to be processed. It is a fairly general formula for waiting time in that it makes no assumptions about the processing or interarrival time distributions involved:[7]

$$W = \text{time in queue} = \left\{ \frac{V(P)/P^2 + V(I)/I^2}{2} \right\} * \frac{U}{1-U} * P$$

Although it looks complicated, this formula illustrates in a concise way the factors that create waiting time. And if you know waiting time, you can easily determine the lead time. Note that average lead time, L, for a single machine is simply the sum of the time to process a batch and the time the batch waits in queue; i.e., $L = P + W = S + rQ + W$.

The formula for W has three components. The first shows that the waiting time in queue depends on the variability of the process and interarrival times. The second term shows that waiting time depends on utilization (U) and, therefore, on process and interarrival times. Finally, the third term indicates that waiting time depends on the average time to process a batch.[8] In essence, waiting time is determined by the processing and interarrival times.

Insights regarding waiting time in queue

You can derive some very important lessons from the waiting time formula above. Although we will discuss most of these lessons later, some that are by no means obvious or intuitive are stated here.

- *Waiting time depends on the utilization, but in a nonlinear way.* Specifically, when utilization goes up by a certain percentage, waiting time increases even more (an effect that can be traced to the U/(1-U) term). In other words, the closer utilization comes to 100 percent, the faster the waiting time increases. Figure 7-1 illustrates this by showing waiting time as a function of utilization. This relation points to a basic trade-off in manufacturing: *everything else equal*, you will either have short lead times or high utilization—but not both! You can also conclude from Figure 7-1 that a system operating at a low level of utilization will have more stable lead times in the face of load variations than will a system operating at a high utilization level.

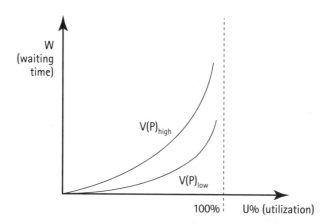

$V(P)_{high}$, $V(P)_{low}$ = high and low processing time variance, respectively

Figure 7-1. How waiting time depends on utilization

- *Waiting time can increase or decrease by changing the processing time or interarrival time variances while the utilization is held constant.* As

Figure 7-1 illustrates, you can reduce waiting time by reducing utilization, either by slowing down the rate by which batches are sent to the machine (i.e., increase I) or by reducing batch processing time (i.e., lower P). If you increase I while batch sizes are fixed, you will produce less output per day. And if you maintain the job input rate but use smaller batch sizes, you will again produce less output.

However, the formula above shows that you also can reduce waiting time, W, by making the P and I variances smaller, *without lowering utilization—and, therefore, without lowering output*. This happens because U = P/I; that is, utilization depends only on the processing and interarrival time means, but not on their variances V(P) and V(I). The end result is that a machine can, depending on the variances, operate at the same utilization level with different waiting times (or lead times). This can be seen from Figure 7-1 by comparing the curves for high and low processing times variances. It is possibly the most nonintuitive insight derivable from the waiting time formula.

Bottlenecks in Manufacturing Systems

The term *bottleneck* is used to signify a workstation that slows down material flow and makes the manufacturing system "choke." The results are long waiting times and inventory build-up at this station. Bottlenecks can be of two kinds, hard or soft.

A *hard bottleneck* is a workstation that actually limits the output of a system. Let us take the simple case of one machine where batches arrive at a rate of 1/I per hour and it takes P hours to process each batch. As before, the machine utilization U = P/I. How many batches can this machine process per hour? If the station is constantly busy processing batches, the highest rate at which complete batches leave the machine is the inverse of the processing time:

Max output rate = 1/P

For example, if P = 0.2 hours (12 minutes), the machine can, at the most, produce 1/0.2 = 60/12, or five batches per hour. In general, *the hard bottleneck is the machine in the system with the smallest maximum output rate*.

For the bottleneck to produce at its maximum level, its utilization must be 100 percent—in other words, P = I. To accomplish this there must always be an inventory of parts in front of the workstation (otherwise, the machine could become idle). Of course, if processing times were known and fixed, it would be possible to control arrivals so precisely that the station was always busy while, at the same time, queues did not build up. This would happen if jobs arrived at exactly the same rate as that at which they were processed, something that is exceedingly difficult to accomplish in practice.

In reality, all workstations are at some point in time *temporary hard bottlenecks* and will limit output. Thus, the utilization of a workstation is sometimes 100 percent and it is busy processing parts. During that time, its output rate is 1/P. While the machine is busy, batches that arrive will have to wait in the queue. At other times, no new jobs arrive, the queue is empty, and the station may be idle for some time (and its output is zero). On average, then, the utilization will be less than 100 percent. Therefore, workstations don't operate in the long-term as hard bottlenecks, and the maximum output rate (1/P) is really a theoretical (not achievable) long-term limit on output.

The more common use of the term "bottleneck" is that it is the workstation with the largest long-term utilization in the system. We call this a soft bottleneck, or simply the bottleneck. For example, if two stations have utilizations of 75 and 89 percent, respectively, the latter is the soft bottleneck. The soft bottleneck is the station that most frequently becomes fully utilized and serves as a hard bottleneck (in this case, 89 percent of the available time). As such, it constrains output and causes the largest waiting times, lead times, and inventory build-ups. This means you want to pay attention to the soft, and also the near-soft, bottlenecks. If high output or fast throughput times are critical, you must take great care to protect the bottleneck station from downtime, delays, and wasteful utilization. Thus, this is the most important station to protect from yield losses, equipment down time, waiting for labor or tools, high setup times, or idle time due to lack of inventory.

REDUCING MANUFACTURING LEAD TIME

Let us now return to the problem of reducing lead time. Based on the waiting time (W) formula, and generalizing from one machine to a system of machines (like a cell), here are some ideas for reducing waiting time and, therefore, lead time:

- *Reduce average batch processing times, P.* Since $P = S + rQ$, you can achieve this by reducing setup time, by lowering batch sizes, or by more efficient processing (lowering unit run time). Note, however, that if you reduce batch sizes while interarrival times remain the same, less output will be produced.

- *Increase average batch interarrival times, I.* This will slow down work to the system and reduce utilization. You can accomplish this by scaling down the production schedule and releasing fewer jobs to manufacturing each day or week. Of course, with lot sizes unchanged the result is less output.

- *Reduce average batch processing and batch interarrival times in equal measures.* If you reduce lot sizes, the number of units produced over time will decline unless you also reduce the batch interarrival time in the same proportion. For example, if you cut the lot size (Q) in half, you must process twice as many batches as before not to lose output (that is, I must be cut in half as well). The increased number of batches will double setup time, but if you manage to reduce the time per setup by 50 percent you can keep $U = P/I$ constant (also see the section "*Lot size reduction alone*" below). In this way the output rate stays constant while waiting time is reduced.[9]

- *Reduce variability in processing times, V(P).* The processing time variance for a batch, V(P), comes from three sources: variations in the time it takes to set up the machine (S_i), variations in the time it takes to process a single unit

(r_i), and variations in the size of the lots used by the family members (Q_i). You can reduce V(P) by grouping similar jobs and/or standardizing product design (as normally happens in cells). This will reduce the variances in setup times and unit run times. In addition, you can stabilize batch sizes for all members in the family. You also can reduce variability by assigning sequential tasks to the same operator. The process time variance for a job consisting of a set of tasks is smaller than the sum of the variances for each of the individual tasks. Job enlargement, with resulting lower variances, is one advantage of using cells with multi-functional operators.

- *Reduce variability in batch interarrival times, V(I).* You can do this through stable schedules and/or controlled releases of jobs to the cell (as discussed in Chapter 11).

- *Increase effective resource capacity.* Clearly, this is the most straightforward way to achieve lead time reduction. By adding more equipment to the system's bottleneck area, while keeping job arrival rates the same, you can reduce the utilization of the bottleneck and thereby lower lead time (Figure 7-1). However, this solution requires that you use more resources while output remains constant (note that utilization for a group of m machines is $P/(m*I)$). This may therefore be a costly solution where the trade-off is between inventory investment (and long lead times) versus equipment investment (and short lead times).

    Many plants that complain of long lead times are simply short of capacity. This mismatch between capacity and market demand will only worsen if a company plans to grow without taking other actions. Cellular manufacturing can improve lead time through setup time reduction, lot size reduction, move time reduction, and operation time improvements. You typically also get the variance reduction that comes from family processing and order schedule stabilization. However, although these changes will increase the plant's effective capacity, there are clearly situations where you *must* inject new capacity (i.e., through additional equipment and labor) in order to meet growing demand.

In the discussion above we have ignored move times. Obviously, as stated earlier, if you reduce move time you reduce lead time. Since a material-handling resource can be thought of as another machine in your plant, everything stated so far applies to move times as well.

Little's Law

There are two additional ways to reduce waiting and lead times. The first, a highly obvious one, is to ensure that resources are available when needed.[10] There are many ways to do this, such as using preventive maintenance to eliminate equipment downtime, or improving job safety and the quality of the work environment in order to reduce absenteeism. You should also try to coordinate simultaneously needed resources, like equipment, tooling, and labor.

To explain the second way to control lead time, we will use another very important relationship that you should be familiar with. In fact, it is one of the very rare laws that exist in the area of manufacturing management. Let's first define terms:

L = lead time = average time in the system for a batch

WIP = average number of batches in the system (i.e., WIP inventory = batches in process on machines or waiting to be processed)

I = average batch interarrival time

Now, *for any system in steady state* the following relation, referred to as *Little's Law*, holds true:[11]

WIP = L/I

Remember that we are talking about systems in steady state. For such systems, the job input rate to the system equals the job output rate. In other words, what comes in must go out at the same rate. Further, since the input rate is the inverse of the time between job arrivals (i.e., input rate = 1/I), Little's Law can be stated as:

WIP = Lead time * Input rate = Lead time * Output rate

Alternatively, we can rearrange terms and state this law as:

Lead time = WIP/Input rate = WIP/Output rate

Applying Little's Law

You can use Little's Law to estimate the average lead time for a system if you know its WIP and average input or production rate.[12] Consider a situation where batches are processed at a workstation at a rate of 1 per hour and there are an average of 5 batches in the queue and in process at any time. The time it takes to get through this station, therefore, is 5/1, or 5 hours.[13] Likewise, you can estimate WIP if you know the two other parameters. Let's say batches leave a cell every 12 minutes, i.e., at a rate of 5 lots per hour. Further, you know that the lead time for a batch, from arrival to the cell to its departure, is 2 hours. The average WIP inventory in the cell is then 2*5, or 10 batches. If each batch consists of 5 pieces, WIP is 10*5, or 50 pieces.

As you can see, Little's simple formula is fairly intuitive. It also applies to *all systems in steady state* (whether it is a single machine, a cell, an assembly area, a planning department, or a whole factory). It is therefore a very powerful formula for predicting one of the three variables *once the other two are known*. You can also use the formula to verify factory performance data. For example, if someone claims that a plant operates with an average WIP inventory of $50,000 (material cost only), while producing $100,000 worth of goods per week (again, material only) with an average throughput time of 2 weeks, you can be sure that this is not possible. With WIP = lead time*output, your calculated WIP is 2*100,000 = $200,000. But WIP was claimed to be $50,000—thus, at least one of the three variables is incorrect.

Little's Law is not a wish list but a relationship between three actually realized system variables. Therefore, you cannot arbitrarily set two of the variables to values of your choice and then calculate the third. For example, you cannot say: "If I keep the input rate to a cell constant but limit WIP in the cell to 50 percent of current levels, average lead time will be cut in half." In fact, if *the only thing* you did was to constrain the space in the cell available for WIP while the jobs kept coming into the cell at the previous rate, there must be a build-up of inventory at the entry to the cell instead.

Controlling lead time by controlling inventory

We stated earlier that if you increase the average time between batches, i.e., slow down the job input rate to the system, lead time will decline. Since WIP = Lead time*Input rate, it follows from Little's Law that reducing the input rate will lower not just lead time but also WIP inventory. But what if you begin by setting a goal for WIP? Batches cannot come into the system unless there is space for them. Thus, the input rate is constrained by the available space for WIP inventory. You then may reason as follows: "If I limit WIP to a certain level, and find a lower input rate that makes WIP stay within that limit, according to Little's Law I should have put a bound on lead time." In fact, this idea of *controlling lead time via inventory caps* is one of the characteristics of pull systems. A lid is here kept on WIP inventory through the use of kanban squares or by limiting the number of circulating containers. The pull mechanism then adjusts the input rate to maintain the WIP inventory (see Chapter 11).

Is there a downside to limiting WIP inventory? Yes, since the input rate—and therefore the output rate—is affected by WIP, you buy lead time reduction at the price of lowered production. Figure 7-2 illustrates how limiting the buffer space between workstations in a cell constrains its output.[14] By successively increasing WIP space, you can off-load workpieces more frequently from machines that previously sat idle (i.e., the "blocking effect" that prevents operators from passing on the workpieces to the next station is reduced). Ultimately, output becomes constrained by resource capacity rather than by buffer space.

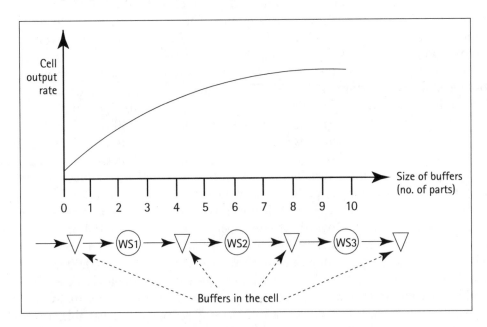

Figure 7–2. The impact of buffer space on output rate

Remember, though, that you need not lose output in order to compress lead time. The section "Reducing Manufacturing Lead Time" provided several other ways to lower lead time, for example by reducing the variances in process (P) and interarrival times (I). If you follow those suggestions, you can operate with the same output rate as before but at lower levels of both WIP and lead time.

SPECIAL PROBLEMS IN DESIGNING AND OPERATING CELLS

During cell design you are likely to encounter many situations where the right choice is not immediately apparent. At the end of Chapter 6 we gave several examples of such "design dilemmas." Some of these are addressed in this section. Specifically, we look at the following issues:

- Where to reduce setups, and how to set lot sizes and transfer batches.
- Whether it is better to share machines between cells or duplicate them.
- Whether it is better to have one large or several small cells.
- Whether it is better to group machines in one place in a cell or locate them according to the flow sequence to avoid backtracks.
- How to assign operators to stations, and the degree to which they should be cross-trained.

The Impact of Setup and Lot Size Reduction

Setup and lot size (batch size) reduction is closely associated with just-in-time systems and lean manufacturing. When you create cells, the time spent on setup tends to decrease due to the formation of families. However, you should still continue to drive setup times down in the cell via more efficient changeovers (see Appendix K for how to accomplish this). You also should lower the lot sizes. We noted earlier that reducing either one will reduce lead time—directly through the setup or operation time component in the lead time formula, and indirectly through the waiting time component.

Here are a couple of interesting questions:

a) Is it always worthwhile to reduce setup time? If so, on what machine should you perform setup time reduction? Also, for what magnitude of setup time reduction should you aim?

b) Is it always worthwhile to reduce lot sizes? If so, for what parts/products should you reduce the lot sizes, and for what magnitude of reduction should you aim?

Setup time reduction alone

Previously, we noted that utilization is the ratio of the average time to process a batch to the average time between batch arrivals, i.e., U = P/I. As before, the average batch processing time is:[15]

$$P = rQ + S$$

where,

> Q = size of the average batch
>
> r = average operation (run) time per unit (including any load and unload times)
>
> S = average time to set up the equipment for a new batch

It is now easy to see what will happen when you reduce setup time at a machine. Since S will go down while r and Q remain unchanged, P will be reduced. Accordingly, utilization will decline.

Figure 7-3 shows the time a batch has to wait at a single workstation as a function of machine utilization and illustrates that a lowered utilization means a smaller wait time for the batch. It follows that setup time reduction reduces lead time. But consider points A-A′ and B-B′ on the graph. If a machine is highly utilized (at point A) and you perform setup time reduction so that the utilization is lowered (to point A′), the impact on waiting time is fairly large (it drops from a to a′). However, if you perform setup time reduction on a machine with a low utilization (see points B and B′), the effect on waiting time is quite small (it drops from b to b′). We can therefore conclude the following:

- Reducing setup time will reduce lead time at a workstation.

- To have the greatest impact on lead time, reduce setup time on the bottleneck or near-bottleneck equipment in the cell since these have the highest utilizations.

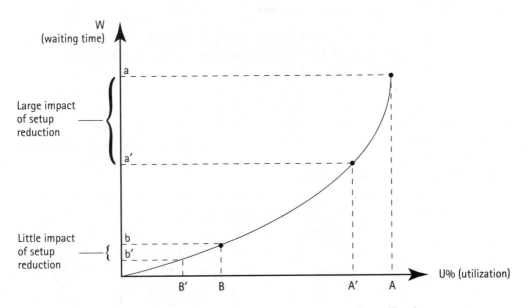

Figure 7-3. The impact on waiting time from lowering utilization

Lot size reduction alone

Assume now that you decide to reduce the batch size while keeping the setup time constant (i.e., you have not performed any setup time reduction). To maintain the same output as before, you must increase the frequency by which you produce batches by the same degree by which you reduce the lot size. What will now happen to lead time? Let's demonstrate using a simple example.

Assume that you modify the original lot size Q by a factor of n (i.e., the new lot size Q' is Q/n). If you change the time between successive batches to I/n, the "before and after" utilizations at a machine will be:

$$\text{Before lot size reduction} = \frac{rQ + S}{I} = U^0$$

$$\text{After lot size reduction} = \frac{rQ/n + S}{I/n} = \frac{rQ + S + (n - 1)S}{I} = U^0 + \frac{(n - 1)S}{I}$$

Consider this example: Q = 100 units, r = 1 minute per unit, S = 20 minutes per setup, and time between job arrivals = I = 140 minutes. The utilization of the workstation is then:

$$U^0 = (1*100 + 20)/140 = 0.857, \text{ or } 85.7 \text{ percent}$$

What if you now reduce the lot size by 25 percent (i.e., $Q' = (3/4)*Q$, and n = 4/3)? According to the second formula, the new utilization is:

$$U' = 0.857 + ((4/3 - 1)*20)/140 = 0.857 + 0.048 = 0.905, \text{ or } 90.5 \text{ percent}$$

Thus, utilization has gone up because you spend more time setting up. What if you now decide to cut the lot size by 50 percent instead (i.e., $n = 2$)? According to the formula above, you get:

$$U' = 0.857 + ((2 -1)*20)/140 = 0.857 + 0.143 = 0.999, \text{ or } 99.9 \text{ percent}$$

In other words, you are dangerously close to 100 percent utilization, a situation where the waiting time will be very large. *If you make a batch size smaller while increasing the batch frequency to keep production output constant—but keep the setup time constant—the system will sooner or later choke and the waiting time and lead time will explode.*

We can illustrate this by calculating lead time as a function of the lot size by using the waiting time formula introduced earlier. If we ignore move time, the lead time for a batch of size Q is L = W + rQ + S. Figure 7-4 shows what happens when you successively diminish the size of the batch.[16]

There are four things to note from this graph:

1. Smaller lots typically have shorter lead times.

2. There is a "best lot size" that will minimize lead time—see point Q* in Figure 7-4.[17]

3. When the initial lot size is "large," the reduction in lead time is directly proportional to the reduction in lot size—see the curve for lot sizes between Q^1 and Q^2 in Figure 7-4.

4. When the lot size reduction is "too large," lead time starts increasing rather than decreasing. A critical situation can develop rather abruptly— see the curve left of point Q* in Figure 7-4.

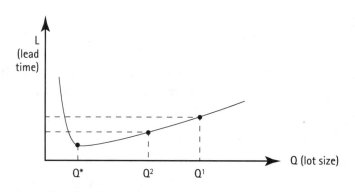

Figure 7-4. How the size of a batch influences lead time (demand is constant)

Lot size reduction is probably the easiest and most cost-effective way to cut lead time. A major reason to perform setup time reduction is to lower the load to allow for small batches. Figure 7-5 illustrates what happens if the setup time is cut in half. Since you have increased the effective capacity by lowering setup time, lead time has declined for sizes of the lot. In addition, the critical turning point also has been lowered, from Q^* to Q^{**}, making it possible to operate safely with smaller lot sizes than before. You may also note from the formula for "utilization after lot size reduction" above that if setup time is modified to the same extent as the interarrival time and the lot size (i.e., S is divided by n as well), utilization as well as output will remain constant.

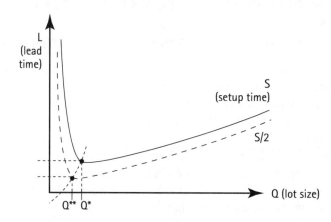
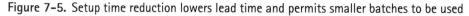

Figure 7-5. Setup time reduction lowers lead time and permits smaller batches to be used

For what parts should lot sizes be reduced?

If you produce more than one part, for which should you reduce the lot size? Obviously, due to market pressures, you may need to reduce lead time for some parts more than for others. However, if you have no reason to treat the parts differently and simply are looking for lead time reductions, you can find a general answer to the question by looking at the waiting time formula (W). This formula indicates that you should not just try to reduce the processing time, P, via setup times and lot sizes, but also that you should set these values to minimize the variances for batch processing and interarrival times.

Let's illustrate using a simple example of just two products. You can minimize the processing time variance (i.e., V(P)) by making sure that the time to process each type of batch is the same. In other words, you want $S_1 + r_1Q_1$ to equal $S_2 + r_2Q_2$. Likewise, you should minimize the batch interarrival time variance (i.e., V(I)) by ensuring that the batches of both types are being processed with similar interval, i.e., $Q_1/D_1 = Q_2/D_2$. You can extend this principle of equalizing batch processing times and order intervals to any number of products in the cell.

Of course, as you can see from the formula for W, it is possible to minimize the variances and still increase the total waiting time. This can happen because lot sizes affect both utilization (U) and the processing times (P). Thus, you do not want to increase utilization or the average process time when you set the lot sizes, unless you deal with a non-bottleneck—further proof that setting operating parameters for manufacturing systems is not trivial, and that insightful answers require computer modeling (discussed later).

The Impact of Move (Transfer) Batches

So far, we have focused on lot sizes for complete batches. The implicit assumption, therefore, has been that when a batch arrives at a workstation it remains there until all items in the batch are processed. This is the typical situation when workstations are located far apart (as in traditional job shops) or when material is sent to subcontractors for processing. You can easily understand that keeping a large batch together will make for long lead times. For example, if you have 500 parts in the batch, 499 parts will have to wait for the last part to be processed before you can move on to the next station. The way to minimize waiting time, therefore, is to process an item and immediately move it to the next workstation (like we do on assembly lines). This suggests that the *ideal* transfer batch is one unit. Whether you can actually operate with such small transfer lot quantities depends on several factors:

- What setup times do successive batches face at a workstation? If setup times are "too large," small lot production can actually have a *negative* impact on lead time (as discussed above).

- How much effort is needed to move small batches between stations? If the transfer batches are very small, and moved by hand, you may have to devote a lot of human effort to material handling.

- To what extent do you need to keep track of batches moving in the system? Small batches, floating all over a factory, could create an administrative headache.

Consider a cell where closely located stations produce a small number of similar products. If the cell processes one model at a time, the changeover times between individual items within a product family are small or nonexistent (on the other hand, if the cell processes several product models simultaneously, transfer lots must be carefully sequenced to avoid excessive setup times). When workstations are placed next to each other, operators can move products easily. Alternatively, with mechanized material handling (like a conveyor), the effort to move products is inconsequential. And because production takes place within the confined space of the cell, the tracking problem is moot. These factors point to the use of very small move batches inside cells—ideally of size one (also referred to as "one-piece flow manufacturing").[18] Typically, the batch sizes by which material is moved to and from the cell are larger than the batch sizes inside the cell due to material-handling efforts and the problem of tracking small lots throughout the entire factory.

It is intuitive that one-piece transfer batches will minimize lead times in cells. In fact, *the ability to use very small transfer batches in cells is, in itself, a very important reason to choose cellular manufacturing over traditional batch manufacturing which, for setup, move time, and tracking reasons, requires large move batches.* (Chapter 11 provides a more detailed discussion on transfer batches, their impact on lead time, and how they should be scheduled.)

The Pooling of Machines

In a functionally organized plant, a job arrives at a work center, waits in a queue, and is served by the first available machine. This is identical to the system commonly used in banks, where customers wait in a single line for the first available teller. In a cell, however, the arriving jobs typically only face a single machine at each step of the process. That is, there are typically no alternative machines to use. What impact do you think this has on throughput time performance? As we indicated in Chapter 6, you inevitably will wrestle with the problem of selecting machine group size during the cell design process. We call this choice the *machine pooling dilemma*. There are at least three situations where the pooling dilemma will or should be addressed:

- Should you choose one large cell or several small cells?
- Should you group similar machines together in a cell or place them according to process sequence?
- How is the factory as a whole affected by pooling losses when cells are formed?

We discuss each situation below.

One large versus several small cells

During the cell design process you identify product/part families whose members are similar in some respect. The stricter your definition of similarity, the smaller the resulting families. Assume that you are choosing between having one large cell, consisting of several machines of each type, and a group of smaller cells, each with one machine of each type. To create the smaller cells, you simply break up the family and the machine groups in the large cell and distribute the parts and the machines among several small cells (see Figure 7-6). Which alternative is best with respect to lead time and inventory?

To gain insight into this problem, we again rely on queuing theory. The waiting time formula we used earlier, however, only applies to a single machine and must be revised for the multi-machine case. Due to its complexity, we will not show it here.[19] Rather, we simply will demonstrate what happens to the waiting time in queue when we pool identical machines into groups. We compare the following cell configurations:

One cell

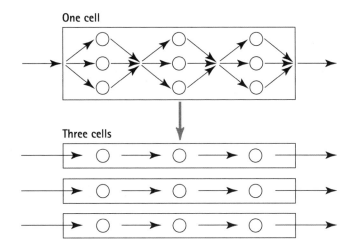

Three cells

Figure 7-6. Breaking up a large cell into several small cells

- A single-cell system with four identical machines.
- A two-cell system with two identical machines each.
- A four-cell system, where each cell consists of a single machine.

Figure 7-7 illustrates the relationship between the batch arrival rate and the waiting times for these systems (setup times are assumed equal in each case). You can derive four important insights from this figure:

- *All else being equal*, the breakup of a machine pool *increases* the average waiting time for a batch.
- The smaller the resulting pool of machines, the larger the impact of a breakup (i.e., the impact on waiting time when switching from two machines in the pool to one is greater than switching from four to two machines).
- The impact on waiting time from a breakup of a pool increases as the batch arrival rate (and, thus, utilization) increases.
- The waiting time for a system with a large machine pool is less sensitive to changes in the batch arrival rate (utilization) than is a system with a small machine pool.

In essence, the smaller the machine group, the worse—and less stable—is the throughput time performance. Thus, if nothing else changes, breaking up a pool of resources will decrease throughput time performance. Since cells are often created by breaking up existing machine groups, this result does not favor cellular manufacturing in general, and certainly not small cells. The key phrase in the first bullet point above, however, is "All else being equal." This implies that *if you can find ways to counteract the lost ability to choose among multiple machines in a pool, you can improve performance.*

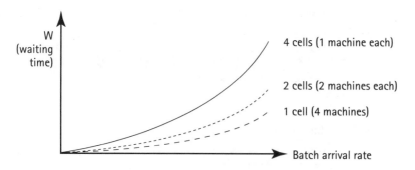

Figure 7-7. The impact on waiting time from pooling machines

When you break up a part family and its cell into smaller entities, you are likely to achieve several benefits. Specifically, you can expect cells with:

- Lower changeover times and changeover time variances due to part families with greater geometric similarities.

- Lower run times due to greater part similarities (labor productivity improvements).

- Improved flow patterns in each cell due to smaller families and more similar part routings.

- More efficient teamwork due to smaller teams and greater cohesion.

- More efficient material handling due to more compact layouts.

- Less complex control problems due to smaller sized cells.

These benefits, however, do not mean that you can ignore the pooling effect. *If you cannot anticipate clear benefits from breaking up a large cell, you should think twice about doing it.* Computer modeling can be extremely helpful in evaluating alternative solutions for any specific cell design project.

The above discussion does not apply to the situation where you turn a long assembly line into several smaller assembly cells. In that case you do not break up resource pools. Rather, you actually move in the opposite direction, creating a system that pools tasks and labor resources. This case is further discussed below.

Placement of machines in the cell

You may face a second pooling dilemma when you decide how to place equipment in the cell. Consider the case where you have formed a family for a part production cell and determined the required number of machines. Assume that two machines of the same type are required to meet capacity, and that this machine type is needed at different places in the part routings. You then have the choice of: (a) putting the two machines together and forcing some of the parts to backtrack to this machine group, or (b) putting the two machines in different positions to eliminate backtracking and making the materials flow linear. These situations are illustrated in Figure 7-8 (also see Figures 6-13 and 6-14).

If you only consider the local impact, alternative (a) is the best choice. The pool of two M1 machines will lower throughput time *at this station* when compared to the longest throughput time at either of the two separated M1 machines in alternative (b). Another advantage is that the same operator can handle both machines, rather than having different operators assigned to the same machine type (which may be preferable if the machines are located far apart). On the other hand, pooling the machines may increase the move times inside the cell. You also need to consider the loss of visual clarity and control by letting parts backtrack in the cell (and then jump forward to the next operation). So alternative (b), placing the machine in the operation sequence, also has advantages. Let's take this alternative as the base case. Grouping two machines in that cell becomes more advantageous (1) the more uneven the utilizations of the machines considered for pooling, (2) the shorter the current distance between the two machines in the cell, (3) the lower the resulting backtrack volume if the machines are pooled, and (4) the larger the savings in tooling if this resides at one machine only. Again, computer modeling can assist here if the choice is not obvious.

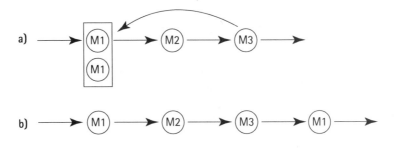

Figure 7-8. Placing machines of the same type in a group vs. process sequence

The pooling effect's impact on the factory as a whole

In Chapters 4 through 6 we mentioned that companies typically design and implement cells one by one. Here we want to raise a warning flag about the potential danger of implementing and evaluating single cells without also considering the larger picture. If we extend our analysis of the pooling effect to the plant as a whole, it suggests that—*all else being equal*—the breakup of a complete factory into cells may not result in lead time improvements. You may say, "Wait a minute! Doesn't this imply that a functionally organized plant, where we do use pooled equipment, is preferable to a cell system?" The answer is "No, not always; but, yes, it can be true under certain conditions."

Consider the common situation where you convert a portion of the plant into a cell while the rest of the plant continues to operate in the functional mode. Assume also that you are not acquiring any new machines to support the cell. What is likely to happen? To reflect on this, we assume that only three part families, P1, P2, and P3, are manufactured. These families are currently processed on machine groups M1, M2, and M3, where each machine group consists of three machines. You then decide to create a cell for part family P1 by pulling one machine out of each of the three machine groups and putting them in the new cell (see Figure 7-9). What will happen to the lead times for the three part families? Will they all improve or all get worse? Or will some get better and some worse?

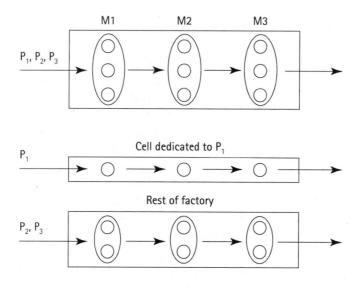

Figure 7-9. Removing equipment from a functional area to create a cell

Unfortunately, this is quite a complicated problem with no easy answers. However, let's make some simplifying assumptions. First, we'll ignore setup and move times. Further, let's say that each part family contributes an equal load on each machine. For example, the machines operate 40 hours per week, and each family contributes 30 hours of weekly load on each machine type. The utilization of each machine type is total workload divided by total available capacity. Thus, utilization is 3*30/3*40, or 75 percent for each machine group in the original system (Figure 7-9a). After the cell is created, the utilization of each machine type will be 1*30/1*40 and 2*30/2*40, or still 75 percent in both the cell and for the machine groups processing part families P2 and P3. Then, if you have made no improvements to the two systems, *average lead times for all three part families will increase.* This effect follows directly from our observation that a breakup of machine pools will increase throughput time, as was shown in Figure 7-7.

Let us now change the load balance in the system and see what happens. What if you decide to change the product mix so that you schedule only 20 standard hours of family P1 per week while increasing the production of families P2 and P3 by 10 standard hours per week? In this case, the utilization of the cell machines will be 20/40, or 50 percent, while the utilization of the machines in the rest of the factory will increase to (30+30+10)/(2*40), or 87.5 percent. What happens now? Clearly, lead times for P2 and P3 will grow even further because machine utilization has increased (see Figure 7-1). However, P1's lead time will now decline below its original value (i.e., the lead time it had when it was processed together with the other two part families; see Figure 7-9a) since the utilization of the cell machines has been lowered.

The preceding discussion, although stylistic and simple, serves to highlight the following points, the first of which we have stressed several times already:

- You must take measures to overcome the loss of machine pooling if you are to achieve lead-time improvements for parts processed in a cell.

- Creating a cell by removing parts and machines from existing groups can cause lead time performance for the remaining parts to deteriorate. To counteract this, you may have to lower the load on the remaining machines or create new capacity for these resources.

Cells can overcome pooling effects through a combination of lowered workloads, reduced setup times, shorter batch operation times, smaller move times, improved setup, operation, and move time variances, and through controlled order releases. New and more efficient processing technology will contribute in this regard. It is possible, however, that these improvements may be insufficient to compensate for the loss in lead time performance due to smaller machine pools. If you already operate with small lot sizes, short setup times, and stable production schedules for the parts you intend to put in cells, you are less likely to achieve performance improvements than if you start from a situation with large lots, long setup times, and erratic job arrivals.

Our key message in this section, however, is that while you can build cells with excellent performance, the remainder of the factory may demonstrate worse performance unless you improve the processes there as well, acquire more capacity, or shift workloads. Simply put, local performance for a cell is not the same as global performance for the factory.[20] Performance evaluations should therefore cast a wide net (also see Step 13 in Figure 4-1).

Multi-functional and Cross-trained Labor

So far in our analysis of cell behavior we have looked only at the role of equipment. However, the performance of a cell depends also on the availability of other resources, the most important being labor. A cell, according to our definition, is a production unit that performs several distinct operations. While in traditional factories operators specialize on one task, cells lend themselves to the use of *multifunctional operators* who can master more than one process. The most obvious reason for having operators in charge of more than one type of operation is that they may have time available to perform other tasks. This is obviously the case if the cell uses (semi-)automatic equipment. A second, related reason is that by assigning multiple tasks to operators you can reduce time wasted due to process imbalances. This means you may be able to run a cell with fewer operators than before. Job enlargement also tends to reduce processing time variance and, thereby, lead time. A third and very important reason is that when multiple operators are *cross-trained* on several of the same processes, they represent movable and flexible capacity. This makes it possible to meet varying demand with varying staffing levels.

To illustrate, assume a two-operator flow-line cell where the average process time per unit is 15 minutes for the first station and 10 minutes for the second. The maximum output rate for the cell is 60/15, or 4 units per hour. In this mode, the second operator is always idle 5 minutes for every part cycle. Assume now that the operators are trained to perform the tasks at both stations. This means, first of all, that you can run the cell with a single operator. The workload for an operator is then 25 minutes per unit, and maximum output is 60/25, or 2.4 units per hour.

Note, thus, that even if labor capacity was cut in half, output declined only by 40 percent. Second, you could also run two separate one-operator cells (of course, to do this you need more equipment). The combined output for these cells would be 4.8 units per hour, or 20 percent more than for the two-operator cell without cross-training.

What exactly is cross-training?

The term *cross-training* is frequently used in connection with cellular manufacturing. In the case of a single-operator cell it means that an operator can master all tasks required to process a part in that cell. A task in this case can be to set up a screw machine, to inspect a workpiece, to assemble a gear box, to test a completed subassembly, and so on (we are here ignoring administrative tasks; see Chapters 12 and 13).

In a multiple-operator cell, cross-training can mean two different things: (1) that each operator is capable of doing more than one type of task, i.e., is multi-functional, but that each set of tasks is *independent* of those assigned to other operators; and (2) that each operator can perform more than one task, and that some or all task sets assigned to operators *overlap*. In the first case, you simply have distributed the tasks among the operators in the cell. The operators' ability to handle more than one process means that you can run the cell with fewer operators than machines. However, since there is no overlap in tasks, this type of cell is vulnerable to absenteeism: if one operator is missing, no one can do his or her tasks in the cell. Likewise, without overlapping tasks, an operator cannot help others in times of need. These two situations motivate the use of the second type of cross-training.

The second definition of cross-training implies multifunctional operators who are *deliberately* trained to have *overlapping skills*. In this way, operators can assist each other if needed, and the cell can operate with different levels of staffing. Henceforth, it is to this definition of cross-training that we refer when we use the term. Table 7-2 shows some possible labor assignment strategies for a pinion cell at the Falk Corporation in Milwaukee, Wisconsin, when three operators are used.[21] In the first strategy, there is no task overlapping, while for the second and third strategies, some operators are assigned to both main and secondary (overlapping) operations.

How should you allocate tasks to operators?

When you dimension a cell, you must determine both the number of machines and the number of operators needed to meet demand. The latter decision depends on the type and degree of operator cross-training (as we discussed in Chapter 6). Thus, there are two related issues of importance: (1) *how many* process steps (operations) should you assign to each operator, and (2) *which* processes should you allocate to each operator?

To address these issues we cannot use the basic waiting time models we have relied on so far. Instead, we need to use either more sophisticated queuing models or rely on stochastic simulation. Rather than introducing such models here, we will provide guidance into the allocation of tasks to operators simply by discussing some known effects of cross-training (also see Chapter 12, especially Figure 12-1):[22]

1. *A cell's output increases when the number of tasks that each operator can perform increases.* Figure 7-10 shows the simulated output from Falk's pinion cell when the task assignments go from a nonoverlapping situation (base assignment) to one where each operator is fully cross-trained on all equipment. As can be seen, output increases with cross-training.

2. *You should allocate tasks among operators to level their workload.* A skills chart, like the one in Table 7-2, does not indicate the load that each machine imposes on the cell. However, for any level of cross-training, you should try to assign tasks for which the operators have main responsibility in such a way that you level the operators' workload. Not only is this fair,

Table 7-2. Three labor allocation strategies for a pinion cell

Strategy	Machine ID	Operator 1	Operator 2	Operator 3
1 Basic	Lathe	●		
	Lathe	●		
	Hobber		●	
	Hobber		●	
	Gear Shaver			●
	Okuma VA Mill			●
	Cylindrical Grinder			●
2	Lathe	●		
	Lathe	●		
	Hobber		●	
	Hobber		●	
	Gear Shaver		⌒	●
	Okuma VA Mill		⌒	●
	Cylindrical Grinder			●
3	Lathe	●		
	Lathe	●		
	Hobber	⌒	●	
	Hobber	⌒	●	
	Gear Shaver		⌒	●
	Okuma VA Mill		⌒	●
	Cylindrical Grinder	⌒		●

● operator's main responsibility
⌒ operator shares whenever possible

but it also maximizes output and minimize lead time. The more tasks each operator is capable of performing, the easier it is to level workloads. In an ideal state, when all operators know all tasks in the cell, the operators' workload can be completely balanced.

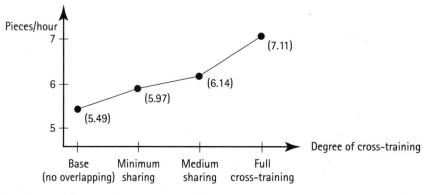

Based on 3-shift operation (4–3–2 strategy)

Figure 7–10. The influence of cross-training on cell output

3. *You should ensure that each task can be performed by at least two operators.* The term redundancy refers to the number of operators that can perform a specific task. Labor strategy 3 in Table 7-2, for example, has a redundancy of 1 for the two lathes (no overlapping), while the hobbers have a redundancy of 2. To protect against absenteeism, the minimum redundancy for all tasks should be 2 (thus, the labor allocations in Table 7-2 are not ideal because some have a redundancy of 1).

4. *You should create a degree of task overlapping that is proportional to the workloads.* Operators should be cross-trained so that redundancy varies with workload. This means you want the highest degree of redundancy for bottleneck or near-bottleneck operations in the cell to ensure the highest protection against "waiting for labor." This will minimize lead time.

5. *You may consider the location of the workstations when determining task allocations.* From an operator movement perspective, the primary location of an operator can dictate what other operations he or she should be able to master. In high-volume assembly cells, in particular, training operators to handle the process steps before and after a primary station is very effective.

Why does cross-training work?

Cross-training is effective because it creates a labor pooling effect similar to the one we discussed in connection with machines. That is, when an operator increases his or her skill set so that it overlaps with that of another operator (they cross over), you create a *labor pool for each of the overlapping tasks.* Therefore, whenever you need to execute that task there is a choice of operators rather than just one. Also, because cross-trained employees are multi-functional, there tends to be less efficiency losses due to load imbalances and task hand-offs. Both effects dynamically increases that cell's effective capacity and improves lead times and output.

We demonstrated in Figure 7-7 that when you increase the size of the machine pool, lead time declines—but at a diminishing rate. That is, machine pooling gets to be less and less effective. Although not shown in Figure 7-10, the same thing tends to occur for labor pooling. The reason why increasing the degree of cross-training gradually reduces its effectiveness is that the cell cannot take advantage of the increased flexibility that additional task overlapping provides. The lesson from this is that although firms often want operators who are fully capable of handling all processes in a cell, this may be neither necessary nor cost effective due to training and recertification costs. Rather, due to its declining effectiveness, a little cross-training goes a long way. Note also that cross-training needn't be uniform across the operators. However, as stated above, each operator should ideally be able to handle at least two tasks, and if possible the number of operators trained on each task should be proportional to its workload.

Other issues in cross-training

So far we have discussed only the case of operators handling multiple tasks inside the same cell (referred to as *intracell* mobility). However, you can also take advantage of cross-training by letting operators temporarily move to other cells when their skill sets are needed due to "emergencies." This type of *intercell* (i.e., between cell) mobility can be very effective in enhancing the performance of a cell system. In one group of companies we studied, 39 percent claimed to have operators move between cells when capacity was needed elsewhere.[23]

Finally, there is a host of other concerns regarding cross-training, most of which deal with human nature or behavior. We are referring to the operators' willingness and/or ability to be trained in multiple tasks and use their skills by rotating inside the cell (see Chapters 12 and 13). For example, some operators do not appreciate the loss of unique skills that comes with cross-training because this diminishes their sense of identity.[24] Further, just because operators are cross-trained for certain tasks does not mean that they will perform them. In fact, there is evidence that operators in some cells—even when fully cross-trained—favor certain processes and stay with these rather than rotating among all operations in the cell.[25] Of course, there also are cells where operators are required to move with the piece and visit all stations in the cell. Such cells obviously require both full cross-training and full use of the operators' skills.

Designing Cells: Considering All the Factors

When dimensioning a cell you determine the number of machines or workstations of each kind, as well as the number of operators and their station assignments. In Chapter 6 we looked at the simplest form of cell dimensioning where you calculate the expected load on the resources and then make sure that the available personnel and equipment exceed the workload. We have found that about two-thirds of companies involved with cell projects undertake this most basic form of modeling at the design stage.[26] As long as utilization is below 100 percent, you will be able to produce the targeted volume. However, this perspective ignores the issue of time: that is, although you can meet the rate of expected output (in units produced per day or week), you do not know how long the lead times will be.

Recall that lead time is largely made up of waiting time, and that waiting time in queue is a nonlinear function of utilization (see Figures 7-1, 7-3, and 7-7). Thus, lead times in manufacturing cells (or office cells) are not constant but depend on the load that is imposed on employees and equipment. *Checking load versus capacity is therefore a necessary but insufficient step in cell dimensioning.* It also is important to get a feeling for expected lead times for parts and products. In the previous sections we noted that setup times are part of the workload and that lot sizes have a large and direct impact on lead times. We also noted that cross-training and variations in processing and job interarrival times play a part as well. Obviously, multiple factors influence lead time and thus need to be considered simultaneously. The next section discusses advanced modeling tools that can be used for this purpose.

QUEUING AND SIMULATION MODELS—AN OVERVIEW

Using the simple expressions for lead time, waiting time, and Little's Law, we have been able to develop several powerful insights into the behavior of manufacturing systems. Based on these insights we also formulated actions that can reduce lead time. Although some of the guidelines were based on a single machine that never breaks down, and for which move times and/or operators were ignored, they are general enough to apply to all systems, including cells. What you don't know in any specific case, of course, is *how much* you should change a parameter and *how much impact* this will have. To get answers to those questions before the cell is built, you must model it.

There are two important dimensions of a model. The first is whether it considers any variations in the model variables. For example, are job processing times, demand, job arrival rates and the like constant, or are they assumed to fluctuate over time? If there are no random variables, the model is called *deterministic*. Otherwise, it is a stochastic model. The second dimension classifies models based on the influence of time. A model whose output depends on time is called a *dynamic model*, while a model whose solution is unaffected by time is referred to as a *static model*. For example, a spreadsheet model that determines workloads is a deterministic and static model; a queuing model is a stochastic and static model; and a simulation model typically is both stochastic and dynamic (see Figure 7-11).

	Deterministic Models	Stochastic Models
Static Models	Basic spreadsheet models	Analytic queuing models
Dynamic Models	Deterministic simulation models	Stochastic simulation models

Figure 7-11. Classification of models

Simulation Models

Obviously, the real world is both stochastic and dynamic. You know it is characterized by variability in all factors that matter, and that those factor combinations change over time. Therefore, the most realistic models are stochastic simulation models. Setting all variances in a stochastic simulation model to zero makes it a deterministic model. Because we often lack knowledge of the statistical distributions, simulation models frequently combine deterministic and stochastic variables.

Stochastic simulation models come closest to modeling reality and therefore provide the most detailed answers. However, they suffer from a few drawbacks, the biggest being the inordinate amount of time it takes to collect input distributions and build and validate the model. Furthermore, since simulation incorporates stochastic variations and dynamic phenomena, you must use statistical techniques to evaluate the significance of the output. And to derive answers with an acceptable degree of reliability, you have to run these models many times and/or for long periods.

On the other hand, the advantages of modern simulation software are that almost anybody can build simple models after a short training period, and that small models can be up and running quickly. In addition, software often provides animation capabilities so that you can view the modeled system on screen and observe dynamically changing variables such as location of people and workpieces, levels of inventories, or machine uptime. Many companies use animation to demonstrate proposed manufacturing systems to managers and employees. These visual and colorful demonstrations are an important complement to the change proposals and tend to be very effective in selling the reorganization concepts—a picture is worth a thousand words.

Queuing Models

Queuing models fall in the static/stochastic category of models. For example, you can easily see from the waiting time model used throughout this chapter that it is "static." That is, neither input nor output data are linked to any specific points in time. This means that you can get a solution to the model simply by plugging in parameter data such as mean and variance of processing time. The great advantage of queuing models is that they are "quick and dirty." In other words, while their solutions most often are only approximate, they are suitable for rapid "what-if" evaluations of system behavior when you are less concerned with details in the model or accuracy in the results.

Queuing models provide you with information on utilization levels, lead times, waiting times, and output rates. Since they assume steady-state situations, you cannot get information on performance variations over time. This means queuing models cannot answer questions such as, "Will job F4693, due next Monday, be ready on time?" or "What is the highest inventory level predicted for January?" For such time-dependent questions, you must rely on stochastic simulations.

However, given that factories are constantly evolving, and that building and analyzing simulation models is time consuming, queuing software has the advantage of allowing you to build and evaluate a system quickly. There are only a few commercial software packages based on queuing theory. The one with which we are most familiar, MPX, is a PC-based product developed by Network Dynamics, Inc.[27] MPX provides output data in both numerical and graphical form, showing, for example, lead times for product groups broken down into productive time and waiting time (see Figure 7-12).

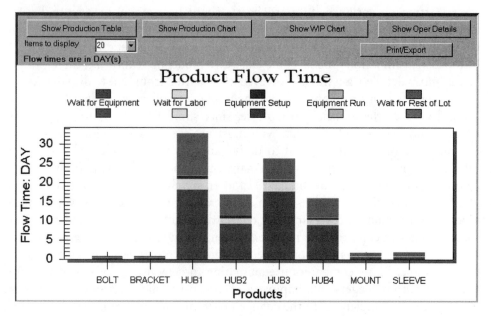

Figure 7–12. MPX screen showing product flow time (i.e., lead time)

Building Queuing Models—Some Illustrations

To give you an idea of what it takes to build an MPX model, here is a list of required input data:

- Bills of materials and routings for each family, showing the equipment groups visited.
- Setup and operation times for each family at each equipment group.
- Reliability of each machine group (in mean time between failure, and mean time to repair).
- Lot sizes and transfer batches per family.
- Number of machines in each equipment group.
- Labor time spent on setup and operation for each family at each station.
- The labor pool to which each equipment group is assigned.
- Percentage of time labor is unavailable.
- Hours of overtime allowed.
- Scrap rates per equipment group (in percent).
- Total number of hours available in a year.
- Demand per family per year.
- Degree of variation in job arrival times and processing times.

Although you can model move times between stations, these are often ignored to simplify the model-building process. Next, we will revisit the Deltrol Controls (discussed in Chapter 5) and Ingersoll Cutting Tools (discussed in Chapters 4 and 5) to illustrate how you can use MPX for cell design and evaluation.

Deltrol Controls

If you recall, Deltrol wanted to know whether a switch to cells would have a favorable impact on the production of general purpose relays. This broad product group was broken down into four different model families that were used for the analysis (Figure 5-10 shows the routings for these families). The original setup times, lot sizes, and transfer batches were used together with other data to build an MPX model. This model then determined the lead times for each component as well as for the final assemblies (see the light bars in Figure 7-13).[28]

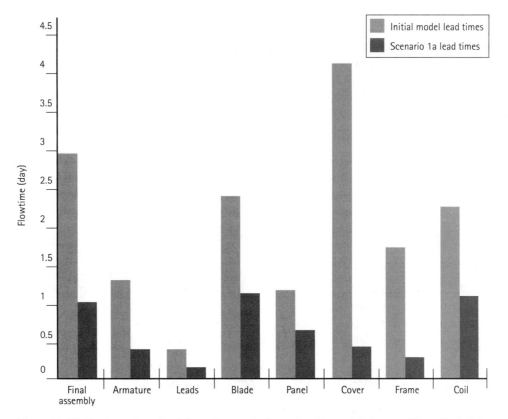

Figure 7-13. The impact on lead times from reducing setup times, lot sizes, and transfer batches

After the analysis team tried out various scenarios and consulted with company personnel, it recommended the revised setup times, lot sizes, and transfer batches shown in Table 7-3. In addition, it suggested operating the coil-winding machine during the lunch break to gain greater effective capacity. The MPX model was rerun with this revised input. The dark bars in Figure 7-13 show the resulting impact. As noted, the model indicated that Deltrol could dramatically reduce lead times based on the recommended changes.

Table 7-3. Proposed lot and transfer batch sizes for the relay manufacturing area

Part Name	Current		Recommended	
	Lot Size	Transfer Batch	Lot Size	Transfer Batch
Final Assembly	509	509	500	24
Armature	772	772	500	24
Leads	8,884	8,884	1,000	100
Blade	7,877	7,877	4,000	24
Panel	990	990	1,000	24
Cover	8,484	8,484	1,000	24
Frame	15,562	15,562	1,000	24
Coil	1,109	1,109	1,000	24

Other "what-if" scenarios were also investigated. What if we acquire one more coil-soldering machine and one more molding machine? What if we run two shifts per day rather than one? Investigating such alternatives can be done rapidly and provides you with good insights into the kind of performance levels you potentially could achieve. In Deltrol's case, the model indicated that, with additional changes, the company could ultimately reduce WIP inventory by 91 percent, from 70,000 pieces down to 6,000 pieces. Likewise, the lead time for final assembly could be reduced by 88 percent, from 2.97 days down to 0.35 days (i.e., 0.65 days beyond what is shown in Figure 7-13).

Ingersoll Cutting Tool Company

Ingersoll Cutting Tool is a manufacturer of cutting tool bodies. At the time of this study, it operated a functionally oriented shop that made 75 percent of its products to order (MTO) and 25 percent to stock (MTS). Lot sizes were quite small, averaging three units for MTO products and eight units for MTS items. The company was interested in pursuing a strategy of cellular manufacturing in the machine shop after having had a positive experience of the cell concept in the office (see Chapter 18). A primary goal was to reduce lead time by about 50 percent.[29]

The analysis team developed an MPX model after collecting the following data:

- The routings for 800 released orders during a two-month period. These were used to develop the routing structure for the model.

- Setup and run times gathered either from actual data collected by the labor-reporting system over a five-month period, or, if actual data were not available, from standards. These data were used to determine equipment workloads.

- Downtime and repair time data for a 10-month period. These were used to estimate mean time between failure (MTBF) and mean time to repair (MTTR).

- Demand data for one year, which were used to illustrate how demand varied over time and to drive the MPX model.

A few interesting observations from the modeling analysis at Ingersoll are described next.

The impact of utilization. If you want to understand how to increase output or reduce throughput time, the first step is to determine utilization levels and locate the bottleneck operations. The MPX model automatically calculates utilizations for each machine group based on demand data. Figure 7-14 shows that utilization levels exceeded 100 percent on some machines. That, of course, is not possible. In reality, Ingersoll outsourced work in order to handle the demand, so the actual utilizations of the equipment were in fact lower. However, they were still very high on some equipment (in the upper 90s). Figure 7-14 also shows that the utilization levels in the shop varied greatly: many machine groups operated at low levels, and some at very high levels. This is typical for many plants.

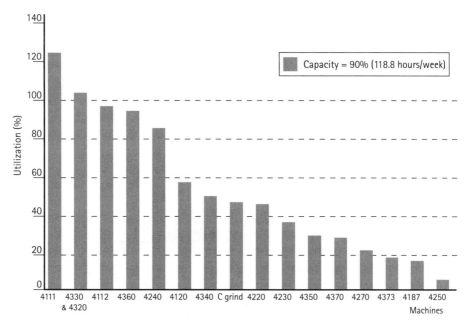

Figure 7–14. Machine utilization chart for Ingersoll Cutting Tool

To deliver more rapidly, Ingersoll needed greater control over manufacturing. In effect, this would require shifting subcontracted work back to an already overloaded in-house manufacturing operation. Furthermore, because lot sizes at Ingersoll already were quite low, lead time compression due to reductions in batch size was not going to be very effective. Both factors suggested that more capacity was needed for the bottleneck machine groups.

Adding one machine each to the two highest utilized groups in Figure 7-14 and rerunning the model revealed that average lead time would decrease from 24 days per batch down to 2.5 days. This assumed the plant brought *all* outsourced work back in-house. The reason lead time could be reduced so drastically can be explained by looking at the waiting time/utilization curves (similar to the one in Figure 7-1). In Ingersoll's case, this curve was quite steep for the highly loaded equipment, indicating that even a small reduction in load would generate a large reduction in waiting time. The MPX model confirmed that duplicating the bottle-neck and near-bottleneck machines—but doing nothing else—would reduce lead time substantially.

Cells and the impact of machine pooling. The analysis team finally recommended that the company should produce three product families in two cells, and that the two new machines discussed above should be made part of the cells. However, the MPX model indicated that the functional shop with the same added machines could produce the cell parts faster than could the dedicated cells. Figure 7-15 shows the average lead time for the three families before (i.e., in the current shop, with additional machines) and after (i.e., in the planned cells).

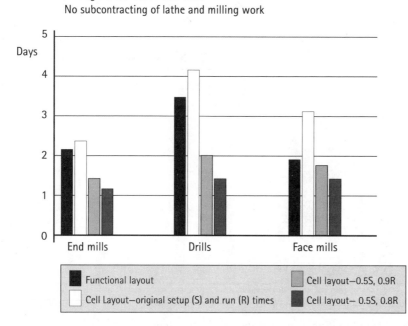

Figure 7-15. Average batch lead times for part families at Ingersoll: functional layout vs. cells

The anticipated increases in lead time after a conversion to cells ranged from less than 15 percent for the combined end mills/drills cell to almost 50 percent for the face mills cell (see the left two bars in the figure). These increases in lead time for the cells, which assume "all other things equal," can be explained by the pooling effect we discussed earlier. However, you can always expect both setup times and operation times to improve in cells. Figure 7-15 therefore also shows what happens if Ingersoll could cut setup times in half, and lower run times to 90 percent and 80 percent of their original values, respectively (see the right two bars). As can be seen, the average lead times for the cell part families are now much shorter than in the functional shop. Based on this analysis, management decided to proceed with cell implementation.

Final Comments on Deltrol and Ingersoll

In both of these analyses, the MPX model omitted some factors that contribute to lead time. First, the material-handling systems were ignored because their contribution to overall lead times was judged to be quite small. The possible gain in enhanced model accuracy did therefore not seem to outweigh the increased effort of incorporating move times in the model. Second, the models did not consider the impact of reduced variations in processing times that product families often yield. Such reductions, as discussed, would lower lead times further. This omission, again, was based on effort exceeding the need for accuracy.

Finally, you may wonder why we predicted the improvement at Ingersoll to be so low. After all, you probably have read many accounts of firms lowering their lead times by 70 to 90 percent after switching to cells. Remember, however, that companies often add new equipment to their cells but compare the cells' performance to the situation in the plant without new capacity added. Figure 7-15 provides a more accurate and fair comparison. It shows the performance in the functional versus the cell shop after adding an equal amount of capacity in both cases. If you compare lead times in cells with capacity added, with the average in the original shop without capacity added, lead time reduction is dramatic (from 24 days to about 3 days).

You also should note that much of the radical lead time improvement at Deltrol is due to large lot-size reductions. Because Ingersoll already had very small batches in place, lot-size reductions played no role in shortening lead time. Accordingly, lead time reduction at Ingersoll must come from productivity improvements, variance reductions, or more favorable capacity/load ratios.

THE VALUE OF MODELS AND MODELING

Here are some questions that often surface during the cell design phase, and later, while operating the cells:

- What happens to throughput time if the product mix changes?
- What is the effect on WIP inventory if we run the cell with one less operator?
- How will the output rate be affected if we manage to reduce scrap by 20 percent?
- What will happen to the average lead time if we add one more part to the cell?
- Should we reduce setup time on the lathe or the mill to get the largest performance improvement?
- What happens to the cell's productivity if we can train Shyam, Neil, Wenhui, and Lori to master three operations each?
- Given our growing demand, when do we need to add equipment and operators to the cell in order to maintain the same level of response time as before?

To predict what may happen in situations like these, you can turn to queuing theory or stochastic simulation.[30] There are numerous commercial software products on the market, and you may want to consult the annual software reviews published by professional magazines or posted on web sites in this regard. In one of our studies, only about 10 percent of the cell users relied on simulation modeling.[31] If you don't use modeling, however, you have to rely on intuition or general insights when designing your cells, and on other companies' experience when it comes to predicting performance improvements. This could be adequate in many cases, but there are still situations when you definitely should take advantage of modeling.

When to Use Modeling

Modeling projects can be costly. If done in-house, you need software and the skills to use it. You also need to devote time to digging up the data required for the model. If you outsource the modeling project to a consulting firm, there are direct out-of-pocket costs which do not include the time in-house personnel spend gathering data. Either way, the benefits of modeling must outweigh these costs. In general, modeling efforts are likely to pay off when these three characteristics are in place:

1. There is a large investment in new equipment or facilities involved.
2. It is difficult to change the new system once it is built.
3. The planned system is complex, and its behavior is difficult to predict.

When a lot of money is involved, and the new factory will be difficult to reconfigure, you must be more concerned with system performance than if you can rearrange equipment and facilities easily. Thus, in light industries such as electronic assembly, where you can create a cell within an hour—to have it change in the next—you can use trial and error rather than modeling. This is not possible in the mechanical industry where heavy equipment requires solid floor foundations and extensive utility connections, and is difficult to move.

In addition, manufacturing systems whose behavior you really don't understand are better candidates for modeling than are simple systems. Complexity is a function of both size and interconnections. For example, a small cell that is labor-driven is easier to understand than a large, automated cell where machines are linked via a mechanical material-handling system. Your ability to predict the behavior of a cell also declines when the number of interacting resources increases. For example, compared to a cell that is solely machine constrained, it is more difficult to predict the performance of a cell (1) if the equipment utilization also depends on the effective use of labor, or (2) if cell machines must share a limited inventory of tools with equipment inside or outside the cell.

Figure 7-16 shows the simulated output for a three-shift pinion cell operation at the Falk Corporation.[32] The simulation demonstrates that while the cell output increases with increasing staffing levels, it is maximized for nine operators per day. At that point, the cell becomes constrained by machine rather than labor capacity. Also note that output depends on how each of the three shifts is staffed. With 8 operators, for example, only the 3-3-2 staffing policy (i.e., 3 operators on first and second shift, and 2 on the third) is able to meet the target output level of 6.5 pieces per hour for the cell. This example demonstrates that simulation is an excellent tool for evaluating various policies when the outcomes by no means are obvious.

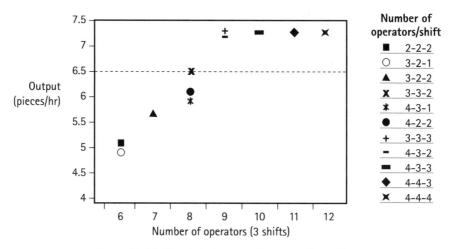

Figure 7-16. Simulated output from a pinion cell

Modeling as a Learning Tool

The value of modeling is not limited to "merely" being able to predict how a specific manufacturing cell, or office cell, will perform. There is also a great learning benefit embedded in the modeling process. First, the output of a model run provides you with concrete numbers on performance. With these as starting point, the discussion in the team will inevitably focus on the design of the system by examining the assumptions of the model. This is an excellent way to learn how the plant's current processes really work. Second, by playing with the model, i.e., using different demand patterns, lot sizes, staffing levels, and the like, you can learn how the system behaves. This may cause you to consider alternatives you had originally not thought about.

Third, modeling can be a powerful tool for educating reluctant managers about the current state of the firm and convincing them to reorganize and improve. This is especially true for simulation software that has the ability to depict the dynamic behavior of the system in an animation mode. For example, many managers—even quite experienced ones—fail to believe that the batches travelling through their factories spend up to 95 percent of their time in a waiting mode. Many are also not aware of the role that lot sizes play in determining lead time. Queuing or simulation models can be good vehicles for creating such insights. Finally, modeling can provide data for the economic justification of cell projects (see Chapter 8).

Can Models Incorporate the Human Side of Work?

You may wonder how well models can capture reality when they exclude the soft, human side of work. Even if we include labor in the models, isn't there something missing? Can we really embody the way people behave in quantitative models? Granted, people are often unpredictable and behave in surprising ways—ways that can be both positive and negative. And the exact behavior is impossible to model. *But we are only interested in people's behavior if it affects variables that have an impact on system performance.* For example, people determine the number of available hours that makes up a cell's capacity, influence the part processing times (the statistical properties of the distributions) through their behavior and skills, and modify job schedules. And of course, they can directly influence the way in which they assist each other in the cell.

You can consider all these factors in models in one way or another. But since in most cases the actual system you build will be in constant evolution, it is futile to try to design *the perfect system* using modeling. A better use of models is to help designers and decision-makers to fairly quickly hone in on good cell designs that can be rapidly implemented.

KEY INSIGHTS

Table 7-4 summarizes the guidelines for reducing lead time and inventory that we have discussed in this chapter.[33] The effect of these changes is cumulative; that is, the more factors you modify, the greater the impact on lead time. Your point of departure also matters. Thus, lot size reduction can be very effective if you begin with large lots. Likewise, setup time reduction leads to lower lead time on machines with high utilization than would be the case with low-utilization machines. Leveling the product mix influences lead time more if it is highly unbalanced to begin with than if it is almost level, and so on. The fact that firms have varying points of departure can explain, at least partly, why some companies show large improvements with cells while others do not (also see Table 1-1).

Our message in this chapter is simple: modeling tools, especially easy-to-use tools such as MPX, can be very helpful in estimating lead times, inventories, and output rates for cells. Furthermore, queuing formulas, even if they are too simplistic to predict the performance of the cell you are designing, still can provide valuable insights into the fundamental behavior of systems. You can rely on these for designing and operating cells.

Below we summarize some key insights for understanding cell behavior and determining cell performance:

- *Lead time is dominated by waiting time.* The time a batch waits during its time in the factory can make up 70 to 95 percent of lead time.

- *Lead time is related to utilization in a nonlinear way.* The more you load a resource, the greater the output. At the same time, however, lead time grows longer. In fact, the more you increase utilization, the more rapidly lead time increases. Thus, more capacity will lower lead time.

- *To reduce lead time, you can reduce setup times, batch operation times, and move times.* Although waiting time dominates lead time, it cannot be attacked directly. Rather, you have to manipulate the three other components of lead time: setup, operation, and move times. Perhaps the most effective way to shorten lead time is to use small batches.

- *Reducing variations in processing times and the job arrival stream is an effective way to shorten lead time without losing output.* You can accomplish variance reduction through batch size and schedule stabilization.

- *Cross-trained operators will improve performance.* Make sure that at least two operators can handle each key task in the cell. Also, the larger the workload a task requires, the more operators should be trained to perform it.

- *Focus on the bottlenecks.* The bottleneck resources, whether equipment or labor, dictate output, inventories, and lead times. Thus, an effective way to reduce lead times is to reduce the load on the bottlenecks and the near-bottleneck resources. This can be done through scheduling (controlling input) or through productivity improvements (such as setup time reduction).

- *Resource pooling improves performance.* The lowered routing flexibility (reduced pooling) that comes with cells is the only factor that can make cells perform worse than the functional shop. You can overcome this loss of flexibility by adding capacity or by increasing the efficiency and stability of the cell.

- *Consider using simulation or queuing models to predict cell performance.* Modeling is appropriate if cells are complex, difficult to reconfigure, and/or require large investments.

- *It is easier to achieve lead time improvements with cells than in functionally organized work centers.* All of the ideas for how to reduce lead time that we have discussed in this chapter are applicable to any type of manufacturing system. However, most are easier to accomplish with cells. Thus, the changes listed in Table 7-4 are facilitated by the complete processing of similar products with dedicated equipment and labor in a compressed space.

Table 7-4. Factors with established influence on lead time

Factor	Needed to Reduce Lead Time
Setup time	Decrease
Setup time variability	Decrease
Unit processing time	Decrease
Processing time variability	Decrease
Lot size	Decrease*
Lot-size variability	Decrease
Move time	Decrease
Move time variability	Decrease
Transfer batch size	Decrease
Order schedule variability	Decrease
Labor flexibility (cross-training)	Increase
Routing flexibility (machine pooling)	Increase
Capacity/work load	Increase/decrease

* Setup times may have to be reduced jointly with the lot sizes.

8

Determining the Economic Value of Cells

If your cell project requires outlays for capital equipment, you will probably be asked to submit a formal capital acquisition request. If, on the other hand, no new investment is needed, you may not need to do an economic justification. In one of our studies, more than two-thirds of all firms installed at least some new equipment when they established cells. Furthermore, in about one-sixth of these firms *all* equipment for the cells was new.[1] Similarly, another study found that while about 70 percent of the firms rated their investment as "small or none," the remaining firms considered their investment significant.[2] Thus, it seems that between one-third to two-thirds of all cell projects require a financial justification.

There is no doubt that the majority of cell users feel they have achieved economic value from the reorganization, regardless of whether they perform an economic analysis or not. For example, *every* firm participating in one study claimed that their cell projects had been successful. In another study, only 1 percent of the respondents had considered abandoning their cells.[3] We also know that most cell users (between 69 to 87 percent) have plans to continue to establish cells and perceive that the benefits exceed the costs involved.[4] That cellular manufacturing delivers economic value is also supported by statements like these: "Our ability to schedule, plan, and produce in this environment is considerably enhanced in comparison with conventional layouts," and "I didn't realize that you will get continuous improvement with the same operators in the same cell day after day."[5]

Such positive responses to cells should come as no surprise, given the range and magnitude of performance improvements documented in the literature.[6] However, cell projects have been terminated because they could not demonstrate a sufficient return on investment.[7] So it is important that you are familiar with commonly used justification procedures and how to apply them. In particular, we address the following issues in this chapter:

- What roles should strategic and economic justification play in decisions about cell projects?
- What costs and benefits should you include in your justification, and how do you estimate them?
- What methods can you use for economic justification?
- How should you handle intangible benefits in your justification?

- How much justification is really needed?
- What else (apart from a solid justification) should you do to sell the cell project to decision-makers?

STRATEGIC VERSUS ECONOMIC JUSTIFICATIONS

An investment is economically viable if it increases the value of the firm. However, a project must also be judged on its strategic merits. Therefore, you must ask questions such as, "Will it improve the competitiveness of the company?" and "Does it fit with other strategic initiatives within the firm? Table 8-1 illustrates the potential dilemmas that can occur when projects are regarded from both an economic and a strategic point of view. Clearly, there is no conflict if either situation 1 or 4 occurs—these cases represent clear and easy choices because the strategic and economic perspectives conform. Situations 2 and 3, however, are more problematic.

Table 8-1. Strategic vs. economic justifications

		Economically Justified?	
		Yes	No
Strategically Justified?	Yes	1. Project is justified both from a strategic and an economic viewpoint.	2. Project is economically justified, but not from a strategic perspective.
	No	3. Project is strategically justified, but not from an economic perspective.	4. Project is neither economically nor strategically justified.

Projects that Show Economic But Not Strategic Value

In situation 2, the costs and benefits for a project have been estimated, and the calculations show that the investment should be accepted (e.g., because the expected payback time is less than two years). So, what is the problem? Shouldn't management always look favorably on a project that promises to increase the value of the firm? Isn't the company in business to make money? The simple answer is that projects can "look good on paper" but still be wrong for the firm.

For example, assume that you propose a machining cell designed around a narrowly defined component family. The cell is to feed an assembly line used by several product families. You may well be able to justify new equipment for this cell, but what if the marketing strategy calls for one of the product lines to serve a market segment that demands increasingly customized products? A cell that is not flexible enough to manufacture an increasing variety of components can become an obstacle to this customization strategy. Thus, although the cell may be economically sound from a limited, part-manufacturing perspective, it may look inappropriate if you take a strategic, market-oriented view. In short, implementing such a cell may be "doing things right"—i.e., increasing efficiency—but would not be "doing the right thing."

Projects that Are Strategically Sound But Show Insufficient Economic Value

Investment proposals in situation 3 are of strategic importance but do not show a positive economic value. But pushing ahead with a change project based on "strategic reasoning" alone is potentially risky.[8] To quote a noted expert almost 50 years ago: *"the idea that there is such a thing as strategic value, not ultimately rooted in economic worth, is demonstrably wrong."*[9]

Thus, although projects need to be strategically justified, they must sooner or later also be found economically viable. Therefore, you must move projects from quadrant 3 to quadrant 1 in Table 8-1. This sometimes requires that you assign economic values to more of the predicted benefits, essentially turning so-called intangible benefits into tangible ones. For projects new to the firm, this may call for pilot implementations so you can better understand the underlying costs and benefits. (We return to the issue of tangibility later in the chapter.)

Begin with Strategy

Reorganizing the plant or office into cells in order to improve your firm's competitiveness goes way beyond simply replacing an obsolete machine or computer. It is a project that changes and upgrades processes, systems, technologies, and the way people work. These changes will affect the organization in very substantial ways for a long time to come. Therefore, when you justify a cell project, you need to start with a review of the firm's strategy and how cells can help achieve it.

The following example illustrates this. In the mid-80s, Electrolux, the Swedish manufacturer of household products, decided to invest heavily in the Italian company Zanussi. In particular, one facility was to be transformed—to the tune of $90 million—into a state-of-the-art refrigerator plant supplying the Italian market. The plant would also serve as a laboratory for new technologies. Management decided to design the plant using cellular manufacturing (CM) principles:[10]

> ... the strategic ramifications of implementing CM outweighed the operational or tactical consequences. The focus was long-range, emphasizing strategic advantages such as improved flexibility, ability to respond to customer demand, decreased time-to-market, and improved product quality. One manager summarized thus: "We were faced with business pressure and foreign competition able to deliver not the same product but an equivalent product at a significantly lower cost with a significantly reduced schedule. It was felt there was no way we could compete without implementing cellular manufacturing."

In this case, the detailed economic analysis of the investment took place after the $90 million had been set aside for the project and after the decision to adopt the cellular manufacturing philosophy had been made.

A similar sequence of events took place in one firm exploring the use of the group technology philosophy not just in cellular manufacturing, but also in areas such as design and process planning.[11] Top management approved the GT project from a strategic perspective and based on a rough cost justification. However, all subsequent investment phases had to be justified in the traditional economic sense. Caterpillar's large "Plant with a Future" project in the 1980s reportedly followed the same approach.[12]

The Three-Step Justification Process

The above examples illustrate that there is a strategic-economic justification sequence. The strategic perspective steers a project early on and is instrumental in its approval. Later, the economic aspects become more important as the project digs deeper and deeper into implementation planning. So, *Rule 1* of project justification is that you should make sure a cell project meets *both* the strategic and the economic expectations. *Rule 2* is that you should *first* check whether the project conforms to the strategic plan. Only after passing this test does it make sense to justify it economically.

In between these two steps, however, comes a third checkpoint. Recall that in Chapter 1 we looked at a cellular manufacturing project in terms of its impact on the company's "current processes, technologies, organizational structure, management systems, people, and the informal organization" (see Figure 1-4). Our message was that all these areas affect, and are affected by, the cell project, and that you therefore need to consider them for a successful implementation. Since an economic justification is simply a forecast of the future, it is critical that you fully understand how to change the organization in order to make that forecast a reality. *Rule 3*, then, is that you should develop a clear picture of the future organization, and how it will work with the cells in place, before you undertake the economic justification. The credibility and reliability of the justification depend on this. Figure 8-1 illustrates how the three rules determine a three-step sequence of project justification.[13]

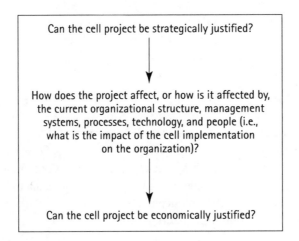

Figure 8-1. Strategic, organizational, and economic justifications

HOW TO COST-JUSTIFY CELLS

In this section we present a brief overview of how you can determine the economic value of cells. For now, we ignore tax implications or the time-value of money. Those issues are covered later, after we have discussed the determination of costs and benefits in more depth.

Relevant Costs and Revenues

A relevant cost (revenue) is an expected future cost (revenue) that depends on actions you take.[14] In other words, if you compare two alternative solutions to a problem, such as how to organize work processes, the relevant costs (revenues) are those that differ among the alternatives. *You should base a decision whether to adopt cellular manufacturing only on relevant costs and revenues.* Here's an example of how a Fortune 500 automotive parts manufacturer used relevant costs to justify cells:[15]

> Six synchronous cells have been established over the course of the past 18 months. Each of the cells began with a specific product-related proposal describing the cell plan, approved by a joint union-management team. A rough pro-forma cost savings estimate was generated for each cell, projecting cost savings as a result of *reduced supervision, increased labor efficiency, lower inventory levels,* etc.

In this case, the company expected cost savings in inventory and direct and indirect labor. In general, savings are typically estimated in areas where firms have solid knowledge of activity levels and activity costs (e.g., the number of employees and their compensation, or the level of inventory and the cost of carrying it).

A company in the lawncare industry that planned to implement an assembly cell limited the benefit estimation to three areas:

1. Lowered cost of moving parts. Both the distance and the number of moves (affected by smaller transfer batches) were considered when the number of miles moved was calculated. The "before and after" distances were multiplied by a transportation cost per mile.

2. Lowered WIP inventory holding cost due to smaller batches.

3. Lower labor cost due to reduced rework.

Included in the planning and implementation cost for the cell were:

- Expenditures for new containers.
- Charges for the planning team.
- Charges for the crew that would move equipment and install lighting and air.
- Other costs for preparing the facility.

The company compared these expenditures against the avoided costs and concluded that the project would pay for itself in less than two years. In the section on "risk" in the firm's Capital Appropriation Request document, the cell planning team stressed that the charges for in-house personnel did not represent out-of-pocket cost. The team also listed "improved quality" and "reduced lead time" as intangible (non-quantified) benefits.

In general, an economic justification based on relevant costs and revenues considers any incremental net revenues from sales, as well as any avoided costs, and compares the result with the investment due to the change. Table 8-2 shows a limited example for a planned cell system. Sales are anticipated to increase due to improved response times. Accordingly, the additional sales minus the manufacturing costs for these products are included as a benefit. Due to a move towards assemble-to-order manufacturing, finished goods inventory as well as WIP inventory will go down. The reduced costs of holding these inventories are included in the justification. Finally, the impact on labor and scrap is considered.

The justification approach in Table 8-2 is to compare the net benefits over time with the required investment and expenditures. If the latter capital can be paid off within a reasonable time, the cell project is accepted. The economic value of cells may also be demonstrated by comparing the production cost per piece with and without cells. This approach runs into problems because standard cost data—especially the overhead portion—hide the relevant cost needed for a proper justification. We comment on the use of standard cost data in Appendix A.

Table 8-2. Pro forma cost justification of a cell using relevant costs and revenues

Cost Justification of a Cell System	
Increased revenues due to cell manufacturing	
Additional sales revenues	575,000
Incremental manufacturing costs	415,000
Net sales revenues per year	**$160,000**
Costs avoided with cells	
Less finished goods inventory (holding cost)	95,000
Less WIP inventory (holding cost)	120,000
Less material scrap	62,000
Less storage room personnel	55,000
Less material-handling labor	110,000
Less planning and control personnel	65,000
Total cost avoided per year	**$507,000**
Net benefit per year	**$667,000**

The cost of implementing the cell system is estimated at $875,000.
Thus, the payback time is 875,000/667,000, or 1.31 years.

ESTIMATING THE COSTS AND BENEFITS OF CELLULAR MANUFACTURING

As indicated in the previous section, to justify a project economically you must specify the following data:

1. The investments, and when they occur. These are *cash outflows*.

2. The relevant costs associated with the project, and when they occur. These are also *cash outflows*.

3. The net revenues, and avoidable costs, linked to the project over the planning horizon. These are *cash inflows*.

In this section we discuss the issue of estimating these cash flows in more detail.

Estimating Cash Outlays—The Cost/Investment Side

Table 8-3 shows a general list of costs and investments (cash outflows) that you may incur in connection with a cell project. It is straightforward to estimate the cost of "hardware" that is purchased from the outside, like a lathe, a barcode scanner, or containers in which to move parts. The same holds true for services purchased from vendors, such as consulting services, constructing an office for a new order-processing team, pouring new floor foundations for punch presses, putting up ventilation ducts over a welding cell, or sending future cell leaders to training courses.

Table 8-3. Costs/cash outflows associated with establishing cells

Cost Categories	Examples
Cost of planning the conversion	Lost work time for project team (core and extended)
Cost of consultants	To assist with planning, education, etc.
Cost of analysis tools, software, etc.	Purchase of classification and coding system, simulation
Cost of preparing the plant	Floor foundations, heating/cooling ducts, power, plumbing, storage racks, meeting areas, etc.
Cost of moving equipment	Moving existing machines into a cell; moving equipment remaining in the functional group
Cost of new equipment (incl. control systems)	New machinery, tools, fixtures, gauges, workbenches, hardware/software
Cost of new material-handling system	New systems for moving products, new containers
Cost of product redesign	Redesigning products to fit the cell equipment
Cost of process planning	Revising all affected process plans
Cost of new management systems	Adjustments to, or development of, new production planning, scheduling, measurement, compensation systems, etc.
Cost of education and training	Upgrading knowledge and skills of managers, supervisors, operators, and other employees
Cost of lowered productivity	Lost output due to installation, learning, multitasking, and unplanned disturbances
Cost of higher wages	Increased direct wages due to multiskilled workers and task variety

You need to include these items in a cost justification because they represent out-of-pocket costs for which the firm will be billed (thus, they represent true cash outlays). A review of Table 8-3 shows, however, that there are many activities for which a firm will never be invoiced. Most of these involve the use of employee time to plan for the cell conversion and modify existing processes and routines to fit the new system, or for the employees themselves to adjust to the new operating environment. The cost of in-house training, and the associated loss of production, also belongs to this category. It is not uncommon that companies ignore these costs when they justify a project. There can be several reasons for this.

First, these activities may be considered a normal part of the employees' jobs. For example, adjusting and documenting the process plans for products assigned to a new cell can be viewed as part of the regular responsibilities for a process planner. Redesigning tooling or part features so these fit a proposed cell can be seen as normal duties for a tool designer or a design engineer. And having supervisors or cell managers educate future cell operators about lean manufacturing and pull systems can be regarded as normal responsibilities for supervisory personnel.

If your view is that some (or even the majority) of an employee's time regularly should be spent on process improvement, time "lost" when engaged in such activities should not be charged to the cell project. The rationale is that the employee, if not engaged in this project, would spend his or her time on other projects or participate in other training programs. Since cellular manufacturing frequently is introduced in connection with corporate improvement programs mandated by management, such as TQM or JIT, expenses other than equipment may not require formal justifications.[16]

There is some merit to this argument. It is no doubt difficult and impractical to charge each employee's time to a project. This is especially the case if the whole organization is dedicated to continuous improvement "everywhere and all the time." On the other hand, if the improvement project is of a type new to the organization, involves many employees, and/or requires a fairly large investment, you'll want to keep close track of resource usage and outside expenditures. This will better prepare you for future projects. *Specifically, this means you want to assess the cost for your plant's first venture into cellular manufacturing with some accuracy, even if it does not involve a large investment.*

A second reason some companies may exclude certain costs in their economic justification is because they believe they are too difficult to estimate. For example, it can be hard to determine the cost of change-oriented activities that require employee time, such as restructuring bills of materials or developing a new team-based compensation system. You may find it equally hard to put a dollar value on lost production due to the plant rearrangement or lowered productivity due to the operators' lack of proficiency in running the cell. As a result, the associated costs are not made part of the justification. We will return to the issue of ignoring costs after discussing the benefit side of economic justifications.

Estimating Cash Inflows—The Benefit Side

A cell project must generate economic benefits in order for it to have value for the firm. Thus, you need to translate the predicted operational benefits into positive cash flows. This is where many economic justifications run into problems.

The largest and most frequently reported operational benefits of cells—and also the common reasons for pursuing them—pertain to shortened lead times and setup times, and lowered work-in-process (WIP) and finished goods (FG) inventories.

Other areas include lowered scrap and rework rates, improved direct and indirect labor productivity, less use of space, and enhanced job satisfaction.[17] These and other benefits reported for cells are summarized in Table 8-4. We have partitioned the table into two parts. Benefits 1 through 11 are based on variables for which you probably already have, or could easily construct, measures of performance. The remaining benefits, 12 through 17, are not easily measured, although firms often attest to their achievement. (We discuss such "intangible" benefits later.)

Table 8-4. Benefits of cellular manufacturing

1. Reduced lead time.
2. Reduced move distances.
3. Reduced setup times.
4. Reduced customer response time.
5. Improved on-time delivery.
6. Reduced raw material, WIP, and finished goods inventories.
7. Lowered scrap and rework rates.
8. Improved direct labor productivity.
9. Reduced need for indirect/support personnel.
10. Reduced use of space.
11. Lowered unit costs.
12. Improved employee job satisfaction.
13. Improved manufacturing flexibility.
14. Improved labor flexibility.
15. Improved job status visibility.
16. Simplified planning and control procedures.
17. Increased operator improvement efforts.

Besides being more or less difficult to measure, you can think of benefits as being of two kinds. *Revenue-enhancing benefits* are those that generate an increased stream of cash due to the investment in cells. *Resource-reducing benefits*, on the other hand, lower the cost to produce. In other words, these are "cost-avoiding" benefits.

It is easier to estimate a cell project's impact on cost than on revenues because the firm is in control of its manufacturing resources (i.e., its costs), while market forces dictate revenues. For example, a lower manufacturing lead time translates into lower WIP inventory holding cost. But its impact on revenues is not that obvious. It is especially difficult to estimate a cell's influence on revenues if it produces components that go into many different final products. As a consequence, cell justifications commonly rest on estimates of costs that are avoided rather than on revenues that are increased.

Cost reducing benefits

For any area of improvement, you can express the cost avoided due to cellular manufacturing as:

Cost avoided = (Cost for a resource or activity *before* cells) –
(Cost for a resource or activity *after* cells)

A *resource* in this regard can be equipment, people, space, and so on. An *activity* is something that resources do, such as move material, hold inventory, inspect parts, and enter data on a terminal. The resource or activity *level* describes the usage. For example, the resource level could be "two operators," and the activity level could be "700 units of inventory."

In order to simplify our formulas below, we drop the term resource and mainly use the term activity. We can now express the before and after costs in more detail:

Cost avoided = (Activity level before the change)*(Cost for the current activity per unit of time) – (Projected activity level after the change)* (Projected cost for the activity per unit of time after the change)

Activity levels after a change are sometimes estimated using "improvement factors" expressed as percentages. For example, if you estimate that WIP inventory will be reduced from $100,000 to $45,000, the improvement factor is (100-45)/100, or 55 percent. Thus, cost savings can also be stated as:

Cost avoided = (Activity level before the change)*(Cost for the current activity per unit of time) – (Activity level before the change) (1- Improvement factor)*(Projected cost for the activity per unit of time after the change)

If the cost of the activity *remains the same* before and after, this can be simplified to:

Cost avoided = (Activity level before the change)*(Cost for the activity per unit of time)*(Improvement factor)

We will illustrate these calculations by looking at avoided costs for labor, inventory, and scrap. You can apply the same approach to many of the other benefits listed in Table 8-4.

Labor savings: If you anticipate that a cell implementation project will generate savings in labor, the resource levels are the current and future number of employees needed in a year. The cost for the resource is the annual cost for this personnel category, including fringe benefits, before and after the change. If the employee compensation is the same after the conversion, you can use an improvement factor to estimate the resource level. This factor is the percentage by which you expect the labor requirements to decline after switching to cells.

For example, you believe that by switching to cells you can reduce the need for schedulers in the production planning and control office by 30 percent (i.e., the improvement factor is 0.3). If the salary for schedulers averages $50,000 per year, and there are currently three schedulers, the annual savings amount is 0.30*50,000*3, or $45,000 per year. You could also determine this saving as 3*50,000 – (1-0.3)*3*50,000. Note that the required number of future schedulers is (1-0.3)*3, or 2.1. If you find that this capacity is not needed to handle future growth in order volume, and that you cannot use the equivalent of 0.9 schedulers for productive work elsewhere, then you cannot avoid any costs.

Here is another labor savings example: You expect a machining cell to operate with two employees. Currently, the parts to be shifted to the cell require the equivalent of 3.2 machinists. Because of the need to cross-train the cell operators, you estimate that the wages for each of these employees will be $58,000 per year. This is in contrast to the machinists in the job shop who are currently paid $52,000 annually. The savings in direct labor cost is then 3.2*52,000 – 2*58,000, or $50,400 per year. Again, this is under the assumption that you can use the equivalent of 1.2 operators elsewhere in the plant, or that they will not be on the payroll (e.g., due to voluntary severance, transfers to other divisions, or layoffs).

By the way, most companies will indeed experience staffing reductions as they move to cells. In particular, the reduced need for support/indirect personnel can be a major advantage: "... the benefits obtained *off* the shop floor are usually several times what is achieved on the shop floor."[18] Table 8-5 shows the percent of firms reporting decreases or increases in personnel after switching to cells, based on a study of 109 Australian manufacturers.[19]

Table 8-5. Impact of cellular manufacturing on direct and indirect/support personnel

Labor Category	Percent of Firms Reporting a Reduction	Percent of Firms Reporting an Increase
Indirect labor	57	5
Supervision	61	5
Production planning	37	10
Mfg. engineering	17	23
Direct labor	48	14

Inventory savings. If savings from cells are anticipated in the form of inventory reduction, the activity level is the average inventory expressed in dollars. The cost for the activity is the annual cost of holding inventory, expressed as a percentage per year (the carrying charge). Finally, the improvement factor is the percentage by which you estimate the inventory will be reduced when switching to cells. Table 1-1 provides improvement factors for inventory and other variables experienced by various firms we have surveyed.

For example, if you anticipate that cells will reduce work in process by 40 percent, and the average WIP level for the parts to be made in the cell was $40,000 in the last year, the expected WIP reduction due to cells is 0.4*40,000, or $16,000. This is a one-time addition to cash flow if inventory will remain low in the future (also see Table 8-8; this benefit was not included in Table 8-2). If the inventory carrying cost for WIP inventory is 20 percent per year, the cost avoidance benefit, or saving, is 0.20*16,000, or $3,200 annually.

Scrap savings. Finally, if you anticipate that quality improvement activities will reduce material scrap cost, the current activity level is the average scrap rate expressed in percentage of material cost. Likewise, the cost for the activity is the annual cost of materials, expressed in dollars. Assume current scrap rate is 2.5 percent, but you think it will go down to 0.5 percent with cells. If the annual material cost for the parts to be manufactured in the cell is $267,000, the cost avoided is (0.025-0.005)*267,000, or $5,340 per year.

Revenue-generating benefits

Many companies implement cells to lower their response time to the market. In fact, this "time-based benefit" usually tops the list of reasons why firms convert to cellular manufacturing. The belief is that lower lead times will increase a firm's competitive advantage and maintain or increase sales. But what is the economic value of time? You will not know the impact of lead time on sales without conducting a special investigation. Table 8-6 illustrates how you can gather this type of knowledge.[20] Clearly, Step 4 is the critical one in this estimation process.

Table 8-6. Assigning economic value to time reduction

1. Identify products for which slow response to inquiries and or booked orders is perceived to be a problem.
2. Assess whether manufacturing cells or office cells can reduce response time.
3. Estimate the potential magnitude of the response-time reduction, possibly with a range (e.g., 4 +/- 2 weeks).
4. Estimate the sales revenues attributable to the expected response-time reduction.
5. Convert the sales revenues into net contributions (revenue minus variable cost). Treat these as positive cash flows associated with the project.

There are a couple of ways to estimate the impact on revenues. One way is to ask sales representatives to guess how customers will react to a change in response time. Will they increase their purchases and, if so, by how much? You can get better estimates by asking customers (actual and prospective, and preferably the important ones) directly about such changes. The accuracy of any data you collect this way, like any polling results, is no doubt uncertain. Not until you are able to deliver more rapidly will you know the customers' true reactions. But it is useful to get an advance feeling for how customers look at this issue. In addition, you will get a quantified notion of how much a change in response time is worth to your firm.

Because of the difficulty of estimating the value of time reductions, companies often decide to ignore this benefit. Remember, however, that a reduction in lead time impacts both costs and revenues. A shortened lead time in manufacturing leads to lower inventory.[21] As discussed above, this represents both a one-time cash flow due to a lowered asset level, and an annual cash flow saving due to less holding costs. So even if you neglect the revenue-generating aspect of lead time you should at least consider its cost-reducing aspect in the justification.

DISCOUNT RATES AND TAX CONSIDERATIONS

Capital budgeting techniques are formal methods used to determine the economic value of investments in long-term assets. Well-known techniques include *payback time, internal rate of return (IRR)*, and *net present value (NPV)*. In many countries the first two methods are the most popular, and both are frequently used within the same firm.[22]

All capital budgeting techniques require that you estimate and quantify anticipated future cash flows. That is, you must develop estimates of the size of the investment itself, associated expenditures, and asset depreciation over the planning horizon. You must also determine the inflow and outflow of cash directly linked to the investment in question.

The very simplest technique, the payback time approach, determines the time it takes for the cash inflows to exceed the sum of the investment and the ensuing cash outlays (i.e., to break even). For more sophisticated procedures, such as NPV and IRR, you also need to determine either a discount rate (for NPV) for converting cash flows into current dollars, or a hurdle rate (for IRR), which is the lowest rate of return for a project that the firm finds acceptable. In the example below, we illustrate the use of payback time, NPV, and IRR.[23]

A Large Investment in a Machining Cell

Here is an example of how to cost justify a machining cell with traditional capital budgeting approaches. Table 8-7 shows the assumptions we are using. We plan to take advantage of the cell project to upgrade equipment technology. In addition, we need new tooling, new material-handling equipment, and new containers. Further, we estimate that savings will occur in terms of people, inventory, materials, and space. Table 8-8 presents the calculations. It shows that the net cost incurred at the beginning of the project is $805,000, assuming we can sell the old equipment for $40,000. The new equipment is estimated to be worth $90,000 after five years, the time horizon that we use. For simplicity's sake, we disregard the impact of inflation.

There are two rows related to inventory in Table 8-8, *Inventory investment reduction* and *Savings in inventory holding cost.* As we have already mentioned, a lowered inventory can be seen as equivalent to an infusion of cash to the firm. In this case, we expect to reduce inventory by $300,000; thus, a $300,000 cash flow is assigned to the end of Year 1. Once the inventory has been reduced, the annual carrying cost charges, estimated to be 10 percent of each dollar stored in inventory per year, will also be reduced in the future. Accordingly, we now have a cost saving of $30,000 per year. However, we assume that the inventory reduction takes place gradually over the first year. Thus, the savings in carrying charge in Year 1 is set at 50 percent of the savings for subsequent years.

The rows *Total negative cash flows* and *Total positive cash flows* show the size and timing of the costs and the savings associated with this cell project. The sum of the negative and the positive cash flows over time determine the *Accumulated net cash flows.* This row indicates the year in which this project is expected to show profit. In this case, the payback time is less than three years since the accumulated cash flow first turns positive sometime during Year 3.

The calculations below the bold line in the table consider both tax implications and the time-value of money (i.e., discounting). We have assumed that $500,000 of the $675,000 for new equipment will be depreciated linearly over a five-year period. Since depreciation is tax deductible, the *Taxable income stream* equals the

Total positive cash flow minus the *Depreciation*. The tax rate is set to 40 percent. The resulting *Net cash flow after tax* amounts to *Total positive cash flow* minus *Taxes paid*. To find the year in which the project is paid back after considering the tax effects, sum up the Net cash flows after tax, starting with Year 0. The row *Accumulated net cash flows after tax* in Table 8-8 shows that the payback now occurs sometime in the fourth year. If you compare this row with the *Accumulated net cash flows* row a few lines above you can see that the tax implications make this a less profitable undertaking than if taxes are ignored.

Table 8-7. Assumptions used for the machining cell justification example

Investment and Expenditures	Amounts
Vertical lathe and horizontal milling machines	
Work tables, material racks, and roller conveyor	
Family tooling, new part containers	
Total new investment	$675,000
Travel and time spent by planning team	
Total planning cost	$ 30,000
Training in team, cellular, and JIT/TQM concepts: operators, supervisors, and managers	
Total training cost	$ 10,000
Adjustments to B/Ms, process plans, planning and scheduling procedures, measurement and compensation system, and accounting	
Total system cost	$ 30,000
Moving and installing equipment, facility preparation	
Total installation cost	$100,000
Net Savings	
Reduction in direct labor	
Reduction in material handlers, inspectors, and supervisors	
Reduction in planning and maintenance personnel	
Total personnel savings	$180,000
Reduction in WIP and FG inventory	
Total savings in inventory investment	$300,000
Reduction in scrap and rework	
Total quality–related savings	$ 25,000
Reduction in space used for manufacturing	
Total savings in space	$ 110,000
Salvage value—old equipment	$ 40,000
Salvage value—new equipment	$ 90,000

Discounted Cash Flows

The net present value (NPV) method considers the time value of money by discounting the cash flow stream over time by an interest rate (the cost of capital). Assuming that the discount rate is 20 percent, Table 8-8 shows both the annual discount factors and the resulting cash flows. For example, a dollar due three years from now is only worth $0.579 in present value, turning a $181,000 cash flow into the equivalent of $104,799 today.

The last row in Table 8-8 shows the *Accumulated discounted net cash flows*. The last year of the planning horizon, Year 5, shows the net present value of this cell project.

Table 8-8. Discounted cost/benefit calculations for a machining cell

Year in Planning Horizon	0	1	2	3	4	5
Investment in equipment	-675,000					
Planning, training, systems, installation	-170,000					
Salvage value—old equipment	40,000					
Total negative cash flows	-805,000					
Salvage value—new equipment						90,000
Savings in personnel		90,000	180,000	180,000	180,000	180,000
Inventory investment reduction		300,000				
Savings in inventory holding cost (charge = 10%)		15,000	30,000	30,000	30,000	30,000
Material-related savings		12,500	25,000	25,000	25,000	25,000
Space-related savings		110,000				
Total positive cash flows		527,500	235,000	235,000	235,000	325,000
Accumulated net cash flows (years 0–5)	-805,000	-277,500	-42,500	192,500	427,500	752,500
Depreciation		100,000	100,000	100,000	100,000	100,000
Taxable income stream		427,500	135,000	135,000	135,000	225,000
Taxes paid (tax rate = 40%)		171,000	54,000	54,000	54,000	90,000
Net cash flows after tax (including depreciation)	-805,000	356,500	181,000	181,000	181,000	235,000
Accumulated net cash flows after tax (years 0–5)	-805,000	-448,500	-267,500	-86,500	94,500	329,500
Discount factor (20%)		0.833	0.694	0.579	0.482	0.402
Discounted net cash flows (years 1–5)	-805,000	296,965	125,614	104,799	87,242	94,470
Accumulated discounted net cash flows (years 0–5)	-805,000	-508,035	-382,421	-277,622	-190,380	-95,910

A project should be accepted if NPV is positive. Unfortunately, the calculations demonstrate that this cell project should be rejected because NPV is a negative $95,910.[24]

The internal rate of return (IRR) is defined as the interest rate at which NPV is 0. Although we don't show the calculations here, IRR is in this case 14 percent.[25] If the company requires a return of at least 20 percent (*the hurdle rate* that IRR must exceed) for any project to go forward, we again should reject this cell project. Does this mean that it is a money-losing proposition, as the negative NPV value indicates? No, it simply means that the project will not return 20 percent within the five-year planning horizon—only 14 percent. You must decide whether this return is acceptable for this particular project.

To summarize, this example shows that the impact of taxes and discounting (a dollar is worth more today than tomorrow) can change the time it takes for a project to show economic value, if it does it at all.

TANGIBLE AND INTANGIBLE COSTS AND BENEFITS

Benefits that are quantified—expressed as numbers—are commonly referred to as *tangible*. Conversely, benefits that are not quantified are called *intangible*. Lowered lead times, for example, often are treated as an intangible benefit. However, benefits are not inherently tangible or intangible. Rather, *whether a benefit is tangible or not depends on your willingness to provide a quantified estimate* (a task that seems to have been made easier with the advent of activity-based costing systems).[26] The habit of failing to quantify benefits has eloquently been chastised as follows: "Conservative accountants who assign zero values to many intangible benefits prefer being precisely wrong to being vaguely right."[27]

Besides struggling with determining the *value of time*, companies also find it difficult to assign economic value to benefits such as increased job satisfaction, improved flexibility, or simplified planning and control (see the bottom half of Table 8-4). Such improvements are frequently described as "additional benefits" in companies' project proposals. A better alternative is to try to translate such soft benefits into concrete advantages. For example, job satisfaction should lead to less employee turnover, flexibility should lead to higher sales, and simplified planning and control should reduce the need for support personnel.

Of course, the ease by which benefits can be quantified depends on the availability of data. For new technologies or systems, performance data are not available. The experience at the Zanussi plant mentioned earlier, where special machinery and automated material-handling systems were part of the investment, is typical in that regard:[28]

Many difficulties were encountered. In the first place, invariably, some factors had been overlooked and were responsible for additional costs during project implementation. Moreover, given the complexity of the project, it was difficult to identify and quantify all benefits, both tangible and intangible. Some participants said: "It was a new technology for us. We did not know what it was going to do for us. We didn't know if it was even going to work."

However, it is not necessary for you to turn *all* intangible benefits into tangible ones. Rather, you need only to quantify benefits until the project shows positive economic value.

The Strategic/Economic Conflict Revisited

What happens if you can strategically justify a cell project but cannot make it show economic value, even after you have undertaken a very detailed analysis? This outcome may, of course, be a correct one. After all, the project could well be a bad idea that you should abandon. However, if there are additional benefits you feel you cannot directly quantify, there is another way to make the project show value. First estimate the negative contribution the project would make to the firm. Then assess whether the value of the intangible benefits that you believe accompany the project could be sufficient to overcome the quantified negative project contribution.

For example, the cell project discussed in Table 8-8 shows a net present value of –$95,910 over the five-year planning horizon. Assume now that your firm expects to gain an increased foothold in the marketplace due to faster response times. However, the project team has not been able to "dollarize" that benefit. You may then consider whether this intangible benefit could be worth at least $37,521 per year (this is the amount that, if discounted over five years, equals $95,910).[29] If that is the case, the cell project will break even (NPV = 0). If, at the same time, the project is viewed as having important strategic value, this implicit conversion of intangible benefits to tangible ones could be enough to give the project a go-ahead.

Strategic Discount Rates

As demonstrated in Table 8-8, the discount rate lowers the value of future cash flows. Thus, the higher the discount rate, the less a dollar forthcoming in the future is worth to you. Companies sometimes use different discount rates for different types of investments. For example, 15 percent may be used for replacement investments, 20 percent for new facilities, and 25 percent for new product or process investments. These rates are supposed to reflect the different amount of risk involved with each investment category. For example, to simply replace an existing machine carries low risk, while spending money developing new products carries a high risk of failure.

This type of reasoning, however, ignores the strategic question, "What if we don't invest?" Henry Ford allegedly once said "If you need a new machine and don't buy it, you pay for it without getting it." In other words, there is a price to be paid for doing nothing. Just replacing an old machine is a conservative action that does not necessarily improve the firm's competitive stance. On the other hand, investing in new processes and work organizations, such as cellular manufacturing, creates new capabilities. We have seen several companies take the view that the whole cell, and not individual pieces of equipment, must be justified.[30] Such strategic investments should be encouraged, not prevented. This is also the basic idea behind what is called *strategic discount rates*. The premise here is that discount rates used for capital budgeting purposes should be lowest for investments aimed at moving the firm in new directions, and highest for investments aimed at status quo.[31]

JUSTIFYING CELLS "AFTER THE FACT"

We recommend that you do both a pre-audit and a post-audit of the costs and benefits of your cells. This lets you determine whether the cells have lived up to their promise, and helps you do a more informed justification next time. If you don't do an economic justification at the outset of the cell implementation project, a before-and-after comparison, of course, is impossible. However, you can still do a justification "after the fact." Here are a couple of examples. (The example shown in Appendix A illustrates a comparison of unit costs that can be done both before and after the cell implementation.)

The Shalibane Company

Shalibane is a British manufacturer of automotive parts. Its cell implementation generated several large benefits:[32]

> The reduction in throughput times (86 percent) and set-up times (75 percent), and the reduction in run quantities (reduced batch quantities (77 percent)), has reduced both the investment in stocks (58 percent) and the cost of stock holding (75 percent), without increasing manufacturing costs. This has increased the rate of return on investment (24 percent). Profit has increased (21 percent), partly due to reduced stock holding costs, and partly due to increased sales (33 percent). Increased sales have required additional labour (12 percent), but the sales per worker ratio has been increased with the change (19 percent).

Besides these impressive bottom-line results, there were also difficult-to-quantify indirect benefits. These included better accountability, and improved morale and job satisfaction. Plant management saw these benefits as the main drivers of the economic gains.

The cost of Shalibane's cell implementation was one-third of the reduction in the inventory investment. This meant that the cash flow freed up by operating with a lower inventory by itself paid for the cost of the cellular conversion. However, it should be noted that one reason the employees supported the implementation was the introduction of a new group compensation scheme. Shalibane did not consider the additional cost for this bonus scheme in its retrospective justification.

Steward, Inc.

The second example of retrospective justification involves Steward, Inc., a manufacturer of zinc ferrite parts.[33] The company wanted to become more responsive to its customers and, as a consequence, made the unusual move of putting its sales manager in charge of manufacturing. However, the suggestion to look into cellular manufacturing came from General Motors, a major customer that was the victim of Stewart's delivery problems.

Steward did not undertake a formal justification of its cell conversion project. Rather, management so readily approved of the cell concept that it was immediately implemented in one area. Then, without carefully investigating the results of its first cell, the company implemented other cells elsewhere in the plant. These decisions appear to have been driven largely by strategic needs and by direct observations of the common-sense physical changes on the factory floor.

After two months of operation, Steward evaluated the decision to implement its four cells. Table 8-9 shows the before/after results along eight different dimensions. The benefits realized at Steward are quite spectacular, well exceeding the average industry improvements we reported in Chapter 1.

Table 8-9. Improvements due to cellular manufacturing at Steward, Inc.

Performance Measure	Functional Layout	Cellular Layout	Resulting Improvement
Work in process	$590,000	$116,336	80%
Finished goods	$880,000	$353,167	60%
Refractory supplies	$8,333/month	$0	100%
Lead time	14 days	2 days	86%
Late orders	100 (backlog)	4 (backlog)	96%
Scrap	22%	14%	8%
Direct labor	198	145	27%
Manufacturing space	45,000 sq. ft.	20,000 sq. ft	56%

The reduced inventories are a result of smaller lot sizes and a shift from make-to-stock to make-to-order manufacturing. By having less WIP on the floor, the scrap rate went down due to less damage. That, in turn, can lower inventories even further. The reduced need for direct labor is due to improved efficiencies, less material-handling, and fewer inspectors. (Steward claims that there was no reduction in indirect labor. It can be assumed, then, that handling and inspection was carried out previously by direct labor.) Finally, space was freed up due to less WIP and rearranged equipment. This newfound space has both tangible and intangible value. First, the company avoided building a new facility at a cost of $120,000. Secondly, it could now put in a long-deferred employee canteen, a project that had a positive impact on morale.

The Steward Company did not make any new investment in equipment for these cells. However, it did purchase more die sets in order to reduce time spent on setup (which had increased due to lowered batch sizes). If the reported stock levels will remain low (note that two months is an insufficient time on which to base a serious evaluation), Steward will have lowered its inventory investment by a little over $1 million. Assuming a conservative annual carrying cost of 10 percent, the company is saving more than $100,000 per year.

If each direct laborer costs the firm $30,000 per year, another $1,560,000 is saved. Of course, these types of labor savings do not turn into cash flow unless the number of employees is actually reduced due to attrition or layoffs. However, if a firm is short of capacity, and freed-up employees can be transferred to other areas, this sum represents the cost avoided by not hiring more personnel. In Steward's case, both attrition and employee redeployment was used.

Finally, the firm estimates that each percentage point of avoided scrap is worth $55,000. The 8 percent improvement in scrap yields another annual saving of

$440,000. With an additional $120,000 saved in building costs, Steward has avoided a total of $2,220,000 in the first year alone. There also is a permanent reduction in inventory investment of $1 million, a sum that represents a one-time cash flow contribution. Thus, the conversion to cells looks like a remarkably profitable undertaking for this $10 million a year firm.[34]

SOME PRACTICAL ISSUES IN JUSTIFICATIONS

Regardless of the method you use, many practical and ethical issues must be resolved when you justify cell projects. We discuss some of these next.

Data Sources and Data Accuracy

One of the first issues you have to face is how you can estimate the costs and benefits for the economic justification.

Where Do You Get the Data?

You must secure two basic types of data to make savings calculations. The first type concerns the activities (the levels and the costs), and the second concerns the projected improvements. The *current cost* of an activity is in most cases available from your firm's accounting system (e.g., labor rates, material costs, space charges). The *future cost* for an activity, if different, will not be available but you can determine it with the current cost as a basis.

For example, assume you expect to have fewer material handlers in the cell shop. In this case, the cost for the remaining handlers will be the same as it is now. Thus, current and future rates are identical. However, if you plan for a cell to run with operators handling multiple processes, the cost per labor hour may increase due to the need for extra skills. Since compensation issues commonly are unresolved at the time of a cost justification, the project team must estimate future labor costs. Those costs, of course, depend on the type of compensation system that is put in place after the change. If it involves group compensation or bonuses, the ability to project future cost is certainly more difficult than if compensation is based on just hourly rates.

Current activity levels, such as number of labor hours, material usage, number of production planners, and inventory levels are recorded by the cost accounting system or other measurement systems in the firm. Thus, you can usually find such data without too much difficulty. That leaves the search for the improvement factors. This information is not part of a firm's standard performance measurement system. Table 8-10 lists various ways to gather data on improvement factors.

Of course, it is ideal if you and your firm already have experience with cells and can use that knowledge to estimate the improvements from future cells.[35] These may be the most credible and reliable data sources because the experience is from the same organization. You also can get insights into the type and magnitude of expected benefits by communicating with, and preferably visiting, other plants. When you can, study plants that have products and technology similar to your own.

You may elect to base your estimates on computer modeling. Whether done in-house or by a consulting firm, we recommend extensive modeling only in cases where the investment is large and the complexity of the system makes it difficult to fully understand how the cell will function. Often, this is the situation when automated cells with material-handling systems are involved. For other cases, easy-to-use modeling software is available that fairly quickly can give you a feeling for system performance (see Chapter 7).

Table 8-10. Sources of improvement data

- From in-house experience
- From other plants (inside or outside the firm)
- From modeling (simulation or queuing theory)
- From consulting firms
- From software and equipment vendors
- From published case studies
- From published large-scale research studies

Consulting firms, whether specializing in modeling, plant reorganization, process reengineering, or other forms of organizational improvements, accumulate data from past clients. Those improvement experiences are accessible to future clients. The same is true for software and equipment vendors, especially if they get heavily involved with their clients during implementation (as is the case with ERP vendors and those selling shop-scheduling software or advanced process equipment).

The final sources of improvement data are books, articles, professional magazines, and research reports, which often include accounts of companies that have implemented cells. However, while the results frequently are spectacular, you are not privy to crucial details surrounding the cell implementations, so you should view such accounts with some skepticism.

Improvement data can also come from research covering large sets of plants. Data from such studies have been cited previously in this book (see, for example, Table 1-1 and Table 8-5). Although the true and complete stories behind the numbers are not available from these studies, they have one advantage over anecdotes from single plants. They typically demonstrate that while individual plants may report impressive results, such as lead time reductions of 90 percent, the *average* improvements across a range of plants are more modest, often 40 to 50 percent. Such findings suggest that you should not uncritically borrow improvement results from other firms. These results are convincing evidence that savings most often *do* materialize, but you must think through how you will achieve enhanced performance given your plant's particular situation. Only then can you finalize the improvement factors and use them to justify your own cell project.

Double-counting the benefits

As discussed, you can classify benefits (and also costs, for that matter) as *tangible* or *intangible*. The latter are benefits you believe will occur, but which you are unable or unwilling to quantify and "dollarize." In our experience, justification proposals often include lists of intangible benefits, sometimes even without any accompanying explanations. If you rely on intangible benefits, be wary of the fact that some of these may already have been accounted for elsewhere in the justification. A mild form of double-counting occurs when several intangible benefits refer to the same thing, although they simply are worded differently.

It is more serious when tangible and intangible benefits overlap. For example, assume you include "simplified planning and scheduling" as an intangible benefit but also include reduction in support personnel as a quantified benefit. If the latter is due to the delegation of planning and control tasks to operators, you are in effect double-counting the benefits (i.e., the "simplified planning" is already reflected in the personnel reduction). Similarly, if you include "reduced setup times" as an intangible benefit while at the same time predicting a labor time reduction of 25 percent when the cell is in place, you have double-counted the impact if the reduction in workload already considers the shorter setup times.

Is this type of double-counting a serious problem? Well, to begin with, you might be tempted to approve a project just because it has a long list of intangible benefits. The economic calculations, on the other hand, will produce only one or two numbers; for example, payback time and internal rate of return. Thus, you say to yourself, "These intangibles may not all come true, but if some do, this project will look even better and have a lower risk." However, you will be fooling yourself if the benefits are double-counted. Second, if the quantified benefits, as in our example above, do not convincingly demonstrate that you should go ahead with the project, the list of intangibles can serve that role. Thus, a deficit in the economic calculations may be held up against the list of intangible benefits (increased job satisfaction, more time for strategic planning by managers, increased sales due to faster response, etc.), and used to compensate for the quantified deficit. This is a legitimate approach. However, you should again be aware that such deliberations are not valid if the intangible list includes benefits already considered in the cash flow calculations. Note, finally, that double-counting can take place both *within* a single project and *between* two project proposals. For example, if you are planning a cell project jointly with a TQM project, and separate cost justifications are required, listing "fewer mistakes" in both places could well be double-counting the benefits.

Fudging the numbers

Besides adding intangible benefits to the proposal, there are other ways to make an appropriation request look more favorable. One way is to exclude the tangible costs. Another is to overstate the tangible benefits. Both have the result of increasing the economic value of the proposal.[36] Resist the temptation to do either.

Areas Affected By the Cell Project

When you create a cell by moving equipment and people from an existing job shop, the latter is depleted of resources. Accordingly, while the performance of the cell may look good, the same may not be true for the rest of the plant. By having less equipment and fewer people, it may now show *worse* results than before the cell was created (as also discussed in Chapters 3 and 7). Thus, a proper justification should include all affected areas of the plant.

Furthermore, the difficulty of planning the change, and estimating its operational and economic consequences, increases with the scope of the project. Companies with little or no previous experience with new technology or organizational transformations (like cellular manufacturing) tend to overestimate the benefits and underestimate the required time and resources.[37] If you are a newcomer, you are advised to rely on gradual implementations (one cell at a time) and learn as you go. You can then use the experience gained to generate better predictive data for the next phase (see Chapters 4 through 6).

How to Sell the Project to Management

"I just wish my boss was here to listen to this!" We have heard this lament many times when speaking to industry groups about cellular manufacturing. Typically, such outcries are followed by stories about how these individuals couldn't convince their superiors to go ahead with their pet cell projects. Of course, we cannot be sure that these projects were not poorly conceived to begin with and therefore would not have benefited these companies. But it is more likely that the job of *selling the idea* of cellular manufacturing was not effective.

How upper management assesses project proposals

An objective analysis of the value of a cell project is just one aspect of the approval process. As with many endeavors, there is both a message and a messenger—and the latter can be just as important as the former. Let's begin by considering the steps that are included in a justification process. Earlier in the chapter, we let Figure 8-1 summarize our discussion of the relationship between strategic, organizational, and economic assessments. Figure 8-2 is an augmented version of that figure that captures the essential steps in the project approval process.

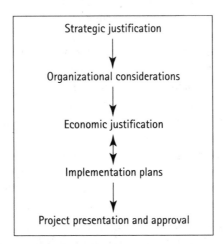

Figure 8-2. The justification and approval process

Although not shown in Figure 8-2, many project justifications go through a two-stage process. The first phase is usually limited to the approval of a further investigation of the concept. This is because it is difficult to perform a detailed cost justification for a project on which you have not spent much time, and for which no specific blueprint exists. Thus, the outcome of the first justification phase will be either a decision to drop or modify the project, or to continue with design and development work (see Step 5 in Figure 4-1). During the second phase the team will do a more detailed cell design, develop specific cost and benefit estimates, and prepare a preliminary implementation plan. At the end of phase 2, the team should be ready to present both justification calculations and implementation plans to management (see bottom part of Figure 8-2; also see Step 9 in Figure 4-1).

To gain approval to commence planning may require only that you prepare a presentation on the first, and possibly the second, step in Figure 8-2. If you fail to convince management of the strategic advantages of cellular manufacturing, it is unlikely the project will proceed. As part of your presentation it is also important to show the cell project's impact on the organization in terms of reporting relationships, compensation, labor relations, training issues, and so on. Management needs to understand early on that there are many serious issues to consider that can affect both the duration and the economics of the project.

Once you have had adequate time to ponder the fit between the cell concept and the company's current structure and culture, and have collected sufficient information to enumerate costs as well as potential benefits, you are ready to do a detailed economic justification. Firms involved in large projects sometimes do rough, broad-based justifications in the first phase, followed by detailed justifications for each subproject in the second phase.

Estimated future cash flows represent an economic forecast. Such forecasts must rest on scenarios (i.e., your vision of the future). If these scenarios do not materialize, your financial forecasts will be incorrect. So you must think carefully about implementation, or you may seriously underestimate such matters as the time and expenditures needed to prepare the facility, the type and cost of the material-handling equipment that must be replaced, and the time needed to prepare the workforce for the new way of work.

Note that the arrows connecting economic justification and implementation plans in Figure 8-2 point in both directions. This is to emphasize that how—and how well—you plan for implementation will affect the cash-flow streams. A good justification document should include a discussion of the future implementation, have a Gantt chart that outlines the timetable and milestones, and indicate who is responsible for each activity. It also should outline clear metrics and goals.

All decisions are economic decisions, whether expressed in financial terms or not. That is, every decision has economic consequences. Since management is responsible for the financial performance of the company, the economic aspects are obviously of great interest. How, then, do you sell a project to management? By emphasizing those aspects that are of greatest interest. *A project proposal that neglects to capture the cost of the undertaking, or fails to express at least some of the benefits in financial terms, runs a great risk of being rejected or ignored by management.* This is true even if the idea came from management to begin with. Thus, sooner or later, all great ideas need to be translated into money streams.

The role of the messenger

Decisions are not taken based on the content of the message alone. Who delivers the message, and how it is conveyed, will both influence whether the project is approved. Advocates of a particular project or solution tend to be biased in their advocacy. The bias is revealed by their emphasizing a favorite alternative, overestimating benefits, ignoring risks, and so on.[38] At the same time, management is usually not as well informed and has to rely on the project team for its information. As a result, the *confidence* management has in the team and its leader affects the decision to approve or reject a proposal. Therefore, it is important to eliminate from documents and presentations any exaggerated claims that may come across as unsupported or biased.

Furthermore, when uncertainty surrounds the project—for example, when little previous experience exists—management's perception of the confidence that the team members have in their own proposal will affect its decision. This works in reverse as well: employees affected by a change project need to trust management in order to be sold on the idea. This appears to have been the case for the $90 million change project at Zanussi, which was met by great suspicion by many middle managers: "'the interpersonal component' played an important role in winning approval for the project. A combination of credibility and commitment by top management and its hand-picked team was used to convince everyone to go ahead."[39]

As a consequence, the cell project team should be composed of respected individuals with strong track records. It is especially important that the team leader have the trust of both management and staff (for more on this, see Chapter 15).

To help you prepare and present your proposal to management, we have included guidelines for structuring and delivering effective presentations in Appendix B.

KEY INSIGHTS

Some might argue that due to the difficulties of estimating cash flows, detailed cost justifications of cell projects are unnecessary and irrelevant. However, the less care you take in estimating costs and benefits, the more vulnerable you are to criticisms directed towards your project proposal. In our view, the pragmatic approach is to do "just enough justification." Thus, if a calculation based on a few reliable variables shows a clear economic value, you do not need to seek other benefits or derive more precise estimates. However, if the calculations show very narrow—or even negative—economic margins, you must put more care into the justification process.

Here are some key points to keep in mind when determining the economic value of your cell project:

- *First, justify cells based on strategy.* To be viable, a cell project must support the organization's strategic objectives for competing in the marketplace. Do not proceed with economic justification unless the strategic justification is a "go." The project should also be checked for its compatibility with, and impact on, the organization's systems, structure, processes, people, and culture. This will help you make better estimates of the financial and operational implications of the cells.

- *Then, justify cells economically.* Early in the planning process, it may suffice to justify the cell concept strategically. However, you should justify the cells economically once detailed planning has begun.

- *Base your justification on relevant costs and revenues.* Avoid using the cost accounting system's overhead charges for this purpose.

- *If the investment for the project is large, and the payback is likely to take several years, your justification should consider both the time value of money and tax implications.* This means using a capital budgeting technique that considers discounted cash flow streams.

- *Focus on a few major benefit areas in your justification.* If the tangible benefits are insufficient to show economic value, pick some important intangibles and turn them into tangible benefits.

- *Carefully consider both the anticipated benefits and the potential pitfalls.* Prepare a careful justification by describing in full what you expect to encounter both during and after implementation. You must understand how cells actually will work in order to derive realistic estimates of their costs and benefits.

- *Be honest.* All justifications are shrouded in uncertainty. It is fairly easy to "fudge the numbers" to make cost justifications look better. However, a flawed financial projection is not helpful to anyone.

- *Carefully plan and execute the "selling" of the project.* Management approval of cell projects is not based solely on the strategic and economic value to the firm. How you sell the project, and the credibility of the messenger, are important factors that influence management decisions. They can make or break a project. Think about the audience and how to reach it, anticipate questions, focus on issues of importance to management, and follow the rest of the guidelines in Appendix B.

DESIGNING THE CELL SYSTEM INFRASTRUCTURE

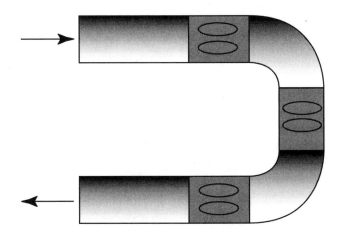

9

Performance Measurement for Cells

Over 200 years ago, Lord Kelvin said: "When you can measure what you're speaking about, and express it in numbers, you know something about it; but when you cannot measure it, when you cannot express it in numbers, your knowledge is of a meager and unsatisfactory kind." Kelvin, the originator of the absolute temperature scale, was involved with science but his ideas apply to organizations as well. The absence of measures leaves us uncertain as to what is going on and incapable of acting rationally. Or put more concisely, "If you cannot measure it, you cannot control it. If you cannot control it, you cannot manage it. If you cannot manage it, you cannot improve it. It is as simple as that."[1]

Fundamentally, performance measures focus your attention on important tasks and, in particular, on reaching goals. Performance along certain dimensions becomes important when you measure it. Conversely, dimensions of performance that you do not measure become less important. Also, measured results often influence rewards. Individuals and groups tend to pay most attention to those aspects of their work that are measured. This underscores the importance of designing a performance measurement system that is consistent with your goals.

For most organizations, cells are part of a customer-oriented strategy that emphasizes speed and quality. Determining the effectiveness of this strategy calls for new measures. A study of 800 small and medium UK firms found that organizations emphasizing quality and quick response had put in place performance measurement systems to assess progress toward these objectives.[2] Similarly, as illustrated in Table 9-1,

Table 9-1. Performance measures used at 42 plants before and after cell adoptions

Type of Measure	Before Cells (%)	After Cells (%)
Productivity	93	79
Schedule performance	81	71
Quality	33	93
Lead time	31	64
Inventory	24	74
Preventive maintenance	5	24
Utilization	2	2
Cell completeness	0	5
Other costs	7	21

Note: Percentages exceed 100% since plants use multiple measures.

a study of U.S. firms showed that companies that adopted cells put stronger emphasis on quality, lead time, and inventory turn measures.[3] In short, if you implement cells as part of a revised strategy, you need to rethink how you assess performance.

The move to cells represents a departure from previous ways of organizing work. Specifically, cells have different organizational boundaries than the functional systems they tend to replace (see Chapter 2). This means that the points at which data are collected, who collects the data, the type of measures that are used, and who uses the performance metrics will all change. To put it mildly, cells disrupt existing performance measurement systems.[4]

In this chapter we address the following key issues related to cells and measurement:

- What is a performance measurement system?
- What principles or guidelines should you use when you create or revise performance measures?
- How do you best present measures to cell operators and supervisors?
- How do you evaluate a measurement system for completeness and effectiveness?

At the end of the chapter we present a longer example of an organization's performance measurement system, and analyze it using a diagnostic tool.

WHAT IS A PERFORMANCE MEASUREMENT SYSTEM?

Performance measurement helps you *understand*, *control*, and *improve* performance. First, measures help you *understand* what is going on by answering questions like: What are our current output rates? Are our customers satisfied with our products? How does the productivity of Assembly Cell 1 compare with the productivity of Assembly Cell 2? Thus, measures give you a sense of where you are, often relative to other companies, departments, or cells.

Second, you can use measures for *control* purposes. It is well known that performance measures drive behavior: people do what they are rewarded for. To use measures for control, you need targets against which you can compare current performance. The measurement system can then signal out-of-control conditions, identify performance that should be either rewarded or corrected, and communicate performance objectives throughout the organization.

Finally, you can use measures to track *improvements* and motivate further improvements. In fact, one of the most important purposes of measuring may be to support performance improvement.

Organizations frequently struggle with the question of how to assess performance. They get bogged down in the process of identifying a detailed set of measures that makes sense. But identifying measures without guidelines is the wrong way to start. You first need to appreciate what a performance measurement system looks like, where measures should be taken, and the types of measures that exist. In the next two sections we discuss the basic structure of measurement systems and, more importantly, provide a framework for thinking about measurement that you can use as a foundation for either creating new measures or analyzing your existing measures.

Elements of a Performance Measurement System

In its simplest form, a complete performance measurement system consists of three components:[5]

1. *An organizational unit.* For example, a cell or a group of cells that supplies data for the measurement process.

2. *A measurement system.* A manual or computer-based system that collects data, translates these into metrics, and presents them to target audiences.

3. *One or more decision-makers.* These are employees who evaluate performance data and decide whether or not to take action, such as cell operators, cell leaders, support engineers, or plant managers.

Figure 9-1 shows the quintessential measurement-action cycle for control and improvement. That is, you observe an activity or process within a defined organizational unit, collect selected performance data, compare them with targets, and decide whether to intervene. As Figure 9-2 shows, the measurement system itself consists of three subsystems:[6]

1. *A data collection system.* This system ensures that necessary input data are collected so that performance metrics can be constructed.

2. *A metric creation system.* This system takes the collected input data and converts them into metrics.

3. *A metric presentation system.* This system displays the metrics to the intended audience.

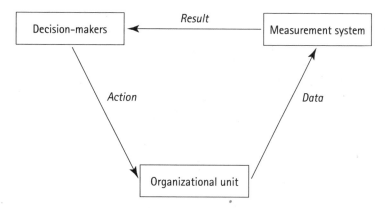

Figure 9-1. A simple representation of a performance-management system

We will use an order-processing office cell to illustrate the subsystems in Figure 9-2. Both the cell employees and the manager supervising the cell are decision-makers. Suppose that one key metric for this cell is the average elapsed time between the cell receiving a customer order and the time a complete job is submitted to manufacturing. To construct this metric, you need to collect data on customer order arrivals and manufacturing order submissions. As part of this data collection process, cell employees might log in the time and arrival date for each order in a

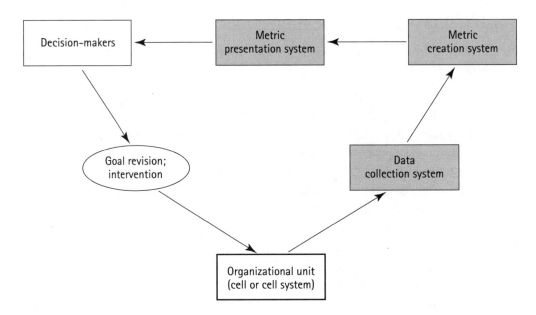

Figure 9–2. Key components of a performance-management system (measurement-action cycle)

database. At regular intervals, say weekly, a computer program scans the database and identifies completed customer orders that arrived since last week. The extracted data are then fed to a software module that calculates the order-processing time for all new orders and determines the average processing time for the last week. This is the metric creation system. That average is then entered into a database containing average order-processing times for the last six months. Finally, a cell employee may convert the measures for average order-processing time into a line graph or histogram, print it for display on the cell's bulletin board, and also submit it via e-mail to the cell manager. This is the metric presentation system.

As you can see from this example, the data collection system simply collects raw data (order entry and exit times). Such data are commonly not the same as the performance measures themselves (average order-processing times). Further, the time intervals involved may differ; for example, you may collect data daily but choose to develop a weekly measure.

Metric creation can take many forms. In our example above, a simple weekly average was added to the database of averages determined for the last six months. The elapsed time data also could have been fed to a statistical process control (SPC) module that can signal whether the data come from an unstable process. A third alternative could be to link the order-processing time data to another set of data. For example, you could collect the dollar value of each order, match each order's dollar value with its elapsed time, and create a *value vs. time* plot of orders processed in the last six months. In other words, you can create a large number of possible measures based on one set of raw data.

You can also express the final measure in many different ways. For example, based on data on number of units scrapped per day, you could express scrap as dollars of scrapped material per month, units scrapped per batch, and so forth. To turn raw data into a measure requires clear *operational definitions* that specify the type of input data to collect and how to construct the metric. Without detailed operational definitions, your performance measures may not be accurately determined and will, therefore, be less meaningful.

Metric presentation can also take many forms. Written reports, graphical displays prominently posted in the area, websites, and email updates on performance are all possible options. Later in the chapter we present helpful guidelines for metric presentation.

Finally, from an organization-wide perspective, *measurement consistency* is important. For example, you may want to construct an assembly department quality index by combining a cell's defect measures with quality measures taken at other cells. Obviously, this aggregate measure is meaningful only if the individual cells are measuring defects in the same way.

HOW TO GENERATE PERFORMANCE MEASURES

Creating a performance measurement system that helps you understand, control, and improve performance is a complicated undertaking. As Figure 9-2 suggests, you must determine why, what, where, when, and how you will measure, as well as who will take the measures, analyze the data, and report the results. While this is a very involved process, there are a number of important principles that can help guide your efforts. We discuss some of these next.

A Process Perspective on Measurement

As a starting point for performance measurement you need to define the organizational unit whose performance you want to assess (see Figure 9-2). The formal boundaries traditionally used in organizations—e.g., individuals, departments, or the plant—are not always helpful in determining what to measure and where to measure it. This is because those boundaries may not correspond with how work actually is performed in the organization. Instead, we prefer to use *process thinking* as a basis for performance measurement.

All companies rely on processes, i.e., the basic sequences of activities that accomplish the work the organization is in business to perform. Processes take material and/or information *inputs*, and through the application of *resources*, such as machines, computers, and labor, *transform* these inputs into *outputs* (see Figure 9-3). Examples of processes include receiving and storing incoming goods, verifying order

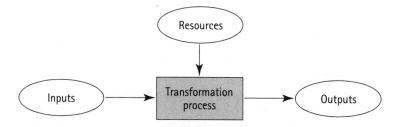

Figure 9-3. Simple process model

entry data, assembling PCB boards, inspection and testing of finished computers, and developing new products.

Cells, ideally, are process-complete operations. They consolidate work by pulling production activities (and often nonproduction activities) from functional departments and grouping them under one roof. Assessing cell performance can be simpler and more timely, accurate, and useful than measuring activities in functional shops.

Consider the situation where the measurement system reveals a dramatic drop in first-pass quality for a key product. In a departmentally configured firm, this decline in quality might be the result of defects introduced in any of the work centers the part has visited. Since these work centers are located in different departments spread throughout the plant, it is not obvious how and where to begin to remedy the situation. And because of long lead times, you might not discover the drop in quality until long after the errors were made and many defective units have been produced.

Cells, on the other hand, provide clear lines of responsibility and accountability, and facilitate rapid feedback. When there is a drop in quality for a cell, you immediately look to the cell process for causes and remedies. Further, because production lead times are short, measuring cell performance is tightly coupled with the activities that create the cell output. Since all work is performed through processes, it is natural to design measurement systems to track process performance. This is especially appropriate for cells given that they are process-complete operations.

Identifying Performance Measures—The Five-Step Procedure

The starting point for creating measurements is defining the work process. This and other steps required to create performance measures are shown in Table 9-2. The outlined procedure applies to *any* process, whether cell-related or not. Details on each step are provided below.

Table 9-2. A five-step process for creating performance measures

1. *Identify, define, bound, and map the process.* As part of this step, ask yourself, "What is the purpose, what are the key outputs, and who are the customers of this process?"
2. *Determine the critical characteristics of each output from the customers' perspective.* After which completed process step can you collect performance data on these aspects?
3. *Determine the process characteristics that may be critical to customer satisfaction.* This includes incoming material, productive resources involved, and the transformation process. Which aspects affect financial performance? And after which activities in the process can you collect performance data on these characteristics?
4. *Develop metrics for each critical aspect of the process.* State them in both verbal and operational terms.
5. *Establish goals, targets, or standards for each measure.*

Step 1: Map and bound the process

This key step sets the boundaries for the system/process that you want to measure. The process may be within an existing organizational unit, such as a planning department or an assembly cell. It may also be a process that covers only part of the work in a unit or, as often happens, one that crosses organizational boundaries. For example, an order-fulfillment process may include personnel and administrative systems from sales, engineering, customer service, manufacturing, warehousing, distribution, and accounting.

Effective performance measurement is difficult when processes cross organizational boundaries. This is because there is an inherent conflict between vertically structured organizations and horizontal processes that span multiple departments. Measuring work within one department only will not help you improve the overall process.[7] This is one reason why cells—where responsibility for previously separated tasks now falls within the boundary of a single organizational unit—can be so effective.

The best starting point for process identification is defining its purpose and outputs. You should ask, "What products and services is the process producing, and why are these produced?" Starting with the purpose and outputs also forces you to *identify the customers of the process* for whom the work is carried out (alternatively, you may begin by identifying the customers, and then the purpose and outputs). Mapping a process means documenting it in a flow chart. "If you can't flowchart the process you want to improve, a performance measure will offer little insight into what you should do to improve."[8] Specifically, a process is defined by the *entry activities* that first use resources to transform materials, and by the *exit activities* that produce the final outputs that represent the purpose of the work.

In Chapter 2 we made a distinction between manufacturing cells, whose main purpose is to process material, and office cells, whose purpose is to process information. Similarly, we can distinguish between *material-converting* and *information-converting* processes. Of course, these two types of processes are often interlinked; for example, a complete order-fulfillment process requires both material and information processing. However, for the purpose of performance measurement, you first should identify the core process that you are interested in assessing. For a manufacturing cell, the core process is the conversion of incoming raw material into finished parts or products that leave the cell. Conversely, for an order-processing office cell, the core process is the conversion of incoming customer order information into internal order specifications that ultimately trigger shipments of the requested goods to the customer from inventory. An especially close link between material and information-based processes can be seen in make-to-order manufacturing, where the order information process essentially determines the manufacturing process.

Obviously, when you form a cell you have determined, de facto, its core processes and boundaries. Frequently, though, different teams are responsible for the technical versus the infrastructural aspects of the cells. Thus, the team involved with performance measurement must develop a full understanding of the cell process, just as the design team did when it selected parts and equipment and determined the physical layout.

Step 2: Establish the customer perspective

As stated, defining a process inevitably forces you to think about its outputs—part drawings, order quotations, shafts, assembled instruments, and so on. You should identify the output characteristics that matter most to customers of the process. Typically, these characteristics are delineated by dimensions such as quality, timeliness, and cost. Each process output, of course, may have several critical performance aspects.

When you identify a critical process output, note the step at which it is completed so that the data collection system knows where to take output-related measures (e.g., after what process step can you measure the number of completed units ready for shipment?). As a general rule, *most performance measures are taken at decision points along the process* where the outcome of the measurement can influence decisions upstream or downstream from where data were collected.

Step 3: Process aspects affecting output

To fully gauge the efficiency and effectiveness of a process, you need to look beyond customer variables, such as response time or customer quality complaints, and think about *the whole process* that is creating the output. Is it efficient, productive, cost effective, and fast? For example, it may be possible to improve response time to customer requests, but if you must increase inventory levels or enlarge staff to do so, this could be an expensive and unappealing alternative. In short, you must understand how the process affects output performance. As we will discuss later, the four process elements shown in Figure 9-3 (inputs, resources, transformation activities, and outputs) form the backbone of our process measurement framework; each of them is a natural point at which to measure process behavior. But you must decide which dimensions of those resources and activities to monitor for the purpose of controlling and improving the process.

Step 4: Formulate detailed measures

Once you have identified the critical aspects of the process, you need to develop *operational definitions* for those performance dimensions. Operational definitions specify what data to collect and how to manipulate them in order to generate precise measures. You may, for example, decide to measure scrap in the process. But before collecting data you must determine where you should measure, whether you should express metrics in units, tons, or dollars, whether you should use an absolute or relative measure, and so on. For instance, you could measure cell scrap as "the number of defective housings per week found during inspection at test station 3." You might also measure "kilos of metal scrapped per week divided by kilos of metal used by the process per week." The first is an absolute measure stated in units per week, while the second is a relative measure stated in percentage of defective material per week.

Step 5: Set goals or base lines

Finally, you need to generate targets or standards. These are necessary to construct efficiency-oriented measures because *planned* input or outputs are part of the final measure. (For example, one efficiency measure is standard hours divided by actual hours.) You'll probably want to set goals or targets for *all* measures because they help stimulate improvement. But you can—indeed must—revise your targets over time. They should not be set in stone, since raising the bar motivates continued improvement and prevents complacency.

We recommend that you assemble a team to develop cell measures. Include employees who will work, or are already working, in the cell. Doing so helps develop ownership of the measurement system, something that is especially important when metrics are linked to performance appraisals and/or compensation systems (see Chapter 14).

HOW TO EVALUATE AND PRESENT PERFORMANCE MEASURES

How do you know if the measures you have in place, or the ones you generate for a new or improved process, are good or bad? How do you know if they do what they are supposed to do? And how should you best present the metrics you develop? The guidelines below (along with the five-step procedure we just presented) can help you successfully implement and use measures in cell systems. We have separated the guidelines into two areas: (1) are you measuring correctly? and (2) are you presenting your metrics in the best possible way?

Are You Measuring the Right Things, and Are You Measuring Right?

- *Link cell measures to the organization's strategic goals.* A key role of measures is to assess progress toward strategic goals. An organization's strategy tells you where it wants to go and how it plans to get there. Typically, top management develops strategies and then seeks to deploy them throughout the organization. Whatever its strategy, an organization needs measures at all levels that capture how well the strategy is achieved. Ideally, all measures should be linked to, and be consistent with, the firm's *critical success factors.*[9] Table 9-3 illustrates how the corporate strategic goal of cost competitiveness at one firm has been refined into concrete goals at various organizational levels, from corporate management down to individual cells.

- *A set of measures is complete if it reflects resource usage and project improvement progress, as well as inputs, transformation, and output aspects.* As we noted, to take the pulse of a cell, and especially to support improvement activities, requires measures that assess the performance of all process dimensions: material inputs and outputs, resources, and transformation. The Process Performance Measurement Matrix introduced later (see Table 9-7) can help the project team in charge of performance measurement identify relevant measures.

- *Measures should impact behavior in the "right" direction and discourage behavior in the "wrong" direction.* Performance measures "have a profound impact on human behavior, because people are more likely to do what you inspect than what you expect."[10] In other words, *individuals in organizations tend to concentrate their efforts on what is measured and rewarded* and tend to be less attentive to issues and dimensions of work that are not measured and therefore not rewarded.

  One focused factory had a self-managed group running an assembly cell. It was "common wisdom" that this line was the most efficient in the plant. A new director of manufacturing started to measure output per day from each cell in the factory, and to relate it to the number of employees manning each cell. He discovered two things. First, the self-managed cell turned out to be the *least* efficient cell. Second, the output of all cells started to increase immediately after the measurement system was put in place.

  In another plant that makes components, supervisors were rewarded based on machine utilization and labor efficiency. Both measures improved when more parts were produced per period. Producing more output, however,

Table 9-3. Goal/measurement linkages between organizational levels for a company with cells

Organizational Level	Goal	Measures
Corporate headquarters	Improve cost competitiveness	• Market share • Unit sales
VP of operations	Keep product costs stable—no cost increases	• Average product cost • Dollar output per equipment dollar invested • Output per square foot occupied
Manager of all assembly cells	$300,000 worth of cost reductions in assembly to offset increases in inflation, resource and input costs	• Sum of cost reduction in individual cells and support areas (reductions in material, labor and overhead costs) In support of cost reduction, will also measure: • Overall scrap rates in assembly • Number of unplanned schedule changes • Overall machine downtime • Dollars and days of supply in finished goods inventory
Individual assembly cell	$15,000 in cost reduction improvements	• Savings from cost reduction ideas implemented In support of cost reduction, will also measure: • Scrap rates • Unplanned schedule changes • Defective rates on incoming parts and subassemblies • Absenteeism • Changeover/set-up times

meant long production runs, high WIP inventory, long lead times, and poor due-date performance. These were not the outcomes plant management wanted, but were a direct consequence of the measurement system.[11]

The last scenario illustrates a relatively obvious disconnect between goals and measures. Other, subtler inconsistencies are possible. Therefore, to assure that measures motivate desired action, you must (1) think through all possible consequences of the measure itself, and (2) evaluate any possible interactions with other performance dimensions, including those that are not explicitly measured (also see Appendix C). That is, you should ask "What will be the result of scoring very high, or very low, on this measure?" and "Will emphasizing this measure contribute to poor performance on other, possibly unmeasured variables?" For example, measuring and emphasizing high utilization will lead to unwarranted side effects such as large WIP inventories and late orders.

• *Clearly define each measure and provide precise definitions for collecting data.* One company implemented a new measurement system for cells but failed to provide clear definitions for each measure. Management did not articulate what constituted a particular metric or how to collect the required data. Job descriptions did not include anything about collecting, displaying, and analyzing data. Because of these omissions, the new measurement system did not serve its purpose and was later abandoned.

We have said this before, but for any performance measurement system to be effective, each metric must be defined precisely and clearly. Consider production lead time. Does lead time begin when the order is released to the cell, when all the required material has arrived, when the first operation begins, or at some other point? Does production end when the last operation is complete, when the item is entered into work in process or finished goods inventory, when the items leave the cell, or at some other point (i.e., which are the critical activities and events)? *To specify how data should be collected you need to thoroughly understand the production process!* Further, your instructions for data collection should be so clear that two trained individuals observing the same process should capture exactly the same data in the same way. Even in situations where data collection is completely or partially automated, those who will work with the data need to understand the operational definitions. In the absence of this, measures are meaningless.

- *Adopt a limited but important set of measures.* Although the quote by Lord Kelvin at the outset of this chapter suggests the danger of failing to measure, many organizations err on the side of using too many measures:[12]

  All organizations start with an almost overwhelming network of financial measures in place. Add to that measures driven by past problems, shifting emphases of new managers, and new corporate programs of quality, cycle time and customer service. The result is a collection of largely unrelated and unmanageable measures, leading in many cases to "measurement gridlock"—managers in a state of paralysis because they can't move performance affecting one measure in a positive direction without (seemingly) moving two others in a negative direction.

  A component parts plant is a case in point.[13] This plant used to generate 50 to 60 performance reports each month to assess plant performance, many focusing on labor efficiency and cost variances. Due to the complexity of the measurement system, which required large amounts of time and computer resources to maintain, nobody knew how to improve if a report showed unsatisfactory performance. This system was discarded when the plant began to convert to cells. The new system consists of only eight measures.

  The lesson is clear: when measures are too numerous, operators, supervisors, and management all find it difficult to determine the measurement signals to which they should respond. Cell decision-makers need to know the relative priority of various measures. This is extremely difficult to do when faced with a barrage of different, and possibly contradictory, measures. Furthermore, too many measures cause individuals and teams to spend an inordinate amount of time gathering data and tracking activities, and not enough time engaged in their primary work.[14]

The data in Table 9-1 indicate that when companies adopt cells they introduce new measures. Unfortunately, they also retain the old ones. However, *cells must focus only on the most critical measures.* You can track other metrics, but you should not present them on a regular basis. Rather, they should be used as background information when needed to solve performance problems. Displaying only a limited set of key measures ensures that employees know that these are the important ones.

- *Hold cell employees responsible only for measures they can influence.* Do not hold a cell responsible for dimensions of performance that it has little power to influence. For example, a cell may be measured on output quality, but if it is not given authority to inspect and reject incoming material, cell operators do not have full control over the quality measure. (In fact, one reason for measuring the timeliness and quality of incoming material is to establish starting points for accountability.) Similarly, suppose you measure a cell's standard to actual hours. If the cell relies on other groups (such as equipment engineering or machine setters) for key support tasks, this productivity measure depends on other people's actions. Cell measures should assess the cell employees' performance, not the performance of groups that support the cell.

- *Assure that cell measures are based on credible data.* Performance measures are only as good as the data on which they are based. If data are inaccurate or unreliable, the resulting measures will not be meaningful, trustworthy, or used. One company introduced a new performance measurement system to support three recently created manufacturing cells. The cell employees were to administer and use the system. Unfortunately, both managers and operators knew that the underlying data used to determine the measures were unreliable. This contributed to the quick demise of the performance measurement system.[15]

At another firm, test equipment had begun to operate inconsistently. This meant that a cell component might or might not pass its final test depending on which station performed the evaluation. As a consequence, the performance data on first-pass quality provided possibly misleading information and was therefore generally ignored.

- *Continually review and improve the measurement system, but maintain consistency in metrics over time.* Most organizations find themselves operating in turbulent environments that force them to continually adapt to stay competitive. If your organization changes course, the measurement system too will need to change: "When the old performance measures square off against new strategies or actions, the measures often win."[16] Specifically, as strategies change, a company may need to discard old performance measures that are no longer relevant and adopt new ones that capture progress toward the revised goals. Typically, cells are created in support of business strategies emphasizing quick response and high quality. Cell measures should reflect these strategic thrusts. If you continue to base assessments on traditional measures (labor efficiency, utilization, earned hours, and so forth), you create significant inconsistencies between the organization's goals and the measurement system.

Thus, you periodically need to evaluate cell measures to ensure that they are still (1) measuring dimensions of performance that are important to the organization, and (2) helpful in understanding, controlling, and improving cell performance. On the other hand, you don't want to change measures capriciously. Assessing performance over time requires a constant set of measures. Measurements establish baselines and trends that form the foundation for decision making. It is impossible to know whether a cell is doing well or poorly, to compare one cell to another, or to compare this month's performance to last month's, if performance measures are constantly changing. So, while it is important that some measures assess what is important now to the organization, it is also important that other measures provide a basis for continuity.[17]

Are You Presenting the Performance Metrics Effectively?

- *Assign responsibility for data collection and presentation.* Cell operators frequently are assigned responsibility for collecting, analyzing, displaying, and interpreting cell performance data. If this is the case at your plant, you'll need to train the operators in these tasks. Computer software can help analyze data and prepare performance reports and exhibits. However, *employees* must collect and feed raw data to terminals and ensure that final reports are made available; in fact, a description of a measure is incomplete unless it also indicates *who* is responsible for these tasks. Having the cell operators themselves contribute to the design of the performance measurement system is a good way to instill ownership for tracking important dimensions of cell performance.

- *Assure that measures are presented in a timely manner.* Timeliness is a key aspect of a credible measurement system. Since measures can signal problems, they should be reported as concurrently with events as possible. This means that the speed of the process, gauged by flow characteristics such as output rates and throughput times, determines how frequently you need to report the measures.[18] If the cell produces many units every *hour*, learning that *last month's* cell production had an unacceptably high defect rate is not as valuable as learning that *last hour's* production had a high defect rate. In the latter case, it is possible to investigate and remedy the situation much sooner. In general, long gaps between the time critical quality variables are measured and the time they are reported may be costly. Continued defective output, and the consequent increase in material scrap, rework labor, overtime, late orders, and rescheduling efforts, are all possible consequences of delayed reporting.

- *Display data in ways that communicate performance effectively.* Cell performance measures should be displayed in a clear and conspicuous manner. Specific guidelines for showing data include:[19]
    - Use graphs instead of tables.
    - Avoid complicated charts.
    - Be sure to label clearly all axes, and provide a title and legend on each graph.
    - Where possible, use color displays rather than black and white.

    "Visual scoreboards" represent one mechanism for displaying cell performance information. The "why, what, and how" of scoreboards for cells are discussed in the following section.

- *Use a unit of measure that motivates improvement.* If you report a defect rate as 2,000 parts per million, it suggests there is room for improvement. A reported defect rate of .2 percent, on the other hand, may be interpreted being so low that making gains is practically impossible. Similarly, expressing the time to change between product families as 12 minutes can be more effective in motivating improvement than referring to it as 0.20 of an hour.[20] In other words, make the number you want to reduce as large as possible in order to motivate improvement.

- *Display measures so they reveal underlying trends in the data.* An important role of cell measures is to assist in improvement efforts. This requires that you compare performance over time. Therefore, do not report data as a single point (e.g., number of defects this week), but rather as a series of points over time (e.g., number of defects per week for the past 30 weeks). This permits you to draw conclusions about improvements or degradations in performance. Trend data are best displayed in graphical form (SPC and run charts, of course, exemplify this guideline).

- *Design measures that are simple to calculate and easy to interpret.* If cell workers will be analyzing much of the performance data themselves, it is important that the measures be relatively simple to calculate and straightforward to interpret. Overly complex measures that no one understands will not be used for very long. In one precision machining cell, for example, workers simply quit collecting data on a couple of metrics because no one in the cell understood how the measures contributed to cell operations.

    Be cautious when you interpret measures expressed as *ratios* or *averages*. Suppose you measure labor productivity in a cell as units produced divided by actual labor hours, and that productivity rose by 15 percent in the last month. That increase in productivity might be due to either (a) more units produced with constant labor hours, or (b) the same number of units produced as in the previous month but using fewer labor hours. Thus, a ratio measure doesn't reveal the causes of the change. To understand those, you also need to track each of the variables that make up the ratio (in this case, output and labor hours). However, those measures should not be regularly displayed, but be only relied on when a deeper understanding of changing performance is necessary.

Likewise, suppose you compute an overall lead time by averaging all recorded part lead times in a cell. This can be very misleading if the parts are produced with different frequencies. Parts produced only once a year would have the same impact on the average lead time measure as parts produced every week. In this case, it is better to use a *weighted average*, where the weights are the number of orders processed of each part per time period.[21]

Finally, avoid measures that are sums of multiple variables. Such measures can be of questionable value when you need to understand why a metric is increasing or declining. For example, suppose you measure scrap as the sum of the cost of defects in incoming material plus the cost of scrap in the manufacturing process. Based on that measure you cannot tell whether an increase in scrap is due to the suppliers or to the in-house process. Thus, combined metrics hide data and make problem-solving and improvement efforts more difficult. If they are used in order to reduce the number of key measures regularly monitored, we suggest that you also maintain more detailed performance data for cause and effect investigations.

Table 9-4 summarizes the above guidelines for performance measurement. In Appendix C we provide a checklist of questions to ask when you are analyzing new or existing performance measures.

Table 9-4. General guidelines for performance measurement

Measure the right things the right way:

- Link cell measures to the organization's strategic goals
- Measure inputs, outputs, transformation, resources, and project improvement
- Design measures to impact behavior in the right direction and discourage behavior in the wrong direction
- Clearly define each measure and provide precise definitions for collecting the data
- Adopt a limited but important set of measures
- Hold cell employees responsible only for measures they can influence
- Assure that cell measures are based on credible data
- Continually review and improve the measurement system, but maintain consistency in metrics over time

Present the performance metrics effectively:

- Assign responsibility for data collection and presentation
- Assure that measures are presented in a timely manner
- Display the data in ways that effectively communicate performance
- Use a unit of measure that motivates improvement
- Display measures so they reveal underlying trends in the data
- Design measures that are simple to calculate and easy to interpret

Presenting Cell Performance Measures Effectively—The Visual Scoreboard

Those who work in manufacturing and office cells are responsible, on a day-to-day basis, for delivering low-cost, high-quality products or services on schedule. In addition, cell employees are often assigned the task of improving performance.

With these responsibilities comes the need for information. In a traditional hierarchical information flow, higher-level managers inform lower-level managers, who in turn inform supervisors who, at last, inform operators. This is neither efficient nor effective in an environment where operators are expected to make decisions and not just follow directions. You need to rethink information flows. In particular, cell employees need *self-service information*—information that is available when needed.[22] And, as Jan Carlzon, the former CEO of Scandinavian Airlines Systems viewed it, if you provide information to people, they will *assume* responsibility. If that information is publicly available, it can serve as an additional inducement for performance improvement.

A *visual scoreboard* is a physical display (a wall, a freestanding board, etc.), located in or near the cell, which shows information important to cell operations (see Figure 9-4). The scoreboard data might also be available to cell employees via database software or a Web site. These vehicles, though, prevent the data from being easily visible to other employees and visitors. This is why the use of visual scoreboards is referred to as "glass wall management," indicating that information should be shared openly inside the firm.[23]

A visual scoreboard should highlight targets, recent performance compared to goals, ongoing projects, and a host of other cell performance information. It answers everybody's primary question: How is the cell doing, and what needs to be done better? Ideally, the scoreboard includes both "flash" (quick or summary) and in-depth (detailed or back-up) information.[24] For example, a flash indicator might be the number of products that failed final test last week. In-depth information might be a Pareto diagram summarizing the historical reasons for failure, such as bad parts or assembly errors.

In addition to performance on key process measures, the scoreboard also includes background information. This might include the cell's name, its mission, its business plan, pictures of those who work in it, a list of suppliers and customers, and a training matrix indicating who can do what jobs. The board should also indicate the status of current improvement efforts. Reference materials and documents, such as manuals, monthly reports, and minutes from cell team meetings, should be nearby.

The guidelines for effective cell measurements, shown in Table 9-4, can help you design a visual scoreboard. A few important ones are repeated below, along with additional guidelines.

- Scoreboards should include measures the cell operators "own" and can influence. Specifically, corporate sales figures and stock price are inappropriate for the cell scoreboard. Daily output levels, production lead times, work in process levels, and defects (and other specific cell performance measures) are more relevant.

- When several cells use visual scoreboards, there should be a general agreement among the cells on what data to display. This allows operators and managers to understand each other's scoreboards, facilitates cross-cell com-

Cable Team Members:

[Photo here]	[Photo here]	[Photo here]	[Photo here]
Shyam	Hadrian	Brook	Dennis

	Prev. 6 months	July	Aug.	Sep.	Oct.	Nov.	Dec.	6-month goal
Injuries	1	0	0	0	0	0	0	0
Missing items	793	16K	2K	0	0	0	0	950
Setup time	OK	OK	OK	OK	OK	OK	OK	<15 min.
Non-attend %	2.8	1.9	1.5	.9	2	3.2	2.5	2.52%

Weekly Schedule Date/Product/Quantity

Weekly Output

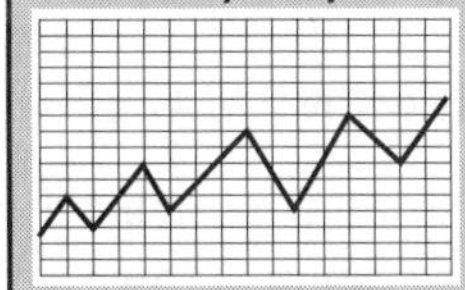

TRAINING MATRIX

Operations	1	2	3	4	5	6	7	8	9	10	11
Shyam	x	x		x		x	x	x		x	x
Hadrian	x	x	x	x	x	x	x	x	x	x	x
Brook	x	x	x	x	x			x			x
Dennis			x	x	x	x	x	x	x		

HOT ORDERS!

Quality Performance

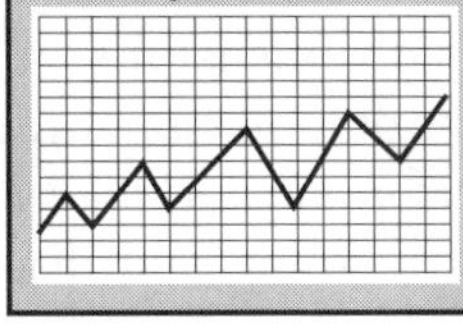

Our Mission

Only a sample of performance measures are included:
* Injuries = recordable injuries
* Missing items = total number of items missing from boxes ready to ship
* Setup time for changing from product to product (ok if less than 15 minutes)
* Non-attendance percentage = total hours not worked/total hours available to work based on planned staffing levels

Figure 9-4. Visual scorecard for cable specialty products cell

parisons, and stimulates improvements. Obviously, some metrics can be unique to each cell.

- Displays should be large, colorful, prominently located, carefully labeled, and not too busy.
- The scoreboard should indicate who is responsible for updating the displayed performance data.
- The scoreboard should be located in an area accessible to both cell employees and visitors, and which can serve as the meeting place for the cell team as well. Such an area has been dubbed a *green area*—"a place where ideas grow." The advantages of a green area, including a visual scoreboard, are listed in Table 9-5.[25] Referring back to Figure 9-2, you can see that the visual scoreboard is a core part of the *metric presentation system*.

Table 9–5. Advantages of "green areas"

---

1. The high level of visibility of performance measures on display facilitates control.

2. The system increases the involvement of all team personnel.

3. It improves communication, providing a forum for discussion about work and business related issues.

4. The system clearly assigns accountability, enabling team and individual performance to be determined.

5. The cross measurement system [i.e., measures of performance determined by the cell's suppliers or customers] ensures that the workflow is accurately controlled from cell to cell.

6. The system provides a shop window for the team, enabling it to clearly show its performance to people visiting the team.

7. The system places a responsibility on the business manager to facilitate development of a new working culture and to respond promptly to issues raised and shown on the display boards.

8. The Green Area becomes a focus of contact for the team and people visiting the team.

THE PROCESS PERFORMANCE MEASUREMENT MATRIX

The guidelines we have presented so far should be helpful in creating or assessing any cell-related performance measurement system. However, we want to introduce one last tool, the *Process Performance Measurement Matrix*. You can use this matrix to diagnose a measurement system from the perspective of emphasis, completeness, and redundancy. The matrix looks at two dimensions of measurement: (1) the *process dimension*, which identifies the key components of the process whose performance you want to track, and (2) the *performance dimension*, which contains the critical measurement variables. After first defining and discussing each dimension separately, we combine them to create the Process Performance Measurement Matrix. We then show, via an example, how you can apply the matrix to assess a measurement system for cells.

The Process Dimension

As mentioned earlier, the main process components—the inputs, the resources, the transformation itself, and the outputs—are the critical areas of performance measurement (Figure 9-3). A process is designed to handle and/or convert material. For convenience, we use the term *material* to denote anything the process transforms (i.e., material, in terms of its properties and/or location, is what the process was designed to change). Thus, steel used in a sheet fabrication cell, components put together in an assembly cell, information processed in an order-fulfillment cell, finished products moved to a warehouse, or an employee undergoing a training process are all examples of material.

Input measures track various attributes of the material as it *enters* a particular stage somewhere along the process. "Raw material quality" is an example of an input measure. Conversely, *output measures* assess characteristics of the material as it *departs* a particular stage in the process (usually at the end) and moves on to subsequent processes. "Units produced" is an example of an output measure.

We like to think of the incoming side of the process as the *supplier side*, and the outgoing side of the process as the *customer side*. That is, measures taken to characterize the input material tell you something about the suppliers to your process, while measures taken to characterize the outgoing material are of interest to internal or external customers. In fact, your customers can be the ones who collect performance data for your process (e.g., customer complaints).

In order to understand, control, and improve the process you also need to assess the characteristics of the conversion process itself. We call such internal process measures *transformation measures*. Many transformation measures are constructed by comparing data collected at different places in the process. These data collection points are typically located at the input and output side, but could also be in the "interior" of the process. Manufacturing lead time is an example of a transformation measure based on the tracking of process start and end times. Although this type of measure is internal, it is often of interest to customers as well (e.g., "customer response time").

Finally, to get a complete understanding of the process, you need to assess various aspects of the productive resources used in the process (like labor and equipment) and the workplace environment in which these resources perform their activities. This "resource measure" category also includes consumable resources, like perishable tooling or printing supplies, which support the conversion of the material. In this vein, scheduled overtime is an example of a capacity-oriented resource measure. Figure 9-5 illustrates the process-based input/output thinking that underlies the types of measures just discussed.

The process measures are intended for the routine, ongoing tracking of operations. Thus, they help you monitor regular process performance. In addition, you

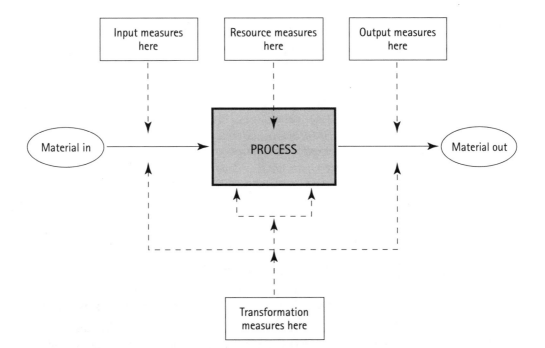

Figure 9-5. Where measures are taken

also need a fifth measurement category related to processes—*project status*. Cell teams are frequently engaged in non-routine projects aimed at improving processes. One electronics firm, for example, requires that all its cells track progress on initiatives such as implementing SPC and developing a five-year technology plan. At another plant, which has high levels of repetitive-motion injuries and cumulative trauma disorders, cells track the number of ergonomic audits performed each month. Although improvement projects are not the cell's core processes, these projects seek to improve the performance of the core processes. Thus, the measurement system should capture all types of activities carried out by the cell, including temporary project work.

The Performance Dimension

The input, output, resource, transformation, and project status categories direct your attention to different stages in the process and to supporting projects. In other words, they tell you where to measure. But they don't tell you *what* measures to use to assess performance. Based on the guidelines we proposed in Table 9-4, you know that you should link at least some of the measures used at the cell level to the firm's strategic goals. Apart from that, the guidelines do not tell you specifically what type of measures to use.

Table 9-6 shows the broad measurement categories used at three well-known manufacturing companies. All three firms consider quality, cost, and delivery to be key strategic variables. Beyond that, the measurement categories are not consistent. This illustrates that even when you categorize performance measures at the very highest level you typically will find a great deal of variation among companies.

Table 9-6. Performance-measurement categories for three manufacturing companies

Hewlett-Packard	Harley-Davidson	Delphi-Harrison
1. Quality	1. Quality	1. Quality
2. Cost	2. Cost	2. Cost
3. Delivery	3. Delivery	3. Delivery
4. Responsiveness	4. Safety	4. Safety
5. Technology	5. Employee development	5. People

We use a slightly different set of measurement categories. In our view, the categories below can capture all relevant aspects of work in cell systems:[26]

- *Quality*. How well do our materials and resources meet expectations and standards with respect to things like defect levels and skills?
- *Work environment*. What is the quality of the work environment in terms of safety and employee well-being?
- *Productivity*. How productive is our process in converting inputs to outputs?
- *Flow*. At what rates does material flow into, out of, or through the process? And, from a resource perspective, on what activities are we spending our time?

- *Inventory*. How much material or how many resource units do we have available at various stages in the process?

- *Timeliness*. How well do we meet given due dates? For example, how timely are the responses of our suppliers? How is our delivery performance with respect to our internal/external customers?

- *Financial aspects*. What are the cost (and, in some cases revenue) characteristics of the process?

Notice that most measure categories apply to both material and resources. For example, you can assess the quality and flow of material as well as the quality and flow of resources. Likewise, you can measure the cost of material and the cost of using people and equipment. The specific metrics you use, of course, will differ in each case. Second, because the core process in a manufacturing cell focuses on materials, we use three categories that relate to materials movements—flow, inventory, and timeliness. Note, finally, that although you take measures on material and resources, like parts and equipment, the purpose is to learn about the performance of the complete process, not about the material or the resources themselves.

For the sake of creating a more compact measurement system, we collapse some of these measurement areas. We combine productivity with quality into a "quality and productivity" category. We do so because labor productivity can be seen as an aspect of process quality (e.g., the fewer problems in the process, the higher the productivity). We also combine flow and inventory measures into a single category because of the close connection between these two types of measures (e.g., inventory is created by differences in input and output flow rates). We call the new category "flow and inventory." These changes leave us with five performance measure categories.

Applying the Five Performance Measure Categories

The five measure categories in the *performance dimension*—quality and productivity, flow and inventory, timeliness, workplace environment, and financial aspects—make up the rows in our Process Performance Measurement Matrix. The *process dimension*—input, output, transformation, resources, and project status—make up the columns. Table 9-7 shows a Process Performance Measurement Matrix with various measures entered. Before we illustrate how the matrix can be used, let us take a closer look at the five measurement categories.

1. Quality and productivity. You can measure material quality at the output side of a process. Quality output measures tell you something about material leaving the process. Based on that, you can draw conclusions about the process. Specifically, the measures can tell you the degree to which a product or service fails, meets, or exceeds customer expectations. In one firm, the number of returns—defective parts returned from an assembly cell—is an output material quality measure for a machined parts cell. Also, when defective parts are returned to the supplying cell from the assembly cell, they prompt a "corrective action" procedure. The component cell tracks the number of such investigations underway each month and uses this number as one indicator of output quality.

Table 9-7. The Process Performance Measurement Matrix with sample measures (*measures in bold come from one specific company*)

	Resources (productive and consumable resources)	Input (incoming material)	Transformation (material, internal focus)	Output (outgoing material)	Project Status
Quality and Productivity *How well and how productive?*	• Percent of employees trained on cell operations • **Std hours produced per actual labor hour**	• Scrap rate, incoming material	• No. units failing test • **Scrap rate**	• No. of customer complaints per month • **No. of customer returns**	• ISO 9000 preparation
Flow and Inventory *How much, what rate?*	• **Hours spent on rework per period** • Hours of unscheduled maintenance	• Units received per week • **Raw material inventory** • Order backlog	• **WIP inventory** • Manufacturing lead time • Response time to customer inquiries	• Units shipped/week • Fluctuation in daily output	• Lead time reduction project
Timeliness *How timely?*	• Scheduled maintenance projects completed on time	• Percent shipments received on time	• Order completion status at milestone	• **Orders completed on time**	• Project aimed at understanding causes of late orders
Workplace Environment *How safe and satisfying?*	• No. of work stoppages due to accidents				• ISO 14000 preparation
Financial Aspects *How much (in monetary terms)?*	• Monthly cost of supplies	• Dollars of raw material lost to obsolescence	• Dollars of waste in process per month	• Total manufacturing cost per unit leaving cell	• Activity Based Costing (ABC) implementation

Similarly, the percentage of defects found in incoming material is a quality indicator of material input. Quality aspects of the *transformation process* include conformance measures taken internally to the process. Thus, first-pass quality is a transformation quality measure.

Resource quality measures assess various aspects of productive and consumable resources. For example, labor skill ratings, tool breakages per shift, and equipment uptime belong here, as do various measures of manufacturing flexibility (although there are no easy ways to measure this, and most firms do not assess it directly). *Resource productivity* measures relate *material output* to *resource input*. These measures express how efficiently people and equipment contribute to the transformation process. A common productivity measure is number of standard labor hours of output divided by number of actual labor hours used.

2. Flow and inventory. These measures consider how much material or resource time the process uses as input, and how much material is leaving the process as output. Thus, average equipment utilization (a resource measure), units shipped per week (a material output measure), and labor hours spent on rework per week (another resource measure) are all examples of measures in the flow/inventory category. By the way, "rework" could also be used as an indicator of resource quality, but only if you know that resources are the root cause of the rework.

The time it takes for material to be processed is also a flow measure. At one company, measures focusing on time are averaged over 11 precision cells on a monthly basis. The reported performance data are shown in Table 9-8. The two turnaround time measures and the lead time measure are all flow measures focusing on transformation. Note, though, that the quote turnaround time is associated with a different process than the other measures since the "material" here consists of information only.

Table 9-8. Aggregate flow and timeliness measures for a system with 11 cells

Measure	Target	Actual	Comments
Total production lead time with work	20 days	58.7 days	Cells are overloaded
Prototype turnaround time	10 days	11 days	30 prototypes: 16 early, 8 late, 3 on time, 3 in process
Prototype due dates met	100% on time	73% on time	
Quote turnaround time	10 days	0	No quote requests this month

Finally, the flow/inventory category also includes measures that express inventory levels of materials and resources at the time of measurement. Inventories increase or decline with differences between the material input and output rates. Thus, WIP inventory is an example of a transformation flow/inventory measure.

Backlogged work (i.e., unfilled demand), whether measured in units or hours, is also a flow/inventory measure since it represents "negative inventory." Finally, the rate of absenteeism is a resource-based measure that tracks the flow of labor into this non-productive category.

3. Timeliness. These measures capture on-time performance (i.e., were the materials or resources available *when scheduled or requested?*).[27] The "prototype due dates met" measure in Table 9-8 is a timeliness metric for the output of a manufacturing process. Likewise, the percentage of customer calls answered within three minutes is a timeliness measure for an order entry process in an office cell. Another example of an input timeliness measure is the backorder-to-pull ratio measured for all fabrication cells at one plant. This ratio tracks the percentage of successful raw material pulls from the storeroom into the cell (e.g., if this ratio is 90 percent, then raw material was only available 90 percent of the times it was requested by the cells).

4. Workplace environment. This category includes safety-related measures such as incidences of accidents and injuries, and quality-of-work-related measures such as job satisfaction.

5. Financial aspects. Financial metrics assess the monetary aspects of resources or materials used in the process. However, it is not always clear to an observer whether a measure is financial or not. For example, is dollars of scrap per month a quality metric or a financial metric? If you express measures in monetary terms, you need to decide how to classify them based on the *intent of the measure*. One electronic firm combines dollars of wasted material with labor dollars spent on rework into a single measure that is compared monthly to a target.[28] The intent here is to assess manufacturing quality, not to measure financial performance. On the other hand, a cell system may, for the purpose of cost control, track a variable called "labor and overtime" in dollars. This metric, thus, is a financial aspect measure. Another example of a financial measure is cost of goods transferred out of the cell.

The financial aspects of cell operations are typically of greater interest at the cell-system level than at the individual cell level. In fact, the higher the organizational level, the more likely that the metrics will be expressed in dollars. Although financial information can serve as a warning signal of declining performance, it is not a useful guide to improvement. Other measures must be in place to understand what to do to turn financial performance around: "Everybody watches cost, but mercilessly attacking cost, rather than the drivers of cost, will not win the game."[29] In other words, you need to monitor quality, productivity, flow, inventory, and timeliness to understand why costs and revenues may be failing and what to do to improve them.

The Process Performance Measurement Matrix as a Diagnostic Tool

You may be familiar with the *balanced scorecard* concept.[30] This well-known framework for measurement suggests that an organization needs to assess performance from four different perspectives: (1) financial, (2) customer, (3) internal business processes, and (4) learning/growth. In that vein, the process perspective and the measure categories that we introduced above, and combined into the Process Performance Measurement Matrix (Table 9-7), form a similar balanced framework. The essential point is that you should design a broad-based cell measurement system to help employees and managers see the "big picture."

You can use the matrix to gain insight into your current performance-measurement system. The matrix also can help you create measures for a new cell. Either way, you begin by entering your existing or proposed measures into an empty matrix. By carefully analyzing the resulting matrix, you may find *measurement gaps*—aspects of performance that are not being monitored. These will show up as "white areas" in your matrix. Similarly, you might discover *measurement redundancies*—aspects of performance that are overmeasured. To form a complete picture of redundancies and gaps, you also should look at measures outside the cell, particularly measures used by your (internal and external) suppliers and customers. For example, your cell might not measure incoming material quality levels because your suppliers' thorough quality assurance practices make this unnecessary.

The Process Performance Measurement Matrix is a tool for critically analyzing your existing or planned measures. When combined with the measurement checklist in Appendix C, the matrix can prompt you to raise probing and important questions about your measurement system.

MEASURING THE PERFORMANCE OF CELLS AT TURNER PRODUCTS

Turner Products makes electrical equipment.[31] In 1989, as part of an overall plant modernization effort, the company began converting to cells. Currently, about 700 direct employees work in more than 40 different manufacturing cells. In total, the cells produce 350 different products, 1,250 product accessories, and over 14,000 service parts. Output in 1998 was in excess of two million products.

Early in the transition to cells, management recognized that appropriate performance measures would be a critical factor in the success of the new manufacturing organization. Effective measures would connect individual cells and workers to company strategy, and provide a mechanism for assessing improvement. Through linkages to the compensation system, the performance measurement system would motivate actions in the right direction and reward groups for their contributions to achieving company objectives. Consequently, management focused considerable attention and energy on performance measurement design. In 1993, Turner launched a major program that laid the foundation for the current system.

The company's overall strategy of expanding distribution and improving cost competitiveness drove its manufacturing strategy, which in turn drove the selection of cell measures. To support the enlarged distribution network, manufacturing needed to increase both order fill rates and inventory turns. To track progress towards these goals, individual cells would measure variables related to delivery. To support improved cost competitiveness, the manufacturing goals included aggressive cost reductions and a 10 percent minimum annual improvement in product quality. At the cell level this meant measuring product quality as well as progress toward cell-specific cost improvement targets.

Performance measures for each cell cover five key dimensions: safety and housekeeping, quality, cost, delivery, and progress toward various project goals (see Table 9-9). Some cells use inventory as a sixth category. With the exception of project goals, which tend to be cell-specific, each of the four core categories includes some standard measures that all cells track. Under safety and housekeeping, for example, all cells monitor recordable injuries, number of ergonomic ideas implemented, and completion of required safety audits. However, cells can include additional measures that target particular issues or problems. For example, some cells track tooling expenses as part of their cost measures, while others track overtime hours in the same category.

Table 9-9. Measures for a steel components cell at Turner Products

	Measure	Explanation	Six-Month Goal
Safety and Housekeeping	• Recordable injuries • Ergonomic ideas implemented and documented • Timely safety audits • Number of Group 1 violations	• Injuries that require more than first aid • Ideas that reduce the risk of workplace injury from cumulative trauma disorders • Audits of workplace housekeeping/safety practices • Safety/housekeeping problems identified in the audit deemed direct, blatant, or serious	• Zero injuries • 8 ideas • 1 audit per month • Zero Group 1 violations
Quality	• Weekly demerits • Demerit improvement percentage	• Customer cells give the supplier cell demerits for poor quality • (Average weekly demerits last 6-month period – average weekly demerits this 6-month period)/ Average weekly demerits last 6-month period	• 1.52 demerits per week • 5% improvement
Cost	• Scrap percentage • Cost improvements • Direct labor productivity • Perishable tooling expense • Absenteeism	• (Dollars of material scrapped/Dollars of material used)*100 • Reductions in product costs through improvements in material, labor or overhead expenses • Output/hours worked as % of standard • Percent of department budget spent on perishable tooling • Cell man-hours absent per month/cell man-hours worked per month	• 1.33% /month • $18,750 • 100% • 16.7% (5% improvement) • 2.24%
Inventory	• Cycle days	• Days between counts of in-area material (cycle days are the days between successive counts of the same item)	• Reduce from 49 to 47
Delivery	• Component availability • Service part availability	• Percent of shifts that end with components complete for the next 8 hours' assembly • Percent of service parts delivered to stockroom by due date	• 91.5% • 90%
Project	• ISO preparation	• Prepare log books of history (maintenance records, part production history) • Find, arrange store, audit, and calibrate all gauges	• Complete for 3 machines • 100% complete

Project goals are unique to each cell team, although in some cases they reflect overall company initiatives as well. Preparing for ISO-9000 certification is one such example. During the period preceding the initial certification and re-certification audits, virtually all cells' project goals included milestones related to ISO training or documentation.

Target values for the cell measures are developed annually and revised every six months. Each cell team proposes a set of measures (including the measures that all cells track) to a coordinating group made up of managers, supervisors, and key support personnel from engineering, maintenance, quality, and human resources. For each measure, the team proposes a target for the next six months. Team bonuses are based on the team's success in achieving these goals, so the targets are very important. The coordinating group reviews each cell's measures and targets, and either accepts them or negotiates with the cell team for a revision.

Once measures and targets are set, the team tracks its progress. A visual scoreboard at the entrance of each cell prominently displays a measurement sheet indicating the past six months' performance as well as the current goals (similar to Figure 9-4). Although these measures are formally only reported monthly, cell teams collect data in support of them on a weekly, daily, and sometimes hourly basis.

Every month the coordinating group reviews each cell's performance with respect to its goals. Every six months this same group also formally grades the teams. For each measure, the coordinating group determines if a team missed the goal (0 points), reached part of the goal (1 point), made the goal (2 points), exceeded the goal (3 points), or far exceeded the goal (4 points). Total points, coupled with overall company performance, determine team members' bonuses.

Analysis of Turner's Cell Measures

Table 9-9 shows the measures used by one Turner cell that supplies steel components to several assembly cells. Table 9-10 maps these cell measures onto the Process Performance Measurement Matrix that we introduced earlier. In completing that matrix, each metric's definition was considered. The transfer of the metrics from Table 9-9 to Table 9-10 reveals some inconsistencies in Turner's labeling. For example, scrap percentage is categorized by Turner as a cost measure but is not measured in dollars. It may be more appropriate to think of it as a quality indicator. Likewise, "cycle days" is categorized as an inventory measure, but the measure tracks an administrative activity (cycle counting) rather than inventory itself.

You can analyze the matrix in Table 9-10 vertically or horizontally, and with respect to what is versus what is not measured. Let's begin by looking at the column entries. A quick glance reveals that there are no measures assessing material input. The company's extensive supplier certification program and elaborate incoming inspection procedures explain why this cell does not measure incoming material quality. Rather, material that arrives to the cell has already been checked out fully. However, the absence of input measures focused on flow/inventory, timeliness, and costs has no immediate explanation.

In terms of pattern, the majority of measures assess timeliness, cost improvement, and quality performance. This focus is consistent with the company's overall strategy. According to one director of operations: "We are not the low-cost supplier. We distinguish ourselves in the marketplace through our delivery performance and our high

Table 9–10. The Process Performance Measurement Matrix for a Turner Cell

	Resources (productive and consumable resources)	Input (incoming material)	Transformation (material, internal focus)	Output (outgoing material)	Project Status
Quality and Productivity *How well and how productive?*	• Direct labor productivity		• Scrap percentage	• Weekly demerits • Demerit improvement (%)	• ISO, gauge quality • ISO, machine maintenance
Flow and Inventory *How much, what rate?*	• Absenteeism				• ISO, machine output
Timeliness *How timely?*	• Timely safety audits • Cycle days			• Component availability • Service part availability	
Workplace Environment *How safe and satisfying?*	• Recordable injuries • No. of Group 1 violations				• Ergonomic ideas
Financial Aspects *How much (in monetary terms)?*	• Perishable tooling expense (%)			• Cost improvements	

quality." Given this strategic intent, you would expect the cell-level measures to emphasize timely responses and customer quality. At the same time, the cell's emphasis on cost reduction explains why perishable tooling is a resource cost receiving special scrutiny. This too is consistent with the overall company objective of maintaining stable product costs by offsetting increases in inflation with internal cost reductions.

There is a strong emphasis on resource-oriented measures. These run the gamut from measures considering the workplace environment, like safety and housekeeping (note that the latter metrics are supplied by customer cells that perform workplace audits of supplier cells), to labor productivity and absenteeism, to checks on whether administrative routines (like inventory counts and safety audits) have been performed. The cell tracks the number of ideas aimed at bettering working conditions via ergonomic improvements (see the project status column in Table 9-10). Taken together, these metrics paint a picture of a cell concerned with a safe and clean work environment, but which still may have some problem with absent operators. Also note that the Turner cell does not monitor resource quality, such as the skill level of its workforce or the reliability of its equipment.

The material-transformation process is assessed using a single measure, scrap material. Notably missing are measures like inventory and throughput time. You may argue that it is not necessary to monitor manufacturing lead time if you measure due-date adherence, as is done here through the component and service part timeliness measures. However, the ability to meet due dates does not tell you anything about the length of the manufacturing cycle or a cell's ability to respond to schedule changes. Finally, Turner Products, like many other firms, is involved with seeking ISO 9000 registration. Accordingly, it has several ongoing projects aimed at satisfying those demands.

KEY INSIGHTS

"If the organization changes and the measurement system doesn't, the latter will be at best ineffective or, more likely, counterproductive."[32] During cell implementation you should reconsider and probably revise your performance measurement system. This is because cells often reflect new strategic initiatives and certainly a new type of organizational form. As we have emphasized, both call for a careful examination of existing performance measures. Those who will manage and/or work in the cell need to think through the measures they will need in order to understand, control, and improve cell operations. Without an appropriate measurement system in place implementation is incomplete, and the cell's contribution to achieving company goals may never be fully realized.

In this chapter we focused primarily on measurements at the cell level, although we also discussed linkages to measures both downwards and upwards in the organization (i.e., at the level of individual employees and at higher organizational levels such as a cell clusters, departments, or the organization as a whole). We emphasized the problems faced by all managers and self-managed teams: how do you generate performance metrics, and how do you know if they are effective?

Here are some special insights to keep in mind when setting up your performance measurement system:

- *Understand the structure of the performance-measurement system.* To create an effective measurement system, you need to develop one system that collects the data, one that converts the raw data to a set of measures, and a third that transform the measures into a format that decision-makers (who in many cases are cell operators) can use. In particular, consider the visual scoreboard for presentation purposes.

- *Make sure that the chosen measures drive behavior in the right direction and discourage behavior in the wrong direction.* The "right" behavior is one that leads to fulfillment of the company's overall goals. Conversely, "wrong" behavior will detract from meeting those goals. At lower levels, right behaviors help employees or teams do their work and meet the stated goals for their processes. *Be especially careful with measures that connect directly to the company's compensation system.* Monetary rewards are powerful incentives that may override other desirable behavior (see Chapter 14). In general, use the guidelines provided in this chapter (Tables 9-2 and 9-4), and the measurement checklist in Appendix C, to create, present, and assess performance measures.

- *Think "process."* A process perspective is very useful when you are faced with the question of what to measure. You cannot answer this question in a vacuum; the solution must be related to your work activities and the purpose behind those activities. You create *material-converting* and *information-converting* processes when you form cells. Make these core processes the foundation for the measurement system as well.

- *To control, understand, and improve cell processes fully, measure material or information at the supplier and customer side, as well as internally to the process. Also assess resource performance.* Some management experts and consultants advocate a customer focus, rejecting the notion of measures unrelated to customer expectations. We do not subscribe to this view. A focus on a single metric is always dangerous when a combination of materials and resources contributes to performance. Improved performance on one dimension can be accomplished at the expense of lowered performance on another dimension. Second, output depends on input—if you can't control incoming material, you can't control outgoing material either. Finally, in order to improve process performance you need to have primary and secondary measures in place. Primary measures typically are linked to strategic goals, while secondary measures help you understand why certain variables behave the way they do. For example, response time may be a key variable, but resource utilization can help explain why response time has increased or decreased. For these reasons we advocate the use of a full set of process measures.

- *Review performance measurement systems for consistency.* You should review the cell measurement systems at regular intervals (at least annually). Doing so will help ensure that they are (a) consistent with current strategic priorities, (b) consistent with the systems of other cells and departments, and with measurement systems at higher organizational levels, and (c) consistent with the measurement and reward systems used for individuals and teams inside the cells.

10

Cost Accounting and Cellular Manufacturing

In the previous chapter we stressed that a sound cell measurement system should be balanced to include both financial and non-financial measures. Financial measures tend to be aggregated and also reported later than operational performance measures. Thus, they are not very helpful in making day-to-day operational decisions or avoiding problems in real time. Neither do financial measures fully capture whether the firm is accomplishing its strategic goals.

That said, you cannot ignore the financial performance measurement system, i.e., *the accounting system*. In fact, in practically all firms, the accounting system is the only formal system that tracks performance and presents metrics at all levels in the organization. Because of its formality, prevalence, and strong roots, the accounting system plays an important role in organizations, and you have to pay attention to it.

This chapter focuses on the relationship between cells and *cost accounting*. As indicated in Chapters 4 through 6, cost accounting is part of the cell system infrastructure that should be reviewed for possible modification quite early in the planning process. Cost accounting systems have been criticized in recent years as being inadequate and not well suited to deal with the many changes that have taken place in manufacturing. Two changes, in particular, stand out: the increased use of automation, and the adoption of management philosophies like cells and lean manufacturing. The first change has removed direct labor from the manufacturing process. The second has expanded the role of direct labor in the work process, lowered inventories, and increased process speed. The use of automation is not related to cellular manufacturing specifically. It is the second transformation of the production process, and its impact on cost accounting, that we are interested in this chapter.

One of the most puzzling problems in manufacturing occurs when the cost accounting system and the non-financial performance measurement system (see Chapter 9) give contradictory signals:[1]

> ... a production manager who successfully implements a JIT work cell and witnesses dramatic improvements in quality, cycle time, and WIP inventory may nonetheless get blamed for poor financial performance because of large volume variances and underabsorbed overhead.

The lack of congruence between a plant's operational measures and the accounting system's performance measures is one of the issues we address in this chapter.

Broadly, we look at the following important questions related to cost accounting and cellular manufacturing:

- Does your cost accounting system support the adoption of cellular manufacturing?
- Can your cost accounting system motivate behavior that will support your cellular strategy of lead time and inventory reductions?
- How can you increase the accuracy of product cost data after a cell conversion?
- Is it possible to make cost accounting systems for cells more efficient? That is, if you have lean production, shouldn't you also have lean accounting?

We assume you are involved with the operations side of the company and are not an accountant. Our purpose is to alert you to issues linked to costs and cost-performance measures that may be raised by accountants and top management. Specifically, we want to equip you with a foundation in cost accounting so that you can participate in such discussions by asking the right questions and even forcefully push issues based on an operations perspective. Due to their dominance in industry, we concentrate in this chapter on standard costing systems.

If you already are well acquainted with terms like COGS, expensing, standard costing, two-stage overhead allocation, cost drivers, variances, and the like, continue reading. However, if you are unfamiliar with these terms, need to brush up on the definition of "earned standard dollars," or want to understand the difference between financial and cost accounting, you should first read Appendix D at the end of this book. This appendix contains vital background information for this chapter. Finally, economic evaluation of projects, cost accounting, performance measurement, and compensation systems are strongly related. Thus, besides this chapter, you may want to consult Chapters 8, 9, and 14 to get a complete perspective on these interrelated areas of cell management.

STANDARD COSTING SYSTEMS AND PROCESS IMPROVEMENT— ARE THEY COMPATIBLE?

A *costing system* is a system for determining the manufacturing unit cost of a product. A *standard costing system* is one where all cost rates and usage rates are predetermined and referred to as "standard rates" (for details, see Appendix D). Standard costing systems are frequently used in industry. In a study of 85 American manufacturing firms, 74 percent had this type of costing system.[2] Of these users, 73 percent allocated overhead using direct labor as a cost driver. Other studies indicate that 80 percent (or more) of firms use standard costing systems, and that 80 percent of those users base overhead allocation on labor. The use of standard costing systems in Europe and Japan appears to be slightly lower, ranging from 65 to 76 percent.[3]

As mentioned, standard costing systems have been criticized for being unsuited to "modern manufacturing environments." Table 10-1 lists some specific problems associated with these systems.[4] The first two problems, which involve the use of labor as a cost driver for overhead allocations, are discussed next. The last four problems, dealing with variance analysis, standards, and measurement focus, will then be addressed in the context of the experiences at two firms.

Table 10-1. Problems with standard costing systems

1. They often allocate overhead based on direct labor usage even if direct labor hours spent have little or nothing to do with the use of various resources.

2. Because labor hours are used as an allocation base (cost driver), great effort is devoted to the tracking of labor hour usage even though it represents only a very small portion of total manufacturing costs.

3. Variance analysis focuses on achieving standards, not on improvement (and may in fact prevent improvement activities that cause short-term unfavorable variances but promise long-term gains).

4. Variances often are too aggregated and reported too infrequently to be helpful to operations managers.

5. Reliable and credible standards are difficult to determine in situations with rapidly changing product mixes and short product life cycles.

6. The focus is on resource utilization, efficiency, and cost—at the expense of strategic measures that matter to the customers (quality, response time, etc.).

Allocating Manufacturing Cost Based on Direct Labor

In this section we look at the use of direct labor as a cost driver, beginning with a brief overview of how indirect costs are allocated.

Overhead cost allocation

To determine product cost, you need to identify the direct labor cost, the direct material cost, and the manufacturing overhead cost. Since you cannot trace manufacturing overhead directly and uniquely to products, as you can with material and labor costs, you must *allocate* it to products (this is why overhead cost also is referred to as *indirect cost*). Most costing problems are due to the difficulty of allocating overhead costs in an accurate, relevant way.

Costing systems use a *two-stage approach* to manufacturing overhead allocation. This means that accumulated overhead costs are first allocated to cost pools, and from these cost pools to products. These allocations can be done using either actual or budgeted overhead costs. The process is illustrated in Figure 10-1 and further explained below.[5]

Manufacturing overhead costs that are related to production over some period (e.g., a week, a month, a year) are collected in various accounts. These accounts include salaries for management and supervisors, equipment depreciation, supplies, plant utilities, insurance, and so on. Costs from these accounts are assigned to one or more manufacturing overhead *cost pools*.[6] Cost pools are classified as either *production departments* or *support departments*. Traditional production departments include assembly, machine shop, sheet metal, paint, packing, and the like. Manufacturing cells represent another type of "production department" to which costs can be assigned. A support department performs service activities for several production departments but is not directly responsible for manufacturing conversion.[7] Examples of support departments include manufacturing engineering, materials management, scheduling, and quality assurance.

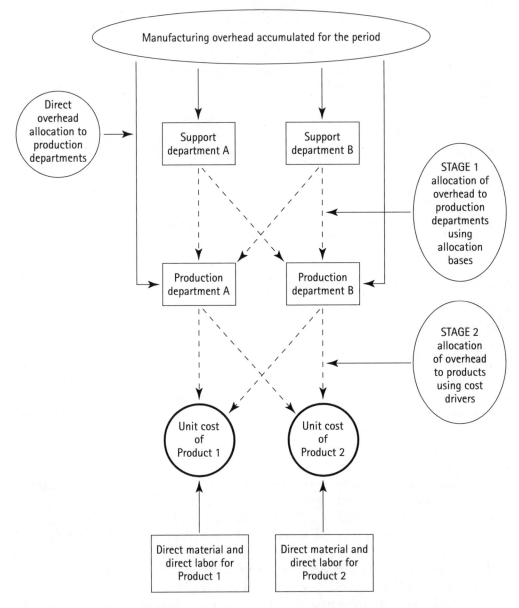

Figure 10-1. Two-stage cost allocations

Accumulated overhead costs per period that are traceable to production departments are assigned to these directly. However, costs incurred by support departments are distributed to the production departments they serve using allocation bases as weights (see Figure 10-1). Common *allocation bases* at Stage 1 include floor space, head count, percentage of total expenses or activities, and direct labor hours. For example, the annual cost for scheduling the plant—a support activity—could be allocated to the machine shop—a production department—based on the number of jobs processed in the machine shop per year relative to all jobs processed by all production departments in the plant in a year. Likewise, general and administrative costs for the factory could be allocated to production departments in proportion to the fraction of the floor space each one occupies.

At Stage 2, the production departments' overhead costs per period are allocated to individual products using *cost drivers*.[8] While companies use many different allocation bases at Stage 1, the dominant cost driver at Stage 2 has historically been, and still is, direct labor hours. Thus, budgeted (or actual) department costs for a period (often a year) are divided by the planned (or actual) number of labor hours to generate a manufacturing overhead cost per direct labor hour. For departments where labor has little influence on production rates or production cost, manufacturing overhead is sometimes allocated to products using *machine hours* or *materials dollars* as cost drivers.

The problem with labor as a single cost driver

Traditional standard costing systems use labor as a cost driver for manufacturing overhead allocation. This is a problem with two components. First, direct labor in many cases has little or nothing to do with the use of the resources included in the overhead charge. For example, plant insurance or the salaries for purchasing personnel have no immediate link to the use of labor hours but may still get allocated to products based on the products' labor content.

Second, direct labor cost as a portion of manufacturing cost (COGS) has been declining in all industries for many decades. The overhead rate—the ratio between manufacturing overhead cost and labor hours (or labor dollars) spent—has thereby increased to sometimes very high levels. For example, manufacturing overhead rates can be in the range of 300 to over 1,000 percent in extreme cases (i.e., for every labor dollar spent, 3 to 10 dollars in overhead is budgeted). Because of the important role direct labor plays in determining product costs, much effort is devoted to tracking labor. However, when you consider that labor only accounts for 5 to 10 percent of manufacturing cost, much of this effort may also be seen as wasteful. We will revisit this issue in a later section.

Companies have addressed the weak link between labor and manufacturing overhead usage in various ways. Some have found more relevant cost drivers. For example, the more industries automate, and labor serves an increasingly supporting rather than direct processing role, the more sense it makes for manufacturing cost to have a driver based on machine hours rather than labor hours. Likewise, in some cases the usage of materials may be a more relevant cost driver.[9] The most radical change is to adopt a system that differs in fundamental ways from the traditional accounting systems. Activity-based costing (ABC) is one such approach that has been suggested in recent years. (We will return to the issue of ABC systems and cells later.) An intermediate solution is to use several cost drivers simultaneously within the existing costing system, as described next.

A manufacturing overhead allocation scheme using multiple allocation bases and cost drivers

Figure 10-1 showed the basic principles behind an overhead allocation scheme. In Figure 10-2, we illustrate the costing system at a tool manufacturer that accumulates

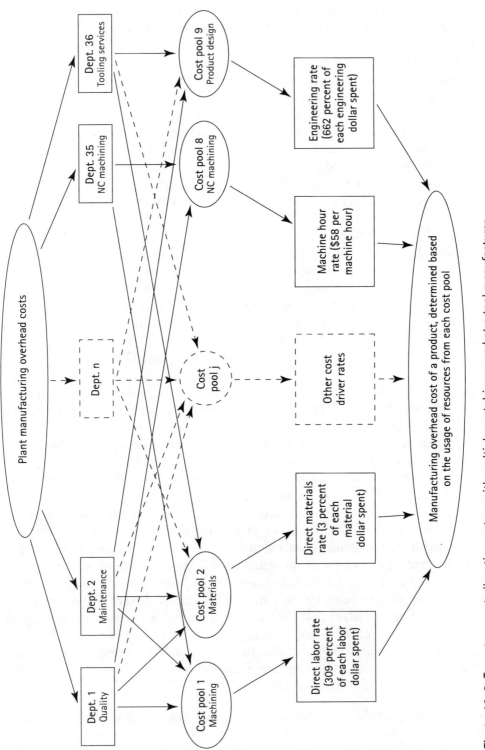

Figure 10-2. Two-stage cost allocation system with multiple cost drivers used at a tool manufacturer

overhead costs in 36 different production and support department accounts (including quality, maintenance, machining, NC programming, production administration, etc.). These 36 accounts are aggregated into nine cost pools so that each pool can have its own cost driver. The aggregation into cost pools is based on percentage figures negotiated between all department managers. For example, if the annual expenses for the quality department is $340,000, then cost pool 1 (machining) may be charged 16 percent of these expenses, cost pool 2 (materials) may be charged 13 percent, and so on until all costs are distributed across the nine cost pools. Some of the cost pools are assigned names that are identical to the 36 production and support departments (see, for example, department 35 and cost pool 8 in Figure 10-2).

This company uses a rather complex costing system in that the second-stage allocation of manufacturing overhead to products relies on *not just one but four* types of cost drivers:

1. Direct labor dollars.
2. Direct material dollars.
3. Machine hours.
4. Engineering labor dollars (engineering time is primarily charged to make-to-order products).

Costs are allocated to products directly from both production and support cost pools, and not only via production departments, as is typical (see Figure 10-1). Each of the nine cost pools is linked to a unique cost driver. For example, to allocate the engineering costs from the cost pool "product design" to products, an engineering labor rate of 662 percent is used. Thus, if the engineering time required by a customer order is charged at $50, then the engineering overhead cost allocated to the products is 50*6.62, or $331.00.

The Case of the Brice Plant

The last four problems with standard costing systems listed in Table 10-1 focus on standards, variance analysis, and performance measures. We approach these issues by recounting the experiences of two companies, Brice and Office Machines. We begin with the Brice plant.

An automotive supplier issued a corporate mandate that all plants needed to reduce throughput times to one week (equivalent to having annual WIP inventory turns of 52) and scrap dollars in manufacturing to 0.5 percent of cost of goods sold (COGS).[10] At the time the goals were introduced, inventory turns at the company's Brice plant averaged 10 per year and the scrap rate was at 4.5 percent. The plant employed a typical standard costing system, with manufacturing overhead allocated down to products using direct labor hours as a cost driver. Overhead's portion of COGS was 62 percent, while direct labor was 8 percent. Each department was measured on earned standard dollars per period, and cost variances were discussed in weekly meetings.

For a whole year there were no improvements in inventory turns or scrap. The corporate president then strongly reemphasized the goals to the various plant managers. After this decree, the Brice plant started to spend money on both direct and indirect labor. It hired employees to run equipment, move material, and inspect products. Management also authorized overtime and reduced batch sizes (which led to increased setup costs). During the five months following the spending increases, inventory turns went from 14 to 25. Dollars shipped remained fairly steady, while inventory fell by about 40 percent. In addition, the scrap rate was reduced to 1.9 percent.

During the same period, however, the monthly direct labor dollar variances (i.e., the difference between earned standard dollars and actually expended labor dollars) had turned unfavorable. The same was true for the variance measuring indirect spending for labor, supplies, maintenance, and so on. The corporate vice president of manufacturing and the corporate comptroller told the plant manager that these unfavorable variances would not be tolerated, especially since dollars shipped had not increased (and in fact had declined slightly). As a result, the plant manager cancelled all overtime, and ensured that the old lot sizes were reinstated and that orders were released early. These actions caused indirect spending to decline while the inventory and earned standard dollars increased. The outcome, therefore, was more favorable variances but fewer inventory turns (now down to 12 per year).

After a few months, corporate management again stressed the need to reduce inventories. And, again, plant management caused them to go down while at the same time creating unfavorable spending variances. And, as before, corporate management emphasized the need to control the variances. After almost two years, the inventory turns were back close to the starting point (12 turns) while the variances were hovering around zero.

Analysis of Brice

At Brice, the battle between signals from the costing system (in the form of variances) and operational measures (in the form of inventory turns and scrap as a percentage of COGS) is clearly visible.[11] You could argue that corporate management was wrong in that it put too much emphasis on cost variances relative to the two non-financial metrics. However, you also could argue that the inventory goals for this firm were being achieved in the wrong way—in fact, a costly way. That is, the Brice plant hired people, worked overtime, and reduced lot sizes without also reducing setup time. Thus, the inventory reduction was to a large extent based on an increase in capacity. There is no indication that Brice had a deliberate strategy for achieving long-term performance without additional resources. There was no adoption of a new philosophy, like cellular manufacturing, that would lead to sustained, long-term improvement. Although possibly unintentionally, corporate management may have acted correctly and responsibly to prevent spending that was not aimed at leading to permanent change.

The most important lesson from the Brice experience, however, is that if a company seeks to reduce inventory and lead times, management should not retain measures that seek to maximize output. As we discuss in Appendix D, a metric such as earned standard dollars can lead to favorable labor variances, but it contradicted Brice's new strategy. The company could have put in place more direct performance metrics. Specifically, since throughput time reduction was a goal, it would have been more transparent to employees and managers alike if lead time had been measured directly. In another company, a $30 million FMS was installed to machine engine blocks. Due to an emphasis on direct labor efficiency, the number of operators assigned to this system was kept constant even when product mix changed. The result was that, in order to keep labor utilization high, the system was periodically idle because of insufficient staffing to load and unload pallets. In general, any measure based on standards, like cost variances, should be viewed with great suspicion in periods of organizational change. Unless you update your standards to reflect "the new mode of operation," a comparison with previous performance standards is likely to be irrelevant.

The Case of Office Machines

Office Machines is a Swedish manufacturer of office equipment.[12] It used a traditional costing system with manufacturing overhead costs allocated to products based on direct labor hours. The main measure of performance in manufacturing was productivity, defined as actual labor hours spent divided by standard labor hours earned per period. The company had adopted a lean manufacturing philosophy, and changed its functional layout to one where manufacturing was organized around part and product families. Initially, three flow-lines were put in place as pilot cells. As part of this change, the company implemented cross-functional operators and let the cell teams take over indirect tasks such as production planning, material handling, purchasing, maintenance, and quality control.

While the company made major changes to the physical and organizational structures, they left the cost accounting system and its measures intact. Very soon after the implementation, management noticed a decline in productivity. The shifting of indirect tasks to the workers had caused the actual direct labor hours to increase. However, the labor standards—the standard hours per unit produced—had not been adjusted. Accordingly, the productivity ratio had increased, indicating lower efficiency. After a few months, the company increased the standard times per unit as a way to compensate for the enlarged task times. The productivity measure was retained, however. It had for a very long time been *the* measure of performance, and was familiar to both operators and managers throughout the company.

After about one year's experience of running the three flow-line cells, productivity had begun to show improvement, as had WIP inventory and quality. Based on these developments, the company board approved the continued adoption of family-organized production for the firm (13 more flow-line cells had been planned). A few months later the managing director observed that total production costs were down, operating margins were higher, on-time delivery was better, and quality had improved. However, mysteriously, productivity was now lower than before the change to cellular manufacturing.

The event that led to a review of the cost accounting system was the discovery of a 32,000-hour labor variance. Initially, management attributed these hours to the decline in productivity due to the cell project (even if the variance was for the production department as a whole). However, analysis showed that changes to the product mix and the introduction of new products, factors that had not been considered in the budget, were the likely causes of the overrun. Essentially, products requiring more labor had replaced products using less labor. However, the managing director was most concerned, and puzzled, about the actual production costs, which now were below budget. In short, while the measures based on standards—variances and productivity—showed declining performance, total costs and several non-financial measures showed improved performance. These conflicting results were disturbing and called the whole cost accounting system and its metrics into question.

An ensuing investigation identified the use of standards as one of the culprits, and found several instances of flawed standards. One suggestion was to replace the old productivity measure with one that, for each flow-line cell, simply related the number of products produced per period to the number of hours spent in that period. Another proposed change was removing the distinction between direct and indirect costs on the lines (except for materials cost). This would mean using a fixed conversion cost per cell. This suggestion was based on the difficulties of associating labor hours spent with specific products in cells where multi-functional operators perform both direct and indirect tasks for the whole cell family.

In the proposed system, the *conversion costs* (i.e., the sum of direct labor and manufacturing overhead) per period would be distributed equally over the products produced. Because the products are similar by definition (they belong to the same families), this would cause little distortion to the product costs. However, some people resisted these proposals because they felt that by abandoning the old productivity measure they would lose control over production.

Analysis of Office Machines

A major lesson learned from Office Machines' experience is that a shift in strategy also requires a shift in performance measures, a point we stressed in Chapter 9. Companies, understandably, want to retain old measures to keep a link to the past. This way they can detect the impact of an organizational change. But herein lies a problem—the change itself may invalidate some of the old measures.

Previous measures may not capture the new strategic intent. For example, measures like productivity or variances against standards do not tell you whether quality has improved or if you now deliver more rapidly. In this case, Office Machines started to pay attention to previously "unimportant" measures such as inventory, delivery, and quality. The positive developments in these measures, as *actual* costs declined, made the company question the use of standards and variance analysis.

Furthermore, if processes change, the way you measure work needs to change as well. (This is another key lesson from Chapter 9.) In the case of Office Machines, as in most firms that adopt cells, the shift of indirect work from support staff onto floor operators radically changed the process: old standards were no longer meaningful, and there was no continuity between old and new performance measures.

As you can see, traditional accounting systems do not automatically support the strategy upon which cellular manufacturing rests. But what can happen, as it did at Office Machines, is that the new strategy is questioned when old measures show no improvement. In fact, retaining old measures is a tactic that "change resisters" can use to justify the abandonment of a new strategy. To prevent reverting to the old ways, it is critical that you adjust the measures to capture the intent of the new strategy. This does not mean that you abandon the cost accounting system—you still must prepare budgets, track costs, and determine unit costs. However, as also illustrated by the Brice case, you may run into problems if the measures linked to the accounting system contradict the new strategy.

HOW TO MODIFY YOUR COSTING SYSTEM FOR CELLULAR MANUFACTURING

There are obvious weaknesses with standard cost accounting systems, as you saw from Table 10-1 and the analyses of Brice and Office Machines. If you are considering "going cellular," or have already done so, you must ask yourself whether these problems will occur in *your* cellular environment. If so, you may want to switch, or at least modify, your existing accounting system when you adopt cells.

Consider the basic system choices indicated in Table 10-2. We assume that you start in Quadrant 1. That is, you are operating a plant without cells, you use a traditional (standard) costing system, and you are considering implementing one or more cells. The question before you is whether adopting cells without also modifying the cost accounting system is a sound idea. This would mean moving from Quadrant 1 to Quadrant 2. Alternatively, you can consider changing the cost accounting system *before* you implement cells (i.e., move from Quadrant 1 to Quadrant 3), and then proceed to Quadrant 4.

Table 10-2. Aligning manufacturing and cost accounting systems

	Existing Manufacturing System (w/o cells)	After Cell Implementation
Existing Cost Accounting System	1	2
Modified/New Cost Accounting System	3	4

The issues of why and how to modify your cost accounting system take us back to the questions we raised at the beginning of this chapter:

- Issue 1: Does the cost accounting system support the adoption of cellular manufacturing?
- Issue 2: Does the cost accounting system motivate the right employee behavior?
- Issue 3: How can you increase the accuracy of the product cost data?
- Issue 4: How can you remove waste from the cost accounting system and its administration?

We address each of these in turn.

Issue 1: Does the Cost Accounting System Support the Adoption of Cellular Manufacturing?

In Chapter 8 we discussed the economic justification of an investment in cellular manufacturing. An important issue that links economic justifications and accounting systems is whether, in retrospect, you can compare before/after production costs to see if cellular manufacturing actually leads to lower unit costs.[13] In other words, is it possible to compare unit costs from Quadrant 1 in Table 10-2 with those from Quadrants 2 or 4 in a meaningful way?

Before and after unit costs

If you choose to not adjust the accounting system (i.e., you move from Quadrant 1 to Quadrant 2 in Table 10-2), you will operate with a system that is not well suited to capture the cost of producing in the cellular system. Most likely your costing system will overstate the "true" manufacturing cost for the cells because labor time will increase as operators take on more tasks in the cell, both direct and indirect, than what they previously performed (see the discussion in Appendix A). Office Machines discovered this problem after the conversion to cells, and it led them to temporarily increase the standard time used for their productivity calculations. However, as we discuss later, you also need to adjust the overhead rate in order to get a more accurate cost picture for the cell.

A more "fair" comparison, then, is between costs in Quadrants 1 and 4. This comparison, however, may suffer from the problem that the products before the change (i.e., while in Quadrant 1) may have used a costing approach that was not well suited for that production system. In other words, the original unit costs may not be as accurate as they could be.[14] However, since you are unlikely to change the costing system before the cell conversion in order to increase the accuracy of the current product costs (i.e., move to Quadrant 3 before you move to Quadrant 4), the next best before/after comparison involves using a costing system that is modified to suit the cellular system you have implemented.[15] We discuss such modifications under Issue 3 below.

The role of volume and product mix variations

Differences between standard and actual unit costs depend on differences in material, labor, and manufacturing overhead costs (see Appendix D). Of these three cost elements, the overhead category is most directly influenced by changes in production volumes and mix.

The common approach is to divide fixed overhead for a period by a "budgeted" (or "expected") production volume. If the actual production volume for the period differs from the budgeted volume, an actual unit cost can be determined by distributing the overhead cost over the volume actually used (e.g., if volume goes down, actual overhead cost per unit goes up compared to the budgeted overhead cost). If the company monitors actual unit costs, these can thus vary due to circumstances beyond the manufacturing function's control. For example, a decline in the overall market, or shifts in demand among products, will affect period unit costs. This not only makes manufacturing look bad but may also influence product pricing. In the latter case, customers suffer from management's inability to link capacity to demand. Another disadvantage with the use of budgeted capacity for overhead rate determination is that there is no clear mechanism for tracking the cost of unused capacity with this system.

One way to deal with these problems is to determine manufacturing overhead costs based on "normal" or "practical" capacity rather than on budgeted capacity.

This means that a capacity level is established for a production area, like a cell, by considering the activity level that normally can be accomplished given the available resources for the period. Thus, this approach takes a supply-oriented rather than a demand-oriented perspective on capacity. Since available capacity tends to be larger than used capacity, the unit cost according to practical capacity is lower then the cost determined by budgeted capacity. Any unused (i.e., unabsorbed) capacity costs are not assigned to products but instead tracked in a capacity variance account. For example, if you (a) estimate that normal capacity is 40,000 machining hours, (b) the overhead rate based on that usage level is $75 per hour, and (c) the actually used capacity for a period is 32,000 hours, the cost of unused capacity is (40,000–32,000)*75, or $600,000. By monitoring unused capacity variances, management can determine whether idle capacity is increasing or decreasing and act accordingly.[16]

The notion of practical/normal capacity has emerged as part of the activity-based costing (ABC) approach. However, U.S. tax authorities do not allow this method to be used for inventory evaluation purposes.[17] Instead, the denominator in the overhead calculations should be based on the budgeted volume for the next period. Furthermore, differences between budgeted and actual overhead costs, as tracked by overhead variances, are allocated to cost of goods sold or distributed between COGS and unsold inventory. Because of the problem of having two sets of unit cost calculations, there are probably few firms that take advantage of the very useful "practical capacity" idea. Again, financial accounting restrictions drive the internal costing system.

Volume and mix variations affect actual versus budgeted costs. Thus, be aware that if you face volume and mix changes after cells have been implemented, unfavorable cost variances may be caused by these factors rather than by the cell implementation itself. Regardless of the reasons, the cells themselves may unjustifiably be seen as the culprit. The volume/mix problems are general to all standard costing systems and independent of whether you operate cells or not. Luckily, they also are the easiest problems to detect and correct.

Inventory holding costs

The cost of holding inventory includes items such as storage facilities, insurance, material handling, product obsolescence, breakage costs, and so on. Also included, and sometimes the largest portion of it, may be the *opportunity cost* of carrying inventory. This is the income you could have earned had you invested the value of the reduced inventory elsewhere. While the other components of holding costs are recorded in various accounts and ultimately included in the manufacturing overhead cost, opportunity cost is not a cash outlay. It is, therefore, not a part of manufacturing cost. *This means that the full benefit of lowering inventory does not get reflected in the cost of the product.* This is another reason why comparing before and after unit costs does not give you the complete benefit picture for cells.

In summary, cost comparisons are always problematic in the face of organizational change. If you have to compare costs before and after cells, make sure that the costing system in both cases determines costs in a reasonably accurate way. A particular problem can emerge in such comparisons if production volumes and mixes are not kept constant. Another problem is that costing systems do not include opportunity costs for holding inventory or keeping space. Accounting data therefore will understate the benefits of reducing inventory by converting to cells.

Issue 2: Does the Cost Accounting System Motivate the Right Employee Behavior?

As we suggested in Chapter 9, one of the most important guidelines for designing performance measures is to verify whether they impact behavior in the "right" direction, and discourage behavior in the "wrong" direction. In a cellular system, any behavior that drives inventory, lead time, and defects and mistakes down is the right behavior, while the opposite is the wrong behavior.[18] That is, the right behavior helps your organization reach its goals.

A standard costing system doesn't always cause the desired behavior. At the Brice plant we saw that a measure like earned standard dollars led managers to produce as much as possible without considering the resulting inventory build-up. We also saw that direct and indirect cost variances turned unfavorable, even in the face of improved inventory turns.

In general, we would argue that all measures that encourage inventory build-up, and therefore increase lead time, should be used with the greatest care. Such measures, including earned standard hours, equipment/labor utilization, and efficiencies, should never be the prime metrics driving decisions or employee rewards. However, you can use these measures to help explain system dynamics. Utilization, for example, is closely linked to lead time (see Chapter 7). Measuring utilization gives you an idea of bottleneck locations and helps you understand why lead times are increasing or decreasing over time.

Financial vs. non-financial measures

Cost variances are not helpful to managers or cell employees in their quest to deliver quickly and on-time.[19] In general, and especially with cells, the focus on financial performance measures should diminish in favor of operational measures that better reflect the strategy of the firm. We saw at both Office Machines and Brice that the operational measures reflected the improvements made, while the cost-related measures and variances went the opposite directions. One reason for this is that the measures linked to the accounting system often cannot keep pace with operational changes. For example, labor standards do not get updated, or the manufacturing overhead costs per unit or hour do not reflect the correct resource usage. This deficiency suggests that the reporting of financial data should be less frequent.[20] They should serve as checkpoints rather than as measures that you must monitor and react to every week or month.

In the previous chapter, we also advocated the use of both financial and non-financial measures. One reason is that this allows you to measure the accomplishment of non-financial strategic goals. Non-financial, or operational, measures represent the basis for all cost measures and precede these in time (e.g., you can get immediate feedback on scrap in a cell, while a cost of scrap measure typically is reported less often). Accordingly, non-financial metrics must serve as the real focus of control and improvement activities.

In short, operational measures are more complete and timely than are cost-based measures, and will therefore more accurately reflect changing manufacturing performance (our italics):[21]

> Many of the savings in reduced working capital, factory storage, and materials handling from reducing WIP will eventually be reflected in lower total manufacturing costs. But many of the savings that arise from transactions *not* taken—less borrowing to finance inventory, for example, or less need to expand factory floor space—will not be reflected in these costs. *Therefore, such direct measures as average batch sizes, WIP, and inventory of purchased items will provide much more accurate and timely information on a company's manufacturing performance than will the behavior of average manufacturing costs.*

Complementing this view is the fact that an increased use of non-financial measures is associated with higher organizational performance in both JIT and non-JIT firms.[22]

Using the costing system to motivate behavior

All performance measures affect behavior. An interesting issue, then, is whether you deliberately should use a measure that you believe will drive behavior in the right direction—even if that measure may not be accurate. *Target costing* involves determining standard costs based on what a product *should* cost in order to be salable (after a reasonable mark-up). Unfavorable variances, therefore, imply that you have not met the target costs. The main purpose of target costing—a concept frequently used in Japan—is to encourage product and process innovations that can reduce resource usage.

Another way to motivate behavior through the costing system is to allocate overhead costs based on an activity you want to reduce. This approach has also been used in Japan, and has been reported for some well-known U.S. firms as well.[23] For example, at Tektronix Portable Instruments Division, 50 percent of the manufacturing overhead cost was allocated to products using "number of part numbers" as a driver. In other words, the more parts a product contains, the higher its allocated overhead cost. The intention was to make design engineers reduce the number of parts and focus their attention on simplifying the design of new products.

Since the prime goal for cells is to reduce lead time and inventory, allocating overhead costs based on lead time would be a way to stimulate time (and inventory) reduction. In fact, companies like Tektronix and Zytec have considered or adopted systems that use time as a cost driver. The argument for using time as basis for cost allocation is that charging products for the time they spend in the cell is more intuitive and relevant than charging overhead based on the labor time expended.[24] If a product can go rapidly through a facility, it will by necessity use fewer resources—less energy, less effort by support personnel, less space (due to less WIP), and so on. Although the link between overhead costs and lead time is not always clear, and the precision may be lower than if you use a multiple cost driver system, the use of lead time as a single driver highlights it as the variable you want to drive down. It also fosters congruence between the non-financial measures, like inventory and lead time, and the financial measure, product cost.

However, there are clear practical difficulties with this approach. For example, you would have to estimate a "normal" lead time (L_j) for each product going through a cell, based on a "normal" schedule and "normal" resource levels. Based on all these lead times, you can determine the total sum of lead times for the cell products (i.e., $L_{TOT} = L_1 + L_2 + \ldots + L_n$). The allocated cost for a single product j would be the manufacturing overhead cost for the cell multiplied by the fraction of the product's lead time relative to the sum of all product lead times (i.e., L_j/L_{TOT}). Lead times, of course, are very much dependent on the volume of parts being processed relative to available capacity. Therefore, this method is susceptible to the volume and mix problems we mentioned earlier.[25] Further, to use it, you must make sure that lead times for linked production units in the facility are defined so that intermediate inventories are not left out of the lead time measures. You also should ensure that the cells' lead times are not dependent on previous production units, for example, in terms of part deliveries or part quality.

A simpler alternative approach to measuring lead time for the purpose of overhead allocation is to rely only on the processing times (setup and run times) at the bottleneck in the cell. The rationale for this approach is that it is the bottleneck operation that determines cell lead times (see Chapter 7). For a flow-line cell with three stations, and with processing times for a product being 15, 20, and 17 minutes respectively, the *minimum* lead time is 3*20, or 60 minutes. You can use these minimum lead times, rather than the actually measured lead times (which include waiting times), to allocate overhead costs to products.[26]

Although these ideas are intuitively appealing, there are few industry applications and little evidence to demonstrate how well they work. Also, when should you use a cost system that you know or suspect may produce less accurate costs than what you can determine by other costing systems? Only in cases where you have already determined your strategy, like lead time reduction, and want to implement it.[27] However, if you are still trying to understand your cost situation, and do not yet know what the best strategy is, then an accurate picture of your costs would certainly be desirable.

Determining appropriate usage costs for equipment

A PCB testing facility used three types of insertion technologies: manual, automatic dual inline package (DIP), and surface mount.[28] The cost to use each process was set to $30.00, $133.59, and $362.43 per labor hour, respectively. The surface mount technology was quite recent, and only a few items had been designed to take advantage of it. As a result, the predicted volume for surface mount was low, with the result that the cost per hour was high. A "death spiral" then set in where the engineers saw the high cost per hour and avoided the new technology in favor of older, low-cost, inefficient, and overloaded technology.

The ideal solution to this problem is to determine a normal or "practical" activity level for the new equipment, based on what can be accomplished with the given capacity, and then determine the cost per hour (see our earlier discussion of "practical capacity"). This will lower the overhead rate and stimulate an increased usage. The level of unused capacity, of course, needs to be tracked.

In summary, four points are important when it comes to cost systems and behavior:

1. Don't use performance measures that contradict the firm's strategy.

2. Always use both financial and operational measures.

3. It is possible to select a cost allocation base to motivate simultaneous reductions in both costs and the cost driver. This idea, although intuitively appealing, requires more industry experience before it can be recommended.

4. Finally, be aware that the determination of overhead costs depends directly on estimated production volumes. An inappropriate use of overhead cost can prevent new technology from effectively being used inside and outside cells.

Issue 3: How Can You Increase the Accuracy of Product Cost Data?

The major criticism against standard costing systems has been their reliance on direct labor as a basis for overhead cost allocation. The main argument is that there is little or no relationship between an additional hour of direct labor and the use of resources like equipment, support personnel, space, and supplies. In response to this criticism, some companies have changed cost drivers to use machine hours or materials dollars, or are relying on more than one cost driver (as we illustrated in Figure 10-2).

If your firm has adopted, or is thinking of adopting cellular manufacturing, the question of cost driver relevance certainly applies. More broadly, you should ask whether your current costing system will provide a fair and accurate picture of the lowered resource usage that you expect will occur with the reorganization to cells (again, see Table 10-2). There are several ways you can change the costing system to achieve this:

- Modify the labor standards.
- Modify the burden rate.
- Change allocation bases/cost drivers.
- Adopt an activity-based costing system.
- Increase direct allocations.

Modify the labor standards

In cells with fewer operators than machines, previous standards from a "one man, one machine" situation may no longer be valid. If cell workers take on indirect tasks, such as maintenance, scheduling, and so on, the old labor standards used for costing become irrelevant. As we saw at Office Machines, one way to adjust the costing system is to increase the standard time per piece to reflect this change. Since the labor (dL) and manufacturing overhead (MOH) portion of the standard cost per part is "Std dL cost/hr*Std dL hrs/part + Std MOH cost/hr*Std dL hrs/part," the effect of increasing the standard labor time per part is that the cost per part increases (see Appendix D). Although this change may reduce or eliminate unfavorable labor variances, it does not truly reflect the new work processes. Specifically, if cell workers now perform indirect tasks, that means somebody else is not doing them. This needs to be reflected in the overhead allocation. *Therefore, you need to modify both the labor standard and the manufacturing overhead rate* (see below for a discussion of overhead rates).

There are always problems with setting standards, and in cellular environments additional complications creep in. When an operator responsible for several workstations in a cell moves freely between them to process different parts from a family, determining a standard rate per piece that reflects the total use of labor is difficult to do using direct observation. A related complication is that the operator also may be engaged in assisting other operators in the cell and performing indirect tasks such as scheduling or problem solving.[29] In addition, cells are collections of people and groups of workstations. In a functional manufacturing environment, one operator runs a group of one or more identical machines. In a cell, however, there are several pieces of different equipment—usually only one of each kind. The output rate from the cell is determined by both the staffing level and the bottleneck machine. If the cell is constrained by the machine, then you probably should use machine time as an allocation basis. If the cell is constrained by labor and you vary the number of operators in the cell according to capacity needs (see Chapter 11), the cell's output rate will vary as well. In such cases you may want to develop one labor standard time per unit for each staffing level. Alternatively, you can determine a standard labor usage rate based on a long-term average staffing mix over time. All three factors—movable operators engaging in indirect tasks, bottleneck resources, and a varying number of operators—suggest that the way you determine standard time per piece must change when cells are adopted.[30]

Modify the burden rate

Modifying the manufacturing overhead cost per hour is probably the most common change to the costing system because it is one of the easiest to undertake. The argument for this change is that cells do not use as many resources as other departments. For example, you may expect that material handling, maintenance, quality assurance, production planning and control, supervision, and other types of support personnel will be reduced with cells. The magnitude of this reduction comes as a surprise to some managers, as evidenced by this reaction by Mike Vrcelj, Head of Manufacturing Engineering at Raychem's Interconnection System's Division:[31]

> I had read about how the JIT system required many fewer overhead workers than traditional batch operations, but I never internalized the magnitude of the differences until we started the detailed planning—how material would be handled, how production would get scheduled, where and how information needed to flow, and so on. [...] in the batch system there are a *lot* of people working on information problems—figuring out and communicating where each batch of parts should go next; where orders had gotten held up in the process; where bottlenecks were cropping up; and so on. In the cell system, all this information is embedded in the process flow itself—so much of the information flow problem is permanently solved. There literally was *no need* for a lot of those people who had seemed so indispensable just a few months earlier.

A reduction in the manufacturing overhead cost, of course, depends on the elimination of tasks, or the transfer of the tasks from indirect personnel to cell employees. The latter transfer, as we have just pointed out, will lead to increased labor time per unit. Therefore, when you move to cells you must recalculate the manufacturing overhead cost per part (i.e., Std MOH cost/hr*Std dL hrs/part). Changing the MOH rate for the cell requires that you reset the rates for other departments in the plant as well, since you will be shifting costs away from the cell and to other areas. This change may affect the whole factory.

What are the implications if overhead rates are not modified? It means that you move from Quadrant 1 to Quadrant 2 in Table 10-2 and, therefore, determine manufacturing costs using data that do not accurately reflect the new reality. The likely result is that *actual* direct labor costs will increase and efficiency variances will become unfavorable. In that light, those who monitor cost performance may view cellular manufacturing as a poor strategy for the firm.

Change allocation bases and cost drivers

In response to the deficiencies of using direct labor as a way to allocate manufacturing overhead to products, you could adopt an expanded set of allocation bases and drivers (as shown in Figure 10-2). This solution will generate costs with greater "accuracy" for cell and non-cell products alike. However, it is a rather major modification to the costing system and one that is not likely to be adopted just because cells are being implemented. On the other hand, if you are thinking of expanding the number of cost drivers you might also consider adopting a whole new cost system. This is discussed next.

Adopt an activity-based costing system

Activity-based costing (ABC) was devised as a way to develop more precise product cost estimates than those available from a costing system using a single driver. Thus, while the direct labor and direct material components of product cost are the same, ABC relies on multiple cost drivers to assign indirect costs (i.e., manufacturing overhead) to the products. The basic idea is two-fold. Resources are consumed, and thus overhead costs are incurred when activities are performed. This means you should identify the major activities that "create overhead cost." Second, you should allocate manufacturing overhead costs to products based on the rate at which they consume various resources. This means each identified activity should have its own cost driver and cost driver rate. ABC systems typically categorize activities into four groups:

1. *Unit-related activities.* These are activities whose levels or volumes are directly proportional to the number of units produced or to measures that themselves are proportional to units produced.

2. *Batch-related activities.* These activities consume resources every time a production batch is issued and processed.

3. *Product-sustaining activities.* These activities support the production of specific products. These activities cannot be linked to units produced or to batches issued.

4. *Facility-sustaining activities*. These activities support the plant and its administration at large.

Table 10-3 shows examples of the four types of activities and related cost drivers.[32] Note that the difference between an ABC system and more traditional costing systems is not just that ABC has multiple cost drivers. More importantly, ABC relies on cost drivers that are not merely unit-related (i.e., based on a driver, like labor hours, that is proportional to production volume) but also linked to more intermittent activities—like batches released or products launched.

Table 10-3. Activities and cost drivers

Activity Type	Representative Activities	Representative Cost Drivers
Unit-related	• Every item inspection • Supervision of direct labor • Consumption of power and oil to run machines	• Number of units • Direct labor hours • Machine hours
Batch-related	• Machine setup • First item inspection • Purchase ordering • Material handling • Production scheduling	• Setup hours • Inspection hours • Number of orders • Number of material moves • Number of production runs
Product-sustaining	• Product design • Parts administration • Engineering • Expediting production orders	• Number of products • Number of parts • Number of ECOs
Facility-sustaining	• Plant management • Accounting and personnel • Housekeeping, lighting • Rent, depreciation	• Square feet of space • Number of workers

To adopt an ABC system you must identify a set of activities and then link each activity to a cost pool that accumulates indirect costs. For example, you may have cost pools for materials handling, quality inspection, setup, scheduling, and so on. Each activity cost pool has a cost driver and a cost driver rate used to assign cost down to the product level. For example, for the batch-related activity "setup," you may choose the cost driver "number of setup hours," and the cost driver rate may be $36 per setup hour. If the setup time for a batch is 15 minutes, products in a batch are assigned a setup cost of 36*(15/60), or $9 per issued batch.

In general, the cost per unit of activity is found as the budgeted cost of the activity per period divided by the available activity volume per period. It could also be directly found as a cost per hour. For example, the cost driver rate "setup cost per hour" could simply be the labor cost per hour. To avoid variations in cost due to volume swings, ABC systems rely on the practical capacity of each activity to determine cost driver rates (see our earlier discussion on this topic). Practical capacity is the activity level, such as number of setups or number of orders processed, that a firm is capable of handling in a period. This is distinct from the actually used capacity that in traditional cost systems determines actual overhead and product unit costs.

With an ABC system there could be a large number of activities and drivers. In a study of 166 firms using such systems, 53 percent of the firms relied on more than 100 activities. Of the same firms, 66 percent used more than 10 cost drivers (the same type of driver, although with a different rate, may be used for different activities).[33] Clearly, ABC is much more detailed than the traditional costing system, which uses a rather small number of cost pools and often a single driver.

Activity-based costing (ABC) and cells. Is activity-based costing worthwhile in a cellular manufacturing system setting? The argument in favor of ABC is that it leads to more precise unit costs, and that the identification of an enlarged set of cost drivers helps put the spotlight on activities that drive cost. Thinking about those activities, the argument goes, should help you improve your work processes by reducing or eliminating the activities. Let's say you have identified "setup" as a batch-related activity that causes costs, and you select "setup hours" as a cost driver. Thus, the total activity cost per period for setup is:

$$\text{Setup cost/period} = (\text{no. of batches per period})*(\text{setup time per batch})*(\text{cost per setup hour})$$

You can reduce setup cost by reducing any of the three elements on the right-hand side in the cost equation. However, if you reduce the number of batches by increasing the lot sizes, you will increase inventory. This means you are acting against the lean manufacturing strategy that caused you to adopt cells to begin with. This simple example shows that ABC does not necessarily lead to desirable improvements.[34]

Increasing the number of drivers, however, is likely to lead to a more accurate costing system. The example we showed in Figure 10-2, by the way, is a traditional cost system that has adopted a few more drivers—beyond labor hours—without becoming a full-blown ABC system. This goes to show that there are many ways to modify a costing system. *We are not convinced that ABC is the right thing for cells.* Implementing and operating such systems can be a complex undertaking.[35] Since cell products are similar to each other, and the amount of overhead allocated to them may be small (due to direct allocations—see below), it is doubtful that an ABC system can significantly increase the precision in product cost estimates compared to those generated by a *modified* standard cost system. By this we mean a system with corrected labor standards and overhead rates and where a large portion of overhead costs are allocated directly.

Increase direct cost allocations

Costing systems allocate overhead cost in two stages, as shown in Figure 10-1. Since "errors" or "inaccuracies" in product cost determinations largely depend on the allocation of the indirect costs, you can minimize such errors if you can avoid Stage 1 cost allocations. It is natural to let each cell be a "production department" or "cost pool" to which indirect costs (i.e., everything beyond labor and materials) can be allocated at the first stage rather than first going through a support department. *In essence, indirect resources can be dedicated to the cell rather than being shared with other production departments.* In the second stage, costs are then allocated from the "cell cost pools" to the products using cost drivers.

If the cell is organized as a fairly independent, self-managed cost center, you can assign both direct and indirect personnel to the cell on a permanent basis. In effect, the cell becomes a mini-factory. At the Raychem plant cited earlier, one quality control inspector, one maintenance person, and one manufacturing engineer became members of each cell team. In doing so, costs normally considered manufacturing "overhead" became directly allocated to the cell. By using such direct cost allocations you reduce the portion of the plant's overhead costs that need to be distributed using cost allocation bases. Consequently, you get a better grip on the true resource usage for the cell. Furthermore, by assigning the cost—and therefore the responsibility for the cost—directly to the cell, there will be greater incentive for the cell manager and supervisor to reduce this cost than if it is simply allocated from a larger cost pool.

Of course, you still have the problem of allocating cell overhead costs down to the products to determine unit costs. However, because cells produce families with high internal similarity among products, this last-stage allocation will create less distortion in product cost than in a functional organization where a wide variety of products are manufactured.

Direct cost allocations may have a downside. For example, if you buy a new machine for a cell, the cell products must bear the total cost for this equipment. This may cause unit costs to escalate. The alternative, making the machine a part of a larger cost pool to which many cells and departments belong, could in fact reduce the equipment cost charged to the cell products. Similarly, if support labor is dedicated to the cell, you expect a high degree of involvement and improvement as a result. However, if the indirect employees are not adequately utilized, they become a burden on the cell and can increase product cost. Thus, unit cost accuracy may come at a price.[36]

Issue 4: How Can Cells Remove Waste from the Cost System Itself?

The use of cells falls squarely in the "eliminate waste" paradigm of manufacturing. It makes sense to look at the cost accounting system from the same perspective. That is, can you simplify the costing system so that the effort in determining costs is reduced? Also, since accounting systems focus on control, and control can impede the manufacturing process, are there ways you can change the cost accounting system to better fit a rapid process? *In short, if you have lean manufacturing, why shouldn't you also have lean accounting?*

It has been argued there are four types of waste associated with the cost accounting function: (1) tracking direct labor for the purpose of overhead allocation, (2) tracking machine utilization as a measure of performance, (3) tracking WIP inventory for the purpose of full absorption costing, and (4) variance reporting to gauge performance.[37] We discussed variance reporting earlier and concluded that it is of little help to cell management. Some argue that tracking machine utilization is a waste since it is a measure that contradicts JIT manufacturing. That is, if you increase utilization, inventory and lead time will increase as well. Although this is correct, we see a need to measure both machine and labor utilization. This need is due precisely to the important role utilization plays in determining cell performance. For the remainder of this section, we concentrate on wastes in the form of labor and WIP tracking.

Tracking direct labor

The most clearly identifiable form of waste in an accounting system is the transaction. A transaction is the entry of a piece of data into a data collection system (see Figure 9-1). Tracking is particularly time-consuming when it comes to direct labor. Harley-Davidson found out long ago that while direct labor accounted for only 10 percent, and overhead for 36 percent of manufacturing cost, the company spent 62 percent of their "administrative effort" focusing on direct labor but only 13 percent on overhead.[38]

The detailed tracking of direct labor in manufacturing requires that transactions be submitted every time a worker starts or completes a particular task. Often, this involves operators recording the time data, supervisors reviewing it, clerks entering the data in computer systems (unless this is done automatically via barcodes or floor terminals), and accountants reviewing the costs. The data recorded are also used to construct variance analysis reports that then occupy financial executives' time.

The prime reasons why you need to collect detailed data on direct labor are: (1) to determine a product's manufacturing cost—both directly through the labor cost and indirectly by using labor as a cost driver for overhead allocation, and (2) to use the data for compensation purposes. It is evident that the value of such labor data declines the less labor you use in the manufacturing process, the less relevant labor is as a cost driver, the less the compensation system relies on individual efficiencies in the process, and the more similar the products are from a manufacturing perspective. In particular, if there are great similarities among the products, you don't need to determine how much time an operator spends on one versus another. *This suggests that in many cells there is little need to track labor.*

To bolster this argument, you may recognize that there are clear difficulties with monitoring labor in cells. It may simply not be possible (or at least not practical) to record the time an operator spends on a particular batch since he or she switches between different batches and between direct and indirect tasks throughout the day.

But what happens if you abolish the tracking of direct labor usage? The operators, of course, do not have to worry about recording their time, so they can be more productive. But what is impact on the costing system? An immediate effect is that you can no longer determine the actual labor time per job in a detailed way. But this also means that determining labor standards for products in the cells will be difficult. How, then, can you determine unit costs for inventory valuation and other purposes? This issue requires a discussion of various types of costing approaches.

Job, process, and operation costing. You may be familiar with the difference between *job order costing* and *process costing*. In the former system, labor/machine and material usage is tracked and linked to each individual work order issued to the shop. Job order costing, therefore, is most suitable for shops where there is great variety in the types of jobs processed and the routings they follow through the plant. In process costing systems, on the other hand, job work orders are not used and resource usage is not linked to individual products (process costing has its origins in pure process manufacturing systems, like chemical plants or oil refineries, where there are no discrete products.) Instead, material and labor/machine usage is recorded for each stage in the manufacturing process. The cost per period is then allocated to the product quantity manufactured in the period.

When production includes discrete but similar products, *operation costing* can be used.[39] In this hybrid costing system, individual work orders are used to charge material cost and conversion cost associated with each operation during the process. The main difference between this system and pure process costing is that under operation costing the various products do not have to go through the same stages in the process. This is the reason work orders are used to track the individual jobs' material and operation conversion costs. And the difference between operation costing and job costing is that the conversion cost, i.e., the sum of the labor and manufacturing overhead costs, in the latter case is the same for each operation visited, regardless of the product. This is because of the similarity between the products.

As discussed in Chapter 2, cells come in many forms. Some are more like small job shops, and the products in the cell can follow different process paths. The volumes of each can be low, and there may be little similarity among the products. For such cells you have to stick with a job costing system and track labor and/or machine hours per work order. However, when products are similar and many process steps are repeated, operation costing is more appropriate. In the extreme, you have flow-line cells producing a single family using just one process path. For the latter type of cell you would not be interested in the differences among individual products, because they are small or nonexistent. Accordingly, a process costing approach is ideal for such cells.

As indicated, companies that use operation or process costing rely on conversion cost, i.e., a combined labor and overhead cost that is applied to products. The conversion cost for cells can be determined per process stage (cell operation) or for the combined process (the whole cell). This depends on whether all products go through each stage. For a flow-line cell, for example, you can have a conversion cost rate per labor hour of production based on a specified staffing level. Assume you run a cell with two employees for eight hours a day for 20 days while producing 2,380 units, and that the conversion cost for this staffing level is $180 per hour. The manufacturing conversion cost for this month is then (20*180*8)/2380, or $12.10 per unit.

Note that you are not tracking the time individual operators spend on individual products. Instead, you are simply averaging the period cost over the number of units produced. Harley-Davidson was one of the first companies to abandon labor tracking and switch to the conversion cost approach. The main rationale was the cost/benefit perspective—simply, too much time was spent tracking labor relative to its portion of total manufacturing cost. In addition, labor tracking in cells can be difficult, and Harley at the time had begun experimenting with cellular manufacturing. Office Machines also contemplated a shift towards process costing to simplify its costing system. Table 10-4 shows the extent to which a job order, process, or hybrid costing approach is used by companies that have moved towards JIT manufacturing.[40]

Table 10-4. Job order and process costing practices

	Before JIT	After JIT
Job Order Costing	14 (70%)	6 (30%)
Process Costing	4 (20%)	12 (60%)
Hybrid System	2 (10%)	2 (10%)

Data based on 20 firms.

Although the sample is small, the data show a clear tendency to switch from job costing to process costing in lean manufacturing environments.

Tracking WIP inventory

Besides tracking labor, determining the value of WIP inventory just so that all manufacturing expenses can be inventoried can also be considered a form of waste in accounting systems, particularly when inventory levels are low. Backflushing is a way to reduce or eliminate the tracking of WIP inventory. It is used for cells operating *without* work orders. Thus, backflushing is especially suitable for high-volume, high product similarity, fast-cycle, low WIP inventory cells.[41]

Backflushing (also called "post-deduct costing") works as follows. Consider inventory points A and G in Figure 10-3. Assume you are making two products and have standard conversion costs of $10 and $20 per unit. Likewise, the material costs per product are $75 and $100 per unit, respectively. You record the purchase of raw materials for every month (assuming the period length is one month). Thus, if you bought material for $150,000, the raw materials inventory (point A) is increased by that amount. During the month, as each product is completed and entered into finished goods inventory (point G), its standard conversion cost—including material—is recorded. This is the backflushing point. Up to this point in the process, no costs have been recorded except raw material purchases. At point G, however, the material used by the completed product is "post-deducted" from the raw materials inventory at point A using the bills of materials.[42] In other words, there is a delay between the time the inventory is pulled out of raw material inventory and the time when this usage is recorded in this inventory account.

At the end of the month you sum up the total conversion cost as well as the number of units produced. If you made 500 of Product 1 and 1,000 units of Product 2, the total manufacturing cost for the month is $500*(10 + 75) + 1,000*(20 + 100) = $162,500$. This is entered into a finished goods control account. The total account balance can then be entered, together with the raw materials inventory, on the company's balance sheet.[43] If you sold 600 and 750 units during the month, respectively, COGS is $600*(10 + 75) + 750*(20 + 100) = $141,000$, which is entered on the income statement. Since there may be differences between actuals and standards, you can apply material and conversion cost variances to correct the COGS account.

In a more extreme case, appropriate for high-velocity processes, you may record cost only at the entry and exit points in the cell system, as raw material is coming in and goods are shipped out (see points A and H in Figure 10-3). In this case, the cost

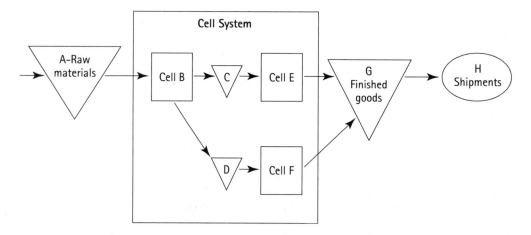

Figure 10-3. Possible backflushing points in a cell system

of conversion is directly expensed as COGS in the period of shipment and there are no entries into a finished goods inventory account. This is a more radical approach than to backflush at the time of product completion (i.e., at points A and G in Figure 10-3), which is more appropriate if there is a time delay between completing a product and shipping it. An advantage of using shipments as a trigger for backflushing is that it removes the incentive for building inventory. Operating income can increase if you produce beyond budgeted amounts and add to your inventory (for an example of this, see Appendix D).[44]

If you backflush at the point of shipping, you would have to base the inventory valuation for the external reporting purposes on raw materials only (since there is no WIP or finished goods inventories). However, the only restrictions on cost accounting systems are those regulating inventory valuation, specifically that inventory must include direct material, direct labor, and manufacturing overhead (see Appendix D). How, then, can a costing approach that ignores the conversion cost be allowed? The answer lies in something called "materiality." In essence, this means that if the number of units kept in WIP and finished goods inventories is very low, and, therefore, the value of this inventory is very low (say, less than 2–5 percent of sales, if it was to be measured), then you may ignore the WIP/FGI in the external inventory reporting system as well (i.e., on the balance sheet).

If you feel there is a greater need for cost control, you can backflush at multiple points. Consider again the three cells in Figure 10-3. If you are reluctant to abandon WIP tracking, you could backflush first at points C and D using one conversion rate for each cell. You then simply add to the WIP account at points C and D, and subtract the corresponding raw material cost at point A. When products are complete at point G, the same thing happens. That is, the conversion cost rates for cells E or F are multiplied by the number of units completed at point G and the WIP costs for the corresponding units are subtracted from the inventory accounts at points C and D.

In the study of job order and process costing systems mentioned earlier, 36 percent of the firms had adopted backflushing. This switch to a system with fewer transactions, together with an increased use of process costing, helps explains why almost three-fourths of these JIT firms claimed that their cost accounting system had become "less complex."

In summary, if you can accept less detailed control over expenses and assets in your cell system, then avoid tracking labor and inventory. This will lower the cost of operating your costing system and, at the same time, increase the efficiency of the manufacturing process.

A "NEW" COST ACCOUNTING SYSTEM FOR CELLS

We have now looked at how costing systems can be modified to better fit with cellular manufacturing in terms of (1) supporting the cell strategy, (2) delivering enhanced costing accuracy, and (3) motivating desired behavior so performance goals can be achieved. We have also discussed how the costing system can be simplified to take advantage of the product similarity that is the very foundation of cells. Table 10-5 summarizes these modifications.

Table 10-5. Possible modifications to the accounting system

Retaining the standard costing system
• Modify labor standards to accommodate indirect tasks
• Modify overhead rate for cells to exclude activities now terminated or performed by cell
• Change cost driver from direct labor or machine hours to lead time or bottleneck time
• Increase the degree of direct cost allocation to the cells
• Apply conversion cost using process costing; possibly track materials using job orders
• Apply backflushing either at product completion stage or at point of shipment
• Reduce emphasis on variance reporting and analysis
• Reduce emphasis on efficiency and utilization measures
Replacing the standard cost system
• Adopt activity-based costing system

By now you should recognize that there are many ways in which you can design a costing system. It is up to the financial executives and the operations managers to jointly find a system that satisfies all needs. You can meet the requirement to assign value to inventory and COGS for external reporting purposes fairly easily; the rest comes down to a battle between the inertia to change the accounting system versus the benefit of doing so.

Most companies that have implemented cells typically have portions of their plants still operating in a functional mode. Most plants also have a mix of make-to-stock and make-to-order manufacturing, with volumes ranging from high to low. An obvious question, then, is whether a single costing system can adequately satisfy such diverse characteristics, or whether you should run several systems side by side.

If you operate a high-volume, linked flow-line cell system you can use direct cost allocation, process or operation costing, conversion cost application, and backflushing. If you have cells with more varied production volumes and mix, you may use operation costing per process stage or, if less change is allowed, a system with modified overhead rates or multiple cost drivers (see Table 10-6). All these changes should be doable within existing standard costing systems and their supporting software.

Table 10-6. Fitting the cost accounting system to the cell system

Low-Volume, Make-to-Order Cells	High-Volume, Make-to-Stock Cells
• Maximize direct cost allocations to the cell	• Maximize direct cost allocations to the cell
• Use job order costing, or possibly operation costing	• Use operation costing (with work orders) or process costing (without work orders)
• Adjust standard labor and overhead rates to truly reflect the cell's role in carrying out indirect tasks	• Apply conversion cost to units produced
• Do not rely on earned hours or other efficiency or utilization measures (unless for problem-solving purposes)	• Use backflushing at inbound and outbound points of cells, or for larger processes (linked cells)
• Adopt (simple) activity-based costing system if there is a need for accurate unit costs	• Do not rely on earned hours or other efficiency or utilization measures (unless for problem-solving purposes)

The key issue in choice of costing system is to balance the need for "accurate" product costs with the need for "efficient" accounting procedures. Activity-based costing, with its new structure, requires a radical change. However, if products in a cell are very similar and the amount of direct cost allocation to the cell is high, the amount of manufacturing overhead allocated to the products is low. Therefore, how this allocation is done is less crucial since the potential "error" in product cost is small. We could combine ABC with process costing and backflushing, but this means we fail to take advantage of the power of the ABC system to determine accurate product costs. On the other hand, if the amount of direct overhead allocation to the cell is low and there are pronounced differences between products, you need a costing system that not only "fairly" allocates costs to products but also provides more detailed cost data. Here, you may be able to justify the expense of implementing an activity-based costing system. However, given the scope of this change, a decision to adopt must consider the needs of the plant as a whole, and not just the needs of the cells.

KEY INSIGHTS

Cost accounting, the internal reporting system, is the oldest, most formal, and most powerful source of performance data in the firm. Although you can design it any way you like, it is a system run by financial executives who also are in charge of the external reporting system (i.e., financial accounting). Since the business of business is to make money, these are influential people in the firm. But you should not forget that it is the operations side that makes the money, not the accounting system.

Too often, accountants don't understand the operations side, and operations people don't understand accounting. So it is to your advantage to be conversant in the area of accounting. In particular, you need to understand that the costing system should be adapted to the cellular manufacturing system. In this way you can avoid situations where you "get no respect," even after you have achieved impressive time and quality results, just because the costing system tells a different story. If you cannot advocate for cells in a language that your accountant colleagues can understand, you may find that your pet cell project gets killed. *So make accounting and the accountants your friends!*

In this chapter we raised many issues, and tried to answer several important questions about the interplay between cost accounting systems and cellular manufacturing. Here are some important points. For basic accounting terms, concepts, and formulas, see Appendix D.

- *Ensure that a "balanced scorecard" system is in place.* Make sure that cost-based performance metrics are complemented by measures that more frequently and rapidly provide feedback on the cell processes and their resources.

- *Don't automatically believe reports about increased costs due to cells if you know that operational performance has improved.* The implementation of cells can drive up the unit cost per manufactured item unless you adjust manufacturing overhead cost pools, standards, and cost rates, or even adopt a new costing system. In the short term, rely on non-financial measures to tell you if cells are better able to support the firm's strategy than the work organization you left behind. In the long term, of course, financial metrics are the ultimate arbiters of success.

- *Market-related changes may adversely affect product costs, while the cell system gets the blame.* Product mix and volume changes can have a powerful impact on overhead cost allocations. Keep this in mind when analyzing cost developments.

- *Abandon performance measures, such as earned standard hours or utilization, that lead to increased lead times and inventories.* Cells are adopted to accomplish lean manufacturing and rapid response. Avoid metrics, used in traditional accounting systems, which may steer behavior in the opposite direction.

- *Cost systems should be adapted to the manufacturing process, not the other way around.* Specifically, if you implement cells, your costing system should be adjusted to fit the new manufacturing process. If you retain the standard costing system, there are many ways in which you can fit the system to the cell (see Table 10-5). In particular, drive waste out of the accounting system where possible by simplifying the data collection system. Use conversion costs, process costing, and backflushing principles for short-cycle, high-volume cells (see Table 10-6). Activity-based costing systems may not be worthwhile for cells with highly similar products and a high degree of direct cost allocation.

11

Manufacturing Planning and Control Systems for Cells

Most companies adopt cells in an attempt to improve their internal and external response time to orders and order changes.[1] Although cells represent essential building blocks in efficient organizations, they are incomplete without a system that regulates material flows. This is why a cell system, and the plant as a whole, requires a *manufacturing planning and control (MPC) system* that plans, coordinates, and controls the two basic elements required to manufacture and move products: material and capacity.

The MPC system, which may be part of a larger supply chain management system, assists you in deciding when and in what quantities you should order parts and components from suppliers; when and in what quantities you should issue manufacturing or product assembly orders; and when and in what quantities you should move batches of parts from one work area or plant to another. The MPC system also supports resource-related decisions, such as determining the number of operators you should assign to a cell per day or week, when you need to buy new equipment, how to allocate incoming orders to various cells and work centers, and when an operator should begin on a new job or move to another workstation or cell.

An assortment of MPC systems is available to manufacturers: ERP/MRP, reorder point systems (ROP), pull/kanban systems, and finite/constraint-based schedulers. All plants have some form of MPC system in place—whether sophisticated, formal, and computerized, or simple, informal, and manual. For a plant that reorganizes itself fully or partially into cells, the important question is whether it should replace or adapt its MPC system and, if so, how.

In this chapter we cover some of the basic aspects of materials/capacity planning and control, and discuss how cellular manufacturing influences these activities. In particular, we look at these important issues:

- How do cells affect master scheduling, materials, and capacity planning?
- How is job execution at the shop floor level affected by cells? How can you lot-size and sequence jobs in cells?
- In general, how should you choose an MPC system for your cell system?

Since space does not permit us to provide details on each MPC procedure, we assume that you have a working knowledge of planning and control systems, especially MRP.[2]

AN OVERVIEW OF CHANGES TO MPC PRACTICES DRIVEN BY CELL ADOPTION

A recent study of MPC techniques in 57 firms shows how cells drive MPC practices.[3] First, the introduction of cells increases the likelihood that firms will operate multiple MPC systems simultaneously. Table 11-1 shows that while 82 percent of the firms only had one system in place before cells, that percentage declined to 49 percent after cells had been adopted. At the same time, the percentage of firms with two or three MPC systems in place after cells was 36 and 15 percent, respectively. If we generalize from this study, it appears that about half of all firms with cells have two or more MPC systems running in parallel.

Table 11-1. Percentage of firms simultaneously operating multiple MPC systems

Number of MPC Systems	Before Cells	After Cells
One	81.8%	49.1%
Two	16.4	36.4
Three	1.8	14.5

Second, before cells were established, 75 percent of the firms used MRP, 10 percent used ROP, 7 percent used pull/kanban systems, and 20 percent used other planning and control methods (which could include finite schedulers or simple materials planning systems that do not rely on netting). Table 11-2 shows that these figures changed to 71 percent for MRP, 13 percent for ROP, 56 percent for kanban, and 18 percent for other techniques after the cells were implemented. The fraction of firms using MRP does not vary much, while there is a large increase in the adoption of pull systems. This indicates that many firms with cells operate MRP and kanban together. In fact, the percentage of firms running both techniques increased from 3.6 percent before cells to 32.7 percent after cells were in place.

Table 11-2. Type of MPC system usage before and after cell implementation

MPC System	Before Cells	After Cells
MRP	74.6%	70.9%
ROP	10.2	12.7
Kanban	7.3	56.4
Other	20.0	18.2

This study also confirmed changes in MPC practices that we have observed in earlier research.[4] Firms that adopt cellular manufacturing have been noted to:

- Reduce lot sizes.
- Introduce smaller move (transfer) batches between workstations.

- Release jobs more frequently due to smaller lot sizes.
- Develop flatter bills of materials.
- Release jobs to cells rather than to individual machines.
- Perform capacity planning by concentrating on the cell bottleneck.
- Schedule jobs inside cells by operators or supervisors.
- Shift job tracking from the machine to the cell level.
- De-emphasize the use of alternate routings (stay within the cell).

In subsequent sections, we touch on many of these modifications to MPC systems and practices. Given that most firms use MRP/ERP systems as a foundation for their MPC activities, we begin by providing a very brief overview of those systems. We then discuss various changes to the MRP/ERP systems due to cells.

MRP/ERP SYSTEMS

Modern-day enterprise resource planning (ERP) systems grew out of the manufacturing resource planning (MRP) systems of the past, and MRP-based planning and control modules in ERP systems still regulate materials and capacity to, from, and inside the plant. Accordingly, we use the acronym MRP to refer to the core planning and control activities in ERP systems.

A General MRP-Based Framework for Materials and Capacity Planning

Figure 11-1 shows an overview of a traditional MRP-based planning and control system.[5] We call this the *disaggregation framework* because the process begins with plans established for families of products (aggregate planning level) and breaks them into master schedules for individual products (for make-to-stock items) or groups of parts and subassemblies (for assemble-to-order items). The master schedules are product-build schedules based on forecasts and accepted customer orders. These schedules are disaggregated into orders for parts and components via the materials requirements planning explosion process.

The explosion process uses the bills of materials, quantity on hand, open purchase and manufacturing orders, lot sizes, and lead times to determine quantities required and respective order release dates. The demand and order data for all items in the product structure are presented in MRP records (for a simplified example, see Figure 11-2). Order schedules for purchased items are sent to the supplier system, while schedules for manufactured parts are sent to the internal shop floor control (SFC) system. The SFC system releases orders into manufacturing. Operations are processed at various workstations, and the job status is monitored by the SFC system until the orders are completed. Likewise, the supplier/purchasing system sends plans and releases orders to suppliers, and monitors their status and arrivals.

When you move from top to bottom in the disaggregation framework, and from planning to execution, the time aspect changes. Specifically, if you consider the planning horizon (the length of time over which you plan), the planning period (the

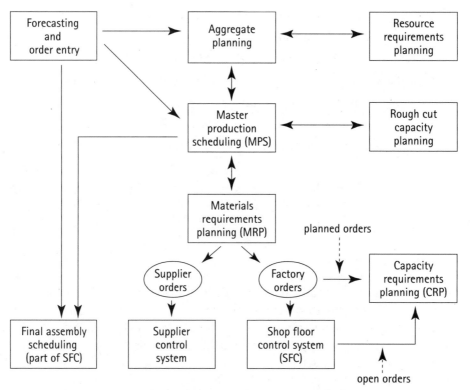

Figure 11-1. Disaggregation framework for MRP

smallest unit of time used for planning), and the replanning frequency (the frequency at which plans are revised), you will find that:

- *The planning horizon gets shorter*—from a year or more at the aggregate planning level to a week or day at the shop floor control level.
- *The planning period gets smaller*—from a quarter or a month at the aggregate planning level to a day or an hour at the SFC level.
- *The replanning frequency gets higher*—from monthly or quarterly at the aggregate planning level to daily or weekly at the SFC level.[6]

The MPC framework in Figure 11-1 shows that each planning level has both a materials and a capacity planning component. Thus, aggregate planning focuses on materials, while resource requirements planning is the corresponding capacity plan. Likewise, the rough-cut capacity planning procedure translates the master production schedule into machine or labor hours. Similarly, the capacity requirements planning (CRP) system turns time-phased manufacturing order schedules generated by MRP, and open orders from the SFC system, into detailed capacity plans.

MPC MODIFICATIONS DRIVEN BY CELLS—PRODUCT STRUCTURES AND PLANNING HORIZON

Cellular manufacturing does not principally change materials or capacity planning at the product or product family levels, unless accompanied by a switch from make-to-

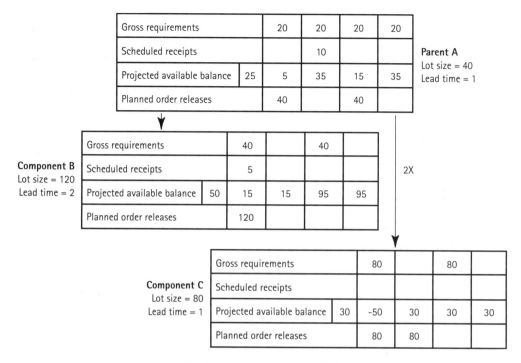

Gross requirements		20	20	20	20	
Scheduled receipts			10			**Parent A**
Projected available balance	25	5	35	15	35	Lot size = 40
Planned order releases		40		40		Lead time = 1

	Gross requirements		40		40		
Component B	Scheduled receipts		5				2X
Lot size = 120	Projected available balance	50	15	15	95	95	
Lead time = 2	Planned order releases		120				

	Gross requirements		80		80		
Component C	Scheduled receipts						
Lot size = 80	Projected available balance	30	-50	30	30	30	
Lead time = 1	Planned order releases		80	80			

Figure 11–2. Parent-component MRP records

stock to assemble-to-order (see the end of this chapter). However, two issues related to master scheduling are of special interest: the impact on product structures and the impact on the length of the planning horizon.

Product Restructuring

The MRP explosion process takes master schedules, bills of materials, current inventory levels, open orders, planned lead times, and lot-sizing policies and determines the order schedules for manufactured and/or purchased materials.

Key to this process is the *bill of materials* (BOM), which will need to be modified for cells. The BOM identifies the parts and components used to make a product. It also specifies the "per" quantities of lower-level items required by each higher-level item (e.g., we need three shafts per gear box). A *product structure tree* is a graphical illustration of a bill of materials. You can create many different bills or product structures for any given product. The exact configuration, however, should satisfy the needs of the materials planning function. Each node in the structure tree corresponds to an item, and that item has its own MRP inventory record. *How you structure the bills of materials, therefore, depends on which items you want to produce and control using inventory records.*

It is often necessary to produce component parts to stock. This is the case when the same part is used in several different products, when its lot size is larger than the immediate demand, or when it is manufactured both as a spare part and as a component in a currently manufactured product. In situations like these, MRP records are used to control production and track material usage. However, when an item is produced and used almost immediately in the manufacturing process, you do not have to move the item from the work area to a stockroom. Neither do you need to assign it a new identifier (part number) and control it via an MRP record. This situation, common in cellular manufacturing systems, serves as an opportunity to streamline bills of materials to fit the revised manufacturing process.

An example of bill restructuring

Figure 11-3 shows the manufacturing process for an assembled product that is made to stock, as well as the corresponding product structure. Assume now that you create two fabrication part cells, and collapse the subassembly and final assembly operations into a single assembly cell. The process flows would then look as shown in Figure 11-4. The corresponding product structure is changed to match the revised manufacturing process.

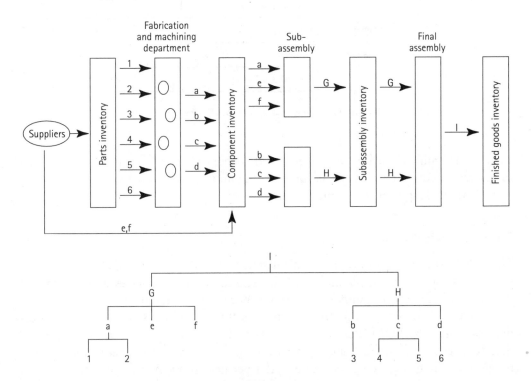

Figure 11-3. Production process and associated BOM—before cells

Because the subassembly and assembly processes have been combined, you no longer need to store and control the intermediate items G and H. Accordingly, these have disappeared from the product structure and their MRP records no longer exist. However, the intermediate items a, b, c, and d remain in the product structure. These items are not moved into the component inventory location in anticipation of the assembly process, but rather stored in buffers right on the floor. You can use MRP records to track their inventory balances and issue orders for the assembly process.

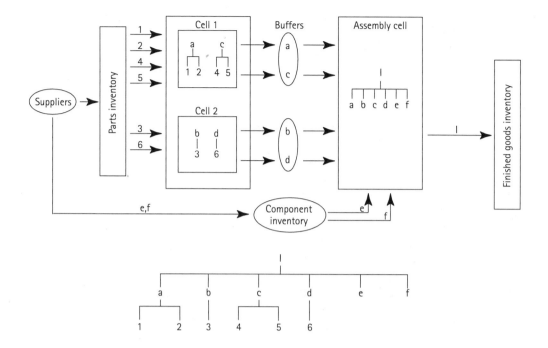

Figure 11-4. Production process and associated BOM—after cells

However, if there is no need to track the inventory of these components either, you can designate them as "phantoms."[7] This means that the MRP explosion "goes right through" these items' MRP records—without performing lot-sizing, lead time off-setting, or order releasing—and simply transfers the parts demand down to next level in the BOM (the effect is the same as if the structure for product I now consisted of only one level, with items e, f, and 1 through 6 directly below it). This feature is useful if, for example, you use the MRP system only for ordering purchased material and not for internal scheduling.

The point is that you can remove levels in the bills of material and simplify the product structures with cellular manufacturing. With a rapid manufacturing process there is less need to track and control inventories of intermediate items inside a cell. Ideally, you want only single-level bills of material associated with each cell product (see the product structures inside the cell boxes in Figure 11-4). This means that the need to produce a parent item causes the release of orders for all components of this parent. If you have a series of cells feeding each other, the order schedules for one cell—determined by the planned order releases (POR)—become the gross requirements (GR) for the preceding cells (see Figure 11-5).

Cells' Impact on the Planning Horizon

If you implement cells so that the longest lead time in a product structure tree is shortened, you can reduce the planning horizon used for master production scheduling as well (the minimum planning horizon is determined by the longest total cumulative lead time found among all products manufactured). You will then be

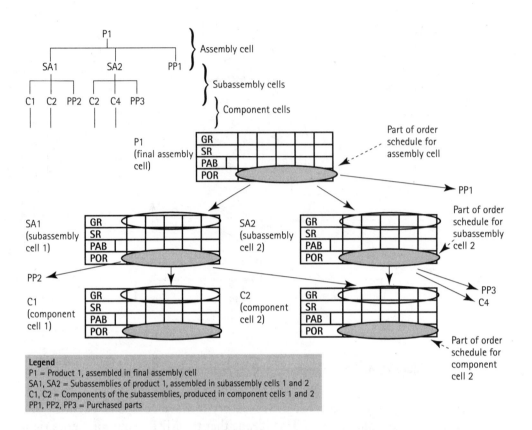

Figure 11-5. The use of single-level bills inside cells—the effect on MRP records

able to react faster to forecast and customer order changes in periods outside the planning horizon. Assume, for example, that cells can compress cumulative lead time from six months to one month, and the planning horizon from eight months down to three months (see Figure 11-6). Any change to the master schedule within the cumulative lead time affects both purchased and manufactured materials. Outside this horizon, no purchase orders are affected since none have been issued. Thus, while in the past you may have needed to issue supplier orders at least six months in advance, you now can make changes outside the one-month horizon without any impact on supplier schedules.

An additional benefit is that forecasting only three (rather than eight) months into the future will reduce forecast errors. Further, with compressed lead times you may be able to change from being a make-to-stock (MTS) manufacturer to an assemble-to-order (ATO), or even a make-to-order (MTO) firm.

MPC MODIFICATIONS DRIVEN BY CELLS—CAPACITY MANAGEMENT

Capacity management is the translation of forecasts and/or production schedules into capacity requirements, the determination of available capacity, and actions taken to align capacity needs with capacity availability.[8] In this section we discuss the use of capacity bills, load imbalances within and between cells, and cell staffing.

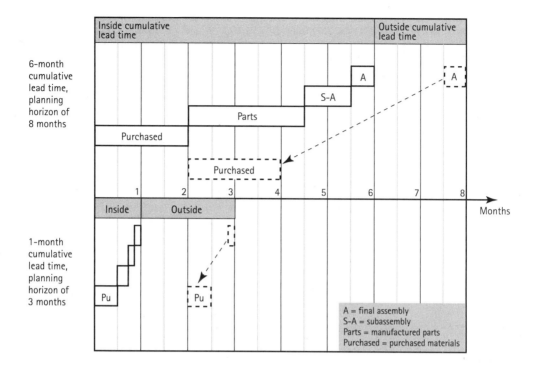

Figure 11–6. Impact of lead time reduction on MPS planning horizon

Capacity Bills

Master schedules are crucial in MRP systems because they drive the gross-to-net explosions (see Figure 11-1). Master schedules must be executable, i.e., sufficient capacity must be made available. The capacity requirements planning (CRP) technique is most often too complex to use with cells. You can check capacity needs more easily using a rough-cut capacity planning tool called a capacity bill. A capacity bill is derived from the product's routing data and bill of materials, and translates one unit of a master scheduled item into hours of load on people or machines.[9] Multiplying the master schedule (MPS) by the *capacity bill* gives you an estimate of the work hours needed at each workstation to execute the MPS (see Figure 11-7).

For items produced in cells, such capacity checks can be fairly reliable—despite the fact that capacity bills ignore both inventories and lot sizes (however, they can be modified to consider lead times). This is because cells typically operate with small lot sizes (could be the same as the MPS lot sizes) and have low WIP levels. If the cells have stable bottlenecks, it may suffice to include these and the near-bottlenecks in the capacity bill. The master schedules must then be adjusted to match the bottleneck capacities.

Managing Load Imbalances in Cell Systems

Load imbalances, which show up as different levels of backlogs at workstations or cells, represent one of the most frequently mentioned problems for firms involved

Assume we make 3 products (A,B,C) in an assembly cell. One work station in a previous cell, WS42, is the bottleneck for the complete product routings from raw materials to end item. Based on products A, B, and C's bills of materials and routings, we can determine the capacity needs at WS42 for making 1 unit of each product.

Product A	Product B	Product C
Work hours required at WS42 = 0.4	Work hours required at WS42 = 0.3	Work hours required at WS42 = 0.5

Assume further that the master schedules (MPS) for the three products are as follows for the next 6 weeks:

Product	W1	W2	W3	W4	W5	W6
A	15	15	17	15	14	16
B	30	30	32	32	30	30
C	37	37	41	41	36	37

Multiplying the master schedules by the capacity bills then yields the capacity requirements, in hours, at the bottleneck over the planning horizon (e.g., in Week 1 we have 15*0.4 + 30*0.3 + 37* 0.5 = 33.5 hours):

Capacity vs. work load on WS42	W1	W2	W3	W4	W5	W6
Load from MPS	33.5	33.5	36.9	36.1	32.6	33.9
Available hours	34.0	34.0	34.0	34.0	34.0	34.0

Figure 11-7. Use of capacity bills to determine workload

with cellular manufacturing.[10] Load imbalances can appear within or between cells, and are a function of both system design and system operation.

To begin with, process equipment comes only in integral units. This means you have to buy a whole machine even if you only need a fraction of it to satisfy capacity needs. The same, of course, is true for human capacity. The resulting problem is that when you put resources together within a cell, the output rate from one station may not match the need of the downstream stations. The result of such mismatches can cause *blocking* and *starving*. Starving occurs when a station runs out of work due to its operating at a faster pace than preceding stations, while blocking occurs when a station cannot pass on its work to a downstream station (this can only happen when there is a limit on WIP inventory).

For example, you may have one machine that spits out parts at a rate of 500 per hour, while the subsequent machines produce at a rate one-fifth of that. You could, of course, operate a cell with these machines by running the fast machine at the same rate as the slower one. Whether this is feasible depends on the technology and the cost of the machine. In general, such problems get less serious the larger the cell. If you have enough demand to operate a cell with an output rate that is several times the processing rate of the slowest machine, you can duplicate that machine. Likewise, if you can combine several smaller cells into one (normally, though, with less ideal flows and higher setup times as a result), you can increase the utilization of the high-speed machine by having it feed several slower machines. These situations are illustrated in Figure 11-8.

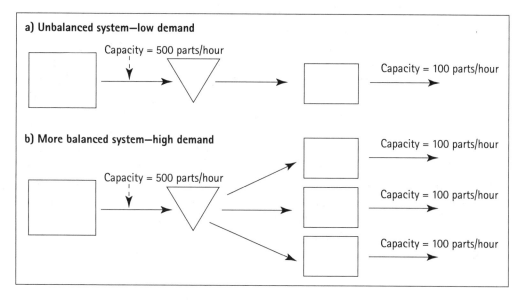

Figure 11-8. Capacity imbalances from combining machines with different output rates

When the batch output rates between machines differ greatly, cells may be inappropriate. Processes with *fixed cycle times*, like heat treatment or oxidizing, represent a special problem. These processes typically must operate in batch mode. They are not suited to be put in cells based on the one-piece flow principle since batching will interrupt this flow. Instead, they may have to be placed as independent "service centers," supplying parts to multiple production units in the plant. (Chapter 16 contains a detailed discussion of how to deal with such "monument" processes.)

Load imbalances can also be caused by changing demand patterns. When you dedicate resources to product families, you prevent those resources from being used to produce other products. This can result in either over- or underutilized cells. You can control the load distribution by:

- Selecting different routes through a cell.
- Moving the jobs to other cells.
- Changing lot sizes.
- Controlling the mix of orders released into the cells.
- Moving operators (e.g., to different workstations inside a cell, or to different cells).

The actions suggested here are short-term, compensating measures to alleviate the build-up of backlogs in the system. If serious load imbalances persist, it is a sign that you need to redesign the cells.

The role of labor in cell capacity management

In one of our studies, approximately 39 percent of the firms moved operators between cells. Also, 87 percent had cells with cross-functional operators who moved inside the cells.[11] Obviously, such flexibility in capacity assignment will better equip cells to handle variations in demand, late orders, or equipment breakdowns. However, although flexible labor can be a great advantage, moving operators between or even inside cells can potentially mean a loss of both quality and individual operator productivity.

The impact of cross-training is discussed in more detail in Chapters 7, 12, and 13. Two facts are worth emphasizing here, however. First, the greater the degree of cross-training, the greater the cell's output capacity at any particular staffing level (although the increase in output diminishes marginally when operators learn more tasks, due partly to loss of operator productivity and partly to the inability to take advantage of the added flexibility). Second, the greater the extent of the cross-training, the greater the cell's ability to handle increasing or decreasing demand levels by varying the staffing level. Figure 11-9 illustrates the flexibility to modify the output rate for a cell where operators are fully cross-trained on all processes. Detailed capacity planning in these situations requires that you know the skills of the cell operators and the stations inside their primary cell (or in other cells) to which they can be moved. This information can be used together with the load from the capacity bills to plan for proper output and staffing needs.

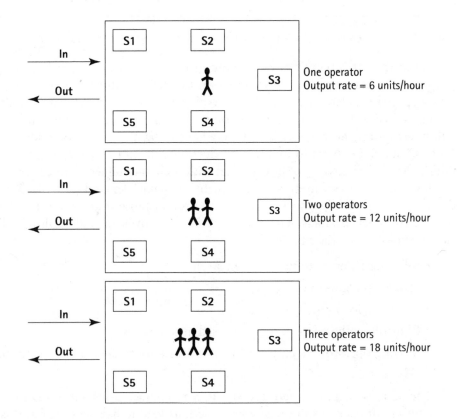

Figure 11-9. Effect of varying staffing levels

A cell capacity management system based on labor flexibility

An appliance manufacturer solved its capacity problem in a fairly unique way.[12] This make-to-stock plant has a sheet metal fabrication area that feeds 11 assembly cells. Low-value parts are controlled using a visual ROP system, with the operators faxing their suppliers when refilling is needed. However, the MRP system orders most of the purchased materials and also schedules the sheet metal area. The components from that area are pushed to the cells. Orders for the cells are then executed based on final assembly schedules.

Although this firm had an absenteeism rate of only 1 percent, the available vacation days turned the effective absenteeism into 6 percent. To handle the peak demand, eight "standby operators" were permanently employed. These roving operators had lower skills than their permanent counterparts. Accordingly, quality and output problems arose. More serious was the impact on employee pay. Each team received a group bonus of 40 percent of base pay if they met the weekly schedule. However, the standby operators prevented the cell teams from receiving this bonus. After a failed attempt to coordinate employee vacation schedules, the company devised a totally new scheduling/staffing system.

The system with standby operators was eliminated. All regular operators are now cross-trained to perform all jobs in a cell. Further, each cell is required to have a maximum and minimum staffing level (for example, Cell 3 may operate with between 5 and 8 workers), and must meet the minimum staffing level each week. Vacation policy was also changed so that employees must firmly plan 7 of their 13 vacation days by February 15 each year. The company now tracks attendance at each cell and uses the historical pattern to schedule output over the nine-week master schedule horizon. Operators that come to work unexpectedly are assigned to cells with unexpected absenteeism or to "off-line" work.

The company views this form of capacity planning and scheduling as being very effective. They have saved the wages for the standby operators, quality has improved, and on-time shipment has increased from 95 to 97 percent despite a 43 percent increase in number of product variants produced. In addition, sales-per-employee has improved and is now the highest in the industry. At the same time, the cell teams regularly meet schedules and receive their bonuses. Morale has increased and grievances have gone down. The agreement with employees regarding vacation scheduling and minimum staffing levels, along with the powerful incentive of the weekly bonus, have reduced the planning and execution headaches by stabilizing the capacity and reducing the uncertainty regarding schedule completion.

MPC MODIFICATIONS DRIVEN BY CELLS—THE SHOP FLOOR CONTROL SYSTEM

Although MRP systems came to the fore in the early 70s (then called material requirement planning systems), they are still the main building block for most companies' MRP/ERP systems. As indicated, studies show that between 70 and 90 percent of all plants with cells have MRP systems in place, and that MRP remains in place after adopting cellular manufacturing.[13] However, firms usually do not operate these systems in the same way before and after a cell conversion. Rather, they are augmented with other systems and procedures, especially pull systems, and their operating parameters are modified to better suit the new cell environment. *It is the "lower end" of the MPC system—where the shop floor control activities reside—that is most affected by the conversion to cells.*

Shop floor control (SFC) is the "doing" subsystem within a larger MPC system. It deals with the execution of materials and capacity plans.[14] It is at the shop floor level where people are allocated to perform production tasks, where equipment breaks down and quality problems occur, and where immediate decisions are needed to counteract well-laid plans that have become impossible to carry out. At this level, the MPC system must be closely tailored to the processes and events on the floor. It is therefore natural that it is here the impact of cells on the MPC system can most clearly be seen.

In our MRP-based planning and control framework (Figure 11-1), the SFC module is depicted as a "black box" at the bottom of the structure. There are three key activities performed by the SFC system: (1) scheduling, (2) order releasing, and (3) reporting. These activities, applied to both cells and functionally organized departments, are shown in Figure 11-10.[15] We discuss each of these activities below, as they would be executed in traditional, push-oriented environments. The use of pull systems is discussed in the following section.

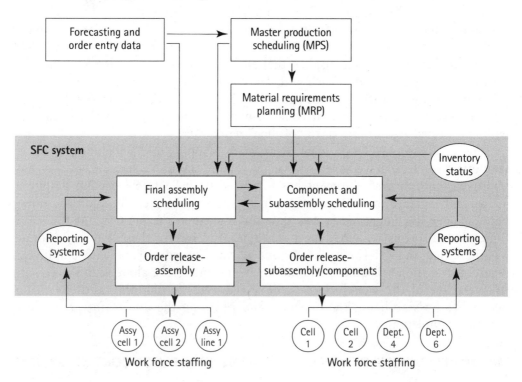

Figure 11–10. Shop floor control system

Scheduling

To *schedule* an order or operation means to assign it a start time and a finish time. For example, the planned order release (POR) row in an MRP record shows the start dates for a set of orders, while the completion dates are given by start dates plus the planned lead times (Figure 11-2). In contrast, a *sequence* is simply a list of jobs ordered according to some priority rule. The rule tells you in what order to process the jobs. A sequence, therefore, does not have any start or finish times. Note, however, that any schedule can be turned into a sequence. For example, if you take all jobs in a schedule and order them according to their start times, you now have a sequence of jobs.

Orders for assembled items are scheduled through the creation of the master schedule (MPS) and/or from customer order data, while orders for manufactured items are generated from the MRP explosion. The traditional SFC system schedules the *operations* required by each order. Operations scheduling can take two forms: infinite operations loading and finite operations scheduling. In contrast to infinite loading, which usually is performed through backwards scheduling and without consideration to capacity, finite scheduling is forward-looking and schedules each operation while taking recognized capacity limits into account. In so doing, finite schedulers *calculate* manufacturing lead times rather than relying on fixed, planned lead times.

The scheduling system relies on the planned orders from MPS and MRP, usually by considering a limited set of orders within a short time horizon.[16] Schedule creation also takes into account the status of the open, already released orders and the amount of inventory at hand. For the SFC system in Figure 11-10 we have separated the final assembly scheduling activity from the component/subassembly scheduling. Although the same scheduling system can be used for both types of orders, there are many SFC systems for which detailed scheduling of component orders never takes place. Rather, the planned orders from MRP are sent directly to the order release function. Also, if you want to control cell components with pull systems, there may or may not be any MRP schedules for lower-level items. (Due to their importance in cellular manufacturing, we discuss pull systems in a separate section below.)

Most firms develop final assembly schedules (FASs) that cover a relatively short time horizon (one to four weeks). For firms producing products to inventory, there are relatively small differences between the MPS and the FAS. But for companies operating in the assemble-to-order mode, the master schedule's role is limited to ensuring that kits of components are available for assembly. The FAS then takes over and schedules the final product configurations based on customer specifications.

Order Releasing

In traditional MRP systems, component orders are processed through the plant using prioritized dispatch lists. These lists are created on a daily basis for each work center. They show the orders that are present at the work center at the time of the list creation, and *the sequence* in which these orders should be processed. A "work center" can be a group of similar equipment, or it can be a cell. You should avoid using dispatch lists *inside* cells, though you can use them to prioritize the orders at the *entry point* to the cell. In this way you do not need to track job status inside the cell, a necessary activity to keep priority lists updated for each machine. Thus, orders can be released to the cell, but the cell employees should be responsible for the detailed execution of the orders inside the cell (assisted by the priority list generated by the SFC system).

Treating the cell as a "black box" or single operation for the purpose of scheduling and order releasing greatly simplifies both the part routings and the scheduling activity.

Input/output control

Order releasing is an activity where capacity management, inventory management, and lead time management merge. Oliver Wight, one of the early MRP gurus, proposed in 1970 the use of a simple technique called *input/output control*. This technique tracks incoming and outgoing work at the machine or work-center level. You can use that information to increase or decrease capacity, or increase or decrease scheduled workload, in order to regulate WIP and lead times.[17]

Figure 11-11 shows an input/output control report for a cell. The unit of measure is "standard hours of work." Thus, the planned input and planned output rows track the anticipated workload in hours arriving to and departing from the cell. The planned input data can come from the MRP system's planned order release row multiplied by the work content of the parts (possibly after adjustment for setups).

Input

Week	14	15	16	This week	18	19
Planned input	73	75	83	71	71	71
Actual input	75	72	91			

Output

Planned output	68	68	76	76	76	68
Actual output	62	74	73			

WIP Inventory (target WIP = 80 hours of work)

Planned WIP		72	87	85	91	86	89
Actual WIP	67	80	78	96			

Demonstrated capacity (without overtime) = 68 hours/week

Figure 11-11. Input/output control report

Planned output, simply put, is the number of standard hours of output the cell has historically been able to produce (effective capacity without overtime). In the same vein, the actual input and output rows show the amount of work arriving at and leaving the cell. These quantities are also stated in standard hours. Finally, at the bottom of the report is the information of most interest: WIP inventory tracked over time, in terms of both planned and actual levels.

The calculations for the I/O control report follow the basic "bath tub" analogy. That is, the water level in the tub is determined by the difference between the rate by which water comes into the tub via the faucet and leaves through the drain. Or, to use manufacturing terms:

Ending inventory = beginning inventory + production – shipment

For example, if the actual WIP is 67 hours at the beginning of week 14, and the planned input for the following week is 73 hours while the planned output is 68 hours, the planned WIP level at the end of week 14 is 67 + 73 – 68, or 72 hours. Similar calculations apply to the actual WIP row in the report.

You can see that both planned and actual WIP have been rising steadily and now exceed the target level of 80 hours. This indicates that there is more work coming into the cell than it can process. As a response, the cell manager has scheduled overtime for weeks 16, 17, and 18 (see the planned output row). She has also been able to slow down the rate of incoming work in future weeks (see the planned input row). Even so, she does not expect to reach the target WIP level by the end of week 19.

In the past, the cell has been able to deliver 68 standard hours of work per week, without working overtime. A target WIP level of 80 hours means that each new hour of work arriving to the cell can expect to spend 80/68 or 1.18 weeks in queue (waiting) and in process (being worked on) before departing the cell. Of course, jobs do not necessarily consist of a single hour of work, but this doesn't change how you calculate the average throughput time. Assume that an average batch processed by the cell requires a total of 2.56 standard hours. The target WIP then consists of 80/2.56 or 31.25 batches, while the average demonstrated output per week is 68/2.56 or 26.56 batches. Accordingly, the average lead time for a batch is 31.25/26.56, i.e., 1.18 weeks. Clearly, input/output control thinking can be quite useful in estimating and regulating inventory and lead time for a cell.[18]

As an aside, a more advanced planning approach that can be used by cell employees is to rely on a queuing model or a simple simulation model. As we discussed in Chapter 7, such models can predict lead times and WIP, given specified demands, lot sizes, and staffing levels. A cell team can then make mid- to short-term decisions regarding staffing assignments, overtime, and lot-sizing in order to met lead time targets.

Reporting

One task for the SFC system is to monitor and report on plant floor activities. When you create cells you should critically review the existing reporting system. For example, is it necessary to *track the location of a job* inside a cell? This is required only if the cell is very large, the throughput time long, and the flow pattern erratic. Even then may it be unnecessary since the opportunity for visual control is present when a cell is located within a dedicated, compressed area (as one cell user told us: "parts do not get lost" in cells).[19]

Also, you don't have to track order completion status unless cell throughput time is very long. Order completion status is required to use capacity requirements planning (CRP), but this complex capacity planning technique is "overkill" in most cell applications. Likewise, some sequencing rules, like order slack or critical ratio, require order status information to calculate job priorities. However, it does not make sense to use these dispatch rules inside the cell unless it has long lead times and an erratic flow pattern. And if this is the case, you probably need to rethink the cell's design and operation anyway. You want small cells with uniform flow patterns and short throughput times, and where internal order sequencing can be avoided.[20]

Finally, perhaps the most contentious issue regarding SFC reporting relates to the tracking of labor hours for the purpose of product costing. This is unnecessary in cells with highly similar products with stable demand. We discussed that issue in detail in Chapter 10.

Cellular Manufacturing Driving MPC System Changes at Applicon

It is primarily at the shop floor control level—the Achilles heel of MRP—where we see changes to MPC practices when cells are established. Firms that have adopted cellular manufacturing, and especially those that run these cells in a more or less repetitive mode, find that the use of MRP-generated work orders and dispatch lists are unnecessarily complicated when a much simpler system can work well. Before continuing our discussion of MPC modifications, let's look at one company's experience of transitioning from classic MRP to a lean environment using cells.

Applicon makes software and terminals for the CAD/CAM market.[21] The firm had an MRP system in place and was making products to stock. An inefficient process and a poor quality system had created long lead times and high costs. The ratio of indirect to direct labor was high, with 83 material handlers and 60 quality inspectors for only 160 operators. Material went in and out of stockrooms, and inspectors checked the products after each operation. After ignoring growing competition, the company found itself with large inventories of unsold products, WIP, and raw materials—not an ideal situation in a market characterized by rapid technological change.

As part of a new operations strategy, the company created four assembly cells. Each cell performs assembly work, as well as testing, burn-in, clean-up, and packaging operations. A central area that performs manual insertion, wave soldering, and PCB testing feeds these cells. As part of the conversion to cells, lot sizes were reduced from monthly to daily quantities. Furthermore, purchased material was delivered directly to the cells, and the central stockroom was eliminated.

A big change to the MPC system was the adoption of an assemble-to-order (ATO) philosophy. This involved restructuring the bills of materials from standard to planning bills.[22] The old work-order driven SFC system was also removed and replaced by a daily final assembly scheduling system. Thus, the MRP system is now ordering purchased materials only.

Figure 11-12 shows the key aspects of the new MPC system. Based on forecasts, the MRP system issues orders to suppliers. Upon receipt, the material is taken to the point of use at the PCB area or the four cells. Customer orders for products are entered into a backlog report that is updated weekly. Based on the order backlog, the production schedule for the coming week is posted, for each day of the week, on a production board near the cells. Each cell also receives a stack of production cards specifying the product quantities to be built that week. As can be seen from Figure 11-12, the product backlog is also translated into daily PCB requirements and converted into production cards, indicating the types of PCBs required. To consider the time to manufacture the boards, the daily requirements for PCBs are offset by four days from

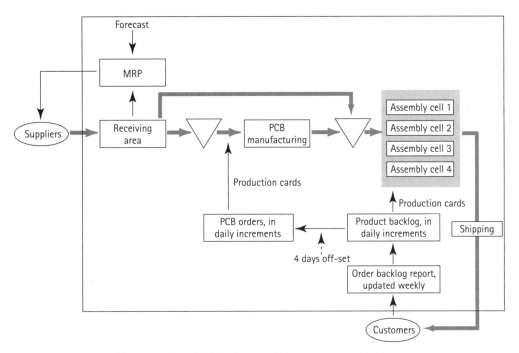

Figure 11-12. Applicon's materials management system

the need date. Thus, PCB manufacturing begins four days before the assembly operation begins. The boards are then pushed through the PCB manufacturing work areas and delivered to the input storage area for the respective assembly cell. Thus, nothing is built on speculation—all production is tied to actual customer orders.

The rapid manufacturing process allowed Applicon to simplify inventory accounting procedures. The old system required an inventory transaction each time material was received from suppliers, removed from the stockroom for use in manufacturing, or returned to inventory after completion. The new system involves only "wall-to-wall" backflushing, requiring two transactions only. This means that material is simply added to inventory when it arrives from suppliers and deducted from inventory when a complete product leaves an assembly cell (see Chapter 10 for details on backflushing).

Moving to cells and simplifying the MPC system, along with a strong emphasis on process quality and the introduction of more reliable equipment, led to a reduction in manufacturing lead time from four months to four days. These changes also reduced total space needs at Applicon by close to 75 percent. In particular, the large area previously devoted to various forms of inventory (about one-third of all factory space) was reduced by 93 percent.

MPC MODIFICATIONS DRIVEN BY CELLS—CONTROLLING MATERIAL FLOW THROUGH PULL SYSTEMS

MRP systems were developed to be work-order driven planning and control systems operating in job shop environments with long lead times and varying time demands. Through the net requirements calculations, MRP determines when to release orders to suppliers and the internal factory. Typically linked to standard MRP is a *job costing system* where materials used and hours worked are tracked and reported against each issued work order. Once an order is closed out, the job costing system uses this information to determine actual product cost.

This work-order based system becomes cumbersome and impractical when manufacturing is repetitive and rapid, and output levels are high and stable. The emergence of the JIT approach to manufacturing led software vendors to modify MRP to be rate-based rather than work-order driven. In *rate-based MRP*, where a narrow set of products with stable designs is produced constantly in fairly fixed volumes (say, 100 per week), work orders are not used and *process costing* replaces job order costing (see Chapter 10). In such repetitive manufacturing environments, traditional shop floor control systems become less useful. However, regardless of whether rate-based MRP is used or not, companies that have reorganized into cells, and now keep material on the shop floor rather than moving it back and forth to stockrooms, have discovered that simpler mechanisms exist for controlling material flow inside, and even between, plants. These mechanisms are universally referred to as *pull systems*.

Pull Systems Defined

Pull systems initiate material movement or production activities through the removal or depletion of inventory.[23] In essence, consumption triggers replenishment ("use one, make one"). This is in contrast to *push systems* where material is sent along to the next stage in the manufacturing system once it has been processed, and where orders are initiated not based on actual usage but on a schedule.[24] Standardized containers, in which material is moved and stored, are integral to pull systems. Containers, which can differ in size for different materials, serve the purpose of stabilizing batch sizes, protecting material from damage (especially if the containers are designed with holders for the parts), and simplifying the visual estimation of WIP if all stored containers are required to be full of parts.

The basic pull system idea has been around for a long time in the form of reorder point systems. However, it didn't become popular worldwide until its role in the Toyota Production System became public knowledge in the early 1980s. There are several different forms of pull systems. In the sections below we discuss only some of the most important variants.

Product-Specific Pull Systems

Pull systems are frequently referred to as kanban systems. *Kanban* means "card" or "display" in Japanese. A kanban system, therefore, is a production control system that uses some form of card as an information carrier (the card can be made of cardboard, plastic, metal, etc.). The cards circulate between points of storage, are attached to full containers of parts, or hang on "kanban boards." A *move card* signals the need to move material from one work area or storage point to another. Likewise, a *production card* signals the need to produce (i.e., to replenish inventory that has been removed).

The information displayed on cards usually includes: part name and number, station or cell where the part is produced, container type, lot size (which could be expressed in number of containers), number of cards or containers in circulation, identification number of each specific card (e.g., card no. 3 out of 5 issued cards), and number of accumulated cards needed before production or movement can begin (specifies the lot or move batch size). Figure 11-13 shows an example of a move card used by the cells at Milwaukee Electric Company, while Figure 11-14 shows a corresponding production card.

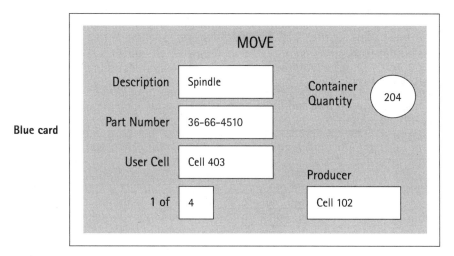

Figure 11–13. A typical move card

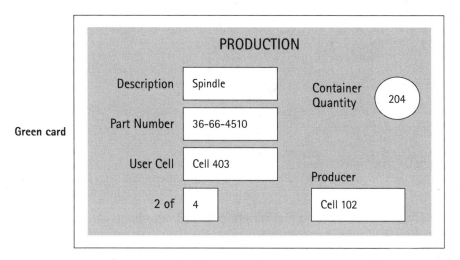

Figure 11–14. A typical production card

A product-specific pull system, as the name implies, is one where the production or move signals identify specific products to process or transfer. In both dual and single card pull systems, cards serve the purpose of identifying the products.

Product-specific pull systems are "pure" pull systems in that they lack forward-looking capabilities. Thus, they are control systems only and must operate together with a material- and capacity-planning system to form a complete MPC system.

Dual-card pull systems

The original Toyota pull system is a dual-card system in which each work area has production cards circulating *inside* the area to trigger production, while move cards circulate *between* work areas to move material into and out of production. The term *dual* comes from the use of two card types. It does not mean there are only two cards at each work area.

While most plants using pull systems have in place both production and move cards (or, as discussed later, rely on other forms of trigger signals), the use of dual cards is necessary only if two consecutive work areas are far apart and separated by *two* buffer locations. For example, the assembly cell in Figure 11-15 gets material from the two distant subassembly cells. Material is pulled from the output sides of

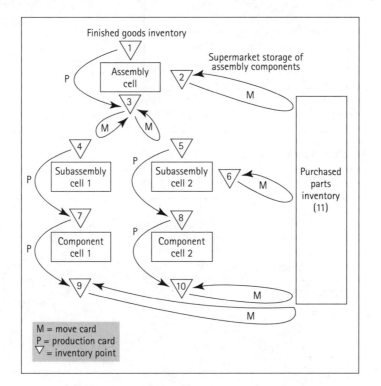

Figure 11–15. Single and dual card systems

the subassembly cells to the input side of the assembly cell using move cards. A complete cycle is as follows. Removal of a product from the finished goods inventory (FGI; point 1) will send an associated production card to the assembly cell's input side (point 3) to signal that replenishment is needed. The card may be sitting in a queue of production cards (or hanging on a kanban board), waiting its turn. When the time has come to act on the card, and the material needed to assemble the product specified on the card is available (thus, there must be a match between the information on the production cards and the move cards), the appropriate move cards are removed from these containers and sent back to the subassembly stage (points 4 and 5). The production card is then attached to a container and travels with it through the final assembly process. Thus, containers sitting in the FGI location all have production cards attached to them. Although widely known, dual-card systems are rare in industry—at least in the United States. Accordingly, we focus most of our attention on other types of pull systems.

Single-card pull systems

If work areas are close to one another, it is sufficient to maintain a single buffer between them. Move cards are then unnecessary and the card system can operate with production cards only. Consider subassembly cell 1 and component cell 1 on the left-hand side of Figure 11-15. When a container of subassemblies has been picked up from point 4 and moved to the assembly cell (point 3), the removed production card (P-card) is hung on a kanban board at subassembly cell 1. When a subassembly operator is idle, he or she will take a card from the board, go to the input side of the subassembly cell (point 7), and pick up a container of the material specified on the card. If available, that container will have a P-card associated with component cell 1 attached to it. This card will be removed and put on the board for the component cell, and later be used as a trigger to replenish the material just taken to subassembly cell 1. The P-card for the subassembly cell is then attached to the container and travels with it through the process, until the container arrives at the output side of the subassembly cell (point 4). When work areas are closely located, and material handling is performed by operators rather than by designated material handlers, single production cards are sufficient.

Note also that if work areas are in fact separated by two buffers, and these are close, a single card can serve as both production and move card. For example, if component cell 1 had an output buffer and subassembly cell 1 had an input buffer, the operator could take the latter cell's P-card directly to the component cell's output buffer, pick up respective container, bring it to the input side of the subassembly cell, and begin processing. In essence, the P-card serves the additional role as a move card between the two buffers.

Finally, material is often moved between distant storage areas in the plant. For example, raw material arrives from suppliers to a central storage area but is then moved to a supermarket buffer area next to a cell. In such cases, move cards are used to control material transfers between the storage areas, like the use of M-cards on the right-hand side of Figure 11-15. Here you are moving material from the purchased parts inventory (point 11) to "supermarket" storage areas close to production (points 2, 6, 9, and 10).

Determining the Number of Production Cards

How do you determine the number of production cards (or, alternatively, the number of containers that hold WIP) in a pull system? Toyota has developed a formula for this:[25]

$$y = \frac{D*L*(1+\alpha)}{c}$$

where   y = number of cards (or WIP holding containers)
D = demand per day (in units)
L = lead time, in days, to replenish one container (including
wait time)
α = safety factor
c = container capacity (in units)

The use of this formula requires that you have determined the container size (see the section "Lot-sizing in Pull Systems" below). Assume now that for a specific cell $\alpha = 0$, the container size is set to 10 units, demand is 20 units per day, and you have estimated the lead time for one container to be one day. The number of containers needed inside this cell is then 20*1/10, or two containers. Thus, within each one-day cycle you fill two containers and consume them, and the cycle repeats itself. The lead time (L) to replenish a container includes:

1. The time the production card waits on the kanban board before it is removed.
2. The time from the moment the card was removed to the point when production begins.
3. The time to set up and process the batch.
4. Any waiting time during this process.
5. The time the container with finished parts sits in the output buffer (with the card attached) before it is removed by a downstream pull.

In short, container lead time consists of all the time elements that make up a complete cycle for a production card.

While you can easily estimate the container's processing time (setup and operation time), waiting times are problematic as they depend both on the size of the container and the number of cards used in the cell (either waiting to be processed or attached to complete containers). This creates a circular situation—a trial-and-error scenario wherein you must guess a reasonable lead time, determine the number of cards, operate the system, refine your lead time estimate, and then recalculate the required number of cards.

In poor manufacturing systems, lead time can be 20 to 30 times the batch processing time. In lean systems, lead time—at best—may be twice the processing time. Since you will not be in an extreme lean position when you launch a cell, and you do not want to starve the cell of inventory, your lead time estimate should be high—perhaps three to five times the batch processing time.

Instead of guessing, you could set a goal for lead time and then determine the required number of cards. Thus, if in our example demand is 100 units per day and you want the lead time to refill a container to average one day, the number of cards will be 10. By the way, the safety coefficient (α) is in the formula to create an extra buffer inventory to compensate for variations in both the demand and the lead time estimations. But it may not be needed if y comes out as a fractional number and must be rounded upwards to nearest integer. For example, if y is 2.26 when α = 0, the required number of containers is three. In effect, then, the safety factor is 3/2.26–1, or 0.327.

What may be the basis for Toyota's formula? Let us rewrite it as follows (we ignore the safety factor):

$$y*c = D*L$$

Now, $y*c$ is the maximum amount of inventory in the cell, while D should equal the average production rate for the cell. Accordingly, we can restate the formula as follows:

$$WIP\ inventory = Output\ rate\ *\ Lead\ time$$

You may recall that we discussed the same formula in connection with the input/output calculations in the shop floor control section (you may also recognize this as Little's Law; see Chapter 7). Thus, if you think of lead time L as the time it takes to process an inventory of size $y*c$ at a rate of D, then Toyota's formula makes sense. Obviously, estimating the number of cards required becomes more complicated when multiple parts are involved—each with different processing times, lead times, and demand rates. However, the formula still holds, with D and L being averages for all parts produced in the cell. For assurance, you can always verify card counts, and resulting lead times, using simulation modeling.

Determining the Number of Move Cards

The Toyota formula also applies to move cards. The lead time (L) is now the time required to complete a cycle with a move card. It includes:

1. The time the card waits at the inbound side of a cell, attached to a container, waiting to be removed by an operator and put on a kanban board.
2. The time the card waits on the board to be picked up by a material handler.
3. The move time back to the preceding work area.
4. The time it takes for the material handler to locate the right material at that buffer point and bring the card, and a full container, back to the original production area.

Thus, for both production and move cards, the lead time is the total time required to circulate a card, whether inside a cell or between two stocking points.

The Limitation of Product-Specific, Pure Pull Systems

A product-specific pull system replenishes each container that has been removed from a storage location and pulls the material through all stages of the production process for all items controlled by the system. That is, the "manufacturing pipeline" will always be full. An effective use of these pure pull systems, therefore, rests on two conditions. The first is that only a limited number of items are controlled this way. This is because each item requires storage space on the factory floor at each stage of the process (e.g., if a cell makes 100 parts, and you have two production cards per part, there could be up to 200 containers of parts at the output side of that cell alone!). The second condition is that item usage is relatively steady. If it is not, replenished material will just sit as idle inventory on the floor along the manufacturing process. In short, *product-specific pull systems are best suited for high-volume, low-mix, repetitive manufacturing cells*. Deviations from those conditions call for other types of pull systems, as we discuss next.

Generic (Non-Product Specific) Pull Systems

If you do not want to automatically refill inventory that has just been removed from a buffer location, you have to control production via a schedule that tells you what to produce. Most pull systems are in fact controlled by at least one schedule—the one for the final assembly stage. Although material may be pulled throughout the process, from raw material up to final assembly, the assembly schedule decouples production from external demand and stabilizes production rates (if there is no assembly schedule, then pull signals come from distribution centers or from customers). To avoid automatic replenishment at other places along the manufacturing process, you must use schedules *for each production* unit (such as cells).

It is possible to combine pull signals and schedules into a hybrid pull/push control system. The role of the schedules is to indicate to each stage the items that are needed for the coming time period (an hour, a shift, a day, a week, etc.), and the order in which they should be made. The role of the pull signal, on the other hand, is to indicate *when* production of the next item can begin. Since each stage has a schedule telling it what items to make, it is not necessary to use kanban cards that are product-specific (i.e., that display the type of item to produce). Rather, the pull system is "generic" in that the cards that signal production don't include product information.

Illustration of a generic pull system with schedule

Consider the two cells in Figure 11-16. The target production for a specific week is shown by the sequence below each cell. These sequences could be derived from the MRP system by taking a week's worth of planned order releases for each item in a cell and arranging them in a prioritized order (e.g., according to order start date; see Figure 11-5). We assume in this simple example that each product requires a unique component (product A requires component a, product B requires component b, etc.). The arrows underneath each weekly sequence indicate the type of item each cell is to work on next, once inventory has been removed and the generic production cards have been freed up. The finished goods inventory after the assembly cell currently holds three containers of product types A, B, and C—each with a generic production card attached—while product D is in process in this cell. Likewise, the buffer area between the cells holds two containers with items e and f, while the component cell has item g in process.

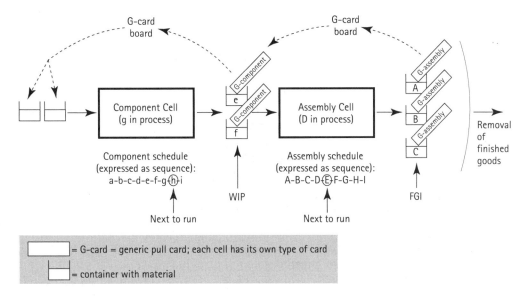

Figure 11-16. Generic card system with schedule

Assume now that all three containers in the finished goods inventory are removed. The generic cards (G-cards) are then detached from each container and put on a G-card board for the assembly cell. After this cell has completed product D, the freed up G-cards signal that the cell can begin on the next product in its sequence (product E). The operator will, therefore, look for item e in the buffer. Once this component has been brought into the cell, the G-card is removed from its container and brought back to the board for the component cell. The G-card from the assembly cell is then attached to the component container, and it is ready to be used for assembly. If the assembly cell works rapidly, it may complete products E and F before the component cell has finished item g. In that case, there will be two G-cards waiting on the board for the component cell. These then signal that the next two components in the sequence (h and i) can be produced.

The output from this hybrid control system can be changed as often as cell schedules are revised. This prevents unnecessary production and storage of products with irregular demand patterns. Thus, *generic pull systems are suitable for cells in assemble-to-order or make-to-order environments characterized by varying volumes and product mixes.*

Cardless Pull Systems

The kanban card serves as an information carrier. Its primary function is to signal that it is time to move or to produce (this is the only function for a generic card). Its secondary function is to specify which item is in line to be produced or moved, the quantity involved, and, in case of move cards, the starting and ending locations for the containers. The use of cards is definitively simple and low-tech. Of course, the necessary information can be transmitted in many other ways. A fabrication cell could send faxes or e-mails to suppliers, or post orders on its suppliers' websites, should the incoming buffer inventory run low.

When it is unnecessary to communicate information, other than to indicate that material has been removed, several alternatives are available. For example, the empty containers themselves can signal the need for material. Another common *cardless system* is the use of "kanban squares" or "kanban lanes." These are marked areas on floors or tables designated for containers (or for carts or racks of materials). An empty area is a signal to replenish inventory. Conversely, when an area is full, the previous processes are prevented from producing more.[26]

Consider the assembly cell in Figure 11-17. Here we have kanban squares inside a cell, each with a WIP limit of two containers. If the operator at workstation 2 pulls material from the preceding buffer area into her station, a space opens up. This open space represents a pull signal for workstation 1 to produce, since inventory has been removed from a downstream station. Once work on a product is completed at workstation 1, the container—if there is open space—can be pushed into buffer area 1. The determination of what to produce next (i.e., what material to pull in from incoming material) comes from a sequence or schedule at station 1. Thus, kanban squares can be viewed as a generic pull system with schedule.

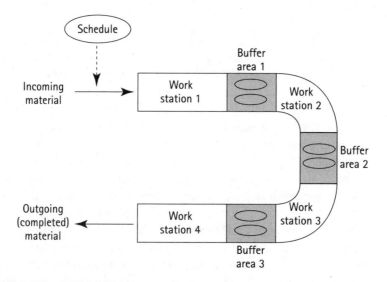

Figure 11-17. Using buffer limits to control production and material movements inside cell

Order Releasing with Pull Systems

There are two important features of pull systems. One is that they maintain a fairly constant inventory in the system controlled by the pull loop. The second is that they control order releases to meet either demand or the maximum production capacity.

Controlling WIP inventory

Pull systems have been endowed with almost mythical powers, and large-scale lead time and inventory reductions have been single-handedly attributed to the implementation of these systems. Actually, it is not the use of pull signals per se, but the enforcement of WIP limitations that fosters lead time and inventory reductions. We discussed in the section on input/output control, as well as in Chapter 7, how you can regulate and stabilize manufacturing lead time by controlling WIP inventory. In pull systems, controlling the number of cards, containers, or buffer spaces controls WIP. For example, by designating kanban squares you limit the maximum possible WIP inventory. If a buffer space is full, production stops because there is no place for the preceding workstation to put completed material—a phenomenon called *blocking*.

In short, if inventory is not depleted, production signals will not be issued, and no more inventory will be built up. (Thus, the addition or removal of cards, containers, or buffer spaces in the system will increase or decrease inventory.) In this respect pull systems operate differently than most schedule-driven systems. In the latter, WIP inventory typically is unlimited, and production continues according to the schedule regardless of whether or not there is demand.

Releasing to the bottleneck rate

Any productive system has one or more bottlenecks that dictate the possible output. There is no sense in releasing work into manufacturing at a rate greater than what the bottlenecks can handle. This will only lead to excessive inventory build-up, resulting in a choked system with long lead times. The latter situation often happens when MRP is used to regulate order releasing, because the order schedules from MRP are created without detailed consideration of shop floor capacity.

Consider the flow-line cell in Figure 11-18a. This cell uses a generic card system to regulate the start of production. Each time a batch is removed from the buffer at the end of the cell, a signal is sent to the beginning of the cell to launch a new batch. Since there is a limited number of cards (or circulating containers), a signal to produce will not be sent unless inventory is removed at the end of the cell. If demand exceeds the capacity, orders will, effectively, be released at pace with the rate of the bottleneck in the cell. In essence, the average output rate adjusts itself to either the consumption rate or the bottleneck production rate, whichever is the smallest. In order to prevent the line from overproducing, it needs to be controlled by a schedule or a sequenced backlog. Thus, this is the generic card system we discussed earlier (sometimes referred to as CONWIP).[27]

In the system in Figure 11-18a, the pull signal comes from the buffer inventory at the end of the cell. Accordingly, the demand rate is the primary device that controls production releases. An alternative method is to release a card as soon as a unit has been completed at the end of the line.[28] Since the signal now is sent without a unit being consumed from a buffer point, this is not a pull system in the traditional sense. However, it can be viewed as a pull system if we consider the inventory on the line. Thus, rather than being a system that controls inventory on and after the line, this approach limits WIP on the line only. As before, this system needs a schedule in order to prevent unnecessary inventory build-ups (although a specified limit on the line plus buffer WIP inventory will have a similar effect).

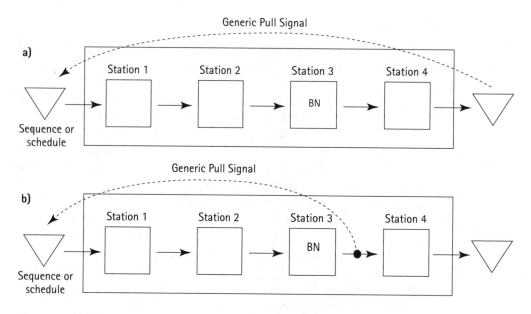

Figure 11-18. Pull signals from inventory vs. from bottleneck (BN)

A signal to pull a new job into the cell can also come directly from the bottleneck, as shown in Figure 11-18b. The system now sends a signal to start production as soon as a batch has been completed at station 3 and continued down the line. In this way, the release rate will always equal the cell's production rate (however, if the bottleneck location is not stable you may as well pull from the end of the line).[29] One advantage of sending signals from the bottleneck is that this station can operate even if any station further downstream is malfunctioning. Since those stations are not bottlenecks, they can catch up once the problem has been fixed. This is not the case if you let the bottleneck station starve for work, something that can happen if the signal is sent from the end of the line.

For generic card systems to work well, i.e., to keep WIP relatively constant, the generic card should signal the release of approximately the same work content. If the parts/products on the line differ with respect to processing times, the card could represent standard hours of work rather than units. The idea is then to lot-size released work so that each release to the cell contains about the same amount of work (also see Chapter 7).

Robert Dowden's drum-buffer-rope system for cells

One way to schedule against bottlenecks is to use the *drum-buffer-rope* (DBR) methodology. In brief, the *drum* is the master schedule that sets the beat based on the bottleneck output rate. The *buffer* refers to the inventory created in front of the bottleneck station to ensure its uninterrupted operation, and the *rope* is a pace-setter mechanism that releases orders to match the capacity of the bottleneck. The details of DBR go beyond the scope of this book.[30] It should be noted, though, that the "rope" principle in DBR is essentially also used in systems controlled by a pull mechanism. We illustrate this through an example.

Robert Bowden, Inc., is a small manufacturer of commercial building products.[31] Its millwork operation, consisting of 20 workers, makes custom doors and windows. The lead time for the products hovered around six to eight weeks, while the competition could deliver within three to five weeks. Bowden reorganized the facility into five cells, each with four workers. Each cell team was designed so that a range of skills existed in each cell.

It was estimated that a team could complete an order in one day, so the drumbeat was set by a daily master schedule. Further, a buffer of three weeks was necessary to prevent the teams from going idle while at the same time precluding delivery times from getting too large. Accordingly, when the backlog of orders gets beyond three weeks, any new orders are subcontracted out. The rope, finally, is simply a generic pull signal; a new job is released into a cell once a previous job has been completed (see Figure 11-19). Therefore, WIP and lead time are kept constant. The result of these changes has been a substantial improvement in due-date performance, a lower defect rate, and a 20 percent increase in labor productivity. Also, response times have gone down to between two to three weeks.

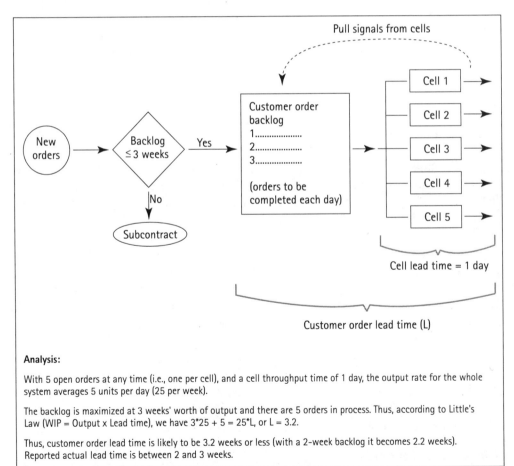

Figure 11-19. The drum-buffer-rope system at a millwork operation

The Issue of Loop Length—How Detailed Should the Pull Control Be?

You may have noticed that Figures 11-15 through 11-19 (with exception for Figure 11-17) all show how pull signals control the movements of material *into and between cells*, while we have not said much about how material movements are controlled *between workstations* inside each cell. By definition, a cell will have closely located workstations. Typically, these are separated by buffer spaces. Now, can you, and should you, use a pull system inside a cell as well?

Consider again the assembly cell in Figure 11-17. The flow inside this cell can be controlled in several ways. First, as we already discussed, you can limit the buffer spaces between stations so they can serve as kanban squares. Second, you could use a pull system that links all inventory points. That would mean that pull signals come from the outgoing material inventory to buffer area 3, from buffer area 3 to buffer area 2, and so on all the way back to the incoming inventory buffer. A third alternative is to send pull signals from the outgoing material inventory directly to the incoming material inventory. The material, once pulled into the first station, is here pushed from station to station until the product is complete. Note that the kanban square system is a generic but cardless pull system with a schedule. For the last two types of systems, the cards may be either product-specific or generic. Also, they do not operate with physical limitations on the buffer inventories in the interior of the cell.

There are two key features that separate the systems we just described:

1. Whether we have a pure pull system with product-specific cards, or a generic system with schedules, and

2. Whether we control WIP inventory at each workstation or only at the cell level.

Let's again consider the use of pull systems inside a cell. First, the number of products controlled, and the variability of their demand, are critical issues. If you have few products and stable, continual demand, a product-specific pull system could work fine inside the cell. On the other hand, with only few products you would not need a card system; kanban squares would suffice. That would limit the use of a card-based pull system to one that links the exit and the entry points to the cell. Likewise, if you have many products—even if their demand is relatively constant—you would not want to use a product-specific card system inside a cell. That would mean that you would have to store containers of each type of product at each station in the cell, waiting for the next pull. This would clutter the work area in the cell.

Accordingly, most cells should use either a kanban square system inside the cell, with production controlled by a schedule, or a pure or generic card-based pull system where the control loop runs from the outgoing to the incoming buffer point of the cell. Note, however, that kanban squares control WIP inventory tightly in the cell and are equivalent to a card-based system that controls each station. The issue of the length of the control loop therefore requires more discussion.[32]

The impact of control loops

Consider the two systems in Figure 11-20. Think of them first as a cell with three workstations. In that case, the cell in Figure 11-20a is controlled by a detailed "station-to-station" pull mechanism, and the one in Figure 11-20b by a "cell-to-cell" pull system. However, you could also think of the three workstations in the figure as cells. Now, the top figure would be a cell-to-cell pull system, where the jobs are pushed through each cell, while the bottom figure shows a "department-to-department" pull system where the jobs are pushed both to and through the cells. This points to the fact that an analysis of pull system performance has less to do with how we draw the boundaries for the smallest production unit we consider—station, cell, department, and so on—than with *the lengths of the control loops* we apply to those production units.

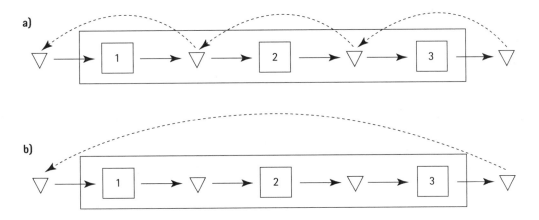

Figure 11-20. Control loops in linear systems

Look again at Figure 11-20. While in Figure 11-20a each inventory point following a workstation is controlled by the number of cards (or the physical number of buffer spaces), there are no restrictions on the buffer inventories inside the cell in Figure 11-20b. Based on our discussion in Chapter 7, we would expect that a system with less restrictive WIP inventory control would be better suited to situations where product demand and mix are erratic. This is because a system with short control loops would not adapt to such variations, resulting in either blocked or starved stations in the cell. Thus, unless demand is very stable per product, and each product has very similar lot sizes and processing times, a pull system where the loop runs from the exit to the entry point of the cell is preferable to one where the loop runs between workstations. Furthermore, if product demand is sporadic you would not want a product-specific pull mechanism, so a generic pull system with schedule and long loop would be the choice.

Let's take this one step further and consider a production system with more complex routing patterns. Figure 11-21a shows a system with five connected cells where the pull control loops span one cell each (again, if you like, you could also view this as one cell with five workstations). Figure 11-21b shows the same cell system controlled by a single loop going to the two gateway cells. Because the routing patterns are complicated, we can assume that the product demand and mix varies, and that the processing times differ from product to product. We will therefore probably rule out the use of a pure pull system in this case. But, again, should you control each cell

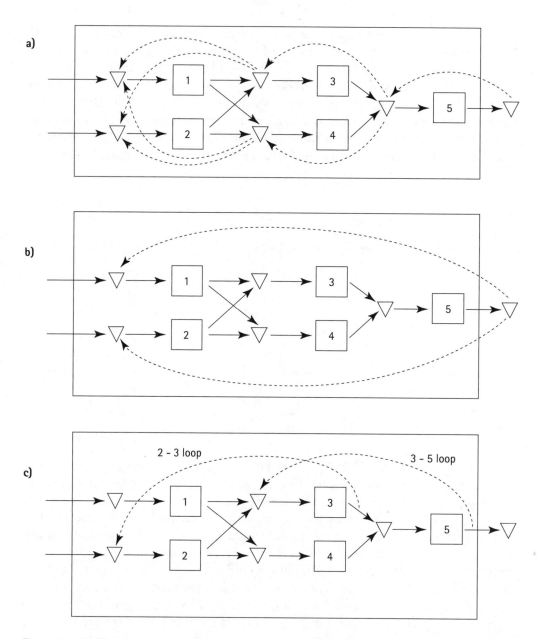

Figure 11–21. Control loops in complex systems

or use a longer loop? How well can you estimate the need for WIP at each cell in the face of varying demand? This raises the issue of how many cells should be controlled by each loop. One? Two? All? This is a difficult and intriguing question.

The POLCA system. The pull system design dilemma can get more complicated. For example, should each product be controlled by a single loop or multiple loops? Figure 11-21c shows a pull system where each loop covers two cells. This system, referred to as *paired-cell overlapping loops of cards with authorization* (POLCA) has been proposed for high-variety, MTO production but could also be used for MTS production.[33] POLCA is a generic card system, with cards being circulated as soon as a product leaves the last of the two cells in a loop. A free card indicates that capacity is available and that a new product can be brought into the cell. This is done according to each cell's schedule (generated by the MRP system). Also, there is one generic card type for each possible loop. Thus, the loop between cells 3 and 5 has a 3-5 card, the loop between cells 2 and 4 a 2-4 card, the one between 1 and 4 has a 1-4 card, and so on.

The POLCA system works as follow. Consider a product that requires processing in cells 2, 3, and 5. When a complete product leaves cell 5, and that product previously came from cell 3, a generic 3-5 card becomes available (if the product came from cell 4, a 4-5 card becomes available). That card is returned to cell 3. If cell 3's input buffer holds subassemblies destined for assembly cell 5, and the schedule indicates that this job along the 3-5 route can start, the subassemblies could be brought into cell 3 to be processed. When that happens, the 3-5 card is now added to the 2-3 card that was already attached to the product. Thus, when processed by cell 3, an item holds two cards. When work is completed in cell 3, the product is transferred to the input buffer of cell 5. At the same time, the 2-3 card is freed and sent back to the beginning of cell 2. When cell 5 has completed work on any product, it will—because it is the last cell in the system—simply look at its input buffer and pull in next available job.

To repeat, cell 2 does not get authorization to work until a product that follows the cell 2/cell 3 route has been completed in cell 3. Likewise, cell 3 does not start work until a product that follows a cell 3/cell 5 route has been completed in cell 5. Therefore, one difference between the POLCA system and the generic card system with independent (nonoverlapping) loops shown in Figure 11-21a is that a free card in POLCA indicates that the next cell ahead in the routing has just completed work, while a free card in the single-cell generic card system indicates that the same cell that completed the work is idle. But since any generic card system can be adjusted to loop over multiple cells, the major difference between those systems and POLCA appears to be the overlapping loops.

A Brief Comparison of Pull and Push Systems

At this time, fairly little is known about the design and operation of pull systems and their variants. However, based on a few simulation studies, it appears we can observe a few things about their performance, and also that of purely schedule-driven push systems. The following results, based on comparing output or service-level performance with the inventory needed to sustain that performance, appear to hold under a variety of demand conditions:[34]

1. A pure pull system may carry more inventory than a schedule-driven push system. This is because of the minimum WIP inventory in pull systems dictated by the number of cards per product.

2. A generic card system with schedule (including POLCA) always outperforms a pure pull system (that is, it generates the same output while

requiring less inventory). The assumption, of course, is that the schedule is always correct.

3. A pull system with longer loops most often equals or outperforms a system with shorter loops.

4. A generic card system with independent loops that cover three cells (or more) equals or outperforms POLCA.

5. In production systems with machine breakdowns, POLCA does better than large-loop generic card systems.

The last result indicates one possible advantage of shorter control loops. If a cell stops producing due to problems with a resource, WIP inventory does not build up ahead of it. However, if the loop extends from the end of the cell system to the beginning, material can continue to flow into the system, building unnecessary inventory in front of the problem cell. Finally, let us emphasize that the performance of a pull system very much depends on the setting of its parameters, i.e., the lot size (container size), the number of cards, the length of the loop, and the schedule (if applicable). Thus, pull systems can be much more complicated than one might expect. More theoretical and practical insights are needed before we fully know the best practices regarding design and operation of all pull system variants.

The Pros and Cons of Pull Systems

Pull systems, through their tight WIP control, can reduce inventory and stabilize lead times. They also have the advantage of being simple to use, require relatively low maintenance, and can be operated without computers (it is rather common today, though, to send electronic pull signals using computers or to record job completions using barcoded cards for the purpose of inventory control). The complexity of MRP-based order schedules, coupled with a frustration with their poor performance, has led many companies to disconnect the traditional shop floor control system in favor of a pull system.

Pull systems, however, can have clear disadvantages. For example, some companies have experienced problems with missing cards, or cards that are turned in late or hung incorrectly on the boards. The use of electronic move and production signals can alleviate some of those problems. In other cases, the limit on WIP—set by kanban squares—is not respected. Thus, pull systems require discipline to operate successfully. The most obvious disadvantage, as we discussed earlier, is the philosophy of "replenish upon use" which prevents product-specific pull systems from being applied effectively in situations with greatly shifting production volumes and product mixes. The problem of unnecessarily filling the pipeline with inventory you don't need, or being unable to anticipate forthcoming demand, can of course be handled by combining the pull system with a job schedule at each production stage. As indicated, these types of pull systems tend to perform better than pure pull systems.

A final comment pertains to disturbances. In situations with problems such as missing parts or failed tests, production will be held up since cards are attached to the problem units. To avoid this, temporary cards can be issued to start production of new items. These cards are removed once the problems are rectified.

PLANNING AND CONTROLLING SUPPLIER ORDERS

Pull systems are merely execution systems, so you must also have a system in place that (1) plans overall production output for the firm, (2) secures capacity in the factory, and (3) arranges for raw materials to be shipped from suppliers and final products to be sent to customers and distribution warehouses. Most companies therefore use an ERP/MRP system for order entry/order fulfillment and for material and capacity *planning*. However, as we discussed above, you can replace the practice of using MRP-controlled dispatch lists by relying on pull systems. Disconnecting the MRP system from manufacturing execution means that only purchased items are ordered via MRP schedules while internal manufacturing is controlled via pull systems. However, the use of pull mechanisms to trigger orders can be extended to sourced material as well. An example is presented below.

Example of a Supplier-Based Pull System

Pull systems in internal manufacturing tend to be of the *fixed order quantity, variable time interval* type. This is in contrast to pull systems between plants and suppliers, which tend to be based on the *variable quantity, fixed time interval* principle. In other words, trucks may arrive at the supplier's plant for pick up on a regular basis, say every third day, though the exact part mix and quantities requested can vary depending on the manufacturing plant's own demand.

Waterville TG, Inc. (WTG) is a Canadian-based manufacturer of weather strips for the automotive industry.[35] WTG has expended much effort in recent years to become a world-class manufacturer. Although it makes a fairly simple product, the company has around 100 suppliers providing close to 400 purchased items. In recent years, it has implemented both an MRP system and a kanban system for managing 65 percent of the procured materials. WTG uses 23 dedicated extrusion cells. However, the focus here is on the external MRP/pull system involving the suppliers.

An MRP system was first put in place to generate purchase orders. At the same time, a card system was instituted simply to promote "post-deduct" inventory control (see Chapter 10). The ordering process worked as follows. A weekly master schedule was developed based on customer orders (see Figure 11-22, no. 8). This schedule drove the MRP explosion, and a 12-week order schedule was sent to suppliers (nos. 9 and 10 in Figure 11-22). When material arrived at the plant (no. 1), inactive cards (no. 2) were first activated with a barcode scanner (no. 3), scanned to record the addition to the inventory (no. 7), and attached to the material.

Material is mostly stored at the point-of-use (no. 4). Once it was consumed in the manufacturing process and the associated cards were released (no. 5), the cards were again scanned (no. 6) to record the depletion of inventory (no. 7). For control purposes, each card was sequentially numbered to track active, inactive, lost, or discontinued cards.

Two years later, WTG switched to a pull-based system. The new system is very similar to the old one (see Figure 11-23). As before, the suppliers receive each week an MRP-generated order schedule covering the next 12 weeks (no. 9 in Figure 11-23). But they also receive a daily fax—appropriately called a faxban (no. 11)—which

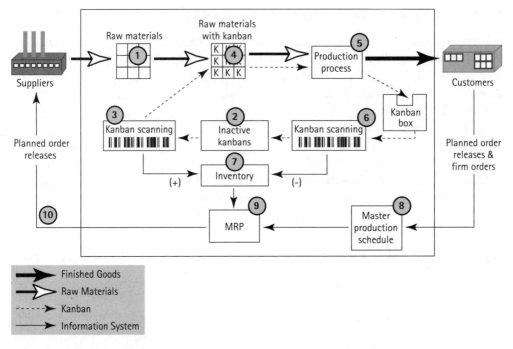

Figure 11–22. Original card system at WTG

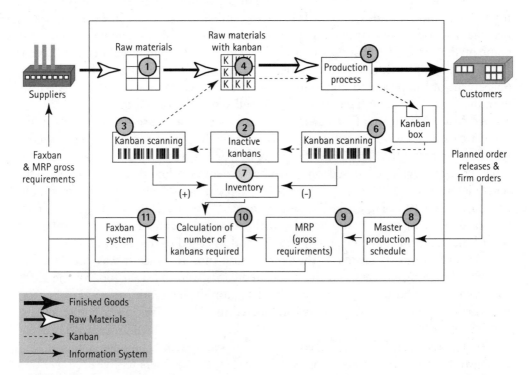

Figure 11–23. The faxban system at WTG

informs the supplier of the most current need for the next shipment stated in number of containers. On a predetermined day of each week, the faxban contains a final and official order request, again stated in number of containers. The amount ordered is the difference between a precalculated maximum inventory level (which includes safety stock) and the inventory at the day of ordering (no. 10). For the rest of the stages in the card loop (i.e., nos. 1 though 6), the activities are the same as in the previous system.

A crucial feature of this system is that WTG receives orders from its customers on a weekly basis, covering the next 8 to 16 weeks. Likewise, WTG transmits to its suppliers a schedule for the following 12 weeks. It also keeps the suppliers up to date through the daily need reports (the faxbans). Thus, there is extended information on both sides of the process, assisting the manufacturer as well as the suppliers in their planning process.

MPC MODIFICATIONS DRIVEN BY CELLS—LOT-SIZING AND TRANSFER BATCHING

A lot size or batch size is the amount you manufacture of one product before you switch over to another kind. Existing lot-sizing techniques, like EOQ and Period Order Quantity, ignore "the reality of the shop floor." Specifically, they ignore capacity and WIP inventory. Parts or products do not exist in a vacuum in the manufacturing system. Therefore, you should view batches as customers who compete at each workstation or material-handling station for service. Given that capacity always is limited, some batches have to wait (this is the WIP inventory). The magnitude of this wait time depends on the size of the batch. The smaller the batch, the faster it can be processed, and the shorter the wait time for all items in the batch. In addition, since the time to process one batch affects the waiting time for all other batches in the system, *small batches tend to have shorter waiting and throughput times than large batches.*

We say "tend to" because a qualifying factor here is the time to change over between two different batches. Let setup time be S. With a demand of D and a lot size of Q, the time spent on setups per unit of time is $S*(D/Q)$. Thus, the smaller the lot size, the more time is devoted to changeovers between products. Since capacity is limited, there will be less and less time left over for producing when the lots get smaller. Ultimately, the waiting time will explode (we discussed this phenomenon in Chapter 7).

Setup times, therefore, play a major role in determining lot sizes. If setup times are large, lot sizes must be large as well. Conversely, if you reduce time per setup, you can safely reduce lot sizes. But even if you do not reduce the lot sizes, shorter setups will still have a positive impact since they create more productive capacity on the equipment. In cellular manufacturing, the use of part and product families facilitates the reduction of setup time.

Unfortunately, there is no simple lot size formula that considers lead time or other items in the system competing for capacity. *As a rule, however, lot sizes are often too large, and you should probably reduce them to achieve improved throughput times.* You can always use modeling to test the impact of various batch sizes (see

Chapter 7). If you do not want to resort to modeling, trial-and-error goes a long way. In any event, you should reduce the lots for parts that have excessive lead times and for which there is no good reason to maintain large lots.

In the rest of this section we discuss the use of small transfer batches in and between cells, and the relationship between lot-sizing and container size in pull systems.

The Transfer Batch Concept

A transfer batch is the number of units moved between workstations or production areas. A transfer batch is typically equal to or smaller than the production lot size. The use of transfer batches (also called lot-splitting or overlapping operations) is an extremely powerful way of reducing throughput times. As you can see from the flow-line example in Figure 11-24, breaking the lot quantity into three, equal-sized transfer batches compresses the total elapsed time for the jobs from 630 to 370 time units—a reduction of 41.3 percent.

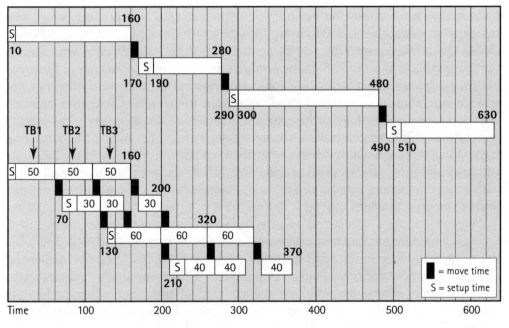

Figure 11–24. Impact of transfer batching in a flow shop

The application of transfer batches differs depending on whether you apply them in cells with linear or jumbled flows. We treat each situation separately below.

Transfer batches inside flow-line cells

In a flow-line cell, the workstations are arranged in process sequence. Batches move from station to station, and the sequence between transfer batches applied to the first station is maintained throughout. Here are some important insights regarding transfer batches in flow-line cells:[36]

- The time to complete a set of jobs declines when you use transfer batches (as shown in Figure 11-24).

- The effect of transfer batches is marginally decreasing. That is, splitting a lot into two transfer batches has the greatest impact on the time to complete the jobs. Splitting the lot into three transfer batches will reduce time further, but the additional reduction is less than the first, and so on (see Figure 11-25).

- Machine utilization, measured over the time it takes to complete a job set, increases as the number of transfer batches increases. This is because smaller batches make each station wait less time for work.

- A bottleneck in the cell diminishes the effect of transfer batches. This means that the more unbalanced the line, the less impact transfer batches will have on the time to complete a schedule. To complete a job set in the shortest time, you should ideally balance the cell both in terms of the load from each individual item as well as in terms of the total workload on each station.

- The smaller the setup times, the larger the impact of small transfer batches.

- A transfer batch of one provides the shortest schedule. This assumes that material handling does not constrain the schedule.

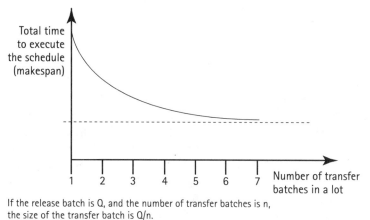

If the release batch is Q, and the number of transfer batches is n, the size of the transfer batch is Q/n.

Figure 11–25. The marginally decreasing effect of splitting lots into transfer batches

Small transfer batches are easy to use in flow-line cells. A transfer batch size of one (one-piece flow) is, of course, the norm in assembly cells, but you can also it in serial part-fabrication cells where the operators move with the parts from station to station. *In general, there is no reason not to apply small transfer batches in flow-line cells.* This is one of the easiest and most effortless ways to reduce lead times. Slicing the release quantity into just five sub-batches typically accounts for the majority of the time compression available from transfer batching (see Figure 11-25).

Transfer batches in dominant flow shop and job shop cells

A *job shop cell* has internal material flows that follow a highly irregular pattern. A *dominant flow shop cell* is one where materials follow an almost linear pattern, but where jumps between stations occur. When material moves around in patterns that deviate from strict linear ones, transfer batches of one product may get mixed with transfer batches of other products. Keeping track of the job status in the cell can therefore become a problem. Second, when transfer batches get mixed together, the need for changeovers increase. This negates some of the lead time advantages with transfer batches. You can deal with this problem, however, by using *family-based sequencing procedures*. We discuss this approach later, in connection with sequencing in cellular systems (for details, see Appendix E).

Lot-sizing in Pull Systems

Is the container size in pull systems the same as the lot size or the transfer batch? And how do you determine the size of the containers in the system?

The availability of cards or containers serves as the *order release mechanism* in pull systems. However, a single available production card, or an empty container, should not necessarily trigger production. You may want to operate with release rules such as "production should not be initiated unless there are three production cards or empty containers available." Such a rule is typically used in order to prevent excessive changeover efforts. Another variation is to let the pull system serve as a classic ROP system by releasing a card when the buffer inventory reaches a certain level. The card then signals a lot size, which consists of multiple containers.[37]

Second, even if production cannot start until a certain number of production cards have accumulated, the size of the lots moved *inside* the cell can be smaller than the container size. At one extreme, the transfer batch can be a single unit. At the other, of course, it can be equal to the production quantity (which could be multiple containers).

Third, you can have fixed or dynamic transfer batch sizes for movements *between* cells. For example, you may require an inventory of four full containers at the output side of a cell before you move them to next cell or functional work area. Alternatively, the material handler may move all the containers that are available at the time of the move. Here, the intercell transfer batch changes over time.

In summary, the size of the container often determines the *minimum* transfer batch to be moved between work areas, and also the *minimum* production lot size. The container, then, represents the smallest number of units that will be produced and moved between work areas.[38] *There is no simple rule for determining container size, except that small is preferable to large.* This is because you can always accumulate containers, but you cannot reduce their size. At Toyota, the container size typically holds around 10 percent of average daily demand, but that may be too small in less repetitive situations. Also, since you don't want too many types of containers around the plant, you must find a compromise between the needs of all the different parts/products manufactured.

MPC MODIFICATIONS DRIVEN BY CELLS—PRODUCT SEQUENCING

To sequence jobs, or batches, means to arrange them in order for processing. Job sequencing is a necessary activity since jobs can only be handled one at a time by an operator or a piece of equipment (except when simultaneous processing of parts is possible, such as with heat treatment, cleaning processes, and certain machine tools.). In this section we look first at general sequencing rules. Then, since cells are designed to process families of parts or products, sequencing procedures that consider families are also discussed. Finally, we look at sequencing in pure pull systems.

Sequencing in Push Systems

Let's consider the traditional ERP/MRP system first. Once orders have been released into manufacturing based on their MRP-determined due dates, the shop floor control (SFC) system takes over. For each work area in the plant, it will create—typically on a daily basis—a prioritized sequence of orders to be executed. Among the most commonly used priority rules are:[39]

- First come, first served (FCFS). Arrange and process jobs in the order in which they have arrived at a work station, with earlier arrivals coming before later arrivals.
- First in system, first served (FISFS). Arrange jobs in the order in which they were released into manufacturing at their gateway operation, with those released first put first in every queue in the system.
- Earliest order start date or due date (EORSD or EORDD). Arrange the jobs using the order dates from MRP, with jobs with the earliest start dates, or due dates, coming first (this rule can be used with generic card systems, for example).
- Earliest operation due date (EOPDD). Arrange jobs using the operation due dates established by either an infinite scheduler (like CRP) or by a finite scheduling program. Operations with early due dates precede those with later due dates.
- Shortest processing time (SPT). Arrange jobs based on the sum of their operation and setup times at the station where they are waiting. Process jobs in order of increasing processing times.
- Various "home-grown" sequencing rules, based on physical, monetary, or customer-based properties (smallest size first, light colors first, largest dollar value first, most important customer first, etc.).

Some companies choose not to use daily dispatch lists, but rely on *finite or constraint-based scheduling software* instead. These typically take planned and open orders from MRP, and then schedule their operations against pre-established capacity limits for each workstation. A whole cell can here be treated as a single workstation, unless it has a highly erratic internal flow pattern. In that case each workstation inside the cell may be scheduled. Companies often find that the schedules determined by finite scheduling software cannot be executed due to time delays (i.e., a late job will delay the start time for the following job). However, because each schedule is also a sequence, these companies may retain the job sequences created by the finite schedulers and use them to process jobs waiting in queue. In effect, the schedules default to daily dispatch lists. Despite such experiences, software that combines finite scheduling principles with infinite capacity scheduling may completely replace MRP in the future.

Sequencing of Product Families

The general sequencing rules listed in the previous section—referred to as *job sequencing procedures*—can be applied to any type of production unit, including cells. However, since cells produce one or more families of similar parts or products, the use of special sequencing techniques should be considered. A *family sequencing procedure* incorporates information about part or product family membership in its structure, and one of its main purposes is to avoid setups.

Family sequencing procedures typically follow a two-stage process where you (1) first determine the sequence among families waiting in a queue, and (2) then determine the sequence among the items within each family. All waiting jobs in a family are processed before you switch to the next family. For family sequencing to be effective, switching between families should require a *major* setup, while switching between jobs within a family should require only a minor setup. You can reduce lead time for all items in a queue by arranging the jobs in a sequence so that unnecessary major setups between families are avoided.[40]

Examples of family sequencing rules

With the *FCFS-Family rule* you establish the family sequence by first choosing the family who had a batch which arrived the earliest to the queue. You then run all waiting jobs in that family according to the order in which they arrived (i.e., in FCFS order). The family whose members arrived second to the queue is processed next, and so on. FCFS-Family (illustrated in Appendix E) is probably the simplest of all family sequencing rules. Another simple but effective rule is *minimum setup-shortest processing time* (MSSPT). Whenever the queue is to be prioritized, you inspect the waiting jobs and select first the family that requires the smallest amount of setup time. Note that family setups can be sequence-dependent; i.e., if family 3 is processed before family 1, the setup may be 20 minutes. If the sequence is reversed, it may be 12 minutes. Once you choose a family, you run the jobs inside the family according to the SPT rule.

The impact of family sequencing

In almost all situations, family sequencing procedures outperform job sequencing rules (which ignore family membership) with respect to throughput time and lateness.[41] In addition, our research shows that production output can increase at one machine by over 20 percent simply due to family sequencing.[42] A very nice feature of family sequencing procedures is that they "create capacity" when it is most needed. When a queue is small, family sequencing does not have much impact. However, when queues grow large and the risk of long lead times increases, sequencing to avoid setups results in shorter throughput times. Thus, the beauty of family sequencing procedures is that they "kick in" in times of need. They tend to lower both average throughput times and their variances, which makes them more robust than job sequencing rules.[43]

In general, family sequencing rules are more effective than job sequencing rules when:

- The number of different families is low.
- Family setup times are large.
- Resource utilization is high.
- Processing time variability is high.
- Batch interarrival time variability is high.

These conditions make intuitive sense. If utilization and variability are high, you will have larger queues in front of the resources. In these queues, the likelihood of finding jobs from the same families increases if the number of families is small. Finally, the setup time saved by combining jobs from the same families, and processing them together before switching to a new family, is greater if the family setup times are large.

Although family sequencing can be very effective in reducing average lead times and meeting due dates, there is a risk that altering the job sequences can cause delays for certain jobs and also cause mismatches between components going into assembly processes. Appendix E provides a more in-depth discussion of family sequencing and also gives an example of its use at J.I. Case Corporation.

Family Sequencing and Production Coordination at John Deere

John Deere's tractor manufacturing plant in Waterloo, Iowa uses family sequencing within an MPC system that relies on MRP, pull mechanisms, and a schedule-based signal system.[44] The material flow goes from two foundries that make iron castings to Department 500, which machines the castings into "transmission casings," onto the transmission assembly department that builds the transmissions, and finally to the tractor assembly division, which finalizes the tractors (see Figure 11-26).

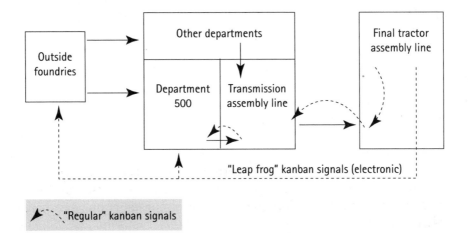

Figure 11-26. Information and materials flows in Deere's tractor manufacturing system

Department 500 makes 23 different versions of casings in seven manufacturing cells. The transmission casings weigh between 100 to 150 pounds (45 to 68 kilos) and pass through an average of six machining centers before completion. A master schedule for tractors drives MRP explosions and generates delivery schedules for both Department 500 and the foundries. The machined casings are pulled from Department 500 into the transmission assembly line (located in the same building), delivered via truck to the tractor assembly plant, and then pulled into the assembly line according to the final assembly schedule.

Both the foundries and the cells in Department 500 face long changeover times. For example, the setup times for casing families range from two to four hours, though within each family the setup times are small. Recognizing that the prudent sequencing of raw and machined castings can avoid setup time, planners manually grouped jobs. The planners' perspective, though, was that further setup reduction in Department 500 required new equipment technology. However, management decided that this investment could not be cost-justified based on setup reduction alone.

The leapfrog kanban

An internal team then developed a system called "the leapfrog kanban method." In this system, electronic pull signals are sent simultaneously to Department 500 and to the foundries (see Figure 11-26). This is done by scanning barcoded assembly documents as soon as a new tractor is launched on the final assembly line. While the department-to-department pull system is still in place, the leapfrog system means that the preceding departments now know at an early stage the exact future sequence on the assembly line. Knowing the product requirements in advance, rather than waiting for pull signals from the transmission area, gives the manufacturing cells extra time to sequence casings according to families to minimize setup time. Likewise, the foundries have more time to batch their orders to meet the firm delivery schedule. This example illustrates that reactive pull systems, in an effort to be "just in time," may generate signals that come too late to allow for efficient sequencing. The leapfrog system in place at Deere helps overcome this limitation. It should be noted that although it is called a kanban system, the leapfrog mechanism is not a pull system in a strict sense but rather a short-term coordination system based on the final assembly schedule.[45]

Sequencing in Product-Specific Pull Systems

Although the discussion in the previous sections applies to pull systems as well, a few comments on sequencing in these systems are in order. We focus here on product-specific pull systems (i.e., pure pull systems without schedules). It is sometimes assumed that only one sequencing rule applies to pull systems—namely first come, first served (FCFS). This notion probably derives from the belief that since the main purpose of product-specific pull systems is to refill what was just consumed, this replenishment automatically follows the sequence of consumption. But this is not necessarily the case.[46]

Assume that you make a variety of parts and have a pull system with product-specific cards. As containers are removed from the cell, the production cards will be placed on the kanban boards to signal need to replenish. If a FCFS sequence is followed, the jobs are processed according to the order in which the cards arrived at the board. In the pull system (called CAR, for "components as required") at one of APV Crepaco's plants, for example, operators write down the container arrival date and time on a sheet on the kanban board in order to maintain the FCFS sequence among the jobs.[47]

For firms that do not rely on FCFS sequencing, another system—based on actual need—may be used. Here, the kanban boards have one row (or column) designated for each part type. Furthermore, each row (or column) is partitioned into colored sections where each section indicates the urgency to refill the containers. Red is "hot," yellow is "warm," and green means "no particular hurry" (see Figure 11-27). Each part has a different number of production cards, depending on its average demand, lead time, and container size (see our earlier discussion). If part A has 10 cards, and 4 hang on the board at a particular time, this means there are 6 filled containers in the system. Part B, on the other hand, may have 6 cards, of which 4 are on the board. Thus, for this part there are only two full containers.

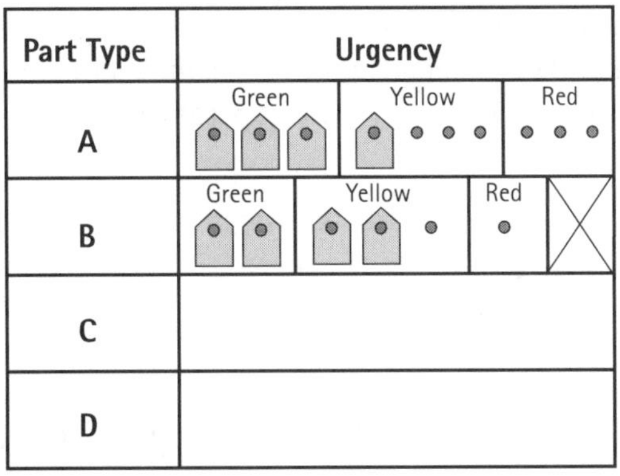

Figure 11-27. Kanban board indicating priorities

Now, let's define *run out time* (ROT) as:

ROT = (total number of production cards issued − number of cards currently on the board)*(container size)/(demand)

The inventory for each part in the cell is a function of the current card count. Dividing the inventory, in units, by average demand gives you the predicted time you will run out of inventory. For example, if part A has a demand of 50 units per day, part B has a demand of 30 per day, and the container in both cases holds 10 parts, then the ROT for part A is (10−4)*10/50, or 1.20 days. Likewise, part B's ROT is 0.66 days. So, you have less inventory to cover part B's average demand than you have for part A.

The board in Figure 11-27 does not indicate the arrival time of the cards, so FCFS cannot be applied. Rather, the colored fields have been determined based on run-out-time reasoning. For example, for part A: red = number of cards for which

ROT ≤ 0.40 days, i.e., 8 or more cards; yellow = number of cards for which ROT ≤ 1.20, but > 0.40 days, i.e., between 4 and 7 cards; and green = number of cards for which ROT > 1.20 days, i.e., 3 cards or less.

In the example in Figure 11-27, parts A and B both have the same number of cards on the board. Furthermore, the cards extend into the yellow priority area. However, since part B is closer to the red zone, you should give this part priority over part A. (Although this is not evident from the board, B's ROT, as we showed above, also indicates a higher priority.) The sequencing system described here does not follow the FCFS principle, but chooses the next job to run based on need rather than on the arrival time of the production card. In this way you can avoid spending capacity refilling inventory of low-priority parts and instead produce according to actual usage rate. Thus, sequencing in pure pull systems is a soft way of mitigating the strict "replenish when used" philosophy.

CHOOSING AN MPC SYSTEM FOR A CELLULAR WORK ORGANIZATION

After this review of planning and control procedures, you may ask: "How do I decide what type of MPC system to use with a cellular organization?" This is quite a complex issue, and the answer depends on the specific characteristics of your firm. In this regard, there are four aspects of a firm's operations that are closely intertwined and affect each other:

1. Operations and market interaction strategies.
2. Product characteristics.
3. Manufacturing process characteristics.
4. MPC system design.

As illustrated in Figure 11-28, market characteristics shape the operations and market interaction strategies. These, in turn, affect the design of the MPC system, as do the product and process characteristics. They also influence each other. In general, you should think of MPC system design as a reactive activity; i.e., one that is shaped by the firm's strategy and molded to fit its products and processes. The strategies and product characteristics determine the overall capabilities you require of an MPC system. However, it is the process characteristics, together with selected product characteristics, that most directly dictate the detailed MPC applications.

Operations and Market Interaction Strategies

Two related strategies are of critical importance to MPC system design. The first is the firm's *operations strategy* and the second is its *market interaction strategy*. The operations strategy specifies the plans to make the firm more competitive. As we discussed in Chapter 4, the need to deliver more rapidly, and at a lower cost, motivates firms to adopt cellular manufacturing. Such performance expectations also dictate the capabilities expected of an MPC system, since cells must work in concert with this system to become responsive. The operations strategy, together with market characteristics and competitive pressures, drives the company's choice of market interaction strategy.

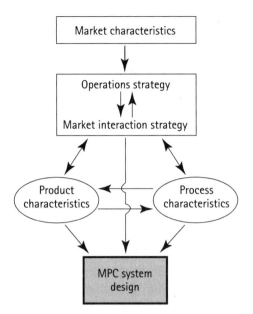

Figure 11-28. Areas influencing MPC system design

For any segment of its product lines, a manufacturing company can operate in three different manufacturing modes depending on its market interaction strategies:

1. *Make-to-stock (MTS)*. Essentially, an MTS company builds products on speculation and stores them, in advance of sales, in a finished goods inventory and often throughout a distribution system. There is no direct customer interference in either the product design or the manufacturing processes.

2. *Make-to-order (MTO)*. An MTO firm, on the other hand, makes products only after a customer has negotiated with the firm about the design, production, price, and delivery of a product. The product is customized in that it is designed fully or partially for that particular customer. Some raw material, however, may be ordered to forecast (e.g., commodities, steel, plastic, and other materials frequently used). Accordingly, the contact between customer and firm is close. Although any firm can take advantage of cells, due to varying demand and product specifications they tend to be least common in MTO companies.

4. *Assemble-to-order (ATO)*. An ATO firm purchases and manufactures parts and components, and possibly subassemblies, based on market predictions. However, it waits until a customer order is received before building a specific product. Although products are configured and assembled especially for each customer, the product is not "customized" in the typical sense of the word. The customer selects product options from a limited menu, and these options translate into modules of already manufactured, stand-alone subassemblies or kits of parts.

The need to handle planning bills of material for modular products (required for ATO), track customer orders throughout the manufacturing process (required for MTO), or deal with rate-based schedules (useful for MTS) are all examples of how market interaction strategies influence MPC systems. Table 11-3 shows the major characteristics associated with each of the three types of manufacturing modes.[48]

Product Characteristics

Product characteristics affect the scope and nature of the MPC system. The more product variants that are offered to the market, and the more components that these products require, the more complex is the planning and control process. One way to control growing complexity is to adopt an ATO strategy. This requires that the products can be modularized. The modules can be assigned to individual cells for manufacture (i.e., product affecting process). In addition, modularization can strongly influence a firm's decision to outsource.

Outsourcing can simplify MPC efforts by shifting the headache of planning to the suppliers.[49] Consider the product structure in Figure 11-29. If your firm performs all the purchasing, part fabrication, subassembly, and assembly operations in-house, the planning and control effort can be very large. Compare that with the situation where all components below the dotted line in the structure tree are outsourced. The number of purchased and manufactured components will then be reduced, as will the required number of manufacturing processes.

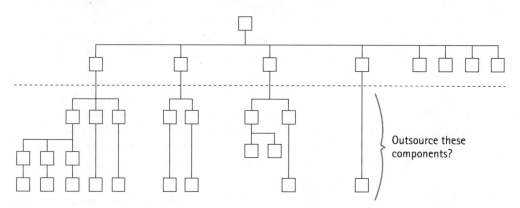

Figure 11–29. Reducing MPC complexity by outsourcing

When products can be modularized, the opportunities for outsourcing are enhanced. More specifically, suppliers that before only made individual components can now be given responsibility for complete module design and manufacture. This has been a clear trend in recent years, especially in the automotive industry. Here is an example from Mercedes-Benz:[50]

When managers at Mercedes-Benz planned their new sports utility assembly plant in Alabama, for example, they realized that the complexities of the

Table 11-3. Market interaction strategies: characteristics associated with MTS, ATO, and MTO firms

Dimension	Make to Stock (MTS)	Assemble to Order (ATO)	Make to Order (MTO)
Volume per unit	High	Medium	Low
Product mix variety	Low to medium; stable	Medium to high; unstable	High; unpredictable
Order promising	ATP via product MPSs	ATP via module MPSs	Eng. and mfg. capacity checks
Customer response time	Short	Medium	High
Manufacturing lead times	Short	Short to medium	Medium to high
Changeover times	Short	Short to medium	High
Manufacturing lot sizes	Small to large	Small to medium	Very small
Work-in-process	Low to medium	Medium	Very low
Finished goods inventory	High	Low or none	None
Central/decentralized planning	Central or decentralized	Centralized	Centralized
Central/decentralized shopfloor control	Decentralized	Centralized or decentralized	Centralized
Basis for planning	Product forecast	Module forecasts/backlog	Confirmed order backlog
Forecast accuracy	Medium to low	High	Low (if done at all)
Bills of material	Standard bills	Planning bills	Gradually created for order
Master production schedule unit	Product (sales unit)	Module (subassemblies, kits)	Prototype product
Final assembly schedule	Products, based on FC+orders	Products, based on orders	Products, based on orders
Schedule variability, MPS	Low (i.e., level schedules)	Medium	Medium to high
Schedule variability, components	Low (i.e., level schedules)	Medium	High
Shopfloor control approach	Pure pull or with schedules	Pull system, with schedules	Schedules or pull w. schedules
Inventory accounting	Backflushing possible	Backflushing or perpetual inventory	Perpetual inventory accounting
Manufacturing process dedication	Flow-line cells likely	Flow or job shop cells likely	Cells less likely
Supplier relations	Few and close	Close	Less tight; can vary
Supplier material control	Pull w. or w/o schedule possible	Pull with schedule possible	Schedule driven

Note: ATP = available to promise, MPS = master production schedule, FC = forecast.

vehicle would require the plant to control a network of hundreds of suppliers according to an intricate schedule and to keep substantial inventory as a buffer against unexpected developments. Instead of trying to manage the supply system directly as a whole, they structured it into a smaller set of large production modules. The entire driver's cockpit, for example—including air bags, heating and air-conditioning systems, the instrument cluster, the steering column, and the wiring harness—is a separate module produced at a nearby plant ...

In short, the number of different products, and their complexity, determines the scope of the MPC system (i.e., small versus large). A product's design can also strongly influence decisions to outsource and/or to adopt an ATO strategy. Outsourcing reduces the scope of the MPC effort as well as the scope of the manufacturing system, while ATO manufacturing can reduce finished goods inventory.

Manufacturing Process Characteristics

The top half of Figure 11-30 depicts an input-output model of a manufacturing system. Here, material flows from suppliers to customers via a series of production areas. Within each such area—receiving, part production, subassembly, final assembly and test, and shipping—there are one or more "production units." A production unit is the smallest organizational entity that is considered for planning and control purposes. A work center composed of a group of similar machines can be one type

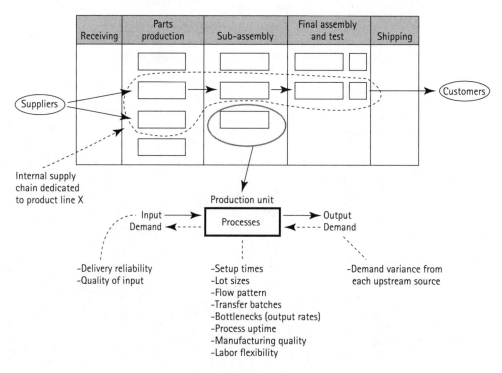

Figure 11-30. Analyzing MPC systems

of production unit, a paint line another type, an assembly cell a third type, and so on. Thus, you may view a complete manufacturing system as being composed of several smaller production units (as shown in Figure 11-30).

One way to approach the design or choice of MPC systems is to first "decompose" the complete manufacturing process. Taking on the whole plant is too difficult. Instead, if you can partition the plant cleanly with respect to related production units along a *value stream*—the internal supply chain—you can simplify the analysis (also see the discussion of focused production in Chapter 5). This is indicated by the dotted line for product line X in the upper half of Figure 11-30.

Inside the internal supply chain you then need to consider individual production units and their interactions. The smallest production unit we have focused on in this book is the cell. You can view each cell as a process that converts inputs to outputs (see the lower half of Figure 11-30). The cell's production depends on the demand signals it receives (in the form of schedules and/or reactive pull signals). In turn, the cell requires material to produce and therefore sends demand signals to the previous step in the supply chain. This could be a feeder cell or an external supplier.

Factors that Influence the Choice of MPC System

As we stated earlier, the characteristics of the manufacturing process heavily dictate the choice of the MPC system for a cellular system. The lower portion of Figure 11-30 lists process factors we think are especially critical to MPC systems. However, the figure also shows some product-related factors, like demand, which we also have included because of their strong influence on process design.

These critical factors also appear in Table 11-4. As can be seen, many product/process factors can affect your choice of MPC system. It is obvious that each factor can have a large number of different settings (in fact, there are no limits to most of the factors). However, when all factors are set in one extreme way or the other, the choice of MPC system is typically easy. In Table 11-4 we show (in the second column) all critical factors having a best and a worst setting (high versus low, large versus small, etc.). We then suggest, in the third and fourth columns of the table, the ideal MPC system when factor settings are at their extremes.[51] The fifth and last column, applicable to the gray area where factor settings are mixed, shows the characteristics of an MPC system appropriate for those "murky" situations.

While you may find Table 11-4 intuitive and self-explanatory, a few comments are in order. When all factors are at their *worst settings*, i.e., when setup times are high, the flow pattern is complex, bottlenecks are severe, manufacturing quality is poor, demand variability is high, etc., you also have the most difficult planning and control situation. Nothing is simple here. The most obvious conclusion is that you must rely on a system capable of *scheduling* production. Reactive pull systems, operating in the "replenish what was just consumed" mode, would be highly inappropriate. By the way, this "worst-case" situation, with all factors at their upper levels, is not suitable for cellular manufacturing. In fact, you are unlikely to adopt cells for this environment, and if you do you will find it difficult to design and operate them effectively.

On the other hand, when all factor settings are at their *best settings*, i.e., when setup times are low, flow patterns are simple, bottlenecks are balanced, manufacturing

Table 11–4. Selecting MPC systems

Factors Affecting Choice of MPC System	Factor Settings	If All Factors Are at Their Worst Levels (high, large, complex, etc.)	If All Factors Are at Their Best Levels (low, small, simple, etc.)	If Factor Settings Are Mixed
Setup times	High	*For materials and capacity planning:* • Use ERP/MRP *For supplier control:* • Use MRP for supplier material *For shop floor control:* • Use centralized SFC • Use MRP & priority lists, or finite schedules, to control manufacturing orders • Use part family scheduling at machine level • Report per machine and/or individual operator	*For materials and capacity planning:* • Use rate–based ERP/MRP *For supplier control:* • Pull supplier material *For shop floor control:* • Use decentralized SFC • Use product-specific pull systems • Part-family scheduling not beneficial • Report per cell	*For materials and capacity planning:* • Use ERP/MRP *For supplier control:* • Use MRP and/or pull for supplier material *For shop floor control:* • Preferably use decentralized SFC • Use MRP and priority lists or generic pull systems with schedules • Use part-family scheduling unless tight links between units • Preferably report per cell
	Low			
Lot sizes	Large			
	Small			
Flow pattern	Complex			
	Simple			
Transfer batches	Large			
	Small			
Bottlenecks	Severe			
	Balanced			
Process uptime	Low			
	High			
Manufacturing quality	Low			
	High			
Labor flexibility (cross-training)	Low			
	High			
Demand variability (output side)	High			
	Low			
Delivery reliability (input side)	Low			
	High			
Material quality (input side)	Low			
	High			

quality is high, demand variability is low, etc., planning and control can be relatively easy. These are also the ideal conditions for cellular manufacturing. Note, by the way, that if you compare Table 11-4 with Table 11-3, you can see that when all factors in Table 11-4 are at their upper level, you are most likely to operate in an MTO mode. On the other hand, when all factors are at the low level you probably operate in an MTS mode.

"High" and "low," or "worst" or "best," of course, are relative terms. Therefore, it may not be clear to you whether the factors for your production units, including cells, are at high or low settings, or in between. For making such subjective decisions we recommend that you employ benchmarking data and a high degree of common sense.

FACILITATING PLANNING AND CONTROL BY REDUCING COMPLEXITY

Many firms have found that material- and capacity-planning and control are simpler and easier for cells than for a functionally organized plant. This "simplicity" can be traced in large part to the use of decentralized control. With cells, you can change the order release points from the machine to the cell level, and transfer the responsibility for executing work schedules to the cell operators. By delegating planning and control tasks to the cell, you reduce the centralized MPC efforts. Figure 11-31 illustrates the simplified information network that is possible with cells.[52]

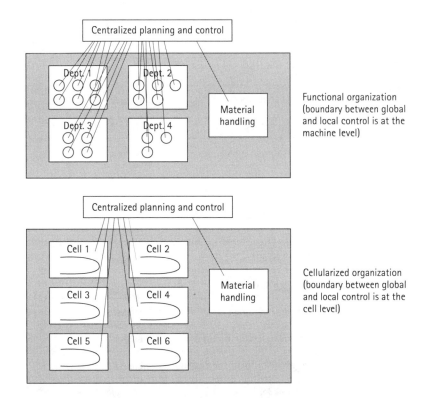

Figure 11-31. Information flows in functional vs. cellular organizations

Some cells are easier to plan and control for than are others. This has very much to do with the same factors that determine system choice. In other words, it is easier to manage cells in environments characterized by the best rather than the worst settings in Table 11-4. *Therefore, whatever the starting conditions, you should always try to reshape the manufacturing environment to make it smaller, simpler, and with less variability.*

The most important factor in reshaping the environment is the size (and, therefore, the variety) of the part and product populations. Product and component proliferation can be a serious impediment to MPC effectiveness. One automaker once offered customers 87 different styles of steering wheels, 300 ashtrays, 437 dashboard meters, 1,200 carpets, and 110 possible radiator models.[53] *If you standardize parts and increase the commonality among your company's products (a classic application area for group technology), you will reduce your MPC efforts, stabilize your schedules, lower your inventories, and reduce your costs.*

Variability in demand is another critical factor that lessens performance and increases MPC efforts. Demand variability tends to escalate as you move down the product structure (because of lot-sizing and shared components in products). This is why it is so important to stabilize the master schedules and use small lots. Furthermore, pull systems in their pure form (i.e., those that use product-specific signals) will not work well in environments characterized by variation. In fact, you should not install these for cells until the manufacturing environment is right. Specifically,

Table 11-5. Actions needed to reduce lead time

Factor	Needed to Reduce Lead Time
Setup time	Decrease
Setup time variability	Decrease
Unit processing time	Decrease
Processing time variability	Decrease
Lot size	Decrease*
Lot-size variability	Decrease
Move time	Decrease
Move time variability	Decrease
Transfer batch size	Decrease
Order schedule variability	Decrease
Labor flexibility (cross-training)	Increase
Routing flexibility (machine pooling)	Increase
Capacity/work load	Increase/decrease

* If preceded by setup-time reduction.

pull systems should be implemented only after you have worked hard on housekeeping, improved the flow, stabilized the schedules, reduced setup times and lot sizes, and improved quality.[54] Many of these changes, of course, will take place when you implement cells, though you should still try to continually improve on all these factors even after your cells are in place.

Interestingly, there is a close connection between cell system performance and the factors you should consider for MPC system selection. Table 11-5 shows the factors, discussed in earlier chapters, that will improve lead time performance for cells if changed in the proper directions.[55] These changes all move the factors towards settings favorable to the MRP/pull system combination (see fourth column in Table 11-4). You should note that such changes typically take place when cells are created—in some cases automatically, but mostly through your concerted and continual efforts.

KEY INSIGHTS

Some companies make the mistake of believing that cells can improve performance without adjusting the manufacturing planning and control (MPC) system. However, well-designed cells have the ability to react much faster than "the rest of the plant" and may be slowed down by MPC procedures tailored to other types of processes. Therefore, an integral part of cell adoption and implementation is to conduct an MPC review. Depending on the extent of cellularization of your plant, modifications to existing procedures can be large or small. Here are some key insights to keep in mind as you think through the MPC options for your cells:

- *You can simplify the MPC task with cellular manufacturing.* By turning the responsibility for detailed scheduling and control over to the cell, you can reduce the central MPC effort.

- *Responsive cells require responsive suppliers.* Cells are key elements of lean manufacturing. However, for them to operate well, you must ensure that the cell suppliers—whether internal or external—are as responsive as the cell itself. This is the only way you can achieve truly reactive systems. You should develop close information- and knowledge-sharing relations with your suppliers.

- *Flexibility and capacity in the process facilitate MPC efforts.* The more capacity, and the more flexible the resources in the system, the easier the planning and control, and the better the performance. You can create "extra" capacity by reducing setup times and by clever setup-avoiding scheduling. Mobile capacity can come from operator cross-training.

- *Shop floor control for cells can be simplified with pull systems.* Pull mechanisms work well with most cells, unless these are subject to large product mix and volume variations. If you use pull systems, you can dismantle the order execution portion of the MRP/ERP system.

- *You should seek to minimize the size of transfer batches inside as well as between cells.* Cells are ideal for one-piece transfer batches. Also apply small transfer batches between cells. This is an easy way to reduce lead time.

- *You may consider family sequencing in order to reduce setup times.* Scheduling jobs according to part or product families is a good way to avoid large setups in certain situations. You should use this approach if flow patterns are irregular, and for creating extra capacity at severe bottlenecks.

- *Always consider reducing the size and complexity of the manufacturing system, and the variability in the demand.* Smaller, simpler, and more stable processes are easier to manage. In addition, they tend to provide better performance. Note, though, that the downside of small cells is a loss of routing flexibility.

- *MPC system selection for cells is influenced by product, process, and market characteristics.* Of these, the process characteristics may be most important. See Table 11-4 for guidance.

12

Job Design and Daily Work
in Manufacturing Cells

In the past several chapters we have focused on fairly technical dimensions of manufacturing cells—how to select cell products and equipment, how to create an effective layout, how to measure cell performance, and the types of production planning systems that will best support the cell. While these technical decisions form the backbone of the cell architecture, decisions about people in the system are equally important. In fact, our work with companies over the years suggests that people issues are frequently a stumbling block to efficient and effective implementation and operation of cells.

Designing a cell's "people system" is a vital element of your effort to create a supportive cell infrastructure. Chapters 5 and 6 pointed out where in the cell design process you should address the infrastructure issues (see especially Figures 5-1 and 6-2). We also identified the key areas (e.g., job design, selection, training, compensation, change management) you need to address. In the next few chapters we take a much closer look at various dimensions of people in cells.

In this chapter we examine jobs in cells by addressing the following questions:

- What is work like in cells? What do operators actually *do*?
- When companies adopt cells, do jobs automatically change?
- How should companies decide what types of jobs are best suited for their cells?
- What does cell work mean for task allocation, cross-training, teamwork, job classifications, ergonomics, and other job-related issues?
- How do supervisors' jobs change with cells?

WHAT WORK IS LIKE IN CELLS

The examples below describe daily work in three different cells. Based on actual companies' experiences, the examples highlight important dimensions of cell work and illustrate the different ways in which jobs can vary from cell to cell.

Life in a Supervisor-Led Multi-Operator Cell

Pedro is one of about 15 operators who work in an assembly cell that puts together subassemblies for air conditioning units. When Pedro arrives in the morning, his supervisor assigns him to one of the three stations he is qualified to staff. His co-workers have been similarly trained on a subset of the cell's many tasks. Pedro works at this station all day or until the supervisor assigns him to another location.

A central conveyor moves units from one station to the next and helps determine the pace of work in the cell. Small buffers decouple Pedro's work area from the preceding and following stations. The documentation accompanying each unit tells him exactly which components to attach. Several hours into the shift, Sally, an adjacent worker, is having difficulties and asks Pedro for help. A part will not insert properly. Together, they discover that the component has a distorted flange. Pedro tags that part as defective and alerts the supervisor of the problem. In the meantime, Sally inserts a defect-free duplicate.

Pedro and his co-workers are responsible for direct labor tasks only—converting material inputs into material outputs. Apart from recording defective parts and helping to solve on-line production problems, Pedro and his fellow workers do not perform any *indirect* labor tasks (activities that support production but do not involve the physical transformation of material). In this cell, indirect tasks are left to the cell supervisor, who determines work assignments, coordinates schedules, interfaces with supplier and customer cells, and intervenes when workers cannot solve a production problem. The cell supervisor is also, jointly with the human resource department, responsible for selecting replacement workers when the cell has a vacant position.

Pedro's job is quite similar to the work he did before the cell was formed. The major difference is that he and the other operators now are trained to perform several tasks. At least two workers are trained in each process step. This means they can assist each other when problems occur at a station.

Life in a Self-Managed Single-Operator Cell

Steve is the sole operator assigned to the plastic components cell at a large precision machining shop. The cell produces several families of like parts. Before the cell, setup times ranged from 8 to 12 hours. Part family sequencing and dedicated tooling have cut setup times to about 3 hours in the cell. Specialized family tooling has also reduced run times from between 4 and 5 minutes down to 2. Processing in the cell consists of turning and counter boring, cleaning, deburring, miscellaneous second operations, and packaging (parts are packaged in quantities before being transported to the central inventory storage area). Early in the life of the cell it became apparent that the counter bore operation could be done as part of the first operation on the turning equipment. This change streamlined the production process and reduced part costs. No one thought of combining these tasks before. However, once the cell was put together, it seemed like an obvious improvement. Deburring is handled by an operator in an adjacent area and takes place while Steve is running other parts.

Each Monday morning, Steve's first task is to review the schedule spreadsheet. This document provides demand and inventory information for the cell. For each part, it lists the family to which it belongs; the quantities needed by the assembly area during the last four months (recorded as material pulls by the assembly lines from central inventory storage); the MRP-generated expected usage, by week, for the next three months; the projected annual usage; and the projected number of days of inventory left in stock. Based on this review, which takes about half an hour, Steve determines what parts to run for the upcoming week, and in what quantities. He uses the spreadsheet information and his own knowledge of the parts to make these decisions. Steve tries to avoid backorders, keep finished part inventories low, and keep only a few work orders open at a time.

Prior to opening a work order, Steve goes to his terminal and reviews the on-line documentation (drawings and process plans) to be sure they match the hard copy documentation on file in his area. If they do not, he obtains the current hard copy drawing and process plan from the manufacturing specifications department. Once Steve has the correct documentation in hand, he opens the work order.

Steve spends the next three hours preparing a setup on the CNC equipment. He can make part program adjustments directly on his terminal. Once the setup is complete, he starts the production run. Typically, the CNC equipment can run four hours turning a single piece of plastic bar stock without requiring new tooling. (From his tool analysis, Steve knows how many parts this operation can produce before he will need to replace the cutting tool.) While the CNC machine is running, Steve performs the second operation on the parts using other machines in the cell. Whenever a part operation ends, Steve cleans and checks the parts. He might also have time to inspect and package the finished parts, and complete the paperwork to place these items in the inventory storage area (where they sit until pulled from the assembly lines).

Because quantities are large and run times are long, Steve has trained swing shift personnel, who work from 3:00 P.M. to 11:00 P.M. (15:00 to 23:00), to load the CNC machine with new bars of raw material and restart the process. (These workers are assigned to areas outside Steve's cell.) When Steve arrives the following morning, he unloads the machine.

As part of his cell responsibilities Steve participates in process improvement teams for the assembly areas that use his parts. He also works on new product introductions. This involves modifying CNC programs to produce prototype parts, and identifying and obtaining any special materials. If a part does end up in full-scale production, Steve prepares all the necessary setup documentation and adds this to his in-cell files. Steve maintains his own stocks of raw materials and tooling. Once a week he reviews these inventories and, if necessary, contacts the buyer to place orders.

Steve also works on odd projects assigned by his supervisor, and is a member of the "medical preparedness team." This means he could be called at any time to respond to a medical emergency in the plant. Steve also spends time updating the ISO 9001 documentation for his cell. Finally, Steve tracks his own hours, and schedules his own breaks and vacations. In short, Steve has almost total ownership of his cell and its parts.

Prior to being assigned to the cell, Steve had been responsible for setting up and operating a single piece of equipment. Obviously, his job as cell operator is more varied, more complex, and carries with it significantly more responsibility. According to Steve, "I get to stay real busy and I like that."

Life in a Self-Managed Multi-Operator Cell

Nicole works in a cell that makes subassemblies for electronic instruments. Processes in the cell include component part insertion, pressing, soldering (both oven and hand soldering), epoxying, oven curing, cleaning, and packaging (for internal transportation to subsequent work areas). The equipment, arranged to create a linear flow through the U-shaped cell, consists of microscopes, arbor presses, oven, leak tester, cleaning station, and various hand tools and workbenches. The cell has 18 stations and occupies about 1,300 square feet (around 121 square meters).

While Nicole is one of nine full-time employees who work in the cell, temporary workers are also used. At present, five such "temps" work in the cell, but this number changes in response to capacity needs. Each operator (permanent and temporary) is on a job rotation and training plan that is intended to eventually result in all operators being fully trained on all operations in the cell. A training matrix located on one of the cell walls indicates who has been trained to work at the various cell stations.

When Nicole arrives in the morning, she puts her personal belongings in her locker (she does not have a designated "home workstation" in the cell). She then checks the electronic pull system on the cell terminal for any new build orders, and surveys the work in process located throughout the cell to decide where to work first. Nicole has several favorite stations. If there is work to be done at one of them, and no "hot" orders elsewhere, Nicole begins to build products. Each station is equipped with all the needed materials, instructions, and tools, many of which are ergonomically designed and power-assisted. Part bins are carefully arranged and color-coded to make assembly efficient.

Over the next half an hour, Nicole's co-workers arrive, select starting stations, and begin work. (The plant uses flexible-time scheduling, so workers arrive at different times within a set window. Initial station assignment follows the "first to work, first to choose" rule.) Once everyone is present, the supervisor assembles the entire cell team to review workloads and production targets for the day.

Nicole returns to her assembly station and continues working for another half-hour. Her supervisor may intervene and ask her to move to another station in response to a production build-up or the need to process an urgent order. Normally, though, Nicole and the other operators are themselves responsible for assessing the work situation and moving to the stations where they are most needed.

Nicole often decides to change stations for ergonomic reasons. Repetitive motion injuries/cumulative trauma disorders (RMI/CTD) are a significant issue in this assembly cell. Nicole and the other operators are well aware of the risks involved, and they rotate stations frequently. They also take mandated RMI exercise breaks performed to music played for that purpose over the public address system.

At mid-morning, Nicole discovers some in-process items with workmanship errors. She completes a rework tag and places the assemblies at a designated rework station. She also alerts the other operators of the defects she has discovered. Nicole and her colleagues have received substantial training on how to communicate effectively with one another, including how to provide constructive feedback.

After lunch, Nicole moves to the packaging station after noticing that a backlog of completed parts has accumulated at this work center. She packages the parts and places them in part bins located at the outbound side of the cell. Nicole next moves to the rework area. For some items she removes components that have been incorrectly attached and then reintroduces these subassemblies (minus the incorrectly inserted components) into the workflow at the station where the first needed component is inserted. She also discovers that a few parts cannot be reworked and must be scrapped. For all parts she handles at the rework station, she documents the nature of the defects and the actions she took.

Prior to leaving at the end of the day, Nicole attends a second brief team meeting led by the cell supervisor. The team reviews its progress and problems encountered during the day. Hadrian, another operator, has discovered an inefficiency in the documented build process for one cell product. The team reviews Hadrian's proposed change and agrees to try it out during the coming week. Issues requiring more focused problem solving will be discussed at a formal team improvement session later in the week.

In summary: Nicole and her fellow cell operators are responsible for inspection of incoming materials, all component assembly operations, material movement within the cell, final inspection of completed subassemblies, and rework of defective items. They also purchase consumables, interface with upstream and downstream processes—such as plating, milling, and final assembly—update process documentation, and are responsible for continual process improvement. Compared to operators who work in the traditionally organized part of the plant, Nicole and her team members have many more responsibilities.

DO JOBS CHANGE AUTOMATICALLY WHEN YOU IMPLEMENT CELLS?

Cells can have a significant impact on operator and supervisory work. Cells often mean different responsibilities, more tasks, and more teamwork. But these changes are not automatic. Jobs don't change on their own just because the physical layout changes. It is management that determines whether and to what degree jobs will change.

Consider these examples, reminiscent of the three cases we just discussed. Three mid-sized manufacturing companies in the UK each introduced cells.[1] In two cases, jobs changed dramatically: cell workers were given broad responsibilities, performed a wide variety of different tasks, and collaborated with their co-workers in performing indirect and direct labor tasks. The number of job classifications was reduced. Cells at these two plants were, in effect, part of management's strategy to create "a cooperative, flexible and skilled workforce." In the third plant, however, jobs did not change with cells. There was a strict division of job responsibilities within each cell, and each operator performed only a narrow range of tasks. Management's goal was to retain tight control over production. They "designed idiot-proof, low-skill job tasks" and "discouraged shop-floor initiative and discretion."

A number of factors—such as an organization's size, whether a plant is independent or part of a larger corporation, management's values and assumptions, the firm's strategy and performance, the skills and aptitudes of the available workforce, and so forth—can influence whether and how jobs change with cells.[2] The role of management, however, is critically important. In particular, management must be willing to support (e.g., through employee selection and training) and reward (through financial and non-financial means) new ways of working in order for jobs to change with cells.

WHAT IS JOB DESIGN?

Job design is the process of planning and specifying the tasks that a particular job will include, and the way in which this job will be performed.[3] There are two broad goals of job design. One is to create jobs that satisfy the requirements of the organization and its technology. The other is to design jobs that are consistent with the individual worker's requirements; in other words, to make jobs safe, satisfying, and motivating for the individual employee.[4]

Job design is important. It affects how well employees coordinate their work, the degree to which they are committed to the goals of the organization, the extent to which their abilities are tapped, and the extent to which their psychological and ergonomic needs are met.[5] In short, job design influences both performance and employee well being. It follows that job design is at the heart of an organization's human resource management system.

There is a great deal of choice involved in job design. While it is true that work processes and technology (and other factors that we will describe later) place constraints and limitations on available options, much of job design is discretionary. *It follows that there is no single best design for a given job.* Moreover, job design tends to be evolutionary and iterative rather than performed once and once only. Cell job design is, in fact, often *job redesign*. This is because, in most cases, cells are created by reconfiguring existing plants with existing jobs. Furthermore, once the cells are established, process improvement—and thereby job redesign—typically takes place.

Basic Approaches to Job Design

There are four different approaches to job design: mechanistic, motivational, perceptual-motor, and biological (see Table 12-1).[6] While these approaches have different objectives, they are all central to the design of jobs for cells. For example, in any job design you will need to consider *work methods*. These are the procedures and processes used in executing a job or task. The focus is on how the task is done and the tools that are used. Determining work methods may involve time studies, process analysis, and the development of work standards—all elements of the mechanistic approach to job design.

Similarly, you must take into account *physical and mental considerations*, elements that are related to the perceptual-motor and biological approaches to job design. This includes the overall design of the workplace, tools, and equipment to account for the physical and mental capabilities of people. Physical considerations also include other attributes of the work environment, such as noise, temperature, and lighting. Cell design teams need to consider these ergonomic aspects when they plan the detailed cell layout (see Chapter 6). Finally, effective job design takes into account the *social and psychological work environment*. This involves considering the motivational aspects of work, i.e., those factors that make work meaningful and satisfying.

Table 12–1. Approaches to job design

	Origins/Objectives
Mechanistic	• Rooted in industrial engineering. • Goal is to study a job "scientifically" (through time and motion studies, for example) and find the most efficient way to perform it. All workers should then be trained to use this one best way. • Tends to results in narrow, specialized, and highly efficient jobs, which are performed repetitiously, requiring little training or mental ability.
Motivational	• Rooted in organizational psychology. • Goal is to make jobs meaningful for employees. This is accomplished by designing jobs that provide varied work, autonomy, significance (performing a whole piece of work), the opportunity to use varied skills, the opportunity to participate in decision making about work, feedback on performance, recognition, growth, and achievement. Most often this is accomplished through job enlargement (adding more tasks of the same type) and job enrichment (assigning workers planning and control tasks previously assumed by management or support groups). • Tends to result in broader jobs that are satisfying and motivating for (most) employees.
Perceptual–motor	• Rooted in the scientific discipline most commonly referred to as "human factors." • Goal is to design jobs that efficiently and safely use people in human-machine systems. This is done by considering the mental capabilities and limitations of workers, so that jobs do not require more attention and concentration than the least capable worker is able to provide. This approach focuses on making displays, programs, other equipment, and printed job materials easy to see and use, minimizing the information workers must attend to and process, and minimizing the memory requirements and stress associated with the job. • Tends to result in jobs that limit the amount of information workers must pay attention to, remember, and think about. This can reduce errors and accidents, as well as training requirements. Jobs tend to be less stressful and less mentally fatiguing, but may increase boredom and decrease satisfaction.
Biological	• Rooted in the study of biomechanics, work physiology, and anthropometry (study of body sizes). • Like the perceptual-motor approach, the biological approach is concerned with the person-machine interface. The goal is to design jobs that are within people's physical capabilities and limitations, and to assure that they take place in a physically comfortable environment (no excessive noise; comfortable temperature; ergonomically appropriate seating and so forth). Focuses on designing jobs that require fairly little strength, lifting, and endurance, and few wrist movements. • Tends to result in jobs that require reduced physical abilities and produce less fatigue and fewer medical incidents.

CELL WORK CHARACTERISTICS

The four approaches to job design we just discussed, together with other inputs, determine the basic structure of jobs in cells. We will refer to these basic structural factors as "cell work characteristics." These characteristics include four important dimensions of work:

- *Staffing level.* How many operators will work in the cell? This is essentially a capacity and skill-based decision.

- *Task type allocation.* Will cell operators perform direct labor tasks only, or will they also perform indirect labor tasks? As noted earlier, *direct labor tasks* involve the physical conversion or handling of material to produce output. Examples include machining, assembly, machine setup, loading and unloading of parts, material transport, and rework. *Indirect labor tasks* are support activities that facilitate the conversion of material inputs to material outputs. Examples include materials management (such as ordering parts, providing feedback to vendors, counting physical inventories, etc.), maintenance and housekeeping activities, quality assurance, performance measurement, and so forth. These are tasks that traditionally have been the responsibility of managers and other support or "indirect labor" personnel. The number and types of indirect tasks you assign to the cell will determine the degree to which the cell is *self-managed* versus *supervisor-led*. Table 12-2 provides a sample of direct and indirect tasks that can be performed by cell operators.

- *Multi-functionality.* To what degree should operators be trained to perform multiple tasks, whether direct or indirect? Operators who are able to rotate among different tasks will experience more varied jobs, avoid ergonomic problems, and increase their general knowledge of cell parts and processes. In addition, they are able to switch among tasks in response to production bottlenecks. You can measure the degree of multi-functionality for a given cell by considering the number of tasks assigned to the operators. In Figure 12-1, the average number of tasks per employee in Cell A is 1.25. Employees in this cell are less multi-functional than those in Cell B, where, on average, 2.5 tasks are assigned to each employee.

- *Cross-training.* To what degree should operators be cross-trained in overlapping tasks? (A task is "overlapped" if multiple employees are able to perform it.) The greater the task overlap, the greater the flexibility in assigning people to various tasks. You will need to determine the following:
  - *Degree of overlap in direct tasks:* At one extreme is complete cross-training on all direct tasks: each cell operator can perform all the technical work processes that convert cell inputs to cell outputs. At the other extreme is no overlap: operators are trained to perform one or more tasks, but each task can only be performed by one operator.
  - *Degree of overlap in indirect tasks:* When indirect labor tasks are assigned to the cell, and there is little overlap, individual workers or the designated cell leader can be responsible for specific tasks. At the other extreme—in cases of high overlap—most or all indirect labor tasks are shared (or rotated) among operators.

Task overlap offers important advantages. It enables employees to assist one another when needed and replace each other when absences occur (as we noted in Chapter 7, multi-functionality without overlapping is not helpful in dealing with variable workloads). Task overlap also makes it possible for employees to actually "share" a task. Task sharing exists when the level of interaction required to perform

Table 12–2. Direct and indirect tasks that can be performed by cell operators

---

Direct Labor Tasks
- Operating machinery, setting up machinery, loading and unloading parts
- Assembling
- Reworking parts or products
- Material handling between cell machines
- Assisting other operators to perform direct labor tasks

Indirect Labor Tasks

Materials management activities:
- Ordering parts or working with procurement on orders
- Interfacing with suppliers to provide feedback or expedite delivery
- Scheduling and sequencing work
- Providing information to customers on part/product status
- Monitoring raw material and finished part or product inventories
- Tracking material
- Material handling between cell and other units

Maintenance and housekeeping activities:
- Performing routine machine maintenance and repair
- Performing various housekeeping tasks

Manufacturing support:
- Designing and controlling tools and fixtures
- Developing or revising NC machine programs

Quality assurance activities:
- Conducting inspections
- Providing others with feedback on nonconformance
- Managing and revising documentation
- Collecting and analyzing quality data (e.g., maintaining and interpreting process control charts)

Performance measurement:
- Helping to develop process and product metrics
- Tracking process and product metrics
- Interpreting and responding to process and product performance metrics
- Providing performance status reports to others in the organization

Personnel-related activities:
- Providing input to hiring/firing decisions
- Providing input and/or delivering peer performance reviews
- Training other operators

Improvement activities:
- Identifying improvement opportunities
- Participating in team improvement sessions
- Designing and executing data collection and analysis
- Developing and implementing solutions
- Assisting other operators in any of the above indirect tasks

---

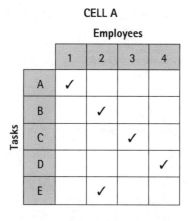

CELL A

Employees

Tasks	1	2	3	4
A	✓			
B		✓		
C			✓	
D				✓
E		✓		

Multi-functionality:
- ◆ Average number of tasks per employee = (1+2+1+1)/4 = 1.25

Cross-training:
- ◆ Average number of employees trained on each task = (1+1+1+1+1)/5 = 1
- ◆ Percentage of tasks on which employees are cross-trained = 100 × (no. of tasks that can be performed by multiple operators/total number of tasks) = 100 × (0/5) = 0

CELL B

Employees

Tasks	1	2	3	4
A	✓	✓		
B		✓		
C	✓	✓	✓	
D		✓		✓
E		✓		✓

Multi-functionality:
- ◆ Average number of tasks per employee = (2+5+1+2)/4 = 2.5

Cross-training:
- ◆ Average number of employees trained on each task = (2+1+3+2+2)/5 = 2
- ◆ Percentage of tasks on which employees are cross-trained = 100 × (no. of tasks that can be performed by multiple operators/total number of tasks) = 100 × (4/5) = 80%

Figure 12–1. Measuring multi-functionality and degree of cross-training

a particular task is high, e.g., when there is a great deal of back and forth in terms of work flow and operators must continually react to one another's inputs in completing work. Many tasks (particularly direct labor tasks) do not lend themselves to task sharing but rather take place in a sequential process where operators hand off work to one another.[7] Other tasks, often indirect labor tasks, do require high levels of interaction and, therefore, task sharing. Examples include group problem-solving and process improvement activities.

You can assess the degree of cross-training (or task overlap—we will use the terms interchangeably) by looking at two related measures: the average number of employees trained on each task, and the percentage of tasks on which employees have been cross-trained. Figure 12-1 shows that Cell A has a degree of cross-training equal to 1, and its percentage of tasks with cross-trained employees is 0. Thus, each task in this cell can only be performed by a single employee. While the cell has multi-functionality, it has no cross-trained operators. For Cell B, however, the same measures are 2 and 80 percent, respectively. Thus, this cell averages two employees trained on each task, and 80 percent of all tasks can be performed by at least two employees.

You can determine some of the fundamental characteristics of jobs in cells by answering certain key questions. How many operators will work in the cell? What types of tasks will cell operators perform? To what degree will operators be trained to perform multiple direct and indirect labor tasks? How much cross-training and task overlap will there be in direct labor tasks? In indirect labor tasks?

We have summarized these basic decision variables in the *cell work characteristics framework* shown in Figure 12-2. To make it simple, the matrix shows only the extreme positions regarding task allocation, multi-functionality, and cross-training (i.e., high vs. low).

Let's illustrate the framework by revisiting the cells we presented at the beginning of the chapter. Pedro's air conditioning subassembly cell is an example of a supervisor-led multiple-operator cell where operators have a low level of multi-functionality and are cross-trained in a limited number of direct labor tasks only. Pedro and his co-workers form a cell team, but operators are not responsible for indirect labor tasks.

Steve's plastic parts cell is an example of a single-operator cell in which the operator performs both direct and indirect tasks. Steve's cell is *self-managed*—a term we use to describe cells in which the employees assume primary responsibility for a large number of indirect labor tasks. Like any single-operator cell, his is also a *craft cell*, i.e., a cell in which each operator performs all the direct labor tasks in the cell. (Multi-operator craft cells are sometimes referred to as "rabbit chase cells" since the operators follow each other around the cell building products start-to-finish.) Note that Steve's cell has high multi-functionality with respect to both direct and indirect labor tasks, but as a single-operator cell, it has low task overlap.

Nicole's electronic subassembly cell is an example of a multi-operator cell with significant responsibility for indirect labor tasks and a high degree of overlap in both direct and indirect tasks. Thus, the cell's operators are extensively cross-trained and cooperate in performing both types of tasks. Although Nicole does have a supervisor, her cell is, in many ways, a self-managed operation. It is also an example of a cell with teamwork, a concept we will discuss in an upcoming section.

One critical issue remains to address: *how do you decide how work should be conducted in any specific cell?* Why, for example, would you elect to create a single-operator cell? How would you determine the number of indirect tasks the operators should perform, or the degree to which tasks should overlap? In general, what steps should you follow in making decisions about cell work design? These are the questions we turn to next.

	Multi-Functionality (Number of Tasks Per Employee)		
	Low level of multi-functionality (number of tasks per employee is low; number of employees per task is also low)	High level of multi-functionality (number of tasks per employee is high)	
		Low overlap (number of employees per task is low)	High overlap (number of employees per task is high)
Direct Labor Tasks	□ Operators have narrow jobs similar to those in a functional organization □ Operators hand off work to one another (no overlap or task sharing; limited interaction) □ Low job enlargement □ **PEDRO'S CELL**	□ Operators are trained in many tasks but cannot replace or assist one another □ Operators hand off work to one another; limited employee interaction □ High job enlargement □ **STEVE'S CELL**	□ Operators are trained in many overlapping tasks and can assist and replace one another □ Task sharing (high interaction) is possible □ High job enlargement □ **NICOLE'S CELL**
Indirect Labor Tasks — *Low number of indirect tasks assigned to the cell*	□ Supervisor-led cell □ Low autonomy □ Limited employee interaction □ **PEDRO'S CELL**	Infeasible	Infeasible
Indirect Labor Tasks — *High number of indirect tasks assigned to the cell*	□ Self-managed cell □ High autonomy □ Tasks are performed by the cell leader and/or selected operators □ Limited interaction due to low multi-functionality and low overlap □ Job enrichment for those performing indirect labor tasks Note: For cells to be self-managing, some operators, and in particular the cell leader if one exists, must be multi-functional. Self-management requires knowledge of the entire process.	□ Self-managed cell □ High autonomy □ Tasks are performed by the cell leader and/or selected operators □ Limited interaction due to low overlap □ Job enrichment for those performing indirect labor tasks □ **STEVE'S CELL**	□ Self-managed cell □ High autonomy □ Tasks distributed among most or all operators □ Task sharing (high interaction) is possible □ Job enrichment for many □ **NICOLE'S CELL**

Note 1: For a given cell with a given number of employees, increasing multi-functionality leads to increasing degree of cross-training. Thus, you cannot have a low degree of multi-functionality and a high degree of cross-training.

Note 2: This matrix is intended to illustrate different types of cells, not to compare the same cell over time.

Figure 12-2. Cell work characteristics matrix

A DECISION FRAMEWORK FOR CELL JOB DESIGN

Figure 12-3 presents a decision process framework for cell job design. The process begins with four critical inputs that influence decisions about the cell work characteristics: (1) the cell's intended strategic capabilities, (2) the cell's processes and technology, (3) the cell's demand pattern, and (4) management's (or the design team's) vision of cell work. We'll discuss each of these below.

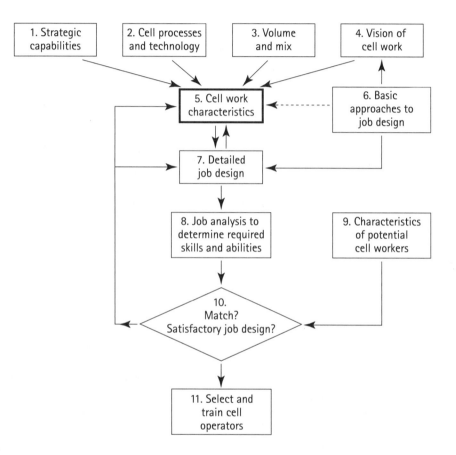

Figure 12-3. A decision process framework for cell job design

Strategic Capabilities

As we have suggested (repeatedly!) in prior chapters, *cell design begins with strategy*. Thus, the cell's intended strategic capabilities (Box 1, Figure 12-3) should help shape decisions about cell work. This means you should establish specific cell performance objectives related to the key strategic objectives (cost, quality, response time, flexibility, etc.) that are important for your competitive environment. Of course, several different job designs are possible for a cell that, for example, is to compete effectively on cost. You might design narrow jobs (limited multi-functionality and cross-training) at which workers specialize, thereby gaining great efficiency and contributing to low cost cell output. However, you might also achieve low costs by cross-training operators so that they can break production bottlenecks, speed up production, and operate with little inventory. Cross-training can also minimize loss of time due to narrow job designs, and may make it possible to staff the cell with fewer operators. This too can have a positive impact on costs.

While thinking about strategy will not necessarily direct you to specific choices concerning the four cell work characteristics (staffing level, task allocation, multi-functionality, and cross-training), you should keep strategy in mind as you make decisions about cell work. The key question you should ask yourself is: *Will the proposed job design support or hinder the ability of the cell to meet its strategic objectives?* Thus, the cell's intended strategic capabilities serve as a backdrop for assessing the various cell work characteristics options suggested by the technology, volume, and cell vision dimensions.

Cell Processes and Technology

The processes and technology used in the cell (Box 2, Figure 12-3) will set natural limits on your job design options. First, consider *staffing levels*. If the cell consists of equipment capable of running unattended for long periods of time (as was the case in Steve's cell), a few operators, or even a single operator, can staff it. If the tasks have a high manual labor content and/or the equipment can't run unattended (as was the case with Pedro's cell and is generally the case in assembly), higher staffing levels are called for.[8]

Similarly, technology also influences *task allocation*—the degree to which you elect to have cell operators assume indirect labor tasks in addition to their direct labor responsibilities. When equipment can't run unattended there is simply less opportunity for employees to take on indirect work. Technology and work processes will also affect decisions about multi-functionality and cross-training. There are far more opportunities to train operators on multiple and overlapping tasks in assembly cells, where process steps are relatively easy to learn, than in machining cells. For example, in a precision machining environment, where equipment is difficult to operate and the required skills can take years to develop, the amount of multi-functionality and cross-training you can consider is limited. In this situation, training cost and skill availability may motivate you to let cell workers specialize in a limited number of tasks that they alone are trained to perform.

Volume and Product Mix

Production volume and mix issues (Box 3, Figure 12-3) also influence cell job design. Volume, first of all, is the most important determinant of overall staffing levels. For example, the expected production volumes may be insufficient to support more than a single operator in the cell. Higher volumes might require multiple operators to meet demand. Volume (and technology, as noted above) also influences task allocation; high volumes may make it more attractive to have operators focus exclusively on direct labor tasks.

With respect to multi-functionality and cross-training, ask yourself how flexible cell workers need to be to match your product type and volume variability. In situations where volume variability requires that operators and staffing levels flexibly adjust to changing requirements, you want to train the operators in many overlapping tasks.

Vision of Cell Work

The processes and technology the cell will use, and the volume and mix of work it will produce, establish the boundaries for decisions regarding the cell work characteristics. For example, let's suppose that you have concluded that volume and cell technology require a multi-operator cell. Let's also assume that the processes and technology are such that workers can master multiple and overlapping direct labor tasks (e.g., the tasks are relatively easy to learn). Finally, let's say that the workload makes it possible to assign some indirect tasks to the cells. Does this mean you *should* design cell work so that operators perform varied and overlapping direct and indirect tasks? Not necessarily. It simply means that you *can* do so within the limitations created by technology and volume. The job structure you actually design for the cell will depend ultimately on your "vision of cell work" (Box 4, Figure 12-3), as well as the strategic capabilities the cell needs to meet.

You probably already have a vision of what work in cells is all about—or should be all about—even if this vision is not well articulated or well thought out. This vision has likely been influenced, either consciously or unconsciously, by the four approaches to job design shown in Table 12-1. In particular, a vision "takes a stand" in the apparent conflict between the mechanistic and the motivational aspects of work. With that in mind, answering these three related questions can help you form or refine your vision:

- Do you envision cell work as a way of making jobs more satisfying and motivating for employees? In other words, do you view cells as a way to create jobs that are "enlarged" (include more and varied *direct* labor tasks) and "enriched" (include responsibilities for planning and controlling work, i.e., include *indirect* labor tasks)?

- Do you see cell work as a way to introduce or sustain team-based operations?

- Is your plant currently constrained by a narrow job classification system?

We discuss each of these issues in turn.

Job enlargement and enrichment

Job enlargement—also called horizontal loading of tasks—involves increasing the number or variety of tasks a worker performs.[9] Training a machinist to operate a second piece of equipment, or adding setup, loading, and unloading to the machining tasks he or she already performs would be examples. Compared to the work they did before they went into cells, Steve, Nicole, and Pedro each have enlarged jobs (Steve and Nicole more so than Pedro).

Job enrichment—also called vertical loading of tasks—involves adding more decision-making authority to a job.[10] It means giving employees responsibility for some of the planning, controlling, and evaluating duties that managers/supervisors used to perform. The jobs that Nicole and Steve perform were enriched when they moved to cells. Pedro's job, on the other hand, was not.

An extensive body of research exists on job enlargement and enrichment (see Appendix F for more details). In summary, enlarging and enriching jobs will, with great likelihood, create jobs that employees find motivating and satisfying. This should lead to higher employee involvement, lower absenteeism and turnover, and improved quality performance. However, studies show a more mixed picture when it comes to productivity. For some firms, productivity has been shown to increase; for others it stays the same or even declines. Any positive outcome from enlargement and enrichment assumes that you have in place, or will introduce, other human resource practices (e.g., appropriate training, supervision, compensation) that support these broadened jobs. It follows that the notion of enlarged and enriched jobs also has economic implications for the firm. Finally, it should be noted that the outcomes are partly dictated by individual preferences. That is, some individuals prefer to have broader and more challenging jobs, while others are satisfied with "more of the same." This highlights a dilemma in job design: finding the right balance between *skill depth* and *skill breadth*.

Skill breadth versus skill depth. The trade-off between breadth and depth of skills is an important issue. For example, one machine shop's distinctive competence was its ability to machine tight tolerances that few facilities in the world could replicate. If cells were created, they had to protect these strategic capabilities. Furthermore, the machinists were highly compensated; making them responsible for a wide range of activities was not a good option from an economic point of view. Multi-operator cells, where skilled machinists worked primarily on their specialty while other operators did less complex tasks, were a better choice. So, as you articulate the cell's desired strategic capabilities, consider whether skill depth is important and factor this into your decisions about cell work characteristics.

You also should consider the consequences for job satisfaction of making everyone in a cell a "jack of all trades." Highly skilled employees value their unique contribution to the company. It is a source of status, self-esteem, and satisfaction. These employees might experience lower job satisfaction if anybody could do their job and they no longer possessed special skills. They might also resent having to perform simple tasks that they believe are "beneath" them. You need to consider how cell job design and other human resource policies (compensation, career ladders, etc.) can address this. For example, you might promote and recognize their expertise by making highly skilled employees responsible for training others in their specialty. (Of course, the cost of doing so may be prohibitive; thus, the sophistication of modern technology can work against multi-skilling.)

In summary, if you view cells as a venue for job enlargement and job enrichment, then you want to train workers to perform multiple and overlapping direct labor tasks (for job enlargement) and allocate significant indirect labor tasks to the cell (for job enrichment). However, be aware of the depth versus breadth trade-off.

Teamwork in cells

The second question we raised above pertained to the use of teams. You may see cells as a way to introduce or reinforce the use of teams in your company. Employees working together form a team when:

- They perceive themselves as a unique group within the plant (e.g., the 8510 cell team).
- Others can clearly identify who is a team member and who is not.
- They are responsible for producing a whole and distinct part of a product or service.
- Their work tasks require them to work closely with one another.[11]

Virtually all multi-operator cells satisfy these criteria.[12] However, it is the way in which team members interact with one another and the scope of their responsibilities that determine the degree to which the cell team is able to capitalize on the significant advantages that can accrue to the use of teams.

We devote a separate section to the use of teams later in the chapter. However, at this point we suggest that you reflect on the set of criteria presented in Table 12-3.[13] This list can help you determine if a work team is right for your environment. The greater the extent to which these criteria match the characteristics of your desired work environment, the more likely is it that a cell team structure will provide a satisfying work environment for employees, as well as strong performance for the organization. You can also use Table 12-3 to decide whether you should adopt cells or not. That is, some firms come to establish cells not by first forming product families (as we outlined in Chapters 5 and 6) but through their desire to introduce teamwork to the organization. Once this idea seems right, the search for suitable families around which to organize work can begin.

As the list of characteristics in Table 12-3 suggests, you must think carefully about the nature of your business strategy, competitive environment, tasks and technology, worker preferences and capabilities, and current organization to assure that work teams are an appropriate choice. Specifically, cell teams with extensive amounts of direct and indirect task overlap make the most sense when flexibility and responsiveness are important. This will most likely be the case in uncertain or unstable environments where employees need to make quick, on-the-spot decisions.

The impact of job classifications on job design

Many factories categorize jobs into classes or job grades (e.g., level 11 assembler, level 12 assembler, machinist I, machinist II), each of which is typically linked to a wage rate or range. Companies with classification systems that narrowly specify job tasks often find they need fewer and broader job categories when they establish cells. This happens when cell operators are to be cross-trained to take on tasks that in the past were performed by individuals in separate job classifications. As the types and variety of tasks performed expand, there will be fewer distinctions between operators and less need for narrow job classifications. For example, one unionized plant that converted to cells went from 160 job classifications to 12.[14] This reduction of job classes is not an isolated phenomenon. One large survey study found that plants with cells had 38 percent fewer job grades than plants without cells.[15]

Of course, whether you need to modify job classifications depends on where you start and the degree of labor flexibility that you want for the cell. In one corporation, the plants that introduced cells made no changes to the existing job classification system, which already stratified operators by the number and type of different tasks they performed. The broader jobs that cell employees were asked to undertake

Table 12-3. When to consider a cell team

Factors related to tasks and technology:
- When cell tasks require a variety of knowledge, skills, and abilities so that combining individuals with different backgrounds would make a difference in performance.
- When the cell work tasks are interdependent (they are linked sequentially or there is a lot of back and forth among tasks). If work in your cells is not interdependent, you may want to rethink your cell design.
- When it is technologically possible for a group of people to perform the cell work tasks in a meaningful and efficient way.

Factors related to strategic capabilities and performance:
- When breadth of skill and workforce flexibility would help the cell meet its goals.
- When increased worker motivation and interest in work would make a difference in the effectiveness of the cell.
- When increased communication and information exchange could improve cell performance, not impede it. Increased cooperation among workers would improve cell performance.
- When the cell team could reach decisions in a time frame that would not be detrimental to performance.
- When you can come up with meaningful group performance measures that could be used to assess the cell team as a whole.

Factors related to workers' preferences and capabilities:
- When individuals are willing to work in a cell team and do not have a strong preference for independent work.
- When individuals would be willing and able to be trained in interpersonal and technical skills required for the group to perform well.

Factors related to the organization and its culture:
- When teamwork is compatible with the organization's culture, norms, policies (especially other human resource policies), and leadership styles.
- When labor-management relations would support teamwork.
- When top management would support the creation of cell teams.

---

simply pushed some workers into higher job classifications. The number of job grades and their definitions, however, remained unchanged.

On the other hand, some plants actually *increase* the number of job categories when cells are introduced. One forklift manufacturer created an additional (and highest paid) job category that required proficiency on multiple types of equipment. Because only a portion of the plant was being converted to cells, the company wanted to leave the existing system intact. We have seen the same strategy followed in both unionized and non-unionized facilities in different industries.

In summary, your views on the assignment of direct and indirect tasks to operators, and the use of teams in cells, coupled with your perception of whether the job classification system is a hurdle or not, all will influence your vision of cell work. Together with strategy, technology, and demand pattern, these factors determine the cell work characteristics that shape cell jobs.

Detailed Job Design

Once you have specified the key characteristics of cell work (Box 5, Figure 12-3), you can determine in more detail the tasks and work methods that will constitute each job

(Box 7, Figure 12-3). To do so, you need to look closely at the specific direct and indirect labor activities that will take place in the cell. Decisions at this detailed level, which consider mental and ergonomic aspects of work, are determined by the perceptual-motor and biological approaches to job design discussed in Table 12-1 (see Box 6, Figure 12-3).

Cells have proven to reduce many job-related injuries. In one company operators were strained by moving and handling heavy products in and out of storerooms between operations. Cells reduced the need for excessive lifting by completely processing the products in cells. Further, many companies design cell jobs to reduce the risk of repetitive motion injuries. These injuries are caused by repeating the same movement (like turning a screwdriver) over extended periods of time. In the United States, injuries of this type account for about 60 percent of all workplace injuries and about $20 billion in workers' compensation claims (payments to workers for disability income, medical care, and rehabilitation services) annually.[16]

In one company, assembly work required the use of fine motor movements. Before cells, workers assembled batches of product start-to-finish and moved with their batch from station to station. They used equipment in a central "job shop" area that was organized by type (e.g., all the auto bonders were in one location). Typically, workers would spend several hours at each station repeating the same work sequence on the units in a batch. As a result, many suffered repetitive motion injuries. To address this problem, a U-shaped craft cell was created to process a family of circuits. In this way, setups could be dedicated and lot sizes could be reduced from 30 to 40 down to 3 to 4 units. Operators still move with their batches, but due to the small lots they now do so about every 15 minutes. Since these changes, the incidence of repetitive motion injuries has dropped dramatically.

Similarly, at one apparel plant, rising injury-related costs was the most important reason for creating cells. Moving to cells where operators could switch between different tasks many times a day and, in some cases, stand instead of sit, has reduced the incidence of carpal tunnel syndrome and lowered the company's injury-related expenses by "tens of thousands of dollars."[17]

Job Analysis to Determine Required Skills and Abilities

Once you have determined the tasks that will be part of each cell job, you need to identify the knowledge, skills, abilities, and other characteristics (KSAOs) that cell workers must possess in order to perform these jobs (Box 8, Figure 12-3). This process is generally referred to as "job analysis" (we defer an in-depth discussion of this step to Chapter 13).[18] Your next step (Box 10, Figure 12-3) is to compare the KSAOs cell workers need with those of "potential" cell employees (Box 9, Figure 12-3). Because most cells are formed in existing plants, potential cell workers are primarily found among the current workforce. However, should these not meet your expectations, the potential workforce might also include hires from the local community labor pool.

At this stage, you need to know if you can find and develop employees for the cell. To do that, ask yourself these questions:

- Can the potential operators, at this point in time, perform all the direct and indirect labor tasks required by the cell design?

- Will the potential operators be capable of acquiring those skills if they don't have them now? How long will this take?
- Are individual worker preferences (to the extent that you can assess them) likely to be at odds with the preliminary job design? (For example, a prevailing plant culture of independent work might impede plans to create cell work teams.)

Since you can expect the cell, with the help of employee training and education, to improve and evolve over time (see Step 12, Figure 4-1), you may develop two sets of cell work characteristics—one for the near term and one for the long term. For example, many organizations we have worked with have planned, in the long run, to make cell operators responsible for the majority of indirect labor tasks. Their vision of cell work included self-managed cells with high degrees of multi-functionality and task overlap. For most organizations this represents a dramatic change in worker and, as we will discuss, supervisory roles. Their short-term vision, however, was cells with moderately multi-functional and cross-trained operators, and a focus on direct labor tasks. Over time, as the team matured, management would shift indirect labor responsibilities from support and supervisory staff to the cell workers.

Referring back to Figure 12-3, box 10, you must determine if training and development of the potential workforce can, *in both the near term and the long term*, produce the workers you need for the cell. If the answer is *no* for the near term, then you need to rethink the cell work characteristics or the detailed cell design for the start-up phase (Boxes 5 and 7, Figure 12-3). If the answer is *yes* for the near term, you can proceed to select and train cell employees (Box 11, Figure 12-3)—two topics we discuss in our next chapter. If you find that the long-term vision does not seem to match the qualifications of the potential workforce (*after* skills training), you will need to revise your long-term goals for cell work.

Balancing Objectives and Constraints in the Job Design Process

As you work through the process shown in Figure 12-3, you may discover areas of conflict between the job design that best satisfies the decision constraints and the job design that best expresses your cell vision. For example, you may want cells to serve as a venue for expanding operator skills, but technology, volume, job classifications, and economic considerations support narrow job designs and limited overlap in cross-training. You'll then need to find some common ground that will satisfy both the constraints and your organization's objectives with respect to people in the system.

This balance underscores the relationship between the technical and social dimensions of any work system, including cells. In creating cells, your goal should be to jointly optimize the social and technical systems.[19] Although our book discusses technical issues first, we do not want you to think that you should complete the technical design before you turn to issues involving people (also see our discussion of sociotechnical systems in Chapter 2, as well as the discussion in Chapters 5 and 6, especially Figures 5-2 and 6-2). Optimizing the technical system first and then "force fitting" the people system into it can lead to problems. Early in the cell design process you must consider both technical aspects *and* the roles people will play in the system. One way to accomplish this is to involve those who will ultimately work in the cell in the design process. This is a prescription that we have offered earlier, and one we will repeat when discussing managing the cell implementation project (see Chapter 15).

CELLS AND TEAMS

We have now completed our discussion of the cell job design process outlined in Figure 12-3. Before we consider how a conversion to cells affects the jobs for supervisors, we will (as indicated earlier) return to the topic of teamwork in cells and review when and how teams can be advantageous in production.

As mentioned in Chapter 2, "cell" and "team," though often used interchangeably, are two distinct concepts. It is possible to have cells without teamwork (for example, single-operator cells) and teamwork without cells. This said, cells *with* teamwork are a common and often powerful combination.

A team is a collection of people who can be identified by themselves and others as a team, who work closely together to complete a whole and distinct part of a product or service, and are jointly responsible for meeting a set of shared goals.[20] In Chapter 2 we defined a cell as:

> A group of closely located workstations where multiple sequential operations are performed on one or more families of similar raw materials, parts, components, products, or information carriers. The cell is a distinctive organizational unit within a firm, staffed by one or more employees, accountable for output performance, and delegated responsibility for one of more planning, control, support, and improvement tasks.

As we have seen, cells and teams share many common features. In fact, virtually all multi-operator cells are teams: they are a collection of individuals, they can be identified as belonging to a particular team, and they work together with the shared goal of producing a family of outputs.[21] However, not all cell teams are alike. Cell teams can work together in different ways and can have widely varying responsibilities. Differences between teams are largely a function of differences in the type of tasks allocated to the cell team and the degree of cross-training—and more specifically task sharing—among cell operators. These two key cell work characteristics, task allocation and cross-training/task sharing, determine the amount of autonomy a cell team has and how closely operators must work together.

Task Allocation and Autonomy

The more indirect labor tasks the cell assumes, the more autonomously the team can operate. Obviously, in order for teams to operate effectively, they must be given some authority to apply their ideas and use their judgment. Cell teams, however, vary in the amount of authority they have to make decisions and take action.

Some cell teams are *externally (manager/supervisor) led cell teams*, where the teams execute work that others design, monitor, and manage.[22] Pedro's air conditioning subassembly cell is an example. Here, management retains tight control over cell administration. Operators perform very limited indirect labor tasks (e.g., reporting and recording quality problems, contributing to the solution of problems that arise on the line), but most decisions are in the hands of management. Thus, in this cell, operators have few indirect labor responsibilities.

At the other extreme are *self-leading* (sometimes called *self-governing*) *cell teams*, which have virtually unlimited authority to choose goals, select new members, and determine the best way in which to carry out work. All (or nearly all) indirect labor tasks are managed within the cell. In our work with companies we find truly self-leading teams to be rare. However, the cell teams at one manufacturer that builds medical products on a contract basis for other equipment manufacturers provide an example. These cell assembly teams own, start-to-finish, the design and execution of production. They work closely with support staff to determine the equipment and layout for their cell, select the best assembly sequence and methods to use, decide on staffing levels (including decisions to increase or decrease the size of the cell team), and manage virtually every aspect of production. In some instances they even travel to customer sites to become more familiar with product needs and to advise design engineers on manufacturability issues.

Between these two is the *self-managed cell team*. Here the cell team has significant responsibility for indirect tasks, including managing the work, but others (managers or support personnel) make decisions about goals, team structure, and organizational support.[23] Quite a few of the cells we have worked with (and many of the cells described in the literature) appear to be self-managed. Nicole's component assembly cell described at the outset of the chapter is one example. Sometimes individual workers (who, of course, have enriched jobs) handle the indirect tasks assigned to a cell team. In other instances, these tasks are the joint responsibility of the team. When this is the case, members must interact closely to accomplish their work.

Advantages of Cell Work Teams

A cell work team where operators interact closely in performing both direct and indirect labor tasks (e.g., a high level of task sharing in a self-managed cell), may offer a number of advantages over job designs where work teams are not used.[24] This section describes the benefits likely to accrue to these teams.

First, team members will have ample opportunities to learn from one another. This will improve skill levels as well as create greater flexibility in terms of job assignments. Sharing broad responsibilities also creates opportunities for team members to develop interpersonal, problem-solving and decision-making, and management and administrative skills. This may be particularly important to employees who value growth and learning.

Furthermore, jobs on a cell team—compared to the jobs the cells displace—will be enriched and enlarged, attributes that have been shown to have a positive effect on job satisfaction (again, see Appendix F). In addition, team members often develop a sense of cohesion, and feel loyalty and commitment to the team. They may work especially hard to avoid letting the team down. Because of their commitment to the team, members may feel that they must attend work, be on time, and perform well. This can translate into less absenteeism and lower turnover, both of which can mean lower costs. (Note, however, that peer pressure can develop in teams and have a negative effect on team members, especially in terms of stress.)

Creating a cell team that combines individuals with different original skill sets (e.g., milling operators and assembly workers), also can lead to the productive cross-fertilization of ideas, better problem solving, and creative solutions to cell issues.[25] Worker proximity and task sharing can also mean improved communication about work tasks. This can have a powerful impact on quality because the cell team is able to resolve problems and identify improvement opportunities more rapidly. As we pointed out already, this is particularly important in production environments where variations in the production process require quick reactions by the group. Costs may also be lower because the team will perform support tasks previously undertaken by indirect labor personnel and supervisors who are no longer needed for these duties. Finally, there is evidence that productivity can increase as a by-product of flexibility, higher skill levels, better work methods, and the fact that teams set goals and receive feedback on performance.[26]

A skilled workforce, capable of participating actively in problem solving, guaranteeing quality at the source, and mastering new products rapidly can be a source of competitive advantage. If, on the other hand, you have a relatively stable and certain environment, where the decisions to be made are relatively routine and can be anticipated by management, cell team members can accomplish their work with relatively low levels of interaction. Management can develop rules and standards that employees can simply execute.[27] There is little to be gained by giving workers discretion over work activities. Consequently, cell work teams in this setting—where indirect tasks belong to management and there is little need for task overlap—will yield few of the advantages described above.

A recent study of high-performance work systems in manufacturing (defined as the use of production teams, or employee participation in problem-solving or quality improvement teams) found that the use of teams has positive outcomes for both the organization and the employees.[28] The researchers interviewed managers, collected plant performance data, and surveyed workers at 44 manufacturing plants spread across three different industries—steel, apparel, and medical imaging. Teams were found to have a positive effect on performance measures important to managers in each industry: productivity in steel; cost and throughput time in apparel; and work in process and finished goods inventory in medical imaging. The authors also found that workers who are on teams in steel and apparel earn significantly higher wages than those who are not. In addition, the authors found that the use of teams had a strong positive effect on job satisfaction and worker commitment to the organization, and did not increase worker stress. Here we have evidence to suggest that teams can outperform traditional work systems and make work both more satisfying and financially rewarding for individual employees.

Cell team size and performance

The advantages of teamwork depend somewhat on the size of the team. Productive teamwork is facilitated by a team that is neither too large nor too small. We have seen cell teams with as many as 40 participants, and those with as few as 2 (of course, we have seen many single-operator cells as well). Most cell teams we have worked with have been in the 3- to 10-operator range. A general rule of thumb is that cell work teams should be the smallest size possible to accomplish the assigned work tasks.[29] The group should be large enough to include the diverse skills and talents the team needs, but not so large that decision-making gets bogged down.

Laboratory research has found that when group size increases beyond 5, decision quality deteriorates.[30] Some organization development specialists suggest teams of between 8 and 12 members, with outside bounds of 4 and 14. Others who have studied groups include the term "small number" (of employees) in their definition of a team.[31] Still other investigations suggest that when team size exceeds 10 people, task groups become less effective.[32] As group size increases, communication, group cohesion, and job satisfaction may decline, and social loafing, absenteeism, and turnover may increase. All this seems to suggest that cells teams will work best when they are not too big; say, between 2 to 12 members.

We do want to point out, however, that some of these findings are less relevant for teams where a significant portion of the decision-making responsibility rests with the supervisor or cell leader. In one plant, each cell was responsible for the start-to-finish assembly of a family of products, activities that required 15 to 25 people per cell team. These cells still functioned very well, thanks to strong cell leaders and supervisors.

Obviously, team size is not determined in a vacuum. As we have discussed, volume, processes, and technology determine the capacity needs, which translate into staffing levels (Figure 12-3). However, there is always the possibility of redesigning the product family (Chapters 5 and 6) if the required cell team size is undesirable. For example, you may split one large cell in half to reduce team size. You may also assign multiple smaller teams within the boundaries of a physically large cell.

Disadvantages of Cell Teams

It is important to note the possible downsides of adopting cell teams:[33]

- Possible incompatibility among team members.
- Extra effort in selection to match personalities as well as job skills.
- Possible internal group conflicts and competition.
- More time spent on socializing, coordinating work, and building consensus.
- Less flexibility in replacing team workers.
- Possibility of free-riders or loafers.
- Possibility that some team jobs will be less attractive or rewarding.
- Possibility that decision making and creativity may be inhibited.

Although some of these disadvantages can be overcome through learning, good management, and the passing of time, they can be obstacles to cell performance. We have seen companies that have closed down cells due to the unwillingness of employees to conform and work with the team. We also know of firms that have avoided team-based cells in favor of single-operator cells, either due to employee conflicts or because of resistance to group-based pay systems. In one egregious case, the whole self-managed assembly line team was loafing. The team was believed to run the most productive line in the plant. However, when the newly appointed manufacturing manager began measuring the productivity of each cell in the plant, this self-managed cell turned out to be the poorest performer. In reality, the team members had used their self-managed status to spend more time off line than on it. This example indicates that teams are not a substitute for good management—which begins with goal setting and performance measurement. The best point at which ill-performing teams can be avoided, however, is at the time of employee selection (see Box 11, Figure 12-3). Poorly chosen team members can impair the effectiveness of a cell team.

SUPERVISION IN CELL SYSTEMS

The traditional role of a supervisor has been "to assign work, keep people working, expedite parts, and report machine efficiency, absenteeism, units produced, and earned hours."[34] Supervisors in a functional shop are responsible for the performance of operators working on one machine type. Cell supervisors, on the other hand, have a significantly different role. Their specific job responsibilities, the skills and knowledge they need to be effective in their jobs, and their span of control are all broadened with cells.

Cell Supervisors and Cell Leaders

We make a distinction between cell supervisors and cell leaders. A *cell leader* is an operator with leadership responsibilities who works in a multi-operator cell. A cell leader typically reports to a cell supervisor. A *cell supervisor*, on the other hand, does not work in the cell and tends to have more managerially oriented responsibilities than a cell leader. Also, while a cell leader works in, and has responsibility for, a single cell, a supervisor can oversee more than one cell. For example, at a U.S. electrical equipment manufacturer, management appoints a cell leader for each cell team. The cell leader does "real work" by building products, but has other responsibilities as well. He or she trains new people, approves setups, and provides leadership for the team. Several cell leaders report to a single supervisor who is responsible for a group of cells in a particular area of manufacturing.

We note, finally, that some companies have cell leaders as well as supervisors, some have supervisors only, and some have cell leaders only (who report directly to management).

The Roles of the Cell Supervisor and Cell Leader

Just as jobs change for operators when they join a cell, especially if they become cell leaders, supervisors also find their jobs differing greatly from traditional supervision. This section describes four critical dimensions that characterize supervisory work for cells.

Technical leadership in more areas

Cell supervisors often oversee different types of equipment and a broad range of technologies and processes. The supervisor of a connector cell observed that "my job is to support the production of attenuators and switches, and they are assembled right here next to my line." Thus, he saw his role as supporting a particular business by providing a key component and managing a whole chain of process steps. This supervisor—who before managed only a milling area—now needs to understand milling, grinding, buffing, degreasing, plating, heat treating, and assembly operations. He is also much more aware of the problem with delays, specifically of not feeding the assembly area in a timely manner.

Similarly, cell leaders also oversee a wide array of process types. In fact, cell leaders may need even deeper technical capabilities in some areas than do supervisors because they will be building products in the cell as well. Working in the cell also gives cell leaders a way of keeping their technical skills sharp.

Helping the cell team work together

In cells with teamwork, cell leaders and supervisors have another important responsibility—helping team members work together. This may involve leading team-building activities, providing mentoring and coaching, and assisting in problem resolution. Table 12-4 describes the roles and responsibilities of cell supervisors at one particular plant where helping cell team members work effectively together is a major supervisory responsibility.

A broader focus

When cell operators take on more responsibility for managing as well as executing work, the cell supervisor is able to focus less on the issues of direct production, and more on supporting cell members in their work and linking the cell to the rest of the organization. This is particularly the case when cell workers have responsibility for indirect labor tasks, and even more so when there is also a cell leader.

The supervisor of Nicole's electronic assembly cell saw his role as "monitoring and directing the process and people to meet all cell objectives, manage expenses, and assist and train operators." Table 12-5 lists the tasks performed by this supervisor in a typical day at his non-union facility. This list includes many traditional supervisory tasks. However, the supervisor of Nicole's cell spends little time expediting parts, redirecting the flow, and assigning work, and much time training workers, facilitating team activities, and interfacing with the rest of the plant. He also coordinates activities between his cell and other cells, serves as a customer and supplier liaison, and is more involved in new product introductions—a time-consuming and critical activity in this particular manufacturing environment.

A larger span of control

The supervisor's span of control is typically larger in cells than in traditionally organized facilities. When cell leaders are in place, or when the cell itself manages indirect labor activities, supervisors often oversee several cells. We have seen this in a number of organizations. One large-scale survey confirms our impression: it found that supervisors and managers in factories with cells had significantly larger spans of control than their counterparts in factories without cells.[35]

Table 12-4. Roles and responsibilities of cell supervisors at a plant with self-managed cell teams

Provide leadership in establishing self-regulating behavior:
- Model and train team-building leadership
- Facilitate goal setting
- Help empower team to establish ownership of inputs, throughputs, and outputs of team
- Establish and facilitate team meeting structure to ensure good flow of information and safe environment for open communication
- Establish and facilitate cross-shift communication
- Help the team establish metrics and performance feedback system
- Facilitate continuous process improvement activities

Provide administrative support for the team:
- Participate in the selection of new employees
- Provide or negotiate to get resources for the team
- Monitor and control the overhead budget
- Resolve team member conflicts
- Plan team manpower needs
- Facilitate team performance evaluations
- Provide disciplinary actions if necessary

Manage issues and information outside the team boundaries:
- Represent the team as an informational interface with the larger organization
- Bring organizationwide issues to the team
- Manage boundary issues for the team
  - Borrow/lend manpower across teams as required
  - Interface when upstream or downstream problems occur
  - Obtain needed support from various support groups

Deciding the Best Supervision Model for Your Cell System

How do you structure cell supervision and reporting relationships so they best suit your environment? Should you have cell leaders, supervisors, or both? And what should be their responsibilities? The decision depends, in part, on the size of the cells, the number of cells, and the degree to which operators themselves are responsible for indirect tasks.

Very simply, the bigger a cell, the more there is to coordinate and oversee, and the more you need a supervisor. You may also want a cell leader inside the cell. The smaller the cell, the less there is to coordinate and oversee. A single supervisor might therefore manage several small cells easily. If the supervisor will manage a large number of cells, however, you may also need a cell leader in each cell who reports to the supervisor.

Similarly, the more indirect tasks cell operators perform, the less you need a supervisor to undertake these activities. You can assign these tasks to a cell leader or let them be shared among the cell operators. On the other hand, if operators are not given responsibilities for indirect tasks, a cell supervisor must take these on.

Table 12-5. A day in the life of a cell supervisor

- Review the workload for the day with the team, noting any late parts or orders requiring special attention.
- Provide training for any new permanent or temporary worker, or for current workers who are learning a new skill.
- Deal with any technical or interpersonal problems that the cell operators themselves cannot resolve.
- Lead team meetings at the beginning and end of each day.
- Collect and log pertinent performance and problem data (operators also engage in this activity).
- Adjust the number of temporary workers by reviewing expected demands and comparing them with current staffing levels. This may involve borrowing/lending manpower from/to other areas.
- Interface with other groups (e.g., engineering, production planning and control) to get the cell the support it needs.
- Represent the team to the larger organization.
- Work with the R&D department on new product introductions involving the cell.
- Attend meetings related to business issues important to the cell.
- Work with cell customers or suppliers to resolve or avoid problems.
- Communicate to the cell team any key information from elsewhere in the organization.

One alternative for cells with operators responsible for indirect tasks is to have supervisors, but not cell leaders. This seems to make the most sense when cells are small and can coordinate work easily without a formal leader. It may also be a viable option for large cells that have considerable experience working together and performing "supervisory" tasks. Supervisors of large cells that have not yet matured and are without cell leaders may need to assume more traditional supervisory functions. The matrix in Figure 12-4 shows how the combination of two major characteristics, cell size and operator responsibility for indirect tasks, point to various supervisory models.

Transitioning to New Supervisor Roles

Not all cell supervisors embrace their new roles. In fact, supervisors typically find the transition to cells difficult.[36] Sometimes the roles are not clearly spelled out because management has failed to think through the change in supervisor activities, and sometimes supervisors are unwilling to give up responsibilities that operators want to assume. Overt, but usually covert, supervisor resistance has slowed or stalled cell implementations at some companies. The problem is further complicated because of its dynamic nature—as cell workers gain experience working together, they need less and less traditional supervision. A supervisor who was very comfortable with her role at the outset of the cell's life may feel the rug pulled out from under her as the cell matures. We discuss general guidelines for such transitions in Chapter 15, and the specific problem of supervisor resistance in Chapter 16.

Cell Size (number of operators)	Degree to which operators have assumed indirect labor (management and support) tasks	
	Low	**High**
Large	**Cell supervisor** • Responsible for a single cell • Focus is on traditional supervisor resposibilities	**Cell leader and supervisor** • Cell leader provides day-to-day management of cell tasks • Supervisor focuses less on material flow and more on managing the cell's relationships with the rest of the organization, training and team development, and providing administrative support **Cell supervisor only** • Cell operators manage day-to-day activities themselves • Supervisor focuses less on material flow and more on managing the cell's relationships with the rest of the organization, training and team development, and providing administrative support
Small	**Cell supervisor** • Could be responsible for multiple cells • Focus is on traditional supervisor responsibilities	**Cell leader but no supervisor** • Cell leader provides day-to-day management of cell tasks • Cell leader reports directly to manufacturing management **Cell leader and supervisor** • Cell leader provides day-to-day management of cell tasks • Supervisor may be responsible for several cells • Supervisor focuses less on material flow and more on managing the cells' relationships with the rest of the organization, training and team development, and providing administrative support **Cell supervisor only** • Cell operators manage day-to-day activities themselves • Supervisor may be responsible for several cells • Supervisor focuses less on material flow and more on managing the cells' relationships with the rest of the organization, training and team development, and providing administrative support

Figure 12-4. Types of cell supervision

KEY INSIGHTS

In this chapter we presented a decision process framework for job design in cells. We discussed the role that strategy, technology, vision, volume, teamwork, and other considerations play in job design decisions. We also described how cells affect the job of the supervisor. Below, we offer several prescriptions for job design in cell systems:

- *Jobs don't change automatically when you implement cells.* If you want jobs to change with cells, you have to make it happen. Depending on the starting conditions in your plant, this may mean reducing the number of distinct job categories (while broadening job content) or adding new job categories for cell work, providing cross-training, and redesigning supervisor roles. It also requires that you change other policies to make them compatible with broadened operator and supervisory roles. Specifically, your firm's selection, training, and compensation policies must be made consistent with new jobs in order for the latter to be effective.

- *Determine the key cell work characteristics.* Your strategy, cell processes and technology, volume/mix and cell vision, along with various perspectives on job design, will help you make decisions about key characteristics of cell work. These are the staffing level (will you have single- or multiple-operator cells?), task allocation (will cell operators perform only direct labor tasks, or indirect labor tasks as well?), multi-functionality (to what degree will operators be able to perform multiple tasks?), and cross-training (will operators be cross-trained in overlapping direct and indirect labor tasks?).

- *Consider broad jobs for cell workers.* Research suggests that most employees respond positively to enriched and enlarged jobs. In a competitive environment where there's a need for operators to make real-time decisions, and cell technology and volume don't constrain you, designing broad jobs for workers can also have a performance payoff. In particular, work quality will most likely improve, although the impact on productivity is less certain.

- *When it fits with the strategic intent, technology, volume constraints, and cell work vision, cell teams where operators share direct and indirect tasks can offer distinct advantages.* Cells bring people together in close physical proximity and focus them on the production of a set of similar items. Teams in cells offer the greatest advantages when your competitive environment calls for rapid response on the shop floor. In this scenario, creating jobs that facilitate high levels of interaction between cell team members (e.g., jobs with a high degree of overlap and task sharing), will allow you to reap the benefits often associated with the use of teams.

- *Evaluate current job classification systems for their impact on cell jobs.* Rigid job classification systems are the enemy of broadened jobs. If your goal is to develop a flexible, adaptable workforce that is capable of learning and change, narrowly focused job categories will stand in the way. They are at odds with job designs where operators perform many overlapping tasks.

- *Don't overlook ergonomics—physical and perceptual-motor dimensions—as you design cell jobs.* Jobs need to be safe and not unduly taxing in order for workers to perform them well day after day. Because they closely locate a variety of work processes and equipment, cells can address ergonomic concerns through job rotation and small batch processing.

- *Carefully think through the role of supervision in the cellular organization.* Companies sometimes overlook changes to supervision when they are planning cell systems. Think through the roles supervisors and/or cell leaders should play given the nature of cell work.

- *Don't make job design an afterthought.* The social and technical systems are inextricably linked. While you may develop the outline of the cell's technical system first, this is simply the starting point. Involve operators early on as a way of grounding the technical design in the realities of work on the shop floor. Further, as you proceed with the detailed job design, be prepared to modify the technical system, if needed, to better accommodate people in the cell.

13

Selecting and Training Cell Employees

In the previous chapter on job design we described how cells sometimes lead to fairly radical changes to operators' and supervisors' jobs. In this chapter we explore how to select and train employees for these new roles. We begin with an example that illustrates why you need to rethink selection and training when you introduce cells. Then we address the following important issues:

- What criteria and methods should you use to select cell operators and supervisors?
- What type of start-up training do cell operators and supervisors need?
- What is the best way to deliver this training?
- What are the potential pitfalls in preparing operators and supervisors for cell work?
- What role does ongoing training play in cell operations?

WHY SELECTION AND TRAINING ARE DIFFERENT WITH CELLS

Let's look at what happens when cells replace a traditional manufacturing system in the apparel industry. The old system, commonly called the "progressive bundle" system, is classic batch production in a functional organization where similar operations are located together and the operators each man a single piece of equipment. Operators work independently and are paid on a piece-rate basis. Once a bundle is complete, it sits near the operator's machine waiting to be transported to the next process. Large queues of work in process before each station decouple successive operations and assure that operators will not be starved for work. Bundle operators are isolated at their workstation and have little knowledge of production activities and problems elsewhere in the system. Supervisors typically oversee a single step in the process and are responsible for the efficiency of their department. They spend much time expediting work and solving other day-to-day production problems.

Now consider a typical cell (also called "module") in this industry. Equipment is closely located in a linear or U-shaped layout, and operators pass their completed items directly to an adjacent worker. There is little inventory between connected tasks. A module worker will perform some of the prior worker's duties if the latter falls behind. Workers inspect the piece they receive and provide quick and direct feedback to one another to correct workmanship errors. By switching tasks to alleviate bottlenecks and keep work moving, module operators are involved in determining the pace and flow of production. Off-line, they may perform minor maintenance, contribute to decisions about how to arrange equipment, and participate in goal setting, problem-solving, and conflict resolution. Referring to our cell work characteristics model (see Chapter 12), apparel modules are multi-operator cells where operators have been assigned overlapping direct and indirect labor tasks.

Jobs also change for the supervisors. They now manage an area that includes many different types of equipment and focus on total process output, not on individual machine or labor utilization. They train new workers, liaison with other areas, provide coaching, and assist the team in solving problems. However, workers, not supervisors, manage the workflow through the cell and are primarily responsible for solving day-to-day production problems. Under the bundle system, these issues were among the supervisors' major responsibilities.

Modules of the type just described have significant implications for employee selection and training. The old progressive bundle system can tolerate high levels of turnover, typical in the apparel and footwear industry, since selecting and training employees to perform single tasks can be quick and inexpensive. And, given the large work in process that decouples successive operations, a worker who is performing slowly because he or she is learning a task will have little immediate impact on overall output. Nor will the reduced output affect other workers' pay as long as there is WIP inventory.

A high level of labor turnover, on the other hand, could cripple a modular system. The time and cost (including lost production) to select and train a new cell worker can be significant. Therefore, when you select employees you must evaluate their ability to learn and perform multiple processes, as well as their ability to work in a group. Where new workers are deficient, training must fill the gap. Selecting and training supervisors will also change. As discussed in Chapter 12, cell supervisors need all the same skills that traditional supervisors need. Beyond that, they also must be proficient in a variety of technical work processes and have coaching and team facilitation skills. Again, where skills are deficient, training must be offered.

As this example emphasizes, cell jobs require different skills than do traditional jobs and thus call for changes in employee selection and training processes. In fact, you need to align *all* your firm's human resource management practices with the new way of working. As we discussed already in Chapter 1, changes in job design, selection, training, and compensation need to work in concert with one another in supporting the cell system.

SELECTING CELL EMPLOYEES

Employee selection is the process of identifying qualified people who can help an organization meet its objectives. It is an important activity. Accurately selecting people who are well qualified to perform assigned job tasks can make a substantial difference in productivity.[1] Inattention to people issues, including selecting employees who are ill-suited to cell work, can mean the difference between a successful implementation and one that has problems.[2] Since most cells are created by converting existing plants, most cell staffing decisions involve selecting cell workers and supervisors from an existing workforce.[3]

Figure 13-1 presents a decision process framework for the selection and training of cell employees. To select employees for cell work, you need to identify the knowledge, skills, abilities, and other characteristics (KSAOs; see Table 13-1 for definitions[4]) that cell workers need in order to perform their jobs well. Thus, the starting point for selection is the detailed job design (Box 7, Figure 13-1). This is because KSAOs will be inferred or derived from the specific tasks operators will have to perform in their jobs (attach components using non-mechanized tools, operate a five-axis milling machine, reorder material, document quality problems, etc.).

Table 13-1. Foundations for cell staffing decisions: knowledge, skills, abilities, and other characteristics

Term	Meaning
Knowledge	Body of factual or procedural information that is necessary for performing a task. Examples: knowledge of manufacturing processes, knowledge of what constitutes a defect, knowledge of key manufacturing concepts such as lead time and inventory.
Skills	Level of proficiency at performing a particular task. An "observable competence" for working with or applying knowledge to perform particular tasks or a closely related set of tasks. Skill requirements are directly inferred from observation or knowledge of tasks performed. Example: skill at component attachment, skill at operating a five-axis milling machine.
Ability	A more general and enduring trait that is useful for performing a wide range of different tasks. There are four different types of abilities: cognitive, psychomotor, physical, and sensory abilities. Examples: ability to read written work instructions, ability to follow oral instructions, ability to use arithmetic to calculate inventory levels, "ability to quickly and repeatedly bend, stretch, twist, or reach out with the body, arms or legs."
Other characteristics	Any other characteristic that does not fit neatly into knowledge, skill, or ability, but which is a requirement or otherwise important for performing the job. Examples: availability (e.g., start date, hours available per day), legal requirements (e.g., citizenship, licensing, age), character requirements (e.g., work ethic, conscientiousness).

The process of determining the tasks that together form a "job" and then determining the KSAOs important for its effective performance is referred to as *job analysis* (Box 8, Figure 13-1).[5] There are two main outputs from job analysis. The first is a job description, which focuses on characteristics of the job. It lists the tasks, duties, and responsibilities (observable actions) that the job entails. It can also include a description of the work environment and regulations in place to avoid injuries or accidents.[6] The second output is a job specification, which focuses on characteristics of the individuals who will perform the job. It lists the KSAOs that an individual must demonstrate to successfully perform the work. (The job specification and job description can be combined in a single document. Figure 13-2 shows a combined job description/job specification for a cell operator position).

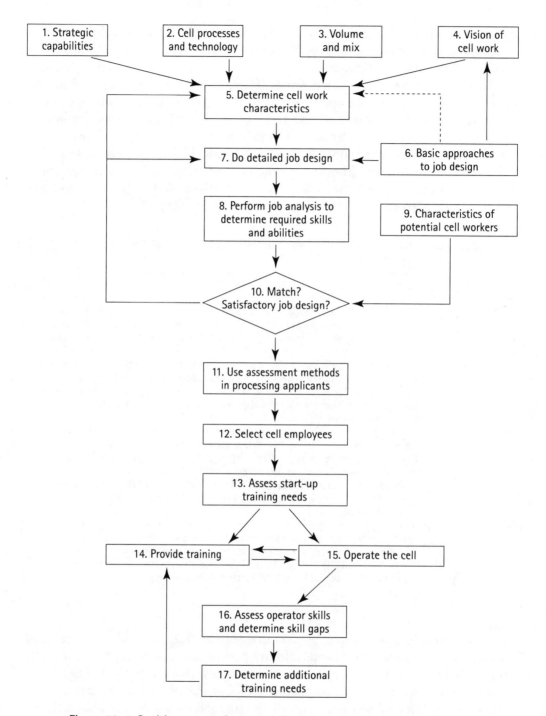

Figure 13-1. Decision process framework for cell employee selection and training

The mechanics of a job analysis are beyond the scope of this book. Your human resource professional should be well equipped to undertake this analysis. Indeed, you need the HR group to be your partner in designing and executing cell employee selection.

JOB TITLE: HVAC Unit Assembler
Department: Assembly
Manager: Bill Christie

JOB SUMMARY: The assembler is responsible for putting together parts and components into final products.

PERFORMANCE DIMENSIONS AND TASKS:
Phase I: Initial duties
- Sets up parts and equipment for the job
- Installs parts on components according to work procedures
- Informs stock movers when parts are needed
- Informs line leader when short of purchased sheet metal parts
- Informs the line leader when having a problem with parts or components
- Assists other assemblers
- Fills out P-chart when required
- Writes up rejected parts
- Writes up over-pull incidents
- Uses computer workstation to search for part information
- Orders own parts
- Performs area housekeeping duties
- Other job-related duties as assigned by supervisor

Phase II: After experience on the job
- Reads blueprints
- Performs the job swiftly and without assistance
- Identifies and corrects mistakes and prevents them from happening in the future
- Uses SPC charts
- Experienced with all stations in this cell and minimum of three other cells

JOB SPECIFICATIONS
1. Education: high school
2. Experience: assembly experience preferred, but not required
3. Skills and abilities: speaking ability, mathematical ability, judgement, dexterity, alertness, initiative, good attitude (must be willing to perform the job in a thorough manner so that internal and external customers are satisfied; must be willing and able to understand and abide by the company's Code of Business Conduct)
4. Physical demands: must be able to lift minimum of 25 pounds; must not have medical restrictions for twisting and bending
5. Equipment used: rivet gun, air drills, tape measure, calculator, silicone gun, torque wrenches, grinder, hand truck, Big Joe lift, wide range of handtools
6. Other: Attendance requirement of 97% (emergencies do not apply); responsible for quality, productivity and safety

WORK ENVIRONMENT: Indoors, temperature-controlled factory environment; see Safety and Dress Code Policy for information on job hazards and expected dress

---

Figure 13-2. Sample job description/job specification for a cell operator position

KSAOs and the Key Cell Work Characteristics

Although you do need to conduct your own job analysis, several KSAOs seem to be important to *all* cell work. The cell work characteristics introduced in Chapter 12 (also see Box 5, Figure 13-1), and our related discussion of job enlargement, enrichment, and teamwork, point to six categories of KSAOs that are critical to effective cell operations:[7]

- Technical skills in multiple areas (multi-functionality).
- Interpersonal skills and abilities.

- Problem-solving and decision-making skills.
- Administrative and management skills.
- The ability to learn.
- The willingness to learn.

Table 13-2 shows the relationship between each of these skills and the nature of the work assigned to cell employees. We'll examine each of these areas before we look at the selection process itself.

Technical skills in multiple areas

With rare exceptions, workers in cells need to be technically multi-functional, i.e., able to perform a variety of technical operations. The demand for skill variety is obviously the largest for single- or multi-operator craft cells where operators perform all tasks from start to finish. In fact, for most cells, this multi-skilling criterion—being proficient at many tasks—is more important than deep expertise in a single task.[8]

Interpersonal skills and abilities

Interpersonal skills are those skills that enable workers to "communicate, cooperate, and coordinate their efforts."[9] In particular, interpersonal skills refer to both communication skills and the ability to work with others. These skills and abilities are important in any environment where work is designed to be done collectively. This means that in environments with teamwork, interpersonal skills are critical for performance.[10] With respect to cell teams, interpersonal skills are especially important in cells where there is high task overlapping. Cell operators in these settings need to communicate effectively and work together when they share responsibility for task execution.

Ideally, you would like to select cell workers who *already* have good verbal communication skills (speaking, listening, questioning, clarifying, confirming, and so forth) and who can work well with others. Good negotiating, feedback, and conflict resolution skills are a plus as well.

Problem-solving and decision-making skills

In cells where operators perform certain indirect labor tasks, they need problem-solving and decision-making skills. This is the case, for example, if operators will be responsible for tracking quality problems, analyzing the collected data, taking corrective action, and developing long-term solutions to problems. As part of the job analysis process, you need to consider the specific indirect labor tasks that have been assigned to cell workers, and their implications for problem-solving/decision-making skills. In addition, cell operators who are jointly responsible for many indirect labor activities need to have the skills to solve problems in a group (related, of course, to interpersonal skills as well).

Administrative and management skills

Cell operators who have responsibility for indirect tasks also may need to master the specific skills required to *administer and manage* the cell (see Table 12-3 for an extensive list of indirect tasks performed by cell operators). Examples include scheduling, ordering supplies, record keeping, monitoring and reporting performance, and

Table 13-2. Importance of various skills and abilities in cell worker selection

Skill or Ability Type	Direct Labor Tasks (DL)			Indirect Labor Tasks (IL)			
	Low level of multi-functionality in DL tasks (tasks per employee is low)	High level of multi-functionality		Low amount of indirect tasks assigned to cell	High amount of indirect tasks assigned to cell		
		No task overlap	High overlap		Low level of multi-functionality in indirect labor tasks	High level of multi-functionality	
						Low overlap	High overlap
Technical skills in multiple areas	Of limited importance	Very important where operators perform varied DL tasks on their own	Very important where DL tasks overlap	Very important where focus is on DL tasks only	Not applicable to IL tasks	Not applicable to IL tasks	Not applicable to IL tasks
Interpersonal skills	Of limited importance	Of limited importance where DL tasks do not overlap	Very important where DL tasks overlap	Importance depends on degree of overlap in DL tasks	Of limited importance when individuals work alone on designated IL tasks	Of limited importance when IL tasks do not overlap	Very important where IL tasks overlap
Problem-solving and decision-making skills	Of limited importance	Somewhat important for DL tasks	Somewhat important where DL tasks overlap	Somewhat important where focus is on DL tasks only	Very important for operators who take on IL tasks	Very important for operators who take on many IL tasks	Very important where IL tasks overlap
Administrative and management skills	Of limited importance	Of limited importance for DL tasks	Of limited importance where DL tasks overlap	Of limited importance where focus is on DL tasks only	Very important for operators who take on IL tasks	Very important for operators who take on many IL tasks	Very important where IL tasks overlap
Ability to learn	Of limited importance	Very important where operators must learn new DL tasks	Very important where new DL tasks overlap	Of limited importance	Very important for operators who take on IL tasks	Very important for operators who take on many IL tasks	Very important where IL tasks overlap
Willingness to learn	Of limited importance	Very important where operators must learn new DL tasks	Very important where new DL tasks overlap	Of limited importance	Very important for operators who take on IL tasks	Very important for operators who take on many IL tasks	Very important where IL tasks overlap

so forth. Of course, basic problem-solving and decision-making skills are a prerequisite to taking on any of these indirect duties. Beyond this, the specific expertise required depends on the specific duties that have been assigned to cell operators and whether or not these duties will rotate or be the responsibility of a single operator.

Cell operators also may need general business knowledge. This could include, for example, a basic understanding of profit and loss statements, product cost determination, and the nature of the organization's strategy. Basic knowledge of this type is important whenever cell workers, alone or in concert with others, will be planning, executing, and evaluating the cell's work.

Ability to learn

Given the diversity of the above skill sets, you will likely discover that potential employees have some, but not all, of the required skills. For example, most workers are unlikely to possess all the technical task skills they need for cell work, so the ability to learn new technical skills is important. (Candidates who already are multi-skilled have, de facto, demonstrated their ability to learn.) Likewise, operators who are not already skilled at working together, performing administrative and management tasks, or making decisions and solving problems must acquire these skills. In short, the ability to learn is among the most important KSAOs for cell work.

Willingness to learn

We make a distinction between the ability to learn and the willingness to learn. Not all individuals who are able to learn new skills are *willing* to do so—and being able is not enough. You want to select employees who are motivated to acquire new skills, open to new experiences, and willing to vary routines as circumstances dictate. This willingness to learn is important not only during the cell start-up phase, but over the life of the cell as well. Ongoing efforts to improve cell operations (see Chapter 17) most likely will require employees to continuously learn new skills and take on additional tasks. Thus, selecting employees who are open to learning is critical to the success of cells in many environments.

Techniques for Selecting Cell Employees

Once you have determined the knowledge, skills, abilities, and other characteristics that cell operators will need, you must ensure that your candidates have or are able to acquire these attributes. As noted in Table 13-3, you have a number of options when it comes to assessing potential cell employees.[11]

Many companies combine several approaches in selecting cell workers. The methods you select should meet certain criteria.[12] First, your selection method should be *reliable*, i.e., free of random error. Thus, if applicants perform well on a test just by chance, the approach is not reliable. Second, your selection approach should be *valid*. That is, it should help you distinguish between applicants likely to perform well on the job and those who are unlikely to do so. One way of achieving a valid selection test is for the problems or questions that are part of the test to represent the types of situations that occur on the job. Third, your selection methods should offer *high utility*, that is, be cost effective.[13] Basically, utility is about

Table 13-3. Selection assessment methods

- Interviews
- References and biographical data
- Physical ability tests
- Cognitive ability tests
- Personality inventories
- Work-sample tests
- Performance evaluations, direct information from peers and supervisors, and work histories (for internal hires only)

balancing the costs and benefits of your selection method. If, for example, you and your human resource specialists spend weeks to develop a battery of selection tests and/or these are costly to administer (e.g., individuals must participate in days of interviews and simulations, which tie up plant personnel as well), but these costs are not offset by savings due to having selected better employees (such as reductions in scrap, man-hours per product, product quality, rework costs, or turnover), then your selection system has low utility.[14] Finally, you need to make sure the selection procedures are *legal*. For example, it is important that the tests you use for selecting employees are job-related. If they are not, you open yourself to possible allegations of discrimination. Because of the legal issues surrounding personnel selection, you should not take any action without the involvement of your plant's human resources staff.

Let's now discuss each of the specific methods listed in Table 13-3. Keep in mind that you may want to combine various approaches.

Employee interviews

Interviews are a common selection method for cell workers, even though there can be problems with personal bias in this approach.[15] For example, you may be inclined to select candidates you "like" or who are "just like you." But people you like or who are similar to you in some way won't necessarily be best in the job for which you are assessing candidates. Your evaluation needs to focus, first and foremost, on the needs of the job. In addition, interviews can be time consuming if candidates meet with several people (you, the HR specialist, current operators, a supervisor) and if you interview numerous candidates. Finally, because of their subjective nature, interviews can create legal problems. An individual who is denied a job because of an employment interview might claim the process is biased and take legal action.

On the other hand, job interviews are easy and familiar. You probably have participated in several job interviews yourself, both as a candidate and as an evaluator. Most importantly, a well-designed, disciplined approach to cell job interviews can be effective.[16] Interviews should be structured, standardized, and focused on achieving a few (possibly three or four) goals.[17] It is useful to ask questions about specific situations that are likely to arise on the job. For example, if operators will share indirect tasks, you would like to know about candidates' abilities to resolve conflict. You might ask, "What kind of conflicts have you had with coworkers? How did you work them out?"

In comparison with other selection methods, the unique contribution of the interview is the ability to evaluate the job applicants' goals, values, and interpersonal skills.[18] By values we mean an applicant's "preferences for aspects of the work environment (e.g., supervisory style), and organizational culture (e.g., teamwork) or applicant attitudes about work (e.g., possessing a strong customer service orientation)" that you believe are important for performance.[19] This information can help you determine whether or not the individual will "fit" in the cell, and in the broader organization.

Interviews can also help you determine whether candidates have other necessary KSAOs to perform the job (for example, technical skills). However, if you will be using other types of selection tests (e.g., work-sample tests to assess technical skills), you can structure the interview around the dimensions (values, goals, and interpersonal abilities) to which interviews are particularly well suited.

Appendix G provides detailed guidelines for structuring effective interviews. By following these prescriptions, you can avoid (or minimize) some of the common problems with selection interviews.

References and biographical data

In addition to interviews, many companies use *references and biographical data* in selecting cell workers. Unfortunately, references often prove to be poor predictors of job performance.[20] The problem is that those who provide references are reluctant to share candid assessments, sometimes due to fear of legal action by the candidate. Biographical data provided by the candidate are more useful, particularly for predicting certain outcomes such as length of employment.[21] Further, such data are also free and can be subjected to background checks. Biographical data should be available at the time of the interview so that your questions do not duplicate the data collected on the job application, but rather go deeper and beyond the provided information.

Physical ability tests

Physical ability tests are appropriate when abilities such as muscular strength, cardiovascular endurance, or movement quality (e.g., balance, flexibility) are important for job performance.[22] Screening candidates for physically demanding jobs can help reduce work-related injuries. Of course, as we pointed out in Chapter 12, the best approach is to design jobs so that they are not physically demanding. Physically demanding jobs can be discriminatory (e.g., women, older workers, or those with disabilities may not be able to perform physically demanding tasks) and can increase the risk of injuries. There is a well-developed body of literature to consult when determining the physical abilities required for industrial work and the types of tests to use to assess workers' physical competencies.[23] Ideally, you will not need to rely on physical ability tests in your selection process for cell employees.

Cognitive ability tests

Cognitive ability tests assess the mental capacities of job applicants, typically their verbal comprehension (ability to understand and use written and spoken language), quantitative abilities (speed and accuracy with which an individual can solve a variety of arithmetic problems), and reasoning ability (capacity to develop solutions to diverse problems).[24] There are many highly reliable tests for assessing cognitive abilities, several of which are relatively inexpensive.[25] Examples include the Employee Aptitude Survey, a battery of 10 tests—each of which takes no more than five minutes to administer and focuses on a particular cognitive ability (e.g., numerical ability, verbal comprehension)—and the Wonderlic Personnel Test. Wonderlic, probably the most widely used test, is a 50-item, 12-minute multiple-choice test that has been administered to over 2.5 million job applicants. The test assesses vocabulary, commonsense reasoning, arithmetic reasoning and comprehension, and other areas of cognitive ability.

The hundreds of studies that have looked at the validity of cognitive tests (e.g., does strong performance on the tests translate into strong performance on the job) indicate that they have some validity for all jobs, but particularly high validity for complex jobs.[26] The reason is that some degree of intelligence is important for *all* jobs, even very simple ones. Further, research has also found that cognitive ability tests have high validity in predicting training success. This is probably "due to the substantial learning component of training and the obvious fact that smart people learn more."[27] We want to point out that while there are readily available commercial tests, as we already described, it is also possible to develop simple tests in-house, particularly for basic math and verbal skills.

What are the other implications of cognitive ability tests for cell worker selection? First, in a choice between two applicants who are equivalent on other dimensions, you should select the employee who performed better on cognitive ability tests. In addition, the more complex the cell work, the more important cognitive abilities will be to job performance. For example, if cell operators will be responsible for the managing the cell, cognitive tests will help identify workers well suited to the intellectual demands of the job. Finally, because they tell you something about an individual's ability to learn, cognitive ability tests may be particularly useful if you anticipate that cell operators will need to master new skills in any of the areas we noted above (e.g., technical, interpersonal, problem-solving and decision-making, or administrative and management skills). Cognitive ability tests may help you select employees for whom training is more likely to be successful.

Finally, be aware that research suggests that using cognitive ability tests to choose among candidates may result in some "adverse impact" on certain groups, most often race related. This too can have legal ramifications.[28] Again, we suggest you partner with your HR group in designing and validating your selection procedures to assure that they are appropriate as well as legal.

Personality inventories

Personality inventories attempt to measure "what an individual is like." There are five behavioral traits that capture a significant percentage (as much as 75 percent) of an individual's personality (see Table 13-4).[29] Standard tests that measure these personality traits are readily available. Examples include the Personal Characteristics Inventory, the NEO Personality Inventory, and the Hogan Personality Inventory.[30] Each is a multi-item questionnaire that employees complete.

Research suggests that of the "Big Five" listed in Table 13-4, "conscientiousness" is a "valid predictor of job performance across all types of jobs and organizations."[31]

Table 13-4. The "Big Five" major dimensions of personality

Trait	Traits Associated with This Dimension
Extroversion	Tendency to be sociable, gregarious, assertive, talkative, active, and upbeat
Emotional stability	Tendency to be calm, optimistic, secure, non-depressed, content, and well adjusted
Openness to experience/ Inquisitiveness	Tendency to be imaginative, broad-minded, cultured, artistically sensitive, intelligent, original, and playful, and to have intellectual curiosity and independence of judgment
Agreeableness	Tendency to be trusting, sympathetic, cooperative, flexible, good-natured, courteous, tolerant, and forgiving
Conscientiousness	Tendency to be purposeful, determined, organized, thorough, responsible, achievement-oriented, persevering, dependable, and attentive to detail

Thus, other things being equal, you should select cell applicants who score high on conscientiousness. In addition, "extroversion" and "agreeableness" are important in team settings.[32] Similarly, "emotional stability" can be important in team settings.[33] Finally, the trait "openness to experience/inquisitiveness" may be particularly important if problem-solving and troubleshooting are expected to be important job responsibilities. Moreover, individuals who score high on "openness to experience/inquisitiveness" and "agreeableness" (which includes a flexibility component) may be more willing to learn new skills and take on additional responsibilities—a critical KSAO in many cell environments.

Personality tests can provide you with data for selecting cell workers who will work effectively with others. Keep in mind that "one bad apple can spoil the whole barrel"; specifically, "one highly disagreeable, introverted, or unconscientious team member can ruin an entire team."[34] Also, be aware that job applicants can skew their responses to appear more conscientious and agreeable than they really are. To prevent this from being a problem, use a combination of selection methods (i.e., personality tests and interviews) to assess personality-related KSAOs.[35]

Work-sample tests

Work-sample tests involve observing an individual doing some (i.e., a sample) of the work that will be required for the job.[36] Examples of work-sample tests relevant for cell work include having a candidate follow instructions to assemble a product or operate a piece of equipment. One organization lets candidates for cell jobs work as a team in conducting a meeting. The candidates are provided with an assigned agenda and relevant background material. As a group, they must then decide the order in which to discuss the agenda items and the amount of time to spend on each. After that, they conduct the meeting. Figure 13-3 shows the evaluation form that an observer uses to assess the performance of candidates as they participate in this simulation.

Work-sample tests tend to be good predictors of job performance.[37] That is, candidates who perform well on the work-sample tests are likely to perform well on the job. In addition, well-designed work-sample tests provide job candidates with a realistic preview

---

Candidate _____   Date _____

Assessor _____

Team Interaction Exercise

Circle the statement that best describes the candidate's behavior in the exercise. If there was no opportunity for a behavior to occur, use the symbol N/A to address the behavior

Low Skill
- does not participate
- fights team decisions
- dominates conversations
- rude to or critical of others
- takes the team off track
- generates solution alone
- presents confusing ideas
- avoids/escalates conflict
- reacts angrily if contradicted
- prematurely closes discussion
- rejects/ignores feedback

Medium Skill
- actively participates
- inputs & agrees with team
- asks for other inputs
- respectful of others
- checks for team agreement
- adds to other ideas
- presents ideas clearly
- recognizes conflict
- seeks to understand contradictions
- listens & contributes to discussion
- listens to feedback

High Skill
- provides team leadership
- offers creative input to team
- draws out quiet individuals
- encourages others
- repeatedly monitors process
- integrates diverse ideas
- explains ideas clearly
- accepts & resolves conflict
- re-frames if contradicted
- restates & seeks consensus
- solicits & gives feedback

Supporting comments:

Figure 13-3. Form used by one company to assess a cell operator candidate's team interaction skills

of some aspects of cell work. This could be particularly important when the cell requires interpersonal and problem-solving skills that operators might not have used in previous jobs. Candidates who do not appreciate, or feel that they are not right for, this kind of work may self-select out of the process once they realize what the job will be like.

The disadvantage of work-sample tests is that they can be difficult and expensive to develop and use.[38] Considerable effort may be required to create a work-sample test that is representative of job activities. You will need to identify representative tasks and develop test instructions, test situations, and scoring procedures, as well as train those who will administer and evaluate the tests. Plus, depending on the type of work-sample test, you may need to devote equipment and materials to selection testing. All this can be costly. Moreover, there are jobs for which it is difficult to develop a work sample; for example, for cell tasks that require significant training, work-sample tests are not practical.

Performance evaluations, direct information, and work histories for internal hires

One of the advantages of selecting cell workers from in-house employees is that you generally will have access to verifiable data on the candidates' *work history* and prior job performance. *Performance evaluations* are an excellent source of information, particularly if the prior work is similar to what the candidate will perform in the cell. In addition, you can gather *information directly from supervisors and peers*, informally through conversations or formally by having peers rate their colleagues.[39] Combining opinions will permit you to form a more complete picture of a candidate's qualifications.

If you are selecting candidates internally, and you are a union shop (particularly in the United States), you may be obligated to rely on seniority as the basis for your selection decisions.[40] Unfortunately, seniority (length of service) is a not particularly valid predictor for selection decisions. Seniority is, for the most part, unrelated to job performance. Experience (length of service in various positions in the organization *and* the types of activities performed), on the other hand, has somewhat greater validity as a selection method, particularly if the jobs a candidate has held in the past are similar to the job for which he or she is now being considered.[41]

How to Use the Selection Techniques

We have now discussed a variety of methods for assessing the suitability of candidates for cell operator positions. As we suggested earlier, your choice of assessment method should depend, in large part, on the types of knowledge, skills, and abilities you seek. Figure 13-4 indicates which selection methods are suitable for assessing each of the six major KSAO areas important for cell work.

You should consider using certain tests (e.g., biographical data) as a screening device to eliminate candidates who don't meet minimum standards (e.g., no high school diploma, or a history of job hopping). You can then use other tests (such as cognitive ability tests, work samples, and interviews) to select from the pool of remaining candidates.

Once you have collected information on candidates, you must determine how to consider the results of various selection tests in order to reach a decision.[42] An approach where the results of the tests are scored quantitatively and then combined using some numerical weighting technique is better than using intuition and judgment to make the selection. This approach requires that assessments using methods for which quantitative data normally are unavailable—as is the case with interviews—be turned into numerical scores.

The weights you assign in combining various sources of information should depend on the importance of the various job components. Explaining how to do this is beyond the scope of this book and underscores the importance of involving your HR specialist in the selection of cell employees.[43] As you very well may suspect, using a mathematical combination of results, rather than judgment and intuition, is not a strategy that most managers embrace. But you should be aware that numerous studies have shown this approach to result in better hiring decisions.[44]

Who does the selecting?

The decision-making process for employee selection can be controlled in different ways. The first is to use a manager-led process. Here, managers and/or supervisors,

	Interviews	References and Biographical Data	Physical Ability Tests	Cognitive Ability Tests	Personality Inventories	Work-Sample Tests	Performance Evaluations, Work Histories, Peer Assessment
Technical skills in multiple areas	○	○	○	○		●	●
Interpersonal skills	●	○			●	●	●
Problem-solving and decision-making skills	○	○		●		●	●
Administrative and management skills		○		●		●	●
Ability to learn		○		●		○	●
Willingness to learn	●				●		○

● This assessment method very useful in assessing this KSAO.

○ This assessment method somewhat useful in assessing this KSAO.

Figure 13-4. Linking desirable cell skills and abilities with selection assessment methods

often working with human resources specialists, select cell employees. This option is the only one available when you are selecting employees for your first cells. A common practice is to select cell supervisors first and then have them assist in evaluating candidates for cell operator positions (we discuss supervisor selection below). When selecting cell operators from an existing workforce, management may ask for volunteers and then make their selections from the volunteer pool. About half the respondents to one of our surveys indicated that they had selected cell operators using this approach.[45] In addition, depending on the situation at your firm, union representatives may also participate in selection decisions.

A second alternative is to let cell workers, again with assistance from human resource specialists, decide who will join their team or, in the case of single-operator cells, who will staff a new cell. This approach makes most sense in situations where you have mature cell teams or experienced operators who are comfortable making weighty selection decisions.

A third alternative is to have current cell workers and managers/supervisors, and the union (if applicable), collaborate in selecting cell employees. For example, one alternative would be to give the current cell workers the right to veto management's choices of new cell operators although they cannot themselves suggest candidates.

Examples of How Companies Select Cell Employees

The following examples illustrate different ways of selecting cell workers. The first case involves single-operator cells. In the remaining examples, the companies created cells where teams of workers would collaborate in performing direct and indirect labor activities.

Selecting operators for cells in a precision machining shop

A precision machining shop created a number of single-operator cells. Given part family processing requirements and volumes, small clusters of equipment staffed by a single employee were seen as the best cell design alternative. The equipment was quite complex, requiring considerable skill and expertise to operate. The critical KSAOs for cell operator jobs pertained to technical skills, experience with the parts and equipment, and verbal and mathematical skills to take on indirect labor tasks. Because the operators would continue to work relatively independently, interpersonal skills were not critical.

Management wanted to staff the cells with operators from the existing workforce. Key operators had in fact been involved in the cell design process as members of the analysis team. Once the cells were designed, worker selection was essentially a matching process: which operator was best qualified to machine each family of parts? In many cases, an operator who before ran a critical piece of equipment processing these parts was simply selected to work in the cell containing that equipment (this is a rather common selection approach). Of course, the scope of job responsibilities did increase—operators were required to master other operations, as well as assume administrative tasks. Because management felt confident that the potential cell operators had the mathematical and verbal skills needed to take on administrative work, there was no explicit test for these skills. (These machinists had substantial work histories within the organization and were well known to the managers making selection decisions.) Thus, this plant relied on employee experience and past job performance as the primary selection methods.

Selecting cell workers at an electronics assembly plant

Table 13-5 presents the dimensions one assembly plant uses to evaluate operators for positions in existing and new multi-operator cells. As you can see, critical KSAOs include team-interaction skills, problem-solving skills, openness to change and learning, and employee work orientation/values. Management believes these broad competencies are important predictors of how well an employee will work out in a cell environment. Technical KSAOs, such as how to assemble a product, what constitutes a defect, and so forth, are easily taught; employees do not need to have these capabilities coming into cell work. What is harder to instill, the company believes, is an openness to change, a basic desire to meet customer expectations, and a disposition to work well with others.

Table 13-5. Skills and characteristics used to select cell workers at an electronics assembly plant

Team Interaction Skills
- Respect for others
- Team orientation
- Interaction skills
- Communication skills

Problem-Solving/Continuous Improvement Skills
- Prioritizing and planning
- Analytical reasoning
- Creativity

Openness to Change/Learning
- Openness to new methods, processes, and technologies
- Flexibility
- Initiation of improvement
- Tolerance of ambiguity

Work Orientation/Values
- Customer orientation
- Working independently
- Personal integrity

This organization relies on a combination of interviews (to assess work orientation and goals, as well as interpersonal skills), questionnaires (to assess personality traits such as flexibility and tolerance for ambiguity), discussion with past coworkers and managers, and work-sample tests (various exercises aimed at assessing interpersonal, team-interaction, and problem-solving skills) to screen candidates. Human resource and organization design specialists worked with plant management to develop the selection process, and they jointly conduct the screening and select the workers. Here we see the use of multiple selection tests: interviews, personality tests, information about past work performance, and work-sample tests.

Overcoming union resistance to non-seniority-based selection

Union-based rules that require selection by seniority can present a hurdle in selecting cell employees. At one British plant, management had trouble convincing the union to permit selection based on the results of interviews rather than on seniority.[46] After postponing implementation twice, the union reluctantly agreed to interviews as the main selection tool. Management posted job descriptions, and 40 internal candidates applied for the 25 positions in the pilot cell area. A newly chosen cell leader conducted the interviews. (As mentioned, this is a common approach to selecting cells workers: first select and train the cell leader or supervisor, and then have that person assist in selecting the cell workers.) In terms of KSAOs for cell operator jobs, work orientation and values ("attitude") were considered most important. In screening the candidate cell workers, the company also looked for employees who met basic intelligence and skill requirements, understood what the new jobs would be like, and had a good attendance record. Thus, prior work history with the organization, in addition to interviews, played a role in selection.

In finding workers for subsequent cells, management used personality and aptitude tests, as well as interviews. However, some employees did not read or write well enough to take the tests, and others simply refused the testing. Therefore, interviews remained a staple of the selection process.

Focusing on personal behavior at a textile manufacturing plant

A British manufacturer of textile equipment made a complete conversion to cells.[47] Managers first used role-playing (a form of work-sample test) and psychometric tests (personality testing) to select 24 team leaders from internal applicants. All the 200 manual labor employees who currently worked at the plant were then required to apply for the cell jobs. Management and the cell leaders reviewed the applications and assigned workers to cells of about 10 people each. Each cell was to become a self-managed work team with multi-functional operators collectively responsible for direct and indirect labor tasks. Teams would "set their work standards, decide production levels," and be "responsible and accountable for the quality and operation of their own work." Obviously, in selecting workers for these types of cells, varied technical skills, problem-solving skills, administrative and management skills, as well as interpersonal skills, would be important KSAOs. About 40 of the 200 workers elected to leave the company rather than apply for a cell job because they either did not believe they would be selected for a team or did not want to change to the new way of work.

The company looked externally for workers to fill the remaining positions. In terms of KSAOs, the company was most interested in the behavior and energy of applicants (which may be closely linked to extroversion, one of the five major personality traits in Table 13-4), and their willingness and ability to learn. They also wanted workers who would fit in the team environment. To these ends, potential employees were required to take a basic intelligence test, a technical skills test, engage in role-playing (work-sample tests), and participate in an interview. Previous experience was not a factor.

Cell employees have final say in selection of new team members

One company maintains a pool of "roving" workers. A group of supervisors and human resource specialists selects these roving workers from external applicants, based on interviews and job application information. The driving criteria are to select people who will work well in a team setting and have a strong work ethic. The roving workers have the primary task of filling in for absent employees; thus, they work in a variety of cells. However, when a permanent cell vacancy occurs, a roving worker will join that team on a trial basis.

At the end of the trial period, the team decides whether to accept the roving worker as a permanent member. Being a "team player" and a "hard worker," and having "good skills," are important criteria for this selection. However, the degree of formality in making these decisions is largely dictated by the cell leader or supervisor, who facilitates the decision-making process. Some teams have developed a scoring matrix that identifies key criteria, their relative weights, and a numerical rating scheme. Other teams just discuss among themselves how well a given rover is "working out."

According to one manager, the more formal system of explicit requirements made it easier to focus the discussion on what the team really needed in a new member. Cell operators must work well together to be effective—and to achieve team bonus pay. If the team decides against the temporary worker, another rover joins the team on a trial basis while the rejected rover moves on to another assignment. Roving workers are not eligible for the team bonus, so they are highly motivated to become regular cell team members.

Summary

Several themes emerge from the above examples. First, virtually all companies used a variety of the selection methods we described earlier, reflecting the fact that no single selection method can "do it all." Some approaches are well suited to assessing certain types of KSAOs but poor at measuring others. This is why spending time up front determining which KSAOs are critical to job performance, and then matching them with the most appropriate selection method, is so important (see Figure 13-4). Second, the companies in our examples all relied on interviews at some step in their selection process. This underscores the importance of properly conducting interviews. We direct you again to the guidelines in Appendix G. Third, for several of these companies, work-sample tests were an important element of operator selection. Interestingly, these work-sample tests were not used to verify technical skills, but rather focused on interpersonal abilities and skills. Finally, a number of the companies incorporated assessments of cognitive ability or intelligence in their selection process.

SELECTING CELL SUPERVISORS AND CELL LEADERS

In Chapter 12, we made a distinction between two leadership positions: cell leaders and cell supervisors. A cell leader provides leadership for a cell, but also works in the cell. A cell supervisor, on the other hand, does not work in the cell and may be responsible for more than one cell. Some companies have only cell leaders; others have only cell supervisors; and still others have both (see Figure 12-4).

Cell leaders and supervisors should be selected before cell operators. The starting point for their selection is a clear understanding of the jobs they will perform. What you demand of your supervisory staff depends, obviously, on the tasks that you assign to cell operators. For example, if cell workers are responsible for scheduling work, troubleshooting line problems, and expediting work, supervisors should have other responsibilities. Armed with a clear understanding of supervisors' and cell leaders' jobs, your human resource specialist can help you conduct a job analysis that identifies the KSAOs needed for these positions. You should then use appropriate selection methods to find individuals who have these attributes.

Next, we describe important KSAOs for supervisors and cell leaders, and then discuss the selection process itself. Let us emphasize at this point that cell leaders and supervisors are critical to the effective performance of a cell. Their selection, accordingly, is of utmost importance.

Selection Criteria for Cell Supervisors and Cell Leaders

There are five categories of KSAOs to consider as you assess candidates for cell supervisory and leadership roles:

- Technical skills in several areas.
- Interpersonal skills and abilities.
- Problem-solving and decision-making skills.
- Administrative and management skills (traditional supervisory responsibilities).
- Coaching, mentoring, and facilitating skills.

The relative importance of these attributes depends on the roles and responsibilities cell supervisors/leaders are asked to assume in the cell environment. Furthermore, as we noted in our discussion of KSAOs for cell operators, in situations where potential supervisors and cell leaders do not currently have all the required skill sets, the willingness and ability to learn are important KSAOs (see our earlier discussion).

Technical competence

Cells combine a variety of process steps often drawn from different functional departments. This means cell supervisors and leaders must be knowledgeable about a range of technologies and processes. You should select cell leaders and supervisors who already understand, or can learn, the technical work processes that are part of the cell.

Interpersonal skills and abilities

Cell supervisors and leaders need strong interpersonal skills. Good verbal communication skills (speaking, listening, questioning, clarifying, confirming, and so forth) are essential, as is the ability to work with cell operators and others in the organization. In addition, supervisors need good negotiation, feedback, and conflict resolution skills. You want supervisors who have basic abilities in this area already, and who have the ability and willingness to develop more sophisticated interpersonal skills.

Problem-solving and decision-making skills

Traditional supervisory jobs often are focused on problem solving. For example, expediting work, keeping material moving, and dealing with interpersonal and equipment issues all require problem-solving skills. Most cell supervisors and leaders still will need good problem-solving skills. Even in situations where operators themselves are actively solving problems, cell leaders and supervisors may be called upon to help lead these efforts, offer advice, review solutions, or contribute ideas. Specifically, cell leaders and supervisors need a solid knowledge of group (collaborative) problem-solving processes and techniques.

Administrative and management skills—traditional supervisory responsibilities

Traditional supervisors are responsible for planning, directing, controlling, and evaluating the work of an area. We refer to these as basic administrative and management skills. Supervisors need to understand profit and loss statements, product costs, the nature of the organization's strategy, and so forth. They also need to be able to develop plans, keep records, organize work, direct activities, and evaluate output. When cell operators have not been assigned these tasks, and when there is no cell leader, cell supervisors need to assume these traditional supervisor responsibilities. Thus, in these cases you need the same planning, directing, controlling, and evaluating skills in a cell supervisor that you would seek in a supervisor for a non-cellular work area. If a cell leader provides day-to-day cell management, he or she needs these same basic skills—although perhaps to a lesser extent than the supervisor.

When cell operators (with or without the help of a cell leader) manage the work-flow internal to the cell, supervisors often assume responsibility for multiple cells. This too requires basic administrative and management skills. Although the supervisor will spend less time handling issues within a single cell, he or she will spend more time coordinating the activities of multiple cells and addressing issues that cells cannot handle on their own.

Coaching, facilitating, and mentoring skills

In cells where operators perform indirect tasks (self-managed cells), the supervisor should be skilled at helping the cell team accomplish its work. This calls for coaching, facilitating, and mentoring skills rather than "directing" skills. Of course, excellent interpersonal skills are the foundation for effective coaching, facilitation, and mentoring. In particular, supervisors and cell leaders for self-managed cells need conflict resolution, negotiation, and mediation skills, as well as basic interpersonal abilities. The ability to work one-on-one with operators (in a coach or mentor role), and the skills to orchestrate productive group sessions (the facilitation role) are both important. You want to look for people who already have, or you believe can acquire, these skills.

One aspect of facilitating cell activities involves working across the organization to obtain needed cell resources. Examples include arranging training, securing engineering resources to support cell improvement activities, and working with design groups to help assure that new products will fit into existing cell processes. You want supervisory candidates who can work effectively with diverse groups of employees at different organizational levels.

The Process for Choosing Cell Supervisors and Cell Leaders

In selecting supervisors and cell leaders, you may choose from the array of selection approaches listed in Table 13-3. In addition to these approaches, companies sometimes use a more elaborate approach to selection known as the *assessment center*. An assessment center is a collection of tests used to forecast success, primarily in managerial positions.[48] (This approach can also be used to select cell operators.[49]) Thus, assessment centers formally combine many of the selection approaches we noted earlier into an assessment "event." Typical activities might include work-sample tests (such as an in-box activity where participants must determine the actions to take on a set of incoming correspondence), unstructured group discussions, and written tests of general abilities and personality. Commonly, these tests take days, not hours, to complete and are administered to candidates who go through the testing as a group.

Trained observers (sometimes psychologists, but frequently other managers) evaluate the participants. Assessment centers can be very effective in predicting performance.[50] The major disadvantage is the cost and time to develop and administer the battery of tests and evaluate the results.

Just as was the case with selecting cell operators, interviews are often the staple of the selection process for cell supervisors and leaders. Plant management may announce the supervisor job, candidates apply, and interviews follow. In other cases, a more targeted approach is used. Management may directly contact candidates that seem to have potential for the job, and ask them if they are interested in the position. Managers, human resource personnel, and other supervisors typically interview the candidates and provide input to the decision. For supervisory positions (as opposed to cell leader positions), you may want to have representatives from non-manufacturing groups (e.g., quality, materials, or new product development) interview the candidates. For an existing cell, it is also a good idea to solicit input from the cell's operators. Selecting a supervisor that cell workers themselves strongly reject can cause problems later on.

Choosing from in-house candidates offers certain advantages with respect to the depth, relevance, and verifiability of data. Many companies we've worked with select cell supervisors and leaders from the existing workforce. This means managers typically have observed cell supervisor candidates in their current roles for some time and can provide rich information for making decisions. On the other hand, there is always the risk that selection decisions will be less objective. A manager at one plant observed that "we have had a number of 'bubba net' promotions—cases where someone becomes a team leader or supervisor because they are good buddies with other supervisors." The guidelines we presented in Appendix G are helpful in assuring effective supervisor selection interviews. In addition, highly structured processes, such as the one used at Delphi Saginaw Steering Systems (described below), can also help assure an objective selection.

Selecting Cell Leaders and Supervisors—Examples of Company Practice

Below, we review the processes by which supervisors and cell leaders are chosen at an electrical equipment manufacturer, an auto components manufacturer, and a plant making batteries. These examples illustrate some of the different ways you can structure the selection process.

Using past performance to select from internal candidates

At a plant making electrical equipment, managers and current supervisors choose cell leaders from current cell employees. Management looks for cell leaders to be "well liked and respected, respectful of others, take ownership, have technical competence (understand the parts and products), and have good organizational abilities."

When the plant first transitioned to cells, existing supervisors became cell supervisors. Now, however, outstanding cell leaders move into supervision. The company posts the positions internally and those interested apply. Managers, human resource specialists, and current supervisors participate in selecting new supervisors. They rely on the same criteria they use when selecting cell leaders:

respected and respectful, willing to take ownership, good organizational abilities. Thus, KSAOs related to interpersonal abilities and administrative and management skills are particularly important. Technical abilities are also a factor, although past performance as a cell leader is perhaps the most important consideration in selecting new cell supervisors.

A structured assessment process for the selecting cell coordinators

At Delphi Saginaw Steering Systems each cell has its own coordinator. The cell coordinator is responsible for scheduling material flows, scheduling overtime, maintaining and updating records, institutionalizing housekeeping procedures, scheduling vacations, organizing the training of new workers, facilitating team meetings, interacting with other work units, maintaining and improving quality control systems, organizing daily inventories, and coordinating manpower. As this list suggests, administrative and management KSAOs are particularly important for the coordinator role. Delphi's coordinator role falls somewhere between a cell leader and a cell supervisor. Most of the responsibilities are of the supervisory nature, yet the individual is an hourly representative and does not have the authority to correct behavior or performance problems.[51] On the other hand, the cell coordinator, unlike a typical cell leader, does not build products.

Cell coordinators are selected using a procedure designed jointly by labor and management:[52]

> Whenever a vacancy for a coordinator's position opens, management posts the job in the plant. The candidates are graded out of a possible 100 points and the worker with the highest score is awarded the position. The points are awarded based on seniority, attendance, the employee's infraction record, a quiz on the QNMS [Quality Network Management System—the company's manufacturing system which includes cells], and a preselection class that all potential team coordinators must complete successfully.

The rotating cell leader

We know of a few plants where the cell leader role rotates among the employees. At a German electronics facility, for example, the cell leader is elected by cell members and serves a term lasting several months. When the leader's term expires, the team votes again and selects a different individual to fill this role. The intent is to give multiple operators an opportunity to develop management and administrative skills. At other companies, all cell members rotate through the cell leader position; others select the cell leader from among those cell members who express an interest in the position.[53]

At one battery plant with 33 cells in place, operators elect their cell leader from among the cell team members. Elections occur whenever the current leader resigns or another team member asks to be considered for the role. Some cells have had the same leaders since their inception; others have had several different leaders. Interestingly, at the outset, leaders tended to be elected because they were popular. However, teams seemed to quickly discover that "the best leaders were those who had organizing, planning, interpersonal, and conflict resolution skills." Popularity thus became a less important criterion for cell leader selection.[54]

The practice of rotating cell leaders has both pros and cons. On the positive side, it gives different workers an opportunity to develop management skills. One large-scale study of teams concluded that:[55]

> With the experience of being a team leader, team members will experience firsthand the problems and challenges that must be addressed to perform the leadership role. They will have an opportunity to learn firsthand the concerns of management and to gain more understanding of financial matters, organizational constraints, and the complexities involved in leading others.

Disadvantages include a possible lack of continuity from one cell leader to the next, and poor cell performance if a recently elected cell leader is not effective. Rotating cell leaders probably makes the most sense if you place a high priority on developing leadership skills among many employees, and if the cell team is mature and can adapt to different leaders while maintaining good performance. Letting workers elect their own leader is advisable when you have a strong culture of workplace democracy, where an influence on leader selection is expected. This practice is also a way to create involvement and ownership among cell team members.

TRAINING CELL OPERATORS, LEADERS, AND SUPERVISORS

Training is the planned effort by a company to bring about employee learning of job-related competencies. The goal of training is for "employees to master the knowledge, skill, and behaviors emphasized in training programs and to apply them to their day-to-day activities."[56] *Education*, on the other hand, refers to the development of more general knowledge, skills, and abilities "related—but not specifically tailored—to a person's career or job."[57]

The distinction between education and training can become blurred. For simplicity, we use the term "training" to refer to both the training and the education that equips cell employees with the knowledge, skills, and abilities they need to perform their jobs well. We'll talk first about start-up training, offer some general training guidelines, and then briefly discuss ongoing training for cell employees.

Start-Up Training for Cell Employees

As shown in Table 13-6, there are seven basic areas in which cell employees may need start-up training. We describe each type in the sections that follow. Which of these seven areas you need to address, and how much training you need to provide, depends on how cell work and supervision are structured, as well as on the current skill levels of the employees. In particular, the information you gathered about the new employees as part of the selection process (Box 11, Figure 13-1), coupled with knowledge of the KSAOs needed to perform cell jobs (Box 8, Figure 13-1), will help you identify the gap between what employees know now and what they need to know. This gap helps you determine the type of start-up training to provide (Box 13, Figure 13-1) and the objectives you want this training to accomplish. Obviously, certain start-up training needs to happen in advance of operating the cell (Box 14, Figure 13-1); other types (for example, skills training) may be best delivered "on the job" while the cell is up and running (hence the double arrow running between boxes 14 and 15 in Figure 13-1).

Table 13-6. Types of training for cell employees

- Basic literacy and mathematical skills training
- Cell concepts training
- Technical process skills training
- Interpersonal skills training
- Problem-solving and decision-making skills training
- Administrative and management skills training
- Coaching, mentoring, and facilitation skills training (for supervisors and cell leaders)

Basic literacy and mathematical skills training

Reading, writing, and math skills are important in all manufacturing environments, but particularly where jobs require planning, data analysis, problem solving, and process improvement.[58] Literacy and mathematical skills training, which is more appropriately classified as "education," is absolutely essential if you discover that workers have deficiencies in these areas. No additional training will have much of an impact unless fundamental reading, writing, and mathematical skills are in place.

Furthermore, cell workers from diverse linguistic backgrounds may be unable or reluctant to pass on important information (on defective parts, for example) to employees and supervisors who speak other languages. To rectify this, you may need to provide language training (e.g., English as a Second Language, ESL, in U.S. plants).

Cell concepts training

All cell employees need training on cell concepts, i.e., training that explains the "what" and "why" of cellular manufacturing. Operators, cell leaders, and supervisors who understand the principles and objectives of cell manufacturing will be better able to contribute to its success (in fact, managers and HR personnel also should get this training so they are better equipped to participate in cell employee selection).

We suggest you begin by training supervisors (and cell leaders if you have them) on cell concepts. The objectives of this training are to thoroughly ground supervisors in all issues surrounding cell implementation and operations, to help them understand their role, and to prepare them to answer questions the workforce might raise. This last objective is especially important. Supervisors play a key role in helping workers understand and accept new roles. If supervisors do not understand cell work themselves, they will be of little help during (and may actually hinder) the implementation.

Management at an aerospace firm brought together supervisors and middle managers from several locations for a day of intensive cell training. The course introduced the fundamentals of cellular manufacturing and covered technical issues such as cell design, production planning and control for cells, the role of setup reduction, and the changes in infrastructure that cells require. The course also explored the benefits of cells and the risks involved in the transition. By increasing the supervisors' knowledge level, management hoped to prepare them to be active contributors to the transformation and to equip them to respond knowledgeably to questions from their workers. They also hoped to reduce supervisor resistance. Table H-1 (in Appendix H) presents the objectives and the outline for this one-day course.

It is also important that operators, supervisors, and cell leaders understand the company's motivation for creating cells. As our upcoming discussion of change management suggests, people are more likely to support a change if they understand its underlying reasons (see Chapters 15). Three companies in one British study, for example, each provided focused training to help cell workers understand and embrace the company's goals.[59] Managers believed that a committed, cooperative workforce who understood the overall business objectives would be "more flexible, cooperative, self disciplined and productive."

Based on our work with several plants, we suggest that introductory cell training emphasize the following:

- The concept of cellular manufacturing.
- How cellular manufacturing supports the plant's goals (e.g., reducing costs, increasing quality, shortening lead times).
- The impact cellular manufacturing will have on the work area.
- What jobs will be like in the cellular environment.

Appendix Table H-2 provides an outline for such a course targeted at operators (but suitable for supervisors and cell leaders as well). At one plant, cell concept training began with a half-day course organized around these objectives. After this introduction, workers participated in a daylong physical simulation game in which they worked in a non-cellular system, redesigned the system to create cells, and then experienced work in the cells.

From a change management perspective, reinforcing the case for change through early training is very important. However, when operators arrive for formal training on cell concepts, it should *not* be the first time they hear the term "cell." There should be an ongoing and broad-based communication effort *throughout* the cell design and implementation project. This means that prior to any formal job posting, employees will have heard about the transition to cells and be familiar with basic cell concepts.

Early in the planning process, before employees were given an opportunity to apply for cell jobs, a manufacturer of aircraft components provided hour-long "introduction to manufacturing cells" sessions for all salaried and hourly workers. The audience included workers who would eventually staff and supervise the cells, as well as indirect labor people who would interface with the cells. The term "cells" had a negative connotation at this plant that management wanted to overcome. The hour-long education sessions, presented repeatedly to small groups of employees, answered basic questions about cellular manufacturing and the company's motivation for adopting it. A brief question-and-answer period followed each session. Plant management reports that exposing everyone to the same message about cells helped ease the implementation. Also, having an objective and credible outsider deliver the plant's message helped make the sessions effective. Follow-up training was primarily the responsibility of plant personnel who attended external seminars to gain a deeper understanding of cellular manufacturing prior to training the plant workforce.

This example underscores an important point about cell concepts training. While you may want to have external consultants assist you with training start-up, it makes sense to have in-house personnel do a significant portion of the cell concepts training for operators. Doing so serves several purposes. First, it sends a strong message to participants about the importance of cells to the company. Second, it is generally less expensive to have training delivered by internal personnel than by external consultants. Finally, it assures that you develop internal cell expertise, something that we feel is important for a successful foray into cells. To assure that your employees are adequately prepared to teach operators about cells, you may want to send cell leaders and supervisors (and managers and support staff too!) to external training courses. In terms of in-house training, one useful strategy is to pair a manager or supervisor with an internal training specialist to deliver the training.

Technical process skills training

Most workers who move to cells must master new technical skills. This is especially so with craft cells (with single or multiple operators) where operators are responsible for all production tasks.

Training to create multi-functional workers can be provided in different ways. One is through *on-the-job training*. A trainer, typically a supervisor or operator already skilled at the task, explains the task, observes the trainee's performance, and offers feedback. The disadvantage of on-the-job training, however, is that it may interfere with production—or that production may interfere with training![60] The former can happen when an experienced worker is taken away from his tasks to train a new worker, or when a new operator who is still learning the tasks slows down production. Similarly, training may not be thorough if the trainer (e.g., an experienced operator) is distracted by the need to get product out the door.

An alternative is to provide hands-on technical skills training through *off-line* (and, possibly, *off-hours*) *training*. One facility, for example, has set up a special training cell where operators can learn a variety of skills. Other companies simply maintain training areas equipped with a variety of equipment, but not arranged in cells. Special hands-on classes can also provide task training (e.g., new soldering techniques).

Multi-functionality has many benefits for both the organization and the individual.[61] For the individual worker, the benefits include reduced boredom (by virtue of multi-tasking), reduced risk of repetitive motion injury, and increased opportunities for growth (and more pay). There are a number of benefits for the organization as well:

- *Increased understanding of work processes and their problems:* Training in multiple tasks increases the depth and breadth of operators' understanding of work and its problems.

- *Increased flexibility among the workforce:* Multi-functionality that leads to cross-training increases the cell's total pool of skills. Operators will become flexible and able to shift tasks in response to shifting product demands.

- *Increased communication and team cohesiveness:* Cross-training strengthens team relationships and fosters higher levels of work-related communication.

What is the appropriate level of cross-training? The amount of cross-training that you provide depends on the objectives of the cell, the capability of the workforce, and the nature of the technical work itself.[62] With this in mind, we offer five issues you should consider—besides the cost of training (also see the related guidelines we offered in Chapter 7):

1. *How flexible does your workforce need to be?* How much product design variability should you plan for, and how will this impact the tasks you need operators to perform? Will shifts in product mix call for more operators to perform certain tasks within the cell?

2. *Where is cell work likely to get bogged down?* Which steps or processes are likely to become bottlenecks? These tasks are good targets for cross-training since operators will then be able to help each other out on these critical tasks. Also keep in mind that cross-training that gives operators broader knowledge of cell activities will be helpful with troubleshooting, problem solving, and process improvement.

3. *How will the cell adapt to an absent worker?* We recommend that you train at least two operators on each task. If you do not, an absent worker will bring the cell operation to a halt.

4. *Are there worker safety issues to consider?* When work is repetitive and requires fine motor skills, be sure that multi-functionality and frequent job rotations are part of a comprehensive program to prevent worker injuries.

5. *How many different skills can operators comfortably master?* This will depend on workers' abilities and the nature of cell work. It is not practical or economical to cross-train all operators on equipment that requires highly specialized skills that take years to master (e.g., precision turning or milling of extremely tight tolerance parts). Neither is it practical to train operators with such skills on many other tasks in the cell. Accordingly, cells where work tasks are relatively easy to learn are better suited for extensive cross-training. An example might be light assembly work that requires only simple process steps (join, solder, press, and so forth).

Thus, technical work tasks that require very high skill levels or take a lot of time to master might not be good candidates for cross-training. Thus, let's dispel the notion up front that you must have a fully cross-trained workforce, one where every cell worker knows how to perform every cell task (also see Chapter 7). While this might sound impressive, it can be costly. Training is expensive not only in terms of preparation and delivery, but also (and more importantly) in terms of time spent away from work. Further, in pay-for-skill environments, a fully cross-trained workforce means higher labor costs as well (see Chapter 14).

Finally, many mature cells do have fully cross-trained workers. However, they did not start this way. Over time, you can increase the flexibility of the cell through additional training. In fact, as we will describe later, you will want to have a long-term training plan for the cell and for each individual cell worker.

Administrative and management skills training

Cell operators need an understanding of administrative and management fundamentals if they are responsible for performing indirect labor tasks. What they need to learn depends on the types of responsibilities they will assume. For example, if operators are responsible for tracking the cell's performance and reporting key metrics, they need to understand what measures to take (e.g., to track quality, lead time, and inventory), when and where to take these measures, and how to record key data, compile information and analyze it, and then present the results (also see Chapter 9). Similarly, operators who are responsible for maintaining their own stocks of consumables must understand basic inventory management. In short, the more indirect labor tasks operators perform, the more management and administrative skills training they need. Of course, supervisors and cell leaders must master these same administrative and management fundamentals, although in more depth.

Interpersonal skills training

Cell workers who have overlapping responsibilities need to work effectively together. If operators are coming to cells from jobs where they worked relatively independently, interpersonal skills training will be especially important. Of course, interpersonal skills are even more important for supervisors and cell leaders than for operators.

Interpersonal training should emphasize basic listening, questioning, and responding skills. It should also provide a basic framework for giving and receiving constructive feedback—a major theme in intracell communication. This type of training should have the goal of assuring that cell members, leaders, and supervisors understand the basics of working in a group: the structure of meetings, how to be an effective meeting participant, and so forth. Appendix Table H-3 provides a sample agenda and objectives for training aimed at developing interpersonal skills among cell employees and their supervisors.

Problem-solving and decision-making skills training

All cell leaders and supervisors need problem-solving and decision-making skills. However, when operators are assigned responsibilities for performing indirect tasks, such as inspecting work and resolving quality problems, they too need the same type of skills. Appendix Table H-4 presents learning objectives and an agenda for training aimed at developing problem-solving and decision-making skills among cell supervisors, leaders, and operators.

Coaching, mentoring, and facilitation skills training for supervisors and cell leaders

Supervisors and cell leaders may need to help the cell team get its work done. The more self-managed the cell, the more coaching, facilitating, and mentoring skills supervisors require, and the fewer directive skills. Often, supervisors are more experienced, and far more comfortable, with the conventional directing role; in this case, training to help them understand and be effective in their new roles is particularly important. Appendix Table H-5 provides an outline for a course aimed at strengthening cell supervisors' facilitation, coaching, mentoring, and team leadership skills.

Guidelines for Conducting Cell Employee Training

The process of training includes:

- Assessing training needs.
- Setting training objectives.
- Choosing the training techniques.
- Developing training materials.
- Delivering the training.
- Evaluating training results.

The first two steps—training needs and objectives—were discussed in the last section. Here we focus on *how* to train operators, supervisors, and cell leaders for their new roles.

There are a variety of training techniques from which you can choose. Options include readings, lectures, courses and seminars, conferences, audiovisual instruction, programmed instruction including web-based training, plant visits, group discussions, simulations and games, on-the-job training, role playing, and so on. Unfortunately, the choice of instructional method is not clear-cut. Selecting the right training techniques, and administering them effectively, is "more art than science."[63] However, instruction that engages participants in an activity is for many people the most effective learning mode. Passive learning—i.e., listening only—tends to be less effective. Here are some helpful guidelines for structuring and delivering training at your plant:[64]

- *Use shorter training periods, spread out over time, rather than fewer but longer sessions.* Divide the course into meaningful segments that participants can absorb in one sitting. This makes it less overwhelming and provides time between sessions to reflect on the material and experiment with its application. For example, in teaching cell operators how to monitor production lead times and cycle times, operators at one plant attended three two-hour sessions, spread out over three weeks. At another plant, cell operators met once a week for over a year to learn the basics of statistical process control. In Appendix H we present examples of courses where the material is delivered in a single day. Of course, the length of the course segments depends on the topic and the method of instruction. Some cell simulations and games require a full day to play. Similarly, facilitation or interpersonal skills training where you want individuals to practice in the class also require longer class sessions. Generally, the less hands-on and the more complex the material, the more you should consider shorter sessions.

- *Provide opportunities to practice.* While training delivered in short segments over time helps employees retain what they learn, try to arrange this training so that the employees have an opportunity to immediately apply what they have learned. There is a reason why you always had homework in school: learning is cemented through practice. In one cell cycle time training course, for example, homework assignments required participants to measure the cycle time of their cell's parts and identify improvement opportunities. Each cell team reported back to the class at the next session. This gave workers an opportunity to reinforce key course concepts.

The use of homework tightly links training to application. In the same vein, don't complete training on, say, statistical process control (SPC), in January and then have employees wait till June to actually use this tool. Where you can, do *just-in-time training*—training just before employees will use the new knowledge in their day-to-day work.

- *Provide feedback and reward learning.* Let participants discover how much of the material they have learned and can master. Tests are one option, games and exercises another. For example, a course on improvement tools and techniques for cell operators and supervisors concluded with a quiz game. The game reviewed the key concepts and provided feedback on mastery.

- *Make the training as "real world" as possible.* You want participants to transfer classroom concepts to the workplace. They may have a difficult time doing this if they can't see the connection between the training material and their own work environment. Thus, the examples and scenarios you use in the training should be as realistic as possible. For example, process improvement training at one plant included a simulation game that featured an assembly process and problems that mirrored those in the existing cells. Also consider delivering training to teams of employees involved with the same processes. Discussions can then focus on cell-specific applications. At one plant, cell operators and representatives of key support groups (e.g., accounting, production planning, and engineering) jointly participated in a class on managing internal supplier and customer relationships. Class discussions explored the issues of customer service, feedback, and communication with internal partners.

The final step in the training process is evaluating training results. Companies often forget to evaluate the effectiveness of training programs.[65] Evaluation can let you know if the training worked, i.e., did behaviors change and, if so, did these changes have an impact on performance? You may also discover what participants liked and disliked, what they learned and didn't learn, and how to improve the training. We recommend course evaluations at the close of each session and follow-up assessments several weeks later.[66]

Pitfalls and Challenges in Training Employees for Cells

Any number of things can go wrong in preparing operators and supervisors for cell work. Table 13-7 presents a list of potential pitfalls. In addition, we want to emphasize one especially important issue—underestimating the need for training. We discuss this next.

Underestimating training requirements

There are no hard and fast rules about how much instructional time is required to successfully prepare people for work in cells. A general rule of thumb, however, is that "more is better than less" when it comes to training for cells. The agendas we provide in Appendix H give you some idea of the amount of time required to introduce key topics to cell operators, supervisors, and cell leaders in order to *begin* building skills in these various areas. You should treat these as the absolute lower bounds in terms of training times. Depending on where you start, you may need substantial additional training in specific areas. For example, the time required to equip operators with technical task skills can represent a significant training investment. And you will certainly need to reinforce certain key skills and concepts through follow-up and refresher training (see below for a discussion of ongoing training).

Table 13-7. Common pitfalls in training to support cells

Limiting training to operators only
Managers need exposure to the same training and education that operators receive. Supervisors and other middle management groups need extra attention in the training process to support a smooth transition to their new roles.

Training managers and supervisors after operators
To be supportive of the change and in a position to answer operator questions, managers and supervisors need to be trained before cell operators.

Providing only technical training on operating new equipment and processes
Cell operators may require cell concepts, interpersonal, problem-solving, and administrative and management skills training. Mathematical, reading, or writing literacy, as well as language instruction, may also be needed.

Training people far in advance of the conversion to cells
Training should be closely coupled with application of the skills that are being taught.

Providing only on-the-job training
Clearly, some aspects of cell training (e.g., interpersonal skills training, cell concepts training) are best explored in a classroom setting away from the production line.

Training is one-time with no follow-up
Research on learning suggests that exposure to concepts over an extended period of time and with periodic reviews enhances retention.

Having outsiders provide all the training
External consultants can provide valuable assistance in the transformation process. However, developing internal trainers, who will be able to sustain the change on a day-to-day basis, is also important. In addition, when managers and supervisors—and even operators—are involved in the delivery of the training, it can send a clear message about the importance of and commitment to the new way of operating.

Training is not readily available for new workers joining an existing cell
This is a serious problem for any cell and particularly thorny when operator compensation depends on group output. The problem is a persistent one in environments that routinely use temporary workers. Creating a training cell where new workers can come up to speed before being introduced into the cell can help.

One sheet metal manufacturer estimated that during the first two years of their conversion to cells, employees would spend 25 percent of their time in training.[67] While this is excessive, our studies of cell users reveal that many feel they should have invested more time and effort in training.[68] For example, the training manager at one company told us that he dramatically underestimated the amount and scope of training required to support cells. Some areas were unprepared, both technically and socially, to assume their broadened responsibilities. At this plant, inadequate training contributed to worker and manager frustration, an increase in the defect rate, and a slower than expected implementation. The plant went to great lengths to overcome these problems by enhancing their training. It dedicated a special room to be used for formal training classes. It also developed a set of 30-minute training modules focused on a variety of technical and interpersonal skills. Many are video-based and all are available whenever a work group is ready for training. The training manager calls it "McTraining"—short duration, on-demand training.

When new workers join existing cells, under-training can be a big problem. This is particularly true in cells where compensation is based on group output and work is tightly linked (i.e., there are few buffer spaces between workstations). Module workers at one shoe plant complained loudly when insufficiently trained workers joined their cells. In response, the organization developed a training cell that includes all the major production equipment used in the plant. Trainers can reconfigure the equipment to replicate any module in the facility. New employees can now learn sewing skills, and experience the pace and flow of production, before they join an existing module. The instructors are knowledgeable veteran employees. Besides teaching new workers, they also act as "utility workers," filling in for absent employees anywhere in the plant.

Ongoing Training for Cell Employees

As discussed, one mistake companies make is failing to sufficiently prepare cell employees for their new roles. It is also a mistake to assume that initial training is all that is required. Not only is it vital to reinforce key training messages through fol-low-up sessions, but it is equally important to routinely evaluate worker knowledge, skills, and abilities against the current or future job design concepts and skill needs (see Chapter 12) so that you can determine any gaps. Thus, assessment and training should be tightly linked (see bottom part of Figure 13-1).

At one British plant, team leaders assess cell employees on a monthly basis with respect to the company's behavior standards. Based on the discovered skill gaps— "what people are paid to do, what they need to know to do the job and what they actually know"—the team leader and the employee jointly establish and revise indi-vidual training plans. The company's goal is "for the worker to develop their skills through constant evaluation and training so they are a perfect match with those required in the job scope."[69]

At Tellabs, a manufacturer of telecommunications equipment, supervisors assess cell workers with respect to (1) flexibility, (2) contribution, enthusiasm, and pride, (3) productivity, (4) process conformance, and (5) attendance. This assessment fac-tors into decisions about compensation, but also helps guide decisions about train-ing. For example, process conformance refers to an employee's ability to understand and accurately use process documentation, just-in-time principles and related methodologies (kanban rules, inspection of previous workstation outputs, etc.), stan-dard operating procedures, and so forth. Employees who do not meet the require-ments are candidates for additional training in these areas.

Organizational or technological change may also signal the need for ongoing training. New process technology, for example, may require that you equip cell workers with additional technical skills. In addition, corporate-wide initiatives—such as a program to assure that workers understand the basics of ergonomics, or a plant-wide effort to become ISO 9001 registered—call for additional training of cell workers. Events *inside* the cell may also serve as a catalyst. For example, ongoing conflicts among team members may prompt the cell leader or supervisor to arrange specific training aimed at improving workers' interpersonal abilities.

In general, consider providing appropriate training any time you assign additional tasks to a cell. For example, as workers in assembly cells at one plant gained experience in working together, management shifted more and more administrative and management responsibilities to them. In advance of adding these tasks, however, the workers received extensive training to prepare them for their new duties. Thus, an ongoing program of skills training was the foundation for this transition.

We suggest that you develop a training plan for each cell employee that specifies the type of training each employee needs and when they should complete it. You should also consider maintaining a training matrix, such as the one presented in Figure 13-5. This matrix shows the degree to which each operator is qualified to perform various cell tasks. Training matrices are often part of the "visual scoreboard" placed close to the cell (see Chapter 9).

Operator Name	Component Part Insertion	Pressing	Soldering	Epoxy	Cleaning Station	Packaging and Shipment
Bill	FT	FT	FT	FT	FT	FT
Kelly	T	FT	T	FT	T	FT
Xioyan	T	T	FT	T	T	T
May	T	FT	PT	PT	T	T
Alfredo	T	U	T	PT	U	T
Temporaries						
Marty	U	U	T	T	PT	PT
Omar	T	T	PT	U	U	U

FT = Fully trained on this process and can train others
T = Trained on this process
PT = Has completed basic training on this process and can work under supervision
U = Untrained—not yet able to perform this process

Figure 13-5. Training matrix for electronics assembly cell

KEY INSIGHTS

There are several critical "take aways" for managers, supervisors, engineers, human resource specialists, and others who are involved in designing, implementing, and managing cells:

- *If you are serious about cells, be serious about training.* Be willing to spend the money and invest the time to equip employees with the skills they will need for cell work. The success of the cell implementation may depend on this.

- *Determine selection criteria for cell workers and supervisory staff.* Depending on the types of work they will perform, cell operators may need to have varied technical, interpersonal, problem-solving, and management skills. In addition, workers in *all* cells must be able to master basic cell concepts. Cell supervisors and cell leaders need to understand a broader range of technical work processes than do traditional supervisors. In addition, you need to select supervisors and cell leaders who can help the group accomplish their work through coaching, mentoring, and facilitation.

- *A critical capability for most cell employees is the ability to learn.* Most cell work requires that cell employees acquire new skills and adapt to changing conditions. This requires an ability to learn. Cognitive ability tests can give you a preview of a candidate's ability to respond successfully to training. In addition, employees must be willing to learn. Interviews, past performance, and personality inventories can give you some indication of a candidate's suitability in this regard.

- *Go beyond the employment interview in selecting cell workers.* Where possible, use a variety of means (work-sample tests, cognitive ability testing, job applications, etc.). If you must limit selection testing to interviews, be sure to follow the interview protocols in Appendix G.

- *Try to provide realistic job previews.* Cell work will be different from previous jobs. Work-sample tests can provide good information about some aspects of work. In addition, interviews where you ask candidates about specific job situations likely to arise in cell work can be a good way of communicating the nature of the job. You also might have potential workers speak with current cell operators who can give them a realistic picture of what the cell job is like.

- *Prepare supervisors for their new roles.* Changes in worker roles and responsibilities will change supervisors' tasks as well. Be sure to provide supervisors with the training they need, and train them before you train operators. They will then be able to help workers with the transition.

- *Put together a comprehensive training plan.* Training should address the gaps between current employee capabilities and the cell's requirements. Work with your plant's internal training people or with qualified outsiders to design and deliver the needed training (see Appendix H for examples). Involve managers and supervisors in the training, and provide them with the knowledge they need to teach others effectively.

- *Don't overlook interpersonal and group problem-solving skills.* Don't assume that people automatically will know how to work together. Be sure that training equips operators and supervisors with interpersonal and problem-solving skills. These skills are often difficult for people to learn and master.

- *You should regularly assess employee skills to determine training needs.* Don't assume that you can train once and be done with it. Assessment can help identify training needs as well as readiness to acquire more advanced skills. This will help guide training efforts. Also remember that once cells are operating in full-scale production, you will need to have readily available training that prepares new workers to join existing teams.

- *Look at your human resource management policies as a system.* Selection and training, as well as job design and compensation, work together. Make consistent changes, so that *all* human resource policies support cell work.

14

Compensation Systems for Cell Employees

Compensation—the payments organizations make to their employees—includes *direct* monetary payments, such as wages and bonuses, as well as *indirect* payments, such as health insurance and other benefits. Benefits represent a significant component of total compensation (close to 20 percent in the United States).[1] However, our focus in this chapter will be on direct pay to cell employees.

Decisions about compensation are important. Typically, organizations spend somewhere between 10 and 50 percent of total operating costs on employee compensation. In some service organizations, this figure can be as high as 90 percent.[2] Thus, compensation has a significant effect on the bottom line. In addition, compensation may directly influence job satisfaction, retention, and performance, and may indirectly influence the effectiveness of other human resource policies. For example, your efforts to cross-train operators in direct and indirect labor tasks are unlikely to be effective in promoting teamwork in the presence of a compensation system that rewards employees for individual output.

The compensation system should support your organization's objectives and strategies.[3] This means you should measure and reward performance that contributes to achieving strategic objectives. The link between strategy and the pay system underscores the importance of rethinking compensation systems when you move to cells.

This chapter answers several important questions about employee compensation in cellular systems:

- What are the characteristics of an effective cell compensation system?
- What are some alternative methods for compensating cell work? What are their strengths and weaknesses?
- What types of pay systems have organizations with cells adopted?
- How should you choose a compensation system for cellular work?

We want to stress upfront that the relationship between "pay and performance" is uncertain, and that there is little definitive knowledge about the influence of various pay systems.[4] One thing appears clear, however—*there is no "best" compensation method for cells*. As a result, many alternative pay systems can be used. However, for a compensation system to be effective you need to create payment policies that are (1) consistent with your strategy, (2) consistent with your other human resource practices, and (3) viewed by employees as fair and equitable. Most often, this means that the system combines several individual compensation methods, each satisfying a different need.

In the remainder of this chapter we outline the goals and design characteristics of an ideal cell compensation system, then describe the strengths and weaknesses of specific cell compensation systems with respect to these "ideal" criteria. We'll also briefly cover non-financial recognition and reward systems.

GOALS AND CHARACTERISTICS OF AN IDEAL CELL COMPENSATION SYSTEM

Most organizations have specific goals for their pay systems (e.g., to be market competitive, to foster teamwork, to attract and retain good employees). These goals help guide the choice of pay system strategies. In this section we describe, first, some general goals or objectives that cell compensation systems should strive to achieve. Then we identify a set of specific strategies for cell pay systems—expressed as characteristics or design rules—that support one or more of these goals. We will use these goals and characteristics to assess alternative cell pay systems.

Three Goals for Cell Compensation Systems

There are three overarching goals for any compensation system (see Table 14-1):

1. The compensation system should motivate employees to work efficiently and effectively together.[5] Any compensation system should encourage people to contribute their personal best efforts (see goal 3 below). However, in most cells, operators must work effectively and efficiently *together*. (Even single operator cells are part of a larger group—department and plant—and will work with other parts of the supply chain.) Specific strategies, such as linking pay to cell or work group performance and/or rewarding the behavior of acquiring a variety of technical and interpersonal skills, are ways of facilitating working effectively and efficiently together. You especially will need a compensation system that encourages employees to work together in cells where jobs involve a high degree of task overlap and operators have little experience working in groups and are more accustomed to working independently. People need reasons for altering well-established work patterns and the pay system can provide an incentive for doing so.

2. A cell compensation system should attract and retain employees. Some pay systems send strong messages about what a company values and can appeal to employees that way.[6] As Chapter 13 suggested, you want to select workers who will fit the cell environment. The way you pay people is part of this equation. For example, for multi-operator cells you want excellent performers who can work flexibly with others. A group performance bonus system signals to the employees the importance of pulling together, and can help attract and keep employees who like group interaction. Similarly, a pay system where employees increase their base pay by acquiring additional job skills might attract cell workers who value growth and learning. The system may also help retain employees who simply take advantage of the opportu-

Table 14-1. Goals and characteristics of an effective cell compensation system

Goals
1. To motivate employees to work effectively and efficiently together.
2. To attract and retain employees who can help the organization achieve its goals.
3. To encourage high and sustained performance over time.

Ideal Characteristics
1. It focuses on results as well as on employee behaviors.
2. It rewards both individual and cell accomplishments.
3. It provides a clear line of sight between employee actions and their pay.
4. It links cell employee pay to the larger organization's performance.
5. It includes a component that must be re-earned each period.
6. Employees perceive it as fair and equitable.

nity to increase pay. These individuals, by having mastered company-specific skills that make them more valuable to their current organization than to competitors, are likely to be paid at higher than market rates.[7] This can encourage retention.

3. The cell pay system should encourage high and sustained performance. Although many factors, such as the job itself, contribute to employee motivation, pay systems play at least an indirect role. A system that motivates employees to acquire and use relevant job skills could contribute to achieving this goal. Similarly, a system where employees must re-earn a bonus each pay period can help sustain and improve performance over time. On the other hand, a pay increase that is rolled into base pay (and hence automatically received in the future) does not provide the same kind of incentive since employees do not have to re-earn that pay each period. Also, high and sustained performance may be supported by a pay system that employees perceive as fair. If, for example, low and high performers all earn the same wage, high performers who value money will likely view the system as unfair and may be less inclined to continue to apply their best efforts.

Six Characteristics of an Ideal Cell Compensation System

We have identified six design guidelines that will help a cell compensation system meet the above goals. According to these guidelines, an ideal compensation system has the following characteristics:[8]

1. It focuses on results as well as on employee behaviors. You want a pay system to encourage employee behaviors that will lead to the meeting of the cell's performance objectives. Pay should also be linked to the results themselves. Thus, cell compensation systems should blend a focus on results with a focus on behavior. By results focus we mean that the compensation system should link pay to outcomes or targets for the cell's output, productivity, quality, inventory, or other objective measures.[9]

Focusing on results can help encourage high and sustained performance. However, focusing only on results means emphasizing concrete aspects of performance at the expense of behavioral aspects that, you believe, will create tangible and positive outcomes for the cell in the future.[10] Examples of such behaviors include helping others to learn new skills, contributing ideas to solve production problems, demonstrating flexibility in taking different assignments, improving interpersonal skills, and working with suppliers to develop a permanent solution to a quality problem. These types of behavior are very much part of a pattern of having employees work effectively and efficiently together, another of our pay system goals. To encourage such behaviors in the employees you can link them to pay. This is usually done through supervisors' assessments of employee behaviors (i.e., a performance evaluation).[11]

The connection between behaviors and results means that you should consider carefully the types of employee behavior that results-oriented measures are likely to encourage or discourage (see Chapter 9). Suppose that bonus pay is contingent, in part, on a "zero accidents" safety record for the period. This may motivate employees to cover up accidents rather than behave more safely. In this case, you might want to reward employees for identifying and eliminating unsafe conditions.

Finally, where a cell is in the start-up phase and operators need to learn new technical skills and develop interpersonal capabilities, you may want the compensation system to reward employees for the behavior of acquiring these skills and putting them to work. (At minimum, the pay system should not penalize such behavior). Doing so can attract and retain employees as well as facilitate their working effectively and efficiently together.

2. It rewards both individual and cell accomplishments. A compensation system for cell teams should strike a balance between rewarding employees for their individual efforts and achievement, and compensating them for the performance of the cell team. (For single-operator cells, of course, this is not an issue since cell performance and operator performance are one and the same.) You might argue that individual rewards are inconsistent with a team environment and could generate competition and ill-will between team members. In fact, a study of 203 teams in 11 firms found that the more people were rewarded for their individual performance, the worse was the performance of the team.[12] However, even in team environments, individual incentives do play an important role.[13] Hence, rewarding individual performance can be an important part of cell compensation:[14]

> Organizations and work groups are composed of individual employees. As such, they are limited by the nature of these individuals. If, as suggested [...], high performance employees are more likely to seek out and remain with organizations that provide rewards for high performance, a problem may arise for organizations that do not recognize top performers with top rewards. They may simply choose to work elsewhere, leaving the organization with members of low and average ability levels. Teamwork and cooperation, without ability, is not a formula for success either.

Thus, providing rewards for individual contributions can play a role in meeting our pay system goal of attracting and retaining strong performers who can help the organization achieve its goals. Similarly, rewards based on cell performance may motivate employees to work effectively and efficiently together.

The percentage of pay that should be determined by individual performance (generally measured in terms of employee behaviors) versus the percentage tied to cell performance (which may include measures of both group behaviors and results) is an important question. Unfortunately, research in this area does not have a specific answer to this dilemma. One thing is certain, however: you need some of each in order to have an effective cell compensation system.

3. It provides a clear "line of sight" between employee actions and their pay. An effective compensation system allows employees to see a clear connection between their behavior and the payout from the system.[15] When the compensation system bases rewards on well-understood measures of individual performance, employees will perceive that their actions make a difference in their pay. This can help attract and retain high performing individuals, an important goal for a cell compensation system. While basing rewards on group performance may motivate employees to work efficiently and effectively together, it is harder for an individual to see the link between her work and her pay.

In fact, the "line of sight" between individual actions and group rewards becomes more and more blurred as cell size increases. Therefore, the larger the cell, the less incentive for any one person to work hard, since the impact of his or her work is diluted.[16] This may explain why studies have shown that, when group-based rewards are used, smaller teams tend to generate more substantial performance improvements than larger teams.[17] When group rewards are based on the performance of the plant or the company (as with gainsharing and profit sharing, discussed below), the link between individual actions and rewards is even more blurred. These examples attest to the importance of a manageable cell size, but also to the importance of linking pay to performance dimensions that employees, alone or as a team, feel they can influence. Doing so helps ensure that employees perceive the pay system as fair and equitable (see characteristic 6 below).

4. It links cell employee pay to the larger organization's performance. Cells don't operate in a vacuum. They are part of a larger organization (plant, division, corporation) and contribute to meeting its goals. This means that at least some aspect of the compensation system should connect cell worker pay to the larger organization's performance. Doing so helps integrate the cell with the rest of the organization. Thus, this characteristic supports the goal of motivating employees to work effectively and efficiently together, both within the cell and across the organization. Furthermore, it encourages high and sustained performance in support of the organization's objectives, particularly when employees can see a connection between their work, company performance, and pay.

5. It includes a component that must be re-earned each period. A key goal of a pay system is to encourage high and sustained performance over time. One strategy for achieving this goal is putting a portion of employee pay "at risk." This means that employees don't automatically receive this pay component (such as a bonus) as they would a monthly or hourly wage. Rather, the "at risk" component is earned only by way of good performance.

6. *Employees perceive it as fair and equitable.* This is perhaps the most important of the six characteristics, because employees' perceptions of pay equity influence their behavior and their attitude towards work.[18] If employees feel there are inequities in the pay system (e.g., it is biased for or against certain groups or individuals, is unfairly administered, is veiled in secrecy, or that some part of their work goes unrecognized), their dissatisfaction and lack of acceptance are likely to negatively influence performance.[19]

One common complaint with pay systems, for example, is that low performers ("slackers") get the same pay as high performers. In general, employees are more likely to perceive pay systems as fair if (1) they are applied consistently to all employees within a certain group, (2) employees participate or are represented in the process of determining pay (e.g., they provide input to performance appraisals which determine pay), and (3) pay decisions are based on accurate data.[20] Moreover, when employees perceive that the process by which pay is determined is fair (so-called "procedural justice"), they are more likely to accept the payout as fair (so-called "distributive justice").[21] Thus, whether a pay system is perceived as fair may have as much to do with *process* (how the system is designed, communicated, and administered) as it does with *content* (the payout characteristics of the system itself). Obviously, employee perceptions of fairness are critical to all three of the goals we noted earlier—motivating employees to work effectively and efficiently together, attracting and retaining good employees, and encouraging high and sustained performance.

In the following sections, we describe various ways of compensating cell workers and look at how well these systems fare against our six design characteristics and our three pay system goals. We begin by providing some background information on the basic structure of pay systems.

UNDERSTANDING PAY AND PAY SYSTEMS

Pay is the sum of regular pay and bonus pay. *Regular pay* is determined by pay rates that are known at the beginning of a pay period. The rates are generally a function of the nature of the job and the personal characteristics of the individual performing it. Regular pay is the product of the pay rate and a variable, such as the time worked (number of days or hours) or the number of units produced. *Bonus pay*, the other component of a pay system, is determined by performance and is only known at the end of a pay period. Bonus pay is independent of regular pay and is reevaluated every bonus period. In short, a person's pay is determined by the characteristics of the job, by his/her personal characteristics, by the time spent at work, and by the output produced. The first two determine pay rates, while the last two determine regular and bonus-based payouts.

Striking the right balance between regular pay (also called *base* or *fixed* pay) and bonus (or *variable*) pay is a critical issue in compensation system design. Under some plans, employees can earn as much as 25 percent of their base pay in the form of bonuses, although lower percentages are more common. However, in order to be effective at motivating behavior, bonus pay needs to represent at least 5 to 10 percent of base pay.[22] Many organizations that introduce bonus pay do not reduce base pay as a way to fund the bonuses. Rather, strong company performance creates the funds used to award bonus pay.

Pay Rates

Many organizations use job characteristics, such as required skills, level and scope of responsibilities, and work conditions, to categorize jobs into hierarchical job grades. Each job grade is associated with a pay range. For example, at one plant with cells, pay grade 2 includes the jobs of assembler and finished goods tester/packer. Each of these jobs has a further classification—trainee, regular, or senior. Thus, there are six separate job classes within pay grade 2. The pay range for grade 2 is $8.00 to $11.50 per hour. Thus, a new assembler trainee will have a starting wage of $8.00 per hour, but over time may become a regular or senior assembler earning as much as $11.50 per hour. Thus, within each job grade there may be any number of different jobs, and for each job there will be various job classes. Each job grade is associated with a pay range, with separate pay levels associated with each job classification. In short, when an individual moves between job classes and/or job grades, he or she also moves into a new pay rate.

Since the job classification system defines job responsibilities, an employee cannot take on tasks outside the job class. Thus, a system with many job classes tends to be restrictive and inflexible and, thus, unsuitable for work based on multi-functional employees. A conversion to cells therefore is often paired with a move away from a system with many narrow job classifications and toward one with fewer, more broadly defined jobs.[23] When Delphi Saginaw Steering Systems implemented cells, they collapsed 160 job classes into 12.[24] Likewise, Tellabs, a telecommunications equipment assembler, went from 60 job titles to 2 when they converted to cells.

Fewer job classes may or may not mean higher pay for cell operators. A study of 75 machine cells in 14 Wisconsin metalworking firms showed that cell operators tended to be in higher labor classifications than non-cell workers.[25] However, they earned the same or only slightly higher pay rates than did the non-cell workers. In general, the job classification assigned to employees in a machine cell is often based on the highest rated machine in the cell.

In addition to being linked to job characteristics, pay rates may also be determined by *personal characteristics*. Examples include seniority on the job, number of skills acquired, formal education, interpersonal skills, and quality of work. As will be discussed below, different pay systems use different combinations of job and personal characteristics to determine the pay rate (see Table 14-2).

Alternative Pay Systems for Cells

There are a number of different pay systems from which to choose. Table 14-3 identifies these regular and bonus pay systems, and shows for each how pay rates and pay are determined. Below, we'll describe each of these alternatives and comment on their strengths and limitations with respect to our design characteristics and pay sys-

Table 14-2. Characteristics determining pay rates

Factors Determining Pay Rates	Examples of Characteristics
Job characteristics	Skills required Strain Responsibilities Work conditions
Personal characteristics	Seniority on the job Number of skills or skill blocks acquired Formal education Interpersonal skills Communication skills Quality of work Attendance record

tem goals (Table 14-1). To design a compensation system for cells, you'll need to decide what factors should determine pay rates, as well as strike a balance between regular and bonus pay, and between individual and group pay. These are difficult choices. However, the discussion that follows should help you address these important issues and make well-informed decisions.

COMPENSATION SYSTEMS PROVIDING REGULAR PAY

We separate our discussion of the pay systems in Table 14-3 in two parts. "Regular pay" systems are discussed in this section, while "bonus pay" alternatives are discussed in a following section.

The Individual Piece Rate System

A piece rate system rewards individuals for the number of units produced per period. The intention behind this system is to maximize output per employee, and the "pay per piece" is the incentive for the employee to accomplish this goal. Typically, a standard output rate and an associated guaranteed base pay is established. When a worker produces in excess of the standard rate, she earns the per unit amount. For example, assume the standard is 10 units per hour and the guaranteed minimum wage is $9 per hour. Also assume that the incentive rate for each unit in excess of 10 is $.70. Thus, an operator who produces 10 or fewer units in an hour earns $9 per hour. However, an operator who produces 20 units in an hour would earn $16 (9+10 × $.70) per hour. (This is but one example of many different piece rate formulas.[26])

You can use an individual piece rate system for single-operator cells where operators perform direct labor tasks only. In these cells, employees work independently. Having operators work as hard as they can makes sense for this type of cell if subsequent stages in the manufacturing process, or the market, can absorb the output. You can also use a piece rate system in multi-operator craft cells (rabbit-chase cells). Here, individual operators perform all tasks start to finish, just as in a single-operator cell. Having operators maximize output can be sensible for this type of cell as well (although the operators may run into each other as fast employees catch up with slow ones).

Table 14-3. Alternative pay systems for cellular systems

Pay System	What Determines Pay Rate?	What Determines Pay?
REGULAR PAY		
Individual incentive pay (piece rate)	Job characteristics	Output (pieces produced)
Fixed hourly wage	Job and personal characteristics	Time worked (number of hours)
Fixed monthly salary	Job and personal characteristics	Time worked (number of days)
Cell team incentive pay	Job characteristics	Performance (e.g., output)
Skill-based pay (hourly or monthly)	Personal characteristics	Time worked (number of hours or days)
BONUS PAY		
Individual bonuses	N/A	Individual performance (vs. others)
Cell bonuses	N/A	Cell performance (exceeding targets)
Gainsharing	N/A	Departmental/plant performance (exceeding targets)
Profit sharing	N/A	Company performance (profits)

N/A = Not applicable

However, if cell operators are expected to perform indirect tasks, or if—in the case of multi-operator cells—they are required to work together in any way, the piece rate system does not fit. For example, operators in many multi-operator craft cells engage in joint problem solving, keep quality records, help one another out, and so forth. The individual piece rate system discourages employees from spending time on these activities. Also, why stop and help a team member if it slows you down?

In general, individual piece rates are not a good choice for any cell where operators do not complete items from start to finish. In such settings, measuring output per individual is a major problem. In addition, piece rate systems are inappropriate in paced cells working to a set takt or cycle time. Similarly, piece rates can be at odds with cells that embrace just-in-time and lean production philosophies. In order to avoid "waste from overproduction," employees are to meet but not exceed daily schedules. Clearly, piece rate systems, which encourage maximum production, are incongruent with these operating strategies.

In terms of our goals and characteristics for an ideal cell compensation system, the individual piece rate system fails miserably in most cases. This system *focuses only on measurable outputs*, ignoring desirable behavior. And, as we suggested above, it may actually encourage behaviors that are counterproductive, such as refusing to assist a co-worker or attend to indirect labor activities. Piece rates thus provide *little motivation for people to work together and may not attract employees who will fit in cell environments* (of course, a piece rate system may attract individuals who perform well in single-operator cells). In addition, *there are no rewards for cell accomplishments*, just individual performance. Finally, there is *no link between pay and the organization's performance*—pay is earned for operator output, independent of broader business performance.

There are some advantages with the piece rate system, however. For example, if employees are not held back by factors outside their control (such as machine problems or lack of material), they may view piece rates as fair and easy to understand. (On the other hand, establishing and adjusting the standard output level is a common source of labor management conflict and often gives rise to employee allegations of unfairness.) Also, the line of sight between employees' actions and their pay is eminently clear. Further, a piece rate is structured so that a component of the total pay (earnings above the guaranteed minimum) must be re-earned each period. In this way it may contribute to high and sustained performance.

These positives, however, are not enough to offset the disadvantages of the individual piece rate system that make it unsuitable for most cell work. In fact, in one of our surveys of cell users we found that only about 7 percent of the firms with cells paid cell employees via a piece rate.[27]

Fixed Hourly Wage and Fixed Monthly Salary

A fixed hourly wage or a fixed monthly (or biweekly) salary is among the most common ways of compensating employees. For example, in the study just mentioned, about 50 percent of companies with cells paid operators an hourly rate, and another 23 percent paid an hourly rate in combination with incentive pay of some type.[28]

When cell operators perform indirect labor tasks, they are assuming duties traditionally associated with salaried employees. This work requires interpersonal, administrative and management, and problem-solving skills. Thus, the move to cells can blur the distinctions between thinking and doing, i.e., between white-collar and blue-collar jobs.[29] Consequently, some companies elect to pay operators and supervisors under the same salary system. This sends a symbolic but important message that direct labor employees are equal partners with managers and supervisors in the company's success.[30] In practice, however, salaries for cell employees are probably the exception. In the survey noted earlier, for example, we found no cases where cell employees were paid via a salary.[31]

Pay systems based on fixed wages or salaries do have some strengths. First, they are easy to understand and, given an accurate job classification system, will result in similar jobs earning similar pay (unless modified by personal characteristics). Therefore, employees may view this aspect of the system as *fair*. However, the way in which the fixed-wage systems handle *increases* to the base rate also may influence employee perceptions of fairness. This is discussed next for two different (but frequently combined) approaches: merit-based increases and seniority increases.

Changes to individual pay rates

Individuals may change their rates of pay through (1) changing jobs, (2) changing their personal characteristics (attaining additional skills, increasing seniority through time on the job), or (3) by having aspects of their personal characteristics reevaluated (achieving a positive job assessment score by a supervisor). The last approach is called a *merit rating system*. Under this system, individuals receive pay rate increases based on their individual performance or behavior. Typically, a supervisor provides the assessment, although some organizations with cells rely on input from fellow team members, the individuals themselves, and customers. Merit-based pay rate increases most frequently occur on an annual cycle. The increases are rolled into an employee's base pay rate (an hourly rate or a monthly salary).

Seniority and skill base are other personal characteristics that can influence pay rates. Seniority increases, found mostly in union settings, tie pay raises to the length of time on the job. Specifically, under such systems, employees move through a finite set of pay grades, each associated with a specific wage rate. Movement from one grade to the next happens at fixed intervals, the lengths of which are typically specified in the labor contract. Although an employee's skills can be considered in a merit system, there is also a special type of fixed-wage compensation system—skill-based pay—which determines pay rates exclusively based on the number and types of skills acquired. (We discuss that system in an upcoming section.)

Assessing merit-based increases in fixed-wage/salary systems

One problem with merit-based increases in multi-operator cells is the tendency for all workers in the cell to receive roughly the same annual performance increase. This happens because evaluators tend to avoid low ratings and therefore rate all employees about the same.[32] However, this outcome may be seen as *unfair*.[33]

In addition, fixed-wage systems with merit increases are designed to *reward individual accomplishments, not cell accomplishments*. Similarly, these systems fail to directly *link individual pay to the performance of the larger organization*. Further, merit increases are rolled into base pay and earned in all future periods, and thus *do not include a component that must be re-earned each period*.

In terms of the *line of sight* between employee actions and rewards, merit increases have the advantage of being directly based on the individual's performance or behavior. In addition, a fixed-wage system coupled with merit-based rate increases can be effective in *providing rewards for results as well as for demonstrating important behaviors*. For example, an employee who offers an improvement suggestion (a behavior) that leads to significant improvements in lead time, quality, or cost (all results measures) may be rewarded for this through a larger merit increase.

Compared to individual piece rate systems (suitable only for single-operator cells without indirect task responsibilities), fixed-wage and salary pay systems with merit increases are better suited to *attracting and retaining individuals who fit in a wider array of cell environments*. As the most common approach for compensating cell workers, fixed-wage systems, typically with merit increases, are used in single- and multiple-operator cells, in cells with low and high degrees of task overlap, and in cells where operators are or are not responsible for indirect labor tasks. Such systems also are far more effective than the individual piece rate system at motivating individuals to *work effectively and efficiently together*. However, because prior increases are earned forever and because *there is no component that must be re-earned* each period, fixed-wage and salary systems with merit increases may be less effective at motivating *high and sustained performance*.

Assessing seniority-based increases in fixed-wage/salary systems

The practice of increasing pay rates in fixed-wage systems as a function of an individual's length of service to the company does not fare well against our ideal system (see Table 14-1). Seniority-based pay increases do not *focus on results or desired behaviors* (other than the behavior of staying with the company). Further, this practice *does not reward cell accomplishments* and *provides no link between pay and the organization's performance.* The line of sight between employee actions and pay is also blurred since seniority increases are earned independent of performance. Finally, *there is no component that must be re-earned each period.*

On the positive side, this approach is objective and therefore may be *perceived as fair*: there is little opportunity for personal bias or favoritism to influence pay rates.

With respect to our pay system goals, seniority-based pay may encourage employees, particularly more seasoned employees, to stay with the company. If more experienced workers translate into better cell performers, this will obviously benefit the company. If, on the other hand, younger employees with less time on the job are the ones with better skills and better performance, you may have *problems attracting and retaining employees who can help the organization achieve its goals.* These newer cell employees will earn less and may view the pay system as unfair given their contributions. If money is important to them, they may be motivated to seek employment elsewhere. Further, seniority-based pay rates may be viewed as an entitlement, which may make them *less effective in motivating high and sustained performance.* Similarly, while seniority-based increases may encourage employees to stay with the company, they won't necessarily motivate them to *work efficiently and effectively with others.*

Cell Team Incentive Systems

Some firms pay cell employees on a "group piece rate" (see Table 14-3). One ladies footwear plant, for example, compensates workers based on the number of good pairs of shoes the cell produces per day. Such cell team incentive systems overcome some of the problems associated with an individual piece rate. In particular, they *reward cell accomplishments* and *include a component that must be re-earned each period.*

A group piece rate, however, suffers from many of the same limitations as an individual piece rate. There is a *results-only focus*: it might be hard to get employees to engage in appropriate behavior, such as reporting ergonomic problems, if the payoff is not immediate in terms of more good output. In addition, a group-oriented piece rate system *does not provide rewards for individual accomplishments.* Star performers who value money may feel held back by slower colleagues and seek employment elsewhere. Related to this, *the line of sight* between effort and pay may be blurred if the cell team is large or if strong efforts by one individual are offset by under-performing team members. In fact, any group-only reward systems might lead to social loafing or free riders, which may cause employees to view the group incentive system as *unfair.* Finally, there is *no direct link between pay and the larger organization's performance*: cell pay depends only on cell output.

With respect to the goals we identified earlier, a group incentive may help attract and retain employees who can *work effectively and efficiently together*, but because of the line of sight and associated fairness issues, you may have difficulty *attracting and retaining* really strong performers. On the other hand, cell incentive pay may help attract and retain people who work well in a team environment. Further, group piece rates, like individual piece rates, *encourage high and sustained performance—* the cell team cannot slack off without decreasing everybody's pay.

Skill-Based Pay

Skill-based structures pay employees for the skills they possess, demonstrate, and/or apply.[34] These so-called "pay for knowledge" or "learn and earn" systems provide inducements for employees to broaden and/or deepen their skills and knowledge. Therefore, they support important aspects of cell operations, such as multi-skilling and job rotation. One recent survey of Fortune 1000 companies found that close to 14 percent currently use some form of skill-based pay with some employees.[35] Most companies that have introduced skill-based pay, however, report that it covers only a small percentage of employees (typically 20 percent or less).[36]

To create a skill-based pay system, you must identify the skills you want individuals to acquire. Typically, these skills are grouped into sequential "blocks," each associated with a particular increase in base pay. The skill block structure can be designed to allow for both breadth and depth.

Skill-based pay at an electronics plant

A computer electronics plant with large cells introduced skill-based pay. The system was intended to reward individuals for using critical skills on an ongoing basis, and to provide incentives that would result in a more highly skilled, flexible, and productive workforce. The design team that created the system included representatives from each cell team, the personnel department, and production management.

The skill blocks (see Figure 14-1) focus on four areas: (1) process and job skills, (2) process improvement skills, (3) business management skills, and (4) teamwork skills. The notations in each box describe what a worker must do in order to attain that particular level. For example, consider process/job skills. All new hires "meet the physical requirements" of the job. A worker can achieve Level 1 status by becoming certified at a set of workstations, and can reach Levels 2 through 6 by becoming certified at additional workstations.

A new hire is assumed to have no skills in the process improvement skills area. Operators are certified at Level 1 once they have made two "Level 1" improvements. The significance of the improvement and the process used to make the improvement determine whether an improvement is at Level 1, 2 or 3. (Precise guidelines determine whether an improvement qualifies as Level 1, 2, or 3. Further, in order to attain a given level, operators must first have met the requirements for all lower levels.) Level 2 and 3 improvements must follow the company's Total Quality Control (TQC) process. That is, the worker must document the problem, identify the root cause, develop a solution, pilot the improvement, and collect data to verify the performance impact. In this way workers demonstrate that they know the improvement process and its tools and can put them to work.

With respect to business management skills, new hires are expected to have basic math and English skills and be able to follow written and verbal instructions. They move to Level 1 once they have acquired a basic understanding of the cell's

	Process/job skills	Process improvement skills	Business management skills	Teamwork skills
Level 6	Certified at maximum number of workstations			
Level 5	Certified at additional workstations			
Level 4	Certified at additional workstations			Is a successful certifier (adds pay to any level)
Level 3	Certified at additional workstations	Makes one Level 3 improvement (using TQC), plus has completed Levels 1 and 2		
Level 2	Certified at additional workstations	Makes one Level 2 improvement (using TQC), plus has completed Level 1		
Level 1	Certified at workstations *and* has basic skills	Makes two Level 1 improvements (TQC optional)	Has basic understanding of the cell's business (e.g., customers, supply chain, processes, and performance measures)	Is a successful team member
New hire	Meets physical requirements	No skills	Basic math and English skills *and* can follow written and verbal directions	Works well in a group

Critical Job Skills

Figure 14-1. Skill-based pay matrix for cells at a computer electronics plant

"business"—they are familiar with customer expectations, understand where the cell fits in the supply chain, are knowledgeable about overall cell operations, and are familiar with basic concepts of inventory, lead time, and quality as they apply to the cell. In terms of teamwork skills, new hires must be able to work well in a group. To reach Level 1, the new hire must be a "successful team member."

Moving from one skill block level to another requires certification. There are, therefore, clear operational definitions for what it means to qualify for each block (that is, what is meant by has a basic understanding of the cell's "business" or is a "successful team member"). Once certified in a skill block, additional pay is added to the employee's salary. Cell workers can earn additional pay also by becoming qualified as a "certifier," an individual able to assess the degree to which a worker has qualified for the next level. An individual's highest level in each of the four skill areas, and whether he/she is a certifier, determine the pay. A formal recertification process ensures that skills have not faded. Both management and employees feel that the skill-based pay system offers many advantages. Employees know exactly what they need to do to get more pay. They view the system as fair and easy to understand. They also like the fact that their contribution to the team is objectively verified, with clearly stated definitions of the skills they need to reach each level. In addition, employees can manage their own growth. For the company, the skill-based pay system means more skilled and flexible employees who can respond rapidly to changing production needs.

Assessing the costs and merits of skill-based pay

Creating a skill-based pay system requires a significant effort, and maintaining it can be time-consuming as well. You must define the skill blocks and decide what to pay for them (not a trivial problem, since there is usually limited labor market data on skill-based systems to be used for setting pay levels). You must also provide a formal training program so employees can acquire new skills, and design work so they can use their skills. Finally, a skill-based pay system requires that you have in place objective ways of assessing the degree to which employees have acquired skills. Some companies use certification exams. An employee who passes the exam receives the associated base pay increase. In addition to certification exams, you need regularly scheduled competency evaluations (recertifications) to assure that employees maintain the skills they have acquired. Overlooking any one of these elements can create a situation where employees are not motivated to acquire skills, or where employees earn higher pay but there is no increase in productivity or quality.[37]

Taken together, all these changes can make a skill-based pay system a costly proposition. In addition, as employees learn new skills over time, your labor costs will increase. On the other hand, skill-based pay has been shown to increase workforce flexibility, decrease labor cost, increase product quality, and increase productivity.[38] A recent study, for example, looked at two sister facilities, one with skill-based pay and one without.[39] Both plants had organized production into cells. The study's purpose was to determine whether skill-based pay affects performance. The authors found that skill-based pay was associated with higher quality (82 percent lower scrap percentages than the sister facility without skill-based pay). The plant with skill-based pay also realized higher productivity (58 percent fewer labor hours per part than before the introduction of skill-based pay), and decreased labor costs (26 percent lower wage expenses per good part than before the introduction of skill-based pay). (Of course, keep in mind that the labor cost picture may change over time as employees acquire more skills and earn higher pay.)

Skill-based pay in cellular systems

How does skill-based pay measure up against the six characteristics and three goals for an ideal cell pay system (Table 14-1)? Skill-based pay promotes multi-skilling, a fundamental building block of most cell operations. As such, this system *rewards the behavior* of acquiring various direct and indirect labor skills critical to the performance of cells. It also *rewards individual effort*. Further, the *line of sight* between the effort expended to master new skills and higher pay is short, direct, and clear. Further, a well-designed and easily understood system *may be perceived by employees as fair* because they have greater control over what they earn.

Skill-based pay also performs well with respect to two of our goals. Notably, skill-based pay can help *attract and retain* individuals who want to learn and grow, and who value higher pay. Further, well-designed skill blocks can help *facilitate high and sustained performance*, although they do not directly reward it. Employees always have the opportunity to earn more money by acquiring new skills. This may be particularly important in flat organizational structures where other avenues for pay increases (e.g., promotions) are limited. Of course, employees who "top out," i.e., learn all the skills in all the skill blocks, will have no more skills to master. You can deal with this by designing skill blocks, especially at higher levels, to include a large number of skills that would take a long time to fully master.[40]

Another potential problem, however, is "over-skilling." Unchecked, the skill-based pay system may provide a monetary incentive for every cell worker to learn skills they never or rarely use. You can short-circuit over-skilling by establishing a skill quota that puts limits on the number of people who can learn a particular task. You can also prevent employees from acquiring skills that are not needed inside a cell. Employees, however, may view this as unfair or inequitable.

XEL Communications dealt with over-skilling by creating a skill block of "on-demand skills."[41] When the cell work requires these infrequently used skills, operators with the skill can earn extra pay—they don't earn the extra pay all the time, only when cell work calls for the skill. For example, an operator who has been certified as a trainer (an on-demand skill) earns extra pay when he or she is called upon to train others. Gainsharing and cell bonus pay plans (discussed below) that link compensation to overall costs, including labor costs, may also help offset the individual incentive to add skills (and thereby increase company labor costs) without adding value to the cell.[42]

Closely related to the issue of multi-skilling is the problem of "skill fade," where workers forget, or become less adept at, infrequently used skills. Where job design, production needs, or operator preferences do not take full advantage of worker flexibility, skill fade and paying for unused skills are likely to occur (of course, if a skill is not used, it should be removed from the skill block hierarchy). Skill fading can be addressed by recertifying employees at regular intervals.

Skill-based pay can play a role in an effective compensation system for cells, but we do not think it is a complete solution. In particular, it lacks several important characteristics. Most notably, skill-based pay *emphasizes behavior but not results, does not reward cell accomplishments, and does not directly link pay to the organization's performance*. In addition, there is *no component that must be re-earned each period*. Skill-based pay can also create an "entitlement" mentality in which employees think that every extra task should earn additional compensation.[43] (Of course, this is a general reaction by employees when faced with more to do, and is not necessarily tied to skill-based pay.)

Also consider that skill-based pay does *not provide explicit incentives for employees to work efficiently and effectively together*—it is very individually focused. Thus, if you are contemplating skill-based pay, consider combining it with other compensation systems that can fill in for the weaknesses discussed above. Finally, as we noted earlier, skill-based pay structures can be costly and time consuming to create, administer, and maintain. It is a complicated undertaking, and even "successful" skill-based pay plans (e.g., those that result in employee flexibility and the acquisition of critical skills) can run into problems (such as high costs and over-skilling) that are sometimes so serious that the plans fail.[44]

COMPENSATION SYSTEMS PROVIDING BONUS PAY

In addition to regular pay, the pay system may also include a bonus pay component (Table 14-3). This is a lump sum payment given in recognition of achieving one or more goals.[45] Bonus pay does not affect or increase regular pay and must be re-earned each bonus period. Most large U.S. organizations use some form of bonus pay as part of their compensation system for exempt employees. Among Fortune 1000 companies responding to a recent survey, more than 75 percent used bonus pay for exempt employees, and close to 45 percent did so for nonexempt employees.[46] Further, in a study of 87 manufacturing organizations, plants that had implemented integrated manufacturing (including cells), and upgraded jobs to be more interdependent, were found to be more likely to use group incentives than were traditional factories.[47]

In this section we examine one individual and three group-oriented bonus compensation plans: cell (or team) bonus pay, gainsharing, and profit sharing. The latter three plans differ in terms of the performance dimensions that are tied to pay and in the scope of the group whose performance is evaluated (e.g., cell team, production area, and plant as a whole).

Individual Bonus Pay

An individual bonus system can *reward both behavior and results*, and because the payment comes in the form of a bonus linked to the individual's performance, there *is a clear line of sight between an individual's performance and pay*. There may be less incentive to "rest on one's laurels" and more incentive to continue to pursue high levels of performance since the *bonus component of pay must be re-earned each period*.

Individual bonuses, however, suffer from some potential pitfalls. They focus on rewarding individual contributions, and hence *do not provide rewards for cell accomplishments, nor do they directly link individual pay to the larger organization's performance*. (Individual bonuses sometimes are indirectly linked to work group and organization performance in that if work group or company performance is good, there is a larger pool of bonus money to allocate among employees.) Finally, and possibly most significantly, *if the system is perceived as biased or subjective,* many of the strengths we mentioned vanish. We have seen individual bonuses used as a part of pay systems for single-operator cells, but rarely in team settings.

With respect to our higher-level pay system goals, individual bonuses can motivate employees *to work effectively and efficiently together* and, in some instances, can *attract and retain employees who can help the organization achieve its goals*. In particular, merit bonuses may help attract and retain "star" performers. Finally, a desire to re-earn a bonus each year may help *encourage high and sustained performance*.

Cell Bonus Pay

Under a cell bonus pay system, the cell team as a whole receives a bonus for achieving stated performance goals. Depending on the circumstances in your organization, you may want to define the cell team broadly to include certain support resources that are integral players in the cell's ability to meet performance goals (maintenance, quality, material handling, etc.). The goals are established in advance and may include both operational and financial targets (e.g., quality, cost, inventory, but generally not profits).

Naturally, objective and well-understood performance measures are the basis for an effective cell bonus pay system. When companies link compensation to perfor-mance, metrics take on an added level of importance. Cell operators (and team lead-ers and supervisors) are likely to focus on those measured aspects of performance that are linked to pay, while other dimensions will receive less attention (see Chapter 9 on performance measurement). This means you should carefully design the set of measures that is tied to the bonus system. Consider not only the desirable results, but also the specific actions employees might take (or not take) to attain certain results. Tying cell bonus pay to zero accidents, for example, may lead to no *reported* acci-dents (e.g., an employee who has fallen continues to work rather than go to the nurse), but not necessarily to safer behavior.

Examples of cell bonus pay systems

In Chapter 9, we described the cell bonus pay system for Turner Products, a maker of electrical equipment with over 40 cells in place. Cell operators, in cooperation with a management steering committee, establish six-month goals for a mix of measures. The basic performance categories linked to pay are common across all cells. These include safety and housekeeping, quality, cost, delivery, and progress toward specific project goals (preparing documentation for an ISO 9001 audit, completing ergonom-ics training, etc.). Within this framework, some measures are standard across all cells. Other measures and targets, such as improvement targets, are unique to each cell.

Every six months, cell performance is "graded" by the management steering committee. A team that reaches all its goals for the past period receives a cell bonus. All cell members share equally in the bonus. Teams that "exceed" or "far exceed" their goals receive an even larger bonus, which, again, is equally distrib-uted among team members. Both managers and operators believe that this perfor-mance-oriented pay system contributes to high levels of employee motivation and satisfaction, and to the company's outstanding business success. In addition to cell bonuses, the company pays workers an hourly wage and has a skill-based pay system in place.

Consider also the compensation system at ABB Relays in Västerås, Sweden.[48] This plant makes relay protections and digital substation controls. In connection with a conversion to cells, ABB Relays also began work on a new wage system. At that time, the company had a piece rate system where between 10 and 100 percent of an employee's wage depended on individual or group performance. The system was costly to administer, with lots of time devoted to setting and refining the rates for specific jobs. It also encouraged specialization, which at this plant was linked to repetitive-motion injuries. Absenteeism and employee turnover were high.

A team composed of staff, supervisors, and production workers designed the new system. It has three major components: a job characteristics-based element (about 55 to 60 percent of total pay), a merit component tied to the individual's base pay (about 20 to 30 percent of total pay), and a cell bonus (about 15 to 20 percent of total pay).

The bonus is based on a cell's biweekly performance with respect to quality, service level, lead time, and efficiency. Performance on each dimension is converted into a "performance level" ranging from 1 to 10, as indicated in Figure 14-2. In this bonus matrix, the average performance level on each measure before the work teams were implemented was set to 3. For example, assume that prior to launching the cell teams, product throughput time averaged five days. In the bonus matrix, five days would then be the lead time value associated with performance level 3. The "ultimate objective" for each performance dimension is assigned the value 10. Other levels are assigned relative to these two anchors.

Level	Quality	Service Level	Lead Time	Efficiency
10				
9				
8	x			
7				
6				
5		x		
4				x
3	*	*	*x	*
2				
1				
Achieved Level	8	5	3	4
Weight	.16	.16	.16	.5
Score	1.28	0.80	0.48	2.00

- Average initial performance in each category was set at level 3 (denoted by the *'s in the figure).
- Assume that in one two-week period, the cell's performance was classified as reaching levels 8, 5, 3, and 4, respectively, on the four dimensions (denoted by the x's in the figure).
- Total bonus = (sum of weighted scores) × constant. In this case: (1.28+0.80+0.48+2.00) × constant = 4.56 × constant

Note: The weight for the efficiency component was deliberately set high (0.5) to make for a smooth transition from an exclusively efficiency-oriented piece rate system to the current multi-objective pay system. Over time, the weights for the four performance dimensions will be equalized.

Figure 14-2. ABB Relays bonus matrix

The level of recorded performance for each measurement area is weighted, and the total weighted sum is multiplied by a constant to translate the result into a team bonus stated in monetary terms (see Figure 14-2). The company distributes the bonus equally among the cell team members every two weeks.

A final example comes from an electronics plant. In this system, cell performance is tracked monthly. Depending on their performance, team members can earn up to several hundred dollars in bonus pay every month for meeting "high stretch" objectives in the areas of cost, quality, and delivery. They earn smaller bonuses for only meeting "moderate stretch" or "business basics" goals in each of these areas. In order to earn any bonus pay, a team must meet the lowest level "business basics" goals for all three performance measures. Figure 14-3 illustrates this cell bonus system.

Performance Levels	Cost	Quality	Delivery
Level 3 High stretch objectives	$70	$70	$70
Level 2 Moderate stretch objectives	$30	$30	$30
Level 1 Team meets business basics	$170 Must meet all three goals (cost, quality, and delivery) to earn business basics pay		
Team does not meet business basics	No team bonus		

- Teams must meet all three goals (cost, quality, and delivery) to earn Level 1 team pay.
- Example: Members of a team that meets Level 2 delivery goals and Level 3 cost and quality goals would each earn $340 extra for the month:
  - $170 for meeting business basics goal,
  - $30 for meeting the Level 2 delivery goal,
  - $70 for meeting the Level 3 cost goal, and
  - $70 for meeting the Level 3 quality goal.

Figure 14-3. Cell bonus pay matrix at one company

Key elements of cell bonus pay

The three company examples illustrate several essential features of effective cell bonus pay systems. First, measures and targets must be clearly understood by those who will strive to achieve them. Having employees participate in establishing the performance criteria and targets helps ensure that these are well understood. In addition, achieving the targets must be under the team's control.

Second, the system should guard against unbalanced performance, such as exceptional performance on quality at the expense of lead time. Some companies therefore award a bonus only if all measures reach a minimum level. At Turner Products, a score of 2 ('met goals') must be achieved in all categories before a cell is eligible for the bonus pay (also see Figure 14-3).

Third, transitioning to a cell bonus system may involve putting part of the existing pay at risk. Some organizations reduce base pay, and employees can then earn it back, and more, through the performance bonus and merit raises. Many others simply treat bonuses as an add-on to their existing base pay system. At Turner Products, strong financial performance and the potential for significant market growth prompted management to augment existing compensation (which included hourly wages as base pay, annual individual merit and general cost-of-living adjustments, and a skill-based pay program) with the cell bonus pay system. At ABB Relays, where piece rates had been the dominant pay model before cells, the new compensation system may have actually reduced the amount of pay that was at risk for some employees.

Finally, the potential bonus must be large enough to get the employees' attention. Remember that, in general, bonus pay needs to represent at least 5 to 10 percent of base pay in order to effectively motivate behavior.

Strengths and weaknesses of cell bonuses

When there are well-understood targets, and a connection between the team's efforts and target achievement, a cell bonus system can *motivate cell operators to work efficiently and effectively togethe*r and to be involved in all aspects of cell performance. Both of these factors can contribute to *attracting and keeping employees*, particularly people who will work well in a team environment. In addition, since a bonus must be re-earned each performance period, it *helps encourage high and sustained performance.*

Evaluating cell bonus pay on a more detailed level, using our six ideal characteristics, suggests that the "devil is in the details"—while cell bonuses can support the pay system goals, this depends on how the system is designed and administered. First, on the positive side, the system *does include a component that is re-earned each period*. Second, because the bonus is contingent on what the cell achieves, there is a clearer *line of sight* between group actions and rewards than exists with more macro-oriented bonus systems such as profit sharing (to be described below). However, the line of sight between the individual cell members' actions and rewards is not as clear as with individual bonus or incentive pay, particularly if the cell is large. At Turner Products, for example, problems arose when individuals who made major contributions to breakthrough improvements in a cell earned the same bonus as more "free-riding" team members. The *focus on rewarding cell, but not individual, accomplishments* is a limitation of cell bonus pay.

Likewise, the *primary emphasis on results* may lead to unintended behaviors. For example, at Turner Products, teams must meet a cost reduction target in order to earn team bonus pay. Once the team has met the six-month goal, there is no incentive to continue to pursue improvement ideas in that bonus period. Savvy teams "bank" their ideas so that they can apply them to meeting the next period's cost reduction target.

Cell bonus pay also can create situations where cells operate in their own interest rather than in the best interest of the organization as a whole. Consider the manager who discovered a toolbox full of defective parts that had "disappeared" rather than show up on the cell's scrap parts report, which drove bonus pay.

Because overall business performance depends on factors well beyond the cell, management may be paying a cell bonus at a time when business is poor. This highlights *the absence of a link between pay and the organization's overall performance.*

One company deals with this by considering plant performance when determining team bonuses. In order for cell team members to receive their bonus, overall plant performance must reach certain levels in terms of market share and profitability.

Finally, if employees understand the targets and feel they are reasonable, they may perceive the cell bonus system as *fair*. Claims of unfairness are likely when cells feel they are "held back" by support areas (e.g., maintenance or engineering) that do not respond as rapidly as the cell would like to requests for assistance. While the obvious solution is to include maintenance or engineering personnel on the cell team, this may be impractical if a small staff supports a number of cells and other production units. You'll need to find some other way to give support personnel a vested interest in the cells' success.

More generally, dissatisfaction may arise when a team fails to earn a bonus due to factors that it considers to be beyond its control (e.g., incoming part delivery problems or old equipment). Similarly, establishing targets is a minefield of potential conflict between cell employees, who naturally want easily achievable targets, and company management, who may prefer more aggressive objectives. There is also the issue of maintaining equity in targets across the cells. If members of one cell believe that another cell's targets are easier to achieve, they will probably perceive the cell bonus pay system as unfair.

Gainsharing

Some large U.S. companies have gainsharing programs in place.[49] Gainsharing, like cell bonus pay, seeks to link pay to performance outcomes that employees can influence.[50] However, in the case of gainsharing, the performance of a larger group (e.g., a department, a plant, or even a division) determines the bonus. Gainsharing often applies to everyone in a facility.

Although you can think of cell performance pay as gainsharing applied to the cell, gainsharing at the plant or division level has somewhat different advantages and disadvantages (see our discussion below). Also, the metrics used for plant-wide gainsharing often are quite different from those used to determine cell bonuses. The Scanlon Plan, for example, is a well-known gainsharing program that pays bonuses "if the ratio of labor costs to sales value of production is kept below a certain standard."[51] It would not be possible to calculate the "labor cost to sales value of production" for an individual cell if its output is not sold, but only used as components in other products. Finally, the link between gainsharing pay and the larger organization's performance is tighter. As we noted earlier, this is not always the case with cell bonus pay—this may be paid even when overall plant performance is poor.

There are several essential features of gainsharing programs.[52] First is *group composition*, i.e., the set of employees who will participate in the gainsharing program. Will there be one program for the entire plant or will there be separate programs for each production section or groups of cells? Second, what *baseline performance* will be used as the standard for evaluating future performance, and will this standard change over time as performance improves? Employees must feel that with reasonable effort and within a reasonable time frame, they can produce the gains that will lead to gainsharing pay.[53] The *gainsharing formula*, which determines the payout amount, is a third feature.[54] Both operational and financial performance measures can be the focus of gainsharing payout formulas. The *frequency of payouts* is a fourth feature. From a motivational perspective, more frequent payouts are better, although the amount in each payout needs to be big enough to matter. Some organizations pay a portion of the gainsharing bonus each month or quarter, distributing the remainder as a bonus at the end of the year.

Assessing the merits of gainsharing

Studies have found that gainsharing has positive effects on productivity, grievances (a decrease), and product quality.[55] More generally, "companies who base part of pay on some measure of corporate or division performance report increases in performance of about 4 to 6 percent per year."[56] However, it is important to keep in mind that the way in which such programs are designed, implemented, and administered may in large part determine their effectiveness. In addition, as is the case with all compensation systems, it is possible that other changes companies make when they introduce gainsharing contribute to the positive results attributed to these programs. For example, better labor management relations, increased worker participation, the identification of clear goals, increased feedback to workers, extended training, and so forth, may accompany the introduction of gainsharing and help improve overall performance.

Strengths and weaknesses of gainsharing for cell systems

Gainsharing *links pay to the performance of the larger organization*. In this way, it provides explicit motivation for between-cell and interdepartmental cooperation. This encourages cell teams to work together rather than simply optimizing their individual cells' performances. In addition, linking bonus pay to the larger organization's performance avoids the problem of awarding a bonus to a cell even if overall plant performance is poor. Second, gainsharing plans are typically inclusive—no employees are left out, although multiple plans may be used. Employees therefore may perceive them as *fair*. In addition, subjective assessments do not enter into the calculation of gainsharing pay, a fact that also may contribute to employee perceptions of the plans as fair and impartial.

Countering these two advantages of gainsharing vis-à-vis cell bonus pay is the problem that as group size gets larger, the *line of sight* between individual effort and rewards becomes more blurred. Workers naturally may feel that more aggregate measures are much harder to influence. Thus, group size and metrics only indirectly related to cells are distinct disadvantages of gainsharing programs when compared to cell bonus pay. More explicitly, gainsharing *provides no rewards for cell (or individual) performance*.

With respect to our broader pay system goals, gainsharing *may motivate sustained, strong performance*, or at least not detract from it. Similarly, gainsharing certainly will not detract from your ability to *attract and retain individuals* who can help the firm accomplish its goals (for example, if stronger performers earn higher pay rates, they may perceive that the overall pay system is fair, despite that fact that individual contributions are not reflected in the gainsharing payouts). Finally, gainsharing *may help motivate employees to work effectively and efficiently together* since collective efforts are rewarded.

Profit Sharing

Like gainsharing, profit sharing is a results-oriented payment system. However, unlike gainsharing, where cost and operational performance may influence bonuses, a profit sharing system returns a portion of the profits to employees in the form of annual or semi-annual bonuses. Profit sharing is limited to profit centers (in contrast to gainsharing, which may apply to smaller units). The intent is to make employees feel more like owners, or, at minimum, to make them care about the overall financial health of the organization.[57]

An example of a profit-sharing system

One electronics corporation began implementing cells in many divisions in the 1980s. The company's profit-sharing plan predates the cells by several decades. All employees, whether working in cells or not, participate in the profit-sharing plan, and bonuses are distributed semi-annually. The amount an individual employee receives is in proportion to his or her base wage over the last six months. Interestingly, in several of the divisions within this firm where plants have made *complete* conversions to cells and teams, cell bonus pay has been introduced in recent years to complement the profit-sharing system and provide a more direct connection between cell performance and rewards.

Strengths and weaknesses with profit sharing as a cell compensation system

Profit sharing is a highly indirect way of connecting pay to the efforts of individual employees. This may explain why there appears to be only a weak link between this pay system and improved organizational productivity.[58] Many factors beyond the individual's control influence his or her profit-sharing pay. Thus, the *line of sight* between an individual's actions and rewards is blurred. This is particularly the case when profit sharing is corporate-wide, involving the performance of several organizational units. In addition, there is an *exclusive focus on results (not behavior) and large group—not individual or cell—accomplishments*. As with cell bonus and gainsharing pay, high achievers may perceive that they are undervalued and free riders may be a problem.

On the positive side, profit sharing establishes a *direct connection between pay and the larger organization's performance*. In addition, the profit-sharing bonus *must be re-earned* annually or semi-annually. Finally, because profit-sharing plans are inclusive— no employees are left out of the pay plan—*employees may perceive them as fair*.

With respect to our broader pay system goals, profit sharing *may motivate sustained, strong performance*, or at least not detract from it. Similarly, profit sharing certainly will not detract from your ability to *attract and retain individuals* who can help the firm accomplish its goals. Finally, profit sharing *may help motivate employees to work effectively and efficiently together* since collective efforts are rewarded.

CELL COMPENSATION IN PRACTICE: COMBINING PAY SYSTEMS

We have now discussed eight different compensation systems, and how each one fares against the three goals and six characteristics we listed in Table 14-1. Our discussion is summarized in Figure 14-4. As this figure illustrates, no single pay method meets all our criteria for an ideal compensation system for cells. Because of that, you may find that a combination of approaches works best. Here are some examples of combined pay systems.

Earlier in the chapter we described the skill-based pay program in place at XEL Communications, Inc. In addition to this pay plan, the company compensates employees via quarterly profit-sharing bonuses and annual merit increases based on the performance of the individual and his or her team. To determine merit increases, management ranks all teams based on their performance against quarterly objectives. These objectives are proposed in advance by the teams and approved by management. A team's ranking determines the portion of the annual merit increase budget the team will receive. Within the team, supervisor and peer rankings determine how the merit increase money will be distributed. Typically, top performers will receive more money and most of the team will split the remainder equally. A key motivation behind the new system was to get away from "just because" annual pay increases, where almost all employees received about the same percentage increase.[59]

One Swedish company's cell compensation system evolved over a two and a half-year period. Early in the cell implementation, the organization moved from a piece rate system to straight hourly wages. When productivity fell, management attributed the decline to the elimination of the piece rate system and its motivational power. In an effort to facilitate both individual effort and within-cell cooperation, management introduced a two-pronged compensation system. This system combines skill-based pay with cell bonus pay (see Figure 14-5).[60]

The skill-based pay system includes a competence ladder of technical skills (skill blocks) and a team skills component. The latter assesses how much responsibility individuals have assumed for activities outside building products (e.g., setup, maintenance), for team leadership, and for working outside the team (called "external flexibility"). A portion of the cell bonus is paid for each productivity, delivery, and quality sub-goal being met. However, as seen from Figure 14-5, meeting the latter two goals does not cause a bonus payout unless a minimum level of productivity has been reached. The new compensation system is believed to have contributed to a dramatic rise in worker commitment to meeting quality and delivery goals: operators no longer tolerate bad or missing parts, and take action to identify and resolve problems. Workers also have acquired more skills and become more flexible.

Tellabs, the assembler of telecommunications equipment that we mentioned earlier, combines merit ratings and skill-based pay in their cell compensation system. Operators can move through five skill blocks covering a wide array of light assembly tasks, cell support activities (e.g., quality assurance), and interpersonal/teaming skills (interpersonal communications, problem solving, etc.). By becoming certified in various skills, operators increase their total number of "skill points" (see Figure 14-6).

Merit ratings form the other dimension of cell compensation at Tellabs. Employees complete a self-appraisal in which they evaluate their own performance on five dimensions: (a) flexibility, (b) contribution, enthusiasm, and pride, (c) productivity, (d) process conformance, and (e) attendance. The supervisor then rates each employee (from 0 to 4) on the same attributes and provides specific examples to support the numerical ratings. For the "contribution, enthusiasm and pride" category, for example, a rating of 0 indicates that the employee "does not contribute toward

Characteristics of an Ideal Cell Compensation System	Regular Pay					Bonus Pay			
	Indiv. incentive (piece rate)	Hourly/monthly pay with merit-based rate increases	Hourly/monthly pay with seniority-based rate increases	Cell incentive	Skill-based pay	Indiv. bonus	Cell bonus	Gain-sharing	Profit sharing
1. Focuses on results, as well as on employee behaviors.*	✓	✓	–	–	–	✓	✓	✓	✓
2. Provides rewards for individual accomplishments as well as for cell accomplishments.*	✓	✓	✓	✓	✓	✓			
3. Provides a clear line of sight between employees' actions and their pay.	✓	✓		★	✓	✓	★		
4. Links cell employee pay to the larger organization's performance.	✓					‡	‡	✓	✓
5. Includes a component that must be re-earned each period.	✓			✓		✓	✓	✓	✓
6. Employees perceive it as fair and equitable.**	??	??	??	??	??	??	??	??	??
Number of characteristics satisfied	2	2	0	1	1	3	1	2	2
Pay System Goals									
1. Motivates employees to work effectively and efficiently together.		✓		✓	✓	✓	✓	✓	✓
2. Helps attract and retain employees who can help the organization achieve its goals.		✓		✓	✓	✓	✓	✓	✓
3. Encourages high and sustained performance.	✓			✓	✓	✓	✓	✓	✓
Number of goals supported (or for which the pay system will not be a barrier)	1	2	0	3	2	3	3	3	3

* Must meet both elements of the criterion to count.

** The way in which a pay system is implemented and administered plays a major role in employee perceptions of fairness. Therefore, each of these systems may be perceived as fair or unfair.

★ Depends on the size of the team (larger teams can blur the line of sight).

‡ This bonus payout can be made contingent on satisfactory company performance.

Figure 14–4. Combining pay systems for cells: no one system can do it all!

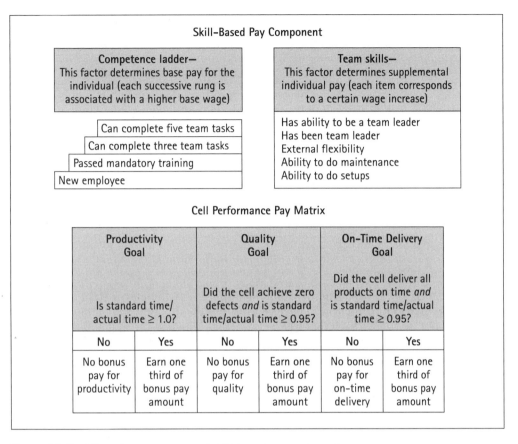

Figure 14–5. Cell performance pay and skill-based pay system at one company

work environment improvement and/or does not exhibit enthusiasm and pride and/or does not share knowledge to assist others." A 4 in this same category indicates that the individual "always contributes toward constant improvement of the work environment, is always enthusiastic, uses Total Quality Control (TQC) methods to improve the process, and always shares knowledge." The supervisor shares the rating with the employee for discussion and approval.

The total average score across the five dimensions makes up the basis for the merit rating. The skill acquisition points and the merit rating are then combined in a formula to determine the individual's salary (the grid in Figure 14-6 illustrates the principle).

Earlier we described the cell bonus pay system in place at ABB Relays.[61] The complete compensation system at this company also includes a job characteristics-based hourly rate and an individual merit increase component. The hourly rate is based on a semi-annual job evaluation that considers the skills, responsibility, strain (physical and psychological), and other work conditions associated with the job. This assessment determines which of several job classifications best matches the job. Each job classification is associated with an hourly rate. The job classification determines about 55 to 60 percent of a worker's pay. In addition, each individual receives a merit component that amounts to another 20 to 30 percent of the

	Skill block 1: 0-10 points	Skill block 2: 11-20 points	Skill block 3: 21-30 points	Skill block 4: 31-40 points	Skill block 5: 41-50 points
Base: 0-2.5	Min. pay level				
Merit 1: 2.51-3.50					
Merit 2: 3.51 - 4.00					Max. pay level

Figure 14-6. Tellabs merit/skill salary grid

pay. Twice a year supervisors rate employees according to their education, experience, flexibility, problem solving, quality of work, and efficiency. This rating determines the operator's merit pay. Finally, the team bonus accounts for 15 to 20 percent of pay.

Combining various compensation methods allows organizations to better encourage and reward cell work. The system at Tellabs, for example, includes dimensions designed to reward *individuals* for developing new skills and increasing their flexibility (the merit system and skill-based pay). There is a *focus on behavior* (skill acquisition, attendance, and flexibility), but also on *results* (productivity). The *line of sight* between individual performance and rewards is short and clear. While there is *no component that must be re-earned each period*, the skill blocks provide a progression aimed at encouraging *high and sustained performance* and the emphasis on multi-skilling, and contributions to the team, *serve to attract and retain employees who will fit in the cell environment and can help the organization achieve its goals.*

The Tellabs system, however, is *short on links to the larger organization's performance* and *rewards for cell accomplishments*. While the system also includes elements that *promote working together* (the "contribution, enthusiasm and pride" dimension of the merit system), the addition of cell bonus pay, gainsharing, or profit sharing might help achieve this pay system goal.

AN IDEAL CELL COMPENSATION SYSTEM

Several pay system combinations possess all the characteristics of an ideal cell compensation system and support the general pay system goals. One alternative we like is to combine an hourly wage (with merit-based increases) with a cell bonus system in which a portion of the bonus is contingent on overall plant performance. As a unit, this combination of pay systems "covers all the bases." Specifically, it focuses on cell results as well as on desired employee behaviors, provides rewards for individual and cell accomplishments, provides a clear line of sight between employees' actions and their pay, links cell employee pay to the larger organization's performance, includes a component that must be re-earned each period, and, when well designed and administered, can be perceived by employees as fair and equitable. This combination also supports the more general pay systems goals of encouraging people to work effectively and efficiently together, attracting and retaining employees, and motivating high and sustained performance. An obvious advantage of such a combination is that you likely already have an hourly wage system with merit increases in place. If so, you simply can supplement your existing system with a cell bonus system.

Creating an effective cell bonus system is no easy task. However, our work with firms suggests that these systems, while not a complete solution, can be a key component of a highly effective cell pay system, particularly when they are paired with other mutually supportive human resource practices (e.g., selection and training). Some of the highest performing cells we have encountered were in plants where there was a well-designed and effectively administered cell bonus system in place.

ISSUES IN ADOPTING AND IMPLEMENTING COMPENSATION SYSTEMS FOR CELL EMPLOYEES

So far we have talked mostly about the "what" of cell compensation systems—the different ways you can structure cell pay, and the strengths and limitations of each approach. What we haven't directly addressed, and what is equally important, are the issues of adoption and implementation. For example, how should you examine your current system for its fit with cells? Why might you elect to leave your current system unchanged, even if it isn't an "ideal" system? And, if you do decide to make a change, what are the elements of a successful transition? These are the questions we turn to now.

Examining Your Compensation System

As part of a cell design/implementation process, you need to determine what changes, if any, would make your current pay system more supportive of cell work. One useful exercise, as illustrated throughout this chapter, is to assess your current pay system with respect to the goals and ideal characteristics we laid out in Table 14-1. If you determine that your pay system falls short in some important way, then you may want to consider changing it and/or adding a new pay system that addresses these deficiencies.

You need to assure that the compensation system is congruent with, or at least does not hamper, work in cells (see our discussion in Chapter 1, and Figure 1-4). From that perspective, only the individual piece rate system is truly unsuited to team-based cells (but could conceivably be used in single- or multi-operator craft cells). All other pay plans are potentially acceptable, and the issue comes down to finding the right balance between regular pay and bonus pay, and between rewards for individuals versus the group.

Why Organizations with Cells May Leave Compensation Plans Unchanged

Administrative systems, such as compensation, are notoriously difficult to change and are characterized by significant organizational inertia.[62] The attractive features of innovative pay structures such as skill-based pay, cell bonus pay, and gainsharing, have motivated some organizations to adopt them.[63] Many organizations, however, are clearly reluctant to experiment with the complicated area of compensation, particularly when policies are long established and firmly entrenched. This is understandable, given that the link between improved performance and any particular compensation plan is difficult to establish. This, in large part, is because compensation systems do not work in isolation. They are but a part of the total fabric of human resource policies that exist in an organization. When the costs of change are large and the benefits uncertain, it is easy to understand a decision to stick with the status quo. However, even when cells run counter to existing compensation mechanisms, organizations can be slow to make changes. For example, an early study of cell practices in Britain reports that managers maintained piece rate compensation systems even though they were aware of their inconsistencies with cell work.[64]

Changing the compensation system to support the new work organization may prove even more difficult if, as is often the case, cells have been introduced in only a segment of the organization. One manufacturer of communications equipment introduced a number of cells that co-existed with assembly lines and traditional batch manufacturing. Workers in all areas of manufacturing were paid in the same way—a salary combined with semi-annual profit-sharing bonuses. Cell operators, for their part, believed that they had more responsibilities and worked harder than did their non-cell colleagues. Accordingly, they did not think they should be paid the same.

Management was reluctant to experiment with the pay system. First, it was concerned about employees' perceptions of equity and fairness. Operators in other parts of the plant no doubt would feel unfairly treated if cell operators had a different compensation system that involved the possibility of additional earnings. Second, management was concerned that the administrative difficulties of operating two different types of compensation systems would outweigh any benefits. Third, compensation decisions were the purview of corporate headquarters, so any experiment would require high-level approval. Finally, managers recognized that while they would like to provide greater inducements for cell performance, the system currently in place (salary and semi-annual profit sharing) did not hamper cell performance. Balancing clearly perceived problems (inequity, administrative costs, and bureaucratic hurdles) against uncertain benefits (what performance improvement would a new compensation system bring?), led to the choice of leaving the existing compensation system alone.

As an epilogue, management recognized the cell workers' broader skills and added responsibilities through job reclassifications. This resulted in higher pay for the cell workers, but no change in the structure of the compensation system. This solution is fairly common in plants with cells.

If You Change Your Compensation System...

Making changes in the pay system is likely to elicit strong reactions from the workforce—how people are paid is a fundamental element of the psychological and economic contract between employees and the company. Most of the companies we have worked with, in fact, have not actually replaced their existing pay systems. Instead they have left the current system intact and added other pay programs (e.g., skill-based pay or cell bonus pay). While this increases the administrative burden (and costs), it does protect the integrity of the original pay structures. If a pay system is abandoned, employees—at least in unionized firms—may have to be compensated for switching pay systems. Such "buy-outs" happen, for example, when a piece rate system is replaced by a fixed-wage pay structure. High-performing operators who will get lower base pay may have to be paid a lump-sum for that type of switch.

Whether you are adding a new program or changing an existing one, the way in which you design and implement your compensation system plays an important role in its effectiveness.[65] Three critical issues are engagement, explanation, and expectation clarity (for more on effective "change management," see Chapter 15).[66] *Engagement* means involving individuals in making decisions that affect them. While this can take different forms, having employees participate in the actual design and implementation of new compensation systems has been shown to lead to higher levels of satisfaction with both pay and jobs (see our earlier ABB Relays example). *Explanation*, or more generally, communication, means keeping the entire workforce abreast of *what* is being contemplated, *when*, and—in particular—*why*. Management must explain why changes are being made and the thinking that lies behind them. This can help employees trust management and its intentions, which is critically important when changes involve such fundamental issues as pay.

Finally, *expectation clarity*, or understanding, means that once the new pay system has been designed, employees need to know how it works and what will be expected of them. Providing clarity is critically important. If pay is tied to business metrics, for example, employees need training to understand basic business performance concepts. Options such as skill-based pay, cell bonus pay, gainsharing, and profit sharing require (sometimes considerable) education to work as intended. No compensation system will be effective unless employees understand how it functions.

The importance of process: an example illustrating radical pay system change

One plant in the computer electronics industry had implemented a number of large work cells over a period of several years. Both managers and operators had expressed concern that the existing compensation system (salary with annual merit increases, plus semi-annual profit sharing) still focused primarily on individual performance. Managers noted that they were "trying to manage team performance, but have a system designed to manage individuals." A top management steering committee sanctioned a design team to review the existing approach and recommend revisions. The design team that developed the new pay system included a project leader, the manufacturing manager, individuals from the personnel department, and representatives from each cell. The operators on the design team were responsible for communicating progress and soliciting input from their fellow cell members.

Working over several months, the design team replaced the old pay system with a new one that combined skill-based pay and cell bonuses. After the steering committee (and the corporate compensation specialists) had approved the specifics of the revised pay system, there was intensive employee communication about the new system and how it would work. Special informational sessions described the intent, expected benefits, and challenges inherent in the change. These sessions always included time for questions and answers. In addition, electronic mail messages and hard-copy postings articulated the "most frequently asked questions" and their answers. Following implementation, the organization launched a monthly newsletter that reported on the performance of various teams.

The company reports significant advantages from changing the compensation system. Designing the system forced management to identify the critical metrics and goals that cell teams needed to pursue. By incorporating critical skills into the skill-based pay system, the company is developing a more skilled and flexible workforce. As a result, individuals and teams now know what they need to do to earn more money, and are in a position to better manage their own career growth. Managers, supervisors, and team leaders report that the cell bonus pay and skill-based pay systems support and enhance the team environment. Last but not the least, the employees think the system is fair, objective, and transparent. The open nature of the process, as well as the efforts to assure employee understanding, have no doubt contributed to these positive results. However, those who designed the system offer these cautions: "it is really hard work," "it will not be perfect," and expect "lots of opinions and lots of criticism." They also emphasize the important role of management commitment and support.

Adopt a Company-Specific Approach

The examples throughout this chapter illustrate that there is no universal approach to cell compensation. As Figure 14-7 illustrates, each organization we have described adopted a unique approach to compensating cell workers. While you want to learn as much as you can from other companies' experiences (whether positive or negative), your compensation system must fit your organization's environment. The culture, management-employee relationships, degree of plant independence in the broader corporate organization, and many other factors will influence what may be possible and appropriate in terms of cell compensation at your plant. In some settings, that means leaving the existing system unchanged.

NON-MONETARY REWARDS AND RECOGNITION

In addition to compensation, you can reward cell workers by recognizing their contributions. *Recognition* acknowledges efforts and achievement through praise, public announcement, and celebrations. For example, recognition may take the form of a "wall of pride" that features photos of cell teams and descriptions of their accomplishments, or simply a visit from a top manager to say "thank you" and congratulate the team on its efforts and accomplishments.[67] Sometimes recognition is accompanied by tangible non-monetary rewards (e.g., plaques, pins, garments bearing the company logo, coffee mugs with inscriptions, sport tickets, the opportunity to participate in educational programs, and so on).

Recognition can play a very important role in creating and retaining a positive work culture in the cell. In fact, it is tough to overdo recognition. As long as you are sincere and are recognizing praiseworthy accomplishments, the more praise the better. Regardless of the compensation system you elect for cells, be sure to supplement it with a healthy dose of recognition.

In traditional organizations, recognition comes primarily from management and is directed at individuals. Cells widen both the source and the target of recog-

Company	Regular Pay					Bonus Pay			
	Indiv. incentive	Cell incentive	Hourly/ monthly pay with merit-based rate increases	Hourly/ monthly pay with seniority-based rate increases	Skill-based pay	Indiv. bonus	Cell bonus	Gain-sharing	Profit sharing
Footwear plant		✓							
Swedish firm			✓		✓		✓		
ABB Relays			✓				✓		
Tellabs			✓		✓				
XEL			✓		✓				✓
Electronics plant			✓						✓
Computer electronics plant			✓		✓		✓		✓
Turner Products			✓		✓		✓		

Figure 14-7. Summary of pay systems exemplified in this chapter

nition. In multi-operator cells, team members are in a position to praise each other's work. They know the work first-hand, are aware of contributions, and can provide immediate positive feedback. Along these lines, one study concludes that "in team-based work environments, most of the rewards for individual effort and accomplishments will have to be administered by the team itself, and a large portion of those rewards will probably be in the form of recognition."[68] In addition, cell teams can self-recognize their work; for example, some teams prominently display their results (e.g., on visual management boards) or publish a team newsletter that describes their recent accomplishments. Others hold celebrations to recognize production milestones (e.g., "10,000th instrument shipped") or project accomplishments (such as the successful introduction of a new product, or a completed ergonomics audit).

That said, management recognition remains a cornerstone of effective non-monetary reward systems. Recognition programs seem to work best when they are inclusive, timely, provide choices, and are perceived as fair.[69] By "inclusive" we simply mean that you should avoid situations where there is only one winner and many losers. Choosing a "cell team of the month" may de-motivate other unacknowledged "runner-up" cells whose performance was close to that of the winning team. Recognizing all teams that achieve a certain level of performance might be a better alternative.

The recognition program also should be timely. You should be able to recognize teams and individuals whenever their performance warrants it, not just on a fixed cycle. This is another potential problem with "cell of the *month*" or "employee of the *month*." In addition, if you are going to recognize people with tangible non-monetary rewards, consider providing them with some choices. Not all employees will value sporting event tickets or a new coffee mug. A manufacturer of barcode scanning equipment recognizes the contributions of cell employees (and others as well) with "Don Bucks."[70] This is paper money that features the Director of Manufacturing's photo. Employees can redeem "Don Bucks" for various gifts and prizes. This example underscores the importance of offering rewards that are valued by recipients.

Finally, recognition programs work best when they are seen as fair and unbiased. In other words, employees should believe that teams or individuals are being recognized for their work, and not because they have a "special connection" with the decision makers.

KEY INSIGHTS

A cell compensation system should be consistent with the design, operational, and strategic objectives of your cells, fit with your organization's other human resource management policies, and be acceptable to employees. It should also help the organization motivate employees to work effectively and efficiently together, attract and retain employees who will help the organization meet its goals, and encourage high and sustained performance. To support these high-level goals, we suggested that a compensation system for cells has certain ideal characteristics (Table 14-1).

Here are some other key "take aways" to keep in mind as you rethink the cell compensation system at your firm.

- *At a minimum, your compensation system should not hamper work in the cells.* Evaluate your compensation system to be sure it does not impede effective cell work.

- *If you elect to make changes in the compensation system to support cells, involve operators, supervisors, management, and human resource management specialists in the process.* The way you make changes in the compensation system will strongly influence the effectiveness of that system. Giving operators a voice in the design of the system can ease implementation ("we support what we help create") and result in a system that helps move performance in the right direction. A compensation system that is unacceptable to employees is not going to be effective.

- *Employees must understand how the compensation system works.* Employees need to know how the system is structured, how performance will be evaluated, how frequently evaluation will take place, who will do the evaluating, what measures will be used, and so forth. In particular, employees need to understand any new performance measures that will assess them, their cell, or the plant.

- *Take a firm-specific approach to cell compensation.* While you can learn from practices at other organizations, your system should fit your environment, support your strategic objectives, and work in concert with your other human resource policies and practices.

- *No single compensation system can "do it all."* Organizations with cells often choose to combine a number of different compensation options, each of which satisfies some limited need.

- *Even if you do not change the compensation system itself, recognize that cell workers with broadened jobs may (rightly) expect higher compensation.* If you ask people to do more—to take on added responsibilities, to acquire and use more skills, to contribute in a variety of ways to cell performance—they will expect to earn more. Think through how you will address this.

- *In addition to compensation, your reward system should include a recognition program.* Non-monetary rewards and recognition can play an important role in creating and retaining a positive work culture in the cell.

IMPLEMENTING AND IMPROVING CELLS

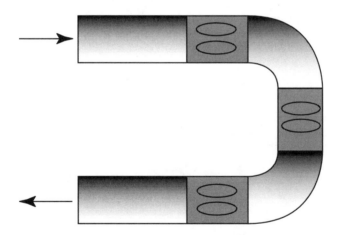

Planning for Cell Implementation and Managing the Change

Chapter 4 provided a high-level overview of the process of adopting, designing, and implementing cellular manufacturing systems, and in the chapters that followed we discussed adoption and design issues in depth. In this chapter we focus on making it happen—managing the details of the cell project. The chapter answers several important questions:

- What techniques and approaches lead to a well-planned, well-executed cell implementation project?
- How can you best prepare the organization for the coming change?
- How do you deal with resistance to change?
- How should you structure a cell implementation project?
- Who should be involved in the project, and who should lead the effort?

In addressing these questions, we emphasize the role of change management and project management in a successful implementation. To set the stage, we begin with a case history.

PLANNING FOR CELLS IN AN ELECTRONICS ASSEMBLY PLANT

The experience of a manufacturer of electronic equipment provides a detailed and large-scale example of the efforts involved in planning and implementing cells.[1] To begin, the manager of the plant's Assembly and Test Center (ATC) convened a small core team to work with him on a strategic analysis. The team's task was to determine the characteristics of an assembly and test organization that would be competitive in the future. The team gathered information from key internal and external stakeholders, and studied competitors and the market. It then developed a vision that defined the new organization.

The team concluded that for ATC to be competitive it would need a committed, flexible workforce that could adapt to changing conditions. The manager further recognized that he should not stipulate what the new manufacturing system would look like. In his words, "I couldn't hope to create a high-commitment workforce by dictating the design."

The Design Process—High-Level Design

The manager pulled together an expanded team (the Core Design Group) that would lead the transformation. This steering committee consisted of the manager, each of his section managers, an internal consultant, the plant's resident cell manufacturing expert, and representatives from key support groups (engineering, accounting, production control). For several months, the Core Design Group struggled with how to proceed. Eventually, it adopted a highly participative approach to work redesign.

Several project teams were formed, each headed by a member of the Core Design Group. These "analysis teams" were to assess the existing work and management systems and identify their shortcomings when contrasted with the characteristics of the future organization. Table I-1 in Appendix I describes the overall team architecture for the ATC cell design process.

The analysis teams worked in parallel for about four months. Each team then generated a set of recommendations that pertained to its area of investigation (e.g., assembly, test, social system, metrics, or business). During the four months of analysis there was considerable cross-team communication via regularly scheduled meetings of the Core Design Group. Team members also communicated progress to the groups they represented.

"Design Week" was an extended off-site meeting that established the framework for the new work organization. The Core Design Group and all the analysis teams (30-plus people in all) participated in this five-day event. During this week the individual teams shared their analyses and recommendations, and the group as a whole made high-level decisions about the structure and operation of the new work system. For example, the group decided to create cells or *"home teams,"* each devoted to assembling and testing a family of electronic instruments. It also agreed to create *business and process councils*, which would identify and communicate best practices across the cells and develop departmental-wide policies. The recommendations developed by the analysis teams would guide the councils in their work. The final output from Design Week was a rough plan for moving forward with implementation. This plan included a communications strategy for announcing the details of the coming change to the plant at large.

The Design Process—Detailed Design

Shortly after Design Week, the Core Design Group met to assign product families and operators to each home team. The process of identifying product families and assigning equipment was fairly straightforward. Assigning operators and supervisors to home teams was more difficult, primarily because many operators had skill sets that made them potential members of a number of home teams. In making final assignments, the Core Design Group considered supervisors' opinions (who would be best at building which products?) as well as operator preferences (with whom would you like to work, and what products would you most like to build?). The Core Design Group also identified some of the initial members and the leadership for each of the councils.

Once created, the individual home teams spent three months working on the detailed design of each cell and some associated infrastructure. In particular, each home team was responsible for:

- Developing its own cell layout.
- Selecting/designing material handling, tooling, and fixtures.
- Establishing, within broad parameters, the job roles and responsibilities of individuals (e.g., who will participate on what councils; what operators will assume responsibility for specific indirect labor tasks that have been delegated to the cell).
- Determining inspection and quality monitoring procedures.
- Determining maintenance protocols.
- Preparing to assume responsibility for material ordering, job tracking, and scheduling procedures.
- Becoming knowledgeable about cost control and reporting procedures (training was provided by the cost accounting group).
- Developing a plan that guarantees customer needs will be met during the transition period.
- Participating in team start-up training.

Appendix Table I-2 describes some of these home team activities in greater detail.

The councils worked with the teams during this period. For example, the Materials Council (which included representatives from each cell and from production planning) helped develop and implement common material supply policies across the cells. Similarly, the Finance Council provided the cell teams with information and training about financial aspects of cell operations. Appendix Table I-3 describes the membership and activities of each council.

There was intense communication in the first months after Design Week. The department manager gave numerous presentations to employees who had not participated in the design process. He described the results of Design Week and shared the plans for moving forward. The analysis team members also presented the new organizational design to the work groups that they represented. Finally, all employees participated in a simulation designed to contrast the current work organization with the new one, giving them a hands-on feel for what work would be like in the future.

Implementation

Two important aspects of ATC's cell implementation were cell team training and project leadership provided by the transition manager.

1. *Training.* Team start-up training was a very significant activity, tightly linked with many of the detailed implementation planning activities. For example, facilitators taught work teams about process flow analysis/functional flow charting (called process mapping in this organization; see Chapter 18 and Appendix L) and then helped the teams map their areas'

activities as a prelude to thinking through detailed layout and job responsibilities. Other sessions focused on team-building exercises, activities to improve team dynamics, and understanding and developing "codes of conduct"—statements of acceptable and unacceptable behaviors for each home team. Still other training events helped the teams define roles and responsibilities in the new work setting. Council representatives from each home team also received additional training (e.g., finance training for the team's Finance Council representative).

2. *Project leadership:* A transition manager coordinated the detailed design work and the preparations for the physical conversion. He was responsible for:

   - Overseeing the planning and execution of the physical reconfiguration.
   - Working with home team representatives to compile a master area layout.
   - Resolving cell coordination issues.
   - Providing leadership for the councils during start-up.
   - Working with support groups to develop an infrastructure that supported the new cell operations.
   - Working with managers to develop delegation plans (which responsibilities to transfer to cell operators, and how to do it).
   - Managing the first several months of start-up.

The physical move to cells took place 18 months after the start of the project and about four months after design week. This was a full conversion in which everyone in the area was placed in cells.

Outcomes

While there were some minor problems in the early days of operation, the cell system proved very successful. By the end of the second year of operation, production per employee had nearly doubled and production lead times had been cut in half. In addition, quality had improved dramatically, spans of control had increased for managers and supervisors, and ESD (electrostatic discharge) damage had fallen. The manager noted that decisions in the cell system were made faster and better, with less management involvement than in the past.

It can be noted that as a result of the increased breadth of direct labor skills, many operators qualified for job reclassification and pay increases (the job classification system itself, however, remained unchanged). So payroll expenses rose, but this was more than offset by the reduction in support personnel for the area: cell operators absorbed the work previously done by eight support people, who consequently were reassigned to other duties.

Comments on ATC's Planning and Implementation Process

ATC followed a fairly elaborate planning and implementation process. In the paragraphs that follow we provide additional comments on selected aspects of this process.

Degree of corporate support for change

Some cell projects are isolated efforts, shepherded along under the watchful gaze of a single manager and unsanctioned by higher levels of management. At the other extreme are cell projects that are part of a well-orchestrated, high-level effort to transform manufacturing. ATC was somewhere in the middle of this spectrum. While it involved a significant portion of the plant's operations, ATC's cell project was not part of a larger plant-wide initiative. The degree to which a project is supported/sanctioned from above will no doubt influence the level and type of resources available to the project team, as well as the goals and objectives of the project.

Total conversion versus pilot cell

As we discussed in Chapter 4, you might plan and implement a pilot cell if you are uncertain about the benefits of cells or believe a successful pilot will help smooth the way for full-scale implementation. This allows you to experiment and learn on a small scale instead of "betting the plant." Because getting a pilot cell up and running will be faster than planning for a total plant conversion, a pilot cell may also appeal to you if your company has a bias for action. ATC did not opt for a pilot cell. The manager of ATC had implemented a successful cell while serving as the manager of another area of the plant. Similarly, many members of the Core Design Group had worked with cells in other parts of the corporation, were very familiar with the concept, and knew it had worked well for manufacturing areas similar to ATC. Thus, there was little need to "prove out" the cell concept. Further, the ATC Manager and Core Design Group were fully committed to a complete "systems" transformation and wanted to avoid "islands of improvement" (or "pockets of enlightenment," as the team referred to them). They firmly believed that the instantaneous reorganization of ATC as a whole was the best way to move toward the vision of future manufacturing.

Extent of planning and involvement

High-involvement design processes that focus on total plant conversion (as exemplified by ATC) take a lot of time. That time is well spent if it eases implementation and promotes acceptance among the workforce. Cell projects also can take just a few months and involve a mere handful of people (typically engineers, managers, and supervisors); however, these projects may meet resistance if the change comes as an unexpected (and unwelcome) surprise to the rest of the organization. Operators are often a main source of process knowledge—for this reason alone, you want to tap their expertise in the design process. If you also want to create self-managed cells where operators perform both direct and indirect labor tasks, operator involvement in cell planning becomes even more crucial. ATC adopted a highly participative approach to cell design. One of the manager's explicit goals for the project was to create a "high-performance" workplace where operators would have significant responsibility for running and improving cells. Remember that people support what they help create.

The amount of advanced planning you need to do depends on the scale of the implementation. Large-scale projects that involve total plant conversions require extensive planning: there is simply more to coordinate when the scope of change is large. This was the case with ATC, where a whole area was being converted.

When sophisticated machine tools or complex material-handling equipment is involved (and, in particular, when new technology is acquired), detailed planning becomes even more important. Getting equipment built, installed, and debugged can be a time consuming process that needs to be orchestrated carefully. Planning missteps, especially in large-scale projects, can carry a hefty price tag. In fact, most unsuccessful cell conversions of this type "are spawned from an incomplete plan that overlooked or deliberately left to chance critical plan elements. It's too late to make critical changes when brick and mortar are cured, machines are on the receiving dock, or customer product deliveries are in arrears."[2] Conversely, in situations where decisions can be reversed easily and inexpensively—making physical experimentation with different alternatives practical—you may elect to invest less energy in detailed planning and more energy in cell improvements (see Chapter 17).

Extent of training

The physical transformation to cells at ATC was accompanied by an extensive effort to train and educate the entire ATC manufacturing and support organization. Recall that ATC was transitioning to a high-involvement organization where significant indirect labor activities would be delegated to operators who would share responsibilities for these tasks. Cell concepts training, interpersonal skills training, problem-solving, and administrative and management skills training were critical for all 100-plus operators who would be transitioning into cells. Managers and support groups needed a solid understanding of cells as well, particularly given the many changes that were needed in infrastructure systems. Note, however, that technical work skills training was not a part of the preparation for cells: ATC workers were already multifunctional, and almost all of them had prior experience building their cell's products. (See Chapter 13 for more on various types of training.)

On the "right way"

The ATC case illustrates but one approach to cell planning and implementation. Other organizations have taken different paths and also been successful. There is no "one right way" to plan and implement cells; rather, the right way depends on your circumstances. Regardless of the specific tactics used, however, we believe that good and sound change management and project management principles should be followed. We discuss change management first.

MANAGING THE TRANSITION TO CELLS

By "change management" we refer to the battle for people's minds and hearts: how do you get personnel in the organization to embrace and support cells intellectually, as well as emotionally? This is an important question for implementers of cell-based manufacturing. The move to cells often means fairly dramatic and far-reaching departures from old ways, requiring new jobs and roles, along with changes in support policies and procedures. The scope and impact of these changes are such that you need to win over *many* hearts and minds in order for the new work organization to be effective.

So, how do you go about doing that? We are going to walk you through a 10-step model for managing the change process.[3]

A 10-Step Change Model

Although the list of steps we prescribe (see Table 15-1) reads like a straightforward recipe, anyone who has been involved in a major organizational change knows that transformations are often messy, sometimes unpredictable, and certainly painful. Thus, although we believe that the following guidelines can help you manage the transformation to cells, you should be aware that change is always "easier said than done."

Table 15-1. A 10-step model for managing the transition to cells

Step 1: Analyze the organization and its need for change.
Step 2: Form a powerful guiding coalition.
Step 3: Create a vision.
Step 4: Communicate and establish a sense of urgency.
Step 5: Line up political sponsorship.
Step 6: Organize the change process and plan the implementation.
Step 7: Prepare for and remove obstacles.
Step 8: Produce short-term wins.
Step 9: Institutionalize the new approach.
Step 10: Change again—go back to step 1.

Step 1: Analyze the organization and its need for change

Every change process should begin with this step—looking broadly and strategically at the organization's strengths, weaknesses, threats, and opportunities. In particular, this step identifies misalignments—elements of the organization that are not well positioned to respond to external demands or to work effectively with each other (see Figures 1-2 and 1-4, and our discussion in Chapter 1). Sooner or later, misalignments will translate into gaps between targeted and actual performance. Therefore, this step focuses on *why* the organization needs to change and *what it needs to become* in order to be competitive.

For example, in the late 80s, a U.S. footwear company's top executive saw modules (cells) in operation at a European competitor's facility. The executive was convinced that modules would enable his plants to compete on customer response time as well as improve quality. This would provide an advantage over lower-wage Asian and Latin American producers who needed five to seven months to fill replenishment orders. To bring home this message, the executive took plant managers on a benchmarking trip to Europe and the Far East. They all returned convinced that modules could deliver the types of performance necessary to remain competitive. They also agreed that without this fundamental change, the company was doomed. Likewise, benchmarking data and customer interviews caused ATC's manager and his staff to conclude that emerging lower-cost competitors represented a significant threat. Furthermore, the group realized that without sweeping changes to assembly and test, the area would be unable to contribute to the division's goal of reducing production cost by 20 percent over the next five years.

Step 2: Form a powerful guiding coalition

The "guiding coalition" is a group of key managers who advocate and support the change. In many cell implementations, this group forms the steering committee. Its members are important to the effort because they have the power to resolve problems and help remove obstacles that stand in the way of transformation. At the shoe plant described above, the plant manager's staff, which included the top people from each function, provided guidance for the design and implementation project. These decisions-makers were deeply involved in the effort and authorized important changes (e.g., a new compensation system) that smoothed the implementation. At ATC, the manager and his direct reports acted as the initial guiding coalition. When representatives from other stakeholder groups joined these managers to form the Core Design Group, the resulting team acted as the steering committee for the subsequent design phases.

Now consider a situation where this level of support did not exist. Individual managers within one manufacturing organization had created "skunk works" cells (more or less "underground" cells, sanctioned by individual area managers but not higher-level management). While the overall plant manager knew of these experiments, there was no powerful coalition backing and guiding them. When the individual areas ran into hurdles (e.g., incompatible material delivery systems, and production control procedures that could not release orders by product family), requests for new ways of doing things fell on deaf ears. There was no high-level group to support needed changes.

Step 3: Create a vision

In Chapter 4, we presented a comprehensive model of the cell planning and implementing process (see Figure 4-1). Step 4 of that model was to *formulate a vision and goals for the new manufacturing organization*. Visions are important because they help people understand, and get enthusiastic about, the direction in which the organization wants to move. "Without a sensible vision, a transformation effort can easily dissolve into a list of confusing and incompatible projects that can take the organization in the wrong direction or nowhere at all."[4]

It is important to have a clear picture of what cells are intended to accomplish. ATC's manager was fond of saying, "It's easier to put a puzzle together if you can see the box cover. Therefore, we need to paint the box cover." Elements of the vision for ATC's new organization included:

- Maintain strong focus on satisfying external customer needs.
- Work easily with internal and external customers.
- Achieve on-time delivery.
- Control variances at the source (solve problems where they occur).

- Ensure a healthy environment.
- Produce low-cost products.

The manager and his four direct reports—who formed the guiding coalition—drafted an initial vision. The larger steering committee, the Core Design Group, worked for over two months to distill, clarify, and develop consensus over the vision elements listed above. The vision was refined in such a way that a large group of people came to understand the vision, bought into it, and could explain it to others. The last point—communicating the vision—is important. "If you can't communicate the vision to someone in five minutes or less and get a reaction that signifies both understanding and interest, you are not yet done with this phase of the transformation process."[5] A consultant friend of ours refers to this as the "elevator speech," signifying that you sometimes only have a few minutes to tell people your vision of the future and captivate their minds (i.e., about the same time it takes to ride the elevator).

Step 4: Communicate and establish a sense of urgency

Making the case for cells paves the way for a successful transformation. You need to make people in the organization feel that there is a compelling reason to consider abandoning current ways of working and embarking on a new path. In the words of one executive, people need to feel that the status quo is "more dangerous than launching into the unknown."[6]

Consider two shoe plants, both of which faced the same markets and the same competitive situation. They used the same work processes and technology, and made similar products. At one facility, top corporate executives and local plant management were convinced that cells offered the best chance for survival. The plant manager, through frank and frequent communication with other managers, supervisors, and the workforce, painted a frightening picture of the organization's future. Learning that workers in the Caribbean earned only a fraction of what they did helped the employees understand the competitive situation and made them realize that things had to change. Consequently, there was very little resistance to cells.

At the other plant, the move to a pilot cell was seen as a minor experiment undertaken for no apparent reason and driven by a couple of managers acting on their own initiative. There was no sense of urgency. Predictably, the exercise did not lead to the implementation of more cells, despite substantial lead-time reductions and better quality. Although experimentation with new technologies and organizational forms is important for successful change, and therefore is common in leading-edge firms, there was in this case no guiding corporate coalition that saw cells in the firm's future. The company has now sold off most of its domestic manufacturing facilities, including the plant where the pilot cell operated.

You need compelling and credible communication to instill a sense of urgency in the organization. This means everyone affected by the change needs to understand the vision of future work and the roles that cells will play. The steering committee sends this message. In addition, the cell implementation team should keep the organization up to date on the project status. In fact, effective communication becomes increasingly important as the project plan unfolds. People need to be aware of the cell implementation project before it directly affects them.[7] Many forms of communication can be used, including large group meetings, presentations, e-mail or website updates, one-on-one sessions for key stakeholders, small group briefings, memos articulating the "most frequently asked questions" and their answers, short videos, and newsletters. The format and frequency of communication depends on the audience and their need to know. In general, small group, face-to-face meetings are the most effective in transferring information and making sure it is received and understood.

Actions, as well as words, communicate. If the steering committee states that cells are an important part of the vision, but then reassigns the project manager to another, "higher priority" task, this undermines the credibility of the whole effort.

Step 5: Line up political sponsorship

At an early stage you need to identify and garner the support of key individuals and groups who can make your change effort a success. These include those who have formal authority, union leaders (if applicable), informal opinion leaders and change agents at various levels in the organization. Use the stakeholder analysis method we present below to determine the level of support you need from these individuals and groups, and the steps to take to acquire it. For example, some key people should be part of the project teams.

Step 6: Organize the change process and plan the implementation

Successful implementations rarely "just happen." They are almost always the result of careful planning, and the execution of those plans, by a committed, capable group of people. At some point you need to create a formal "change organization" including a steering committee and one or more project teams that will be responsible for the cell project (see Appendix I for ATC's change organization). We devote the second half of this chapter to the tools and techniques of project management.

Step 7: Prepare for and remove obstacles

To reach their full potential, cells may require significant changes in the way work is currently done. Job design, employee selection procedures, production planning and control systems, and so on may all need to change. When the leadership group does not clear the way for these changes, the implementation effort can stall. For example, when management in one plant would not authorize changes to the production planning and control system, cell designers had to develop elaborate ways to work around the problems. Other cell implementation teams run into roadblocks created by narrow job descriptions they are powerless to change.

Insufficient training is another common barrier that management must be willing to remove. The manager of one shoe plant that transitioned to modules admits that he and his design team underestimated the work required to get cell operators "to think as a team." Before modules, operators worked in relative isolation, repeatedly performing the same process step on bundles of shoes. This, and the individual piece rate system of compensation, fostered a culture of independence. Modular (cellular) work, on the other hand, called for communication and cooperation. Operators were not well prepared for this. Once they realized the problem, management stepped in and instituted an extensive training program wherein the members of each module team received about 30 hours of training. There were sessions on customers, paradigm shifts, modules in other plants, plant finances, the competitors, and the basics of teamwork, group problem-solving, and interpersonal skills. Supervisors, too, received substantial training. Had management not invested in overcoming this barrier, it is unlikely that the cell transformation would have been successful.

Other barriers include insufficient meeting time, inability to get the right people on the team, and lack of financial support. Hovering over all these, and representing the most common and formidable obstacle to change, is employee resistance. Initial resistance to change—at all levels in the company—is both natural and unavoidable. However, when management does not remove this and other obstacles, the cell effort can falter or, worse, be abandoned altogether (ways to handle resistance to change are discussed in a separate section below).

Step 8: Produce short-term wins

Many organizations we have worked with opted to create a pilot cell in the hopes of creating a rallying point for more extensive change. Often they planned for this "win" by carefully selecting products and people for the first experiment. For example, they chose opinion leaders to work in the cell, and identified an area where a high probability of success existed—typically, one that had a lot of "low-hanging fruit" for improvement. Further, they publicized cell accomplishments widely, thereby creating energy and enthusiasm for a more sustained effort. This, coupled with the opportunity to learn from the experiment, is a very compelling reason to choose the pilot cell route.

When the change process takes longer because it involves a larger conversion (as was the case with ATC)—or even the entire plant—it is even more important to promote and celebrate accomplishments (such as "the successful completion of our Phase I design" or "Team B's successful completion of start-up training"). At ATC, celebrating accomplishments and sharing progress was part of the project landscape. For example, the teams celebrated the close of design week, the completion of introductory training, the completion of the physical move, and other smaller milestones in between. These accomplishments were widely publicized throughout the plant.

This underscores the importance of breaking the project into separate phases, each with expected deadlines and outcomes. As soon as the implementation produces tangible improvements, be sure to highlight them; it helps to convince people that the organization is moving in the right direction.

Step 9: Institutionalize the new approach

One way to "institutionalize change" is to modify the organization's systems and structures so they fit better with the new cellular system. Turner Products, a company we first discussed in Chapter 9, undertook a full-scale change to cells. After the cells were up and running, the company began to work on a team-based pay system. The system would augment hourly wages with cell bonus pay based on each cell's ability to meet specific improvement goals (see Chapter 14). This change reinforced the move to team-based cells and helped convince employees that there was "no going back." Other changes, such as vesting teams with the power to hire replacement workers and remove poor performers from the cells, sent the same message.

Leaders can also reinforce the new way of working by assuring that the next generation of managers supports the new ways. A key manager who spearheaded much of the change at Turner Products was subsequently promoted to a plant management position with broadened responsibilities. Similarly, outstanding cell leaders have moved into the ranks of supervision or have joined the quality department—both are significant promotions. Moving individuals who played a key role in the cell transformation into positions of greater responsibility tells the rest of the organization that the new ways are being rewarded. (Of course, one has to be careful here; if promoting key players leaves the change process in the hands of individuals unprepared or unwilling to continue the effort, this can jeopardize the transformation.)

Step 10: Change again—go back to step 1

The competitive environment is constantly changing. This means that the process of evaluating the organization and its customers and competitors, identifying performance gaps, and working to close them must be ongoing. You should plan for a constant cycle of analysis, experimentation, and strategic change to avoid "active inertia." In particular, continually verify if cellular manufacturing is the best solution for your existing and forthcoming products, or if other types of work organizations are better (see Chapter 17 for a discussion of cell evolution).

Dealing with Resistance to Change

The purpose of the 10-step process just outlined is to ensure that the organization is constantly searching for threats and opportunities in its environment; that it identifies aspects of the organization that need to change in order to remain competitive; and that it plans and implements those changes successfully. A major reason change management must be taken seriously is the natural inclination among employees at all levels to resist change in the workplace. Below, we discuss this important issue in more depth and suggest specific ways to handle resistance (the special problem of labor unions and cells is discussed in Chapter 16).

Sources of resistance

Resistance to change can have many and varied sources, as indicated by Table 15-2.[8] We'll address some of the sources of resistance that have particular relevance to cell work.

Operators, supervisors, and managers may be reluctant to support cells because they fear for their jobs. We recommend that you address this up front. Guaranteeing a place in the new organization for every employee that wants one goes a long way toward dealing with this concern. Employees are more likely to believe statements about job security if you can show how cells will help the company succeed in the marketplace, grow the business, and provide employment opportunities. If people think they will lose their source of livelihood because of cells, the transformation effort will likely suffer from both overt and covert resistance.

Employees may resist cells because they feel their jobs will be less varied. This is particularly the case when the move to cells means a move away from craft production where operators build products start-to-finish. Before cells, operators at one

Table 15-2. Reasons for resistance to change

- Loss of control (change is done *to* you rather than *by* you)
- Lack of facts about the change (what is going on here, and why?)
- Disbelief that change "will work" (based on your knowledge and experience)
- Too much uncertainty (about the future—what is going to happen to me, what is expected of me?).
- Surprise (change is introduced without advance warning)
- The cost of confusion (too many simultaneous changes at once)
- Loss of face (what I did in the past must be wrong)
- Concerns about competence (can I do it—master the change and/or the job requirements?)
- More work (implementing change takes time, energy, efforts, and learning)
- Less desirable job responsibilities (new jobs have less attractive features)
- Ripple effects (new plans disturb old plans still under implementation)
- Past resentments (towards management for unfulfilled commitments from previous changes)
- Real threats to pay, power and influence, position, and job content (change may bring real pain)

electronics plant built batches of subassemblies start-to-finish. Operators were concerned that work in cells would mean they were stuck doing the same tasks endlessly, with no chance for varied work. According to the area manager, "we really had to deal with this up front" by trying to provide realistic previews of what cell work would be like. He also noted that experience was a good teacher and that, after the new system was in place, people realized they could still have variety and could still rotate tasks.

Employees also may resist if they perceive that cell work will be harder. This was the case at one plant where a couple of cells had been in operation for several years. Machinists, who had observed the existing cells, believed that they would have to work harder if they worked in cells. The shop manager responded by placing some of the least enthusiastic machinists on the cell design team. This strategy of inclusion helped, and working in the cells really convinced the operators. After six months, the most outspoken opponents had become avid supporters. They valued the cell's control over start-to-finish processing. In fact, operators were very dissatisfied when some cells were disbanded years later in response to shifting demand.

Operators at an electronics plant disliked job rotation because they liked having their own station. Their attitude was "this is my station, my tools, my space." They considered their work station as their "home at work." Getting operators to accept that "here is a station, but it is not your home" was a big adjustment, according to the manager. In response, some cells developed designated break areas with lockers where workers could "park their soda bottles and pictures of family members."

Resistance to change also may be rooted in a "functional mindset"—a preference for repetitious tasks and independence that characterize work in functional shops. "Everyone thinks they can do the job faster in batches. It seems easier to do the same step 30 times," observed the manager of a medical instrument plant with cells. However, while individual efficiency is greatest when repeating the same task over and over again, the time for the batch to go through the process is much slower. Charles Bearce, plant manager for Reed-Rico, a manufacturer of precision thread rolling dies, notes:[9]

The biggest problem we had was getting people to understand the team concept. They [operators] were used to tending their own machines and you could be a homebody and work by yourself if you wanted. Now that you're working in a cell and there are three machines tended by two people, those two people have to work in coordination with each other to operate that third machine. There were some struggles there, and that was one of the things that had to be overcome.

Similarly, respondents to a recent survey noted problems with operators being unwilling to make decisions or run different pieces of equipment, or with their dislike of task variety.[10] One manager speculated that operators at his plant took pride in being the best at their work and "resented it when others tried to equal their output."[11] We've heard from other managers that the best cell workers complain that they are held back by slower colleagues, particularly if their individual compensation is linked to cell output.

When the functional mindset is not broken, organizations with cells may experience "functional drift."[12] The physical cell exists, but workers drift back to functional ways of operating. In one U-shaped cell, a system of kanban squares was supposed to control the flow of material within the cell by limiting work in process between stations. If the outgoing kanban squares were full or the incoming kanban squares were empty, the cross-trained operators were to move to a different station. Initially, operators followed this new way of operating. However, after the cells had been operating for some time the manager noticed that the work in process inventory was not evenly distributed in the cell. He then discovered that the operators were completely ignoring the kanban squares. Rather, each operator was completing an entire batch of parts at a workstation before passing it on to the next operation. Further, the fully cross-trained workers were moving with their batches from station to station in a craft cell mode. According to the manager, the cell drifted away from one-piece flow because the supervisor and operators were not well trained in the pull method of kanban squares. This was particularly the case for new workers who joined the cell from batch build areas. In addition, both new and experienced cell operators had a strong preference for independent, repetitive work, which they saw as more efficient. The consequence, however, was longer throughput times and higher in-cell inventory levels.

To deal with this problem, the manager provided one-on-one training for the supervisor. The supervisor in turn worked closely with operators, re-emphasizing the performance benefits of one-piece cell flows (e.g., reduced inventory levels, higher quality, shorter lead times). Over the next several months the supervisor spent considerable time on the line enforcing cell discipline. Performance metrics were prominently displayed in the cell so that operators could actually see the benefits of the new way of working.

If the preference for repetitive, independent work is a source of resistance at your plant, there are a number of strategies you can use:[13]

- Design jobs to overlap with the expectation that workers help each other out and rotate assignments.
- Explain why one-piece flow can be superior to larger batch production.

- Base rewards on cell performance, not just individual performance. This can encourage cooperation among employees who might otherwise be tempted to work in isolation at one task, even when needed elsewhere.
- Provide training on technical skills, interpersonal skills, and joint problem-solving so operators can work effectively together.
- Be sure that the cell layout permits workers to see each other's work, communicate easily, and move when needed at another station.
- Provide workers with fast feedback on cell performance so that the benefits of new ways of working are visible.

We discussed these strategies in some detail in our chapters on job design (Chapter 12), selection and training (Chapter 13), and compensation (Chapter 14).

Finally, resistance sometimes exists because managers, supervisors, and operators think that cells are a passing phase—a "flavor of the month." Their attitude is: "I will just hide out under my workstation till this blows over" (see the "ripple effect" in Table 15-2). As we suggested earlier in the chapter, visible, concrete, and substantial actions and support from top management are central to convincing people that cells are here to stay.

At Turner Products, a single incident stands out as the defining moment when everyone knew that cells were "for real" and management was truly committed. One of the teams purchased a new grinder. Billy, the cell leader, and his team decided where to place the new equipment and communicated this to plant maintenance. Plant maintenance, however, decided it would be better to locate the machine in a different spot and proceeded to dig a six-foot wide hole in the concrete flooring. When Billy and his team discovered this, they were livid. Billy walked into the company president's office and said "Are you serious about this team thing or what? Maintenance just dug a six-foot wide hole in a place where we don't want the machine." The president picked up the phone and called the head of maintenance. "Billy says the hole is in the wrong place." The head of maintenance replied, "We already have a six-foot hole in a good spot for the machine." "Well, you better start to fill it up," replied the president. Within hours everyone in the plant had heard what happened. They all knew that it cost money to dig and then fill up a big hole in the concrete flooring. Accordingly, everyone realized that management was committed to the self-managed cell concept. A key manager involved in the transformation noted that "there just wasn't much resistance after this incident."

The concept of "fair process"

Employees involved with change projects often complain about being insufficiently heard, involved, or informed, so they put up resistance. But resistance to change is not *always* bad. In fact, it is often a sign of a need for clarity, and can also reflect a willingness to improve the cell implementation plan. This points to one golden rule in dealing with change: those in charge of change must understand how employees perceive and experience change. In this section we elaborate more on why resistance occurs and provide some general principles for minimizing it.

Frequently, cell design is in the hands of managers, engineers, and consultants. For example, one quarter of the firms in a recent study indicated that they did not involve operators in the design of their workspace.[14] The rationale for such decisions is typically that time is short and that managers, engineers, and consultants probably have the greatest cell expertise and can come up with a good design quickly. While this approach might lead to a good technical solution, it can also contribute to implementation problems. In another study of ours, one manager noted that one of the mistakes he had made was failing to "bring in cell members in the planning earlier."[15] The following example illustrates what can happen when companies do not involve operators in the process.

An elevator manufacturer was under severe pressure to quickly cut costs and operate more efficiently.[16] Management hired a team of consultants to develop a master plan for cells. The consultants were a visible, but unexplained, presence in the plant. Three months after they arrived, the consultants presented the cell plan to operators in a 30-minute session. The presentation did not explain why the firm needed to change or what operators would be expected to do in the new setting. Operators reacted in "stunned silence." Management interpreted the silence as acceptance. Shortly after the equipment began to be rearranged, management told operators they would be judged on group output, but did not make clear how this would work. Management then announced that they were eliminating the supervisor role and that cell teams would be self-directed. But, again, management did not explain how operators were to work through problems that supervisors used to handle. An employee survey revealed massive discontent. "Management doesn't care about our ideas or about our input," "they don't bother to tell us where we are going and what this means to us" and "we don't know what exactly management expects of us in this new cell," were typical comments.[17]

Management in this example failed to observe the principle of *fair process*.[18] Essentially, fair process means that people are more likely to accept an outcome—even a negative one—if they feel they have been treated "fairly."[19] In short, the process can be more important than the outcome. This principle has important implications for cell implementation. Fair process rests on three elements: engagement, explanation, and expectation clarity. *Engagement* means involving people in decisions that will affect them. This requires soliciting input and providing opportunities to comment on ideas and assumptions. Operators in this example were not engaged in the cell design process or asked their views of the proposed changes. *Explanation* means being clear about the decisions that have been made and, especially, why they were made. When workers understand the thinking and vision behind cells, they are more likely to "trust managers intentions" and accept the new system. In the example, management did not explain why cells were needed, and workers were predictably resistant. Finally, *expectation clarity* means making sure people understand what they need to do to be successful in the new system. Management needs to make performance standards, roles, and responsibilities clear. At the elevator plant, employees experienced high levels of frustration and uncertainty because they did not understand what was expected of them in the new, cellular organization.

More generally, expectation clarity assures that individuals in the plant have a realistic picture of how work will change with cells. Where this is not the case, one possible outcome is that people become so enthusiastic about the cell change that they develop very high expectations about what cell jobs will be like. Operators, for example, may envision jobs with far greater flexibility and more self-management than is actually the case once the cells are in place. At one company a manager noted that "operators have accepted change so readily that they want to see more [which] causes friction amongst the operators." Similarly, at another company "operator expectations higher than reality" was a problem.[20] Unrealistic expectations can be countered by providing candidates for cell jobs with realistic previews of the job (see Chapter 13). However, the "rhetoric versus reality" problem is sometimes also the fault of management, who in an effort to create enthusiasm may go overboard selling the cell concept to employees, promising them a level of empowerment that simply will not exist once cells are in operation. The key message here is to carefully manage expectations: be open and honest throughout the planning, implementation, and operation process.

As we have already mentioned, a common complaint from both employees and management is that information sharing during the planning and implementation process is inadequate. As a result, people feel uninformed, left out, or surprised by the changes. This, in turn, can lead to resistance and schedule delays as the cell implementation team does damage control. The solution is to develop and execute a communications plan that emphasizes clear and frequent communication. Or, to frame it in terms of fair process: communication should *explain* (make the case for change and keep the organization informed of progress), *engage* (solicit input and ideas), and *set expectations* (clarify new roles).

Despite all your efforts, some individuals will never embrace the new ways. You need a strategy for dealing with such employees. For example, it might be possible for them to work in, or support, conventional areas of the plant. Early retirement or voluntary severance programs also may be an option. Further, people who are unwilling to work in cells frequently self-select out of the organization and leave the company for opportunities elsewhere. At one company, for example, 20 percent of the workforce left rather than interview for the new cell jobs. Management had provided all workers with realistic job previews and had made clear what they would need to do to be successful in the new system.[21] Those who decided cell work wasn't for them left the firm.

The Change Management Process in Perspective: Avoiding the Pitfalls

Transformation programs are successful when cells become "the way we do things around here."[22] Following the steps outlined in Table 15-1 can help assure a successful transformation. (Note that these steps should all be followed, although not necessarily in the sequence they are presented; also note that many steps take place in parallel, and that some must be revisited throughout the course of the project.) Unfortunately, organizations often skip or fail to thoroughly execute some of these steps. Table 15-3 lists some common reasons why transformations fail. This list, which parallels the 10 steps in Table 15-1, points out what you want to avoid as you transform your organization around cells.

THE ROLE OF PROJECT MANAGEMENT IN CELL IMPLEMENTATIONS

Project management is a set of processes, tools, and techniques used to plan, schedule, and control project activities. Implementing cells fits the classic definition of a

Table 15-3. Why cell transformation efforts fail

Change Management Error	Applied to Cell Implementation Projects
1. Not linking cells to strategic objectives.	• *Failure to understand the strategic importance of cells:* Not linking cells with strategic objectives suggests that cells are "just something we are doing." Cells may be designed to perform well with respect to some measures, but not the ones that matter to overall business performance. Individuals involved don't really understand the purpose or importance. Cell implementation takes a back seat to more pressing projects.
2. Not creating a powerful guiding coalition.	• *An under-powered or under-represented steering committee:* Steering committee does not include managers from key functional areas or representatives lack power to remove barriers. • *No steering committee:* Grassroots project teams may be unable to remove barriers.
3. Lacking a vision.	• *Cells are not part of a compelling vision for the future:* The cell project is not driven by the organization's vision of how it will compete in the future. In such cases there will be little interest in the effort.
4. Under-communicating the vision and urgency by a factor of 10.	• *Failure to communicate the cell vision early and often:* The steering committee/ project team holds a single meeting in which the vision is shared, or holds meetings only after the cells have been designed. This is too little and/or too late. • *No project communication plan:* Project teams work in isolation. Key stakeholders are not informed every step of the way. People feel that the cell "was done to them." • *Supporting the cell vision in words alone:* Management talks about the power of cells, while reallocating resources away from the cell implementation project. The organization knows that cells are not important. • *Failure to communicate a sense of urgency:* Individuals at the top realize the strategic importance of cells, but do a poor job communicating this to the rest of the organization.
5. Lack of political sponsorship.	• *Only "pockets of enlightenment" are committed to the cells:* Only a small cadre of people sees the cell effort as important. They are unsuccessful at getting support from those who do not share this view.
6. Lack of planning.	• *Implementation efforts take too long:* The project team or leader functions poorly and shows lack of project management skills. Implementation efforts drag on without producing tangible results. The organization loses interest.
7. Not removing obstacles.	• *Sacred cows remain:* Narrow job descriptions, individually based compensation systems, inflexible information systems, and other sacred cows are barriers to cell implementation. So are resisting managers and supervisors. Cells do not reach their full potential.
8. No short term wins.	• *Poorly planned or executed pilot operations:* An unsuccessful pilot cell may eliminate any possibility of further experimentation. • *Implementation efforts that take too long without producing short term wins:* Poor planning and inadequate support may be the root causes of the lack of short-term improvements.
9. Not anchoring the changes in the culture of the organization.	• *Changes have not taken roots:* Cells are vulnerable when they have not become institutionalized and part of the culture—that is, they are not yet "the way we do things around here." This happens when the organization promotes people who have not supported the cells or brings in new managers who are not cell advocates. It also happens when cells are not successful because required infrastructure has not been adapted to the cells.
10. Declaring victory too soon.	• *Ignoring the need for continual improvement:* The organization believes that getting the cell up and running is enough. It does not look for better ways of operating— ways that may only become apparent once the physical cell has been created and is operating. Needed infrastructure changes are not implemented, making achieving targets impossible.

project: it is a one-time or infrequently occurring activity involving limited time, limited resources, and a set of performance objectives. In addition, projects generally involve interactions among individuals and teams representing a variety of disciplines. This is certainly the case with cell implementations, where many different groups and functions have input and a role to play.

Regardless of the scope of the cell implementation, the discipline of formal project management can help teams work smarter. Managing activities instead of just "letting things happen" can lead to a more successful implementation. Used well, project management helps avoid the frustrations of cost overruns, unmet deadlines, and unrealized expectations.[23]

Change management and project management are related, overlapping processes. While change management focuses more on feelings and emotions that control behavior, project management deals with more mundane tools and techniques that can improve the quality of the planning process and assist in keeping project teams on track against the goals. Thus, both change and project management are critical elements of successful cell implementations.

The Cell Planning and Implementation Process in Review

We take as our point of departure an organization's formal commitment to evaluate the plant and its products for possible restructuring. Thus, referring to the planning process model presented in Chapter 4 (see Figure 4-1), we begin with Step 6—factory planning. At this point, the vision and goals for the new manufacturing organization exist, a decision has been made to undertake a thorough analysis, and the scope of the design and analysis project has been established (e.g., the entire plant and its products, or some subset). At this juncture the steering committee appoints a project team (or teams) to carry out the analysis and design work, and formal project management begins.

Keep in mind that a progression through the steps in Figure 4-1 may involve a number of small cell projects and associated teams. For example, factory planning, as described in Chapter 5, seeks to (1) identify opportunities for restructuring the work organization into cells, (2) design a new factory layout, and (3) modify the firm's management systems to support cells. Project teams will undertake these analyses and make a recommendation about how best to proceed to the next phase—cell level planning.

If the result is a decision to continue the cell project, you will move to Step 7, initial cell level planning. Here you want to reorganize your "factory teams" (the groups that undertook factory planning analysis) into "cell-based teams," each responsible for developing and implementing a cell. It makes sense at this point to increase operator participation on the design teams, given that detailed knowledge of parts and processes will be important at this stage. In parallel to these technical cell design teams, you want more managerially- and support group-weighted teams looking at existing infrastructure systems and assessing the need for change. Together, these teams will plan and conduct just enough analysis to estimate the detailed costs and benefits of cells.

Finally, detailed cell planning and implementation (Steps 10 and 11 in Figure 4-1), which follows if the rough cost/benefit picture from initial cell planning looks favorable, represents a third layer of the cell project. At this point, you are making the ultimate selection of products, equipment, and people, as well as laying the groundwork for implementation. The teams that did the initial cell planning will continue with this detailed cell design work. However, in terms of composition, you may want to opt for even greater involvement of those who will actually be working in the cell. Thus, at this point, you may add more operators to the project teams.

Each of these cell "projects" will be more successful if it is well planned and executed; that is, if the tools and techniques of project management are brought to bear on the effort. In the discussion that follows, we will talk generally about the "cell project"—the overall effort to design and implement cells—but we want you to understand that different sub-projects with focused goals and varied membership may be involved.

We have organized our discussion on project management around the four major phases of a typical project (see Table 15-4).[24]

Table 15-4. Phases in the cell project

Phase 1: Define and organize the project
Phase 2: Plan the project
Phase 3: Track and manage the project
Phase 4: Close out the project

Phase 1: Define and Organize the Project

To begin a project, you must establish a project organization. This entails selecting the project leader, selecting the project teams, and preparing the teams to work together productively toward an agreed-upon set of project goals. Typically, the steering committee initiates a project, so we will begin by examining its role.

Role of the steering committee

The steering committee is a group of high-level managers, several of whom may have participated in the strategic analysis of the manufacturing organization and made the decision to proceed with the project (Steps 1-5 in Figure 4-1). As mentioned earlier, the steering committee (or steering team) represents strategic thinking, a company-wide integrated perspective, managerial wisdom, and managerial authority. Typically, it is composed of 4 to 10 managers from various areas within the firm. It can include external consultants as well.

At the outset of the project, the steering committee provides vital input by providing teams with "marching orders," laying out as clearly as possible what the team is to accomplish, by when, and with what resources. Thus, the steering committee is responsible for providing the initial project objectives as well as a statement of scope (e.g., whole factory analysis or a more narrow scope). As the project work unfolds, the actions of the steering committee let the project teams, and the organization as a whole, know that the cell implementation effort has management's support. The steering committee (and upper management in general) can demonstrate support in several concrete ways:

- Meet with the project team at the outset of the project. Participate in a segment of the kick-off meeting.

- Provide input to the team's communication plan. In particular, let the team know how to best keep the steering committee informed. Also advise the team on what, how, and when to communicate to others in the organization.

- Meet with the team at significant milestones, and at times when the team requests it. Ask for progress updates. Intervene to help resolve problems when requested and when necessary.

- Provide needed resources in the form of qualified people to work on the project, a strong project leader, adequate time to plan and execute the project, and adequate funding to translate plans into action.

- Serve as an advocate for the project with the rest of the organization. Remain well informed about project status, and discuss the project both formally and informally.

- Participate in any organization-wide events related to the project (e.g., celebrations of significant milestones). Be a visible supporter of the outcomes.

- Reward the team for its work and accomplishments.

One of the steering committee's most important decisions—on which the success or failure of the project may depend—is the selection of the project manager. When a single team undertakes the project, the project manager is typically also the team leader. However, in instances where multiple teams are working in parallel (as was the case with the ATC design), a project manager may oversee the efforts of all these teams, each of which has its own team leader. The project manager or the team leaders report to the steering committee. Alternatively, they are made members of the steering committee itself.

The project manager

Selecting the leader for the cell project is a critical issue. The project manager should have both technical and personal credibility. From a change management perspective, you want a well-respected individual who will be a strong and credible advocate (champion) for the new cell system. From a technical perspective, you want someone who can manage and integrate all the details of planning, scheduling, assessing risk, allocating resources, and revising plans, as well as someone with a solid understanding of the technical work processes. The project manager also needs to be an effective and persuasive communicator. Table 15-5 summarizes personal characteristics often associated with a good project manager, while Table 15-6 identifies the responsibilities of this position.

At ATC, the manager who launched the effort also served as the project manager for the high-level design and analysis work (factory planning). One of his direct reports subsequently became the transition manager—the project manager for the ensuing detailed design work and the subsequent implementation (Steps 7 through 13 in Figure 4-1). The transition manager was in charge of one of several ATC production sections and had a long, positive work history with the department. He was respected and liked by both peers and subordinates. He was generally regarded as an outstanding communicator, had successfully led several other large-scale projects, and had a reputation for paying attention to details. He also had been involved with

Table 15-5. Characteristics of a good project (and change) managers

• Enthusiastic and passionate	• Stubborn
• Creative	• Lobbyist
• Big-picture person (visionary)	• Coalition/relationship builder (understands political reality)
• Catalyst for change	
• Rational (organized, fact finder, administrator)	• Challenger
• Realistic (understands that not everybody will join)	• Delegator (not a micro-manager)
• Trustworthy	• Ownership creator (develops sense of responsibility in others)
• Flexible	• Risk taker (initiator)
• Strong personality	• Role model (walks the talk)
• Communicator	• Competitive (action-oriented)
• Listener (collects ideas; tries to understand how others feel)	• Doer (problem-solver)
	• Durable (stamina to the end)
• Confidence builder (inspires others)	

Table 15-6. Responsibilities of a cell project team leader

- Lead the process of developing or refining the project objective statement, defining project deliverables, and creating the project plan
- Help the team establish procedures and processes for working together
- Provide the structure and facilitation for productive team sessions
- Keep resources focused on developing and executing the plan—keep the team from getting sidetracked or going down "rat holes"
- Integrate individual and team efforts into a cohesive whole
- Resolve conflicts and obtain needed resources
- Report status to various groups
- Contribute technical and process expertise to the team

the cell implementation planning effort since the outset (even during its early, informal planning stage), and had served as team leader for one of the analysis teams. In short, he had considerable technical and personal credibility and was an excellent choice for cell project manager. In this role he coordinated the efforts of the cell teams, each charged with the design of their cell, and the work of various councils, each focused on a set of infrastructure issues.

The project team

The project teams are the "doers." They perform the actual investigative work, collect and analyze data, identify alternative solutions, evaluate the solutions, present their findings to the steering committee, and, in most cases, make detailed plans for design and implementation of the recommended changes.

Getting the right group of people together to work on the project is critical. This may be the most important element of a successful manufacturing cell program.[25] Consider the skills required to plan and execute the project, the personalities and attitudes of potential team members, and the areas or departments that need to be involved for reasons of content/technical expertise, communication, or company politics (see Step 5 in Table 15-1). It is critical that key areas affected by the change have a voice on the project team. Areas that are left out may feel that "the change was done to them." Implementation problems frequently occur when those who did not participate resist, overtly or covertly, the new cell system. The team members' levels in the organizational hierarchy are also important. It sends a strong message to the rest of the organization about the magnitude of the effort: this project is so important that we have assigned some of our best, most knowledgeable people to work on it.

Cell project teams tend to be engineering- and supervisor-heavy, especially at the outset. Other groups often represented in the early design and analysis efforts (i.e., in factory planning) include manufacturing management, operators, production planning and control, and maintenance. This makes sense given that many of the early decisions focus on core work processes. Later, as the focus shifts to detailed cell planning, it is common to add more shop floor representation, especially operators, to the team. Interestingly, some companies—about 25 percent, in one recent survey of cell users—elect not to involve operators in the design process.[26] However, there is also evidence to suggest that even these companies create opportunities for greater operator participation in subsequent cell projects.

At the point where the teams begin to examine infrastructure support for planned cells, other groups (quality control, accounting, human resources) may become more involved. For example, a plant manager at one air conditioning plant that converted to cells assembled a team of engineers and shop floor supervisors to translate a focused factory strategy into a high-level design for the plant. After they completed their analysis it was necessary to add representatives from production control, materials, and other areas to the team. In other cases (as happened at ATC) separate teams will look at infrastructure issues in parallel with technical cell design teams. Representatives for suppliers, customers, and equipment vendors can be tied to the project teams or actually serve as members.

As we have suggested already, the effort to design and implement cells may actually involve multiple teams. As described earlier, the Assembly and Test Center used a multi-team architecture for both factory planning and detailed cell design and implementation (see Appendix Table I-1). By creating several small teams, you can (1) focus groups of key individuals on particular aspects of the conversion, and (2) involve more people without creating a team that is too large to be productive. However, you'll need to coordinate efforts between teams. You may also consider having "core" and "extended" team members; the former are permanent members, the latter are available to the team on a "consulting" basis when the issues at hand directly involve their area of expertise.[27]

Launching the team

A team can be defined as "a small number of people with complementary skills who are committed to a common purpose, performance goals, and approach for which they hold themselves mutually accountable."[28] Labeling a group of people a project team does not guarantee that they will behave as such. Even in companies where group work is the norm and individuals have well-developed interpersonal communication and group problem-solving skills, some groundwork is required to develop a well-functioning team. Naturally, in organizations where group work is less common and communication skills are not as finely developed, even more start-up work is necessary. In particular, you may want to provide basic interpersonal skills training as well as sessions aimed specifically at team building (see Chapter 13 and the agendas in Appendix H).

You must create the right conditions early on for the cell project team to function effectively. We recommend that you start with a kick-off meeting, preferably off-site. Having the session outside the normal work environment demonstrates management's commitment to the effort ("this project is so important that we will send you away from your regular job to get started"). It also allows the team members to focus fully on the project and get to know their fellow team members without distraction. This first meeting should accomplish several objectives:

- Expose the team to the vision and goals for the new work organization that have been developed by the steering committee.
- Give team members an opportunity to discuss/refine these goals and develop a project objective statement.
- Identify and define key project deliverables.
- Begin to build this group of people into an effective team. While simply spending time together aids in team formation, specific sessions focused explicitly on team building can be immensely helpful.[29]

Table 15-7 offers an agenda for a 1.5- to 2-day project kick-off meeting. The larger the project and the team, the more time you need for the kick-off meeting and the more attention you must pay to formal team processes. If you are leading a small team that is focused on a narrow project (e.g., a pilot cell for relatively simple products using existing equipment that is easily reconfigured), you can go with a shorter project kick-off and less formal team processes.

Many of the project launch activities in Table 15-7 involve establishing the parameters for the project and determining how the team will operate. We discuss some of these issues next.

Determining team ground rules. Establishing good work processes and ground rules can help avoid two of the most common complaints about project teams: far too many meetings (because each meeting accomplishes little) and too much difficulty making decisions (because there is no agreed-upon process for working together and making decisions).[30] Table 15-8 provides ground rules for a cell project team.[31]

Defining the cell project objectives. Defining the goals and objectives for the cell project is perhaps the single most important element of the project plan. Generally speaking, goals and objectives should state what is to be done, by when, and with what resources. The more specific, realistic, and measurable the goals and objectives, the smoother the cell planning and implementation process. Cell projects run into trouble when the project requirements are not clearly stated and agreed upon by the involved teams.

Table 15-7. Kick-off meeting agenda for cell project teams

What (Who)	Time (minutes)	Purpose/Deliverable
Review objectives, deliverables, and agenda (team leader)	10	• Agreed-upon plan for the retreat and the desired outcomes.
Introductions (team and leader)	30	• Team members to become familiar with other team members, the areas they represent, and their aspirations for the project.
Steering committee's charge to the team (steering committee or representative)	60	• A clear understanding of what the steering committee wants the project to accomplish and its importance. • Answers to team member questions about the charter.
Team ground rule development (team and leader)	30	• A set of agreements about (1) meeting logistics/preparation, (2) decision-making and participation, and (3) attitude.
Developing the project objective statement (team and leader)	45	• The team's restatement of the steering committee's charge to the team in around 25 words.
Determining success criteria (team and leader)	30	• A set of criteria that will define a successful project…"our team will have been successful if…"
Identifying major deliverables and conducting "Is/Is Not" analysis (team and leader)	60 to 120	• Clear statement of each project deliverable—what will and will not be included. • A set of boundaries for the project—what the project is and what it is not.
Developing the rough-cut plan (team and leader; note: may be delayed till subsequent meeting)	60 to 120	• A brainstormed set of activities the team must undertake to generate the deliverables. • Answers to this question: "What must we do to accomplish this deliverable?"
Developing "issues management process" (leader and team)	30	• Answers to this question: "How will we keep track of problems that cannot be immediately resolved?"
Developing a communications plan (leader and team)	60 to 120	• Answers to these questions: – "How will we communicate between meetings?" – "What is our communications plan for dealing with key stakeholders outside our team? What will we communicate, to whom and via what media? What will be the responsibility of each team member with respect to communicating the team's activities?"
Next steps (leader and team)	30	• Agreements about what individuals on the team will do immediately to make progress on the project. • Plans for the next meeting.
Meeting summary (leader)	15	• Review of accomplishments and action items.

It is useful to have each cell team develop a *project objective statement* (POS).[32] The POS expresses—in as close to 25 words as possible—what the project is to

Table 15–8. Ground rules for effective cell implementation planning teams

---

Meeting logistics and preparation

- We start and end on time.
- We notify the leader in advance if we cannot attend; replacements are (are not) permitted.
- We have expected outcomes, deliverables, and an agenda for each team meeting. This information is distributed to the team in advance of the meeting.
- We begin each meeting by reviewing where we are in the project plan and what we accomplished at the last meeting.
- We have a scribe for each meeting who will be responsible for capturing key points from our discussions on flip charts or white board.
- Each meeting closes with a recap of decisions and statement of action items.
- A designated team member, or the team leader, will prepare and distribute written minutes.
- We come to meetings prepared, and we complete our action items.

Decision-making and participation

- We do not interrupt one another. One person at a time has the floor.
- Everyone participates and no one dominates. We use various meeting processes (such as round robin, brainstorming, etc.) to assure that everyone has a chance to air their views.
- Comments made in the meeting are held in confidence unless explicitly noted as public information.
- We work toward consensus in decision-making, but may rely on other methods for reaching decisions (e.g., majority rules or project/team leader decides) where appropriate.
- We do not attack each other personally.
- We avoid disruptive side conversations—we pay attention during the meeting.

Attitude

- We help each other be right, not wrong.
- We look for ways to make new ideas work, not for reasons that they will *not* work.
- We do not make negative assumptions about one another. If we are in doubt, we check it out.
- We help each other win and take pride in each other's accomplishments.
- We speak positively about the team and each other at every opportunity.
- We act with initiative and courage, as if the success of the team depended on our individual efforts.
- We do the team's work with enthusiasm.
- We respect each other's ideas. We welcome divergent views and constructive debate.
- We don't lose faith or give up.
- We have fun.

---

accomplish, by when, and with what resources. Developing the POS is an excellent exercise for the project launch meeting because it forces the team to clarify project goals and objectives before any work has been done. The steering committee should sign off on the team's POS. Figure 15-1 provides project objective statements for several cell projects.[33]

Some project objective statements include specific goals or targets (i.e., implement a cell that will reduce lead time by 50 percent). We think this is a good idea as long as the targets are based on data. Choosing a number "out of thin air" may either fall short of what is possible or be so aggressive that the team can't possibly achieve it.

Definition:

An effective project objective statement for a cell project meets these criteria:
- Describes the essence of what the project is to accomplish, by when, and with what resources
- Consists of around 25 words
- Is clear, concise, and easy to understand

Examples:

"By June 2002, create a cell from existing machining equipment. Spend less than $3,000. By December 2002, the cell should reduce lead time and cost by 50% while maintaining quality." (30 words)

"Evaluate the feasibility, costs, and benefits of cells in last-through-pack by December 2002, at a cost not exceeding $2,500." (19 words)

"By June 2002, complete high-level design of a high-performance workplace that can compete on delivery, cost, and quality. Spend no more than $5,000." (23 words)

Figure 15-1. Sample project objective statements

Identifying major deliverables and conducting "Is/Is Not" analysis. The cell project team should also establish and define major project deliverables.[34] For a cell project focusing on cell level planning (e.g., Steps 7 through 13 in Figure 4-1), major deliverables might include: (1) a report to management on fit and costs/benefits at the cell level, (2) a detailed implementation plan and schedule, (3) detailed layout plans for each cell, and (4) a project close-out report (a summary of the project and what was accomplished; discussed later in the chapter). The team should clearly define each deliverable in terms of what it does and does not include. The *Is/Is Not* process is particularly helpful here.[35] The team lists what is included in each deliverable (the "Is" list), as well as what the deliverable will not include (the "Is Not" list). An example of an Is/Is Not analysis for a report to management on fit and costs/benefits at the cell level is shown in Table 15-9.

Table 15-9. Sample Is/Is Not analysis

Report to Management on Fit and Costs/Benefits at the Cell Level	
Is	**Is Not**
• A written report and an oral presentation to the steering committee • A rough-cut description of possible cells, including major equipment required and staffing levels • A statement of the financial and non-financial costs and benefits based on cell level analysis • The team's recommendation regarding where to launch a pilot cell • A status report detailing the analysis the team has conducted so far	• A detailed analysis of layouts • Detailed job descriptions • A detailed budget • A set of recommendations about infrastructure changes

The benefit of the Is/Is Not process is that it forces the team to develop a shared understanding of the work involved in each major deliverable. This helps with detailed planning and assures that the team is working toward the same objectives. The Is/Is Not analysis should be shared with the steering committee to verify that the team and higher management have consistent views of project deliverables.

Developing an "issues management process." Among its initial activities, the team should determine how to handle issues. These are problems in any phase of the project that cannot be immediately resolved. We recommend maintaining a "parking lot" of such problems, more formally referred to as an "issues log."[36] This is a formal way of keeping track of issues and their resolution (see Figure 15-2). The log captures when each issue was identified, who identified it, a brief description and the expected impact, the owner (the person responsible for assuring that the issue is resolved), the due date (when the issue needs to be resolved), and the issue's status or resolution. To avoid getting bogged down in too many issues, the project team should agree on what constitutes a legitimate issue. Ideally the issues log should be posted, and the team should review and update it at each meeting. This assures that problems do not fall through the cracks.

Partial issues log as of March 25

Issue No.	Date Logged	Description and Impact	Owner	Due Date	Status or Resolution
11	March 17	Operators are not completing the tracking sheets we developed to log product flow and track lead time. We need this information for our analysis.	Mark	March 22	Resolved— Mark and team have redesigned form; operators are now using it.
12	March 25	Analysis of assembly activities in the 851 area delayed by a week (due date: April 10 in our original plan). The team needs training on analysis methods, and the key trainer is not available till April 10. We will analyze work during the next week and have an off-site scheduled for April 17 to pull everything together. If the work is not complete by April 25 it could delay our Design Week plans.	Anchada	April 25	Pending
13	March 25	Test technicians critical to our analysis work have not attended last two team meetings due to production crises. We are behind by a week in our analysis.	Bogdan and project leader to talk with test technicians and their manager.	March 26	Pending

Figure 15-2. Example of an issues log

Developing a communications plan. Each project team also needs to establish a communications plan. In the words of one plant manager reflecting on his experiences with cell implementation, "you just can't communicate too much." At the outset of the project the team should determine:

- To whom they will communicate project status, and the information they will share.
- The information channels to be used.
- The form and the frequency of communications.
- Who on the team will be responsible for developing and distributing any formal and informal information.
- The role that each team member will play in informal communications about the project.
- How the team should collect feedback from various parties, and how this feedback will be used in further communications efforts.

We are not suggesting that the teams are alone in their efforts to communicate about the project. The steering committee must play a leadership role in promoting the project to various constituencies (see Step 4 in Table 15-1). To do this effectively, it needs frequent status updates from the project teams. The steering committee also should have its own communications plan, conduct a stakeholder analysis (see below), and review and sanction the project team's communication plans. For example, the Core Design Group, ATC's steering committee, had a major communications responsibility. However, each of the individual analysis teams also had a communications plan that detailed how they would communicate with one another, with the areas they represented, and with the steering committee.

One useful strategy for determining appropriate communications is a *stakeholder analysis* (see Figure 15-3).[37] A stakeholder is anyone with a vested interest in the project or its outcomes, who will be affected by the project, or whose support is required in order for the project to achieve its goals. Using this process, the team or steering committee identifies key stakeholders, where they stand in terms of support of the project, and where they need to be for the project to be a success. The output from this process drives the communications plan. The ATC Core Design Group, for example, relied on stakeholder analysis to help plan and execute communication activities throughout the project and found it very effective: it provided a structured process for thinking through communication needs and developing a plan for addressing them.

Phase 2: Plan the Project

As described in Chapter 4 (Figure 4-1), the total plan for a cell conversion covers Steps 6 through 11 and Step 13. (Step 12—Improvement and Evolution of Cells—does not typically involve the project team, but rather is an ongoing and critical activity for cell operators and their management team.) However, recall that within this sequence of steps, there may be several sub-projects; notably, a factory planning

1. Identify stakeholders in the cell implementation. These may be key individuals (e.g., the manager of production planning) or groups of people (e.g., the maintenance department) who can have a real impact on the success of the cell implementation.

2. Identify how you think they feel about the cell implementation. Mark this on the chart below with an "A."

3. Identify the level of support you need from them to assure a smooth and successful cell implementation. Mark this position on the chart below with a "B."

4. As a team, discuss what issues, concerns, or "blocks" you think the individual or group may have with the proposed cell implementation. Examples might include:
   - Cells represent extra work for their area because they will have to support both cells and more traditional areas.
   - They have never received any formal training about cells and are therefore relatively uninformed about what cells are and why you are pursuing them here.
   - They are concerned that their area will lose power—some of the tasks they have done in the past the cells propose to undertake.

5. Discuss what kinds of communication/intervention would help address the issues, blocks, and concerns of each key stakeholder.

6. Develop a communication plan based on the ideas you generated.

Note: this analysis is helpful at various stages of implementation planning.

Name	Range of Support					Issues	Ideas
	Strongly Against	Mildly Against	Neutral	Mildly Supportive	Strongly Supportive		
Mike, Stockroom Manager, and his group		A			B	Concerned that his people will have to support yet another way of delivering material to manufacturing.	Team leader to meet with Mike one-on-one and describe plans; also seek ideas for reducing extra work for stockroom personnel.
						Stockroom people have only heard through the grapevine of the cell effort. There are many misconceptions.	Cell team to make follow-up presentation to entire stockroom group.

Figure 15–3. Stakeholder analysis process

and justification effort, initial cell planning and cost/benefit analysis, and detailed cell planning and implementation.

Specifically, cell level planning takes place at both Steps 7 and 10. Initially, the team will develop a plan for accomplishing Steps 7 and 8 and for preparing to present their findings to the steering committee in Step 9. However, because the project may yet be scrapped, Steps 10 through 13 should be planned, at this point, only at a relatively high level. You need to know enough about these phases to estimate their aggregate time and cost for the cost/benefit picture, but it makes sense to wait for approval in Step 9 before developing more detailed plans for these later deliverables.

There is another reason for delaying the detailed planning of later steps in the process. If the project receives the go-ahead, team composition may change. In particular, you may add more operators and supervisors to the team and eliminate other team members who no longer have a major stake in the project. For example, if the decision is made to pursue cells only in assembly, test technicians who had been involved may step off the team. One of the principles of good planning is that those doing the work should be involved in planning the work, so the team that will carry out certain steps should plan the work for this part of the project. The resulting plan will be more accurate, and the team will feel more ownership for it.

Work breakdown structure and time estimates

The *work breakdown structure* (WBS) is a commonly used project planning tool. In creating a WBS the team identifies and classifies, in a hierarchical structure, all the activities necessary for a project's completion. Figure 15-4 provides part of the WBS from a hypothetical cell project for the task of "understand the current situation," an early step in factory planning. The more detailed the work breakdown structure, the less likely it is that the team will overlook critical activities.

- **TASK:** Understand the current situation.
  - **Sub–task:** Determine which data analyses the team will undertake.
    - *Activity:* Identify key questions that data analysis should answer about our current situation.
    - *Activity:* Review data analysis alternatives (family grouping analysis, product volume analysis, performance analysis, resource and technology analysis—both equipment and people dimensions, capacity–load and bottleneck analysis, space analysis, material–flow analysis, process flow analysis/functional flow charting), including their purpose and the types of output information they provide.
    - *Activity:* Select data analysis options that will provide answers to key questions.

  - **Sub–task:** Prepare for data collection. *For each of the selected analyses:*
    - *Activity:* Determine if the team needs training on the analysis method and, if so, arrange for training.
    - *Activity:* Training.
    - *Activity:* Determine what data are needed as input to the analysis (e.g., for functional flow charting, sequence of steps performed for each part/product family and which department/area performs them).
    - *Activity:* Determine which needed data, if any, are available from existing plant sources/databases (e.g., product routing sheets for functional flow charting). Determine what new data the team will need to collect.
    - *Activity:* Develop data collection plans for new data (how, when, and by whom the data will be collected). Develop draft data collection forms.
    - *Activity:* Consult with areas from where data will be collected to obtain cooperation and assistance.
    - *Activity:* Revise data collection plans based on input from areas.

Figure 15–4. Partial work breakdown structure for step 6 (factory planning)

One useful approach to developing the WBS for a cell implementation is to have the team brainstorm all tasks, sub-tasks, and individual activities needed to accomplish the project goal. Recording each idea on a note and placing the notes on a wall can help stimulate discussion about what must be accomplished. Where appropriate, the team can divide major activities into sub-activities (or vice versa). This can help the team develop a thorough understanding of the project. Once the team has identified the activities, and the manpower that can be devoted to them, it should make a rough estimate of the time required for each. In addition, one or more team members should be assigned responsibility for assuring that each activity is completed.

Risk analysis

Another critical aspect of planning for cell implementation is *risk analysis*. This frequently overlooked step involves reviewing a plan and anticipating problems. What might go wrong? What would we do if this happened? What can we do to help assure that events which will throw us off course do not happen (preventive actions), or to prepare us to recover from them if they do (contingency plans)? By answering these questions, the team can anticipate potential problems and decide how to deal with or avoid them.

For example, early in the planning process, the Core Design Group of ATC determined that there was significant risk that operators might resist the new organization design. It therefore added direct labor employees to each analysis team. In addition, the Core Design Group expanded its original communication plan and agreed to communicate progress more widely and more frequently. As a result, it would circulate meeting minutes, place a project update on the agenda for each section meeting, and make each analysis team member responsible for discussing the design informally within their home area. Analysis team members also were asked to report concerns back to the Core Design Group. The analysis teams and Core Design Group also scheduled formal feedback sessions with various work groups for gathering input on the design as it developed.

Creating the project schedule

To develop a schedule you need to know the precedence relationships among activities. The "early–middle–late method" helps teams determine precedence requirements of cell project activities. The team, as a group, sorts each activity (already recorded on notes) into three categories: (1) those that must be done *early* in the project, (2) those that will happen somewhere in the *middle* and, (3) those that will need to take place *late*. Within each grouping the team makes further refinements using the same early-middle-late process. At the conclusion, the team knows the general precedence and parallel relationships of the various activities.

Armed with activities, their precedence relations, and time estimates, the team can create the project schedule. Most teams find it helpful to create a Gantt chart that shows the projected start and end points for each activity, and also indicates actual project status. Figure 15-5 shows an example based on the partial WBS presented in Figure 15-4. Posting the Gantt chart provides a visual way of communicating project plans and progress to all interested parties.

In addition, the team may want to designate certain activities in the schedule as "project milestones." These represent major project steps whose completion are cause for celebration or whose delays are cause for concern.

Sub-tasks and activities	1	2	3	4	5	6	7
Sub-task: *Determine which data analyses the team will undertake:*					▼		
Identify key questions that data analysis should answer about our current situation.	X						
Review data analysis alternatives.	X						
Select data analysis options that will provide answers to key questions.	X						
Sub-task: *Prepare for data collection* (for each selected analysis, *e.g.,* for functional flow charting):							
Determine if team needs training on the analysis method and, if so, arrange for training.	X						
Training.		X					
Determine what data are needed as input to the analysis (e.g., for functional flow charting need to know the steps performed for each part/product family and where in the plant each successive step is performed).			X				
Determine which of the needed data, if any, are available from existing plant sources/databases (e.g., product routing sheets for functional flow charting). Determine what new data the team will need to collect.				X			
Develop data collection plans for new data (how, when, and by whom the data will be collected). Develop draft data collection forms.					N		
Consult with areas from which data will be collected to obtain their cooperation and assistance.						N	
Finalize data collection plans and forms based on input from areas.						N	N

Current time appears above week 5. *Week* spans columns 1–7.

Bold X activities have been completed. **Bold N** activities are planned, but not yet completed. Any **bold N** activities in weeks 1 through 5 are behind schedule.

Figure 15-5. Partial Gantt chart for activities in Figure 15-4

Project plan sign off

The team should present its plan for cell implementation to the steering committee for approval. The team and the steering committee should then discuss and agree to the plan. Disagreements regarding schedule or cost need to be ironed out at this stage.

Phase 3: Track and Manage the Project

Once the cell implementation project plan has been approved, the real work of executing project activities begins. This means working through Steps 6 through 13 in our model (see Figure 4-1), and actually doing the design and analysis work we have described throughout the book. At this point, the job of the project team (in addition to executing task activities) is to keep the project on track. This means assessing activity status, dealing with issues (problems that cannot be resolved immediately), and managing risks.

Assessing status, dealing with issues, and managing risks

To assess *status*, the team needs to know if activities scheduled to start or finish in a period have actually done so. For example, the Gantt chart in Figure 15-5 shows that while developing data collection plans and draft data collection forms was scheduled for completion by the end of week five, this activity remains unfinished at the outset of week six. The team needs to find out why this activity has been delayed and what can be done to get it started and/or completed.

Dealing with *issues* involves identifying and logging any new issues, as well as reviewing the status of all open issues. Issues might include delays in equipment delivery, problems created by monument processes, or unanticipated training needs. Analysis teams that worked as part of the ATC redesign, for example, discovered that in order to do their work they needed training on cell principles as well as on tools for workflow analysis. Their team leaders, in concert with the project manager, arranged for this training from an in-house expert. The issues log introduced earlier (Figure 15-2) is a powerful tool for staying on top of project problems.

The team also needs to keep an eye on *project risks*. As part of the planning process, the team should have identified the risks that might impact the cell project. As the project unfolds, the team should revisit them. In the ATC redesign, the Core Design Group regularly gauged operator reactions to the new work organization, which the team had identified as a risk and had taken preventive actions to forestall (adding operators to the team and developing an organization-wide communication plan). In addition to revisiting known risks, the team will need to address unanticipated events and their probable effect on the project. For example, in the middle of the detailed cell design for ATC, corporate headquarters announced a major reorganization in which ATC was to move (physically and organizationally) to a nearby sister division. This unexpected "shake-up" meant that there now was a risk that the ongoing project would be scrapped.

Dealing with schedule delays, issues, and risks often requires changing the plan and taking adaptive actions. At ATC the risk of project cancellation prompted the steering committee to initiate extensive communication with the manufacturing leadership of the division ATC would join. This ensured that the planning teams could be kept informed of issues they needed to resolve in order for ATC to "fit" in its new home. As a result, detailed cell planning could continue under less uncertainty. Reorienting activities, delaying activities, changing the project scope (e.g., create fewer cells), or adding resources are common ways project teams adapt to changing conditions.

It is critical that the project teams monitor and adapt to progress, problems, and risks. If possible, create a dedicated "war room" that serves as the hub of cell project activities. This provides a central meeting place for everyone involved in the effort and therefore serves as a venue for formal and informal discussions. To assist with this, project plans and other visuals useful for controlling the project should be on display.

Phase 4: Close Out the Project

A project is not finished until you have completed all activities, reviewed the planning and implementation process, and determined any lessons learned.[38] As part of the close-out, the cell teams should evaluate both the success of the cell implementation and the effectiveness of the process that was used to plan and orchestrate it (see Step 13 in Figure 4-1). To measure success, teams should compare actual performance of the cells to the goals (e.g., actual cell lead time compared to a target lead time). Understanding where and why a cell is under-performing will help guide ongoing improvement efforts (as discussed in Chapter 4, this type of evaluation should not be done too early after "going live" with the cell). The team should also evaluate the project in terms of cost and schedule adherence. Was the project completed on time? What factors explain any delays? Was the project completed with the budgeted resources, or were additional expenses incurred? If so, why?

In evaluating the success of the project process, the perspectives of key stakeholder groups should be considered. How satisfied are they with the results? How satisfied are they with the way the cell project unfolded? Did they feel adequately informed? What problems do they feel could have been avoided through better planning? What could the teams have done differently that would have eased implementation? Questions like these can provide useful information for future cell implementation projects. They also can uncover unresolved issues that need to be addressed in order for the cells now in place to achieve their full potential. It is possible your evaluation will lead you to return to a prior step in the cell planning process (see Figure 4-1).

The project retrospective

With respect to project evaluation, the team may find it productive to conduct an off-site *project retrospective* that focuses on lessons learned from the effort. Table 15-10 identifies key questions to address at such a session.

The team's assessment of the project process and outcomes, as well as a summary of the project itself, should be documented in a *project close-out report*. This documentation is a powerful source of organizational learning and can be immensely helpful to subsequent design and analysis projects. You can be certain that this will not be the last time your organization needs to take a careful look at its manufacturing organization. Don't miss the opportunity to capture both what was done and what was learned.

A final and very important close-out activity is to acknowledge the work that team members have done. Celebrating their achievements and recognizing their work reinforces the new work organization.

Table 15-11 lists the four phases of a cell implementation project, and summarizes key activities and helpful tools and techniques.

Table 15-10. Questions to address at a cell project retrospective

Questions about team effectiveness	• What did we do well as a team in planning and executing this project? • What did we *not* do well as a team in planning and executing this project?
Questions about communication processes	• How well did we communicate amongst ourselves? • How well did we communicate with our key internal stakeholders? • How well did we communicate with key external parties (e.g., vendors) involved in the effort? • What could we have done differently and better?
Questions about the cell design itself	• Did our approach to cell formation work well? What problems did we encounter that a different approach might have avoided? Did we fail to consider any information or factors that proved later to be important? • Was our approach to initial cell layouts effective? What unexpected problems did we encounter? What information or factors did we overlook that we should have considered?
Questions about jobs and people	• Did we staff the cell appropriately? Did we have the right numbers of workers, and did they have the right skill set to best support cell operations? What did we overlook in terms of cell staffing level, skill set, and preparation that we should have considered? • Were supervisors and team leaders prepared for their new roles? Did these new roles support cell operations?
Questions about infrastructure support	• How well are infrastructure systems (maintenance policies, quality procedures, production planning and control, performance measurement, documentation, etc.) supporting the cell? How well did we anticipate needed changes? What modifications would further enhance performance?
Questions about lessons learned	• What are the key lessons learned from this effort? How might we apply these lessons learned to future cell planning projects? To other types of projects? • Who else in the organization needs to know what we learned from this project? How can we best communicate what we have learned?
Questions about project management	• What processes and tools for planning and execution were particularly helpful to us?

Table 15–11. Managing the cell implementation planning project: an overview (*tools/ techniques in italics and parentheses*)

Project Phase	Major Activities (and Tools)

1. Define and organize the project.	• Establish the project organization
	  – Select the project team and project leader
	  – Launch the project (*project off-site*)
	• Define the cell implementation project parameters
	  – Clarify the project objectives (*project objective statement—POS*)
	  – Specify the deliverables (*Is/Is Not analysis*)
	  – Establish processes for handling problems the team cannot solve immediately (*issues log*)
	  – Establish a communications plan (*stakeholder analysis*)

2. Plan the project.	• Establish the work breakdown schedule (*adhesive note brainstorming process*) • Create the project schedule (*early-middle-late adhesive note process; Gantt charts; milestones*) • Obtain steering committee sign off
3. Track and manage the project.	• Do the work described in the project plan • Assess status, deal with issues, and manage risks (*issues log*) • Keep stakeholders informed
4. Close out the project.	• Assess the success of the cell implementation (*performance measurement and stakeholder feedback; project retrospective*) • Assess the effectiveness of the processes used to plan and implement the cells (*stakeholder interviews; project retrospective*) • Celebrate hard work and accomplishments

KEY INSIGHTS

In this chapter we have offered advice on how to plan and execute the transformation to cells, covering various facets of cell implementation planning. We believe that organizations can benefit from applying the discipline of formal project management to cell implementation efforts. However, we also believe that project management skills must be complemented by "softer" change management skills in order for the transformation to cells to be accepted and supported. Here are some important lessons from this chapter:

- *Use the 10-step change management model for managing the transformation to cells.* A focus on change management can help ensure a successful transition.

- *Follow a "fair process" to avoid resistance to change.* The 3 e's—engagement, explanation, and expectation—neatly summarize critical change management principles for avoiding resistance and achieving successful cell implementations.

- *Select a strong project manager.* This individual needs technical and personal credibility, as well as excellent communication skills for working across all levels in the organization.

- *Put together a capable and representative project team.* Select team members who have the technical skills and backgrounds to contribute to the effort. Also make sure the team members represent the areas the cells will impact. Thus, where possible, involve those who will work in, work with, or manage the new system in planning and implementing it.

- *Provide the cell implementation team with the resources and guidance to be successful.* Support the cell implementation with both words and deeds. Talk about the cell effort, support it with your involvement as appropriate, and provide the resources, including time, to make it happen. Teams that do not know what they are to achieve (goals and objectives) or why (the mission) are unlikely to be successful. So are teams that lack resources.

- *Communication is key.* Both the steering committee and the project teams must actively engage in communicating the vision and the urgency for the cell implementation, and update the organization on the status of the project. Use a variety of media, communicate frequently, and be sure communication is two-way. Those receiving the messages should have an opportunity to raise questions and offer input.

- *Apply formal project management techniques to the cell project.* The tools and techniques of project management can contribute to a smoother, more successful implementation effort. Be sure the team leader and the team members are familiar with the discipline of project management.

- *Evaluate the cells and the cell implementation planning process once complete.* Use this information to improve existing cells and to make future cell implementation more successful.

16

Common Problems in the Design, Justification, Implementation, and Operation of Cells

A number of things can go wrong as you design, justify, implement, and operate cells. This chapter looks at the most common problems and suggests how you might avoid or deal with them. In particular, we address these important questions:

- Which are the most common hurdles to successfully designing and justifying, implementing, and operating manufacturing cells?

- What can cell designers and managers do to prevent or overcome these problems?

In a sense, this chapter serves as the capstone to our book. Many of the problems we describe here were introduced in the context of earlier discussions. In short, this chapter underscores the significance of the prescriptions we offered in previous chapters and reinforces the importance of taking a "whole system" view when converting to cells. If you want to avoid the problems we describe, follow the advice we offer herein. These are, mostly, given much deeper coverage in Chapters 1 through 15.

We want to acknowledge up front that it is difficult to clearly separate the design and justification, implementation, and operation phases when we discuss problems that companies may experience. One issue is that many problems are really "design problems" (in the sense that they are a consequence of the cell design), even though they are not detected until implementation or operation. Further, it is difficult to separate implementation and operational problems: problems of the same kind can be detected early (during implementation) or later (during full-scale operation). Despite this, we have elected to adopt a "design/justification–implementation–operation" structure for our discussion.

In the design/justification section, we discuss the issues teams commonly struggle with during the early stages of cell planning, design, and justification. We also consider design choices relating to the core area of cell design: cell processes, layout, and technology. In the implementation section, we deal mainly with issues of managing the cell transformation process: inadequate preparation of employees and (briefly) the potential for resistance to the cell concept. In the operation section, we focus primarily on issues of infrastructure. Although these management systems can (and should) be designed much earlier, project teams often defer this task until later. The problems that arise from not modifying these systems tend to surface during implementation, but become more pronounced during operation. Table 16-1 summarizes the major problems we discuss in this chapter.

Table 16-1. Overview of common problems

Designing and justifying cells:
- Solving the right problem with the right scope
- Selecting initial part families and equipment
- Planning in sufficient detail
- Resolving capacity and work flow issues
- Dealing with monument processes
- Economically justifying the move to cells

Implementing cells:
- Managing the cell implementation project
- Managing the change process and dealing with resistance
- Installing new equipment
- Preparing the workforce for cells

Operating cells:
- Dealing with changing production requirements
- Creating a supportive infrastructure

COMMON CELL DESIGN AND JUSTIFICATION PROBLEMS

In designing and justifying cells, companies may have problems:

- Solving the right problem with the right scope.
- Selecting initial part families and equipment.
- Planning in sufficient detail.
- Resolving capacity and work flow issues.
- Dealing with monument processes.
- Economically justifying the move to cells.

We now discuss each of these in turn.

Solving the Right Problem with the Right Scope: The Issue of Impact

Sometimes the cell design effort is too narrowly focused, and the resulting cells end up having little impact on overall business performance (see discussion of scope in Chapter 4). This is a significant problem. Case Corporation, a Burlington, Iowa backhoe manufacturer, designed cells in the late 1980s to manufacture weldments. These cells performed "wonderfully, with throughput times reduced from weeks to days or even hours."[1] However, there were some 3,000 other required backhoe parts still produced in the functionally arranged part of the shop; these parts, produced outside the cells, had long lead times. Because of this, cells initially improved the production of isolated components, but not overall delivery performance.

The solution was to analyze the remaining parts for their cellular potential. The company implemented an additional cell that could make 80 percent of these parts, and subcontracted the remainder. The result was a leaner, more effective operation. Thus, by extending the scope of the cellular project, the company was able to generate significant benefits.

This example illustrates two important and related points about cell design and issues of scope. First is the importance of looking at the impact cells will have on system performance and, in particular, on the customer. If you intend cells to reduce response time, you need to consider the total manufacturing lead time. Reducing lead time for parts that do not currently constrain your response time will have only local impact. (In project management parlance, you will reduce lead time for parts that are not on the "critical path.") Thus, if reducing response time is one of your objectives for the cell project, you need to identify the critical lead-time parts and evaluate their suitability for cells. It is useful to do this in advance, instead of discovering—as Case did—that the initial cells did not generate the expected improvements.

Second and more broadly, keep in mind that the decision to adopt cells should be part of your overall strategy to increase competitive advantage. "If manufacturing cells are not part of an overall strategy ... they can have a great local success but very little overall impact" commented one manager in a study we did.[2] Similarly, the first cells at Case had great local success, but little overall impact. However, because the company understood the role they wanted cells to play in meeting strategic objectives, it was able to re-scope the project to address this problem. Of course, if you are phasing in a number of cells over time, your early results will not give you the complete performance picture; the full benefits will not be realized until the complete set of cells is up and running.

Selecting Initial Part Families and Equipment

In some cases, identifying and selecting part/product families for cells is straightforward. At one electronics plant, for example, "it was obvious which products belonged together" and what equipment to assign to manufacture each family.[3] Similarly, our recent survey of cell design practices found that "identifying parts/product families for cells was in no case mentioned as a critical problem."[4] There are instances, however, in which part and equipment selection can be a struggle. An engineer in a precision machine shop worked for months trying to find the best part family for an initial cell. The sheer magnitude of the analysis task was overwhelming: there were thousands of candidate parts, and he was working alone sifting through them. At another plant, a team of engineers, machinists, and supervisors visually examined 600 part prints and attempted to sort them into families. According to one of the engineers, "this was a totally random shuffling and arguing process. We could not decide whether to group parts by the function they performed, the processes that were used to produce them, or the product in which they were used. At one point in time, there were actually two people walking around the room arranging parts by products, with two other people walking behind them and rearranging parts by process."

As we pointed out in Chapters 5 and 15, you can avoid a lot of "wheel spinning" for the design team if the vision and direction are made clear up front. Further, management must translate this vision and direction into specific measures of performance that the cell is intended to improve. If design objectives are unclear, the team will have little guidance in determining appropriate cell parts and equipment. Moreover, without clear measures, the team will have a difficult time choosing among alternatives. As we suggested above, in the absence of vision, objectives, and measures, the team is likely to spend a great deal of time engaged in "random shuffling and arguing." Knowing what to accomplish helps to focus cell analysis activities. However, even when the design objectives are clear, companies often struggle with simply getting the data that are relevant to making good decisions about parts and equipment for cells. As we pointed out in Chapter 5, at least 50 percent of the time spent on the project may be devoted to finding data to support the cell formation process. Often, firms don't routinely collect data needed for analysis (e.g., manufacturing lead time), so this task will fall to the design team as well. If relevant data *are* collected, it may still take some manipulation to extract exactly the information you need. This common problem is one factor that contributes to companies chronically underestimating the time required by a cell design effort.

In addition, teams often flounder because they simply do not know how to approach the task. You can help overcome this difficulty by providing those who are performing the analysis with training on how to identify cells and how to use various analysis tools. The guidelines and tools described in Chapters 5, 6, 7, and 17 can be helpful in this regard.

Planning in Sufficient Detail

Companies sometimes fail to plan the cell conversion in adequate detail, overlooking critical details—and, as we all know, "the devil is in the details." At one plant, operators developed detailed layouts of their individual cells. Each group assumed that they should allow for aisle space on the perimeter of their cell. When equipment was rearranged, the area manager realized he had aisles twice as large as necessary, and a lot of wasted space. Planning and coordination among teams cannot be over-emphasized!

Resolving Capacity and Work Flow Issues

Making equipment, staffing, and layout decisions that will minimize load imbalances and ensure a smooth work flow that meets demand is a very common cell design problem. In an early survey, it was one of the two most frequent problems reported by users of cellular manufacturing.[5] More recently, one of our studies asked managers to identify factors that had "great impact on cell performance but which had been given insufficient consideration during cell planning and implementation."[6] Equipment and flow issues (e.g., equipment placement/cell layout, choice of equipment and material-handling system, capacity balancing and product flow) were mentioned frequently as issues to which respondents felt they should have paid more attention. Another of our studies of cell design practices revealed that short move distances within the cell, straight part flows through the cell, and operator considerations (including operator utilization) were three of the four most important cell layout considerations.[7] In the same study, "balanced work flow" was among the most frequently mentioned constraints on overall cell design. Clearly, determining a detailed layout and staffing plan that meets work flow objectives is both problematic and important.

Designing cells that will have a smooth, balanced work flow requires that the design team wrestle with a number of issues. How large should the cell be in terms of people and equipment? Should there be a separate cell for each part family, or should you collapse families into fewer cells based on routing similarity? Is the gain in resource utilization with fewer cells and more resource pooling worth the added complexity of cell flows, the likely increase in setup times, and the potentially longer lead times that are likely to result? Can you justify low utilization of cell equipment? Will you permit non-cell parts to use cell equipment in order to increase utilization and avoid additional equipment purchases? Will you permit cell parts to leave the cell for processing in order to achieve higher utilization and avoid additional equipment purchases? Should equipment be shared between cells? These and similar issues were previously discussed in Chapters 6 and 7.

It is common for design teams to struggle with these questions, in part because answers are difficult to obtain. Conflicting design objectives (i.e., make cells independent *and* minimize equipment investment) place constraints on acceptable solutions and complicate decision-making. In addition, infrastructure decisions (e.g., job design, degree of cross-training, design of job rotation policies) affect flows as well. So there is much to consider, and it gets very confusing, very quickly. Computer modeling often is the best way to evaluate such choices, particularly when the critical performance measures are lead time or inventory. As the following examples illustrate, if you don't get it right at the design stage, you will need to make post-implementation revisions.

Buffer spaces and work flow

At one plant, an initial assembly cell design did not include buffer spaces between successive operations. Units flowed directly from one station to the next. Initial productivity was very low because when problems occurred at a station in the cell— even something as simple as a dropped tool—*starving* (nothing to work on) or *blocking* (no opportunity to pass on completed work because the next station is busy) affected succeeding or preceding stations. The solution was to redesign the cell to include a buffer space between each workstation. After this expensive change, overall productivity improved.[8] Similarly, other plants have reported that determining buffer spaces between machines to handle work in process buildup was a problem they should have resolved in the planning phase.[9] Again, computer modeling in advance of implementation can help you understand the role of buffers on cell performance and permit you to experiment with various potential solutions.

Setup time reduction and work flow

Problems with setup reduction and tooling design also contribute to work flow problems. This was an implementation concern for over 10 percent of the firms responding to one survey.[10] As one manager at a machining plant observed, "we were challenged with the task of reducing setup times so we could ignore them within the cell. This was more difficult than we anticipated." In some cases, companies have actually abandoned cells because they did not achieve sufficient setup reduction. For example, one spring and stamping manufacturer identified families, moved equipment together, and cut batch sizes. However, they neglected to reduce setup times. The result was a clogged shop and reduced output.[11] The company abandoned cells in favor of a traditional functional arrangement. In this case we don't know the extent to which setup reductions could have been achieved had the company pursued them vigorously. What is clear, however, is that without adequate setup reduction, cell performance suffers. (The importance of setup time reduction was discussed in Chapter 7, while Chapter 17 provides tools and a process for tackling this problem.)

Labor issues and work flow

Several respondents to one of our surveys noted that assigning the right number of operators to cells was a critical problem.[12] The direct outcome of inadequately staffed cells is failure to achieve a good physical flow of material through the cells. Further, sometimes cell layouts are inconsistent with how operators need to work in the cell to achieve a smooth work flow. In particular, when job designs call for workers to collaborate, the layout needs to make it possible for operators to see and speak with one another, and to see the status of work at other stations. If operators cannot talk to each other, they will be unable to pass along information about part shortages, tool problems, quality issues, or other work concerns. This will impede the flow of work.

U-shaped cells at one apparel manufacturer initially required that operators work with their backs to each other.[13] With this layout, the cell operators could neither see one another, nor discuss work issues. This made it difficult for them to help one another and balance the work flow. Operators rearranged the equipment so that they were face-to-face with each other and could communicate easily. In another company, operators assembling heart monitoring devices worked on the outside of a four-station U-cell. However, the placement of incoming material on tall shelving units in the center of the cell made it impossible for operators to communicate. Management redesigned the cell layout into a straight line so operators could more easily see the work at several nearby stations and converse with co-workers. The incoming material was located behind them.[14] (Of course, another option here was to keep the U-shape, move material to the outer perimeter of the cell, and retain the relative placement of operators. However, the company felt that a straight line layout would enhance both visibility and communication.)

The layout can serve as a vehicle for preventing situations where social "chatting" distracts people from their work and impedes work flow. One Caribbean apparel plant replaced a cell layout where operators worked side-by-side with one where operators sat behind each other. According to one manager at the plant "the operators made so much noise in the side-by-side layout that output and quality were both affected." Similarly, a manager at a U.S. apparel plant commented to us: "you don't want them to see each other because they will *talk*! The productivity loss far outweighs the ability to communicate easily. They can turn around if it is important."

However, relying on the physical layout to prevent unnecessary communication—as in the examples—must be weighed against the need for the cell to have both visual and oral contact points between employees. This is an issue of both job satisfaction and productivity. Such links are especially urgent in cells that require a high level of employee interdependence. For this reason we feel that managers should be strongly cautioned before making design decisions that will impede the flow of information among operators.

Dealing with Monument Processes

"Monuments" are processes that are difficult to miniaturize, duplicate, or move. They may be expensive, toxic, heavy, or just too large to place in the cell. They therefore complicate the design of an "ideal" cell, where all required processes are closely located within the physical and organizational boundaries of the cell. Because monument processes represent a common problem in cell design (and in cell operation), we will devote quite a bit of space to this topic. Below, we present several typical monument process situations in different manufacturing organizations, as well as some creative solutions for resolving the problem. As you will see, design teams sometimes develop lasting solutions to the monument problem early in the design process. In other instances, initial solutions prove ineffective and must be revisited.

Stamping process: dedication without rearrangement

For an air conditioner manufacturer, stamping was a monument process. The huge stamping presses made parts both for the cellularized and the non-cellularized areas of the plant. The key design question for the project team was, "How can we achieve just-in-time delivery of the right stamped parts, in the right quantities, to the right cells, without incurring unacceptably low machine utilization or moving this equipment, which has deep concrete footings?" The solution was to dedicate two presses to producing the high-volume stamped parts that were common to all products made in the assembly cells. The lower-volume cell parts, unique to each product model, continued to be made in the general stamping area. The company also improved the information flow between the stamping area and the cells. They set up a pull system to convey replenishment needs, and included the manager of the stamping area in the daily cell meetings. In addition, the general purpose stamping area launched an aggressive and highly successful setup time reduction program. This gave it the flexibility to respond more rapidly to demand for cell parts.

Plating process: dedicated plating operator assigned to the cell team

At one plant, plating was the monument process. Due to its toxic nature, technological limitations, and high cost, decentralizing the plating operation to the cell was not considered an option. Consequently, the initial design had parts flow from the cell to plating, then back to the cell. However, batches that left the cell for plating joined a queue of work from other areas. Depending on the length of the queue, the turnaround time from plating varied widely.

Because the company wanted to ensure that cell parts had low, predictable lead times, it changed the organizational structure and made one of the plating operators a full member of the cell team. This individual continued to work in the plating area, but now handled only the cell's components and subassemblies. These came directly to the dedicated plating operator, who took responsibility for moving them through the required processes as quickly as possible. The operator became intimately familiar—through repetition—with these parts. He also had visibility of the future stream of cell parts requiring plating and could schedule the work in advance of its arrival. In addition, he participated in all cell team meetings and reported to the supervisor of the cell. Plating turnaround times for cell parts were shorter and more predictable after this change and, in addition, plating quality improved.[15]

Injection molding: cells come to the monument

At Allsop Inc., a Bellevue, Washington manufacturer of audio cleaning systems, VCR cleaning systems, and accessories for compact disks and computers, injection molding was the monument process.[16] The massive injection molding machines could not be moved easily, nor was there sufficient demand to permanently dedicate any single machine to any product family. The company's solution was to create "roving assembly lines" by putting assembly equipment on wheels. In this way, the molding machines can remain stationary while the assembly lines come to them. At any given time the resulting cell molds, assembles, packages, and readies for shipment a particular product order. When the order is complete, these *phantom cells* (as we called them in Chapter 2) are reconfigured to reflect the next order to be completed.

Curing process: change product/process design

When faced with a monument, you should always consider the possibility of eliminating the need for the process. At a microsurgery device manufacturer, the assembly processes included attaching certain components with epoxy. Partially completed assemblies were then transported to a large centralized oven for curing, and, upon completion, returned to the cell. The company replaced epoxy and cure operations with snap-in components that could be attached in the cell. Thus, by changing the product design, they eliminated the need for the monument process.[17]

Curing process: miniaturize and decentralize to the cell

We have been in a number of electronics plants where the move to cells motivated the decentralization of centralized curing operations. Small, insulated ovens were purchased and placed in each cell. This suggests that some monument processes may be no more than historical artifacts, put in place at a time when a large centralized resource was the only technological and/or economically feasible option. Thus, don't assume you can't decentralize a current monument process and include it in a cell.

Printed circuit board (PCB) loading: outsourcing

As you analyze your operations for their cellular potential, you might decide to eliminate the monument process from in-house production by outsourcing the components (also see Chapter 5). One medical products manufacturer wanted to dedicate certain PCB equipment to the production of families of similar boards.[18] This dedicated equipment would then feed product assembly cells. The idea forced the company to review the boards and the technology required to produce them, and required it to "more carefully analyze the PCB process than ever before." The company discovered that, compared to industry leaders, it was behind technologically with respect to PCB loading processes. Becoming competitive would require a $300 million investment in new equipment. Given this fact, the company opted to outsource PCB loading. Thus, loaded boards became another purchased material input for the cells.

Sheet metal and painting processes: outsourcing

At another plant, a few pieces of sheet metal equipment were considered monuments. After some initial analysis, the design team concluded that sheet metal work would be difficult to place in the product-focused cells: the equipment was big, noisy, dirty, hard to miniaturize, and hard to relocate. While they could have left the sheet metal operations as they were and operated them as a service center to the various cells, further investigation revealed that there were capable suppliers just down the road. The company elected to outsource all sheet metal fabrication and to focus the cells on assembly work alone—thus designing the cells to begin after the monument process. The company now purchases higher quality sheet metal parts at lower costs.[19]

When Case Corporation, the manufacturer of backhoes mentioned earlier, converted to cells, centralized painting was the monument process. Cell planners eliminated the need for this step by opting to purchase pre-painted (and pre-plated) parts. The parts are delivered on an as-needed basis to the cells that use them.[20]

In closing, monument processes can be a significant challenge for cell designers. However, as summarized in Table 16-2, there are a number of creative strategies for dealing with monuments—many of which we have discussed above—that you can consider and adapt to your own situation.

Table 16-2. Strategies for dealing with monument processes

- Dedicate the monument process to the cell but do not relocate it
- Change reporting relationships to dedicate a monument process worker to the cell
- Physically build the cell around the monument process—locate cell equipment, permanently or temporarily, in close proximity to the monument process
- Question assumptions about the need for a centralized monument process—evaluate technological advances that may make it economically and technologically feasible to decentralize the centralized resource
- Share the monument process between cells
- Design cells around monument processes; cells end before or begin after the monument process
- Redesign cell products and their manufacturing processes to eliminate the need for the monument process
- Strengthen communication between the cell and the monument process so that priorities and expectations are clear
- Remove parts from the cell that require the monument process and either (1) produce them entirely in a conventional part of the plant or (2) outsource them

Economically Justifying the Move to Cells

Obtaining the data you need to support a cell analysis can be a significant effort in any cell design process. Similarly, obtaining the data to evaluate your proposed design with respect to the costs it will incur and the benefits it will generate can be a difficult task. However, an economic justification is an important undertaking, and probably a required one if your cells involve outlays for capital equipment. For example, respondents to one of our surveys indicated that financial hurdles, including limitations on purchasing new equipment, were the most frequently noted constraints imposed on the cell design process.[21] And another recent study found that of 44 companies that had elected not to pursue certain cells, 31 percent had done so because of a failure to cost-justify the investment (39 of these 44 plants had other cells in operation).[22] Getting good data for an accurate cost justification is clearly important, and sometimes difficult.

There are several obstacles here. First, while out-of pocket expenses are relatively easy to determine, benefits are far more speculative. You know it will cost $160,000 for a new piece of equipment, but how large a reduction in work in process inventory will the cell generate? In order to answer this and similar questions you will need to delve into details—anticipate what will happen during and after implementation, as well as understand how the cells will actually work. Companies often find it particularly difficult to assign an economic value to time savings. For example, what is the value to customers of reducing lead times by two weeks? As Chapter 8 suggested, sales representatives or customers themselves may be able to help you estimate this.

Companies also find it difficult to assign economic value to benefits such as increased job satisfaction, improved flexibility, or simplified planning and control. As we pointed out in Chapter 8, one good way of dealing with this is to try to translate such benefits into concrete advantages. For example, job satisfaction should lead to less employee turnover, flexibility should lead to higher sales, and simplified planning and control should reduce the need for support personnel. In addition, keep in mind that *it is not necessary to "dollarize" each and every intangible benefit.* You only need to quantify benefits until the project shows a positive economic value.

It is difficult, however, to anticipate *all* the costs and benefits your project will involve; invariably, some factors are overlooked. This is particularly true for cells that involve new technologies. And these hurdles get higher the larger the scope of the project. In fact, as we pointed out in Chapter 8, companies with little or no previous experience with cells tend to overestimate the benefits and underestimate the time and resources required. If you are a newcomer to cells, this is yet another reason to consider starting small—one cell at a time. This allows you to use the experience you gain to generate predictive data. Of course, the experiences of other similar firms, gleaned from plant visits or other sources, can be helpful too.

Finally, be aware that even when the benefit picture looks very good, a cell implementation that involves moving away from established infrastructure systems may be perceived as too risky and therefore too costly to pursue. One large company, for example, spent $50,000 to study the feasibility of cell-based manufacturing for its domestic plants. Despite significant expected benefits and a successful pilot, the company elected not to pursue cells. A major sticking point was the compensation system. Employees at all levels of the organization had misgivings about moving away from the long-entrenched individual piece rate system. Operators anticipated smaller paychecks, while supervisors and managers feared they would not be able to motivate individual performance without the piece rate "carrot." Rather, they believed overall plant productivity would fall. Strong cell support from the recently hired manufacturing manager was not enough to sustain the cell initiative, and top company executives failed to approve implementation.

In general, keep in mind that your justification should focus on relevant costs and revenues. In addition, as we suggested earlier, focus first only on a few major benefits. If these tangible benefits are insufficient to show sufficient economic value, then pick some important intangibles and turn them into tangible benefits.

In this section we have covered several common problems that may arise during either cell design or cell project justification. See Table 16-3 for a summary.

Table 16-3. Common problems related to design and justification of cells

- Not solving the right problem with cells (e.g., sub-optimizing)
- Difficulties selecting initial part families and equipment due to:
  - The overwhelming analysis task
  - Unclear cell design objectives
  - Difficulties obtaining needed data for analysis
  - Inadequate training or analysis tools to support the design effort
- Failing to plan the cell in sufficient detail
- Problems designing the cell (and its operating policies) to resolve capacity and work flow issues, including difficulties:
  - Designing the cell with sufficient buffers
  - Achieving needed setup time reductions
  - Designing appropriate tooling and material-handling systems
  - Satisfying competing design objectives (e.g., minimize equipment investment and achieve complete parts start-to-finish in the cell)
  - Physical layouts that prevent operators from communicating and thereby inhibit work flow
  - Physical layouts that encourage unnecessary conversation that distracts employees from the work task and thereby inhibits work flow
- Difficulties dealing with monument processes
- Difficulties developing an accurate cost/benefit picture for cost justification purposes:
  - Difficulties obtaining needed data
  - Difficulties "dollarizing" intangible benefits

COMMON PROBLEMS IN THE IMPLEMENTATION OF CELLS

In this section we describe problems that are discovered once the implementation process has begun. These often are short-term problems, because the implementation team needs to resolve them quickly to proceed. We discuss problems that fall into several categories:

- Managing the cell implementation project.
- Managing the change process and dealing with resistance.
- Installing new equipment.
- Preparing the workforce for cells.

Managing the Cell Implementation Project

As the cell implementation project unfolds, any number of things can go wrong. Some of the most common problems are also related: failure to manage risks and making unrealistic time estimates. Both can frustrate and delay cell implementation.

Failure to manage risks

Ignoring risks is a common "gotcha." As we noted in Chapter 15, cell planning teams can easily overlook the important step of asking, "What might go wrong, what can we do to avoid it, and what will we do if it happens?" An obvious risk, for example, is employee resistance. Implementation efforts that do not anticipate this, attempt to minimize it, or develop contingencies in the event that it happens may encounter great difficulties getting workers to accept the new ways of operating. Other commonly ignored risks are late equipment deliveries, technical trouble with new equipment, and dramatic shifts in demand for cell products. Project teams that fail to consider potential setbacks often run into unexpected and unpleasant surprises that disrupt implementation.

Unrealistic time estimates

Lack of detailed planning (described under design and justification problems) and failure to analyze risks can both contribute to unrealistic projections about when the cell conversion will be complete. A respondent to one of our early studies of cell users commented that implementing cells takes "three times your most conservative estimate."[23] Similarly, a more recent survey cites users who noted that planning and implementation requires more time than initially expected.[24]

Managing the Change Process and Dealing with Resistance

As you transition to cells you are likely to encounter resistance to the new ways of operating. The way in which the cell planning and implementation process unfolds, however, can have a profound effect on the ease of the transformation and the degree to which those affected by cells resist or embrace them. We devoted much of Chapter 15 to a discussion of how to manage change. We also gave several examples of employee resistance to cell projects (also see Table 16-4 below for a review) and how you may handle it. Therefore, we will not repeat that material here. However, we strongly encourage you to revisit the 10-step model and the accompanying Table 15-8 ("Why Transformation Efforts Fail") as you put together your own implementation plan. We want to reemphasize that you must *manage* the process of building support for cells and a new way of working, for example by following a "fair process." Just "letting it happen" can be a recipe for serious implementation problems and failed performance expectations.

Strong leadership, then, is critical to successful cell projects! Let us also note that we have seen cell implementations flounder due to lack of true management support—even if the cell project had been justified and approved.

Union resistance and cells

The existence of a union in the workplace can pose special problems. Unions may object to the changes that come with cells for many reasons.[25] First, they may believe that cells jeopardize job security in that it will be easier for management to transfer cell production to non-union locations. This is based on the view that decentralizing production to create cells and more thoroughly documenting work procedures could make it easier to move work. (This view is warranted; we give examples of cell relocation/duplication in the section "Organizational and Strategic Change May Require Cell Change" in Chapter 17.) Second, unions may want to retain long-established work rules, seniority practices, and job classification systems designed to protect workers and jobs. Unions may see broader jobs and multi-skilling, for example, as ways of increasing employee work without increasing their pay. Similarly, unions might also fear that older employees will be left behind if seniority practices that govern job bidding are abandoned in favor of merit-based selection methods. Third, unions may feel their role is being radically altered. Involving operators in design and operating decisions can undermine the union's role as "an independent representative of employee interests."[26]

On the other hand, workers may be better off when unions support cells. A study of eleven metalworking firms in Wisconsin found that union leaders unanimously believed that they did not have the option of resisting their plant's move to cells.[27] Doing so, they felt, would have been futile and counterproductive. Because management made it clear that they were introducing cells, unions focused on other issues. They tried to win extra pay and worked to convince management to select cell workers based on seniority. Union leaders also participated, to varying degrees, in selecting, training, and evaluating potential cell employees. This involvement increased the union's stature with both workers and management.

In these cases, the union ultimately saw cells as a way for workers to learn more skills and for the plant to become more competitive. This attitude may not be unusual; in fact, in one of our surveys of cell users we found that resistance to cells was lower in firms with unions than in those without them.[28] In general, unions are more likely to support cells:[29]

- *When they believe there is a strong business reason to move to cells.* If the union believes that cells will help make the organization more competitive, and that this will be good for workers and for the union, they are more likely to support cells.
- *When they believe cells will help assure job security.* Job security is typically a major goal of unions. Cells can mean that workers acquire additional skills. This, in turn, can make the workforce more competitive, which can mean greater job security. If the union views cells as a way of assuring job security, they may be more likely to lend their support.
- *When they believe they can play an important role in the transition and afterward.* Management may encourage union support by making it clear that it too sees a role for the union during and after transition to cells.
- *When there is a give and take.* Negotiation can be an important change management technique. If unions are able to "give" some concessions (e.g., agree to more flexible job classifications) while protecting other elements they view as important, (e.g., selection by seniority), they may be more likely to support a move to cells.

These factors suggest that building partnerships and establishing common goals are at the heart of developing union—and employee—support for cells.

Installing New Equipment

New equipment purchased explicitly for the cell is a common source of implementation problems. It takes time to work the bugs out and reach steady-state production. This is probably why consultants conclude that "cells are easiest to implement when they've made the best use of existing machines and require minimal new or modified equipment."[30] One organization, for example, purchased a sophisticated milling machine to produce a family of critical parts that were difficult to make. Getting the machine up and running, including balancing tool handling and mastering the sophisticated control system, took far longer than cell planners had imagined. Tool breakage, tool sticking, and carousel jams also were unanticipated problems. To deal with this issue, implementers had to develop a maintenance plan to avoid disruptive downtime. These types of start-up problems are typical, but can be avoided.

If your cell design includes new equipment, plan accordingly. In particular, build in time to work out the bugs and don't expect full production during start-up. For this reason, you may want to create some buffer inventory to cover demand during the conversion process.

Preparing the Workforce for Cells

Inadequate or insufficient training can lead to implementation problems. In one of our surveys we found that one third of plants with cells had not provided operators with any formal education on cell concepts, and several plants had provided no training at all.[31] These companies acknowledged that under-training creates problems. In a more recent survey we found that employee training was one of the most important implementation issues.[32] Managers reported that employees, supervisors, support people, and managers alike needed more training in a variety of areas, including overall training in cell concepts. "We didn't realize how much training would be required," commented one plant manager. The manager of a coil-winding cell noted that "we haven't done a very good job training people, especially with respect to cross-training. It's a ticking time bomb."

The manager of a large assembly cell described to us the challenges of preparing cell workers as follows:

> Many of our employees are older generation and come from the time when education and contribution wasn't that important. They just came to work and did the job. We have mostly women and many have an attitude of only working to help out the primary breadwinner. The process of getting these people to embrace broadened responsibilities is really challenging. We have had to provide lots of education, much more than we expected, including one-on-one and group sessions on effective communications, effective relationships, statistical quality control, using the computer and total quality.

The workforce had a really hard time with computer education, but all workers must have this skill to work effectively.

The education level, age, and work ethics of employees, as well as the nature of the work itself, should influence decisions about what training to provide and how to deliver it. (See Chapter 13 for detailed advice on training.)

Getting workers technically proficient can be a problem when cells include a wide array of processes. Workers in one cell were expected to master 30 to 50 separate operations. According to one manager, "this has proved to be an impossible task."[33] In addition, loss of learning may be a problem when operators work only infrequently on certain stations. This occurred at a manufacturer that created a 20-person cell to build a wide array of products. Not only did employees have difficulty mastering all the tasks, they sometimes lost skills they did not frequently use.[34]

Where operators are expected to act as a team, interpersonal skills are particularly important. As one manager described it, "our cells are just like families—there is plenty of interpersonal stuff going on, and lots of family conflicts. We did not provide enough training at first to deal with this." Another company experienced a doubling of employee turnover when they moved to cells. At this plant "employees complained of increased scheduling pressures and felt overwhelmed by the increase in co-worker interdependence that had developed."[35] At yet another company unexpected interpersonal issues cropped up among employees who were simply unaccustomed to working in teams. In response, the company launched a major training program: every employee received eight hours of training each week for 16 weeks.[36]

Language differences can be a problem in cells whose workers collaborate. Where workers are ethnically diverse, English may be a second (and less preferred) language for some employees. In one large cell, operators spoke eight different languages. The supervisor discovered that workers were communicating primarily with those who spoke the same language. This restricted information sharing. In response, the manager instituted an "English-only" policy for on-the-job communication. She also made language training available for employees.[37] While we support the notion of language training, a single-language policy may be problematic. It may be preferable to develop written and graphical process documentation, visual controls, and foolproof mechanisms to ensure that problems do not occur.

Cell versus company perspective

Cell employees very quickly develop a strong identification with their cell and their teammates. Such involvement is a positive aspect of cells. However, operators must understand that cells need to operate in concert with other parts of the organization to meet business objectives. Passing ownership of the process to the cell operators has been "a real plus," according to one manager. "The downside is that, while people feel strong ownership for their work team, they feel no ownership for things that fall outside their area. There is a cohesiveness within but a silo effect between." At another plant, "one team became so good initially, the other teams sabotaged their work." Training should help operators understand how to act in the best interests of the organization, not just in the interest of their individual cell. Of course, performance metrics and compensation systems must support that principle.

Training, compensation, and productivity

Sometimes, training can be a headache for reasons related to labor turnover and compensation. We illustrate this through an example.

In one apparel company, new employees worked in training modules (cells) until they had mastered basic skills. However, the pace of production was slower in these training modules than in the real modules. Thus, new employees, although fully trained, were unable, at least initially, to work at "production" speeds when they joined a module team. "It's like training for combat," remarked a manager. "It's one thing practicing at Fort Benning, Georgia. But it is quite another to land at Normandy." Because the modules were paid on a group piece rate system, bringing in a new employee typically meant lower wages for all the cell's workers. This happened even though management made compensation adjustments to offset the impact of a new employee. For example, during the first several weeks after a new employee joined the team, the cell would be guaranteed their average earnings over the past 52 weeks. However, the constant flow of new workers into the cells, as a consequence of high turnover and absenteeism, meant that more experienced workers felt they were always being held back. As a consequence, their pay suffered. At this company, these types of training-related issues, along with other problems such as "free riders," contributed to low plant-wide morale, high turnover, workplace violence, and, eventually, plant closures. Although this was a dramatic ending, the general lesson here is one that we have emphasized at many other places in this book: you always have to think about the fit between activities and systems in the organization. In this particular case, training and compensation were in conflict.

Training of managers, supervisors, and support staff

Inadequate training for supervisors and managers is a fairly common implementation problem. Sometimes the real problem is that supervisor and manager roles are not well understood. As one manager deeply involved with a cell implementation told us:

> No one at the plant, except one manager, really understood the evolving role of supervisors. Initially, supervisors tried to hang on to power—the "I have your paycheck in my pocket" phenomenon. We needed "ego death training" to convince them they were no longer in charge of the process. We also needed to train supervisors to let the team go headlong into a mistake and then be held accountable for it. This is the only way the teams would learn.

Revamped training on supervisor roles and responsibilities helped the situation at this plant. However, training will not help if supervisors are simply ill suited or unwilling to accept their changed roles. As we noted in Chapters 12 and 13, supervisory roles and responsibilities can be dramatically different with cells. Team-based cells require a facilitative style of leadership that is uncomfortable for supervisors who have operated in a "command and control" mode. Transitioning existing supervisors to cell supervisor positions has proved very difficult for many companies we have worked with.

Finally, companies commonly overlook training for support groups. For example, it is important to include the materials and accounting people in the training. They play an important role in a smooth operation and, as one manager at an electronics plant noted, these groups tend to have a very difficult time with this concept. Of course, the solution to this and many of these training-related problems is, simply, to select the right personnel and train them well. We recommend a well thought-out and executed training plan. Chapter 13 provides additional advice and guidance.

In this section we have covered several common problems that may arise during cell implementation. Table 16-4 summarizes these and clearly shows that most of them have a human dimension.

COMMON PROBLEMS DURING CELL OPERATION

Many problems can arise once cells are in place and operating "at full speed." We think of these problems as "longer term," either because they are driven by gradual changes in product demand, are less urgent, or arise over time and take longer to alleviate than some of the problems we described under the design and implementation sections. We will discuss two major problem categories:

- Dealing with changing production requirements.
- Creating a supportive infrastructure.

In the context of infrastructure we discuss, in particular, issues with

- – Cost accounting.
- – Performance measurement.
- – Manufacturing planning and control.
- – Maintenance and engineering support.
- – Employee compensation.

Dealing with Changing Production Requirements

Dealing with changing product demand, including the introduction of new products, is a common cell operation problem. As we discussed in Chapter 3, this problem occurs because cells tend to be less flexible than the functional environments they replace. Problems with meeting increasing and/or shifting demand often originate in cell design. Thus, the potential shortage of future capacity, and the loss of both routing and product flexibility, must be considered at this stage. One company, for example, reported in one of our surveys that it failed to consider the need for a cell to handle future product line enhancements.[38] This problem became apparent only after the cell was in operation, but it obviously originated in the design phase.

Many capacity-related problems, of course, are solved in the operation stage. One study of 200 cells in 20 companies found that cell organizations rely on many strategies when adjusting cell capacity to meet demand.[39] They may add or delete workers and shifts, off-load or on-load production, use overtime or undertime, and add equipment. Cells are also gradually made to adapt to changing product

Table 16-4. Common problems in the implementation of cells

Managing the cell implementation project
- Overlooking critical activities
- Failure to manage risks
- Unrealistic time estimates

Resistance to change
- Difficulties getting operators to accept the new way of working in the face of:
  - Operator fear of job loss; fear of repetitive, boring work; or that jobs will be harder in cells
  - Well entrenched functional mindset—preference for repetitive, independent work—expressed as:
    - Operator dislike of job variety and job rotation
    - Operator concern (real or perceived) that slower cell workers will impede the performance of more competent operators
    - Operator belief that repetitive batch work is more productive
- Operator "new initiative burnout"—a belief that cells are just another "flavor of the month"
- Resistance among managers, supervisors, and support personnel
- Union resistance to cells based on fears that cells will jeopardize:
  - Job security
  - Long-established work rules, seniority practices, and job classification systems
  - The union's role as an independent representative of employee interests
- Design and implementation efforts that are not perceived as following a "fair process" because of:
  - A tendency to rely only on technical "experts" in the design process
  - Not explaining adequately why cells are needed
  - Not engaging operators and others affected by the design in the design process
  - Inadequate/insufficient communication during implementation
  - Not making expectations clear or failing to manage expectations

Installing new equipment
- Delivery delays; start-up and prove-out problems
- Production shortages during start-up

Preparing the workforce for cells
- Inadequate (or no) technical or interpersonal skills cross-training
- Inadequate (or no) basic skills (math, reading, writing) training where needed; inadequate (or no) language training to support communication in multicultural cell environments
- Expecting workers to master too many tasks; failure to consider "task forgetting"
- Low education levels and high turnover rates
- Inadequate (or no) training on cell concepts
- Training conflicting with productivity and pay
- Supervisor reluctance to relinquish power or adopt different roles
- Failure to clearly define supervisors' role in the cellular system
- Problems developing good supervisors for cells
- Failure to provide cell concepts training for support groups

---

specifications. In general, most cells are quite robust and there is little evidence to support the fear that they may have short life cycles. It appears, rather, that cells are able to stand the test of time through improvements in equipment, processes, and methods that allow them to produce higher volumes and greater part variety.

This is particularly the case when product families remain fairly stable with respect to their basic configuration.[40]

When demand for cell parts falls, some companies try to maintain labor and equipment utilization by redirecting other parts to the cell. As attractive as this may sound, if the parts don't "fit," this course of action can degrade cell performance ("creeping cell decay"). For example, in an effort to deal with capacity load imbalances, one company added non-cell parts to a machining cell. Unfortunately, these parts did not fit well given the current machining and setup capabilities of the equipment. The manager noted that "while this gave us more machining opportunities and a chance to keep equipment busy more of the time, we created a situation where more and more time had to be spent on setup, tooling, training, *et cetera*. We deviated from the cell concept and ended up with a mess."[41]

Similarly, one consultant observes that the second most common error with cells is trying to add ill-fitting components to an existing cell. This results in unnecessary complexity and a decline in cell efficiency. "By the time you get done, the cell becomes just a mini-version of the shop you used to have instead of being a cell focused around doing a few things right."[42]

Other companies deal with shifting demand by creating cells that are "designed to be redesigned." At one footwear plant, fitting cells consist of equipment on wheels. The cell teams (with assistance from engineering and maintenance) rearrange the equipment internal to the phantom cell to match the predominant workflow of the shoes assigned to the cell.[43] Another company has two very flexible cells that can make virtually any product from any cell. When product demand outstrips what the regular, dedicated cells can produce, the two flexible cells accept the overflow. This makes the whole cell system very responsive.

With respect to the problems created by dynamic demand, our best advice is simply to plan for it. As part of the design process, think through how the cell will operate if demand increases or decreases, or if product design changes. What is the next generation of products likely to require in terms of processing requirements (equipment and labor capabilities) or overall capacity (output)? Are there ways to accommodate demand or product changes by building flexibility into the cells? Subtle changes in cell design and operation that increase flexibility may have a big performance payoff later (see Chapters 6 and 7 for further discussion). Likewise, subtle changes in product design may make it easier for existing cells to assimilate new products (see our discussion of group technology and standardization in Chapter 5). Be sure the design engineering group understands the process capabilities of the cells and the cost consequences of deviating from the cell's core processes. Seemingly innocent design changes can lead to the need for new labor skills, more sophisticated equipment (e.g., new features requiring enhanced machining capabilities), new tools, fixtures, and gauges—all of which are likely to increase the cost of operating the cell.

Creating a Supportive Infrastructure

In Chapter 1 we defined "infrastructure" as the subsystems used to plan, manage, and control operations. Cost accounting, performance measurement, production planning and control, and human resource management systems are critical elements of your firm's infrastructure. For cells to reach their full potential, all these management systems must support cellular operations. Organizations therefore invite trouble when they try to operate cells without aligning key infrastructure systems: "Cells simply don't work well, if at all, when they are not part of *an overall strategy of change*."[44] In this section we describe the problems organizations typically encounter when adapting, or failing to adapt, cost accounting and performance measurement, production planning and control, maintenance and engineering support, and compensation systems to support cells.

Problems with cost accounting

Chapters 9 and 10 (on cost accounting and performance measurement, respectively) described in some detail the types of problems companies can encounter when the financial and non-financial measurement systems do not fit the cells. Because these chapters presented a comprehensive discussion, our intent here is to restate only the most common problems companies with cells encounter.

As we discussed in Chapter 10, there is sometimes a lack of congruence between the cost system's performance measures and the operational measures of the cells. One auto components manufacturer, for example, had several cells in place and hoped to add more. But, after 18 months of operation,

> The disappointing truth, and the frustration for cell area managers, was that the planned savings were difficult to translate into dollars. Operational measures showed drastic drops in throughput time, floor space and flow distance, but these savings were not reflected in the plant "Performance to Budget" report. As a result, proposals to expand the scope of the cell manufacturing program came under fire from several quarters.[45]

Operationally, the cells were performing well, but this positive improvement was not captured in the cost accounting measures. And these were the measures that seemed to matter most to decision-makers.

Situations like this happen when companies leave their traditional metric system and cost accounting system unchanged when they move to cells. In another similar case, a medical products subsidiary of a larger corporation converted to cells but retained its corporate-wide cost accounting system. As the plant manager told us, the corporate system, which allocated overhead based on material costs, led to costs that were "ridiculously out-of-line":

> One plastic molded cabinet has a price tag of $8,000. The system allocated $800 worth of overhead to that part. Everyone who works with that part knows that $800 worth of overhead is not spent on that part. Because of these outrageous allocations, products that are really making money for us appear unprofitable.

The plant manager argued that material cost was not the right driver for allocating overhead to products made in the cell. When he asked corporate headquarters to convert his plant to an activity-based costing approach with a more relevant set of drivers, he was denied. An added wrinkle at this plant is that cell workers have full access to financial information. "The people who work with this product see the numbers and get demotivated. They see their area is not making any money, when in fact, they are doing an excellent job."

The problem of overstating the "true" costs of cell products also occurs when companies shift indirect labor tasks to cell operators but fail to adjust standard labor hours or overhead rates to reflect this. When companies fail to make these needed adjustments, cells can look "bad" from a cost perspective. This can make people question the cell strategy.

These examples underscore the importance of the prescriptions we offered in Chapter 10. Most notably, don't automatically believe reports about increased costs due to cells if you know operational performance has improved. These costs may be higher because you haven't adjusted cost pools and standards to reflect the new cell operations. Costs also may be higher due to unanticipated mix and volume changes, so keep this in mind when analyzing cost developments.

Problems with performance measurement

Chapters 9 and 10 both noted the importance of a "balanced scorecard" approach to measurement. This means you should complement your cost-based performance measures with an effective set of formal operational performance measures (see the Process Performance Measurement Matrix in Chapter 9). Unfortunately, companies sometimes make performance measurement an afterthought. At one company, for example, those close to the cells could see that performance had improved. Products were completed sooner, there was less inventory in the plant, and quality was better. However, there were no formal performance measures in place to reflect this, and it was difficult to convince higher-level decision-makers that the change had been effective.

Getting non-financial measures in place that accurately capture performance, and help you plan, control, and improve cells, can take some effort. Operational performance measures need to provide feedback on cell processes and their resources. This makes designing measurement systems a particularly challenging aspect of cell conversion. One manager reported that "developing good, robust measures that will tell us how the cells are doing, how to make them better, and which will drive behavior in the right ways" was among the "greatest challenges" at his plant. This facility replaced the existing performance measurement system with a new set of metrics specifically tailored to cell operations.

Among the most common problems with cell performance measurement systems is the simple failure to align performance measures with cell goals. As noted in Chapter 9, cell supervisors at one plant were measured and rewarded based on machine utilization and labor efficiency. Both measures improved as more parts were produced per period. But higher output meant long production runs, high WIP inventory, long lead times, and poor due-date performance. These outcomes were in stark contrast with cell goals of rapid throughput, on-time delivery, and low WIP inventories. *You simply must rethink not just your strategic goals but also your measurement system when you move to cells.*

Finally, even with an effective *cell* measurement system, the use of different metrics in different parts of the organization may cause operational difficulties. One cell manager complained that the printed circuit board (PCB) area that supplied his cells operated with a "volume mindset." In its defense, the PCB unit's performance was evaluated primarily on cost. The cell's goals, on the other hand, focused on quick response and high quality. These differences in goals created conflicts. Cells strived to assemble boards just-in-time and in small quantities, while the PCB unit wanted long runs of the same boards.

At another plant, different performance measures created similar problems between the stockroom and the cells. The stockroom wanted to deliver in big lots to increase its efficiency, while the cells wanted small lots in support of lean operations. These examples underscore the importance of measures that motivate consistent behavior toward achieving a set of common organizational goals. Frequently, cell measures reflect new organizational thrusts, such as lead-time reduction and responsiveness, but the performance measurement system for other areas remains unchanged. This disconnect leads to inter-organizational conflicts. The solution is to review the firm's performance measurement systems at various levels in order to ensure congruence.

In summary, and as detailed in Chapters 9 and 10, the financial and non-financial performance measurement systems are part of cell planning and cell operation. You need accurate measures to know what the cells have accomplished and how to make them more effective. Deciding how you will measure cell performance and determine product costs should not be an afterthought! It is also important to consider carefully whether or not the cell measures will operate in concert with measures elsewhere in the plant.

Problems with manufacturing planning and control

Although cells can be the foundation for efficient and effective manufacturing, they can only achieve high performance if the system that plans and controls materials is complementary. Some companies make the mistake of believing that cells can improve performance without adjusting the material and capacity control systems. Problems with scheduling, order release and material tracking, and supplier management can result.

Scheduling. Conflicts may arise when production planning and control logic cannot consider part family information. The formal MPC system at one plant was designed for job shop batch production and had no capability for recognizing part families and releasing them together for production. To get around this, the plant developed an operator-based decision tool. This was a simple report that provided cell operators with demand and inventory information for each part made in the cell (current inventory divided by the average demand gives the expected time the inventory will last; also see Chapter 11 for this "runout time" method). Armed with this information, and their knowledge of setup times, operators made decisions about what parts to produce, in what order, and in what quantities. In essence, they created their own family scheduling and order release mechanism inside the cell.[46]

Order release and material tracking. Firms that run cells in a more or less repetitive mode often find that the use of work orders, dispatch lists, and sophisticated material tracking methods are unnecessarily complicated approaches for cell shop floor control. Simpler pull systems with minimal work tracking can work just fine. Sometimes firms have this epiphany only after they have encountered headaches trying to link cell operations to their existing MPC system. The following example illustrates both this problem and the connection to cost accounting problems we discussed in the previous section.

In one plant, work orders were used to authorize an area to build specified quantities of specified items. These work orders were planned in advance based on known assembly schedules. Parts and subassemblies, once completed, were "pushed" between the various departments. For material-tracking purposes, operators scanned a work order barcode before and after processing a batch of parts at their respective station. The made-to-stock system with fixed assembly schedules that had driven work order planning was later replaced by an assemble-to-order system. At the same time, the plant created several subassembly cells to feed the plant's assembly area. Operators were to build subassemblies one at a time, passing single units on to the next step in the cell process.

Initially, the subassembly cells tried to operate using the traditional work order system. However, this system was not set up to provide the flexibility the cells needed. The cell build quantities had become so small that opening a work order for each build created an exponential increase in both the number of open work orders and the administrative effort to track and close them out. Furthermore, the current material-tracking system, which was linked to the work orders, expected a batch of parts to move together. There was no way to tell the system that one subassembly had been completed and moved to final assembly while the remainder of the subassembly work order was still being built. Both production planning and the production areas were massively frustrated. Their desire to improve performance was being hampered by the material planning and control system.

To resolve this, the company first introduced a kanban system that linked assembly production to subassembly production. An empty bin returned from the assembly area was now the signal for the subassembly cell to build more subassemblies. However, because work orders were no longer issued for each order, tracking resource usage against work orders could not be used (i.e., job costing had to be discontinued; see Chapter 10). As a stopgap measure, the planning personnel designed a "process work order" system for the cells. Instead of separate work orders for products, there was now one work order for the entire cell. Material and labor consumed in making any of the cell's products were charged to this single work order (i.e., process costing).

Also, incoming material was stored in bins at the entry to the cell—a change from the previous system, in which work orders signaled the delivery of complete kits of material to the cell. Operators recorded the start of production at the first station and the completion of an item at the last station. The process work order accumulated the work in process costs, while the pull system told operators what to build. When the assembly area removed the completed items from the outgoing kanban bins, they in turn scanned a barcode that credited the cell with the standard cost for the subassembly (post-deduct; see Chapter 10).

The process work order simplified material tracking and gave cells the flexibility to build as needed. But it also created material control problems. The manager of a separate sheet metal cell that also adopted the process work order commented: "We would do a physical inventory at the end of the month to see how we did. We had incredible variances. We were trying to track 175 parts on one work order and it was really a mess. We did not have fine enough control."[47]

The lack of control was due to the fact that a process work order accumulates costs but does not track individual job orders. Thus, when the process work order has a variance, managers can't determine which specific items are responsible. This underscores the importance of identifying the cost accounting requirements of your cells and designing an MPC system that supports them. In this case, the key issue is determining whether knowing variances per job is of real importance.

Material delivery and supplier relations. It is important that internal material delivery policies, as well as procedures for obtaining vendor-supplied material, work in concert with the cells. Managers at several plants have told us that materials personnel chronically overfilled the bins provided to the cells. This increased material delivery efficiency but ran counter to the cells' lean operating philosophy.

Because cells require high-quality levels of incoming parts, suppliers can become a problem. Poor incoming part quality is a serious issue for lean cell operations. Sometimes, just getting vendors to agree to more rapid deliveries of small-quantity, high-quality lots can be a stumbling block. Developing close partnerships with key suppliers is essential, especially when vendor-managed inventories are used.

User-friendly systems. A final problem has to do with the MPC information system itself. When operators assume a more active role in managing the flow of parts through the cell, user-friendly information systems become an issue. Cell operators at one plant complained loudly about the complex and hard-to-understand system for requesting material and reporting status. In response, a team representing operators, information systems, and production control simplified user-interface screens, reduced data input requirements, and provided system training to all operators.

Problems with maintenance and engineering support

Insufficient maintenance can be a problem for cells with minimal buffers. When a machine goes down in a cell, there is typically no duplicate within the cell that can take on its work. Therefore, maintenance issues must be addressed quickly. This can strain maintenance resources and cause cost increases.[48] Also, when cell worker compensation is based on output, maintenance problems can restrict operator earnings. Workers at one plant complained that poor maintenance is "preventing us from earning our pay." Management then sent maintenance workers away for additional training and began paying them for using their new skills on the job (skill-based pay). They also introduced more aggressive preventive maintenance procedures and trained operators to handle minor maintenance tasks.[49]

Engineering support is another potential problem. During cell start-up, and as cell teams work to continually improve operations, they need engineering support. At one plant, teams were to call "their friendly engineer" for assistance in solving technical problems.[50] Management did not anticipate the strong demand for engineering support, and this group became completely overloaded. "Staff up your support groups if you want the cells to be effective," noted the engineering manager.

Finally, the interface between product design engineers and cell operations can be a source of problems. The designers at one plant were accustomed to launching product trial runs on regular production equipment at virtually any time. After cells were implemented, the designers were miffed when cell operators refused to run a prototype that would disrupt the day's production. The design group had not learned about the change to cells and did not understand the new way of operating. Conversely, the cell design team had not thought through the question of how cells would accommodate new product trial runs. The cell manager spent some time educating the product design group and then, together with the operators, worked out a process for planning and executing prototype runs.

Problems with employee compensation

A firm's human resource management policies represent a key element of its infrastructure. These policies must be aligned to support the cell philosophy. One of the most difficult and sensitive issues is the question of how to compensate cell employees. In fact, redesigning the compensation system to fit cell work has proved problematic for a number of organizations we have worked with.

Companies that introduce cells and move from individually based incentives to group incentives may experience problems. Most notably, operators accustomed to working as hard and as fast as they can (and being paid for it), may resent being held back by slower cell colleagues. This can contribute to significant interpersonal problems, low morale, turnover, and in extreme situations, workplace violence.

Often, employee compensation becomes a problem after the cell has been up and running for a while. Here is a typical scenario. An employee survey found that after about a year of operation, assembly cell workers were dissatisfied with their pay. They felt they worked harder and did more than the non-cell workers, yet were paid the same. Cell workers had mastered new skills, learned to work effectively together, and gradually took on more and more responsibility for cell operations. They felt their compensation should reflect this. In this case the company reclassified the jobs, but the pay structure (hourly rate plus corporate profit sharing) stayed the same.

In other cases, companies have radically redesigned pay systems to better reflect cell worker contributions. The compensation system should support cell system objectives. This means that you must think through the interface between compensation and cell operating philosophies and metrics, and do so early. Enlist the assistance of the plant's compensation specialists, and give operators and supervisors a voice in any modifications. As we suggested in Chapter 14, you should be open and above board about any changes and be certain that compensation policies are consistent with other human resource practices. These types of problems underscore the need to step gingerly when making changes to the compensation system.

In this section, we have covered issues that may arise over time during cell operation. Table 16-5 summarizes common cell operation problems.

Table 16-5. Common problems in the operation of cells

Dealing with changing production requirements
- Dealing with product mix changes
- Assimilating new products into existing cells

Problems with cost accounting and performance measurement systems
- Lack of congruence between operational and cost system performance measures
- Traditional cost accounting system overstates the "true" costs of cell parts because of:
  - Failure to adjust standard labor hours or overhead rates to reflect the reality of cell work
  - Use of inappropriate overhead cost drivers
  - Volume or mix changes
- Unwillingness to change cost accounting and performance measurement systems to better support cells
- Using old measures to judge the new cell strategy
- Failure to develop operational performance measures that are consistent with desired cellular outcomes
- Failure to make cell and non-cell measures consistent: measures used in the cells and measures used in the non-cell areas drive behaviors in different directions

Problems with manufacturing planning and control
- Unwillingness to change production planning and control systems to better support cells
- Problems scheduling by part family
- Difficulties adapting the traditional work order system to cells
- Cumbersome and overly complex shop floor tracking systems
- Problems with internal material delivery and external vendor quality and delivery
- Existing production planning and control systems are too complicated and cumbersome for operators to use easily

Problems with other support resources (engineer and maintenance, for example)
- Reluctance of maintenance, engineering, or other groups to off-load activities and expertise to the cell operators
- Support groups not prepared, organized, or motivated to support cell objectives

Problems with compensation systems
- Operator dissatisfaction with compensation
- Compensation system does not support cell work
- Fear of new compensation system—reluctance to change compensation

KEY INSIGHTS

Our work with companies over the years has led us to conclude that much can go wrong as organizations transition to cells. However, many of these problems can be anticipated and avoided. *Being aware* of potential problems is the first step in avoiding them, or in overcoming them, should they arise. Some implementation problems are technical in nature; others have more to do with people and culture. In fact, most cell problems are related to "softer" issues. These organizational issues are often the most challenging and time consuming to resolve. Some important advice for leaders of cell efforts follows.

- *Don't sub-optimize.* Make sure that cells are part of your overall strategy so that a local success with cells translates into improved performance along dimensions that are important for your business. Be sure cells "solve the right problem."

- *Provide the design team with clear directions and sufficient training to undertake a cell analysis.* Without direction and an analysis path to follow, the design team will flounder. Further, don't underestimate the time and effort that will be required to collect or extract relevant data to support cell formation, even when design objectives are clear and the team is well prepared.

- *Carefully plan the cells and their operating policies to assure smooth work flow.* Consider buffers, worker communication patterns, needed setup reductions, tooling issues, and so forth. If workers are collaborating in performing tasks, be sure the layout permits them to see and speak with one another.

- *Deal with monuments.* Note any monument processes early in the design process. Identify the various alternatives, and consequences, for dealing with them. Do not assume that current monument processes must stay that way.

- *Use modeling to help you evaluate alternatives.* You may use computer modeling of cell operations in advance of the physical move to avoid expensive mistakes. This is especially important if equipment and layout are difficult and expensive to reconfigure. See Chapter 7 for information on tools and techniques that you can use.

- *Focus your economic justification effort on relevant costs and benefits.* Follow the guidelines we presented in Chapter 8.

- *Stay on top of project risks.* The project team needs to anticipate what might go wrong and take preventive action and develop contingency plans.

- *If new equipment is required, be sure your implementation plan includes contingencies for (inevitable) delivery delays and start-up problems.* Do not assume you will instantly reach steady-state production. Stockpile product to meet demand during the installation and prove-out period.

- *Develop a training plan that describes who needs to learn what, and how you plan to reach/teach them.* Operators and supervisors are natural education targets, but don't ignore key support groups or upper-level managers.

- *Pay careful attention to selecting and preparing supervisors for their new roles.* Not "just anyone" will have (or be able to develop) the mix of leadership and technical abilities that will be right for your cell supervisor role.

- *Recognize that you are putting in place a system of work that will need to adapt to changing external and internal conditions.* Where possible, design your cell system to adapt to likely fluctuations in product demand, including new product introductions.

- *Evaluate and, where needed, adapt existing infrastructure systems.* Cost accounting, performance measurement, manufacturing planning and control, engineering, and human resource policies must be assessed for their "fit" with cells. In general, the more support areas know about cells and the earlier they are brought into the implementation process, the better.

17

Improvement and Evolution of Cells

We seldom encounter cells that look and operate exactly the way they did when they were first implemented. In fact, as is the case for many other organizational systems, change appears to be a constant for cellular operations.[1]

We should not be surprised that cells change over time. Most companies face a turbulent environment. Customers are demanding, technology is changing, and employee expectations are rising. This dynamic external environment puts pressure on the organization to adapt and change—to do different things, or do the same things, but better, faster, and cheaper. In addition, savvy managers know that it is always possible to improve existing processes. So, not only does the external environment create pressure for change, but the internal reality is that you can and always should improve cell operations.

This chapter answers several important questions regarding the improvement and evolution of cells:

- What is the role of cells in continuous improvement, and what is the role of continuous improvement in cell change?
- What tools and techniques can be used to improve cell performance?
- What are the major external drivers that force cells to evolve over time?

This chapter explores *why* you may want to improve cells, and *how*, and also *why* and *how* cells are driven to change by other forces. The chapter is divided into two parts: (1) managing the continual improvement of cell operations and (2) understanding and responding to sources of cell change.

WHAT IS IMPROVEMENT?

Improvement is the act or procedure of making something better. Applied to industrial environments, improvement means to better the performance of a particular variable while maintaining (or improving) the performance of other important variables. Most improvements have their basis in a problem to solve (e.g., "machine 36 is down for maintenance *again* and we are not going to make shipments") or an opportunity to exploit (e.g., "reducing costs on the 851 product line will increase our margins"). Many improvements involve reducing waste, whether it be wasted time, material, or labor. Others seek to enhance capabilities. Some are incremental modifications to existing methods; others are more dramatic changes.

Whether large or small, however, improvement efforts focus on processes—the way all work gets done in an organization. A process that is not getting better is probably falling behind (since your competitors are surely making improvements, even if you are not). For this reason, organizations are increasingly recognizing that improvement—the constant search for better ways—is essential to both long- and short-term organizational success. In fact, in the best organizations, improvement is an ongoing activity and part of everyone's job.

Eliminating Waste and Adding Value

Continual improvement efforts often focus on eliminating waste.[2] Waste in manufacturing processes can occur in various forms—some obvious, others less so. One common typology identifies the "Seven Wastes": waste from overproduction, waiting time waste, transportation waste, processing waste, inventory waste, waste of motion, and waste from product defects.[3] Table 17-1 presents a revised typology that collapses two highly related categories (waste from overproduction and inventory waste) and adds a category entitled waste from underutilizing human resources.

Looked at more broadly, waste is "anything other than the minimum amount of equipment, materials, parts, space and worker's time, which are absolutely essential to add value to the product."[4] To understand waste, then, you need to understand the concept of value. Essentially, value involves both *doing the right things and doing things right*.[5] Doing the *right things* means engaging in activities that provide customers with what they want, when and how they want it. This suggests that you must first understand the target characteristics of the process output—the attributes and features that customers want and expect from your organization's products or services. Armed with this information you can determine if your processes, and the individual steps that comprise them, produce value.

Specifically, steps in a process have the *potential* to add value when they transform the product in a way that brings it closer to what customers want. For example, the act of attaching the sole to the upper (the body of the shoe) in a footwear cell transforms the incoming material and brings it closer to a completed shoe. This step has the potential to add value. On the other hand, time spent waiting for repairs to the equipment that attaches the sole does not contribute to producing a good that customers want. In fact, no "wait" step in a process has the potential to add value—nothing is being done for the customer while materials are waiting to be transformed or while labor is waiting for work.

To be truly value-added, a step in the process must also be done *right*—i.e., efficiently, using the minimum amount of resources. When this is not the case, waste results. If the sole and upper are not attached properly and must be reworked or scrapped, this activity did not add value. Although the right step was done (attaching sole to upper), it was not done correctly. Because the work was not done right the first time, and rework may be necessary, more than the minimum amount of resources will be consumed.

Table 17–1. Waste and cells

Type	Explanation and How Cells Can Help
Waste from Overproduction and Inventory	*Defined:* Any production in excess of what is currently required to satisfy demand. Unnecessary inventory, unnecessary labor costs in building the inventory, and extra overhead expenses to manage this excess inventory are the result. In addition, overproduction can obscure true priorities, and the resulting inventory can obscure the real causes of problems. *How cells can help:* Cells' tight linkages in terms of space, time, and information mean short production lead times. There is less temptation to overproduce when you can respond to market demands rapidly. This lowers the need for inventory. In addition, small transfer batches are possible, further reducing the amount of inventory in the system.
Waste of Waiting Time	*Defined:* Waste incurred when operators are merely watching equipment run, waiting for a production step to be completed, waiting for work to arrive from another station, standing around because of parts shortages, and so forth. *How cells can help:* Multi-functional cell workers can perform other activities instead of waiting for a machine to complete a cycle.
Transportation Waste	*Defined:* Waste of resources, time, and effort involved in moving material and keeping track of its current location. In addition, damage and rework expenses are always a risk when material is transported. *How cells can help:* In cells, material moves only a fraction of the distances typically associated with job shop production. Further, rapid throughput can eliminate the need for within-cell tracking.
Processing Waste	*Defined:* Extra steps incurred when the production processes themselves are flawed. A machine that will not hold the proper tolerance and requires that parts be inspected and reworked is an example. Bad parts produced as a setup is being verified and adjusted is another. *How cells can help:* Because cell operations are focused, processes can be fine-tuned to do exactly the tasks required in the cell.
Waste of Motion	*Defined:* Movement that does not add value to the product. Looking around for tools, searching for materials, hunting for fixtures, and walking long distances to operate equipment, are all examples of wasted motion. *How cells can help:* The physical closeness of workstations in a cell reduces waste of motion. Storing cell fixtures, tools, and supplies at the cell further reduces motion waste.
Waste from Product Defects	*Defined:* Costs incurred when product defects are discovered in the plant (due to sorting, inspection, rework, scrap, and so forth), or by external customers (which results in warranty and repair expenses, loss of reputation, liability costs, and so forth). This category of waste also includes the cost of the labor that was used to make these defective products. *How cells can help:* The use of small lots and focused families in cells mean that defects are discovered sooner—when they are less costly to fix and before the same mistake has been repeated. Further, operators who are knowledgeable about cell products and processes can identify, correct, and prevent defects.
Waste from Underutilizing Human Resources	*Defined:* Opportunity costs incurred when employees' skills, capabilities, and ideas are not fully used. *How cells can help:* Cells provide opportunities for workers to both broaden and apply their technical direct labor skills as well as take on indirect labor tasks. This more fully uses people's capabilities. Participation in decision-making and improvement of cell operations taps operators' decision-making skills and creative problem-solving abilities. Making cell operators responsible for improvement gives them the opportunity to put ideas into action.

Improvement activities should focus on removing waste from processes as well as on enhancing the capabilities of processes used to meet customer expectations. Often, removing waste and enhancing process capabilities are related. For example, customers may value having products delivered more rapidly, something we can achieve by shortening setups, removing unnecessary steps, and introducing standard operations, each of which removes waste from the process. On the other hand, there are instances where adding value is independent of waste elimination. You may, for example, improve a process by adding new equipment capable of producing additional features that customers want: nothing about the original equipment was wasteful—you have simply improved the process to provide greater value to customers.

Preparing for Continual Improvement—Mastering the Methods and Tools

Anyone who will be involved in cell improvement efforts needs to be familiar with both the steps to follow and the tools to use in making improvements. Figure 17-1 presents a "process model" for continuous improvement. This type of improvement model is a key component of the Toyota Production System, lean manufacturing, and the Six Sigma philosophy of management.[6]

Six Sigma, for example, focuses on "designing and monitoring everyday business activities in ways that minimize waste and resources while increasing customer satisfaction."[7] Specifically, the goal is for every process to perform so well that, with respect to any given critical characteristic, the average incidence of a defect or mistake is only 3.4 per million opportunities. Using the model in Figure 17-1, companies can rethink processes to minimize the possibilities of errors and thereby achieve Six Sigma status. The model may have different names (e.g., Plan-Do-Check-Act, Plan-Do-Study-Act, Focus-Analyze-Do-Evaluate, Define-Measure-Analyze-Improve-Control), but the fundamental steps are the same: define the problem, gather and analyze data to identify the underlying causes, develop solutions, implement the solutions, evaluate the outcome, and refine.[8] We discuss each step in more detail below (also see Appendix K for its application to setup time reduction).

Define the problem and organize the project

The improvement model described in Figure 17-1 begins with *Define the Problem and Organize the Project*. This is the stage at which you determine the focus of the improvement activity and who will be involved. Cell operators are in an excellent position to identify areas that need improvement. However, feedback from customers, both internal and external, performance data, and broader company programs may also be the source of improvement initiatives. The team of operators who run a given cell is a natural group to assume responsibility for cell improvements. Of course, given the nature of the improvement problem, representatives of other groups (engineering, maintenance, accounting, etc.) may also be involved. Depending on the problem the team will tackle and the skills sets people bring to the task, you may need to provide various types of training (e.g., specialized training on setup reduction) as part of this initial phase.

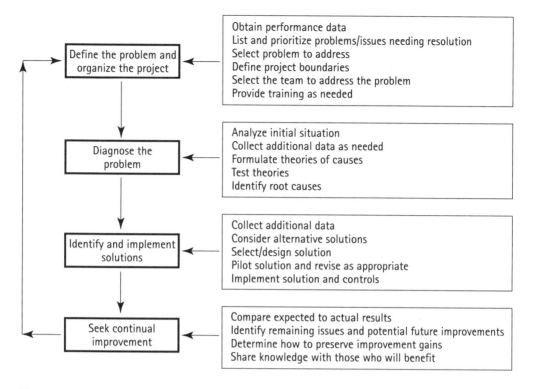

Figure 17-1. A model for process improvement

Diagnose the problem

The next step in the improvement model, *Diagnose the Problem*, suggests that you must thoroughly understand the current system before you propose to change it. Work flow analysis, which is a key part of factory analysis and design (see Chapter 4), can help provide this understanding. You can use different tools for this. *Work flow diagrams* map the flow of materials and/or people overlaid on a layout (see Figure 5-5). *Flow charts*, or process maps, which show the sequence of steps in a process using standard flow charting symbols, can be very helpful in describing the flow of work (see Figure 5-6).[9] *Functional flow charts* show not just the sequence of steps, but also the departments, areas, or individuals responsible for each. Those charts are especially useful for analysis of administrative work (for an example see Figure 18-6; for information on creating functional flow charts see Appendix L).

Storyboards, which depict each step in the process in photos or drawings, are another way of documenting the current process as the basis for subsequent improvement. Freudenberg-NOK posts storyboards for each process right in the production area. As a team makes improvements, it draws a large yellow X through any process step it has eliminated. The company's CEO, Joseph Day, observes that storyboards are "one of those simple visual tools to keep in front of the workers' eyes. It shows them the never-ending opportunity for continuous improvement, and therefore the elimination of cost, in the process."[10]

Once the team has documented the existing process, it can begin to analyze it to identify "root" causes. These are the causes that when eliminated or changed will have the biggest positive effect on solving the problem at hand. Besides the techniques just described, a number of other tools can help teams collect, analyze, and display data, and generate ideas and make decisions as they pursue improvements. These are briefly described in Table 17-2. If you are not familiar with these tools, there are several excellent references that provide in-depth descriptions as well as instructions for their practical application[11] (see also endnote 6).

Table 17-2. Process improvement tools

Purpose of the Tools	Examples of Tools
To collect data	• *Surveys and interviews*, which collect data • *Data checksheets*, which collect and verify that correct and complete data have been collected
To understand the current process ("as is") or to describe a proposed process ("to be")	• *Flow charts or process maps*, which show the sequence of steps in a process (see Figure 5-6) • *Functional flow charts* (also called deployment flowcharts), which show the sequence of major process activities and also the key people/departments that perform them (see Figure18-6 and Appendix Figure L-2) • *Material-flow diagrams*, which show the flow of material imposed on a layout (see Figure 5-5) • *Process analysis charts*, which show the sequence of process steps and categorize them using symbols such as process, storage, transfer, inspection • *Storyboards*, which show the sequence of steps in photographs or drawings (also used to show the process and results of an improvement effort)
To organize and/or look for relationships in data	• *Data analysis and display tools*, such as run charts/time plots, frequency plots, scatter diagrams, Pareto diagrams, histograms, and control charts, which help identify the patterns in data • *Cause and effect diagrams*, which help organize possible causes of a problem • *Affinity diagrams*, which help a team group related ideas and identify major patterns
To generate ideas and make decisions in teams	• *Brainstorming*, which helps generate ideas • *Brainmapping*, another, more structured, method for generating ideas • *Multi-voting*, which helps narrow a long list of items to a few which the team considers to be the most important • *Prioritization matrices*, a more sophisticated method for comparing choices and narrowing down options by selecting, applying, and weighting criteria to produce a relative numerical score • *Matrix diagrams*, which help the team to identify, analyze, and evaluate the presence and strength of relationships between two or more sets of information; particularly useful in making decisions regarding implementation

Identify and implement solutions, and seek continual improvement

Once root causes are known, the team can begin to outline solutions. This activity moves the team to the third phase, *Identify and Implement Solutions*. Finally, once a solution is in place, the team should monitor the impact of the solution, seek to maintain the gain, but also look for other opportunities to improve further. We refer to this phase as *Seek Continual Improvement.*

Improvement as a Way of Life

Creating a culture where everyone strives to continuously improve performance is one of the essential elements of a lean manufacturing approach.[12] In fact, if you've done any reading about lean manufacturing, you've probably encountered the word "kaizen." A Japanese word for improvement (actually, "good change"), kaizen is an essential element of manufacturing philosophies that emphasize eliminating waste. You have probably also heard of "kaizen blitzes." These are events of intense team involvement, typically lasting no more than four to five days, during which you try to accomplish as much improvement as possible.[13] Although compressed into a very short time period, most kaizen blitzes follow the basic model described in Figure 17-1. That is, they begin with understanding the current process and from there diagnose problems, implement solutions, and track performance. Although such events are powerful forces for change, experts agree that "you realize the power of kaizen when all employees are applying it in their work every day."[14]

Some of the most successful cell operations we've seen exist in companies that have fully embraced the philosophy of kaizen. They clearly view getting cells up and running as the starting point, not the end point, of factory transformation. An extreme example of this involves a Japanese plant where explaining the concept to workers, analyzing the existing shop, and rearranging the layout to create a cell consumed only 50 minutes. Working out the details, mastering the flow, and making continual and ongoing improvements followed.[15] Getting the cell in place was, clearly, just the first step in an ongoing journey to improve operational performance.

When the idea of continuous improvement is new to an organization and people are just beginning to work through the steps in Figure 17-1, the process is formal and deliberate and improvement efforts may proceed slowly. However, as employees gain maturity, both in terms of working together and mastering the associated tools, improvement efforts will proceed at a more rapid clip: an issue identified at 9:00 A.M. may be studied and a solution implemented by 10:00 A.M. (or sooner!). Said another way, as continuous improvement becomes institutionalized, improvement becomes less a formal process and more "the way we do things around here." One plant manager we worked with for several years commented that "I'll know when continuous improvement is a real success here when there aren't any formal continuous improvement teams. Instead, problems will be solved on the line every day by people who know how to use data to find and resolve problems and take advantage of new opportunities."

With this discussion as backdrop, we now turn to the subject of cells and improvement. We begin by showing how cells are both a strategy for reducing waste and an ideal setting for continued improvement. Next we discuss some specific improvement methods, primarily for removing waste, and show their use in cells. Then we will describe the actions you can take to help create a culture of continuous improvement.

CELLS: AN IDEAL SETTING FOR CONTINUOUS PROCESS IMPROVEMENT

Waste in manufacturing is both less likely to occur, and more easily identified and eliminated, in cellular systems. Thus, cells are a strategy that companies can use to remove waste from work processes. Consider waste from overproduction and inventory (see Table 17-1). The temptation to overproduce is typically a by-product of long lead times (i.e., we stockpile) and high setup costs (i.e., we run large batches to avoid changeovers), but cells often have short lead times and small setups. Why produce ahead of time if the cell can quickly make exactly what you need in the precise quantities you require? As described in Table 17-1, cells offer similar advantages with respect to each of the other major categories of waste. For this reason, creating cells can be an effective means of reducing waste in manufacturing operations.

Even when organizations take a deliberate approach to cell design and carefully plan each cell in advance of implementation (something we strongly recommend), improvement happens. In fact, participants in a recent survey observed that the most surprising positive outcome from cells was that they kept improving once implemented. Although successful continuous improvement relies on contributions from all employees, operators—because of their hands-on knowledge of the process—play a particularly important role. As a respondent to one of our surveys noted, "I didn't realize you will get continuous improvement with the same operators in the same cell day after day."[16]

Cells have certain job and process design characteristics that make them perfect for operator-based improvement where workers identify improvement opportunities, contribute ideas, and play an active role in implementation. Here, in particular, are five cell characteristics that support process improvement:

- Family focus.
- System's view.
- Pooled expertise.
- Problem visibility.
- Accountability and ownership.

As shown in Figure 17-2, these attributes are tightly linked to the four critical perspectives (resources, spatial, transformation, and organizational) that we used in Chapter 2 to define cells.

1. Family focus: cell operators work with a narrow set of similar parts or products that they come to know well. Compared to job shop work, operators in a cell deal with a more narrow range of parts or products and produce a smaller set of similar items more frequently. This means that cell operators come to know cell products and how to build them quite well. Furthermore, the focus on families enhances individual task learning (e.g., how to insert a particular component or make a particular machine cut better and faster). It also helps operators identify improvement ideas, which once implemented can further enhance performance.[17] And, because any improvement to a process step (e.g., a faster setup) benefits the whole family, not just a single part or product, you get a better return on any process change.

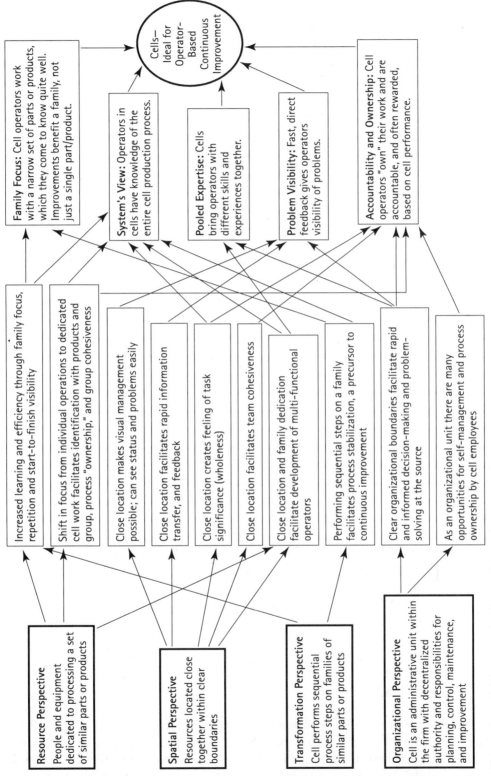

Figure 17-2. Cells as a setting for continuous improvement

Their intimate knowledge of part families puts operators in a particularly good position to contribute to standardization efforts. Cell operators familiar with a family of products can easily identify unnecessary variation in components and build processes. Workers in a subassembly cell, for example, pointed out that current designs called for 12 different bolt sizes where one would be adequate. The cell's focus on building a family of products that *should* be similar provided a great backdrop for identifying unnecessary variation.

2. System's view: operators in cells have knowledge of the entire cell production process. In assembly line or job shop work, employees typically know a single step only. Having all cell tasks closely located "under one roof" means operators can become familiar with the entire cell production process. This "system's view" can be a powerful force for identifying improvement opportunities that were not obvious before the cell was created. Scrap levels for Gelman Sciences Disposable Capsule Filter Cell fell to an all-time low because "members were able to organize their efforts on the entire line to reduce scrap losses, not just at one machine center."[18] Only their exposure to the entire production process equipped operators with the insights to make such broad-based recommendations.

As one manager put it, "when you are just operating a [single] process, the ideas sometimes don't happen, but when your job is 'to make the product' it is different." Operators in the cell he managed worked with equipment engineering to devise a way of decentralizing heat treat to the cell. Their knowledge of the entire cell process had caused them to ask "Why can't we heat treat right here?" Thus, in cells, operators inevitably focus improvement efforts on the big picture—how to create an uninterrupted flow of materials that meets cost, quality, and delivery targets.

3. Pooled expertise: cells bring together operators with different skills and experiences. We have all heard the adage, "two heads are better than one." This is especially true when those heads bring different experiences and skills to bear on a problem. Cell teams are often made up of individuals from different parts of the plant that are skilled in distinct areas. In cells, these operators work side by side, where they can learn from one another. In particular, cells provide an opportunity for operators to pool their expertise, master new skills, and apply ideas and best practices gained from prior work to a different and broader set of processes.

4. Problem visibility: fast, direct feedback in cells gives operators increased visibility of problems. Our spatial perspective on cells holds that operations and those who perform them are located close together. This makes it possible to get an immediate overview of the status of work in cells and to easily detect problems. Moreover, you can achieve near immediate feedback from one operator to another. Marry this with small build quantities, a system's view of work, pooled expertise, and family focus, and you have an environment where operators can quickly detect and correct problems—before the same mistake is incorporated into other parts or products. Operators in one assembly cell discovered that a particular component was often mis-inserted, regardless of who was working at that particular station. They developed a "fail-safe" fixture that prevented incorrect placement of the component.

5. Accountability and ownership: cell operators "own" their work and are account-able for cell performance. A cell is a clearly identifiable place in a facility where an item is made. This means downstream users (including the ultimate customer) can provide feedback directly to the accountable production unit—the cell. This is not the case in job shops, where items are processed in various departments. A footwear plant we know of returns defective shoes directly to the module that built them. Operators repair defects and, as a group, are responsible for corrective actions that will prevent the defect from recurring. Similarly, operators in a small coil-winding cell developed a new way of labeling products for their major customer—an adjacent "celanoid switch" cell. The change came about as the result of feedback from the customer cell.

When operators have a vested interest in performance (i.e., their compensation is linked to cell performance) they may be especially motivated to identify improve-ment opportunities. At Turner Products, for example, each cell is assigned a set of performance objectives (e.g., cost, quality, safety, delivery) for the next six months. They must meet the stated targets in order to achieve the cell bonus pay. This chal-lenges operators to develop and implement improvements that enhance performance. Similarly, operators in footwear sewing cells, whose compensation is based on total good output, asked to be trained to perform minor maintenance and repair. Opera-tors no longer sit idle waiting for maintenance personnel to perform simple repairs.[19]

As these examples illustrate, cells provide a setting where questions about *why* improve, *what* to improve, and *how* to improve are easily answered. A sense of shared mission, teamwork, and accountability, as well as financial incentives for improvement, communicate *why* to improve. The operators' knowledge of products and processes, their skills and experiences, and their access to feedback from within and beyond the cell make clear *what* to improve. Finally, through training and from assistance by support staff, operators know *how* to make improvements happen. All this puts operators in an excellent position to actively pursue the continual improve-ment of cell operations.

SOME SPECIFIC STRATEGIES FOR IMPROVING CELL PROCESSES

In addition to the tools and techniques we mentioned in our overview of the process improvement model (see Figure 17-1 and Table 17-2), there are a number of specific strategies that can help uncover and remove waste in manufacturing. Cell teams can use these to guide the design of the cells, as well as to help refine operations once cells are in place. Here we discuss five strategies: the "5 Ss" for workplace organiza-tion, setup time reduction, mistake-proofing, automatic signaling, and standardiza-tion of work practices. We should also point out that visual display of data and the use of pull systems are other ways of detecting and removing waste from operations (we refer you to Chapters 9 and 11 for these topics).

5 Ss, and 5Ws and 1H

The 5 Ss of workplace organization refer to the Japanese words for separate, straighten, scrub, sustain/standardize, and systematize (see Figure 17-3).[20]

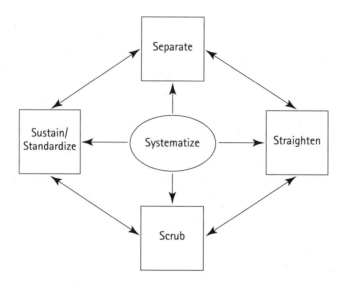

Figure 17-3. The 5 Ss

Separate means simplification through elimination. This involves sifting through the workplace for materials, supplies, tools, papers, folders, and so on, determining what is necessary and discarding what is not. Thus, separate is about getting rid of the clutter that confuses, confounds, and obscures. The team in Western Geophysical Exploration Products' Bay Cable cell, for example, designated and marked space for equipment, supplies, work in process, and other items required to make cable. Anything that was not required was removed from the cell.[21]

Straighten means "a place for everything and everything in its place": assigning essential items to specific locations, having them clearly marked, and making everyone aware of these assignments. A visual approach makes misplaced items obvious. Color coding and clear, big signs are useful ways of achieving this "self-explanatory" status. For example, the Disposable Capsule Filter Cell at Gelman Sciences decided that it was spending too much time looking for tooling. To address this the operators built vertical tool boards for each machine. They designated the location for each tool with a written label and a black outline in the shape of that tool. The board made it visually obvious where to place each tool and whether any tool was missing.[22]

Scrub means cleaning the work environment. Once separating and straightening have occurred, a thorough housecleaning is necessary to assure that everything is clean, neat, and in good working order. *Sustain/standardize* means to make separating, straightening, and scrubbing routine tasks. Thus, equipment, tools, and the workplace need to be maintained in good working order once the initial scrub has occurred. Further, while major maintenance activities may need to be the responsibility of a specified maintenance group, the cell work team can be responsible for sustaining the area through many day-to-day clean-up and maintenance tasks. For example, in addition to cleaning up after machines (discarding chips, keeping equipment free of dust and dirt build-up), the cell team can assure that common break areas are kept neat and orderly. Finally, *systematize* means to expand the use of the previous four steps throughout the organization and continually improve.

Implementing 5 S

5 S efforts often begin with "red tag" campaigns. Employees use a dated red tag to target items for removal from the immediate work area. If, after a specified period of time, no one has used or moved the tagged items, they are either stored in a remote location, away from the work area, or discarded. Items stored remotely are reviewed once a year to see if they should be kept or discarded. Once unnecessary items have been eliminated (separated), you can proceed to straighten, scrub, sustain/ standardize, and systematize.

The use of checklists is another excellent tool for practicing the 5 Ss. Appendix J provides a checklist from a large electronics facility. Teams developed the checklist as part of training sessions on lead-time reduction and waste elimination. They then used the checklist to identify improvement opportunities (note that many of the items included on the checklist pertain to housekeeping; others go well beyond this). Audits by external groups, such as the plant's safety team or industrial engineering group, can effectively reinforce the discipline of the 5 Ss. Such teams can perform monthly audits of all cells, tagging safety or housekeeping violations.

Cells are the ideal setting for applying the 5 Ss since they have finite physical boundaries and a focused mission. This makes it relatively straightforward to identify what is extraneous and what needs to be in the cell to support the work. Moreover, individuals who are familiar with the workplace and accountable for results staff the cells. This means operators have a stake in getting and keeping the workplace clean and orderly. Of course, you need to train operators on the 5 Ss and make explicit the benefits of a more orderly workplace. And keep in mind that while getting people to embrace the 5 Ss can be a struggle, experience is a great teacher. A cell supervisor at Delphi Saginaw Steering Systems explained that he "thought it was crazy that [the location for] everything had to be outlined with yellow tape, including the wastebasket. Now he understands this attention to detail because everything in the cell has a purpose."[23]

The 5W and 1H technique

A related guideline for waste elimination (and problem-solving) is the "5W and 1H" technique. This means asking why (not who!) five times whenever a problem occurs or waste is encountered, and then determining how you can improve this situation.[24] Here is an example applied to workplace organization:

- Today the cell produced fewer units than planned. *Why?*
- Because there was a production stoppage at the auto-bonding station. *Why?*
- Because Jim could not locate a fixture he needed. (He looked in the shelves that hold the fixtures for this machine but could not find it; then he and his supervisor looked in the shelving intended for other machines' fixturing. They found the fixture after a 15-minute search.) *Why?*
- Because the fixture had not been returned to the right shelving the last time it was used. *Why?*
- Because it is easy to make a mistake when putting a fixture back. *Why?*
- Because most operators know where to store the fixtures, but the shelves are not labeled. *How* can we improve this situation?

- Label the fixtures, assign each a specific storage location, and label the storage location. Operators can then easily discern where to retrieve and replace fixtures.

Note the parallel between this series of questions (what's the problem, why did it happen, and what's the solution) and the improvement model we presented in Figure 17-1. The 5W and 1H technique is a simple but powerful tool for teams to use as they go beyond symptoms to determine the true underlying or "root" cause of a problem.

Setup Time Reduction

Setup time is "the time spent between the production of the last part of one lot and the production of the first *good* part of the next lot: the time during which no good part or product comes out of the equipment."[25] Entire volumes have been written on the importance as well as the tools and techniques of setup time reduction. Shorter setups mean more time for value-adding activities, or extra capacity that can be used to reduce lead times (see Chapter 7). Short setups also provide the flexibility for cells to economically produce different items in small quantities. According to the manager of one machining cell, "Setup is the root of all evil. Large setups limit your flexibility to produce exactly what is needed and dictate how fast the production process can change. Once setups are gone, you can do virtually anything in any quantity."

The average setup time for milling and turning operations in a precision machine shop was about eight hours. The shop then created a cell to manufacture families of connectors. Reducing the range of parts helped streamline setups for cell equipment. In addition, engineers and operators collaborated on a number of setup reduction projects over the course of about a year. These resulted in further improvement. Some of the changes made included:

- Standardizing material so the same bar stock could be used for all cell parts.
- Standardizing metric dimensions for all part prints. (This consistency helped operators avoid errors because they no longer had to determine whether the prints were metric or inches, or convert inches to metric before beginning setup procedures.)
- Creating dedicated setups that did not need to be torn down.
- Using insert tooling.

As a result of these changes, setups for the cell's milling and turning fell to about five minutes.[26]

Although we often think of a long setup (or changeover) as a problem in a machining context, setup reduction is useful for all types of cells (including office cells). Creating a family of parts will, by itself, reduce setup time. After all, similar items should have similar setup requirements (unless the similarity is not based on the manufacturing process). However, you may find that additional setup reductions are both possible and necessary in order for cells to perform well. Organizations that attempt to implement cells without reducing setups are likely to find that those cells fail to live up to expectations.[27]

Implementing setup time reduction

Cell operators are often the most qualified group to attack setup time reduction.[28] They have the best knowledge of the machines, are continually dealing with setup and operation problems, may already have ideas for improvements, and will be significantly affected by any changes. In addition, they may be particularly motivated to develop practical solutions because they will be the ones following the revised setup procedures and living with the results. While engineering, tooling, maintenance, management, and other support areas may contribute, operators represent the core team for setup reduction. Frequently, the cell leader or supervisor will provide formal leadership for the setup time reduction effort. In addition, some companies use setup "hit teams"—small groups of workers skilled in setup reduction that act as consultants to other work groups tackling setup time reduction.

Actively engaging operators in simplifying and improving setups taps a powerful source of expertise. But how do you make this effort happen? A few points are worth noting. Active participation in setup reduction efforts may be greater when operators understand "what's in it" for them. If the current setup is "painful"—complicated, difficult, or time consuming—for those who perform it, they may be particularly interested in working toward an improved process. Moreover, when cell rewards are linked to performance measures that are impacted by long setups, operators are likely to be motivated to improve the current process. (The cell concepts education provided to operators—see Chapter 13—should have convinced them of the link between short setups and improved cell performance.) At Turner Products, for example, the team bonus is linked to several performance metrics that are directly impacted by setup time. Consequently, streamlining setup procedures has been the focus of numerous cell improvement efforts.

We provide additional guidelines on how to implement setup time reduction in Appendix K.

Mistake-Proofing the Processes

Poka-yoke is yet another waste reduction and improvement strategy adopted from Japan. The word "poka" means "mistakes caused by carelessness," while "yoke" means "to avoid."[29] You can think of poka-yoke as "mistake-proofing," "error-proofing," or making a process "fail-safe." Essentially, this means designing processes so that mistakes are virtually impossible to make. There are countless examples of poka-yoke mechanisms: templates that guide correct insertion of components, fixtures that only permit workpieces to be attached in the proper orientation, storage areas and material pallets that are color-coded to assure the proper materials in the proper places, color-coding similar looking parts to help distinguish them, and so forth.[30] Figure 17-4 shows the housing for a detector array used in a plastic sorting cell. The asymmetrical slots assure that the housing is inserted in the guide rails properly and is aligned with the ejection system (the system which removes items that the detector has identified).

Cell operators are in an excellent position to identify commonly encountered defects or mistakes that can be avoided through fail-safe mechanisms. In an electronic instrument subassembly cell, for example, final inspections discovered that screws were occasionally too loose, which caused poor connections, or too tight,

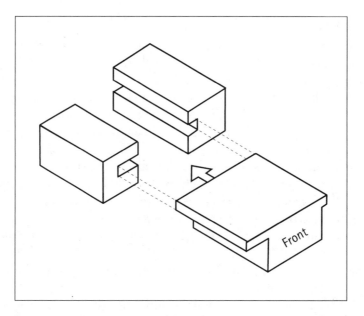

Figure 17-4. Mistake proofing mechanism: keyed detector slide

which caused cosmetic problems. Working with manufacturing engineering, the team suggested using pneumatically controlled screwdrivers adjusted to a pre-set torque level. In a lawn mower assembly cell at another plant, parts were redesigned so that the left and right brackets could not be confused.

Automatic Signaling

Closely related to mistake proofing is another Japanese work design principle, "autonomation," or automatic signaling as we prefer to call it. The point of automatic signaling is to free operators from "babysitting" machines—that is, to design equipment so that it does not have to be watched, but is able to signal when it needs attention. Modern industrial equipment often features this capability. Adding it to older equipment frees operators up for more value-added activities.

Operators in a motor assembly cell at Oriental Motor's Takamatsu factory in Japan suggested that machines automatically stop and signal for human intervention whenever a defect occurs. Factory staff adapted equipment by adding auto-inspection devices that check the motor's characteristics, wiring, and pressure resistance. These devices signal operators whenever they detect an abnormality. These changes, and other automatic signaling and fail-safe mechanisms (e.g., jigs that prevent parts from being mis-inserted; optical devices that signal when part labels have been omitted), reduced manpower requirements, improved productivity per worker, and reduced in-process defects to 0.6 percent, down 80 percent from their previous low level of 3 percent.[31]

The Development and Use of Standard Operations

A *standard operation* is the prescribed and repeatable way of performing a particular task or process step. Standardization offers a number of advantages. First, it leads to reduced variability, which translates directly into improved quality and shorter, more predictable, lead times (see Chapter 7). Further, it is easier to train new people or exchange people between work areas if the process is clearly and completely documented. Finally, adherence to a set of standard operating procedures is the key requirement for organizations seeking ISO 9001 (and QS 9000) registration—credentials that more and more organizations are requiring of their suppliers. In short, standard operations drive out variation in methods and procedures and, as a result, create a repeatable, predictable process that yields high-quality outputs consistently and at lower costs.

There are three critical aspects of standard operations. The first is having the most recently *agreed-upon best way* of performing the task or process documented. The second aspect is *procedural discipline*—assuring that individuals follow the documentation. Finally, there must be a *mechanism for improving* the currently documented "best way." Many organizations discover that the process of creating a cell and focusing on part/product families provides a perfect opportunity for determining and putting into practice standard operating procedures (the checklist in Appendix J can stimulate useful ideas in connection with a process standardization effort).

The case of the connector cell mentioned earlier provides an excellent example. As the cell was being designed, machinists met to decide on the best ways to perform the operations. They developed a flow chart and a lengthy process documentation guide that represented the agreed-upon best way to make each part. This document became the basis for the part programs that control the cell's NC equipment. Before they developed the standard processes, each operator had his own way of performing each operation, captured in separate part programs. Afterward, there was only one way to perform each operation, and the machinists consistently worked to the documentation.[32]

Operators sometimes resist standardized operations, claiming that this practice forces them to work more slowly than they did in the past. In a cell established to manufacture attenuators, the move to standardized operations and sequential flow brought complaints from operators who felt that their creativity had been taken away. According to the manager: "We spent a long time working through this. When operators complained that 'you are not allowing me to take a risk,' we had to get them to recognize that you have to take data if you want to make a change. You must provide a logical reason and be able to back it up."

To deal with resistance to standardized operations you need to clearly communicate their purpose and advantages. You can also make operating to the standard an expectation by measuring compliance as part of regular performance evaluations. In addition, you must have a well-understood mechanism for making process changes. The attenuator cell, for example, has a formal process improvement process. Employees with improvement ideas have a forum (daily and weekly team meetings) in which to propose them. They know that their input will get a fair hearing.

BUILDING A CULTURE OF CONTINUOUS IMPROVEMENT IN CELLS

How can you assure that cells continually improve? Or, more specifically, how do you create "a culture of improvement" that encourages cell operators to constantly work toward bettering the cell? In this section, we offer a number of specific prescriptions for institutionalizing continuous improvement.

Create a sense of ownership. Continuous improvement is more likely to happen routinely when those doing the work "own" the process. Cells, by their very nature, often instill that sense of ownership. The supervisor of one cell at Western Geophysical Exploration Products' plant in Alvin, Texas notes that "If there was a reject, everyone took responsibility. Everybody learned new techniques and taught each other. There was a lot more ownership. They felt part of decision-making. They knew what they had to do. There was a lot more teamwork."[33] Similarly, at Gelman Sciences, it was easier to create enthusiasm about improvement projects once the cell was created.[34]

Make improvement an expectation. Recognize and reward it. To build a culture of continuous improvement you need to set an expectation that improvement is part of the job. As we discussed in our chapters on performance measurement and compensation, if you want to communicate that something is important, then measure and reward it. At Tellabs, cell employees are evaluated regularly on their "contribution toward continuous improvement," and at an electronics plant with cells, "process improvement skills" are one of four critical job skills included in the company's "learn and earn" program (see Chapter 14). Along the same lines, Turner Products links the cell's bonus pay to progress in meeting cost-reduction objectives (see Chapters 9 and 14 for a detailed discussion). In each of these instances, management is sending a clear message that improvement is an expected and important part of the job.

You can also send a message through the use of recognition programs. Many companies use such programs to acknowledge employee contributions to continuous improvement (also see Chapter 14). At Bic Corporation, for example, employees can earn "Suggestion of the Month," a highly coveted award that carries with it a small cash prize and, even more importantly (in the workers' estimation), substantial recognition from peers and management (the winner's photo is prominently displayed on the employee suggestion bulletin board).[35]

Create a structure to capitalize on employees' ideas. For continuous improvement to thrive you need a structure in place that gives employees opportunities to put their ideas to work. Obviously, the use of formal improvement teams is one way of giving employee ideas a forum. Cells at one electronics plant, for example, have weekly team meetings devoted to "problem-solving and improvement." These hour-long sessions address issues that the team has identified during daily meetings and which cannot be resolved immediately. We have seen this structure in place at many other facilities trying to create a culture that embraces continuous improvement. As this suggests, you must be willing to provide employees with the time to propose, evaluate, and implement improvements.

Formal suggestion programs are yet another structure for employees to contribute to improvement. In these programs employees are encouraged to offer ideas for improvement by placing ideas in physical or electronic (web-based) suggestion boxes. While such programs have been around for a very long time (the first documented U.S. suggestion program was at Eastman Kodak in 1898), they have recently gained greater popularity.[36] Corporate leaders have recognized that "workers know more about their immediate surroundings than anybody else, and are smart enough to spot defects in products and procedures and to figure out solutions to them." At Bic Corporation, for example, a cross-departmental team of employees evaluates suggestions submitted each week. When the team endorses an idea, they assign it to an owner (generally the supervisor of the area most responsible for making an improvement happen) who has 10 days to put the change in place. In year 2000, 577 of 684 hourly manufacturing employees submitted 2,999 suggestions, of which 2,368 were implemented.

One hallmark of a successful suggestion program is that employees know that ideas they submit are heard and, if appropriate, lead to action. If employees feel that ideas fall into a "black hole" awaiting management approval and action, the program likely will be unsuccessful and lead to employee dissatisfaction. To assure that good ideas are put into action quickly, some companies permit employees to make changes that cost less than a given amount (say $1,500) without high-level management approval. This practice also underscores another important element of continuous improvement efforts: funds must be available to support them. Some firms accomplish this by making "improvement" a line item in the departmental budget. Other firms have a plant-wide pool of funds available to support improvements.

Be open to new ideas from the workforce. Operators working in a cell will probably come up with new work practices that you haven't anticipated. One manager observed, "there were emergent activities that just cropped up among the teams that the company really never drove for at all." Cell teams at one plant asked to interface directly with supplier representatives. Management hadn't envisioned delegating this responsibility to the teams, but was willing to experiment. In another instance, cells resisted sending completed work in process back to the storeroom, suggesting that it should go directly to the customer cell. Neither management nor stockroom personnel had considered this option, yet in the end it became standard practice.

Provide training. Training is an essential element of continuous improvement. Cell employees must understand the basics of problem-solving and decision-making in order to participate effectively in improvement efforts. They must also be familiar with the tools for data collection and analysis, and be knowledgeable about specific strategies for removing waste and improving efficiency. (See Chapter 13 for advice on designing and delivering this training.)

Make support groups partners in cell-based improvement. The cell team will invariably need support from specialists in the plant. Although their hands-on position makes shop floor personnel the source of many improvement suggestions, engineering and management support often are required to approve and capitalize on operator ideas.[37] Further, support staff may see opportunities or solutions rooted in their own area of expertise and specialization (e.g., engineering or maintenance) that would not be obvious to operators.

Many of the characteristics that make cells foster operator-based improvement also make it easier for other groups to identify ways of improving cell performance. Most notably, bringing cell operations together "under one roof" helps managers, supervisors, engineers, and other support groups see improvement opportunities that simply weren't apparent when equipment and processes were dispersed. When one plant created assembly and test cells, engineers supporting the effort realized there were large opportunities for standardizing testing procedures and tooling across the family. The family focus highlighted operational inconsistencies and unnecessary variation that the test engineers were then able to address.

Collaboration among operators and support groups will, in our opinion, lead to the greatest improvements in cell operational performance. Making support staff available to cell teams on an as-needed basis communicates volumes about the company's commitment to improvement.

Let cell teams make mistakes. Finally, it is important to remember that not all improvements developed by teams will be effective. If you want to build a culture that encourages experimentation and risk-taking by operators and others, you must let teams make a few mistakes from which they can learn. Too much guidance and intervention can stifle initiative and convince teams that they are not really expected to seek improvements. As one manager observes, "when you want your teams to make changes, you have to *let* them. You can't just let them make the changes that *you* want—at some point, you have to trust that they will make the necessary changes." However, there must also be boundaries whenever decision rights are delegated. "Unlimited" empowerment is not a strategy we recommend.

Table 17-3 summarizes elements essential to building a culture of continuous improvement in cells.

Table 17-3. Promoting a culture of continuous improvement in cells

• Create a sense of ownership for improvement among cell operators
• Make improvement an expectation of cell operators; reward and recognize employee contributions to improvement
• Create a structure (e.g., improvement teams, suggestion systems) to tap cell employees' ideas and put them to work
– Provide the time for employees to identify and solve problems, and to put solutions in place
– Follow-up on suggestions
– Provide the funds needed to support improvement efforts
• Be open to new ideas from the cell workforce
• Provide cell operators with training on improvement techniques and strategies
• Make support groups partners in cell-based improvement
• Encourage experimentation and permit mistakes

BEYOND CONTINUOUS IMPROVEMENT—THE FORCES OF CELL EVOLUTION

Continuous improvement is a way of life in many cellular systems. However, cell designs and cell operations often change as the result of forces "beyond continuous improvement." Examples include factors external to the cell, such as *changing market demands, technological advances,* and *shifting business priorities.* In addition, problems at the *interface between the people and work processes* can motivate cell change. In this section we explore these major forces and the ways cells evolve in response (see Table 17-4 for a summary).

Table 17-4. Forces driving cell evolution

Changing market demands • Changes in product mix and overall volume levels • New product introductions **New technology** • New processing technology • New information technology **Organizational and strategic change** • Organizational restructuring (e.g., consolidations, sale of business) • Shifting business objectives **Issues at the interface between people and technical work processes** • Ergonomic concerns • Training issues

Market Demand—A Force for Change in Cells

Rare is the cell that is not forced to adapt to changes in volume and mix (mix changes include discontinuing old parts and phasing in new ones). At one transmission manufacturing plant, 70 percent of the sheet metal parts now made in cells did not exist when the cells were established. And this experience is not unique. Half the respondents to one of our studies reported that their cells produce parts for which they were not originally designed. On average, the number of "new parts" represented about 11 percent of part numbers and 8 percent of total cell volume.[38] "Part numbers come and go," and "volumes will shift based on a multitude of factors" observes another study of cells.[39] As we noted in Chapter 16, this can be a significant issue for cells. When mix changes cause the similarity among cell products to decline, cell benefits are more difficult to realize. The cell will incur more setups, efficiency will fall, effective machine utilization will degrade, output rates will decrease, and lead times will lengthen. Similarly, volume changes may mean demand outstrips cell capacity or leaves cell resources underutilized. To remain viable, cells must find ways to adjust to these changing mix and volume conditions.

You can use different types of strategies when demand changes. For example, you may:

- Use overtime/idle time.
- Perform setup reduction.
- Increase cross-training.
- Modify equipment speeds.
- Adapt tooling.
- Develop alternate routings.
- Outsource parts.
- Change staffing levels in the cell.
- Add/delete shifts.[40]

Some of these responses (e.g., overtime/idle time) leave basic cell design and operations relatively unchanged. Others, such as additional setup reductions, greater cross-training, and changing staffing levels, may lead to incremental changes to cell operations. For example, the routine use of temporary workers (one way of changing staffing levels) to respond to changing demands can motivate (and, in fact, may demand) the development of simpler cell work procedures and greater clarity in documentation. The manager of an electronics cell that uses temporary workers on a regular basis says that "we had to really focus on making our processes easier to do and simpler to teach."

Shifting demands can also lead to more dramatic changes in the way a cell is designed and operated. Large demand changes will sooner or later prompt management to redefine the part/product family and restructure the cell. A fabrication cell was originally established for the complete production of an electronic accessory. The cell performed all operations from raw stock to finished goods inventory, except plating. When volumes declined, management removed all machining equipment, placed it back in the functional area of the shop where it would be more fully used, and focused the cell exclusively on assembly and test. These tasks required only a single operator.[41] Similarly, when demand outstripped capacity for other cells, management broke apart some families and outsourced the parts that were the easiest to make. This left the cells to focus on the higher value-added items.

Of course, increasing volumes can also cause cell expansion. A single operator, who was responsible for virtually all direct and indirect labor tasks, staffed a cell that produced a family of plastic parts. After several years of steady-state operation, demand increased beyond the cell's capacity. Management's response was to add a second major piece of equipment. It also assigned two operators to run the cell during first shift, and used a third operator during second shift. These operators assumed only *some* of the tasks the original operator had performed. Many activities (documentation, parts ordering, scheduling, and so on) were reassigned to support groups so that cell operators could focus on production.

Both increasing and decreasing demand may prompt management to disband a cell. When a machining shop experienced a dramatic and unexpected upswing in demand, plant management eliminated two cells that had been dedicated to low-complexity parts. It subcontracted the parts made in these cells, and reassigned the people and equipment to other cells making more complex parts.[42] Conversely, declining cell demand also may prompt management to eliminate cells. At one plant we studied, management elected to do a lifetime build of an aging product, dismantle the cell, and reassign the equipment and people.

How do you prepare cells for dynamic demand?

Both the magnitude of changes in demand and the flexibility of the cell influence the types of adaptations cells need to make. While we've given a few examples of cells being dissolved in response to dynamic demand, this is, in our experience, relatively rare. This observation is supported by a number of studies that "converge in their findings that a cell can remain relatively intact over an extended period of time with respect to its core processes and product families, although some of the equipment (including tooling) as well as individual products may be subject to change."[43] Thus, most cells are able to evolve, as opposed to getting dissolved, in response to changing demand. But successful evolution is more likely if you have (1) created a culture of continuous improvement (discussed earlier), (2) designed the cell to handle volume and mix fluctuations (discussed in Chapters 6 and 16; see especially "Dealing with Changing Production Requirements" in Chapter 16), and (3) partnered with the design group to promote design for manufacturability. We'll take a closer look at this last factor.

Partnering with the design group. New products may not fit well in existing cells. Accommodating new, ill-fitting products can mean more setups, erratic flow patterns, lower efficiencies, poorer cell performance, costly new equipment, or even cell dissolution. When product designers see this "bigger picture," they may be more motivated to design products "into" the existing cells. Thus, you want to make sure designers know the "what" and the "why" of manufacturing cells, especially that they understand current cell capabilities, and the cost, delivery, and quality consequences of product designs that stray from existing cell processes.

The more product designers attempt to design products to fit cells, the longer the life of the cells. Involving product designers in the original cell design process is one way of providing them with first-hand knowledge of the cell's capabilities. We haven't seen much evidence of this in practice, however. One of our recent studies found that design engineering was involved in cell design efforts only about 20 percent of the time. And, while over half the firms in this study did redesign parts/products in connection with cell implementation, they reportedly made only minor changes. Hence, they may not have viewed design engineering as a key player.[44]

A partnership with design engineering can lead to the development of new, more standardized products that actually improve cell performance. One cell produced a family of oscillators. The build process for these oscillators included circuit assembly, much of which takes place under microscopes. Designers came up with an advanced circuit design for a new product that could replace several circuit types in products the cell already built. Introducing this "universal" circuit allowed cell operators to replace unique fixtures and tools with standard ones, thereby eliminating several process steps and improving cell performance with respect to cost, quality, and lead time.[45]

New Technology as a Driver of Cell Evolution

Technological advances can be a powerful force in cell evolution. In some cases, however, cells easily assimilate new technology, and only subtle changes in cell operations ensue. For example, in one study involving 20 metalworking firms, several companies replaced manual or old, numerically controlled equipment with new NC or CNC equipment.[46] These machine upgrades improved performance but did not change the cells' overall structure and operation.

Sometimes new technology can cause cells to evolve in unanticipated ways. Management at one plant purchased a high-speed flexible milling machine for a cell that was going to produce a family of 18 parts. Once the cell was up and running, "new product introductions came hot and heavy." There was suddenly a big need to turn around lab prototypes quickly. The two cell machinists, along with the department manager, offered to run some of the prototypes in the cell. They were convinced that the new milling machine had more capabilities than were being used. As it turned out, the new mill was perfect for casting simulations, i.e., milling prototypes of what would eventually be cast parts. Typically, the model shop would make these prototype parts on conventional equipment, a process that took several days. Since the cell could do the work in a day, it became the preferred producer of lab prototypes. This made the cell less available for production parts, some of which management off-loaded permanently to other cells.[47]

We have also seen new technology at the heart of decisions to sharply refocus cells. For example, we know of several companies that have removed manual or light-guided printed circuit board loading from existing product assembly cells to take advantage of capital-intensive, high-volume processing technologies (e.g., auto insert and surface mount).[48] In some cases, new cells have been created that focus exclusively on loading families of similar boards using this technology. The original assembly cells now focus on the remaining assembly steps and treat the circuit board as simply another material input.

A study of Dutch firms found that advances in manufacturing technologies (e.g., CNC machining) can reduce the need for multi-machine, multi-operator cells.[49] However, new multi-operation machines also allow organizations to create cells where a single machine and its operator now perform all process steps. Advances in miniaturizing process technologies (e.g., small-scale surface mount) may also make it possible to decentralize current monument process activities. Thus, future technological evolution might lead to an increased degree of cellularization.[50] (We discuss this trend in greater detail in Chapter 19.)

Finally, *information* technology can be a driver of cell change. Advances in information processing and distribution can give operators greater access to key information in support of real-time decision-making. We have seen cells where new information systems replaced ad hoc manual part family scheduling systems. The new systems gave operators more timely and accurate information on what to make, reduced the amount of time operators had to invest in making scheduling decisions, and freed them to spend more time making product. Similarly, the introduction of on-line documentation changed work in electronics subassembly cells and improved performance as well. The new system assured that the single, most current version of product documentation was available to all cell operators. They no longer needed to begin work by verifying that the hard copy documentation at the workstation was the most current version. Also, errors due to wrong documentation declined dramatically.

Thus, in both cases information technology helped improve performance and changed how workers spent their time. The important message here is that technology can be a force in cell evolution and be at the heart of both incremental and radical cell change. You must stay abreast of technological changes that may impact cell operations and look for opportunities to leverage them effectively.

Organizational and Strategic Change May Require Cell Change

Changes in ownership, restructuring, and shifts in organizational priorities are often the catalyst for both cell creation (see Chapter 4) and cell change. Sometimes these factors motivate organizations to expand their use of cells. In other instances, strategic considerations will prompt the organization to move away from cells.

Expanding the cell concept

At one plant, organizational restructuring provided an opportunity to make even greater use of cellular concepts. Two machining shops, each with a number of cells, were consolidated in one location. The broader product line and higher volumes that would be produced by the combined shop prompted a reassessment of all operations for their cellular potential. Management decided to enlarge some existing cells to include equipment and part families that had not previously been made in cells. Other cells were retained in their existing form, and several new cells were created as well.[51]

Strategic initiatives can also motivate management to expand the cell concept by duplicating an existing cell in another location. An electronics company wanted a manufacturing presence in South East Asia. Management looked for a manufacturing process that could serve the growing Asian market and be easily replicated. It selected a large cell that made electronic equipment accessories. Over the past several years, the cell's continuous improvement efforts had focused on developing standardized operations, improving workplace organization, reducing setups, and eliminating waste. Exceptionally clear work instructions meant that process knowledge was explicitly documented, not just tacitly known by those who did the work. These factors contributed to the cell being successfully duplicated in the remote location.[52]

Moving away from cells

Shifting organizational objectives can sometimes underlie decisions to move away from the cellular concept. At an electrical machine shop, management shifted its focus from "the quality of labor and organization" to "financial results."[53] Until 1993, this 140-employee facility had operated with 14 relatively autonomous manufacturing cells. Management's emphasis on cost reduction played out on the shop floor as a desire to better utilize the CNC equipment. In addition, volume was a factor: demand was growing for customized products, but these did not fit neatly into the existing cells. This led to a move towards a more functional arrangement where expensive equipment could be fully loaded. In the machining and turning area, five cells were reconfigured into two larger cells. Likewise, the sheet metal area retained only two cells, and allocated the equipment in the remaining cells to two functional departments.

A Dutch company in the oil tank accessory equipment business implemented four cells, each staffed by 9 to 14 workers.[54] During the first two years, changes in product demand required only incremental changes to the cells. The plant then merged with a functionally organized company that initially adopted cells as well. But over the course of the next three years, management became convinced that the costs and difficulty of maintaining the right level of multi-functionality among operators outweighed the benefits of the cells. The plant reverted to a functional layout.

Another Dutch firm with cells underwent a similar "devolution."[55] After several years of operation, management changed strategic direction and wanted to (1) increase the functional expertise (by having operators who perform the same function learn from one another), (2) make the cells more flexible (by including more and different pieces of equipment), and (3) reduce the cost of supervision. To achieve these objectives, the company's six cells were compressed into three. This change, akin to creating three focused mini-job shops, moved the organization away from the cell concept and back towards a functional arrangement. Operators now focus on a wider range of parts but on a more limited range of equipment (see Chapters 6 and 7 for discussions regarding cell size and performance).

Due to strategic rethinking, another company decided to sell off its sheet metal operations, which included a number of cells. Management wanted to focus on production activities where the company had a distinct competence. There were capable suppliers nearby who could provide quality parts quickly and at costs lower than the company's own sheet metal operations. The company ended up selling the sheet metal equipment to another firm that dispersed it into its functional organization.[56]

Finally, cost pressures may cause a firm to transfer a cell to another location. A manufacturer of automotive components, for example, operates a number of cells. Over the course of several years, continuous improvement efforts had successfully streamlined and simplified operations in a particular cell. As a result, the skill levels required for cell work had decreased. This allowed management to transfer the cell to a plant in a lower-wage country (with lower skill workers). The operators from the original cell were reassigned.[57]

Implications of organizational and strategic change

A firm's competitive situation can have a profound impact on the adoption and evolution of cells. As we described in Chapters 1 and 3, most organizations create cells to help achieve strategic objectives (most often to reduce lead times). But just as there are real business reasons to organize productive resources into cells, there may be compelling reasons for moving away from them. To remain viable, cells must continue to help the organization meet its strategic objectives. Thus, cells need to evolve over time. As the examples above illustrate, cells are sometimes dismantled in response to reorganizations or strategic shifts. However, we haven't seen this happen in very many firms. In fact, at most of the companies we have studied, the use of cells has expanded, not contracted, in the face of evolving competition.[58]

Issues at the Interface of People and Processes

Because work in high-volume cells can be repetitive, it is a logical target for ergonomics. We have seen a number of companies where a heightened awareness of cumulative trauma disorders (CTDs) and repetitive motion/repetitive stress injuries (RMIs/RSIs) has led to initiatives aimed at eliminating work that causes injuries. Cell workers at Gelman Sciences, for example, analyzed videotapes of existing cell operations for inefficient motions that could contribute to repetitive stress injuries. At first, workers did not believe that simple changes such as switching the hand they used could decrease fatigue and increase productivity. However, workers who experimented with the new methods out-produced their peers and were less tired at day's end. Other workers reluctantly adopted the changes, and the new methods became standard operating procedure.[59]

Of course, the solutions went beyond just switching hands. For example, one of Gelman's large assembly cells developed new fixturing devices, installed adjustable tables and chairs, and adopted pneumatic tools to help ease work strain. Other cells moved equipment closer together to eliminate double handling. Management also removed equipment and assembly processes that had been linked to repetitive motion injuries, and outsourced work.[60] At another plant a multi-operator cell that fabricated a family of cartridges was dismantled when changes to operations were unsuccessful in eliminating the risk of injuries. Automated equipment was purchased to produce the parts, and a single operator staffed the resulting cell.[61]

The above examples may make it sound as if cells are a poor form of work organization that causes injuries. However, due to job-rotation, small lots, and multi-skilling, *cell work can actually reduce the risk of repetitive motion injuries*. Chapter 12 gave examples of companies that created cells in part to curtail work that hurt people.

Training issues

Besides ergonomics, another people issue that promotes cell evolution is training, and in particular, training that increases the degree of multi-functionality and cross-training in the cell. As operators acquire more varied and more overlapping tasks, cells may be able to operate with fewer employees, thereby changing staffing levels. We've seen this type of cell evolution at many plants. Similarly, training may facilitate increased job rotation (and thereby job enlargement—see Appendix F), as well as the allocation of additional indirect labor tasks to the cell (job enrichment—again, see Appendix F). Both change cell operating routines, while the latter impacts the types of infrastructure support and supervision that are appropriate for the cell. Thus, operator training can be a force for change in cells.

Implications of people issues

People issues can drive cell evolution. Therefore, be proactive when it comes to people in cells. Carefully consider the way you design or redesign jobs, select people, and train them for cell work. Consider these infrastructure issues as an *integral* part of your cell design and implementation process (also see Chapters 12 through 16).

KEY INSIGHTS

The title of this book, *Reorganizing the Factory*, signifies not only the change from a functional to a cellular organization, but also the constant reorganization that is necessary for the firm to adapt to changing conditions. Our discussion of the improvement and evolution of cells over time makes it clear that cells are not static: change is a reality in cellular settings. An important message of this chapter is that *you should view cell design and implementation as the point of departure for never-ending efforts to enhance manufacturing performance*. The following insights elaborate on this point.

- *Cells are not static.* Cells evolve in a variety of ways and for a variety of reasons. They can change as part of ongoing continuous improvement efforts, or in response to external factors. Cells may expand or contract, be restructured or dismantled. Whatever its magnitude, cell change is constant. Expect it, plan for it, and be open to it.

- *Capitalize on cells as a venue for continuous improvement.* Cells bring people and processes together and focus them on a producing a set of similar items start-to-finish. Product knowledge, a system's view, complimentary skill sets, fast feedback, and ownership/accountability for results make cells a fertile environment for continuous improvement.

- *Create a culture that fosters continuous improvement.* To take advantage of cells as a source of continuous improvement you need also to provide operators (and others) with training, tools, freedom, and incentives to make the cell better and better every day. Create a structure to tap cell employee ideas, and make support groups a partner in cell-based improvement. Bottom-up involvement where *operators* influence the shop floor is one of the success factors for organizations transitioning to a lean manufacturing approach.

- *Staff up your engineering resources and make sure support groups understand the what, why, and how of cells.* Engineering support is essential for the continuous improvement of cells. Don't make the mistake of expecting continuous improvement but failing to provide the staff to support it. However, people outside the cell can contribute to improved cell operations, but only if they understand what the cells are all about.

- *Be aware of the major drivers of cell change.* Cells evolve in response to market pressures (e.g., the need for added flexibility), technological change (e.g., the purchase of monument process equipment that cannot be decentralized to the cells), shifting organizational priorities (e.g., a focus on cost over responsiveness), and issues at the interface between the cells' technical and social systems (e.g., ergonomic issues, costs of maintaining multifunctionality). Recognize that these factors may drive changes to your cells.

- *Consider design and operational policies that will extend the life of your cells.* There are a number of things you can do to extend the life of cells:
  - Where technically and economically possible, design flexibility into your cells through appropriate machine selections.
  - Provide cross-training to support a flexible workforce that can adjust to changes in cell product volume and mix. This will enable you to vary staffing levels in response to demand fluctuations.
  - Promote the design of products that fit cells. Provide the product design group with rich information about cell capabilities and cell requirements.
  - Consider redesigning cells to accommodate changing demand or emerging technologies.

- *Have a strong cell champion.* Visible and vocal management support is important to the successful conversion to cells. The same holds true for maintaining cells once they are in place. If the champion leaves or is not very committed, cells may be abandoned prematurely, simply for lack of an advocate who really understands them and their contribution.

- *Reorganize cells to support your strategy.* We think cells can help many companies achieve their strategic objectives. But for cells to remain viable they need to stay linked to strategy. For most cells this means adapting to changing competitive conditions.

EXTENDING THE CONCEPT—
CELLS IN THE OFFICE

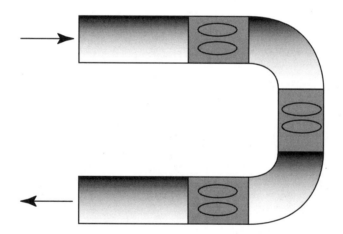

18

Reorganizing Office Work Using Cellular Principles

All manufacturing organizations have office operations for tasks such as taking orders, putting together quotations, and planning and scheduling production. These white-collar activities can be critical to success in the marketplace. In a typical manufacturing organization you are likely to find that over 50 percent of total lead time is consumed by office operations.[1] Moreover, as we point out in Appendix D, administrative overhead is a sizable component of cost of goods sold (COGS), typically representing between 25 and 35 percent. This suggests that a major portion of product costs can be attributed to office operations.

For many organizations, office work represents huge untapped opportunities for process improvement. Over the past 20 years, the net productivity gains in white-collar work are less than one percent.[2] Simply put, companies have not applied the same effort on reducing lead time and eliminating waste in office operations as they have in manufacturing. Much office work, in fact, is still organized and managed in ways that companies now *avoid* in manufacturing.[3] Keep in mind that both office and manufacturing processes are part of the same value delivery chain. This means improved manufacturing lead times may have little overall business impact if administrative processes have not kept pace. For example, a large manufacturer of telecommunications equipment reduced production lead time by weeks, but since pre-production activities—like order entry and specification development—still took months, response time to customers remained slow.[4]

This chapter will show how you can apply cellular thinking to improve office (administrative) work. In particular, we answer these important questions:

- Why should you rethink the way you organize office operations?
- What are office cells?
- How can office cells improve performance? What are the benefits and disadvantages?
- How do you design office cells? What steps should you follow?
- What infrastructure changes will best support work in office cells?
- What are some of the implementation problems you may experience?

Although almost all of the material for manufacturing cells, discussed in Chapters 1 through 17, applies to office cells as well, we have attempted to make this chapter as self-contained as possible. If you have read all previous chapters, this chapter may serve as a high-level, condensed review of cellular manufacturing thinking.

OFFICE OPERATIONS—THE INFORMATION FACTORY

In manufacturing, you are moving, transforming, and storing materials to produce a physical product, while in office operations you are moving, transforming, and storing information. You can think of office operations as an *information factory*. This information factory performs knowledge work; that is, it involves the application of knowledge bases and the processing of information.[5] Some of this work is relatively static and involves a fairly repeatable pattern of activities: we will refer to this as *routine* knowledge work. Processing an order for a product, completing a request for quotation, or preparing a shop order packet would be examples. While such processes may involve simple clerical tasks (e.g., entering information into a database), routine knowledge work often also requires specialized expertise, judgement, and decision-making. Thus, "routine" does not always mean simple or requiring low skill levels. It only means a process that recycles relatively frequently, and where the tasks required to produce a particular type of deliverable (e.g., a completed request for quotation) are relatively stable.

Office operations, however, can also involve *non-routine* knowledge work. New product development is a good example. For any given product development project, the sequence of steps to follow and the time required for each step depends on the nature of the product being developed, the expertise of the players involved, and a host of other factors—many of which are external to the development team (e.g., what the competition is doing, the company's strategic direction, the advent of new technology, and so forth). Non-routine knowledge work often involves considerable uncertainty, and decisions must be made in the absence of complete information. Further, non-routine office work tends to involve many parallel information processes that influence one another (e.g., hardware and software engineers working concurrently), adding another layer of complexity to this work. Finally, non-routine knowledge work (such as new product development) tends to involve temporary teams, which may come together physically only occasionally. And even if such teams are co-located, it is only for the duration of the project. They are not permanent structures.

In this chapter, we focus on routine office work. Given its repeatable and static nature, you would expect that this type of work normally is performed effectively and efficiently. However, the reality is that routine office work is often poorly executed, resulting in long lead times and poor quality. This has much to do with the way in which administrative functions are typically organized.

The Job Shop Nature of Office Operations

Many parallels exist between office operations and traditional job shop manufacturing. Most firms organize office work along functional lines into departments. Instead of milling, drilling, and turning, they have sales and marketing, purchasing, and accounting. However, just like in manufacturing, office work rarely gets completed within a single department. At one organization, for example, order processing activities involved 80 possible steps and 12 different departments.[6] So, while most organizations are structured vertically by department, most work moves horizontally across departments. Let's look at the advantages and disadvantages of organizing work according to department or function.

Advantages of departmentalized office operations

In a functional structure, employees specialize in the work performed by their department, sometimes focusing on very narrow sets of tasks. One clear advantage is that employees will come to know their work quite well. Working alongside others who perform similar tasks, they are also in a position to learn from one another and further develop their expertise. This means that departmental tasks are often performed very efficiently—an advantage further ensured by having departmental managers generally measured on the degree to which they efficiently utilize resources available to the department.

The departmental structure also provides employees the opportunity to progress up well-known vertical career ladders (e.g., from order entry clerk to order entry supervisor to order entry manager) that are consistent with their education and experience. Moreover, functional specialization simplifies management and control; that is, it is easier to supervise, monitor, and control individuals who are performing like activities.

With respect to performance, the big advantage of functionally organized office work is flexibility—work can follow virtually any path through the various departments as needed to complete the job.

Thus, organizing work around functional tasks can yield high task efficiency as well as deep skill development, high resource utilization within departments, overall routing flexibility along the complete process, and focused supervision (e.g., marketing supervisors are only supervising marketing work). As compelling as these advantages might be, they are frequently offset by significant disadvantages.

Disadvantages of departmentalized office operations

The disadvantages of departmentalized office operations are, as in job shop manufacturing, long lead times, quality problems, limited accountability, and fractionalized, "sub-optimal" improvement efforts.

Lead times. You can see the same "batch and queue" phenomenon in office operations that you see in job shops. Batching in office operations happens because individual workers try to avoid mental—or "intellectual" changeovers.[7] An order entry clerk may wait for a day's worth of requests to come from the field before entering them in the system. A sales engineer may wait until the end of the day to fax, phone, or email in the day's orders. While this makes the individual tasks (e.g., entering requests into a database) more efficient, the overall process will be slow. When work is physically moved between work stations (for example, in folders or binders), batching may also take place in order to reduce the number of moves. Besides batching, lead times are also dependent on the amount of rework, the time the job is waiting, and the time the information spends being moved between the people who need it. In a typical information factory process, as in manufacturing, transit (travel) and queue (wait) times consume the majority of the administrative lead time (usually about 90 to 95 percent).[8]

The financing arm of a major computer manufacturer, for example, discovered that only 90 minutes of productive work took place during the six days typically required to turn around a request for financing. Queue and transport time accounted for more than 95 percent of the total processing time.[9] An East Coast bank required ten days to approve or deny credit card applications but processing the application took only about two hours. Here 99.75 percent of the total processing time was consumed by transfer and queue time.[10] You can probably find similar examples among your own office operations.

In office work, as in manufacturing, queue time is the real lead-time villain. Instantaneous information transfer using information systems and technology can make the transit time negligible, but queue time still exists. Just consider your own electronic and paper in-boxes. Unless they are *always* empty, your work is part of a process that includes queue time.

Quality. Traditional office operations are often plagued by quality problems. Every handoff between people, whether inside or between departments, is an opportunity for mistakes, a place where you can lose or misinterpret critical information. In addition, departmental office workers often know only a small part of the process. Therefore they might not recognize errors introduced in previous steps, and if they do, it might be long after the error occurred. Since fixing a mistake often means returning the work to another department, this adds more time and the potential for more errors. Lengthy problem resolution cycles are the norm.[11]

In fact, much office work consists of additional, wasteful steps required to correct errors made at some point in the process.[12] Examples of extra work to deal with mistakes include handling customer complaints about poor-quality products, contacting the customer for more information because the original order data were incomplete, re-quoting a product because the original customer specifications were in error, and redoing an invoice because of an erroneous product number. These activities are "necessary" only because of previously introduced errors. In fact, some jobs exist mainly to correct earlier errors or mistakes. One example is a customer service representative whose major responsibility is to follow up on customer complaints. Another example is a quality control clerk whose function is to inspect outgoing work for errors. If upstream employees performed their work perfectly the first time, these "rework" jobs would not need to exist.

Even in jobs designed to create value, considerable time can be spent fixing mistakes. And, even worse, fixing mistakes may be so commonplace that it *feels* like real work. Marketing associates at a large computer manufacturer spent approximately 65 percent of their time on activities that involved correcting mistakes or dealing with problems in the process. Examples included processing customer returns, converting orders to fix a problem, expediting shipments, and answering questions about order status.[13] Unfortunately, because of the fractionalized nature of office work, mistakes and rework are commonplace and quality is particularly difficult to assure.

Accountability and improvement. In departmental structures, individuals can be held accountable only for the work they actually perform. No one who works in the process "owns" the process. This creates an accountability vacuum: every time work moves from one area to another, it might fade from sight.[14] Further, no one is looking at how all the pieces fit together, or how to make them fit together better.[15] Improvement efforts tend to focus on improving departmental performance, not the performance of the whole process. This is because individuals tend to be measured and rewarded on their contribution to the department's goals, not on the performance of the larger process. Everyone seeks to optimize his or her fiefdom (the "silo mentality"), often at the expense of overall performance.

Table 18-1 summarizes the consequences of traditional routine office work.

Improving Office Operations: Follow Manufacturing's Lead!

Many organizations have streamlined their manufacturing operations but haven't addressed office operations. Why is that? First, office work deals with information flows, not physical goods. It is more difficult to observe the process, pin down the waste, and identify errors when there is nothing physical to see.[16] Since problems aren't obvious, it is easy to assume that the process is "okay."

Second, much of the waste in office operations occurs as a result of required interaction between multiple departments (i.e., work is carried out by different people belonging to different departments). While transit time may not be large (in fact, non-existent in the case of electronic information flow), the time work spends waiting in queue between operations is where the real waste can be found. This waiting time may be invisible to departmental managers who are focused on fully using the resources of their department and not on improving the total process. And upper managers, responsible for managing interdepartmental flows (the "white spaces" on the organization chart), do not know the details of work or how to improve it.[17]

Finally, most organizations—if they measure office work at all—measure *task* performance and rarely *process* performance (such as lead time). One insurance company, for example, launched a project to speed up the new policy approval process. As a first step they studied the existing process and were surprised to discover that the process lead time was about two weeks, while the value-added time was about 7 minutes—customers were waiting two weeks for less than 10 minutes of work to take place. Moreover, the team discovered that about one-fifth of the policy applications had errors or were missing information. Most of these mistakes were introduced early in the process as salespeople worked with customers to complete applications. However, salespeople were measured and rewarded on sales volume, not on the accuracy or completeness of applications. In the current process, these errors and omissions were detected only by downstream steps in the process, who simply sent the applications back for rework but did not track the errors. Management was surprised to learn that lead times were so long compared to the value-added content, and that error and rework rates were so high.[18] But, then again, how could it have known? No one was measuring these critical process performance dimensions!

The recent focus on business process reengineering has motivated many organizations to scrutinize office operations. A major theme in reengineering is process

Table 18-1. Traditional routine office work and its consequences

Characteristics of Office Work	Positive Consequences	Negative Consequences
• The company is organized into functional departments • People work alongside others who are performing similar work within the same functional discipline • Work travels through multiple departments • Individual employees are responsible for tasks that represent only a small part of the overall process • Supervision is by department • Performance measurement is by department • Inspections tend to take place at the functional boundaries • Decisions require higher-level approval	• Individuals can develop deep skills within their functional specialty due to repetition, mentoring, and the ease of sharing "best practices" • Managers can allocate work to any of a number of individuals who can perform a specific activity • Supervisors can provide excellent technical leadership because they need only master one specialty • The system is flexible—work may follow any needed path through the various departments	• There are long lead times due to transport times and large queues of work in process • The large number of handoffs (1) provide opportunities for mistakes, and (2) require that each employee in the flow become familiar with the information (setup time) • Employees may not know how their work fits in and may not be able to see process-wide improvement opportunities • Approval systems are required to control highly fragmented work • Process ownership exists only at the higher levels of the organization—no one working in the process is accountable for the overall process results • There are lengthy problem resolution cycles and lack of timely feedback on performance • Departments involved in the same process may have inconsistent goals • Measures do not focus on improving the performance of the overall process • Expeditors may be necessary to move work through the process • Many checkpoints exist to find and correct mistakes

focus—organizing the work of the enterprise around key business processes and out-comes.[19] This notion of process-complete operations also lies at the heart of office cells.

WHAT ARE OFFICE CELLS?

Office cells organize work, and those who perform it, around key processes. While a manufacturing cell transforms *materials* to produce a physical product, an office cell transforms *information* to produce information deliverables. These deliverables are the "products" or output of information processes. Order processing, for example, yields processed orders as the deliverable. Likewise, a "request for quotation" process yields completed quotes, and a "production planning" process yields schedules.

Based on the general definition of cells we gave in Chapter 2, we present this for-mal definition of an office cell:

> An office cell is a group of closely located workstations where multiple sequential operations are performed on one or more families of similar information carriers. The cell is a distinct organizational unit within the firm, staffed by one or more employees, accountable for output perfor-mance, and delegated the responsibility for one or more planning, control, support, and improvement tasks.

More succinctly, an office cell is a cell whose main task is to process, transform, transmit, and add value to families of information deliverables.

Illustrations of Office Cells

In order to help you visualize the creation and structure of office cells, we provide short examples of three different types of cells. Each example involves order process-ing, perhaps the most common application area for office cells.

Ryerson Tull's order processing cells

Ryerson Tull is a metal distributor with headquarters in Chicago, Illinois. Its East Plant processes incoming metal plate in thicknesses of 1/4 to 16 inches. Processes used include cutting (via oxifuel, electric arc, laser, and circular saw cutting), sand-blasting, and straightening (bending to flatness).

The plant's operations manager was concerned about the time required to process accepted customer orders from the point they were printed from the ordering system until they reached the foremen's offices in the plant. That process was as fol-lows. After customer orders were received, credit checks performed, and the raw material situation verified, the orders were sent electronically to the dispatchers' office. Eight dispatchers released jobs to the next process step—"line-up"—based on backlogs and due dates (see Figure 18-1). After line-up, the jobs went through "plot" and "pre-timing and timing," and then waited in queue to be picked up by a dis-patcher who took the orders down to the plant floor. These process steps (line-up through timing) were performed sequentially by seven workers over two shifts, but each employee only worked on a single task. The office clerks involved, who were paid on an hourly basis, were located in two offices on separate floors.

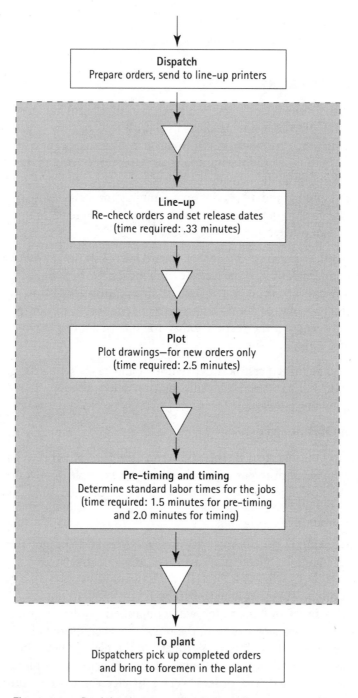

Figure 18-1. Partial order process at Ryerson Tull

Pedro Rodriguez, a summer intern from the Manufacturing and Technology Management (MTM) program at the University of Wisconsin-Madison's business school, was asked by the office manager to reduce order processing lead time to one hour. Although the manager did not know the current lead time precisely, he knew he wanted same-day processing. Pedro analyzed the situation and found the following:

1. The orders moved through the process in Figure 18-1 in an average lot size of 20.

2. The average processing times per step were very low, ranging from 0.33 minutes to 3.5 minutes (see the boxes in Figure 18-1).

3. Although move times were not measured, clerks appeared to spend excessive time moving folders around between offices and floors.

4. Once jobs were printed at the line-up step, all the subsequent process steps handled hard copy documents that were moved around in folders holding drawings and schedules.

5. About 35 percent of the orders needed plotting. There was only one plotter available.

6. Orders were sometimes sent from the dispatchers' office to an office on the same floor, and sometimes to clerks sitting in an office on the first floor (see Figure 18-2).

7. There was a constant need for rework of already-processed orders, stemming from the fact that dispatchers commonly released orders long before they were due. However, customers often changed due dates, or material was unavailable. When this happened, orders had to be reissued so that the printed documents would reflect the most current information.

8. Orders frequently arrived late to the foremen's office in the plant.

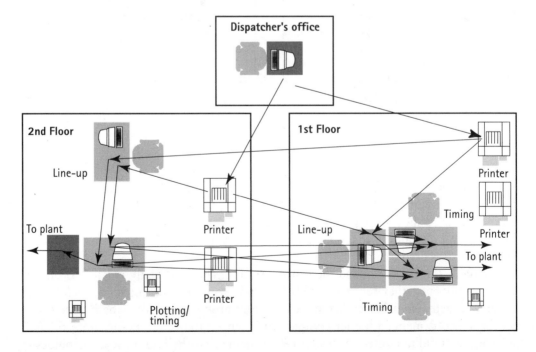

Figure 18-2. Original functional layout

After this analysis, Pedro suggested the implementation of two "process-complete" office cells—one dedicated to orders in need of plotting (i.e., new orders), and another for the remaining jobs (see Figure 18-3). Cell 1 would be staffed by two or three workers; Cell 2 would be staffed by two workers. Both cells would work a single shift. Although dispatchers would continue to process orders in batches, these would be split up once they reached the cells. Thus, the lot size in the cells was to be reduced to a single order. Further, to avoid rework, dispatchers were told not to release jobs early. To move completed orders more quickly to the foremen, dispatchers were also asked to pick up completed folders from the cells every hour.

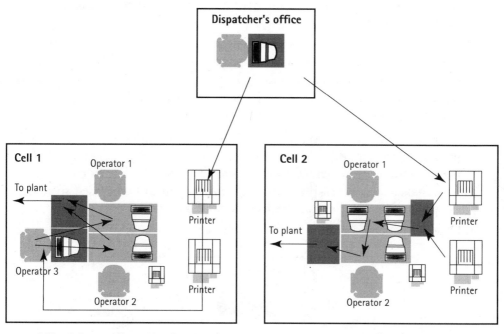

Office Cell 1 processes 35% of orders   Office Cell 2 processes 65% of orders
(those that do need plotting)   (those that do not need plotting)

Figure 18-3. The new office cells

The clerks were trained to perform two tasks in the cells (e.g., line-up and pre-timing), but eventually they will be fully cross-trained. As part of the initial training, employees were shown the principle behind the new system via a visual simulation (a PowerPoint presentation that showed how inventory builds up in systems depending on the lot sizes used).

Initially, the clerks resisted the office cell idea. They especially reacted to the cut in lot size because they felt it would mean they would run out of work (before, the large WIP acted as a buffer behind which true productivity could be hidden). The workers also demanded higher compensation since "they were doing more things." Management did not agree to this request, arguing that the level of responsibilities—or the job titles—had not changed.

Both office cells were implemented and now operate successfully. Due to more efficient processing, two of the original seven clerks were moved to another area, amounting to savings of about $60,000 per year. Although pre- or post-implementation lead times were not tracked directly, orders are now processed very quickly (due in large part to the single-lot principle). This office cell initiative was included as an example of improvement projects on Ryerson Tull's Intranet, making it available to the rest of the company's 70 plants.

While this example dealt with short-cycle clerical work, office cells can also be created for work requiring more sophisticated skill sets and higher levels of judgement and decision-making. This is illustrated by the next two examples.

Aetna's order processing cells

Aetna Life & Casualty created office cells to handle application processing.[20] Prior to creating cells, it typically took 28 days to process insurance applications, while the actual labor content was about 26 minutes. Many different people handled each application: a forms processor would enter the work into the process, a rater would calculate the premium, an input operator would enter this information into the system, another person would type up the policy statement, and yet another would send the policy to the customer.

Aetna has reorganized this work to take place in a number of office cells, each of which consists of a team of customer account managers. Each account manager has been cross-trained on all aspects of the process, so that work is now "one and done"—incoming applications are routed directly to one of several customer account managers who process it, rate it, and input it into the system. From there, the policy is printed and mailed to the customer. Although account managers work in parallel and handle applications start-to-finish, they are organized into teams that share responsibility for performance and improvement. Team members are responsible for training new team members, solving problems, and improving the process itself. Further, team members can earn a bonus based on their individual performance as well as on the performance of their team. By creating teams of case workers and treating them as an organizational unit Aetna encourages joint accountability and ownership, fosters sharing of best practices, and allows work to be routed to one of a number of qualified individuals.

A. Ahlstrom's order processing cells

Problems in order processing, including long and uncertain lead times, many mistakes, and much rework, prompted A. Ahlstrom, a Finnish manufacturer of specialty industrial products, to reconfigure the order processing function into three independent cells.[21] Prior to creating the cells, order processing involved as many as 10 distinct operations performed by individuals working in a number of different departments, including export sales, documents, order entry, finance, spare part sales, domestic sales, and shipping. The office cells brought together the needed specialists from various departments and arranged them in geographically focused cells: domestic sales, European and American sales, and Middle and Far East sales. Each cell team developed a set of protocols to govern their work. The teams also combined tasks so that now only five distinct steps are involved. Obviously, jobs were broadened compared to worker responsibilities before the cell. For example, the role of "sales secretary" and the role of "correspondent" were combined in one. Cell workers pass their work directly to nearby teammates within the physical confines of the cell. Average order entry lead time has fallen from one week to one day, while variation in lead time has fallen from six weeks to one week.

Classification of Office Cells

Figure 18-4 presents a classification system for office cells. Office cells may have single or multiple employees, who may be either physically separated or co-located. This leaves three possible alternative office cells: case worker cells, team-based office cells, and virtual office cells.

	Employees Are Not Co-located	Employees Are Co-located
Single employee	(Infeasible)	Case worker
Multiple employees	Virtual office cell	Co-located, team-based office cell, or simply "office cell"

Figure 18-4. Types of office cells

Physical office cells

Physical office cells bring together in one location the people and technical resources needed for a process-complete operation. Physical cells may consist of either single or multiple employees.

Case worker. A single-worker office cell is also called a "case manager" or "case worker."[22] Here, a single employee performs all the tasks necessary to produce a set of information deliverables. While you might find other case workers in the same physical location, they work independently. (In a manufacturing setting, single operator cells with start-to-finish responsibility would be called *craft* cells.)

IBM Credit arranges financing for the computers, software, and services that IBM sells to its customers. The company created case worker office cells that process all financing applications.[23] Each of these cells is staffed by a "deal structurer" who processes individual applications from start to finish, performing all the necessary steps while supported by an information system. The cell workers can get help from a few specialists (located in the same work area) who assist in the small number of cases that are non-routine. The cells process applications in an average of four hours, replacing a process that involved six different departments and took an average of six to seven days. This represents a 90 percent reduction in lead time. Compared with the previous process, the cell has yielded a 100-fold increase in productivity as measured by the number of finalized deals handled by the workforce.

Co-located team-based office cell. A physical cell where multiple employees collaborate, each performing some but not all tasks, is called a "case team," or simply an "office cell."[24] The order processing cells at A. Ahlstrom fall into this category. Consider also this second example.

Ingersoll Cutting Tool Company, located in Rockford, Illinois, is a manufacturer of replaceable metal cutting tool inserts.[25] It developed an office cell that processes "modified standard orders." These are customer requests for make-to-order versions of catalogue products. An example would be a tool with a slightly longer spindle or a non-standard diameter. In the past, these orders had taken as long as four weeks to reach the factory floor. Requests moved sequentially through 12 major activities (each of which consisted of numerous individual steps), and as many departments. Individual functions had their own information and data analysis systems that supported their part of the process.

In an effort to reduce lead times, the company created an office cell to handle this family of customer requests. The cell was staffed with two multi-functional individuals trained to perform all the tasks required to completely process a modified standard order. The company also enhanced or linked together many of the separate decision support systems. After implementing the cell, the average time to process a modified standard order fell to about two days, down from an average of about 10 days.

Virtual cells

In addition to physical cells, Figure 18-4 also shows that you can configure office cells even where employees are not co-located. As technological advancements increase the speed and capabilities of electronic data capture, storage, retrieval, processing, and transmission, it is possible to relax our "spatial perspective" on office cells. *Virtual office cells* exist where individuals are dedicated in their daily work to processing a family of like information deliverables, but they are not physically in the same place.

Waukesha Bearings is a manufacturer of fluid film thrust and journal bearings headquartered in Pewaukee, Wisconsin. In order to become more market responsive, management wanted to reduce order processing time by about 25 to 30 percent. A team of students from the University of Wisconsin-Madison's business and engineering schools analyzed the order process using process maps, concentrating on a subset of bearings with similar characteristics. The selected families represented a little over 20 percent of all new orders. Collected data showed that only 4.3 days out of about six weeks total order lead time were spent actually working on the order (touch time).

The following personnel were involved in the complete order process: customer service representative, project engineer, design engineer, scheduler, CNC programmer, and manufacturing engineer. Of these, the first three were located at headquarters in Pewaukee, while the last three were at the manufacturing site in Antigo, 200 miles away. Based on task sequences, skill requirements, anticipated workloads, and the difficulty of moving personnel, the team recommended the establishment of a virtual office cell for processing the families of bearings. This office cell would be staffed by one person at headquarters, combining the tasks of the project and design engineers, and by one person at the manufacturing facility, combining the tasks of CNC programmer and manufacturing engineer. The primary mode of communication between the two members of the virtual cell would be daily electronic mail. Through the broadened jobs some review and approval tasks could be eliminated, reducing the process time by between 15 and 20 percent. By using computer modeling (MPX; see Chapters 5 and 7), the future office cell lead time was calculated to be around 11 days, down from the previous average of 40 days.

Virtual cells can be useful when co-location is either too costly or impractical. This basically comes down to labor utilization and whether available, qualified personnel are willing to relocate. Note, however, that virtual cells can face problems—such as lack of team identification and total process ownership—related to people being physically separated. The limitations of current information technology can also be a hurdle. However, improved communication capabilities, using simultaneous picture and data transmission, will probably make virtual office cells more feasible and acceptable in the future.

Choosing between Team-Based and Single-Employee Office Cells

How do you decide which type of office cell—case worker or team-based—best suits a particular process? Essentially, this decision is about the presence or absence of teamwork. In general, you want to select the team alternative when teamwork will benefit performance. The questions below can help you decide if office cells with teamwork are right for your situation.[26] "Yes" answers suggest a team-based office cell.

- *Do the tasks require a variety of knowledge, skills, and abilities so that combining individuals with different backgrounds would improve performance?* If the work requires diverse skill-sets, bringing different people together may offer advantages. Moreover, where mistakes are possible (and a second set of eyes can help assure quality), where individuals can share expertise and raise everyone's skill level, and where there may be a need to dynamically adjust manning levels across different tasks within the office cell, multi-person cells can be beneficial. In short, where workers could assist one another in getting the work done, you would prefer a team to a case worker arrangement.

- *If varied skills are needed, would it be difficult, or prohibitively expensive, for one person to master all the skills needed to perform all process steps?* That is, do some tasks require expertise that is difficult or expensive to acquire? If it will be difficult to train an employee to perform start-to-finish tasks, then choose a team-based office cell where people with diverse skills can contribute to the process.

- *Is the information that must pass from step to step fairly easy to communicate, verbally, electronically, or as part of the physical documentation that travels from each step in the process?* This makes for small setup times as work travels from one cell employee to the next. It also reduces the chance for information loss where handoffs occur. When information is easy to communicate, several people can be involved in the process without creating a negative impact on flow time or quality.

- *Would the use of a team be consistent with the firm's cultural norms, organizational policies, employee relations, and leadership styles?* Will bringing a group of people together, and making them responsible for a process, be culturally acceptable? Will management provide adequate training and support systems? Will reporting structures and compensation be adjusted to reinforce the work of the team? Most importantly, will managers part with good employees who will go into the cell, thereby losing headcount as well as skilled employees?

- *Is the mix of cell work likely to include occasional non-standard requests from internal and external customers?* One of the greatest strengths of teams is their ability to generate ideas and adapt to changing situations. A team-based office cell offers an important advantage if the work may include some non-standard requests.

Obviously, a single-employee office cell makes the most sense when the benefits from teamwork are small. So if you answered "No" to many of the items in the previous list, the process you are considering may best be handled by a single employee. Specifically, case worker office cells are appropriate if you answer "Yes" to the following questions:

- *Do the scope and capacity needs of the work permit it?* Can one individual master all the skills and tasks required, and also have the capacity to meet the demand?

- *Do you want to avoid handoffs?* Are there significant setup times, and potential for errors and information loss, as work passes from one individual to another?

- *Do you want to provide customer contact throughout the process?* Do you want to have a single point of contact for providing information and checking status? Have you ever had to repeat the same information to a series of customer service agents? Or have you been called and asked the same set of questions about an order by different people? Case worker cells avoid this by providing the customer with a single point of contact for providing and receiving information.

Note that some organizations opt for case worker office cells but arrange the case workers in "teams." The Aetna application processing cells described earlier are an example. These "teams" are treated as an organizational unit held accountable for performance and improvement. However, because employees work in parallel (as opposed to in sequence), they cannot spot one another's errors or correct one another's work. You may want to consider this approach when (1) your process is best suited to a "one and done" approach, but (2) you also would like to encourage joint accountability and ownership, be able to route incoming work to any member of the team, and foster continual improvement and sharing of best practices among office cell employees engaged in the same work.

BENEFITS OF OFFICE CELLS

The most fundamental benefit from office cells is lead-time reduction. Companies with office cells also report improvements in process quality. Error rates fall and rework is reduced. Why do these benefits accrue to office cell operations?

In Chapter 2 we introduced four critical perspectives on manufacturing cells: the perspectives of *resources*, *space*, *transformation*, and *organization*. Then, in Chapter 3, we described the linkages between these perspectives, various cell characteristics, and potential performance improvements due to cells. Here, we focus that discussion on office operations. Our discussion might seem overly academic ("who cares where the benefits come from as long as we get them?"), but we think that if you understand the *sources* of the benefits you will make better decisions about office cell design and operation.

The Resource Perspective

From a resource perspective, an office cell is a small group of resources—human and technical—dedicated to information processing. A number of benefits derive from dedication. First, it means that resources focus exclusively on processing a family of information deliverables. Thus, there are no competing activities to tie up these resources. This can mean lower lead times for office cell work.

Second, you can do meaningful cross-training when a group of employees produces a family of information deliverables. This can include adding managerial responsibilities (for example, approvals and inspection) to the tasks office cell workers perform. Increasing the task and skill variety for the employees can mean higher motivation and job satisfaction (see Chapter 12). Further, employees capable of handling several process steps are able to move to where work is backed up and the load is the greatest. This can mean less idle time and higher resource utilization in office cells. Both can contribute to shorter lead time and lower costs.

Finally, cell work, as opposed to isolated tasks, can create a sense of process ownership. It allows employees to identify with the cells' outputs and the cell team, and contributes to a sense of team cohesion. The result can be increased employee motivation and higher job satisfaction, which in turn can have a positive effect on productivity, defects, turnover, absenteeism, and costs.

The Spatial Perspective

The spatial perspective holds that office cell resources are grouped in close physical proximity within clear physical boundaries. In this environment cell employees are able to:

- Move hard-copy work (such as drawings, folders, manuals, and files) shorter distances.
- Transfer small batches of work on an ongoing basis, such as passing along one invoice, instead of waiting until a day's worth has accumulated. This is an important benefit when information processing involves physical documents.

Both of the above contribute to faster throughput and less work in process.

Moreover, closely located employees can collaborate with nearby cell colleagues in making decisions and resolving issues. Co-location makes possible the easy exchange of work-related information. Team members can provide immediate feedback on performance, assist with problem-solving, discuss the nuances of a particular transaction as it unfolds, or step in and help execute a task if needed. They can spot errors and directly communicate instructions to the individual who needs to correct them (or they themselves can undertake the correction). This means faster problem resolution cycles. Such rapid feedback helps reduce defects and improve quality.

Closely located office cell employees can develop a sense of team cohesiveness, thereby increasing job satisfaction and motivation. This may also lower turnover and absenteeism, and so reduce costs. Further, an understanding of the whole process—a by-product of physical proximity—often leads to higher task significance for office cell employees: they can see the importance of their work. This, too, can mean higher motivation and greater job satisfaction. In addition, this whole-process knowledge equips cell employees to both identify problems and improve the outcome of problem-solving activities. This can mean fewer defects, higher quality, lower costs, and improved efficiency.

The Transformation Perspective

Performing multiple sequential steps on a family of like information deliverables is the essence of the transformation perspective. Let's look first at setup. When an employee performs multiple successive tasks on a piece of work, there are fewer handoffs. This eliminates (or nearly eliminates) associated times to prepare to process the job. Case worker office cells, where a single individual does start-to-finish processing of each job, have no handoff setup time. (They may incur other elements of setup: obtaining needed forms, preparing to do the next step, walking to the fax machine, etc.) In team-based cells, handoffs may exist, but the broad knowledge that comes from repetition, cross-training, and familiarity with the whole process helps reduce the "intellectual" changeover time for the employees. In an office cell with short setups, there is less temptation to batch work. The focus is on performing sequential steps, not on repeating the same task "n" times before passing work along. Setup reduction and small batches mean faster throughput and improved quality.

Focusing on a longer chain of operations and on families of information deliverables has a profound effect on stabilization and improvement. The more similar the information deliverables are with respect to their required steps, the more similar will be their processing times. This makes the process more stable (a prerequisite for process improvement) and more predictable: you can state with a reasonable degree of certainty when a completed production schedule will reach the shop floor, or when a response to a request for quotation will be completed. Thus, start-to-finish processing within the office cell can make throughput times more predictable.

In addition, the transformation perspective points to the benefits of repetition. Employees in office cells work on a family of information deliverables that have similar processing requirements and which they come to know quite well. This means enhanced learning, increased efficiencies, faster processing, and lower costs. Further, any changes operators make to improve the process (e.g., design a checksheet to ensure that required information is captured at the source), benefits not just one transaction, but the entire family. Thus, office cell improvements can deliver a bigger punch.

The Organizational Perspective

From an organizational perspective, an office cell is a separate administrative unit within the larger organization. The office cell is accountable—to a single manager or supervisor—for performance, problem-solving, and/or improvement. The organizational dimension of office cells is associated with many benefits:

- As a separate and accountable administrative unit, office cell workers own the whole process. They assume responsibility for functions that management and other groups may have performed in the past, including quality control, approval, improvement and, in some cases, direct contact with customers. For example, at Showtime Networks, which introduced office cells to focus on billing and collection, cell workers "get out of the office and talk to clients. We try to find out from them how we can provide better services. That's the kind of contact we never had before."[27] This whole-process ownership can mean job enrichment and enlargement, which can contribute to higher job satisfaction. Higher job satisfaction can have a positive effect on performance. In addition, for the reasons already noted, office cell workers that own the whole process can contribute to higher quality, lower costs, and reduced lead times.

- Treating the cell as a separate administrative unit can contribute to a sense of team cohesion. This can help the cell team perform more effectively and may be the source of increased job satisfaction and motivation.

- When office cell employees themselves make decisions, they can resolve issues quickly and at the source. This can improve quality and speed.

- Making the cell accountable for improvement can motivate incremental changes that improve quality, lead time, cost, and so forth.

- You can treat the office cell, and not individual departments, as the planning unit. This facilitates output planning (e.g., requests for quotations, completed production schedules). Treating the office cell as an organizational unit can also reduce the need for job tracking—you can simply monitor work coming in and out of the cell. Simplified tracking lowers overhead costs.

- Costing can be simpler and more accurate. All the required resources for a particular process are part of an administrative unit and are dedicated to that process. It's easier to determine the cost to develop quotes, for example, when all the resources required to do this work are part of a single unit dedicated exclusively to this activity.

- You can develop performance measures that focus office cell employees on critical aspects of process performance, such as lead time, quality, and cost.

Linking Benefits to Office Cell Characteristics

The resources, space, transformation, and organizational characteristics of cells are linked to one another, and directly and indirectly to the benefits that cells achieve. Table 18-2 ties these relationships together. We identify the major office cell benefits

Table 18-2. Origins of office cell benefits

KEY BENEFIT	WHY THIS BENEFIT IS REALIZED	DEFINITIONAL PERSPECTIVES			
		Resource Perspective: cell is a small group of resources dedicated to processing similar information deliverables	Spatial Perspective: resources are physically grouped together within clear cell boundaries	Transformation Perspective: cell performs multiple sequential process steps on family of information deliverables	Organizational Perspective: cell is a separate administrative unit within the larger organization
Shorter and more predictable lead times	• Physical transport time is virtually eliminated		X		
	• Cell resources are dedicated to cell work—there are no competing flows	X			
	• People know and perform their jobs better due to repetition			X	
	• Measures can focus workers on achieving these objectives for the cell as a whole				X
	• Setup times are shorter, or there are simply fewer setups			X	
	• Batch (and transfer batch) sizes can be as small as one		X	X	
	• Similar process flows facilitate process stabilization and improvement			X	
Fewer defects/better quality	• Fewer handoffs between employees in different departments			X	
	• Visibility of the whole process facilitates improvement and makes mistakes obvious		X		
	• Ownership—employees are responsible for the process	X			X
	• Rapid problem detection and resolution cycles		X		X
	• Measures can focus workers on achieving this objective for cell deliverables				X

Table 18-2. Origins of office cell benefits, (continued)

KEY BENEFIT	WHY THIS BENEFIT IS REALIZED	DEFINITIONAL PERSPECTIVES			
		Resource Perspective: cell is a small group of resources dedicated to processing similar information deliverables	Spatial Perspective: resources are physically grouped together within clear cell boundaries	Transformation Perspective: cell performs multiple sequential process steps on family of information deliverables	Organizational Perspective: cell is a separate administrative unit within the larger organization
Increased motivation and job satisfaction/lower turnover and absenteeism	• Multi-functionality means employees enjoy greater task and skill variety	X			
	• Employees experience job enrichment, and may be responsible for "managerial" tasks	X			X
	• Greater sense of team cohesion	X	X		X
	• Greater task significance—employees view their work as important		X		
More accurate costing	• All resources involved in the process are part of the cell, and the cell is only responsible for this process				X
Lower costs and higher efficiencies	• Employees can move to where the work is (higher utilization)	X	X		
	• "Whole process" knowledge facilitates process improvement		X		
	• Measures can focus workers on achieving these objectives for the cell as a whole				X
	• Simplified work planning and job tracking				X
	• Improvements benefit a whole family, not just one information transaction			X	
	• Enhanced learning and efficiency through repetition			X	
	• Making employees accountable for performance can motivate incremental improvements				X
	• Delegating managerial/support activities (e.g., approval) to office cells can lower costs	X			X

and the major factors that contribute to achieving each, and we link each factor to one or more definitional elements drawn from our four perspectives.

POTENTIAL DISADVANTAGES OF OFFICE CELLS

Office cells are designed to achieve process completion, but not necessarily flexibility. Thus, they trade off the job shop ability to do "anything" (but not rapidly, nor efficiently) for the ability to do a narrow set of tasks quickly, predictably, and with high quality. As attractive as this sounds, there are trade-offs involved that may degrade performance along other dimensions. Here are some specific disadvantages that may accompany office cells:

- *Low resource utilization due to duplication.* If you have duplicated resources for the cell (e.g., bought another large printer, or hired another person), utilization of these resources may be unacceptably low.

- *Capacity imbalances due to dedication.* Office cells may become over- or under-loaded when the volume and mix of work changes. In general, office cell resources should not be made available to handle non-cell work. This means that these resources may stand idle while similar resources in other parts of the administrative system are overloaded. The opposite is also possible: office cell employees may face large backlogs, while other departments' resources are underutilized.

- *Vulnerability to absenteeism.* The cell may be vulnerable to employee absences. If the individual knowledgeable about cost estimation is absent and no one else in the cell has this expertise, work will grind to a halt. (Of course, cross-training helps mitigate the impact of employee absences, although cell output will fall when fewer cell employees are present.) Job shop office environments enjoy the benefits of resource pooling: there is a set of similar employee resources to which you can allocate work in the face of absent employees.

- *Limited resource flexibility.* An office cell will be less capable of handling work that is outside the employees' skill set or the cell's resource capabilities. This means the cell will be less capable of handling work that requires tasks different from the dominant cell workflow. New work may be harder to fit in the cell.

- *Costs associated with creating office cells.* If you must prepare new office space, integrate existing information systems, or acquire new information systems, office cells will require expenditures or an investment.

- *Loss of skill depth.* Because office cell employees no longer focus on a narrow set of tasks, they may not have the opportunity to develop deep skills in any one area. Thus, office cells trade off depth of skill for breadth of skill. Where deep technical skills provide a competitive advantage, office cells may erode an important strength.

- *People may dislike office cell work.* Some individuals do not like to work in an office cell for a number of reasons. For example, they:

– May not enjoy social interaction.

– May not like the pace of work in team-based office cells where the work of one employee is tightly linked to that of the next employee.

– May not like the peer pressure that can develop among office cell workers.

– May not want to share their expertise with others.

– May not want to learn new tasks.

– May not want to rotate among different office cell activities.

– May not feel office cell compensation is enough for enlarged jobs with more responsibilities.

– May not like being rewarded for group performance and may resent the presence of any "free riders" in the office cell. Because of this, some employees may prefer earning rewards solely based on individual performance.

– May prefer working alongside those in the same profession. Some employees may feel that cell work compromises their ability to develop within their specialty and learn from mentors within their discipline.

– May have concerns about career paths and advancement.

You need to weigh all these potential disadvantages. Ask yourself: Will this be a problem in my environment? If so, how big a problem? Will the potential disadvantages be offset by potential advantages? More broadly, at some point you will need to construct a comprehensive picture of office cell costs and benefits in order to determine whether making this change is worthwhile for your organization. We will revisit this important issue later in the chapter.

AN EIGHT-STEP PROCESS FOR DESIGNING OFFICE CELLS

In many ways, designing office cells is similar to designing manufacturing cells (see Chapters 4 through 6). However, there are some unique challenges created by focusing on information rather than on material flows. This section presents an eight-step office cell design process, summarized in Figure 18-5. In the section that follows we then identify design and operating principles to keep in mind as you work through the design process.

Step 1: Identify Target Information Deliverables

An office cell is created around a *family* of information deliverables that require a similar set of process steps for their completion. But how do you identify such a family? Just as with manufacturing cells, you can start by looking at either products or processes. Thus, you can begin by thinking about "products" (the information deliverables)—the orders, the quotes, the product specifications, and so on. Alternatively, a business process, such as order processing, quote development, or order fulfillment, can be a starting point. Ask yourself, "Who are the customers of this process and what are its key outputs?" This line of inquiry not only clarifies the process, but also leads you back to the information deliverables involved.

Whether you first consider information deliverables or the processes that produce them, there will be many potential candidates from which to choose. You want

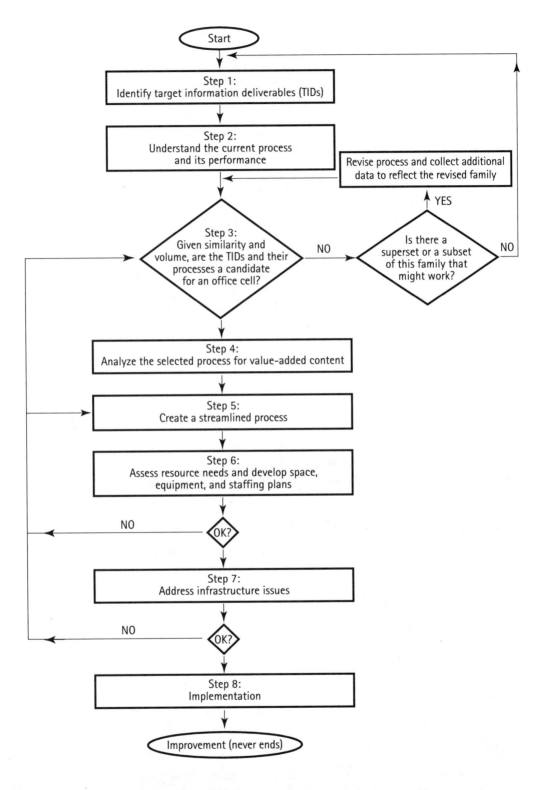

Figure 18-5. A process for office cell design

to select a family where improvements in response time and quality have a market payoff, i.e., a large impact on performance measures important to the customers.

In the physical goods arena, you can get a rough idea of part/product families by looking at product routings. It is not quite as easy when you are looking for families of information deliverables. The steps used to process information are more difficult to observe. There is often nothing physical to see. Further, routing information, *if it exists*, may not help very much: you may find written instructions for departmental tasks, but nothing that ties these together into a whole process.

Given these challenges, how do you get started? In Chapter 5 we pointed out that a great way to begin analyzing manufacturing operations is to segment them based on product focus. The same principle applies to office operations. Thus, partitioning administrative work based on the manufactured product families that office routines support reduces complexity for the subsequent analysis. It also clarifies the link between manufacturing—and manufacturing cells, if they exist—and associated administrative processes.

Furthermore, you'll want to use customer and market information, along with a fair amount of judgement, to identify *target information deliverables* (TIDs). Here is the essential strategic question: For what family of information deliverables would a streamlined and higher-quality process net a real return in the marketplace? Data to answer this question often already exist in the form of customer feedback, market trends, competitor's initiatives, and strategic gap analysis. Ingersoll Cutting Tool Company, for example, targeted orders for their "modified standard" cutting tools as a direct result of a market-driven need.[28] Management recognized that a major portion of the lead time for this order fulfillment process was consumed by administrative activities—tasks that took place before the order ever reached the shop floor. They concluded that the firm was losing business in this market because of long lead times, and that a streamlined office process had become a necessity.

Step 2: Understand the Process for the Target Information Deliverables

In pursuing office cells you need to closely examine the workflow of your TIDs to see if it will meet your criteria for *similarity* (are there commonalties in the required processing steps?) and *volume* (are these flows of sufficient volume to justify dedication?). Your analysis should answer these questions:

- What is the current workflow? What steps and departments are included?
- Do most deliverables follow the same process steps? If not, what variants are there and why?
- What knowledge and skills are required to execute this work?
- What other resources (special plotters, fax machines, reference manuals, etc.) are used?
- What is the current performance of this process (lead time, rework, cost, etc.)?

Two useful techniques to help you answer some of these questions are *functional flow charting* (also called deployment flow charting) and *tagging*. Functional flow charts (see Figure 18-6) show the sequence of activities in a process using standard flow charting symbols, but also use horizontal bands to represent the departments that perform them. They make it possible to see the flows between departments as well as the sequence of activities. Tagging (see Figure 18-7) allows you to track the time required for each process step and for the process overall. Both functional flow charting and tagging are described in Appendix L.

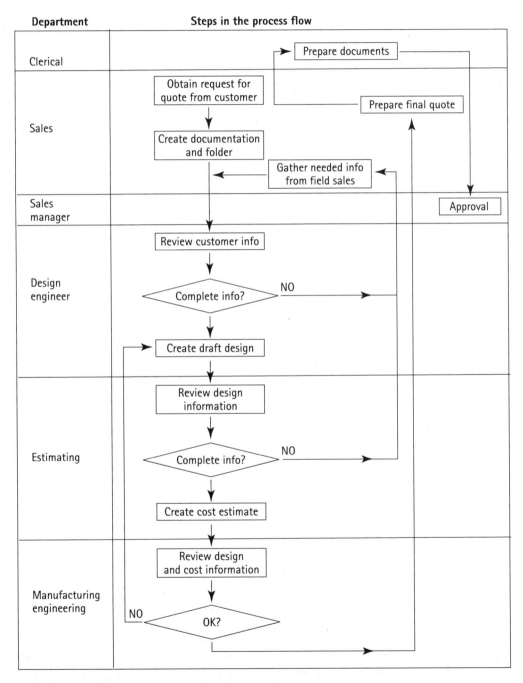

Figure 18-6. Functional flow chart for quote development

Process	Name of process					
Tagging Number	Unique number associated with each tag sheet					
Date Released	Date work began on this information deliverable					
Order Number	Order number associated with this work					
Customer	Name of customer for whom this work is being performed					
Name and Department	In		Out		Tasks Performed	Comments
	Date	Time	Date	Time		
Name of the individual who performed the work and the department in which he/she works	Date this person began work on this item	Time of day this person began work on this item	Date this person ended work on this item and sent it on to the next step in the process	Time of day this person ended work on this item and sent it on to the next step in the process	Specific tasks performed by this individual	Problems encountered during information processing (why the work was routed/ re-routed to this department)
Sally, Design Engineering	May 1	8:30	May 4	10:00	❑ Reviewed order information ❑ Contacted sales for clarification ❑ Drafted design	❑ Called sales on May 1; salesperson not available till May 2 at 11:30 to answer questions

Figure 18–7. Tagging sheet template (*explanations in italics*)

Step 3: Select Deliverables and Their Process for Continued Analysis

Analysis of the tagging data will reveal the average total lead time for this process, and the average time at various steps. It will also show the number of jobs that follow the general routing and its variants, and the quality problems at each stage. This lead-time, quality, and process information, along with volume data and the functional flow chart, can help you determine whether or not this process and its deliverables (or a more narrowly or broadly defined set) remain a good candidate for office cell work. For example, does the family of TIDs have sufficient volume to justify dedicated resources? If the volume is too large (or too small), is there a subset (or superset) of deliverables with sufficient volume to justify an office cell? If, for example, the volume for all "requests for quotations" is too large for a single cell, then you might consider quotes for standard (or non-standard) configurations, or requests from a particular class of customers, as the target office cell deliverables.

Step 4: Analyze the Selected Process for Value-Added Content

Next, you will want to determine the value-added content of your candidate process. Before rearranging employees and preparing them for their new roles, you should identify steps that do not add value. As we noted in Chapter 17, value involves both "doing the right things" and "doing things right." Specifically, you will want to examine each step in the process to determine if it:

1. Transforms the information in a way that brings it closer to the final desired information deliverable (the end product), and
2. Is done right, i.e., efficiently, the first time using the minimum amount of resources.

A process step that fails either of these is a candidate for elimination or redesign.

Suppose documents sit for an average of one day in an approving manager's in-box. This day of queuing does not transform the information in any way, so this step does not add value. (In fact, eliminating queue time is a key objective of the process redesign; see Step 5 below.) Similarly, suppose that an order entry clerk must check with sales for missing information on the customer order sheet. This rework loop suggests that the original step of completing the customer order sheet was mishandled the first time. Here again, we have identified a step in the process that does not add value: while it was the right thing to do (collect information from the customer about their order), it was not done right. Finally, re-entering that same order data several times into different information systems because these are not integrated does nothing to transform the information. Rather, it just replicates work already done. Again, such non-value-added activities are a target of opportunity for your process redesign.

Step 5: Create A Streamlined Process

The office cell process should be as free as possible of non-value-adding steps. But once you have identified these non-value-adding steps, how do you go about streamlining the current process? Your goals are to eliminate those steps that do not transform the information (only do the right things) and to make more efficient those required steps that are presently not well executed (do things right).

We suggest you prepare a matrix that lists the non-value-added steps, the criterion or criteria they fail, and how an office cell will impact each (see Table 18-3). For example, simply co-locating successive operations will eliminate (or severely reduce) non-value-adding transport time for physical information carriers (such as folders, manuals, etc.). Similarly, having cell employees review and approve their own work eliminates transport and queue time; work does not go to a manager's in-box (transit time) or wait for the manager's approval (queue time).

Table 18–3. Eliminating non-value-added work: cellular principles applied to the quote request example from Figure 18-6

Non-value-added process step	What value-added criterion does this step fail?	How can we address this failure in our office cell system?
Specific Examples		
Design engineering reviews customer information to ensure it is complete	Reviewing information to ensure that it is complete does not transform the information in any way.	*Cross-trained workers:* Cross-training helps ensure that needed information will be obtained the first time. This means sales personnel will understand the information to gather now in support of later engineering activities. This encourages quality at the source and reduces the need for checks when work flows from one task to another._x000D_*Other ideas for addressing this step:* We could mistake-proof this process by providing sales with a checklist of information that must accompany each quote as it goes to engineering.
Design engineering contacts sales to fill in missing information	Work is not done right the first time (missing information). This step is a result of failing to perfect the previous step.	*Cross-trained workers:* If sales and design engineering personnel are cross-trained, sales will know the information that engineers need to do their work. If the same individual is performing both steps, there is even less chance that critical information will be overlooked._x000D_*Accountability:* If individuals are jointly accountable for results, there is a great incentive to get the work done right.
General Examples		
Transport time (occurs when physical documents must be routed)	Transport time does not transform the information in any way.	Because office cell employees are co-located, transport times are minimal.
Queue time (occurs when work that has been returned to a previous stage must wait for a reply or for reprocessing; or when work that moves forward to the next step must wait for processing)	Waiting time does not transform the information in any way.	*Co-location facilitates communication:* In an office cell, personnel are located near one another. When questions arise, an immediate exchange between the relevant parties is possible._x000D_*Co-location, dedication, and multi-functional operators facilitate small batches:* In an office cell, one-at-a-time batch sizes are possible. This eliminates work in process between steps and, consequently, queue times._x000D_*Cross-training:* Cross-trained workers are able to answer questions and resolve issues themselves. They do not need to return work to the previous step for problem resolution.

As you work through the list of non-value-added steps, remember that you want to eliminate those steps that do not transform information inputs into desired information deliverables. Where steps are important to perform but are not done efficiently, your efforts should focus on designing these activities to be done right the first time. (The design and operating principles in the next section can help guide your efforts in this regard.)

Keep in mind that it is not necessary at this stage to try to solve all problems and "optimize" the process. As we pointed out in Chapter 17, the essential characteristics of cell work (family focus, system's view, fast feedback, pooled expertise, and accountability/ownership) make cells an ideal venue for continuous improvement. Once cells are in place, employees often make the process better in ways that were not anticipated before implementation.

Step 6: Assess Resource Needs and Develop Preliminary Space, Equipment, and Staffing Plans

After you streamline the process, it is time to prepare a list of required resources. This list outlines the skills, knowledge, and technical resources that each task in the streamlined process will require (this involves job design and analysis; see Chapters 12 and 13). Technical resources include equipment (e.g., computers, desks, phone lines, fax machines), as well as the information/decision support systems (both manual, such as hard copy reference manuals, and computerized). This is where you may come face to face with the problems created by fractionalized and independent information systems. Ingersoll Cutting Tool discovered that it used several different information systems to support the steps in its modified standard order process. As part of the cell design it integrated, as well as upgraded, some of these systems. When IBM Credit designed case worker office cells, it came up against the same type of problem. IBM, too, opted for a more integrated decision support system.

The rapid advances in information system capabilities (such as open systems, database technology, and web-based technologies) permit more integrated solutions that directly support office cell work (and may allow organizations to achieve significant benefits in the absence of physical proximity). As you design the office cell, look for opportunities to leverage information technology.

Armed with a set of resource requirements, you are in a good position to determine space and staffing plans. With respect to space requirements, the data you have collected on equipment needs (desks, plotters, etc.) will allow you to approximate the area required for the office cell. Your preliminary staffing plan, on the other hand, should answer a set of important questions about cell work. Will the cell have one employee (case worker cell) or a team of employees? What tasks will be performed in the cell? Who in the organization may be able to do the jobs, and what training will they require? How will existing or new information systems constrain the way in which work gets done? Keep in mind that you do not need to finalize the details of *how* work will take place. Developing the specific work rules and procedures that will govern task execution is best done as part of implementation and with significant input from those employees who will actually be staffing the cell. However, the design principles we discuss in the next section will guide you in making these detailed decisions.

You may discover at this stage that required equipment resources are in such scarce supply that they cannot be dedicated exclusively to the cell. Or you may determine that an investment in information technology to support the cell is simply not possible at this time. Or you may find that the skill sets the cell requires are not available or are too expensive to develop among the existing workforce (e.g., too much training is required). This may cause you to return to Step 3 and revise the parameters of your office cell process or to Step 5 where you redesign the selected process. Changes in either of these steps will impact the resources required for the cell to work effectively and efficiently.

Step 7: Address Infrastructure Issues

Before you implement the cells, you must consider all infrastructure issues affecting and affected by the cell. Infrastructure refers to the organizational structures, job designs, management systems, and culture that determine the context in which work takes place. Office cells are very different from the departmentally-focused organizations they replace. Unfortunately, most management systems, such as compensation and performance measurement, are designed to support the old job shop approach to administrative work. Efficient office cells require a supportive infrastructure, which means existing mechanisms may need to change. We discussed infrastructure at length in previous chapters, and also briefly review key infrastructure issues for office cells later in this chapter.

Step 8: Implement the Office Cells

Earlier chapters discussed the implementation of manufacturing cells in detail. Our models and advice apply to office cell implementation as well. However, there is one point we want to highlight: the role of future office cell employees and information systems personnel in the cell design process.

We strongly advocate that employees play an active role in the design of manufacturing cells and their operating policies. The nature of office cell work makes this an even more important consideration. In administrative work, you rely heavily on people to "make it happen." Equipment, while important, plays a much smaller role than it does in manufacturing settings—office work tends to be people-paced, not machine-paced, as it often is in manufacturing. Further, many of the dramatic performance improvements that are possible with office cells are closely associated with the "people" aspects of the design: co-location (or, at least, teamwork), cross-training, whole-system knowledge, ownership, and accountability. Those who do the work have a rich experience base and can make significant contributions to design and operation. At the outset of the design effort you should strive for a broad representation that involves the groups most likely to work in an office cell for a particular process (e.g., sales, cost estimators, and manufacturing engineers for a quote development process). As you move into the detailed design phase you can hand off decision-making regarding work procedures and detailed layout to those who have been tapped to work in the cell.

Specifically, cell employees are often in the best position to develop work standards and protocols that team members will follow in executing their work. After all, they will have a vested interest in performance, are closer to the actual tasks, and may be able to develop better ways of working that translate to better performance. Of course, as you prepare people to work in the office cell, you need to provide clear and unambiguous information about work scope, goals, and performance measures. Within these broader parameters, though, you should let those who perform the work have a say in developing and improving work standards and the layout itself. Your initial cell space requirements and job designs should be the point of departure—not the finish line—for operations. If office cell employees have viable ideas to improve cell performance, like revising the initial cell layout or reallocating job responsibilities, you should give them the opportunity to test these suggestions.

We also recommend that you involve information systems personnel in office cell design. Getting them to support the office cell is a key infrastructure challenge in many environments. After all, creating office cells is all about transforming information, and investment in information systems infrastructure (see below) can be a major cost category. Thus, it makes sense to involve information systems personnel in the cell design process.

Economic Justification of Office Cells

Our discussion of steps in the design process (Figure 18-5) has sidestepped the important issue of cost justification—assessing the merits of office cells and determining whether or not to adopt them. The discussion in Chapter 8, which focused on justifying manufacturing cells, can help you assess the value of potential office cells as well. Many of the cost and benefit categories we identified are germane to office cells, as are the strategies we suggested for determining the values to assign to various cost and benefit categories. However, the nature of office cells changes some dimensions of the cost/benefit picture. We'd like to highlight those differences.

First, office cells are less equipment-dependent and more people-dependent. Your out-of-pocket expenses for new equipment and moving existing equipment around are likely to be quite low with office cells. On the flip side, investment in information systems—typically a minor expense in manufacturing cells—can be a major expenditure for office cells.

Second, manufacturing cells are partly justified based on inventory reduction. The backlog reductions that come with office cells do not have a physical manifestation and therefore do not represent an investment in assets. The important savings are in human labor and response times. From that perspective, the assessment of the strategic value of time, and the influence on revenues, may be more important for office cells than for manufacturing cells.

Third, your efforts to assess the merits of office cells may be hampered by the general absence of measurements. You'll need to determine current performance (e.g., for process lead time) as a basis for comparison with your planned cells. This is one reason Step 2 of our model (understand the current process and its performance) is so important. However, as just indicated, you also need to turn the anticipated time reductions into either cost reductions or revenue enhancements.

Fourth, the question of when in the analysis process to conduct a justification and seek approval to proceed is important (also see Chapter 4). Obviously, you need some support at the outset even before undertaking the first few steps. After all, to conduct any kind of meaningful analysis you must involve representatives from the various functions or departments that are part of the original process. Just getting these people together will require support from various managers. Once you have selected a process and analyzed it for value-added content (Step 4 in Figure 18-5), you are in a good position to make a preliminary case for a redesigned process. You'll have performance data on the existing process (i.e., you'll know how good or bad it is) and a sense for the non-value-adding steps (i.e., where the waste is in the process). These data, coupled with information on the strategic importance of the process (part of Step 1), can be sufficient to convince process decision-makers to authorize continued analysis focused on streamlining the process.

After completing Steps 6 and 7 (assess the resources needs, develop preliminary space/staffing plans, and address implementation issues), you are ready to present a more detailed cost/benefit assessment. At this point you can better anticipate what it will cost to put the office cell in place, the likely benefits it will generate, and what it will need in terms of infrastructure adaptations. This cost/benefit picture (or management's reaction to it) may prompt you to go back and redefine the target information deliverables family (Step 3) or revise the office cell process (Step 5).

14 PRINCIPLES FOR DESIGNING AND OPERATING OFFICE CELLS

Now that you have a better understanding of the overall design process, we present 14 principles that you can use to design and run office cells. Many of these will help streamline office work, even when the eventual outcome is not an office cell, but simply a better process.

Principle 1: Organize Work around Outcomes, Not around Individual Tasks

This principle—the essence of process-complete operations—is a restatement of the vertical/horizontal perspective on work organization we discussed in Chapter 2 (see Figure 2-3). Redesign work to move away from fractionalized tasks and toward start-to-finish completion of a whole piece of work. The benefits in terms of speed, quality, cost, and ongoing improvement can be substantial.

Principle 2: Staff the Cell with Skilled and Knowledgeable Personnel

Knowledge work often involves "deliberations,"[29] dialogues between key employees that focus on issues that have to be resolved repeatedly and that provide direction for employees. Deliberations frequently involve trade-offs that require the consideration of various perspectives. One example would be deciding whether to proceed with a particular tool design that will take more time and money but probably be better suited to customers' needs. To make a good decision requires input from sales, tooling, and costing (and possibly others). If the office cell includes these functions, the "right" contributors are present to discuss and quickly resolve issues.

More generally, the office cell should include the various parties with information and knowledge that will allow work to flow smoothly and prevent rework from being necessary. Ask yourself, what are the *issues* that could hold up work in this process? Where do different interpretations and limited information sharing result in delays and rework? Design the office cell to include personnel who can resolve these issues and create a common, shared interpretation.

Another way of expressing this principle is to say that you want to be certain that the office cell is assigned tasks that are interdependent. We talked about interdependencies in Chapter 5 as part of factory layout planning. The driving principle there (and here) is that tasks, departments, and people who are interdependent should be close together. On a micro level, we can use this principle to help design office cells. Tasks and people that are interdependent should be part of the same office cell.[30] Returning to our quotation process, sales and engineering depend on a rich information exchange to do the best job for the customer. They are dependent on one another in this process and should be in the same cell. Identify the key work interdependencies and design the office cell to encompass them.

Principle 3: Design the Process for the Dominant Flow, Not for the Exceptions

If you design the office cell process for exceptional (most complicated) cases, the result will be an overly complex process. For example, work may come along occasionally that is so expensive, or the customer so important, that higher-level management feels obligated to review it. This "exception," however, is not a reason to subject all work to management approval. Don't design an approval step into the basic work flow unless all work needs this review. IBM Credit's old application process was overdesigned, based on the steps that the most difficult applications needed.[31] All applications, even simple and routine ones, followed a complicated series of steps that consumed, on average, six working days. Design the process for the typical, not the exceptional, work flow. This comes back to the careful selection of the family of information deliverables.

But how *do* you handle unusual, exceptional work? One option is to have one cell for standard work and a second for non-standard work. This means identifying families and designing a process for each. If a separate cell for your non-standard work is not an option (e.g., the volume is low), you may simply opt to handle exceptional work using the old process. That is, you send it from department to department as you did before. You may also be able to route it through your office cell, though it will probably take more time and may slow down other work. A final alternative is to let exceptional jobs leave the cell for processing in the functional offices and then return to the cell for completion.

If you are converting *all* your administrative processes to cells (something we haven't seen), you may want to design one or more "cats and dogs" or "remainder" office cells. These cells, designed for lots of flexibility and staffed by people capable of varied tasks, would handle the exceptional work. Our main message here is that you should not try to design one process that fits every possible variant.[32]

Principle 4: Improve the Process Using a Variety of Strategies

A variety of strategies, many borrowed from the manufacturing arena, are useful in streamlining office tasks. You want to reduce both setup and operating times. You can think of setup time in office work as the "intellectual" changeover time—the time it takes to get up to speed on a new piece of work. Operating time, on the other hand, refers the time required to actually execute the task itself.

You can help get rid of unnecessary setup and operation time by eliminating external approvals and having all needed information and equipment (e.g., reference manuals, product catalogues) at the point-of-use. In addition, you can reduce the number of setups and compress operating times by combining steps so that fewer handoffs ensue. This may also involve re-sequencing tasks so that work need not return to a prior station. Quality assurance procedures that help eliminate rework improve task efficiency and eliminate the setups incurred when you send work back to a prior station. Finally, you can use standardized forms or checksheets that gather information at one step and clearly communicate it to the next step. This can reduce the time employees need to be fully prepared to begin real work and can aid in executing work smoothly and efficiently. Table 18-4 summarizes these and other principles for process improvement in office work.

Principle 5: Reduce Batch Sizes

You may not associate batches with office work, but they exist in information processing just as they do in manufacturing. In office work, "batch size" is *the number of distinct information carriers or packages (files) that are processed before work is passed to the next person or step in the process.* Suppose an order entry clerk collects a day's worth of orders prior to entering them into the system. She has then batched her work (also see the Ryerson Tull example in the beginning of this chapter). Ideally, you want the batch size for information transfer to be as small as possible to minimize waiting times. One-at-a-time processing has the same profound effect on lead time and quality in office operations as it does in manufacturing. With electronic processing, a transfer batch of one is the norm. However, when information is moved in physical form, like folders, it is more likely that larger batch sizes will be used.

Principle 6: Consider the Factors that Create Long Lead Times

We devoted Chapter 7 to a discussion of the factors that create delays and backlogs in operating systems. Foremost among them is the relationship between the time to process jobs and the time between the arrivals of new jobs. Capacity and workload factors are as relevant to office cells as they are to manufacturing cells. In essence, don't overload the cell, operate with small batches, pool labor, and reduce variances where possible.

Principle 7: Look for Opportunities to Perform Tasks in Parallel

You can reduce total lead time by performing required tasks in parallel, rather than sequentially. Question your assumptions about precedence relationships. Does the tooling design need to be fully finished before you can begin the cost estimation? Can costing start after only a portion of the tooling design is finished?

Table 18–4. Process improvement tips for office work

General Strategy	Specific Tips
Organize each workstation	• Have a place for everything and everything in its place. • Return items to their correct places. • Label files, folders, forms, and their locations.
Document the work process	• Office work instructions should assure that employees know what is required to begin a piece of work. What information is needed? What documentation is required? What tools will be needed? Further, documentation should accurately describe work steps. • Create checksheets to assure that all necessary information is collected and available; employees who send and receive the information should collaborate in the checksheet design and should periodically review and revise it.
Apply the principles of dedication	• Make sure each workstation has all the tools, information, and so forth that they need to do the job; this may include computers, telecommunications equipment, manuals, and other reference materials. • Store needed materials at point-of-use. • If a resource must be shared among cell workers (e.g., a fax machine, copier, printer, CAD workstation), be sure it is conveniently located for all.
Provide rapid information access	• Be sure that those doing the work have access to all the information they need. This may mean consolidating databases. • When cell employees will need to access different databases, minimize the time to switch from one to another; you may need to create direct links between systems that are transparent to the user. • Design input screens to follow the logical flow of work and to eliminate unnecessary waste.
Avoid revisitation—sending work back to a previous step for reprocessing	• Cross-train employees so they can fix problems introduced in previous steps without sending the work back. This will reduce delays and the possibility of new errors associated with "back flow"—sending work back for reprocessing.
Combine tasks where possible	• Have a single worker perform multiple tasks. This eliminates hand-offs and a significant portion of intellectual setup.

Principle 8: Capitalize on the Power of "One Best Way"

In manufacturing processes involving mid to high volumes, the use of work standards and clearly defined, well-documented procedures is fairly commonplace. It is accepted that having one best way is superior to having each operator develop and use his or her own method. In fact, the benefits of standardization in manufacturing settings are well known: stable, repeatable processes that yield consistent quality outputs and provide a solid bedrock for ongoing improvement. These same benefits are available to office processes if the "one best way" to execute work is identified, documented, and followed (assuming, of course, that sufficient similarity and volume exist).

In knowledge work settings that rely on informal mentoring to pass along best ways of working, the development and use of standardized operations represents a significant target of opportunity. If you have six order entry clerks who each handle their work in a slightly different way, you have introduced unnecessary process variation. Unpredictable lead times, variable quality, and higher costs are likely to result. Granted, it may be difficult to develop standards in cases where employees work with a wide array of different information deliverables, because each piece of work may be "unique" in some way. This underscores the importance of identifying families of like information deliverables in sufficient volumes, documenting the best way to handle them, and then assuring that everyone works to the standard. Standardization can be, and should be, enforced through the information system. This can specify the data used, check data input, control the sequence in processing, and generally prevent many information-related errors (as also discussed below).

Principle 9: Looks for Ways to Mistake-Proof the Process

Mistake-proofing is the use of mechanisms that eliminate the possibility of error (see Chapter 17). Checksheets that itemize work steps and computerized order entry systems that will not accept incorrect part numbers are examples. Other mistake-proofing ideas include on-line process documentation that guides work execution, color-coded fields for data entry, and special forms. An example of the latter can be seen at the order fulfillment office cells at one company. These use specification sheets that travel with the documentation and prompt cell employees to record all essential technical information before the order moves into manufacturing. This has minimized/reduced the number of orders arriving to manufacturing with incomplete or missing information.

Principle 10: Collect Data Once and at the Source

Every time information moves on to another person (a handoff) the potential exists for information to be lost or misinterpreted. Mistakes are also likely when, at successive steps, data are re-entered or transposed from one format to another. Consider this example. A field salesperson sends an e-mail concerning a customer order to the sales office. The salesperson has described the item by name only. The order entry clerk is not sure which specific product number is associated with that product name (because, of course, there are several models known by the same name). The clerk contacts the field salesperson for clarification, or calls the customer (much to the customer's annoyance, in all likelihood). This process is improved if the salesperson provides the product's number as well as its name. It is better still if the salesperson enters the product number directly into a shared database (single data entry at the source). And you will have even higher data integrity if you have mistake-proofed data entry so that the system accepts only valid product information.

The goal is to eliminate all copying, re-entering, or transformation of data. Therefore, provide the persons at the source of the data with all the tools they will need to capture data right there. This idea, of course, is the foundation for data warehouses and enterprise resource planning (ERP) systems.

Principle 11: Design Jobs for Multi-Skilled Employees

You should try to combine tasks into jobs that multi-functional employees can perform. Operating with fewer handoffs decreases the number of setups, reduces processing time variance, lowers idle time due to workload imbalances, and improves quality. Combining tasks also helps you avoid fractionalized work. The resulting, broader jobs can have positive effects on job satisfaction (see our discussion of job enlargement and enrichment in Chapter 12). As noted earlier, the A. Ahlstrom Corporation's order fulfillment cells collapsed 10 distinct tasks into 5, which employees with significantly broadened responsibilities now perform.[33] In Aetna's application processing cells, customer account managers now complete tasks that used to be performed by separate individuals in forms processing, rating, input operations, and document preparation.[34]

Principle 12: Use Task Overlapping to Create Within-Cell Resource Pooling and Promote Improvement

One disadvantage of office (or manufacturing) cells is a loss of flexibility. When you dedicate resources to specific families of work, you decrease your ability to use these resources for other families. Within the cell, however, you can create flexibility through cross-training. The benefits of creating resource pools through cross-training are well known, as we discussed in Chapter 7. Cross-trained employees are able to take on a greater variety of tasks. This helps in balancing capacity, dealing with demand fluctuations, and operating in the face of absent employees. In manufacturing, this generally means employees moving from one piece of equipment to another in response to changing production needs. In an office cell setting, employees may not physically change locations, but the benefits of resource pooling can be just as great

For example, assume that you have created a cell to process requests for quotations for a particular family of customers. Now suppose a customer has requested a quote for work that will require more tooling design work than normal. If your cell includes only one tool designer, and this work outstrips his or her capacity, you have a bottleneck situation. However, if you have cross-trained other cell employees on tooling design, they can help.

When tasks overlap, employees understand each other's work, have a common language, and can assist one another. This helps build a sense of shared responsibility.[35] Moreover, cell employees are by definition jointly accountable for cell performance. Couple this with the cross-training already mentioned and you have a scenario in which employees have both a reason and the skill set for working toward common objectives and continuously pursuing improvement (also see Chapter 17).

Principle 13: Minimize the Need for Tight Controls

Where work flows cross departmental boundaries, you tend to see each department exercise tight controls. Those performing the work in various departments know only a limited part of the process, and are spatially and (often) temporally distant. Inspections to assure incoming work quality, and approvals to authorize decisions regarding the incoming work, are therefore the norm. This slows down work. In office cells, on the other hand, those who perform the work understand the whole process. Because of this knowledge, their close physical proximity, and small batch sizes, cell employees are better able to identify errors and take corrective action sooner. And because jobs are broader, resulting in fewer handoffs, there are fewer opportunities for errors.

Furthermore, because work is performed inside the cell—possibly by the same person—you can eliminate the rechecking of previous process steps.

Greater process knowledge and accountability for results mean that office cell employees have both the skill set and the motivation to make good decisions. This reduces the need for external approvals and makes it possible to push decision-making down to those who do the work.[36]

Principle 14: Consider Linking Office and Manufacturing Cells to Create Focused Factories

The production areas at Telephonics, a Long Island manufacturer of high-tech custom electronics systems, are focused factories.[37] Each consists of all the administrative and manufacturing resources required to complete a family of products start-to-finish, from order to shipment. For many businesses, such "integrated cells" or focused factories provide a tremendous competitive capability. Consider this option when you explore office cell opportunities.

Taken together, these 14 design and operating principles (summarized in Table 18-5) can help you create and operate office cells that improve performance. Moving people and tasks together to create a process-complete operation can generate great benefits. However, there are also significant organizational hurdles, including incompatible management systems and resistance to change. If your organization is not ready to take the full plunge into office cells, these 14 design and operating principles can still help you eliminate wasteful practices and streamline those that remain.

MAKING OFFICE CELLS WORK: INFRASTRUCTURE ISSUES AND OTHER KEY CHALLENGES

We have not yet addressed the key challenges organizations face in implementing office cells and establishing a supportive infrastructure. Chapters 9 through 17 discussed these issues in great detail with respect to manufacturing cells. To a large degree, the advice and prescriptions we provided in those chapters pertain to office cells as well. Thus, in this chapter we mostly highlight those issues that are particularly important or substantially different when cells focus on information rather than on material flows.

Office Cell Infrastructure Issues

As we noted earlier, infrastructure refers to the organizational policies, procedures, systems, and culture that determine the context in which work takes place. Successful office cells require a supportive infrastructure. This means that existing mechanisms may need to change.

Performance measures

In traditional departmentally organized administrative work, performance measures tend to be departmentally focused. For instance, the estimating department might

Table 18-5. Design and operating principles for office cells

	Design principle	Explanation
1	Organize around outcomes, not around tasks.	Create process-complete office operations. Organize work and the people who perform it to focus on whole work, not fractionalized tasks.
2	Staff the cell with personnel who have the skills and knowledge to resolve issues and keep work flowing.	Design the cell to include personnel who can resolve recurring issues that hold up work. People who depend on one another to get their work done should be part of the same office cell. Resources that people depend on to get their work done should also be part of the cell.
3	Design the process for the dominant flow, not for the exceptions	Designing the flow to handle all possible variants will make it overly complicated. Keep it simple. Handle exceptions in a separate area, or handle them as exceptions within the cell.
4	Improve the process through a variety of strategies.	Minimize the time it takes employees to setup and execute their work through the strategies described in Table 18-4.
5	Reduce batch sizes.	Design the process to facilitate one-at-a-time information processing.
6	Consider the factors that create long lead times.	Don't overload the cell. Operate with small batches, pool labor, and reduce variances where possible.
7	Look for opportunities to do tasks in parallel.	Question precedence relationships. Look for opportunities to overlap tasks.
8	Capitalize on the power of one best way.	Find the one best way to perform each step in the process, document it, and assure that people work to the documentation.
9	Look for ways to mistake-proof the process.	Checksheets, on-line process documentation, color-coding, special forms, and the like can all help assure work is done right the first time.
10	Collect data once and at the source.	Eliminate copying, transforming, and re-entering data. Provide the people at the source of the data with the tools they need to capture the data correctly.
11	Design jobs for multi-skilled employees.	Combine tasks into jobs that multi-functional employees can perform.
12	Use overlapping tasks to create within-cell resource pooling.	When employees are cross-trained they can balance capacity, deal with demand fluctuations, and operate the cell in the absence of colleagues.
13	Minimize the need for tight controls.	Design office cells so that decision-making is placed in the hands of those who do the work. They are closer to the action, know the work, and can speed the process along.
14	Consider linking office and manufacturing cells to create focused factories.	Create cells to consist of all the administrative and manufacturing resources required to complete a family of products start-to-finish, order-to-shipment. This can represent a tremendous competitive capability.

measure labor productivity in developing quotes from specifications provided by engineering (e.g., by estimating labor hours per quote). It might, if it is particularly enlightened, also measure the turnaround time for developing the cost estimate once it receives engineering's specifications.

Less likely, however, are measures that encompass the whole process and cover activities that involve multiple departments. For example, most organizations have to launch a special study to find out the time involved in responding to customer requests for quotations (in fact, a special study is frequently needed just to determine the process used to respond to customer requests). As we have pointed out already, measures for processes spanning multiple departments are rare: most businesses lack rigorous *process* measures.[38]

Office cells change all this because they handle a large number of consecutive process steps, not isolated tasks. This makes it possible to routinely measure the performance of the process as a whole (or, at least, a larger piece of it). Office cells allow you to build the measurement system around meaningful process performance metrics that are linked to important company objectives. For most organizations this represents a big change, so these measures will probably be created from scratch.

In Chapter 9 we presented the Process Performance Measurement Matrix which helps organizations think through performance measures for manufacturing cells. Specifically, we suggested that a comprehensive measurement system for cells should assess the quality/productivity, flow/inventory, timeliness, workplace environment, and financial aspects of resources, inputs, transformation, and outputs. The matrix can also help you think about how best to measure office cell performance. In addition, the Measurement Checklist in Appendix C is useful in assessing existing measures or new measures developed expressly for office cells.

We want to underscore the importance of creating meaningful measures for office cells. Departmentally-oriented measures may be virtually obsolete in a process-complete operation that brings together individuals and tasks from many departments. You simply must rethink performance measurement with office cells.

Selection and training

Our design guidelines stressed the need to develop multi-functional employees with overlapping job responsibilities for team-based office cells. Obviously, this has significant implications for employee selection and training. Employees must have the capacity and flexibility to perform a variety of tasks rather than mastery in one area. They also need interpersonal skills to work together, as well as administrative/management and problem solving/decision-making skills to handle the full range of office cell work and to be able to productively engage in—and manage—their own process improvement. Therefore the ability and willingness to learn is also important. You may need to rethink selection processes to ensure they assess these characteristics. Training will need to be broadly based, covering a variety of technical areas, as well as providing people with the interpersonal, administrative/management, problem-solving/decision-making, and cell concepts training important for cell work. We discussed these issues at length in Chapter 13.

Compensation systems

The structure of the reward system sends workers powerful messages about what the organization values. Recent research suggests that process-complete organizations work most effectively when group performance is rewarded. Rewards encourage a sense of collective responsibility, which can have positive implications for performance. "People who feel collectively responsible are willing to work especially hard to avoid letting the team down."[39] A system that rewards people for some combination of office cell performance, plant (or organization-wide) performance, and individual performance may make the most sense. Chapter 14 provides a more complete discussion of this important area.

Reporting relationships, career ladders, and organization structure

Structuring reporting relationships for office cells is a key challenge. To whom should a cell devoted to order-fulfillment report? To marketing? To manufacturing? To the CEO? Consider that previously the individuals working in the office cell reported to different managers representing a variety of functions. This is a challenging problem and one that many organizations struggle with. At Ingersoll Cutting Tool Company, the modified standard order cell included work tasks previously done by manufacturing *and* engineering. After substantial discussion, the company decided to have the cell report outside both of these functional areas, to the manager of technical systems. This manager was part of the product development group.[40]

In deciding how to structure reporting relationships, we offer three pieces of advice:

1. *Have cell employees report to a single manager, not two or more.* This is in full compliance with our view on cells as organizational units. You can't build an effective team if cell employees have different bosses with different priorities.

2. *Provide good leadership.* The manager needs to be able to understand and value the diverse contributions made by office cell employees.

3. *Make sure the reporting relationships are viewed by cell employees as fair and unbiased.* This is closely related to item 2. A sales representative who is part of an order fulfillment cell that reports to the engineering manager may fear that this manager will not understand or value the sales activities. Designing and using objective procedures for performance evaluation of cell employees can help address concerns about bias.

Related to the problem of reporting relationships is the issue of career advancement. In departmental organizations career paths are clear and well known. Formal and informal mentoring, which is facilitated by co-location of people with the same skills (e.g., manufacturing and design engineering), can help employees develop deeper skills and prepare them to move up technically (e.g., from entry level engineer to senior engineer). But what will career ladders look like for office cell employees? Think in advance about possible career paths for these "non-departmentalized" workers so you can address any questions that prospective office cell employees might have. While office cell workers may lose the opportunity to develop deep technical expertise, their new work will help them learn other skills. In addition to broader technical skills, they will have the opportunity to acquire leadership and interpersonal capabilities. Similarly, they can develop an understanding of the whole process and its business implications, perspectives that are particularly valuable in supervisory and management positions. Clearly, however, there will be more lateral career moves in team-based organizations, and employees need to be prepared for that.[41]

Other Challenges in the Design, Implementation, and Operation of Office Cells

In this section we cover three other challenges that are likely to arise when you design, implement, and operate office cells. Monument process issues, dealing with resistance to change, and difficulties creating a supportive culture all can impede a smooth transition. These are issues for manufacturing cells as well, as you know from previous chapters. We highlight them here because there are nuances with office cell applications that deserve special mention.

Monument process issues

Monument processes are resources difficult to place in a cell for reasons of size, cost, or other factors. In administrative work, monument processes can be a special piece of equipment needed by multiple cells, or by both cell and non-cell work areas. An example might be a color plotter, or a "big Bertha" printer. An office monument process can be a human resource; for example, a highly skilled individual who is needed by multiple organizational units.

There are a number of ways to deal with monument issues in office cells. One is to let such resources be shared between cell and non-cell work areas for specified time periods.[42] This assures that everybody has access to the scarce resource while reducing the potential conflicts that might ensue in less structured resource sharing arrangements. If the monument is a highly skilled individual, cross-training to bring additional people up to speed in the monument process task is also an option. Of course, this can be difficult if the expertise you want to duplicate takes years to develop.

Dealing with resistance to change

A key challenge in implementing office cells is dealing with resistance to change. For a number of reasons, creating office cells will likely meet with more resistance than a transition to manufacturing cells. First, change on the shop floor happens much more routinely than does change in the office. Until quite recently, efforts to improve processes have routinely targeted the shop floor, not the office. The notion of doing things differently in the office is likely to be met with skepticism.

Additionally, forming an office cell can be a "bigger" change than forming a manufacturing cell. When you form manufacturing cells, you take people who all worked within the same function (manufacturing) and bring them together in a new work arrangement. Nevertheless, they still are part of manufacturing. This is not the case with many office cells. Here, employees and activities are drawn from different functions, like sales and engineering, and placed in the same cell. Cultural and work style differences may be quite pronounced and difficult to integrate. In addition, professional affinities—the desire to work alongside those doing the same work—may be quite strong. Specialists may complain that they need to work more closely with others in their discipline in order to maintain their technical edge and share best practices.

When Showtime Networks created office cells to handle billing and collections, some employees "never quite understood it and were resistant. The implementation phase has been difficult for a lot of people. Some weren't able to adapt and had to leave the company."[43] Telephonics has experienced these problems with their focused factories, which combine office and manufacturing cells.[44] At this plant, management made administrative activities associated with order fulfillment (including engineering tasks) part of large, integrated cells that also included manufacturing activities:

> Experienced engineers who are used to doing things the old way with the old hierarchies may have problems with the redefined roles, but he [the manager of manufacturing engineering] thinks the new work style is hardest on young engineers. "You go to school for years, and think of yourself as a professional, then you're thrown onto the floor as part of the process," he says. "It's hard to do analyses or computer work. Sometimes the interruptions drive you crazy."

The manager cautions that you can't let this resistance dissuade you: you must focus on the big picture. "We're here to build a product that satisfies the customer. If the assemblers don't get what they need, they can't do that." Telephonics has gone to great lengths to overcome resistance by providing a host of benefits, including an in-house gym, on-site travel agency, on-site tuition-reimbursed MBA instruction, and a 4.5-day work week (9 hours Monday through Thursday, and four hours on Friday.)

In addition, when you move individuals out of departments to create office cells, you must deal with issues of power and reporting relationships. Specifically, managers often do not want to give up employees so they can join an office cell that will report to another manager. This may lead them to reject the idea of creating the cell. At minimum, it means that decisions about office cell reporting relationships may be politically charged, as managers vie for control over this new organizational unit.

Because resistance is likely to be great, your management of the office cell planning and implementation project is critical. In short, you need to pay particular attention to the change process itself. Lining up political sponsorship, clearly articulating the case for change, setting clear expectations, communicating extensively about the plan, and involving those who will do the work in the design of the office cell are key to a successful effort. Because "people make it happen" in office cells, you want to do everything you can to assure that design and implementation are perceived as "fair."[45] The guidelines for managing the change process and the prescriptions for dealing with resistance to change which we offered in Chapters 15 and 16 can help you successfully navigate the transition to office cells.

A supportive culture

Reorganizing around processes can produce faster cycle times, greater customer satisfaction, and lower costs. But to reap these benefits, your culture must support collaboration. This means going beyond "combining the boxes on the organization chart." A collaborative culture develops where (1) the layout lets employees see each other and talk about work, (2) the jobs overlap, (3) the reward structure promotes joint accountability, and (4) the work procedures encourage people to help one another out.[46] Our office cell design and operating principles can help you create office cells consistent with these recommendations for building a collaborative culture.

KEY INSIGHTS

This chapter has presented a compelling set of arguments for adopting process-complete office cells and moving away from the traditional job shop model of office work. We offered an eight-step model for office cell design, as well as a set of 14 design and operating principles for streamlining office operations. We also highlighted infrastructure and implementation challenges that organizations face as they transition to office cells.

We believe that office cells are a breakthrough way of improving white-collar productivity. As you embark on the transition to office cells, keep the following key points in mind.

- *For many organizations office work represents huge untapped opportunities for process improvement.* Most firms structure administrative activities along functional lines into departments. However, most office work moves horizontally across departments. As a result, office processes are often characterized by long lead times, quality problems, limited accountability, and fractionalized "sub-optimal" improvements. Efforts to improve office operations have lagged behind those in manufacturing.

- *Restructuring office work to create process-complete office cells can lead to significant performance improvements with respect to quality, lead time, cost, and other metrics important to the organization.* Table 18-2 illustrates how the resources, space, transformation, and organizational characteristics of office cells are linked directly and indirectly to the benefits that cells achieve.

- *Designing office cells forces a critical analysis of targeted office operations and provides a structured approach for streamlining key information processing activities.* Our eight-step process for designing office cells walks you through the analysis steps and their associated tools. Functional flow charts and tagging (see Appendix L) are particularly useful for understanding the current process, while creating a non-value-added analysis chart (see Figure 18-3) can help you visualize how cells will address current process deficiencies. Our design and operating principles for office cells (see Table 18-5) and the process improvement tips for office work (see Table 18-4) are your guides to creating your new office cell process. As the eight-step process and associated tools suggest, designing office cells is, in many ways, very similar to the process of designing manufacturing cells.

- *Office cells can be linked to manufacturing cells.* In fact, the same product families can be used to design both types of cells. The result is a set of linked cells focused on the information and material transformations involved in designing, selling, producing and distributing a family of products. Consider this option as you explore office cells.

- *People are the key ingredient in a successful office cell design and operation.* Creating an office cell can shake up the organization structure. It won't happen without high-level and broadly-based support. People "make it happen" in office cells. Be sure to:

  - Begin with a compelling, market-driven reason to create an office cell.

  - Involve people who will do the work in the design of the office cells. People support what they help create.

  - Give office cell employees the latitude to improve operations and layout once the cell is up and running.

  - Design (or revise) human resource policies such as performance management, compensation, selection, training, and development to support the new way of working.

WHAT'S NEXT?

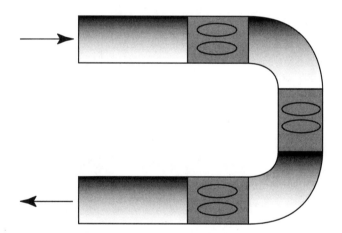

19

Future Changes and Challenges

We have now given you a comprehensive picture of cellular manufacturing. Throughout, our focus has been primarily managerial; that is, our goal has been to provide a set of decision-making frameworks and tools to help you make cells a successful part of your organization's competitive strategy. In this chapter we recap this managerial journey, look at future trends and their impact on cells, and highlight four areas that need more study. In addressing these issues, findings from ongoing research may help you make ever better decisions about designing and using cells in your organization.

A BRIEF REVIEW

We began the book by describing "the new competitive reality." The first chapter set the stage for the book by describing the competitive factors motivating organizations to revitalize their operations. One insight we offered was that the status quo is a recipe for extinction: all organizations must continually reassess their competitive position, and possibly reorganize their operations to more rapidly and efficiently create and deliver the products that customers value. We believe that for many organizations manufacturing and office cells are a viable response to "production under pressure." Therefore, the first section of the book described what manufacturing and office cells are, and why they can improve performance. We detailed the benefits that can accrue to cells, and, more importantly, how cell design and operation produce these benefits. The two are tightly linked: *you have to understand where the benefits come from in order to design a cell that reaches its full potential*. We also stressed that the effective implementation of cells requires attention not just to processes and technologies, but also to organizational and human issues.

The second section of the book focused on the (primarily) technical dimensions of adopting and designing cells. To put that in perspective, we first described the overall planning process in general terms (Chapter 4). We then looked more closely at planning the overall factory (Chapter 5), and developing detailed cell designs (Chapter 6). To create effective cells, you need to understand the dynamics of cell system performance with respect to lead time, inventory, and output. Chapter 7 provided guidelines and tools for evaluating your proposed cells along these critical dimensions. Finally, Chapter 8 in this section looked at the question of economic justification. How do you know, and how do you demonstrate to others, that cells create value for your organization? We provided explicit guidance for working through this important issue.

Successful cells require the right infrastructure. By infrastructure we mean all the systems, procedures, and methods that support a firm's operations. This includes how to measure cell performance (Chapter 9), cost cell products (Chapter 10), plan and control cell production (Chapter 11), design and organize cell jobs (Chapter 12), select and train cell employees (Chapter 13), and compensate cell workers and supervisors (Chapter 14). Every manager who creates a cell must address these issues sooner or later. In this third section of the book we have provided cell-specific descriptions and prescriptions to help you do that. Perhaps the most important point we can leave you with is this: *cells will not work well without a supportive infrastructure!*

The fourth section of the book focused on implementing and improving cells. In Chapter 15, we looked at cell implementation. How do you actually "make cells happen?" What steps do you follow? How do you organize the effort? One of the important themes we stressed was change management. Cells represent a new way of doing things, with far-reaching implications. Depending on your starting point, cells can call for a new culture, one that moves away from a command and control-oriented hierarchy and toward a culture of participation, collaboration, and high performance. It's a big change that won't happen on its own. Then, in Chapter 16, we summarized problems commonly experienced by firms designing, justifying, implementing, and operating cells. We talked about what you and others in your organization can do to make cells succeed, as well as the pitfalls you will need to avoid or overcome. Our hope is that by becoming familiar with other companies' problems, you may learn how to avoid them yourself.

In Chapter 17 we described how and why cells improve and evolve over time, underscoring why this book is entitled *Reorganizing the Factory* rather than *Organizing the Factory*. Cells are not static: their creation marks the beginning of a journey, not the destination. The same pressures for quick response and high quality that drove you to create cells in the first place are ongoing. Staying competitive requires continual incremental improvement and, sometimes, radical cell redesign and even cell dissolution.

The fifth section of the book, a single chapter, extended the principles of cellular manufacturing to office operations (Chapter 18). There are tremendous opportunities to improve office operations by creating process-complete office cells. This chapter described how to do it—the tools to use and the steps to follow. We also considered infrastructure and implementation issues for office cells, highlighting the special challenges you are likely to face when you create cells to process information as opposed to material.

For the remainder of the chapter we will peer into the future of manufacturing and how this may affect the future of cells.

CELLS IN 2020: A PLATFORM FOR COMPETITIVE MANUFACTURING

While we don't generally like to speculate about the future, one trend seems clear: the pressures for speed and flexibility are only going to increase in the years to come (see our opening quote by Skinner in Chapter 1). This observation is more than just our opinion. Groups of scholars and industry leaders who have looked ahead and speculated about the future of manufacturing draw similar conclusions. They believe that the following factors will be the most important in the development of manufacturing in the coming decades:[1]

- The competitive climate will continue to demand rapid responses from organizations. Customers will become increasingly sophisticated and demand higher levels of customization.
- Innovation and creativity in all aspects of manufacturing will be the basis of competition.
- Innovative process technologies will change both the scope and scale of manufacturing and information on all facets of the manufacturing enterprise and the marketplace will be instantly available.
- Environmental protection and the globalization of markets and resources (including labor) will strongly influence decisions about how to organize and operate.

Closing the gap between current manufacturing practice and a future manufacturing enterprise shaped by these factors presents a number of challenges. These include: (1) achieving concurrency in all operations (i.e., conducting planning, development, and implementation in parallel, rather than in sequence—thus, research and development, design engineering, manufacturing, marketing, distribution, and customer support must work "concurrently as virtually one entity that links customers to innovators of new products"); (2) integrating human and technical resources to enhance workforce performance and satisfaction (of course, integration is a prerequisite for concurrency); (3) instantaneously transforming information into knowledge for decision-making; (4) producing with near-zero environmental impact; (5) reconfiguring manufacturing in response to changing market needs; and (6) developing innovative manufacturing processes with an emphasis on "decreasing dimensional scale."[2] These challenges, if met, represent profound changes for manufacturing organizations in the coming decades.

If the pundits have it right, what are the implications for cells? The emphasis on rapid response, innovation, creativity, and customization suggests that successful manufacturing in the future will place a high premium on flexibility. Manufacturing will need to meet high-mix, low-volume demand. Does this call for a return to job shop manufacturing? Although this may happen in certain instances, we do not believe it will be the case in general. In fact, we believe that cells provide an excellent platform for future competitive manufacturing and can help address some of the challenges just noted. We base this belief on three factors:

1. *Advances in process technology will enhance cells' ability to meet high-mix, low-volume demand, and do so rapidly.* Futurists predict that equipment will become much more flexible. It will also be designed for very rapid changeovers. As we discussed in Chapter 2, such developments seem to point to a reduced need for standardized family production in cells. However, flexibility is a form of redundancy that will always cost more,

and be less efficient, than narrowly focused equipment and processes designed to produce similar products. Therefore, outfitting a cell with equipment whose flexibility is tailored to both present and future parameters of the cell family will cost less and be more efficient than equipment with greater flexibility applied to the production of more dissimilar products. Of course, more flexible equipment will permit the cell family to change over time while keeping the basic cell structure intact, thereby increasing cell life. The range of products produced without incurring significant setups will be quite broad, and the physical closeness of cell equipment (along with other operating principles) assures quick response—a hallmark of cellular systems, and a critical requirement for future manufacturing. On the other hand, we expect that job shops, by virtue of their arrangement and operating principles, will always trade off responsiveness for flexibility. Keep in mind, though, that some firms will always need such "unlimited flexibility" to support their make-to-order operating strategy.

Advances in process technologies may also mean that monument process problems vanish. The predicted trend toward small-scale (and scalable) production equipment may make it easier in the future to miniaturize processes and also less expensive to place them in cells.

2. *Cells and focused factories are ideal for integrating human and technical resources, and for expanding the role of employees in decision-making.* Most futurists see front-line employees with far greater responsibilities, more ownership of operations, and more direct contact with customers than what we see today. Advances in information technology will give employees access to data required for making decisions, and higher levels of education will assure that employees can use this information effectively. In many ways, today's self-managed multi-operator cells are a preview of work in the future. Employees in these cells collaborate in performing direct and indirect tasks, manage start-to-finish production, and are accountable for performance and improvement. Thus, cells fit perfectly with the vision of people in future manufacturing systems.

3. *Integration and concurrency are supported by process-complete operations in cells.* In a truly integrated and concurrent organization, traditional functional distinctions (e.g., marketing versus operations) and the associated handoffs that characterize the way work is typically done are blurred or eliminated. Informed decisions concerning one activity (e.g., the design of the product) are based on input from all aspects of the enterprise (e.g., manufacturing, product support, delivery, servicing, end-of-use disposition, and so forth). Creating an organization of this type is consistent with the core principles of cellular thinking. Let us also point out that the creation of cells—because of their focus on product families and process-complete operations—provides an opportunity to review and consider the full environmental impact of both products and processes to be placed in cells.

For the above reasons, we believe the role of cells in manufacturing and office operations is going to increase, not decrease, in the coming years. However, we also believe that the nature of cells will be different than it is today. Table 19-1 identifies the trends we foresee. Below we describe the most important changes.

Table 19-1. Future trends in cellular manufacturing

- Advances in information and process technology will make cells more adaptable and flexible
- Advances in information technology will enable and increase the use of virtual cells in production and office operations
- Cell employees will have expanded management and decision-making roles
- In cells with multiple operators, there will be high levels of operator collaboration in performing direct and indirect tasks
- Single-employee production cells and single-employee office cells (case worker cells) will be more common
- Organizations will link preproduction and production activities to create integrated cell systems responsible for the total process from design to delivery

Technology Will Enable More Flexible and Adaptable Cells

It seems clear to us that of the forces for change we identified in Chapter 17, technological change will be the most powerful driver of cell evolution (and, possibly, revolution). Technological change may eliminate monument processes and position cells to be more adaptable. But couldn't it also drive the organization away from cells? There is no doubt that the more flexible the production process, the smaller the benefits of focus and dedication.

Having said this, we don't predict a scenario where a flexible "supermachine" will make all types of diverse components interchangeably. There will always be boundaries to product flexibility. Also, more flexibility will always cost more than less flexibility. Therefore, as we suggested earlier, product-oriented cells will still play an important role in competitive manufacturing. However, we believe that future cells will be far more flexible than even the most adaptable and reconfigurable cells of today. Advances in process and information technology will make this a reality.

Flexible machine tools will be able to handle more types of operations and less similar parts (and still have low changeover times). In essence, the machine tools in some cases become cells by themselves. In addition, we envision that companies will group similar or identical pieces of very flexible equipment into production units. These units can serve as a new form of flexible cells that dynamically can accommodate different types of product families.

Advances in information technology will also contribute to more flexible and adaptable cells. To begin with, these advances have the potential to transform infrastructure—for example, how you plan and control manufacturing, and your ability to access performance data for improvement purposes. It will allow companies to execute tasks along business processes (design, order management, etc.) in a much more integrated and rapid fashion. In fact, much of the response-time reduction in the future will likely come from reengineered office work that takes advantage of information technology (and some of this work will be done in office cells). Moreover, the availability of instantaneous information will better equip cell employees to rapidly adapt production cells to changing business conditions. Thus, advances in information technology will contribute to increasing levels of cell self-management as well, a trend we explore more fully in the next section.

Clearly, in the coming decades information and process technology will allow you to rapidly reshape or refocus cells in response to changing business needs. This flexibility also has a human dimension. Below we describe some of the people changes that will contribute to cell flexibility.

Collaboration and Self-Management Will Be the Norm in Multi-Operator Cells

In our chapter on job design and daily work in cells (Chapter 12), we observed that cells that make the best use of teamwork—i.e., those with high levels of task overlap in direct and indirect work—are particularly well suited for situations that require adaptation:[3]

> In any situation requiring the real-time combination of multiple skills, experiences, and judgments, a team inevitably gets better results than a collection of individuals operating within confined job roles and responsibilities.

This is exactly the type of situation that will characterize manufacturing in the future. Cells with high levels of internal collaboration and self-management are well positioned to operate in turbulent environments. In fact, most visions of the organization of the future are based on teams replacing individuals as the primary performance unit in the company.[4] Such team-based, self-managed cells, of course, require high levels of education and great access to data for decision-making.

Single-Operator Cells Will Increase in Both Office and Production Environments

Not all cells, though, will be multi-operator cells. Advances in automated production technology suggest that manufacturing cells may increasingly have single operators. Advances in information technology will likewise make it possible for a single individual to perform, start-to-finish, all the transactions involved in information-intensive processes (within the boundaries of a family). Thus, office operations will rely more on case worker office cells—those in which a single employee handles a complete administrative process.

Linked Cells Will Be Responsible for Design to Delivery

Linked cells may be a central organizational form in future manufacturing enterprises. In fact, we envision preproduction and production activities organized as office and manufacturing cells (e.g., order management cells, design cells, and production cells) focused on the same products and linked together via integrated information systems. These value-chain-complete operations would form a focused factory that integrates people and technical resources, facilitates concurrency, and rapidly provides customers with high-value products.

GRAY AREAS: WHERE WE NEED TO KNOW MORE

We readily acknowledge that there are a number of gray areas and unanswered questions about how to best design, justify, implement, and operate cells. Below, we highlight just four selected areas. These are issues that we are beginning to explore ourselves and where clear answers may help you make better decisions about the design and use of cells in your organization.

1. *Multi-stage cell design.* Ideally, we would like to have the whole value chain in a single cell (e.g., order management plus design plus machine and assembly plus packaging, all in one cell). However, there are often technological, physical, and organizational limitations to doing so. But while much has been written about designing single cells, we know less about how to design clusters of linked cells, such as machining cells that feed assembly cells or an order processing cell that submits information to manufacturing cells. Given this, what is a suitable framework and what are useful procedures for approaching integrated, multi-stage cell design? And from a wider perspective, when are cell webs (networks of cells, including both office and manufacturing cells) the best choice, and how do we go about creating them?

2. *Human issues.* As we have already noted, all managers who create cells must make decisions about job design, selection, training, measurement, and compensation for these cells. We have addressed all these issues in this book; however, there is much more to learn about the link between the cell pay system and performance, the ideal levels of cross-training, how and when to involve cell operators in design efforts, what level of self-management is best, and so forth. For cells to reach their full potential we need better answers to these important questions, and the answers are likely tied to a variety of strategic and environmental conditions of the firm.

3. *Measurement issues.* We have devoted much space to the discussion of measurement issues, yet this is a very complicated area that needs further study. It appears that many firms now operate with metrics that prevent cells from being established or lead to resource allocations that contradict quick-response/low-inventory strategies. Part of this syndrome is due to the inability to assign value to time. How do we design measurement systems, and especially cost accounting systems, so they can motivate managers and employees to make the right decisions towards fulfilling the organization's financial and operational goals—in both the short and the long term?

4. *Cells in the supply chain.* While we have tried to emphasize that cells should contribute to meeting corporate objectives, our book has focused on cells within a single factory. We have not explored the linkages between cells and the rest of the upstream or downstream supply chain. What transpires inside a cell may sometimes not be as important, from a time, cost, and profit perspective, as what transpires between the cell and

the rest of the supply chain. For example, due to the growing reliance on outsourcing, a manufacturer's ability to be responsive depends more and more on supplier responsiveness. This begs the question of how organizations best can link cells with other steps in the value creation and delivery chain. As indicated earlier, information technology will play a crucial part here and we foresee cells becoming directly connected to suppliers and customers.

FINAL WORDS

In this book, we have presented much of what is known about manufacturing and office cells (and provided many references in case you want to dig deeper into the material). In discussing virtually every aspect of creating and running cell systems, our goal has been to go beyond description—the "what is"—and provide guidelines and insights that can help you know what to actually do—the "how to."

We can guarantee you, however, that in the process of designing, justifying, implementing, operating, and improving cells you will encounter many issues that evade simple prescriptions. Moreover, the right answer or the best decision will likely depend on the particular circumstances in your organization. For this reason, we have offered frameworks and criteria for making decisions. In essence, we have provided you with a compass and a map. Now it is up to you to survey the terrain and find your own best path. If you have gained some important insights about cellular manufacturing, and we have equipped you with a better sense of the alternative routes and how to choose among them, then our book has succeeded in its mission. We wish you every possible success in your continual efforts to *reorganize the factory*!

APPENDIX A

Using Standard Cost per Piece Data to Justify Cells

Some companies use data from their standard costing system to determine the impact of cells on the manufacturing cost per unit. While we do not recommend this approach, we include it here for completeness. In standard costing systems (see Appendix D), the manufacturing cost of a part is determined as:

$$C = dM + dL + MOH$$

Here, dM = standard material cost per part, dL = standard direct labor cost per part, and MOH = standard manufacturing overhead per part. In systems where direct labor is used as the allocation base, the manufacturing overhead cost per part is determined as "overhead cost/hour*standard labor hours/part." The cost per part can then be stated as:

$$C = dM + (dL \text{ hours/part})*(dL \text{ cost/hour} + MOH \text{ cost/hour})$$

If we break down the labor hours per part into time spent on setups vs. on processing, we get the following relation for the standard cost per part:

$$C = dM + (dL \text{ setup time/part} + dL \text{ operation time/part})*(dL \text{ cost/hour} + MOH \text{ cost/hour})$$

An Illustration Using Cost Data

You can justify cells by comparing the present cost of manufacturing a part with the cost of having it produced in a cell system. This means estimating each factor in the formula above, for both systems. Table A-1 shows an example of this type of calculation.[1]

Table A-1a shows the current situation in the functional shop. The standard cost per unit, as per the formula above, can be found as:

$$C = 52.05 + (0.80/100 + 0.15)*(12 + 12*4) + (1.50/100 + 0.20)*(16 + 16*4) + (1.20/100 + 0.25)*(15 + 15*4) = 52.05 + 1.90 + 7.60 + 3.44 + 13.76 + 3.93 + 15.72 = 52.05 + 9.27 + 37.08 = \$98.40$$

(Note that dL cost is multiplied by the MOH rate of 400 percent, i.e., MOH cost/hour = 4*dL cost/hour.)

Table A-1. Examples of unit cost calculations using a standard cost approach

Table A-1a: Product cost with current operation (lot size = 100 units)

Operation	Setup Time	Run Time/Piece	Avg. Time/Piece	Labor Rate/Hr.	Labor Cost/Piece
Shear	0.80	0.15	0.158	$12.00	$ 1.90
Punch	1.50	0.20	0.215	16.00	3.44
Brake	1.20	0.25	0.262	15.00	3.93
				Total labor cost/piece	$ 9.27
				Material cost/piece	52.05
				Overhead (400%)	37.08
				Total cost/piece	$ 98.40

Table A-1b: Product cost for proposed cell (lot size = 10 units)

Operation	Setup Time	Run Time/Piece	Avg. Time/Piece	Labor Rate/Hr.	Labor Cost/Piece
Shear	0.10	0.135	0.145	$18.00	$ 2.61
Punch	0.15	0.180	0.195	18.00	3.51
Brake	0.20	0.225	0.245	18.00	4.41
				Total labor cost/piece	$ 10.30
				Material cost/piece	52.05
				Overhead (400%)	42.12
				Total cost/piece	$104.70

Table A-1c: Product cost calculation for cell based on modified cost factors (lot size = 10 units)

Operation	Setup Time	Run Time/Piece	Avg. Time/Piece*	Labor Rate/Hr.	Labor Cost/Piece
Shear	0.10	0.135	0.123	$18.00	$ 2.21
Punch	0.15	0.180	0.166	18.00	2.99
Brake	0.20	0.225	0.208	18.00	3.74
				Total labor cost/piece	$ 8.94
				Material cost/piece	47.89
				Overhead (400%)	33.04
*See endnote 2				Total cost/piece	$ 89.87

Table A-1b shows the product cost estimated for the cell under the assumption that both setup and unit operation time will be lowered due to improved efficiencies. As a result, the lot size is reduced as well. At $104.70, the predicted unit cost is now greater than the current cost. This is because the cost of labor has increased to $18 per hour, while the overhead rate is unchanged at 400 percent of direct labor cost. The anticipated rise in labor cost per hour stems from the creation of a new labor grade to accommodate cross-trained cell workers.

Finally, Table A-1c shows the situation where additional cost savings are reflected in the calculations. Material usage, for example, is expected to be 8 percent lower due to less scrap. The time for labor is reduced by 8 percent per part due to scrap reduction, and by 7 percent per part due to less rework. This 15 percent reduction in labor is reflected in the "Adj. time per piece."[2]

In addition, the manufacturing overhead cost per piece is reduced from $37.08 to $33.04 per piece due to an anticipated reduction in material handling, scheduling, and expediting after the cell is in place. With the product cost now lower than the present cost ($89.87 versus $98.40 per piece), and an annual volume of 14,800 units, the savings per year are about $126,000. Since the cost of establishing the cell, including operator training, is estimated at $230,000, the payback time is 230/126 or 1.83 years. Thus, the cell would pay for itself in less than two years.

Comments on Using Standard Cost Data

The above example illustrates several important issues related to cost/benefit estimations for cells. The benefits, in the form of avoided costs, are in the areas of scrap and rework (affecting both materials and labor), direct labor (due to improved efficiencies), and indirect labor and support personnel (less need for material-handling and planning/control personnel). Tables A-1b and A-1c also illustrate the common situation where the labor cost per hour increases in cells due to extended responsibilities. Finally, the calculations take a cost/benefit perspective and use the payback time technique to assess the cell's economic value.

However, these calculations ignore some important factors. For example, they do not take into account the *number of operators*. There are currently at least three operators producing the parts at the three work centers (Table A-1a). But how many operators will be assigned to the cell permanently? One? Two? Three? This is not clear. The calculations based on time per piece assume that labor is divisible, but once operators are assigned to the cell, the parts must bear the full cost of the operators. This affects the economic value of the cell.

The use of standard overhead costs is another questionable aspect of this type of justification. If the MOH rate (as a percentage of labor cost) is left intact while labor cost per hour increases, the produced cost per part may increase in the cell. This can happen even if the time required to manufacture each part decreases (as it did in Table A-1b). Of course, the *actual* costs for space, engineering, planning, maintenance, material handling, and the like—now included in the overhead cost determined by the cost system—*should decline* after the cell is in operation because certain activities are curtailed or no longer needed. However, such a cost reduction will not show up in calculated unit costs until the overhead rates are adjusted. Since this is done only infrequently (on an annual basis in many firms), it may take up to a year before the "true" product cost is known. In fact, you will *never* know unless a decision has been taken to change the overhead rate in the accounting system! We point this out to emphasize that the impact of cells on manufacturing cost is not always reflected in the product cost calculations.

Adjusting Overhead Rates

As we discuss in Chapter 10, the cell should not have the same overhead rate as the rest of the plant. In Table A-1c, the MOH cost assigned to each piece was lowered by $4.04 due to the cell's impact on material handling and scheduling. But how do you adjust the overhead rate? There are two ways to do this. The first, a not fully satisfactory approach, is simply to apply an *arbitrary* improvement factor to the overhead rate. For example, if you believe that there is less need for material handlers and scheduling personnel, a 5 or 10 percent reduction in MOH rate may reflect this reduction.

A more detailed approach would look at the way the MOH rate (in this case the 400 percent charge against each direct labor hour) was determined. To do this, you would need to determine historical expenses for material handling, scheduling, and expediting, and how these relate to all other expenses that make up fixed and variable overhead. You also would need to estimate how the cell would affect each of these expenses, and adjust the MOH cost accordingly. Table A-2 shows how to do this for the example in Table A-1.

Table A–2. A way to determine impact on overhead

> 1. Original overhead rate is 400% of direct labor. Overhead cost per piece is cost is $37.08 (see Table A-1a).
>
> 2. Assume we know that material-handling, scheduling, and expediting make up 16% of the current overhead rate. This means that the overhead cost *excluding* these activities is 37.08*0.84, or $31.15 per piece. Accordingly, a revised overhead cost for parts made in the cell should fall in the $31.15 to $37.08 range.
>
> 3. If we believe that the cell will reduce the need for material-handling, scheduling, and expediting activities by 68.1%, the appropriate overhead charge should be 68.1% less in these areas. The revised overhead cost applicable to these three activities therefore is (37.08–31.15)*(1–0.681) = $1.89 per piece.
>
> 4. The new overhead cost to be used for the cell, then, is 31.15 + 1.89 = $33.04 per piece.

These calculations can get even more complicated. If the operators assume duties previously performed by maintenance and scheduling personnel, the charge to the cell for the latter employee groups should be lowered. You can do this, as just discussed, by adjusting the overhead rate downwards. However, since material-handling and scheduling tasks have not been eliminated, but merely shifted from one group of employees to another, the cost must be charged elsewhere. You can do this partly by increasing the operators' pay per hour. But will multiplying the standard time to manufacture a part by the labor cost per hour now cover the cost of having both the direct and indirect tasks performed by the cell operators? This would be true only if the standard time per piece has been revised to also include indirect tasks.

You may also have noted that the calculations in Table A-1 do not consider the cell's impact on inventories or space. This, again, would require an adjustment to the overhead rate.

In summary, it is difficult to accurately reflect the economic impact of cells using costing systems. In fact, due to all its deficiencies, we do not recommend this approach to justifying cells.

APPENDIX B

How to Make Effective Presentations to Management

At the end of Chapter 8 we discussed how to sell the cell project to management. As part of project planning, the team is likely to be asked to make oral presentations to various parties, especially if the project is large and will affect many people in the firm. Such opportunities can make or break any budding project. Avoiding biases, having a credible team leader and presenter, having an implementation plan, and including financial outcomes are crucial. But there are many other pointers for persuasively presenting your case to a group of decision-makers or participants in a future cell project. The suggestions below provide an excellent summary on how to structure effective presentations:[1]

- *Identify both the decision the team wants management to make, and the key decision-makers.* Design the presentation along the clearest line to elicit that decision. The importance of storyboarding cannot be overemphasized.

- *Make sure the presentation has a beginning, a middle, and an end, and give the audience a preview of its structure.* This will help lead them through the presentation and let them know when to ask questions.

- *Say it with pictures.* Wherever possible, use graphics to illustrate points. Many good texts are available on preparing and making presentations. Inexperienced presenters should take advantage of these.

- *Keep it simple.* Address only one topic per chart, and no more than three or four main themes in a presentation. This doesn't mean that detail doesn't have to be available for those interested. If some points need to be supported by complicated data, prepare this information as handouts and backup material, and use them as necessary.

- *Put the bottom line up-front.* If the project will save $4 million a year, the presentation should make this point early. The presenter will then have the audience's full attention as he or she covers the details. A rule of thumb is that any member of your audience should be able to leave your presentation after five minutes, carrying away the main points and conclusions you intend to convey.

- *Don't ruin a well-prepared presentation by tackling questions that the team can't answer.* A response of "That's a good question, but I don't have the answer right now. Is it all right if we get back to you tomorrow with that?" will earn more respect than an obvious bluff, which could make people question the rest of the information.

- *Don't get bogged down in specific technical discussions of no interest to the audience as a whole.* Allow the concerned person to express his or her thoughts, and address them in general. If a detailed technical debate seems to be developing, arrange for that person to discuss the topic further with someone from the team after the meeting.

- *End the presentation with a summary of the major conclusions, a list of specific recommendations, and a description of the next steps in the project.* Ask that the decision the team is waiting for be made. If it isn't made at this time, find out when it will be made. Make sure no further information is required from the team.

APPENDIX C

Measurement Checklist

Chapter 9 presents principles to assist you with the design of an effective performance measurement system. These principles guide decisions about what to measure and how to collect and display data. Together with the Process Performance Measurement Matrix in Table 9-7 and the guidelines in Table 9-4, the questions below form the foundation for a diagnostic tool for analyzing performance measures.

EVALUATE THE ENTIRE SET OF CELL MEASURES

- Is the underlying process defined, documented, and understood?
  - Has the process been flowcharted?

- Are there missing metrics in the measurement system for this process?
  - Does the Process Performance Measurement Matrix reveal any gaps—areas of the matrix that are empty? Are there any explanations for these gaps?
  - What would be the consequences of adding measures?

- Are any measures redundant?
  - Does the Process Measurement Matrix reveal areas where multiple measures assess the same performance variable?
  - What are the possible consequences of removing these measures? Whose behavior will change? Why?

- Are any measures unimportant to monitor and display on a regular basis?
  - What are the possible consequences of removing these measures? Whose behavior will change? Why?

- Is the measurement emphasis—the degree to which time, cost, or quality measures dominate the matrix—consistent with the organization's strategic objectives?
  - Conversely, does every strategic objective at the organizational level have a companion measure at the cell level?

- How is the measurement system for the cell linked to measurement systems used for individual job performers in the cell, or to those used at the cell system and higher levels in the organization?

EVALUATE EACH PROPOSED OR EXISTING CELL MEASURE

- Is this measure well defined?
  - Is there a clear and unambiguous operational definition?
  - Would two trained employees, observing the same event, record the same data for this measure?
  - Is this measure defined consistently across cells to allow cross-cell comparisons?
- Is this measure linked to a strategic objective?
  - If yes, which one? How is it linked?
  - If no, why is it included? This does not imply it should be discarded, only that its role in the measurement system should be clear.
- Is this measure fully understood and accepted by the cell employees?
  - Do the employees understand what is being measured, how it is measured, and why?
  - Is the measure presented graphically to facilitate easy interpretation?
- Can cell employees influence performance on this measure?
  - What actions on the part of cell operators would lead to enhanced performance on this dimension?
  - What actions would degrade performance on this dimension?
  - What factors outside the cell's control might influence performance with respect to this measure?
- If the cell performs well or poorly on this measure, what are the consequences for cell operations as a whole?
  - What other measured variables may be positively or negatively affected? How?
  - What unmeasured variables may be positively or negatively affected? How?
- Is there a person or group responsible for collecting, calculating, displaying, and analyzing the data for this measure?
  - Who, inside or outside the cell, is responsible for the data collection, data analysis, and performance metrics presentation systems?
- Is there a goal, target, or standard associated with this measure?
  - Who sets the goal?
  - How often is it revised?
  - Do cell employees know about the goal?
- Is this measure linked to a compensation/reward system?
  - Which one? How is it linked?
  - How might this link affect data collection, performance, and intervention?
- What are the possible consequences of changing the time frame associated with the reporting and review of this measure?
  - Would more frequent measurement be helpful and cost effective?
  - Would less frequent measurement lead to an unacceptable loss of information?

APPENDIX D

A Primer on Accounting Systems

In Chapter 10 we discussed cost accounting systems and how these should be modified to fit cellular manufacturing. In this appendix we provide important background information for that chapter in the following areas:

- The difference between cost accounting and financial accounting
- The purpose of cost accounting
- Definitions of manufacturing versus nonmanufacturing costs
- Brief overview of standard and hybrid costing systems
- Cost variances—definitions and formulas
- Performance measures used in standard costing systems—definitions and formulas
- The impact on operating income from building inventory

COST ACCOUNTING VERSUS FINANCIAL ACCOUNTING SYSTEMS

Accounting systems have two emphases. One is to provide financial information about the organization to the outside world. Systems responsible for such *external reporting* are called *financial accounting* systems. The other emphasis of accounting systems is to generate financial information useful for the planning and control of the firm's operations. Systems focused on such *internal reporting* are called *management accounting* or *cost accounting* systems (we will mostly use the latter term in this book). Table D-1 provides some basic differences between these two types of accounting systems.[1] A few of these differences are worth highlighting.

First, cost accounting systems, unlike financial accounting systems, are not regulated by law or accounting standards (at least not in the United States). That is, they may be designed to suit each particular organization's need for data. Second, while the scope of financial accounting is the organization as a whole, cost accounting often looks at smaller units, such as departments, focused factories, or cells, and traces costs down to the product level. Third, and most importantly, the purpose of the financial accounting system is to report on the organization's overall economic performance to external constituencies, while the cost accounting system's main role is to assist in internal decision-making at all levels in the firm.

Table D-1. A comparison of financial and management (cost) accounting

	Financial Accounting	Management (Cost) Accounting
Audience	External: stockholders, creditors, tax authorities	Internal: workers, managers, executives
Purpose	Report on past performance to external parties	Inform internal decisions made by employees and managers; feedback and control on operating performance
Timeliness	Delayed, historical	Current, future-oriented
Restrictions	Regulated; rules driven by generally accepted accounting principles and government authorities	No regulations; systems and information determined by management to meet strategic and operational needs
Type of information	Financial measurements only	Financial plus operational and physical measurements on processes, technologies, suppliers, customers, and competitors
Nature of information	Objective, auditable, reliable, consistent, precise	More subjective and judgmental; valid, relevant, accurate
Scope	Highly aggregate; report on entire organization	Disaggregate; inform local decision and actions

These internal and the external systems, however, are not totally independent. Cost accounting systems must deliver two important pieces of information to the financial accounting system: (1) the value of the firm's inventory on the *balance sheet* and (2) the cost of goods sold (COGS) for the *income statement* (see Table D-2). Thus, the needs of the external reporting system impose some constraints on the internal cost accounting system.[2]

THE PURPOSE OF COST ACCOUNTING SYSTEMS

You can define cost (or management) accounting as "the use of financial information to plan, evaluate, control within an organization, and to assure the appropriate use of its resources."[3] More specifically, cost accounting systems serve the following major purposes:

1. To determine the cost of manufactured products.
2. To determine general administrative costs, and the cost of selling and distributing products to the customers.
3. To assign value to inventories for the financial accounting system.
4. To supply financial (and non-financial) data so that activities and resources can be planned and controlled.
5. To supply data about performance so that organizational units, their managers, and their strategies can be assessed.[4]

Table D-2. Simplified balance sheets and income statements

Balance Sheet, June 30, 2001			
Assets		*Liabilities and Equity*	
Cash	500	Accounts payable	2,000
Accounts receivable	1,000	Notes payable	8,250
INVENTORY	5,000	Shareholders' equity	7,000
Buildings and equipment	10,000		
Other assets	750		
TOTAL:	17,250	TOTAL:	17,250

Income Statement, Period Ending June 30, 2001	
Sales	5,000
COST OF GOODS SOLD	3,500
Gross Margin	*1,500*
Selling costs	650
General & administrative costs	200
Operating income	*650*
Interest expenses	500
Taxes	45
NET INCOME:	105

These five purposes can be distilled into two, since items 1 through 3 deal with *product and distribution cost determination* (and, therefore, profitability), while 4 and 5 focus on *performance measurement and operational control*.[5]

MANUFACTURING AND NONMANUFACTURING COSTS

The *manufacturing cost* of a product consists of three elements: direct labor, direct material, and manufacturing overhead.[6] *Manufacturing overhead* refers to all costs related to production other than direct labor or materials. Table D-3 shows examples

Table D-3. Examples of manufacturing overhead costs

- *Indirect labor*—employees dedicated to material handling, maintenance, quality control, and inspection.

- *Engineering*—salaries for manufacturing, industrial, or other engineers concerned with the design and improvement of the production process.

- *General and administrative expenses in manufacturing*—personnel administration, cost accounting, security, plant managers' and supervisors' salaries, and allocations of corporate expenses for shared services and corporate staff.

- *Facilities and equipment costs*—insurance, depreciation of plant equipment, and tooling; rent, energy, and utility costs.

- *Materials overhead*—costs related to the procurement, movement (excluding indirect material-handling labor), and coordination of material flows and inventories; also the salaries of purchasing, receiving, stockroom, traffic, and manufacturing systems personnel.

of various manufacturing overhead cost items.[7] Typically, direct labor accounts for between 8 to 14 percent of COGS, and direct material for between 51 to 68 percent. The third component, manufacturing overhead, thus averages between 25 to 35 percent of COGS. However, in some extreme cases labor can account for only 2 to 3 percent of COGS, manufacturing overhead for between 8 to 15 percent, while material may represent 82 to 90 percent of COGS.[8]

Besides manufacturing costs there are *non-manufacturing costs* which include costs for marketing and selling, distribution, R&D, and general and administrative costs for the company. Thus, the total cost of a product includes both manufacturing and non-manufacturing costs. However, *to determine cost of goods sold for a period, and to value inventory, only manufacturing costs are considered*. Thus, the non-manufacturing costs are not part of inventory costs. Instead, cost accounting systems treat them as period costs and expense them each period (e.g., each year).[9] Figure D-1 illustrates the role manufacturing and non-manufacturing costs play in determining inventory and operating income for external reporting purposes.[10]

STANDARD COSTING SYSTEMS

In a pure *standard costing system*, all cost factors (prices, rates) used are predetermined and referred to as "standards." The advantage of using standard data is that cost calculations and inventory assessments do not have to wait for actual data to be recorded. Costs typically are classified as fixed, semi-fixed (i.e., some portion of the costs are fixed, others are variable), and variable. This division is based on whether costs are considered to be dependent on changes in production volume. With this perspective, fixed costs are independent of volume, while variable costs vary in a direct way with changes in output.[11]

Assume that a firm has created two aggregated cost pools for each production department— one for fixed and one for variable manufacturing overhead—and that it uses direct labor as a cost driver. The *manufacturing overhead* (MOH) cost per labor hour can then be found for each department as:

- Standard MOH cost/hr. = Fixed MOH/hr + Variable MOH/hr.
- FixMOH/hr = (total budgeted FixMOH cost per year for the department)/
             (total number of budgeted labor hours per year for the
             department)
- VarMOH/hr = (total budgeted VarMOH cost per year for the department)/
             (total number of budgeted labor hours per year for the
             department)

Fixed manufacturing overhead includes depreciation of equipment; internal "rent" for space; personnel in engineering, maintenance, NC programming, etc. Likewise, variable manufacturing overhead includes indirect labor; personnel administration; inspection; material handling; supplies; and other general factory expenses.

The *standard cost per unit for a production department* is then (dM = direct material, dL = direct labor, Std = standard):

- Std cost/part = Std dM cost/part + Std dL cost/hour* Std dL hrs/part + Std
                 MOH cost/hr*Std dL hrs/part

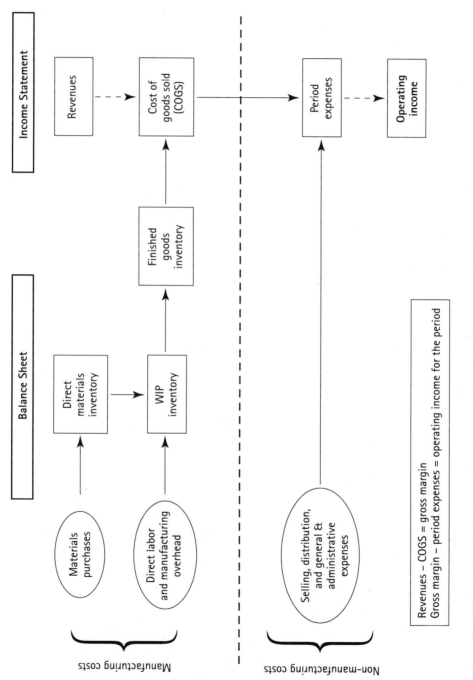

Figure D-1. The relationship between inventory, cost of goods sold, and operating income

This type of calculation must then be repeated for each production department that processes the part. The final standard cost per part is the sum of all department costs.

ACTUAL AND HYBRID COSTING SYSTEMS

Cost systems can also rely solely on actual data. Since you have to wait until the end of a period to know the outcome, these costs systems cannot be used for prediction or planning. The cost per part is (Act = actual):

- Act cost/part = Act dM cost/part + Act dL cost/hr*Act dL hrs/part + {Act MOH cost per dept/(no. of hours actually used in the period)}*Act dL hrs/part

Some systems also combine standard and actual data in different ways. For example, in *normal* costing systems we have:

- Cost/part = Act dM cost/part + Act dL cost/hr*Act dL hrs/part + Std MOH cost/hr*Act dL hrs/part

COST VARIANCES

Standard cost systems use "standards" for material prices, labor and machine costs, and amount of materials, machine time, and labor. These standards can be used to compare expected versus the actually achieved results, typically for a given period but also for an individual job. The differences are referred to as *variances*. There are many types of variances, but the most commonly used labor and materials variances include:

- Materials price variance = (Act price/unit - Std price/unit)*Act quantity/period
- Materials usage variance = (Act usage/period – Std usage/period)*Std price/unit
- Labor rate variance =   (Act rate/hr – Std rate/hr)*Act hours/period
- Labor efficiency variance = (Act hours/period – Std hours/period)*Std rate/hr

These four variances focus on either differences in prices or quantities. These differences are then multiplied by an actual or standard quantity per period or price per hour. The variances above can be derived from the *total cost variances for a period*. Each such variance can be broken down into a sum of price and quantity variances:

- Total cost variance, *material* = Actual cost – Standard cost = (Act price/unit*Act usage/period – Std price/unit*Std usage/period) = Materials price variance + Materials usage variance
- Total cost variance, *labor* = Actual cost – Standard cost = (Act rate/hr*Act hours/period - Std rate/hr*Std hours/period) = Labor rate variance + Labor efficiency variance

Note that these labor variances do not consider idle time. Thus, if during eight-hour days a group of operators regularly produce four hours of direct standard work during five actual hours of direct work per day, the labor variance is based on these two types of times (i.e., actual hours – standard hours). The remaining four hours per day for which the operators are paid could be included in the manufacturing overhead rate (as planned idle time) or in a separate account. At the end of the accounting period, the account balance is either added to COGS or allocated between COGS and inventory.

There are also variances associated with overhead costs. They reflect the fact that the targeted hours for a period differ from the actually produced hours.[12] Variances are *favorable* if actual costs are less than estimated costs, i.e., if they increase operating income. Conversely, variances are *unfavorable* if they reduce operating income (through increased COGS; see Table D-2). For example, a labor efficiency variance is unfavorable if the department spent more hours in manufacturing than were estimated.

PERFORMANCE MEASURES IN STANDARD COSTING SYSTEMS

Firms that use standard costing systems sometimes rely on measures that influence the variances. Among these are various efficiency and machine-utilization metrics. For example, a typical efficiency measure for a department is the ratio of earned standard hours to actual hours used in a period (the inverted ratio is sometimes used as well):

- Efficiency for the period = (Act output/period*Std hours/unit)/(Act hours/period)

Other direct performance measures in manufacturing include earned standard hours or earned standard dollars for a period:

- Earned standard hours for the period = (Act number of units produced/period)*Std hours/unit
- Earned standard dollars for the period = Act number of units produced/period*Std hours/unit*Std cost/hr

Since the standards are fixed for the period, these measures get larger the more units are produced. Thus, they are output-maximizing in their intention. Companies that use earned hours also use a labor variance, as follows:[13]

- Direct labor variance/period = Earned Std hrs/period – Act labor hrs spent in the period.

This variance is different from the labor variances shown earlier. You can rewrite it as:

- Direct labor variance/period = Act units produced*Std hrs/unit – Act units produced*Act hrs/unit = Act units produced*{Std hrs/unit – Act hrs/unit}

You can now see that you get a favorable variance if you can (a) increase output and (b) use fewer labor hours per unit than expected. Another measure of manufacturing performance derived from the accounting system is *inventory turns*, i.e., sales divided by inventory. For example, annual WIP inventory turns could be measured as:

- Annual WIP turns = {(Monthly shipments in dollars)/(Monthly ending WIP)}*12

Inventory turns measure "inventory efficiency" by expressing the amount of output the firm or department can sustain for a given level of inventory. If you keep the right products in inventory and minimize their cycle time through the production process (including the waiting time), you will also maximize the inventory turn measures.

THE IMPACT ON OPERATING INCOME FROM BUILDING INVENTORY

If you use a standard cost system based on *absorption costing*,[14] there is a factor that may seem to work against the adoption and use of a strategy aimed at lowering inventory. The cost system, through the product costs, assesses the inventory value for the balance sheet and COGS for the income statement. If you compare two projected income statements—one for "before cells" and the other for "after cells"— and assume that cells will drive down inventory to a new level, this comparison can make cells look less desirable. Assume, for example, that sales are constant. The only way to reduce inventory is to produce less during a period. Assume further that standard costs and budgeted volumes have not been adjusted. This means that overhead cost will be allocated over fewer units than budgeted. This results in a volume variance that will reduce operating income.[15]

An illustration of how this works is shown in Table D-4.[16] Here you can see that making 250 units *less* than what was budgeted for the period increased COGS and lowered operating income. The reverse is also true. Thus, producing more than budgeted will increase income (as often happens when earned standard hours is used as a performance metric). This is not desirable, of course, because it comes at the expense of an increased inventory. Such projected declines or increases in profit, of course, are temporary. If applied to a cell implementation, you should assume that in future periods—once inventories have been driven down and stabilized—manufacturing costs actually will decline.

Table D-4. Impact of production volume on operating income

Income Statement	CASE 1: Production = 800 units (same as budgeted volume)	CASE 2: Production = 550 units (250 units less than budgeted volume)
Revenues (on 750 units of sales)	$74,250	$74,250
Beginning inventory (200 units at $36/unit)	7,200	7,200
Variable manufacturing cost (at $20/unit)	16,000 (800 units)	11,000 (550 units)
Fixed manufacturing cost (at $16/unit)	12,800 (800 units)	8,800 (550 units)
Available for sale (at $36/unit)	36,000 (1000 units)	27,000 (750 units)
Ending inventory (at $36/unit)	9,000 (250 units)	0 (0 units)
COGS at standard cost (750 units)	27,000	27,000
Manufacturing overhead variance	0	4,000 (unfavorable)*
Total COGS	27,000	31,000
Gross Margin (revenues—total COGS)	47,250	43,250
Non-manufacturing costs	24,650	24,650
Operating income	$22,600	$18,600

Budgeted volume is 800 units for the period, and actual sales are 750 units. Beginning inventory is 200 units. The table compares production volumes of 800 and 550, respectively.

* Manufacturing overhead variance = (actual production – budgeted production)*fixed manufacturing cost per unit = (550 – 800)*16 = -$4,000. It is assumed that this variance is written off to COGS at the end of the period. Thus, total COGS = COGS at standard cost + manufacturing overhead variance.

APPENDIX E

Family Sequencing Procedures

In Chapter 11 we discussed how setup time can be avoided by grouping parts or products from the same families and processing them together. This appendix contains more details on the use of family sequencing, and also provides an additional illustration. For references to the family sequencing literature, see Chapter 11.

PUTTING FAMILY SEQUENCING TO WORK IN CELLS

We will look at the question of where and how to perform family sequencing from three perspectives: (1) initial order releasing, (2) the cell's flow pattern and, (3) the cell system structure.

Order Releasing

MRP systems determine planned order releases (POR) for items independent of their family membership. Planners in charge of order releasing can *override the MRP system* and release orders for parts early so that parts from the same families can be launched together. Figure E-1 shows the MRP records for two parts belonging to the same family in a cell. Part A is targeted for immediate release since its first POR falls in the upcoming week. However, if the MRP schedule is followed, part B would not be released until week 3.

To save setup time, the planner could decide to release parts A and B together in Week 1. When would this make sense? First, the two parts must be processed sequentially inside the cell, operation by operation. This will happen only if A and B follow exactly the same routings. Second, the gain in setup time reduction must compensate for the early inventory build-up of part B.

Internal Flow Pattern

A cell's internal flow pattern affects how sequencing is carried out after orders have been released. Consider the three types of flows in Figure E-2. The pure flow-line pattern is one where all jobs pass through all stations in the same sequence. Accordingly, jobs are ordered only once—at the entry point to the cell. Inside the cell, the FISFS rule is then applied (which, at each station, is the same as the FCFS procedure). Thus, you can use a family sequencing procedure at the entry point of the cell to minimize the time spent on setups once jobs enter the cell.

WEEK		1	2	3	4	5	
Gross requirements		25	10	25	0	28	Part A
Scheduled receipts		30					Family 1
Projected available balance	4	9	29	4	4	6	Lead time = 1 / Q = 30
Planned order releases		30			30		

		1	2	3	4	5	
Gross requirements		10	0	25	35	15	Part B
Scheduled receipts		40					Family 1
Projected available balance	15	45	45	20	25	10	Lead time = 1 / Q = 40
Planned order releases		◄------------ 40					

Release early?

Figure E1. Early order releasing based on family membership

The two other flow patterns in Figure E-2 complicate sequencing and, in fact, require that this activity is carried out *at each station*. Since jobs arrive to the cell in transfer batches, we can connect to our discussion in Chapter 11 to illustrate the need to sequence transfer batches when flow patterns are irregular.

Consider workstation S2 in the job shop cell in Figure E-2. Batches arriving to this station can come from stations S1 or S3, or directly from a buffer outside the cell. If in this situation you release lots to the cell and break them into smaller transfer batches, these batches—unlike the case in a pure flow-line cell—will not arrive in the same sequence to station S2. We illustrate the problem of "out-of-sequence" family members in Figure E-3.

Figure E-3a shows a situation where the first transfer batch of part type D is in process. Waiting in queue are transfer batches of part types A, B, and C (two transfer batches of part A have arrived). These part types may have followed different routes to station S2. Assume now that two more transfer batches arrive, first D_2 and then A3 (see Figure E-3b). The sequence of waiting jobs (including the one in process), therefore, is D_1-A_1-B_1-A_2-C_1-D_2-A_3. If you are processing these transfer batches in the sequence in which they arrived, you will incur six setups (one between each part type). Thus, lot-splitting in cells with non-linear flow patterns causes an increase in the time spent on setups. This may thereby lengthen the throughput times for the parts.

You can get around this problem by resequencing the queue of waiting transfer batches so that the batches of each part type are processed together (see Figure E-3c). We have here used the FCFS-Family rule. This arranges all transfer batches of the same part type into a family by considering the arrival time of the first transfer batch of each type. For example, part type D arrived first, which means that D_1 and D_2 make up the first transfer batch family. Part type A arrived next, and we arrange the three transfer batches within this family according to their arrival sequence. And so on with the remaining transfer batches.

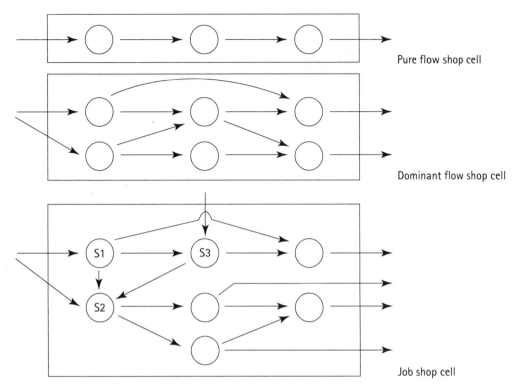

Figure E-2. Flow patterns inside cells (note that the figures do not illustrate the physical shape of the cells)

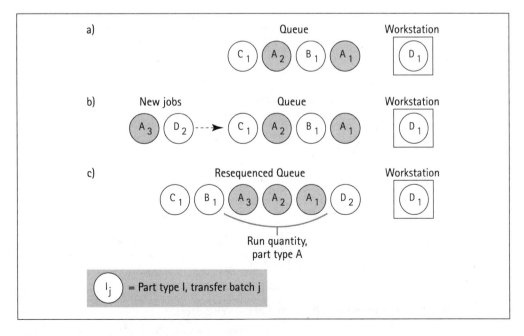

Figure E-3. Illustration of family sequencing

If no more batches of type A arrive, the *run quantity* of this part type consists of the three waiting transfer batches. But if a new transfer batch of type A arrives to the queue while D_2 is being processed, that batch would jump ahead of all other waiting part types and be placed in the queue right after batch A_3. Note, then, that the run quantity dynamically changes over time depending on the jobs in the queue and how they are sequenced.

By the way, many planners, supervisors, or operators apply family sequencing rules on an *informal* basis. That is, although part families may not be formally recognized by the MPC system, the person authorized to chose the next job to run may look at a job schedule and realize that some jobs on that list require the same type of setup. These jobs are then run together to avoid setups, thereby overriding the formal MPC system's priorities.

Cell System Structure

An important consideration when using family sequencing is the way material flows between cells, and between cells and the rest of the plant (or to outside plants). Consider the cell system structure in Figure E-4. The left part of the system, i.e., Cells 1 and 2, together with Assembly Cells 1 and 2 and the uncellularized "Remainder Plant," forms a *buffered cell system*. The supplier and customer cells are somewhat independent in the sense that they are "decoupled" from each other by storerooms. Thus, WIP inventory is removed from the factory floor.

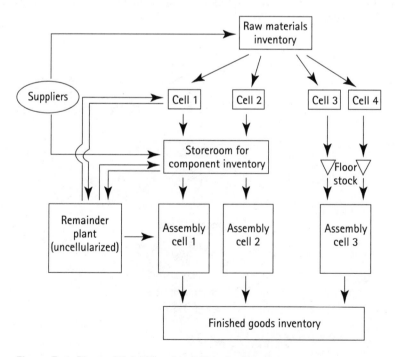

Figure E-4. Plant with buffered and linked cell systems

The right part of the system, i.e., Cells 3 and 4, and Assembly Cell 3, forms a *linked cell system*. Here, Cells 3 and 4 directly feed parts to Assembly Cell 3. Only small point-of-use buffer areas separate these three cells. The internal flow patterns are normally different in the linked versus the buffered systems. The linked cell system is more likely to have a serial, flow shop-like structure internal to the cells, while the buffered cell system is more likely to have cells with irregular flow patterns. This is due to a greater variety of part and components.

Sequencing in linked cell systems

It is easy to see where family-based sequencing procedures would be the least ideal. In the closely linked system you perform fast-paced, lean, repetitive manufacturing. *Here, you want tight connections between assembly cell and feeder cells.* Accordingly, if you apply the same sequence as used in assembly to all preceding production units, you create matching flows of parts coming in to the assembly stage. Using different family sequencing rules, or any type of sequencing rule for that matter, for the different cells will change the order between jobs every time the queue is prioritized. Closely linked systems, therefore, should rely on the FISFS sequencing rule, with the "system boundaries" drawn to cover all the linked cells. This ensures that the same sequence is used at all stages. An example of this type of sequencing was discussed in Chapter 11 in connection with Applicon's MPC system (see Figure 11-12). There, the sequence established for each assembly cell was also applied to the PCB area.

Sequencing in buffered cell systems

What about the buffered cell system? Since the flows between the part and the assembly cells are not closely coupled, it may be less important to apply the same sequence throughout the system. Rather, in a system with a great part and volume variety, you are probably more interested in operating as efficiently as possible. For example, since setup times are likely to be larger in a buffered system than in a linked system, you probably want to avoid changeovers as much as possible. Family sequencing procedures would be most ideal here.

This choice applies to the Remainder Plant as well, since even more extreme conditions are in effect here (otherwise, this area probably would have been cellularized as well). In particular, this part of the factory is likely to have *monuments*, i.e., large, immobile equipment, like 40 ton presses, faced with great volume/mix variety and large setups. Creating families for such equipment to avoid setups makes sense even if you are using these families only for sequencing at that equipment. In general, cells with shared bottlenecks are good candidates for family sequencing. Assume you have two cells sharing a machining center, and each cell processes several families with a varying number of parts in each family. Sequencing work according to the families will help avoid the major setups and reduce throughput time at this shared resource.

FAMILY SEQUENCING AT J. I. CASE

J. I. Case manufactures agricultural and construction equipment. When the company moved production from another facility to its Burlington plant, it reorganized the hydraulic cylinder component manufacturing process. Cylinder tubes and pistons were now made in four cells: two low-volume cells, one cell for intermediate volumes, and one flow-line for high-volume manufacturing (the latter accounted for 80 percent of all cylinders).[1] While these cells operated in a JIT mode and were closely linked to the assembly area, piston rods were produced in large batches in a separate area of the plant.

J. I. Case uses a combined MRP/pull system for the cells, and MRP for the piston rod area. Family sequencing is used to minimize time spent on setups. For example, the final assembly schedule for completed hydraulic cylinders is sequenced in order of increasing diameter. This sequence is then communicated to the cells—after it has been offset for lead time (usually five days). Circulating containers trigger production for the cells, which means the containers serve as generic production cards. J. I. Case chose a generic pull system due to the very large number of components involved (in the thousands).

Creating the Assembly Schedule

Consider the time-phased inventory record for a 3-inch cylinder in Figure E-5. The Demand line shows the daily demand of completed cylinders for the next two weeks. There are 240 cylinders on hand, and the safety stock is set to 200 units. The Available row shows projected inventory levels. On Day 3 in Week 1, the inventory level falls below the safety stock, and a replenishment order must be planned. The lot-sizing policy is a variant of the Period Order Quantity. In this case the order size equals the total net requirement within each five-day period. Given an expected shortage of 25 units in Day 3 (available inventory is below safety stock), and a planned usage of 10 and 20 units for the remainder of the week, the lot size is set to 55.

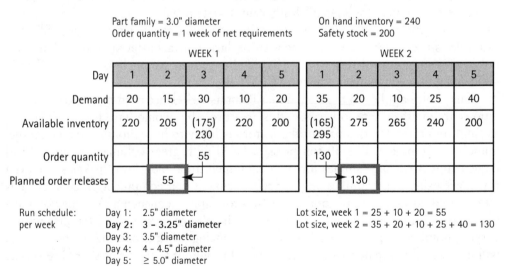

Figure E-5. Family scheduling approach at J. I. Case

Since the record in Figure E-5 looks like an MRP record, you would normally simply offset the lot size by its planned lead time to determine the release date. However, as mentioned, all schedules are constructed so that different-sized cylinders are manufactured each day. As seen at the bottom of the inventory record, cylinders with a diameter of 2.5 inches are made on Mondays, 3.0-3.25 inches on Tuesdays, 3.5 inch cylinders on Wednesdays, and so on. Since the cylinder we are planning for has a 3-inch diameter, the order quantity is entered for the second day (i.e., Tuesday) of the week.

The following week shows that the calculated lot size of 130 units has a need date on a Monday. But since 3-inch cylinders are made on Tuesdays only, the scheduled release date falls one day after it is needed. Because orders in this way can be scheduled up to four days late, the role of the safety stock is to cover shortages. Each cylinder size has a record similar to the one in Figure E-5, so when all sizes have been planned, scheduled quantities will fill every day of the week in the two-week period. The resulting assembly schedule is then communicated to the appropriate component cell using a lead time that varies between one and five days.

You can see that grouping by family is a trade-off between inventory and capacity. Thus, although you can save setup time through family sequencing, and thereby gain extra capacity, you may have to build inventory to be able to satisfy demand. In this particular example, safety stock is used to protect against late production caused by the fact that each cylinder type is only manufactured once a week.

APPENDIX F

Job Enlargement and Job Enrichment

In Chapter 12 we discussed how a desire to expand job enlargement and job enrichment may influence cell job designs. In this appendix we present a deeper discussion of these concepts and their impact on motivation, job satisfaction, and performance. We also take a closer look at the conflict between providing autonomy in jobs and the need to standardize jobs in order to enhance quality and productivity.

Job Characteristics

For the past 100 years *the mechanistic approach* (see Table 12-1) has dominated industrial job design. Rooted in Frederick Taylor's "scientific management," this approach yields jobs where workers perform narrow tasks repetitiously using the scientifically determined "best methods."[1] From management's perspective, jobs of this nature offer certain advantages: rapid training, ease in recruiting new workers, high output due to simple repetitive work, low wages (labor can be easily substituted), and close control over work flows and workloads.[2] From the workers' vantage point, such jobs are easy to learn and don't require much education. On the negative side, it may be difficult to control the quality of highly fractionalized work because no individual is responsible for more than a narrow step in the process. Also, it may be difficult to adapt to changing production requirements, or to tap workers' ideas for improving performance. Furthermore, from a motivational point of view, some workers may find such jobs boring, unsatisfying, frustrating, fatiguing, and a dead end in terms of growth and learning. This may have negative consequences for performance.

In contrast to the scientific management approach, *the motivational approach* to job design focuses on creating jobs that will be motivating and satisfying for employees. Theory holds that there are certain "job characteristics" that are closely related to employee motivation, employee satisfaction, and, as a result, employee performance:[3]

- *Skill and task variety:* The extent to which the job requires that a variety of skills be used to carry out the tasks.

- *Autonomy:* The degree to which the job allows an individual to influence the way work is conducted. For example, does the job allow freedom, independence, or discretion in methods, procedures, quality control, work sequencing, and other types of activities?

- *Task significance:* The extent to which the job is significant and important compared with other jobs in the organization.

- *Task identity:* The degree to which the job requires completing a "whole" and identifiable piece of work from beginning to end.

- *Feedback:* The extent to which a person performing the job receives clear and direct information about how well the task is done (in terms of quality and quantity of output). Intrinsic job feedback is the degree to which the work activities themselves provide information on job performance. Extrinsic job feedback is the degree to which others in the organization (coworkers, managers, supervisors) provide clear and direct feedback on work performance.

The job characteristics determine the motivating potential of a job by affecting various psychological states ("experienced meaningfulness," "responsibility," and knowledge of results").[4] When a job is designed to provide high levels of these characteristics (e.g., lots of autonomy, great task and skill variety, plenty of feedback on performance, the task of completing a "whole" and important piece of work), employees should be more motivated, more satisfied, and more productive.

Worker autonomy and standardization of cell work

Autonomy, as defined above, is the degree to which the job permits freedom and independence in the workplace. *Standardization*, on the other hand, refers to developing and using the one best way to perform a work task or execute a step in the process. Standardization seeks to drive out variation in methods and procedures and, as a result, to create a repeatable, predictable process that yields high quality output consistently and at low cost.

For some individuals, autonomy is an important element of job satisfaction. On the other hand, standardization, by its very nature, reduces an individual's control over work methods and procedures. However, we also know that the use of work standards is a cornerstone of high quality, low cost manufacturing strategies. Accordingly, there is a conflict between the desire of individual workers for autonomy and the need to standardize work. How can you simultaneously accommodate these competing objectives in your cell job designs?

One study of 463 factories found that plants with cells had increased their control over production, making workers less autonomous.[5] This was accomplished by strictly adhering to production schedules (e.g., operators had no discretion regarding the timing of activities) and enforcing the use of just-in-time inventory principles. Operators were also expected to follow process documentation exactly and adhere to standard methods. Because of these changes, operators did not control the pace of work or its content. This reduced autonomy in cell work is a finding borne out by several other studies as well.[6]

Standardized direct labor tasks, which are essential for a repeatable, consistent process, provide little opportunity for operator autonomy. Thus, efforts to create autonomy must focus elsewhere. One alternative is to involve operators in indirect activities, such as monitoring quality or participating in improvement efforts. This enables operators to participate in decisions that affect them and their work. For example, daily team meetings in a microelectronics cell focus on how to improve cell operations. Operators discuss problems they have identified, develop data gathering and analysis strategies, identify solutions, and design implementation plans. Through these activities, operators exercise considerable control over their workplace. However, the cell also has on-line documentation that governs each process step. Thus, once a new work process has been approved and implemented, operators do not deviate from the "one best way" that the documentation describes. Similarly, Steve, the single operator in the plastic components cell described in Chapter 12, has considerable autonomy. Although he must follow precise documentation in his technical work tasks, he has significant indirect labor responsibilities that give him substantial control over various aspects of his work. In addition, as the cell's only operator, he does not need to coordinate his activities with other workers inside the cell. This too is a source of autonomy.

Job Enrichment and Job Enlargement

Job enlargement—also called horizontal loading of tasks—involves increasing the number or variety of job activities.[7] *Job enrichment*—also called vertical loading of tasks—involves adding more decision-making authority to a job.[8]

Job enlargement and job enrichment are frequently used as vehicles for creating jobs with high motivating potential, i.e., jobs scoring high on skill/task variety, autonomy, task significance, task identity, and feedback. A decision to pursue a strategy of job enrichment and job enlargement will have implications for decisions about cell work characteristics (staffing level, multi-functionality, task allocation, and cross-training/task overlap). For example, you can achieve job enrichment by designing cell jobs to include quality control and performance management responsibilities. You can achieve job enlargement by training cell operators on multiple technical work tasks. The key question is whether or not doing so is likely to have a positive impact on motivation, satisfaction, and performance. The matrix in Figure F-1 illustrates the link between direct and indirect labor tasks and job enlargement and enrichment.[9]

Over the past several decades hundreds of studies have assessed the impact of job enlargement and job enrichment in a variety of settings.[10] How have employees reacted? The findings are, for the most part, consistent when it comes to satisfaction. "To a fairly substantial degree, jobs that are larger in scope (that is, in job content characteristics) tend to be more satisfying to many people than jobs that are more restricted in scope."[11] A recent comprehensive review of the research literature reached the following conclusion:[12]

> The direct and indirect evidence is overwhelmingly positive—employees generally prefer to have some say in decisions involving their jobs and work environment and prefer jobs that have greater task variety and autonomy. These trends have strengthened over the years as the general educational level of the workforce has increased.

With respect to the impact that enriched and enlarged jobs have on performance, the evidence is less clear.[13] Some studies show that job performance improves when

Degree of Job Enlargement

		Low	High
Degree of Job Enrichment	Low	Job includes few indirect labor tasks and few direct labor tasks	Job includes few indirect labor tasks and many direct labor tasks
	High	Job includes many indirect labor tasks and few direct labor tasks	Job includes many indirect labor tasks and many direct labor tasks

Figure F-1. The relationship between job enrichment, job enlargement, and task type

employees are given more broadly scoped jobs; others show no positive impact. Looking more closely at the results, experts have concluded that "While most of the research on these interventions has demonstrated that they increase employee satisfaction and performance quality, these interventions do not consistently result in increased quantity of performance."[14] Thus, while the evidence suggests that we can expect increased quality, we cannot conclude that broadly scoped jobs will increase productivity. For example, both enriched and enlarged jobs will almost always include a mix of tasks that for production workers may cause "interruptions in rhythm and different motions when switching from one task to the next."[15] This can reduce output and decrease productivity.

On the other hand, it is easy to see how enriched and enlarged jobs can contribute to higher quality. Cell workers can identify and fix errors at the source before work is passed on to downstream operations. This can increase output quality, eliminate extra work to fix mistakes, and reduce lead times. In one assembly cell, checksheets guide the review of completed work at each station. When an operator discovers a defect, he or she places it in the cell's rework area and informs other operators of the defect. All operators rotate through the rework station; they see the type of errors that are made and help correct them. Therefore, everyone is aware of defect patterns and shares in the responsibility for quality. The number of "line returns"—i.e., circuits which fail the functional test after assembly into finished products—has fallen dramatically. According to the cell's supervisor, these "quality at the source" procedures account for much of this improvement.

The role of the individual

We want to offer an important caveat. Individual differences can influence reactions to job enlargement and enrichment efforts that are aimed at making jobs more motivating. For example, an individual employee who wants to learn new things on the job and develop additional skills will be more satisfied with an enriched job because it provides skill variety, autonomy and responsibility.[16] Employees who are not interested in growth and learning from their jobs will probably not experience greater satisfaction from an enlarged and enriched job. However, they are unlikely to be *more* dissatisfied by such jobs:[17]

Fortunately, even though the cumulative evidence is that individual differences moderate reactions to the motivational approach, the differences are ones of degree, but not direction. In other words, some people respond more positively than others to motivational work, but very few respond negatively.

We also should note that enriched and enlarged jobs are only one of many human resource management practices that, along with individual differences, may have an impact on employee satisfaction and performance. Moreover, it is important to remember that the psychological benefits employees derive from enriched and enlarged jobs "are not likely to outweigh most employees' need of and interest in making a good wage and preserving job security."[18] One study of sewing machine operators, for example, found that these workers were reluctant to accept "multi-skilling and teamwork opportunities."[19] These operators did not believe that supervisors would "protect their rates" (wages). Therefore, they wanted to retain their specialized responsibilities and the piece rate method of compensation in order to control how much they earned. The lesson here is about linkages between human resource practices. The initiative to broaden jobs in the sewing plant was unlikely to be successful unless other human resource practices, most notably pay, were supportive. "We should not expect these workers, or any others for that matter, to take an interest in workplace reforms that come at the expense of their individual or collective earning power or sense of control over their jobs and work environment."[20]

APPENDIX G

Tips for Effective Cell Employee
Selection Interviews

In Chapter 13 we mentioned that interviews, as a vehicle for cell employee selections, could be biased. This appendix provides guidelines for conducting effective interviews.[1]

- *Know the cell job.* Identify ahead of time the attributes (skills, knowledge, abilities, other characteristics—KSAO's) that capable candidates need to perform well in the cell.

- *Focus on attributes you can assess.* Focus on dimensions that are observable (e.g., ability to express one's self) and avoid trying to evaluate dimensions that are better assessed through other means (e.g., cognitive ability tests to assess intelligence). Keep in mind that structured interviews are probably best suited to assessing a candidate's verbal, interpersonal, adaptability, and flexibility skills and abilities, as well as their overall motivation and past experiences.

- *Develop meaningful questions.* Develop one or more questions for each KSAO that you plan to assess via the interview. Link each question to an important skill or ability needed for cell work.

- *Include "situational interview items" in your list of questions.* These questions deal with specific situations that are likely to occur on the job. The intent of these questions is to sample candidates' behavior by asking them to relate what they have done in past situations and what their behavior would be in the future. You can use the answers to assess what the candidate is likely to do on the job. An example might be, "You and a coworker both want to work at the same station. How will you handle this?" Use your knowledge of actual cell issues as the basis for these questions.

- *Create benchmark responses and a rating scale for each question.* You need some way of evaluating the strength of a candidate's answer for each question. For each question you develop, determine what would constitute an excellent, an okay, and a poor answer. Link each of these to a rating (e.g., 7 for excellent, 4 for okay, and 1 for poor). For the situational question posed above (which is designed to help assess interpersonal skills with respect to conflict resolution), you might decide that "tell the coworker to find another station because you were here first," is a poor response, and assign a score of 1. "Discuss the matter with the coworker and agree to let coworker take the station for an hour and then swap," might earn a 7. The benchmark responses should reflect your organization's collective judgments about desirable/undesirable behaviors in cell workers. Furthermore, having a quantitative rating of some sort for each question will help assure that you can combine interview results in a meaningful way.

- *Develop and use a standard interview protocol.* Ask all candidates the same set of questions so you can compare their responses. Have a written "interview document" that lists the questions you plan to ask and has space for you to make notes. This helps you organize the information. Also, as suggested, have a numerical scoring system for each item and then combine your assessments systematically.

- *Provide the candidates with opportunities to ask questions.* These can be revealing. Do they ask good questions? Have they thought about what the work will be like? Do they have good questioning skills? In addition, answering questions about the job can help provide a realistic job preview. This is important for cell work, which can be quite different from the typical industrial job.

- *Be aware of your own potential biases in the interview process.* Watch out for the possibility of bias in the selection process. The race, attractiveness, gender, or attitudes of the interviewee may bias you for or against that individual.

- *Have a number of people interview each candidate.* Compare your assessments in making selection decisions. It helps if you have agreed in advance on the key characteristics you are looking for and have developed a numerical rating system to summarize your assessments. The post-interview discussion of alternative candidates can then center on their strengths and limitations with respect to these key characteristics.

- *Remember that first impressions are sometimes misleading.* Try not to let your initial impression of the candidate overly influence your decision.

APPENDIX H

A Sample of Courses Focused on Basic Cell Concepts, Interpersonal and Problem-Solving Skills, and Coaching and Facilitation

Table H-1. Managing manufacturing cells: A course for cell supervisors

Learning Objectives. *After completing this course, you should*:

- Understand and be able to explain to others
  - what cells are, why companies implement them, and the benefits they can generate;
  - how manufacturing cells are designed; and
  - some of the most significant cell operating challenges.
- Appreciate your role as the manager and administrator of the cell.
- Appreciate your role as coach, mentor, and facilitator for the cell.
- Have acquired some skills and knowledge you will need to act both as a cell manager and cell coach.

Agenda:

Section Title	Content
Course introduction (15 minutes)	Learning objectives Agenda Participant introductions and expectations
Introduction to cells (45 minutes)	What are manufacturing cells? Why do companies create cells—costs and benefits? Where do cell benefits come from? What could cells achieve in our environment?
Manufacturing cell design (30 minutes)	Understanding key objectives of cell formation Understanding the process of cell formation
Operating cells: key challenges I (1 hour 30 minutes)	Setup reduction Scheduling and production control Managing quality
Operating cells: key challenges II (1 hour 30 minutes)	Effective maintenance Job design, supervision, and management Measuring cell performance Generating continuous improvements
Cell supervisor as the manager and administrator (30 minutes)	Business responsibilities of the cell supervisor: managing cell operating issues

An introduction to the cell supervisor as coach, mentor, and team facilitator (1 hour)	Cells, teams, and leadership in our environment
	The new role of the supervisor—coaching, mentoring, and
	  facilitation defined
	The cell supervisor's role in creating a culture of continuous
	  improvement

Cell supervisory challenges at our company (1 hour)	Small group workshop and report outs
Session close out (30 minutes)	Summary, next steps, where to go for more information, session critique

Table H-2. Cell concepts: A course for cell operators, supervisors, and future cell leaders

Learning Objectives. *After completing this course, you should*:

- Understand the concept of cellular manufacturing.
- Appreciate how cellular manufacturing supports the division's goals of reducing costs, increasing quality, and shortening lead times.
- Understand the impact cellular manufacturing will have on the work area and work itself—how are *where* we work and *what* we do likely to change?

Agenda:

Section	Content
Introduction to the course (about 15 minutes)	Learning objectives Agenda Introduction and participant expectations
The case for change: manufacturing cells and the division's strategy (about 15 minutes)	The competitive environment The division's mission and breakthrough objectives Manufacturing's role • Target performance • Current performance Manufacturing cells—bridging the gap between current and target performance
Manufacturing cells (about 45 minutes)	What are manufacturing cells? • Defined/pictured • Demonstration • Examples from sister divisions (or other organizations) Why do companies create cells—costs and benefits? • Where do cell benefits come from? • Table-top simulations/exercises to demonstrate benefits and their sources • What enables cell benefits to happen? What could cells achieve in our environment?
Creating cells (about 45 minutes)	Hands-on exercise Understanding the key objectives of cell formation Understanding the process of cell formation Case studies from sister divisions (or other organizations)
Operating cells (about 45 minutes)	Case examples from around the company (or other organizations) highlighting job changes, flow issues, setup challenges, performance improvement, etc. Small group discussions
Summary and conclusions (about 30 minutes)	Status of our design and implementation effort Next steps and upcoming training Course highlights Your questions Where to go for more information • Internal people who know about cells • Books, articles, and outside help Critique and evaluation

Table H–3. Developing interpersonal skills: A course for cell operators, supervisors, and cell leaders[1]

Learning objectives. *By the conclusion of this training, you should be able to:*
- Use active listening and effective questioning skills in daily communication.
- Effectively give and receive feedback.
- Participate constructively in a meeting.
- Use basic group process tools such as brainstorming.

Agenda:

Session	Section	Content
Session 1 (about 1.5 hours)	Introduction	Agenda, learning objectives Participant introductions and expectations
	Listening skills	Small group exercise and debriefing What is listening? What is active listening? Advantages of active listening Guidelines for active listening Exercise and debriefing
	Questioning skills	Small group exercise and debriefing Types of questions and when to use them Exercise and debriefing
	Summary and close	Highlights Homework Critique and evaluation
Session 2 (about 1.5 hours)	Introduction	Agenda, learning objectives Homework report outs
	Giving and receiving feedback	Small group exercise and debriefing Guidelines for giving and receiving feedback Exercise and debriefing
	Summary and close	Highlights Homework Critique and evaluation
Session 3 (about 1.5 hours)	Introduction	Agenda, learning objectives Homework report outs
	Meetings—good and bad	Meeting disasters and successes: your experiences Key insights
	Meeting structure and roles	The basic meeting structure: beginning, middle, and end Some important roles: leader/facilitator, scribe, participants, timekeeper
	Meeting processes	Some important tools and terms: agenda, objectives, deliverables, brainstorming, action items, "parking lots" (wait lists), follow-up, etc. Exercise and debriefing
	Dysfunctional behavior in meetings	What is it? Role playing exercise and debriefing
	Summary and close	Highlights Where to go for more information Critique and evaluation

Table H-4. Developing decision-making and problem-solving skills: A course for cell operators, supervisors and cell leaders[2]

Learning Objectives. *By the conclusion of this training, you should be able to*:

- Work through the steps of a problem-solving/process-improvement cycle.
- Clearly define problems.
- Develop a data collection strategy for investigating problems.
- Analyze and display data to help solve problems.
- Draw appropriate conclusions; develop, implement and verify solutions.

Agenda:

Session	Section	Content
Session 1 (about 3 hours)	Introduction	Agenda, learning objectives Participant introductions and expectations
	The problem-solving cycle/process-improvement framework	Process problems—examples from your work The problem-solving cycle—steps and examples
	Defining the problem	Small group exercise and debriefing Identifying and selecting problems—the role of data Criteria for a clear problem statement Helpful tools: Pareto diagrams, run charts, the "is/is not" process
	Diagnosis: understanding the current situation and searching for root causes	Small group exercise and debriefing The role of data Helpful tools: flow charts, functional flow charts (deployment flow charts), cause and effect diagrams, tagging
	Summary and close	Highlights and unanswered questions Homework assignment Critique and evaluation
Session 2 (about 2 hours)	Introduction	Agenda, learning objectives Highlights from last time and homework report outs
	Verifying theories of causes	Small group exercise and debriefing Helpful tools: check sheets, Pareto diagrams, run charts, and other data collection, analysis and display techniques
	Drawing conclusions; developing, implementing, and verifying solutions	Small group exercise and debriefing The role of data Holding the gains and sharing successes
	Summary and close	Highlights and unanswered questions Homework Critique and evaluation
Session 3 (about 1 hour)	Introduction	Agenda, learning objectives Highlights from last time and homework report outs
	Review of sessions 1 and 2	Key insights Unanswered questions
	Next steps	Where to go for more information Future training opportunities Critique and evaluation

Table H–5. Coaching and facilitating cell teams: A course for cell supervisors and cell leaders[3]

Session objectives. *After completing this course, you should*:
- Be able to organize, plan, and lead a productive group session.
- Be able to deal with dysfunctional behaviors in your cell team.
- Understand your team's role in the organization.
- Know where to go for help and assistance in building your cell team.

Agenda:

Section Title	Content
Introduction (about 20 minutes)	Learning objectives Agenda Participant introductions and expectations Developing team ground rules
Cell team defined (about 15 minutes)	What's different about cell work Understanding roles and responsibilities of operators, supervisors, and cell leaders
Skills for cell supervisors/leaders as cell team facilitators (about 1 hour)	Facilitation and leadership: wearing two hats The optimal cell team: hands-on exercise Providing the structure for your team Modeling and encouraging effective group behaviors (exercise and discussion) Creating an open and collaborative environment (exercise and discussion)
Structuring a productive group session (about 1.5 hours)	The basic meeting framework The power of preparation: the role of agenda, objectives, and session deliverables Managing the meeting itself: tips and tools for making the most of a group session Tips for closing and follow-up
Dealing with difficult situations (about 1 hour)	Dealing with feelings Listening skills Feedback: giving and receiving it constructively Dealing with dysfunctional behavior (definitions and role playing)
Building your team (about 1 hour)	Coaching defined Getting the team started Stages of team development Team-building activities
Interfacing across the organization (about 1.5 hours)	Mapping your customer contact system Bringing the voice of the customer into the cell Negotiation skills for cell team supervisors/leaders
Creating a network of cell supervisors/leaders (about 1 hour)	Developing action steps for supporting one another—exercise What can management do to support you in your new role—exercise
Summary/conclusions/next steps (about 20 minutes)	Course highlights Unanswered questions Where to go for more information Critique and evaluation

APPENDIX I

One Company's Organizational Change Structure

In Chapter 15, and also in Chapter 4, we told the story of how one electronics manufacturer—specifically, its Assembly and Test Center (ATC)—planned and implemented a cellular organization. This appendix provides details on how ATC organized the various project teams, and the roles and responsibilities it assigned to these teams.

Table I-1. Assembly and Test Center team architecture for cell implementation planning

Name	Membership	Charter/Responsibilities
Core Design Group (steering committee)	• Department manager and his 4 manufacturing section managers • Representatives from operations research, materials control, electrical engineering, production engineering, industrial engineering, accounting	• Develop vision of competitive manufacturing • Plan and lead the design effort • Communicate and coordinate the efforts of the individual analysis teams – Select team members – Set expectations – Review progress • Plan "Design Week" as a vehicle for integrating the analysis teams' recommendations • Lead the efforts to communicate the new design
Assembly Analysis Team	• Industrial engineer (team leader) • Electrical engineer • 2 production workers • 3 supervisors	• Conduct a technical analysis of the assembly processes • Identify performance gaps and key insights about assembly • Develop a set of recommendations regarding assembly processes and organization
Test Analysis Team	• Section manager (team leader) • Electrical engineer • 2 test supervisors • 3 test technicians	• Conduct technical analysis of test processes • Identify performance gaps and key insights about test • Develop a set of recommendations regarding test processes and organization
Social Analysis Team	• Section manager (team leader) • 3 supervisors • 2 production workers • Representative from personnel	• Analyze the current social system • Survey employees to ascertain concerns/desires for the new social system • Develop a set of recommendations regarding the social system in the new organization
Metrics Analysis Team	• Section manager (team leader) • 1 supervisor • 2 production workers • Representatives from production control and accounting	• Analyze the current performance metrics • Identify appropriate metrics to use in assessing the performance of the new factory
Business Team	• Section manager (team leader) • Representatives from accounting, manufacturing and R&D	• Review competitive position of products • Develop recommendations based on gaps and strengths
Design Team	• All members of the above teams	• Integrate the findings of the analysis teams • Develop a high level design for the new organization based on the analysis teams' findings and recommendations • Communicate the new design to the rest of the organization • Lead the implementation efforts

Table I-2. Assembly and Test Center detailed design activities: The role of the home teams in detailed design

---

Layout, tooling and fixtures

- Determined detailed home team layout design (balanced technical needs and desires to create a healthy workplace)
- Established methods for material movement (conveyors, instrument carriers, roller carts, etc.)
- Identified/designed tooling and fixturing (with help of manufacturing engineers)

Job design and job rotation policies

- Determined how to revise jobs to incorporate broader responsibilities including: assembly, cell material handling, working with the product data base, setting and refining reorder points, collecting data, maintaining financial metrics, working with buyers, summarizing and reporting on cell performance, and participating on the various councils
- Determined who would take on which tasks and participate in which councils

Inspection and quality procedures

Maintenance procedures

Learning standard documentation

Production planning and control

- Determined how to work with the new materials information system to order material, track jobs, and schedule work within the cell

Team start-up

- Clarified roles and responsibilities
- Established ground rules and codes of conduct

Table I-3. Assembly and Test Center detailed design activities: The role of each council in detailed design

Materials Council	• Had members drawn from production planning, procurement, and the cell teams • Advised cell teams on materials issues • Worked with the materials department on planning, scheduling, order processing, obsolescence, kanban administration, vendor interfacing, backorders, and materials forecasting tasks • Developed and implemented common policies across the cells
Finance Council	• Had members drawn from the finance department and the cell teams • Provided financial information for the cell teams • Worked with the finance department on asset control, forecasting/targeting, expenses, inventory integrity, capital budgeting, profit analysis, standard costing, and workorder system
Process Councils (Assembly, Test and Button-up)	• Had members drawn from engineering and the cell teams • Looked at process issues common to all cells • Identified and disseminated best practices • Established and implemented standardized process documentation for all cells.
Training Council	• Had members drawn from personnel and the cell teams • Helped plan start-up training which included team-building exercises, team dynamics, ground rules and "codes of conduct" development, understanding roles and responsibilities • Coordinated and oversaw cross-training, job rotation, and capacity balancing through labor reallocation • Assured that team members participating on any of the councils received appropriate training
Performance Measures Council	• Had members drawn from production control, accounting and the cell teams • Helped implement performance measures in each home team—key measures included monthly production volume (in dollars and per employee), electro-static discharge compliance, scrap (in dollars per month), production lead time, rework, customer feedback and complaints

APPENDIX J

Process Improvement Opportunity Checklist from a Large Electronics Plant

This checklist is designed to help you assess opportunities to improve your area's processes. You should complete the checklist as a work group. Answer each question with one of the following: *never, rarely, sometimes, mostly,* or *always*. In most instances, an answer other than "always" identifies a practice, which, if improved, will positively impact the area's performance. Please note that the checklist is not an attempt to grade your area. Rather, the purpose of the checklist is to identify areas of opportunity for your team.

Documentation

- ❏ Is documentation located at the place where the described work takes place?
- ❏ Are instructions in the documentation clear?
- ❏ Is documentation written to the level of the user?
- ❏ Is documentation available when the operator needs it?
- ❏ Is there a process in place for changing documentation when the product build process changes, or when someone has an idea for a better process?
- ❏ Does the documentation accurately reflect the way people do their work?
- ❏ Is there a place at the workstation where documentation can be placed so that the assemblers can easily read work instructions as they work?
- ❏ Could someone unfamiliar with your specific products, but familiar with general assembly practices, be able to follow the documentation (that is, know what to do first, second, third, etc.)?
- ❏ Does the documentation include a flow chart?
- ❏ Do operators receive initial training on the documentation?
- ❏ Are operators retrained when the documentation changes?

Tools and Fixtures

- ❏ Are tools and fixtures located where they are used?
- ❏ Are tools and fixtures available when material is ready for processing?

❏ Do tools and fixtures have designated locations at workstations?

❏ Is it obvious when tools and fixtures are out of place?

❏ Are tools and fixtures color-coded or in some other way made easy to identify?

❏ Are tools and fixtures designed so that parts and products cannot be loaded or attached incorrectly?

❏ Does a process exist for making improvements to tools and fixtures?

❏ Are tools and fixtures routinely examined for wear and tear?

❏ Is corrective action taken when wear and tear is discovered?

❏ Do workstations contain only the tools that are necessary for operations that occur there?

❏ Are tools and fixtures ESD (electro-static discharge) safe?

❏ Are old/obsolete tools and fixtures discarded when new replacements arrive?

Workplace Organization and Layout

❏ Is the area neat and tidy?

❏ Is the area free of unnecessary items?

❏ Are parts, tools, equipment, workbenches, documentation, and so forth free of dust?

❏ Does the layout match the predominant material flow in the area?

❏ Is the physical flow free of wasted motion for operators?

❏ Are stations as close together as possible?

❏ Is the area free of unnecessary storage locations between process steps?

❏ Do all activities required by the products take place in the area?

❏ Are materials, supplies, tools, and fixtures stored at point of use?

❏ Is the layout arranged so operators can see and communicate with one another?

People and Policies

❏ Are operators cross-trained?

❏ Does the area practice job rotation?

❏ Are operators familiar with the production lead-time goals for the area?

❏ When production problems occur, are the key players gathered together within a reasonable amount of time to resolve them?

❏ Is equipment available when it is needed for production?

❏ Does the area avoid keeping people busy by building unneeded product?

❏ Is the area free of jobs that involve simply babysitting equipment to watch for problems?

❑ Does the area practice preventive maintenance?

❑ Does the area engage in a rigorous program of process improvement?

Parts and Processes

❑ Is the process flow free of unnecessary inspection?

❑ Is the process flow free of unnecessary process steps?

❑ Is the process flow free of unnecessary material transportation?

❑ Are setup times zero?

❑ Is the area building and moving products one at a time?

❑ Is the work balanced among process steps?

❑ Does the area look for ways to combine similar activities into a single activity (for example, one operator travelling to the stockroom instead of every operator interrupting their work to travel to the stockroom)?

❑ Does the area look for and adopt best practices developed by other areas?

❑ Does the area communicate part standardization opportunities to the lab?

❑ Does the area work with the lab to take advantage of new technologies that could improve process or product quality?

Process and Quality Control

❑ Does the area utilize bells, lights, and so on to indicate trouble or the need for action of some sort?

❑ Does the area track defects?

❑ Is defect data systematically and routinely analyzed, and used as the basis for improvement initiatives?

❑ Does the area keep control charts for critical processes and process steps?

❑ Has everyone in the area been trained on statistical process control?

❑ Are process control charts prominently posted in the area?

❑ Are process control charts kept up-to-date?

❑ Do area workers know what actions to take when charts reveal out-of-control conditions?

❑ Is it possible to visually determine the level of rework in the area?

APPENDIX K

Guidelines for Implementing
Setup Time Reduction

In Chapter 17 we introduced a process improvement model (Table 17-1) and high-lighted setup time reduction as one specific strategy for waste elimination in cellular systems. In this appendix we take the general process improvement model and its four major steps as the basis for a discussion of guidelines on how you may organize and implement setup time reduction activities in your facility.

Step 1: Project Definition, Organization, and Preparation

Begin by setting project objectives, defining project boundaries, and selecting the team. The team may include all cell operators, or, if appropriate, be limited to a sub-set who work closely with the machine targeted for setup time reduction. You also might include "specialists" who bring focused expertise to the team. If the group is not experienced in setup reduction, then some training may be appropriate.

Setup reduction training should (1) clarify the objectives, (2) introduce relevant tools and techniques, and (3) identify the criteria for evaluating alternative setup reduction solutions (in terms of cost, time to implement, and so forth). It should also provide participants with an opportunity to practice their skills at setup reduction using a sample setup. Videotaped examples of setups before and after reduction can be particularly useful. You can show a tape of the "before" setup and ask participants to develop recommended changes. You might then show the "after" setup reduction tape, stressing the performance improvements yielded and contrasting it with the participants' recommendations. In addition, your training should help operators make good decisions about which equipment to target first (if this has not already been determined). Begin with long-duration, frequent setups on bottleneck equipment. These will provide the greatest potential performance benefits (see Chapter 7).

When Metalsa, a manufacturer of stamped components for the automotive industry located in Monterrey, Mexico, launched their setup training, consultants showed cell operators a videotape of an auto race pit stop.[1] Operators were then asked to look for parallels between the pit stop and machine setup. They recognized that several attributes that contributed to an effective pit stop applied to changeovers in the plant as well:

- All involved knew their individual assignments.
- All involved knew how their activities and positions related to the whole process ("choreography").
- Special tooling helped do certain tasks quickly and efficiently.
- Tasks were "engineered" to be completed with the least effort and time.
- Practice was essential.

Step 2: Diagnosing the Problem

In Step 2 you gather background data for later analysis. Everyone on the team, including those who do not work in the cell, will need to know what parts are made in the cell, in what quantities, with what frequency, and the type and duration of setups required. If possible, videotape the current setup and analyze it frame-by-frame. (This may not be possible in some shops due to union restrictions; in these cases the team will need to observe the setup live, and carefully record each current step and its required time; existing setup documentation may help in this task.) The goal is to dissect the setup and break it up into individual activities, establish the time spent on each, and determine the percentages of time that are spent in various types of activities (e.g., removing a fixture, conducting trial runs, and completing paperwork).

Setup time consists of *external* setup activities—those that can be accomplished while equipment is operating—and *internal* setup activities—those that must be performed when the process is down. Obviously, reducing internal setup time by performing more setup activities externally (while the equipment or process is operating) will decrease the time between successive lots. In addition, simply reducing internal setup times by eliminating adjustments, simplifying attachments and detachments, and adding other resources can help. However, the ultimate objective is to reduce both internal and external total setup time.

Step 3: Identify and Implement Solutions

The third step involves designing and implementing the new setup procedures. Table K-1 provides techniques that the team can use to streamline setup procedures, while Table K-2 characterizes an ideal setup process. The information in these tables can be used to help develop and evaluate the improved setup. The team should then determine the costs and benefits of any proposed changes, and test out various ideas in advance of deciding what to formally implement.

Step 4: Seek Continual Improvement

Once the team has put economically viable changes in place, it can move to the final step, Seek Continual Improvement. Here the team tracks performance, shares results, and identifies further improvements to pursue in follow-up projects.

Table K-1. Strategies for setup reduction

Strategy	Explanation
Analyze operators' activities to minimize time	A number of specific tools can be used to analyze the individual motions used to perform setups. Many are variants of classic time-and-motion studies: examples include operations charts, motion study charts, process charts, and waste elimination tables.
Look for opportunities to do tasks in parallel	Do tasks in parallel, as opposed to sequentially, to save time. When doing so requires additional resources, conduct a cost/benefit analysis.
Perform tasks when the machine is still operating	Do not wait until the machine has stopped to begin the setup. Do as many activities as possible during external time.
Perform the setup for operators from another area	If the areas are not in direct competition with one another, third-party reviews may lead to a productive exchange of new ideas for improvement.

Table K-2. Characteristics of an ideal setup process

Characteristic	Explanation
Workstations, fixtures, and tool storage are well organized	There should be a place for everything, and everything should be in its place. Label storage locations so that it is easy to return items to their correct location and easy to find them in the first place. Arrange items to minimize and ease transportation.
The current "best" way is documented and available at point-of-use	The current "best" way to perform the setup is documented in clear, unambiguous terms. Two operators following the documentation can then perform the setup in exactly the same way. The documentation is available when and where needed.
A checksheet guides the setup process	As part of the formal documentation, a checksheet specifies the sequence of setup activities and assures that tasks are not overlooked.
The setup is planned	For setups that require resources that do not normally reside at the cell, procedures are in place to anticipate when the setup will happen and assure that resources are ready and available when needed.
Dedicated tooling and fixtures are available and verified	Tools and fixtures are dedicated to the equipment. A kit includes all the tooling and fixtures the setup will require. A kit checklist exists and is used to verify the contents in advance of each setup.
Tools, fixtures, and procedures can be used with multiple setups	Standard tools, fixtures, and procedures are used with multiple setups. This saves time.
Setup uses point-of-use storage	Tools and fixtures, setup kits, and other setup materials are stored close to the equipment. This avoids transportation and wait time.
Tools and fixtures are in good working order	Before storing a tool or fixture, operators make sure it is in good working order. Broken or nearly broken tools are never put away, but rather are repaired or replaced.
The setup is reviewed periodically	The principles of continuous improvement are applied to the setup on an ongoing basis. Special team meetings are used to review setups in search of further improvements.

APPENDIX L

A Primer on Functional Flow Charts and Tagging

FUNCTIONAL FLOW CHARTS

Functional flow charts (also called deployment flow charts) show the steps of a process using basic flow charting symbols, but they also indicate who or where in the organization tasks are performed.[1] We like to prepare them with the departments represented as horizontal bands. This lets you see the movement of work between departments (see Figure 18-6). In creating a first-pass functional flow chart it can be very useful to have an objective outsider interview key players and create an initial draft. However, people who work in the process should then jointly review and edit the functional flow chart. Superimposing the process flow on the facility layout can help visually demonstrate the movement of information through the facility (see Figure L-1).

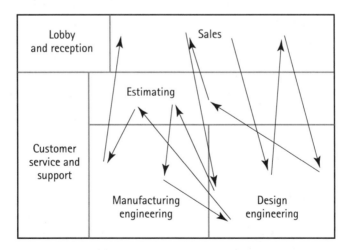

Figure L-1. Mapping the process flow onto the current layout: A quote development example

Several organizations with which we have worked use "war rooms" where they prominently display the functional flow chart and other information related to the analysis. At one company the map of the order management cycle occupied several walls of the war room. This visual display created a shared understanding of the process and highlighted potential problems. The map of the process was a common and concrete frame of reference that helped people communicate more effectively about the process and how to improve it.[2]

One of the biggest problems in creating functional flow charts is deciding upon and then consistently applying the appropriate level of detail throughout. Organizations often struggle with this. Our advice is to start at a fairly high level and then add detail later. Table L-1 presents more guidelines for creating functional flow charts.[3]

Functional flow charts are useful for understanding the steps and departments involved in the current process. What they do not reveal is information about process lead time, volume, or quality. This information can be acquired via a second technique, tagging.

TAGGING

Most organizations do not track office activity performance very well. Thus, information about processing times, delays, rework, and the like is typically unavailable and must be collected to support a redesign activity. *Tagging* involves developing a tracking sheet that indicates the in and out (start and completion) time for each step in the process (see Figure 18-7). The tagging document is attached, electronically or physically, to whatever paperwork or electronic file is associated with a particular information process. Ideally, you should tag all work of a particular type released in a given period. The length of the period depends on the volume of work, but it should be long enough to cover a "representative" part of the job stream. If volume is very high, it may be sufficient to tag only a random sample of the work released in the time period. Overall, you need enough data to assure a realistic and credible picture of the performance of the complete process, as well as its individual steps.

Once you have the data, you can calculate a number of important measures that will help you analyze the process. For example, to understand the time in the process, you may want to determine:

- Average time for each step in the process,
- Average queue time prior to each step, and
- Overall lead time for the process.

You also may want to determine the variability of each of these measures. You can do this simply by finding the data range (i.e., the interval spanning the shortest and the longest times recorded). Alternatively, you can calculate other measures of dispersion (e.g., standard deviation). You can also develop data histograms that show lead-time variation, such as a bar graph that depicts the percentage of deliverables completed in less than 5 days, in 5 to 10 days, and in more than 10 days. The tagging data will also let you examine the degree to which information deliverables followed the same sequence of activities. This is extremely helpful in order to determine if you need to subdivide a family. Thus, you can use tagging data to verify process maps and functional flow charts you may already have developed.

Table L-1. Guidelines for creating functional flow charts

Aspect of Functional Flow Charting	Specific Guidelines
Getting started	• Establish the start and end point of the process to be charted. • Identify the individuals who know the process (or pieces of the process) best—these are the individuals from whom to solicit information on what actually happens. • Identify who will actually participate in creating the chart. Ideally, a small group or single individual will chart the entire process. • Agree on symbols and conventions.
Level of detail	• Try to maintain a consistent level of detail throughout. • Start at a relatively high level by charting the major steps in the process. Then break each major block into sub-blocks if you need a deeper understanding of the process. Your big-block functional flow chart may reveal so many obvious problems that you do not need further detail at this point. • Avoid getting bogged down in too much detail. "Fax order confirmation to the customer" may be sufficient. You don't need to chart "prepare cover sheet, push back chair, stand up, walk with confirmation and cover sheet to the fax machine, place in machine, dial number, press start, etc."
Creating the initial chart	• Have one knowledgeable person or a small team develop a first-pass chart. • Alternatively, have an objective outsider interview experts and create a first pass. • *Do not try* to develop the chart from written documentation, as this may not represent what actually happens.
Tips on formatting	• Represent the main flow as a straight line, with various exceptions flowing off to either side. • Draw the initial chart on flipcharts or a blackboard, and use self-adhesive sticky notes (Post-Its™) for easy editing. • Use color coding, e.g., different color self-adhesive sticky notes (Post-Its™) for each department. • Be sure each activity description conveys the essence of the work at this step by including a noun and a verb. "Fax" is not sufficient, nor is "order confirmation." "Fax order confirmation to customer" does a better job of communicating what is actually happening at this step in the process. • Create a functional flow chart where departments are represented as horizontal bands (see Figures 18-6 and L-2 for examples).
Reviewing the initial functional flow chart	• Assemble those involved in the process and have them jointly review the initial chart. • Verify the process by observing the actual flow and comparing it to the preliminary chart (employees can also keep a copy nearby and note any discrepancies as they work). • Look for inconsistencies (where different steps are followed to reach the same end) and keep a running record of these.
Some general observations	• Flow charting software can be helpful once you have an initial diagram. Don't assume that software can "do it for you." • Chart the process "as is," not as you wish it to be. • Remember that gaining insights on the process and developing a shared understanding of the process are far more important than developing a "perfect" chart. Keep this overall objective in mind. • It takes time to develop useful and complete charts.

You can combine your tagging data with your functional flow chart to create a "time-function" map, as seen in Figure L-2.[4] This figure shows not only the sequence of work and the departments/individuals who perform it, but also the time typically associated with each step. The principle is that each department has both a row and a column in this chart. Figure L-2 also illustrates how you can add detail to the functional flow chart by including transportation (where information must move from one area or individual to another) and delays (where information must wait before getting processed).

Besides information about time, the tagging data can also provide you with rich data on process problems. You should pay particular attention to rework cycles—instances in which information returns to steps previously visited. As Figure 18-7 shows, the "comments" column on the tagging sheet should explain the circumstances. (Of course, you should supplement these insights with quantitative data on quality—if they exist. Those who work in the process also may be able to identify quality problems in the existing process.)

Individuals often, and understandably, resist tagging efforts. They may fear that the results will be used to evaluate them personally. They may also resent having to take time to record their work and may therefore fail to record or may misrecord information. The latter problem can also be due to sheer forgetfulness or haste. You can minimize these problems by doing the following:

- Clearly explain the purpose of the tagging activity.

- Assure people that the results will not be used against them.

- Design data collection forms to be as simple as possible so they are easy and quick to fill out. Solicit input from those who will capture the data; they may have ideas about how to make data collection quick, painless, and more accurate. (In fact, some of these individuals should be part of the investigating team.)

- Stress the importance of accurate data.

- Provide clear instructions on how to record accurate data, and design a process so the tagging sheets are not forgotten in the midst of daily work.

- Keep people involved by sharing any problems with them during data collection, and by thanking them for their efforts once the tagging process has been completed.

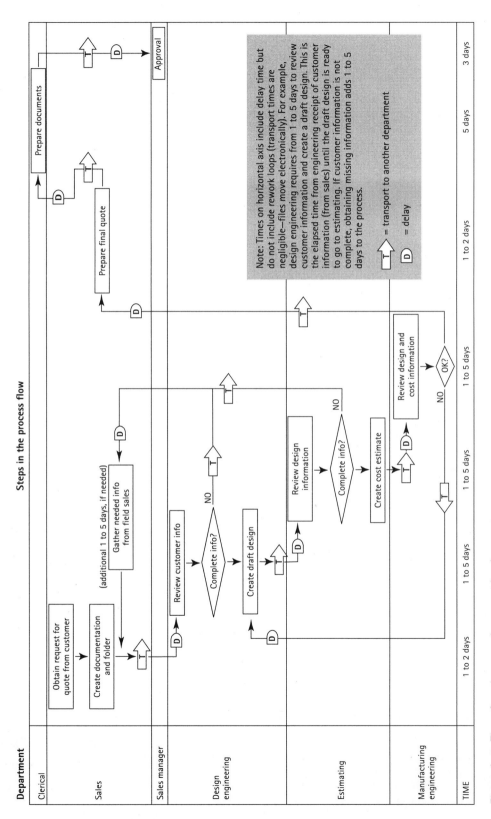

Figure L-2. Time–function map for quote development

Endnotes

Chapter 1

1. This classic quote is from Wickham Skinner, "Production Under Pressure," *Harvard Business Review*, November–December 1966, pp. 139–146.
2. See M. Zayko, D. Broughman, and W. Hancock, "Lean Manufacturing Yields World-Class Improvements for Small Manufacturer," *IIE Solutions*, April 1997, pp. 36–40.
3. Due to the similarity between the basic ideas behind manufacturing and office cells, we will, in order to avoid repetition, mostly refer to the former type of cells in this book. We discuss office cells in Chapter 18.
4. See P. Swamidass, "Technology on the Factory Floor III: Technology Use and Training in U.S. Manufacturing Firms," (Washington, D.C.: The Manufacturing Institute/National Association of Manufacturers, 1998); P. E. Waterson et al., "The Use and Effectiveness of Modern Manufacturing Practices: A Survey of UK Industry," *Int. Journal of Production Research*, Vol. 37, No. 10, 1999, pp. 2271–2292; and R. Montagno, N. Ahmed, and R. Firenze, "Perceptions of Operations Strategies and Technologies in U.S. Manufacturing Firms," *Production and Inventory Management*, Second Quarter 1995, pp. 22–27.
5. The statements related to Falk and Mine Safety Appliances corporations are from *The New York Times,* May 15, 1999, pp. B1 and B3.
6. This is, of course, just a statistical association, and the survey does not shed any light on the contributing factors. However, a supporting piece of evidence is that Gelman Sciences predicts it will achieve an additional $600,000 in sales—without any extra sales effort—once its on-time delivery performance reaches 98 percent (see Zayko, Broughman, and Hancock, "Lean Manufacturing Yields World-Class Improvements for Small Manufacturer," p. 39).
7. This table is from U. Wemmerlöv and D.J. Johnson, "Cellular Manufacturing at 46 User Plants: Implementation Experiences and Performance Improvements," *Int. Journal of Production Research*, Vol. 35, No. 1, 1997, p. 38.
8. See Swamidass, "Technology on the Factory Floor III," p. 4.
9. See Waterson et al., "The Use and Effectiveness of Modern Manufacturing Practices," Figures 4 through 6.
10. See Zayko et al., "Lean Manufacturing Yields World-Class Improvements for Small Manufacturer," p. 37.
11. For this notion, see R. M. Grant, "The Resource-Based Theory of Competitive Advantage: Implications for Strategy Formulation," *California Management Review*, Spring 1991, pp. 114-135.
12. This model of the organization is strongly influenced by, and an extension of, the "congruence model" in D. A. Nadler and M. L. Tushman, "A Model for Diagnosing Organizational Behavior," *Organizational Dynamics*, Autumn 1980, pp. 35–51. Reprinted in Tushman and Moore, eds., *Readings in the Management of Innovation* (Cambridge: Ballinger, 1980), pp. 148–163.

Chapter 2

1. "Modules" and "modular manufacturing" have been adopted by the U.S. textile and footwear industry to refer to cells in a clothing production environment.

2. This apprehension was recently experienced at the Northrop Grumman Corporation: "When workers [...] were first organized into cells last October, they compared it to the cells in the Los Angeles County jail..." (quote from *The New York Times*, March 9, 1999, p. C9).

3. The Langston story can be found in T. C. Karanzalis, "Family Parts Line Production—A New Manufacturing Concept," text of presentation given at Industrial Management Seminar #35, Milwaukee, WI, October 1970, and K. M. Gettelman, "Organize Production For Parts—Not Processes," *Modern Machine Shop*, Vol. 44, No. 6, November 1971, pp. 50–60.

4. For an interesting overview, see J. Benders and R. Badham, "History of Cell-Based Manufacturing," in M. M. Beyerlein, (ed.) *Work Teams: Past, Present, Future* (Boston: Kluwer Academic Publishers, 2000, pp. 45–57).

5. This book, R. Lang and W. Hellpach, *Gruppenfabrikation* (Berlin: Julius Springer, 1922), was written jointly by a Daimler manager and a university professor. See Benders and Badham, "History of Cell-Based Manufacturing," for more details.

6. This quote is from T.A.K. Nimmons, *Improving the Process of Designing Cellular Manufacturing Systems* (unpublished Ph.D. thesis, Cranfield University, 1996, p. 18) and reproduced in N.C. Suresh and J. M. Kay, *Group Technology and Cellular Manufacturing* (Boston: Kluwer Academic Publishers, 1998, p.1).

7. For a complete list of Burbidge's publications, see Suresh and Kay, *Group Technology and Cellular Manufacturing: State-of-the-Art Synthesis of Research and Practice*.

8. For one of the first formal treatment of benchmarking, see R. C. Camp, *Benchmarking* (Milwaukee, WI: ASQC Quality Press, 1989).

9. See the references in endnote 3.

10. See, for example, J. L. Burbidge, *The Introduction to Group Technology* (New York: John Wiley, 1975).

11. See U. Wemmerlöv and N. L. Hyer, "Cellular Manufacturing in the U.S. Industry: A Survey of Users," *Int. Journal of Production Research*, Vol. 27, No. 9, 1989, pp. 1511–1530, and U. Wemmerlöv and D. J. Johnson, "Empirical Findings on Manufacturing Cell Design," *Int. Journal of Production Research*, Vol. 38, No. 3, 2000, pp. 481–507.

12. Quote from *The New York Times*, October 29, 1993, p. C5.

13. For examples of savings due to Group Technology, see N. L. Hyer and U. Wemmerlöv, "Group Technology in the U.S. Manufacturing Industry: A Survey of Users," *Int. Journal of Production Research*, Vol. 27, No. 8, 1989, pp. 1287–1304.

14. One plant we visited after reorganization to cells had re-christened its shipping and receiving departments to the "shipping cell" and the "receiving cell."

15. For more information on virtual cells, see C. R. McLean, H. M. Bloom, and T. H. Hopp, "The Virtual Manufacturing Cell," *Proceedings of the Fourth IFAC/IFIP Conference on Information Control Problems in Manufacturing Technology*, Gaithersburg, MD, October 1982, and V. R. Kannan, and S. Ghosh, "A Virtual Cellular Manufacturing Approach to Batch Production," *Decision Sciences*, Vol. 27, No. 3, 1996, pp. 519–539.

16. For a fuller discussion of the potential disadvantages with resource dedication, see Chapter 7.

17. See W. Skinner, "The Focused Factory," *Harvard Business Review*, May–June 1974, pp. 113–121.

18. See Skinner, "The Focused Factory," p. 115.

19. See Skinner, "The Focused Factory," p. 114.

20. See U. Wemmerlöv and D. J. Johnson, "Cellular Manufacturing at 46 User Plants: Implementation Experiences and Performance Improvements," *Int. Journal of Production Research*, Vol. 35, No. 1, 1997, Table 2, and Wemmerlöv and Johnson, "Empirical Findings on Manufacturing Cell Design."

21. See J. T. Black, *The Design of the Factory with a Future* (New York: McGraw-Hill, 1991).

22. A "production unit" refers to a cell, a machine or a job shop located somewhere else in the plant, another plant owned by the firm, or a subcontractor's plant.

23. See U. Wemmerlöv, *Production Planning and Control Procedures for Cellular Manufacturing Systems: Concepts and Practices* (Falls Church, VA: American Production and Inventory Control Society, 1988).

24. For more information on classification and coding systems, see U. Wemmerlöv, "Economic Justification of Group Technology Software," *Journal of Operations Management*, Vol. 9, No. 4, 1990, pp. 500–525, or section B in Suresh and Kay, *Group Technology and Cellular Manufacturing*.

25. See the preface to Burbidge, *The Introduction of Group Technology*.

26. Note that these three components of the organization are similar to those we introduced in Chapter 1. That is, the "business system" can correspond with the enterprise, strategy, capability, and outcome boxes in Figure 1-4 in that chapter. Likewise, the "technical system" has its parallel in the

process and technology boxes, while the "social system" corresponds with the organizational structure, management systems, people, and the informal organization.

27. This table is adopted from V. Huber and K. Brown, "Human Resource Issues in Cellular Manufacturing: A Socio-Technical Analysis," *Journal of Operations Management*, Vol. 10, No. 1, 1991, pp. 138–159.

28. See J. C. Taylor and D. F. Felten, *Performance by Design: Sociotechnical Systems in North America* (Englewood Cliffs, NJ: Prentice Hall, 1993), p. 3.

28. See B. Shapiro, V. Rangan, and J. Sviokla, "Staple Yourself to an Order," *Harvard Business Review*, July-August 1992, pp. 113–122.

30. It should be noted, though, that the reengineering philosophy is suspiciously void of tools and techniques by which performance improvements can be accomplished.

31. See Y. Sugimori, K. Kusunoki, F. Cho, and S. Uchikawa, "Toyota Production System and Kanban System: Materialization of Just-In-Time and Respect-For-Human System," *Int. Journal of Production Research*, Vol. 15, No. 6, 1977, pp. 553–564 (this seminal paper is reproduced in the book *Toyota Production System* by Y. Monden (Norcross, GA: Industrial Engineering and Management Press, 1983).

32. See pages 12–18 in K. Suzaki, *The New Manufacturing Challenge: Techniques for Continuous Improvement* (New York: The Free Press, 1987).

33. See S. Sakakibara, B. B. Flynn, and R. G. Schroeder, "A Framework and Measurement Instrument for Just-In-Time Manufacturing," *Production and Operations Management*, Vol. 2, No. 3, 1993, pp. 177-194.

34. See J. P. Womack and D. T. Jones, *Lean Thinking: Banish Waste and Create Wealth in Your Corporation* (New York: Simon & Schuster, 1996) and M. Rother and J. Shook, *Learning to See: Value Stream Mapping to Create Value and Eliminate Muda* (Brookline, MA: The Lean Enterprise Institute, 1999).

35. The main proponent was Georg Stalk of the Boston Consulting Group. See G. Stalk, Jr., "Time—The Next Source of Competitive Advantage," *Harvard Business Review*, July–August 1988, pp. 41–51; and G. Stalk, Jr., and T. M. Hout, *Competing Against Time* (New York: The Free Press, 1992).

36. See R. Suri, *Quick Response Manufacturing* (Portland, OR: Productivity Press, 1998).

Chapter 3

1. J. L. Burbidge, *Production Flow Analysis* (Oxford: Clarendon Press, 1989), p. vi.

2. J. P. Womack and D. T. Jones, *Lean Thinking* (New York: Simon & Schuster, 1996), p. 27.

3. Recall the horizontal and vertical process perspectives in Figure 2-3.

4. In this case, "multiple machines" refers to equipment of different types and not to the kind of situation found in, for example, the textile industry, where one operator is assigned to a group of identical machines.

5. Wemmerlöv and Johnson note that two research studies found that between 27 to 78 percent of cells were run by single operators (U. Wemmerlöv and D. J. Johnson, "Empirical Findings on Manufacturing Cell Design," *Int. Journal of Production Research*, Vol. 38, No. 3, 2000, pp. 481–507). Most of these cells performed machining operations. Also see N. Harvey, *The Socio-Technical Implementation of Cellular Manufacturing in American and German Metal Working Firms* (University of Wisconsin-Madison, WI: unpublished Ph.D. dissertation, 1993) for an extensive discussion of labor relations and their impact of cell design and operations.

6. See, for example, M. Fazakerley, "Social and Human Factors in Industrial Systems," *Int. Journal of Production Research*, Vol. 12, No. 1, 1974, pp. 139–147; J. R. Hackman and G. R. Oldham, *Work Redesign* (Readings, MA: Addison-Wesley, 1980); and M. Campion and G. Medsker, "Job Design," in G. Salvendy (ed.), *Handbook of Industrial Engineering* (New York: Wiley & Sons, 1992).

7. See V. L. Huber and N. L. Hyer, "The Human Factor in Cellular Manufacturing," *Journal of Operations Management*, Vol. 5, No. 2, 1985, pp. 213–228.

8. For a more extensive discussion of the use of group technology in change-over and preproduction activities (such as process planning and parts programming), see N. L. Hyer and U. Wemmerlöv, "Group Technology in the US Manufacturing Industry: A Survey of Users," *Int. Journal of Production Research*, Vol. 27, No. 8, 1989, pp. 1287–1304.

9. It was the emphasis on using group technology to reduce setup times and tooling expenditures that occupied many early writers in the field. This also led to the development of classification and coding schemes for part family identification purposes. See, for example, S. P. Mitrofanov, *Scientific Principles of Group Technology* (Yorkshire: National Lending Library for Science and Technology,

1966), and W. F. Hyde, *Improving Productivity by Classification, Coding, and Database Standardization* (New York: Marcel Dekker, 1981).

10. See, for example, K. Suzaki, *The New Manufacturing Challenge: Techniques for Continuous Improvement* (New York: The Free Press, 1987).

11. The idea to display these choices graphically comes from "Production Islands: A Highly Efficient Form of Workshop Organization Making Intensive Use of Workers' Qualifications," undated excerpt from AWF's committee for economical manufacture. (The complete report is published in German under the title "Flexible Fertigungsorganisation am Beispiel von Fertigungsinseln.")

12. In a previous study of cell users, 80 percent indicated that production planning and control was simplified with cells. See U. Wemmerlöv and D. J. Johnson, "Cellular Manufacturing at 46 User Plants: Implementation Experiences and Performance Improvements," *Int. Journal of Production Research*, Vol. 35, No. 1, 1997, pp. 29–49.

13. You may have experienced this effect when you find yourself in the slowest check-out line at the supermarket or after having selected the slowest teller at the bank. In fact, there is a saying related to queuing in service systems that *"The other line always moves faster"* (possibly originated by Richard Larson at MIT).

14. See Wemmerlöv and Johnson, "Empirical Findings on Manufacturing Cell Design," and R. F. Marsh, J. R. Meredith, and D. M. McCutcheon, "The Life Cycle of Manufacturing Cells," *Int. Journal of Operations and Production Management*, Vol. 17, No. 12, 1998, pp. 1167–1182. The cell life cycle is also discussed in Chapter 17.

15. For similar examples of these types of human reactions, see Campion and Medsker, "Job Design"; Harvey, *The Socio-Technical Implementation of Cellular Manufacturing in American and German Metal Working Firms*; and Fazakerley, "Social and Human Factors in Industrial Systems."

16. See, for example, Wemmerlöv and Johnson, "Cellular Manufacturing at 46 User Plants: Implementation Experiences and Performance Improvements," and D. J. Johnson and U. Wemmerlöv, "Factors Influencing the Degree of Cell Penetration in Manufacturing Plants," working paper, June 1999.

17. Of course, if there is no managerial talent available to carry out a cell conversion project, it has to be delayed or shelved. This, however, does not change its relative merits.

18. See D. J. Johnson and U. Wemmerlöv, "On the Relative Performance of Functional and Cellular Layouts—An Analysis of the Model-Based Comparative Studies Literature," *Production and Operations Management*, Vol. 5, No. 4, 1996, p. 316.

19. See Johnson and Wemmerlöv, "Factors Influencing the Degree of Cell Penetration in Manufacturing Plants."

Chapter 4

1. For a nice discussion of organizational inertia, see D. N. Sull, "Why Good Companies Go Bad," *Harvard Business Review*, July-August 1999, pp. 42–52.

2. See, for example, R. M. Kanter, B. A. Stein, and T. D. Jick, *The Challenge of Organizational Change* (New York: The Free Press, 1992); pp. 160 and 172 in D. J. Johnson, *An Empirical Investigation of Factors Influencing Reorganizations to Cellular Manufacturing* (unpublished Ph.D. dissertation, University of Wisconsin-Madison, 1998); and N. L. Hyer, K. Brown, and S. Zimmerman, "A Socio-Technical Systems Approach to Cell Design: Case Study and Analysis," *Journal of Operations Management*, Vol. 17, No. 2, 1999, pp. 179–203.

3. For smaller firms that don't have formal planning procedures, problem awareness typically generates action directly.

4. L. R. Nyman, (ed.), *Making Manufacturing Cells Work* (Dearborn, MI: Society of Manufacturing Engineers, 1992), p. 14.

5. See C. H. Fine, *Clockspeed: Winning Industry Control in the Age of Temporary Advantage* (Reading, MA: Perseus Books, 1998). The make/buy issue is further discussed in Chapter 5.

6. U. Wemmerlöv and D. J. Johnson, "Empirical Findings on Manufacturing Cell Design," *Int. Journal of Production Research*, Vol. 38, No. 3, 2000, pp. 481–507.

7. Also see Nyman, *Making Manufacturing Cells Work*, p. 14.

8. See G. A. Levasseur, M. M. Helms, and A. A. Zink, "A Conversion from a Functional to a Cellular Manufacturing Layout at Steward, Inc.," *Production and Inventory Management*, Vol. 36, No. 3, 1995, pp. 37–42.

9. The same manager may lead the analysis in Steps 3 and 4, joined by a few other employees and/or consultants. Formal teams may or may not be formed until an operations strategy is finalized and a decision has been made to pursue the project in more detail. This takes place at Step 5. To sim-

plify, we will use the term "steering team" to refer to the person or persons doing the continued planning and analysis work.

10. See R. Suri, U. Wemmerlöv, F. Rath, R. Gadh, and R. Veeramani, "Practical Issues in Implementing Quick Response Manufacturing: Insights from Fourteen Projects with Industry," *Proceedings of the Manufacturing and Service Operations Management (MSOM) Conference*, Dartmouth College, Hanover, NH, 1996.

11. To select team members who are all happy with status quo can spell disaster for the project.

12. See R. C. Camp, *Benchmarking* (Milwaukee, WI: ASQC Quality Press, 1989).

13. See, for example, Nyman, *Making Manufacturing Cells Work*, p. 69; also see J. Fox, A. Edwards, J. Watt, and B. Taylor, "Successful Techniques to Realize the Benefits of Cellular Manufacturing," (undated conference presentation by personnel from Boeing Commercial Airplane Group, Wichita, KS).

14. The steering team is alternatively referred to as a steering committee, design team, or guiding team. A project team is sometimes referred to as an implementation team. See, for example C. Beatty, "Implementing Advanced Manufacturing Technologies: Rules of the Road," *Sloan Management Review*, Summer 1992, pp. 49–60; P. Scholtes, B. Joiner, and B. Streibel, *The Team Handbook: Second Edition* (Madison, WI: Oriel Corp., 1996); and Nyman, *Making Manufacturing Cells Work*.

15. See M. Perona, "Cell Formation in a Coil Forging Shop," in S. Irani, *Handbook of Cellular Manufacturing Systems* (New York: Wiley & Sons, 1999), pp. 555–587.

16. See R. Panizzolo, "Cellular Manufacturing at Zanussi-Electrolux Plant, Susegana, Italy," in N. C. Suresh and J. M. Kay (eds.), *Group Technology and Cellular Manufacturing: State-of-the-Art Synthesis of Research and Practice* (Boston: Kluwer Academic Publishers, 1998), pp. 475–490.

17. See D. J. Johnson and U. Wemmerlöv, "Cellular Manufacturing Feasibility at Ingersoll Cutting Tool Co.," in Suresh and Kay, *Group Technology and Cellular Manufacturing: State-of-the-Art Synthesis of Research and Practice*, pp. 239–254.

18. This office cell is further discussed in Chapter 18.

19. See Johnson, *An Empirical Investigation of Factors Influencing Reorganizations to Cellular Manufacturing*.

20. From Johnson, *An Empirical Investigation of Factors Influencing Reorganizations to Cellular Manufacturing*.

21. See Hyer et al., " A Socio-Technical Systems Approach to Cell Design: Case Study and Analysis," Table 3.

22. See Wemmerlöv and Johnson, "Empirical Findings on Manufacturing Cell Design."

23. If the company already has cells, and is going through the planning process assisted by past experiences—see the feedback loops in Figure 4-1—the factorywide analysis may lead to the break-up and dismantling of existing cells. This may be done to return the products to a functional work organization, or due to a need to redesign cells due to a changing part/product family; also see Chapter 17.

24. See U. Wemmerlöv and D. J. Johnson, "Cellular Manufacturing at 46 User Plants: Implementation Experiences and Performance Improvements," *Int. Journal of Production Research*, Vol. 35, No. 1, 1997, pp. 29–49.

25. Levasseur et al., "A Conversion from a Functional to a Cellular Manufacturing Layout at Steward, Inc."

Chapter 5

1. Management systems include planning and control systems, employee selection and training processes, measurement and compensation, quality and maintenance systems, and the like. Also see Figure 5-24.

2. See R. L. Ackoff, "On the Use of Models in Corporate Planning," *Strategic Management Journal*, Vol. 2, No. 4, 1981, pp. 353–359.

3. See M. P. Karle, "Group Technology Paves the Way for a Just-In-Time Manufacturing Philosophy," *Proceedings of the IXth ICPR Conference*, Cincinnati, OH, August 1987, pp. 910–917.

4. See R. Panizzolo, "Cellular Manufacturing at Zanussi-Electrolux Plant, Susegana, Italy," in N. C. Suresh and J. M. Kay, (eds.), *Group Technology and Cellular Manufacturing: State-of-the-Art Synthesis of Research and Practice* (Boston: Kluwer Academic Publishers, 1998, pp. 475–490).

5. See U. Wemmerlöv and D. J. Johnson, "Empirical Findings on Manufacturing Cell Design," *Int. Journal of Production Research*, Vol. 38, No. 3, 2000, pp. 481–507. Firms that did not set quantitative goals simply identified measures and set directions (smaller, better, etc.).

6. See R. Suri, U. Wemmerlöv, F. Rath, R. Gadh, and R. Veeramani, "Practical Issues in Implementing Quick Response Manufacturing: Insights from Fourteen Projects with Industry," *Proceedings of the Manufacturing and Service Operations Management (MSOM) Conference*, Dartmouth College,

Hanover, NH, 1996. Also see P. Mazany, "A Case Study: Lessons From the Progressive Implementation of Just-In-Time in a Small Knitwear Manufacturer," *Int. Journal of Operations and Production Management*, Vol. 15, No. 9, 1995, pp. 271–288.

7. Also see R. J. Schonberger, *World-Class Manufacturing: The Next Decade* (New York: The Free Press, 1996).

8. John Deere regularly documents a part's lead time by breaking it down into its "value-added time," its "required non-value-added time," and its "unnecessary value-added time." The latter is queue time. These data are presented in pie and bar charts as part of what Deere refers to "process mapping" (also see Suri et al., "Practical Issues in Implementing Quick Response Manufacturing: Insights from Fourteen Projects with Industry," and our next section).

9. See M. Rother and J. Shook, *Learning to See: Value Stream Mapping to Create Value and Eliminate Muda* (Brookline, MA: The Lean Enterprise Institute, 1999).

10. For more information on process mapping, see P. Scholtes, B. Joiner, and B. Streibel, *The Team Handbook: Second Edition* (Madison, WI: Oriel Corporation, 1996).

11. You may also use a process map variant, the functional flowchart, to depict both the steps in the process and the department that performs them. See Chapter 18.

12. For more information on the uses and benefits of GT, and the cost of part proliferation, see N. L. Hyer and U. Wemmerlöv, "Group Technology in the U.S. Manufacturing Industry: A Survey of Users," *Int. Journal of Production Research*, Vol. 27, No. 8, 1989, pp. 1287–1304.

13. Charles Fine argues that building the supply chain architecture is one of the most important competencies a firm can have. The sourcing decisions play a critical part in this development. See C. H. Fine, *Clockspeed: Winning Industry Control in the Age of Temporary Advantage* (Reading, MA: Perseus Books, 1998).

14. See T. Hill, *Manufacturing Strategy* (Burr Ridge, IL: Irwin, 1994, pp. 167–171), and Fine, *Clockspeed: Winning Industry Control in the Age of Temporary Advantage*, pp. 165–166.

15. For an example of such a tagging system, see Mazany, "A Case Study: Lessons From the Progressive Implementation of Just-In-Time in a Small Knitwear Manufacturer"; also see Chapter 18 on office cells.

16. Of course, some firms engage only in final assembly; others only in part production.

17. See R. Rössle and R. Züst, "Cellular Manufacturing in Highly Specialized Supply Industries," *Annals of the CIRP*, Vol. 43, No. 1, 1994.

18. For a review of cell formation techniques and their usage, see R. G. Askin and S. Estrada, "Investigation of Cellular Manufacturing Practices," Chapter 1 in Irani, S. (ed.), *Handbook of Cellular Systems*, John Wiley & Sons, Inc., New York, 1999); F. O. Olorunniwo and G. J. Udo, "Cell Design Practices in U.S. Manufacturing Firms," *Production and Inventory Management*, Third Quarter, 1996, pp. 27–33; and Wemmerlöv and Johnson, "Empirical Findings on Manufacturing Cell Design."

19. J. L. Burbidge, *The Introduction to Group Technology* (New York: John Wiley, 1975).

20. The need for formal algorithms and computer support is size-dependent and may be required for problems involving a large number of parts and machines. For overviews of cell formation techniques, for the technically inclined reader, see N. L. Hyer and U. Wemmerlöv, "Procedures for the Part Family/Machine Group Identification Problem in Cellular Manufacturing," *Journal of Operations Management*, Vol. 6, No. 2, 1986, pp. 125–147; S. Heragu, "Group Technology and Cellular Manufacturing," *IEEE Transactions on Systems, Man, and Cybernetics*, Vol. 24, No. 2, 1994, pp. 203–215; and A. Reisman, A. Kumar, J. Motwani, and C. H. Cheng, "Cellular Manufacturing: A Statistical Review of the Literature (1965-1995), *Operations Research*, Vol. 45, No. 4, 1997, pp. 508–520.

21. See B. El-Jawhari, *Lead Time Reduction for General Purpose Relays at Deltrol Controls* (Madison, WI: Center for Quick Response Manufacturing, April 1995).

22. Also see chapter 9 in J. L. Burbidge, *Production Flow Analysis* (Oxford: Clarendon Press, 1989).

23. This chart is adapted from N. L. Hyer and U. Wemmerlöv, "Procedures for the Part Family/Machine Group Identification Problem in Cellular Manufacturing."

24. Without an obvious solution, several "cell blocks" are in fact possible, each representing a tentative cell. Figure 5-15 shows only one possible solution.

25. A "contained" routing is one where a short routing is part of a longer routing. For example, the routing 1-5-7 is contained in the routing 1-3-5-6-7-8 (each number represents a machine).

26. See Hyer and Wemmerlöv, "Group Technology in the U.S. Manufacturing Industry: A Survey of Users," and M. Tatikonda and U. Wemmerlöv, "Adoption and Implementation of Group Technology Classification and Coding Systems—Insights from Seven Case Studies," *Int. Journal of Production Research*, Vol. 30, No. 9, 1992, pp. 2087–2110.

27. D. J. Johnson and U. Wemmerlöv, "Cellular Manufacturing Feasibility at Ingersoll Cutting Tool Co.," in Suresh and Kay, *Group Technology and Cellular Manufacturing: State-of-the-Art Synthesis of Research and Practice*, pp. 239-254.

28. See Wemmerlöv and Johnson, "Empirical Findings on Manufacturing Cell Design," p. 488.

29. See Table 5 in Wemmerlöv and Johnson, "Empirical Findings on Manufacturing Cell Design."

30. The idea for this figure comes from W. Wrennall and Q. Lee, (eds.), *Handbook of Commercial and Industrial Facilities Management* (New York: McGraw-Hill, Inc., 1994), p. 62.

31. See U. Wemmerlöv and N. L. Hyer, "Cellular Manufacturing in the U.S. Industry: A Survey of Users," *Int. Journal of Production Research*, Vol. 27, No. 9, 1989, pp. 1511–1530, and U. Wemmerlöv and D. J. Johnson, "Cellular Manufacturing at 46 User Plants: Implementation Experiences and Performance Improvements," *Int. J. of Production Research*, Vol. 35, No. 1, 1997, 29–49.

32. For statistics on cell sizes, see Wemmerlöv and Hyer, "Cellular Manufacturing in the U.S Industry: A Survey of Users," and Wemmerlöv and Johnson, "Empirical Findings on Manufacturing Cell Design."

33. See J. Slomp, "Design of Manufacturing Cells: PFA Applications in Dutch Industry," in Suresh and Kay, *Group Technology and Cellular Manufacturing: State-of-the-Art Synthesis of Research and Practice*, pp. 153-168.

34. See O. K. Hobbs, "Application of JIT Techniques in a Discrete Batch Job Shop," *Production and Inventory Management*, First Quarter 1994, pp. 43–47. For a similar example, see S. Collett and R. J. Spicer, "Improving Productivity through Cellular Manufacturing," *Production and Inventory Management*, First Quarter 1995, pp. 71–75.

35. See Q. Lee, *Facilities and Workplace Design: An Illustrated Guide* (Norcross, GA: Engineering and Management Press, 1996), p. 14.

36. This and the following chapter provide only a cursory overview of the subject of facility planning. We refer you to other reading materials for more details. See, for example, S. Heragu, *Facilities Design* (Boston: PWS Publishing Company, 1997); Lee, *Facilities and Workplace Design: An Illustrated Guide*; J. A. Tompkins, J. A. White, Y. A. Bozer, E. H. Frazelle, J. M. A. Tanchoco, and J. Trevino, *Facilities Planning* (New York: John Wiley & Sons, Inc., 1996); and Wrennall and Lee, *Handbook of Commercial and Industrial Facilities Management*.

37. See Lee, *Facilities and Workplace Design: An Illustrated Guide*, for this term.

38. See R. Muther, *Systematic Layout Planning* (Boston: Cahners Books, 1973); also see Lee, *Facilities and Workplace Design: An Illustrated Guide*. Although called "systematic," the SLP procedure does not use any algorithms to generate layouts. These are all manually constructed.

39. Figure 5-22 is from Lee, *Facilities and Workplace Design*, p. 82. The order of the space units' entry into the diagram should be determined by the number A-relationships they have, with ties being broken by the number of E-relationships; we then proceed to units with E-relationships, etc. See Ch 7 in Tompkins et al., *Facilities Planning*, for this and other techniques for creating relationships diagrams.

40. See L. R. Nyman, (ed.), *Making Manufacturing Cells Work* (Dearborn, MI: Society of Manufacturing Engineers, 1992), p. 95.

41. See Nyman, *Making Manufacturing Cells Work*, p. 94.

42. This quote is from Tompkins et al., *Facilities Planning*, p. 371.

Chapter 6

1. See M. J. Zayko, D. J. Broughman, and W. M. Hancock, "Lean Manufacturing Yields World-Class Improvements for Small Manufacturer," IIE Solutions, April 1997, pp. 36–40.

2. See D. J. Johnson, *An Empirical Investigation of Factors Influencing Reorganizations to Cellular Manufacturing* (Madison, WI: University of Wisconsin-Madison, unpublished Ph.D. dissertation, 1998); and U. Wemmerlöv and D. J. Johnson, "Empirical Findings on Manufacturing Cell Design," *Int. Journal of Production Research*, Vol. 38, No. 3, 2000, pp. 481–507.

3. See Johnson, *An Empirical Investigation of Factors Influencing Reorganizations to Cellular Manufacturing*, pp. 109, 112.

4. Setup-time reduction is also discussed in Chapter 17 and Appendix K. For good sources on setup time reduction, refer to H. J. Steudel and P. Desruelle, *Manufacturing in the Nineties: How to Become a Mean, Lean World-Class Competitor* (New York: Van Nostrand Reinhold, 1992), or S. Shingo, *A Revolution in Manufacturing: The SMED System* (Cambridge, MA: Productivity Press, 1985).

5. For relatively simple algorithms that construct dominant flow sequences while avoiding backtracks, see R. Hollier, "The Layout of Multi-Product Lines," *Int. Journal of Production Research*, Vol. 2, 1963, pp. 47–57, and A. Carrie, "The Layout of Multi-Product Lines," *Int. Journal of Production Research*, Vol. 13, No. 6, 1975, pp. 541–557.

6. See K. Sekine, *One-Piece Flow: Cell Design for Transforming the Production Process* (Portland, Oregon: Productivity Press, 1992) and K. Suzaki, *The New Manufacturing Challenge* (New York: The Free Press, 1987).

7. We admit that we are speculating here. Also note that some people, even if they are right-handed, prefer to pull with their left hand.

8. See Sekine, *One-Piece Flow: Cell Design for Transforming the Production Process.*

9. For the example in Figures 13 and 14, see Sekine, *One-Piece Flow: Cell Design for Transforming the Production Process,* pp. 79 and 81.

10. See Suzaki, *The New Manufacturing Challenge,* p. 80.

11. Due to space considerations, we do not show the setup and run times for each part on each machine in Table 6-4.

12. When you group items into families and want to determine average run times, average lot sizes, etc., you should preferably determine weighted averages. The best weights are those based on the number of orders issued in a year. Thus, if two parts have lot sizes of Q1 and Q2, respectively, and their annual production volumes are D1 and D2, the weighted average lot size for this part family is $\{Q1*(D1/Q1) + Q2*(D2/Q2)\}/(D1/Q1+D2/Q2) = (D1+D2)/(D1/Q1+D2/Q2)$. However, if the purpose is to simplify calculations, you do not want to determine exact averages; rather, you may simply pick a part from each family and let it represent the family as a whole.

13. See previous endnote for an illustration of weighted average.

14. The reason this works is that "operator utilization" is the same as "average number of operators needed at a machine per unit of time" – although expressed as a percentage of time.

15. See Table 5-3.

16. See Sekine, *One-Piece Flow: Cell Design for Transforming the Production Process* and Q. Lee, *Facilities and Workplace Design* (Norcross, GA: Engineering and Management Press, 1996) for examples of process charts. For line-balancing techniques, see R. G. Askin and C. R. Standridge, *Modeling and Analysis of Manufacturing Systems* (New York: John Wiley & Sons, 1993). Suzaki recommends that the workload allocation—rather than being evenly distributed across stations—be made as uneven as possible in order to drive down the minimum time to zero so that one worker can be eliminated (see Suzaki, *The New Manufacturing Challenge,* pp. 131–132).

17. The examples discussed in Figures 6-11 through 6-13 are modified from Sekine, *One-Piece Flow: Cell Design for Transforming the Production Process,* pp. 49–51.

18. General Motors is using a quantitative model that determines the cost per piece from investing in equipment. The model considers the cost of equipment, labor, setup, and inventory. See D. J. Van der Veen and W. C. Jordan, "Analyzing Trade-Offs between Machine Investment and Utilization," *Management Science,* Vol. 35, No. 10, 1989, pp. 1215–1226.

19. See, for example, J. L. Burbidge, *Production Flow Analysis* (Oxford: Clarendon Press, 1989), and Wemmerlöv and Johnson, "Empirical Findings on Manufacturing Cell Design."

Chapter 7

1. See R. Suri, U. Wemmerlöv, F. Rath, R. Gadh, and R. Veeramani, "Practical Issues in Implementing Quick Response Manufacturing: Insights from Fourteen Projects with Industry," *Proceedings of the Manufacturing and Service Operations Management (MSOM) Conference,* Dartmouth College, Hanover, NH, 1996.

2. See, for example, H. Hirano, *JIT Factory Revolution: A Pictorial Guide to Factory Design of the Future* (Cambridge, MA: Productivity Press, 1988).

3. More specifically, steady state exists when the stochastic distributions that affect the system's performance, such as the job arrival distribution or the distribution of job operation times, do not change over time.

4. $P = \Sigma\{(S_i+r_iQ_i)*w_i\}$, where the weights $w_i = (D_i/Q_i)/(\Sigma D_i/Q_i)$.

5. Thus, $ASUM = \Sigma (D_i/Q_i)$.

6. $V = \sigma^2$, i.e., the variance equals the squared standard deviation, where $\sigma = \sqrt{[\Sigma_i\{(x_i - Ave\ x)^2]/(n-1)}$.

7. See, for example, W. J. Hopp and M. L. Spearman, *Factory Physics: The Foundations of Manufacturing Management* (Chicago, IL: Irwin, 1996).

8. Note, however, that this effect is less evident since P also appears in the first term with the opposite effect. P also appears in U.

9. You can deduce this from the waiting time formula: P is cut in half, U/(1-U) is unchanged, and the first term tends to remain constant or decline when P and I are reduced. Thus, W is reduced.

10. The waiting time formula implicitly assumes that the equipment has 100 percent uptime.

11. See J. D. C. Little, "A Proof of the Queuing Formula *L=λW,*" *Operations Research*, Vol. 9, 1961, pp. 383-387. Little's Law is also discussed in Hopp and Spearman, *Factory Physics: The Foundations of Manufacturing Management.*

12. Note that the arrival (input) and departure (output) rate to the system is equal or lower than the (hard) bottleneck production rate.

13. Imagine you arrive at the end of a line, with five people ahead of you. If only one person can be served every hour, it will take you five hours to get through.

14. For an example, see H. Steudel and P. Desruelle, *Manufacturing in the Nineties: How to Become a Mean, Lean, World-Class Competitor* (New York: Van Nostrand Reinhold, 1992), p. 152.

15. See endnote 4 for a general formula.

16. See U. Karmarker, "Lot Sizes, Lead-Times, and In-Process Inventories," *Management Science*, Vol. 33, No. 3, 1987, pp. 409–418, and N. C. Suresh and J. R. Meredith, "Coping with the Loss of Pooling Synergy," *Management Science*, Vol. 40, No. 4, 1994, pp. 466–483.

17. This best lot size has nothing to do with the economic order quantity (EOQ). EOQ is a "best" lot size from an economic perspective. However, it does not consider lead or waiting times. For calculations of Q^*, see references in the previous endnote.

18. Note that cells also may be staffed by a single operator who moves around in the cell from station to station, carrying the work piece. For further discussion of one-piece flow cells, see K. Sekine, *One-Piece Flow: Cell Design for Transforming the Production Process* (Portland, OR: Productivity Press, 1992), and Hirano, *JIT Factory Revolution: A Pictorial Guide to Factory Design of the Future.*

19. See Hopp and Spearman, *Factory Physics: The Foundations of Manufacturing Management*, p. 277, for the waiting time for a group of machines.

20. For a discussion on this issue, see A. G. Burgess, I. Morgan, and T. E. Vollmann, "Cellular Manufacturing: Its Impact on the Total Factory," *Int. Journal of Production Research*, Vol. 31, No. 9, 1993, pp. 2059–2077.

21. V. I. Cesani, *An Investigation of Labor Flexibility in Cellular Manufacturing Systems* (Madison, WI: University of Wisconsin-Madison, unpublished Ph.D. dissertation, 1998), p. 154.

22. For details, see Cesani, *An Investigation of Labor Flexibility in Cellular Manufacturing Systems*; Steudel and Desruelle, *Manufacturing in the Nineties: How to Become a Mean, Lean, World-Class Competitor*; and E. Molleman and J. Slomp, "Functional Flexibility and Team Performance," *Int. Journal of Production Research*, Vol. 37, No. 8, 1999, pp. 1837–1858.

23. See U. Wemmerlöv and N. L. Hyer, "Cellular Manufacturing in the U.S. Industry: A Survey of Users," *Int. Journal of Production Research*, Vol. 27, No. 9, 1989, pp. 1511–1530.

24. See Molleman and Slomp, "Functional Flexibility and Team Performance," p. 1855.

25. See, for example, Cesani, *An Investigation of Labor Flexibility in Cellular Manufacturing Systems*, and N. Harvey, *The Socio-Technical Implementation of Cellular Manufacturing in American and German Metal Working Firms* (Madison, WI: University of Wisconsin-Madison, unpublished Ph.D. dissertation, 1993).

26. See U. Wemmerlöv and D. J. Johnson, "Empirical Findings on Manufacturing Cell Design," *Int. Journal of Production Research*, Vol. 38, No. 3, 2000, pp. 481–507, section 7.

27. Network Dynamics, Inc., 10 Speen St., Framingham, MA 01701 (*www.networkdyn.com*).

28. For all figures and data in this section, see B. El-Jawhari, *Lead Time Reduction for General Purpose Relays at Deltrol Controls* (Madison, WI: Center for Quick Response Manufacturing, April 1995).

29. For more details on this study, see D. J. Johnson and U. Wemmerlöv, "Cellular Manufacturing Feasibility at Ingersoll Cutting Tool Co.," in N. C. Suresh and J. M. Kay, (eds.), *Group Technology and Cellular Manufacturing: State-of-the-Art Synthesis of Research and Practice* (Boston: Kluwer Academic Publishers, 1998), pp. 239–254.

30. If you are interested in further readings on models and the modeling process, see A. M. Law and W. D. Kelton, *Simulation Modeling and Analysis* (New York: McGraw-Hill, 1991).

31. See Wemmerlöv and Johnson, "Empirical Findings on Manufacturing Cell Design." Even fewer probably use queuing theory based software, although we have no data on this.

32. See Cesani, *An Investigation of Labor Flexibility in Cellular Manufacturing Systems*, p. 180.

33. Also see Table 3-2 from D. J. Johnson and U. Wemmerlöv, "On the Relative Performance of Functional and Cellular Layouts—An Analysis of the Model-Based Comparative Studies Literature," *Production and Operations Management*, Vol. 5, No. 4, 1996, p. 316.

Chapter 8

1. U. Wemmerlöv and D. J. Johnson, "Empirical Findings on Manufacturing Cell Design," *Int. Journal of Production Research*, Vol. 38, No. 3, 2000, pp. 481–507.
2. L. R. Nyman, (ed.), *Making Manufacturing Cells Work* (Dearborn, MI: Society of Manufacturing Engineers, 1992), p. 30.
3. For these results, see Nyman et al, *Making Manufacturing Cells Work*, p. 33, and F. O. Olorunniwo and G. J. Udo, "Cell Design Practices in U.S. Manufacturing Firms," *Production and Inventory Management*, Third Quarter, 1996, pp. 27–33.
4. See, for example, U. Wemmerlöv and N. L. Hyer, "Cellular Manufacturing in the U.S Industry: A Survey of Users, "*Int. Journal of Production Research*, Vol. 27, No. 9, 1989, pp. 1511–1530; D. J. Johnson, *An Empirical Investigation of Factors Influencing Reorganizations to Cellular Manufacturing* (unpublished Ph.D. dissertation, University of Wisconsin-Madison, 1998); and U. Wemmerlöv and D. J. Johnson, "Cellular Manufacturing at 46 User Plants: Implementation Experiences and Performance Improvements," *Int. J. of Production Research*, Vol. 35, No. 1, 1997, pp. 29–49.
5. These quotes are from Wemmerlöv and Johnson, "Cellular Manufacturing at 46 User Plants: Implementation Experiences and Performance Improvements."
6. See, for example, Table 1-1 in Chapter 1.
7. Also see Johnson, *An Empirical Investigation of Factors Influencing Reorganizations to Cellular Manufacturing*, p. 68; and Nyman et al., *Making Manufacturing Cells Work*, p. 22.
8. This issue led Harvard Professor Robert Kaplan to write a widely read article entitled "Must CIM Be Justified by Faith Alone?" (*Harvard Business Review*, March-April 1986), pp. 87–96.
9. This quote is from J. Dean, "Measuring the Productivity of Capital," *Harvard Business Review*, January–February 1954, pp. 120–130.
10. This quote is from pp. 476–477 (our italics) in R. Panizzolo, "Cellular Manufacturing at Zanussi-Electrolux Plant, Susegana, Italy," Chapter I3 (pp. 475–490) in N. C. Suresh and J. M. Kay, (eds.), *Group Technology and Cellular Manufacturing: State-of-the-Art Synthesis of Research and Practice* (Boston: Kluwer Academic Publishers, 1998).
11. U. Wemmerlöv, "Economic Justification of Group Technology Software," *Journal of Operations Management*, Vol. 9, No. 4, 1990, pp. 500–525.
12. See D. J. Dhavale, *Management Accounting Issues in Cellular Manufacturing and Focused Factory Systems* (Montvale, NJ: The IMA Foundation for Applied Research, 1996), pp. 87–92.
13. This exhibit is adapted from S. E. Garrett, "Strategy First: A Case in FMS Justification," *Proceedings of the Second ORSA/TIMS Conference on Flexible Manufacturing Systems: Operations Research Models and Applications*, (K. Stecke and R. Suri, eds.), 1986, pp. 17–29.
14. See C. T. Horngren, G. Foster, and S. M. Datar, *Cost Accounting: A Managerial Emphasis* (Upper Saddle River, NJ: Prentice-Hall, 1997), p. 385.
15. See S. Datar, S. Kekre, T. Mukhopadyay, and E. Svaan, "Overloaded Overheads: Activity-Based Cost Analysis of Material Handling in Cell Manufacturing," *Journal of Operations Management*, Vol. 10, No. 1, 1991, p. 126 (our italics).
16. See p. 146 in Johnson, *An Empirical Investigation of Factors Influencing Reorganizations to Cellular Manufacturing*.
17. See Anonymous, *Survey of Cellular Manufacture: Cellular Manufacturing's Impact on Australian Industry* (Sydney, Australia: Report issued by the University of New South Wales, the University of Wollongong, and IE Management Consultants, 1995); Wemmerlöv and Hyer, "Cellular Manufacturing in the U.S. Industry: A Survey of Users,"; Wemmerlöv and Johnson, "Cellular Manufacturing at 46 User Plants: Implementation Experiences and Performance Improvements."
18. See Nyman et al., *Making Manufacturing Cells Work*, p. 24.
19. See Anonymous, *Survey of Cellular Manufacture: Cellular Manufacturing's Impact on Australian Industry*.
20. Adapted from P. L. Primrose and R. Leonard, "Evaluating the 'Intangible' Benefits of Flexible Manufacturing Systems by Use of Discounted Cash Flow Algorithms Within a Comprehensive Computer Program," Proceedings, Part B (*Management and Engineering Manufacture*), The Institution of Manufacturing Engineers, 1985, pp. 289–294.
21. WIP inventory can be approximated as $D*L*(M+C)/2$, where D = volume, L = lead time, M = material cost, and C = cost at end of process. $C = M+(S/Q+r)*R$, where S = setup time, Q = lot size, r = unit run time, and R = labor cost per hour. See T. O. Boucher and J. A. Muckstadt, "Cost Estimating Methods for Evaluating the Conversion from a Functional Manufacturing Layout to Group technology," *IIE Transactions*, Vol. 17, No. 3, 1985, pp. 268-276 for this formula.

22. See Horngren et al., *Cost Accounting: A Managerial Emphasis*, p. 794.
23. Due to space limitations, and based on our assumption that you have a working knowledge of these techniques, we do not describe them here. For a review of capital budgeting techniques, see Horngren, et al., *Cost Accounting: A Managerial Emphasis*, and A. A. Atkinson, R. D. Banker, R. S. Kaplan, and S. M. Young, *Management Accounting* (Upper Saddle River, NJ: Prentice-Hall, 1997).
24. Another way to look at it is that the payback time, using discounted cash flows, is longer than five years.
25. You can easily find the IRR by trial and error. In this case, IRR must be less than the discount rate of 20 percent in order to increase the NPV from –\$95,910 to 0.
26. For example, at Digital Equipment Corporation, (cost-reducing) benefits that before were considered nonquantifiable became quantifiable because of cost driver data from its ABC system. See Dhavale, *Management Accounting Issues in Cellular Manufacturing and Focused Factory Systems*, p. 77. (Also see Chapter 10 in this book.)
27. See Kaplan, "Must CIM Be Justified by Faith Alone?," p. 92.
28. See Panizzolo, "Cellular Manufacturing at Zanussi-Electrolux Plant, Susegana, Italy," p. 477.
29. 95,910 divided by (0.833+0.694+0.579+0.482+0.402) = 37,521 (see the discount factor row in Table 8-8).
30. Also see Johnson, *An Empirical Investigation of Factors Influencing Reorganizations to Cellular Manufacturing*, p. 420.
31. Also see D. G. Dhavale, *Management Accounting Issues in Cellular Manufacturing and Focused Factory Systems*, p. 79.
32. See J. L Burbidge and J. Halsell, "Group Technology and Growth at Shalibane," *Int. Journal of Production Planning & Control*, 1994, Vol. 5, No. 2, pp. 213–218 (we have inserted the quantitative outcomes in brackets).
33. See G. A. Levasseur, M. M. Helms, and A. A. Zink, "A Conversion from a Functional to a Cellular Manufacturing Layout at Steward, Inc.," *Production and Inventory Management*, Vol. 36, No. 3, 1995, pp. 37–42.
34. Perhaps suspiciously so!
35. See p. 146 in Johnson, *An Empirical Investigation of Factors Influencing Reorganizations to Cellular Manufacturing*.
36. See Wemmerlöv, "Economic Justification of Group Technology Software."
37. See S. R. Rosenthal, "Progress Toward the Factory of the Future," *Journal of Operations Management*, Vol. 4, 1984, pp. 203–230.
38. See D. Gerwin, "A Theory of Innovation Processes for Computer-Aided Manufacturing Technology," *IEEE Transactions on Engineering Management*, Vol. 35, No. 2, May 1988, pp. 90–100.
39. See Panizzolo, "Cellular Manufacturing at Zanussi-Electrolux Plant, Susegana, Italy," p. 477.

Chapter 9

1. See H. J. Harrington, *Business Process Improvement* (New York: McGraw Hill, 1991), p. 82.
2. See A. Neely, J. Mills, K. Platts, M. Gregory, and H. Richards, "Realizing Strategy Through Measurement," *Int. Journal of Operations and Production Management*, Vol. 14, No. 3, 1994, pp. 140–152.
3. See R. F. Marsh and J. R. Meredith, "Changes in Performance Measures on the Factory Floor," *Production and Inventory Management*, First Quarter 1998, pp. 36–40.
4. See L. Nyman (ed.), *Making Manufacturing Cells Work* (Dearborn, MI: Society of Manufacturing Engineers, 1992), p. 312.
5. See S. Sink and T. Tuttle, *Planning and Measurement in Your Organization of the Future* (Norcross, GA: Industrial Engineering and Management Press, 1989).
6. Adapted from S. Sink and T. Tuttle, *Planning and Measurement in Your Organization of the Future*.
7. For a good discussion of the need for process complete measures to drive improvement, see M. Hammer and J. Champy, *Reengineering the Corporation* (New York: HarperCollins, 1993). Also see R. W. Hall, H. Johnson, and P. Turney, *Measuring Up: Charting Pathways to Manufacturing Excellence* (Homewood, IL: Business One Irwin, 1991).
8. See TRADE (Training Resources and Data Exchange) Performance-Based Management Special Interest Group, "How to Measure Performance: A Handbook of Techniques and Tools," Oak Ridge Associated Universities, 1995, pp. 2-3.
9. See, for example, J. Hendricks, "Performance Measures for a JIT Manufacturer: The Role of the IE," *Industrial Engineering*, Vol. 25, No. 1, January 1994, pp. 26–29, and C. Schneier, D. Shaw, and

R. Beatty, "Performance Measurement and Management: A Tool for Execution of Strategy," *Human Resources Management*, Vol. 30, No. 3, 1991 (Fall), pp. 279–301.

10. See R. Hayes, S. Wheelwright, and K. Clark, *Dynamic Manufacturing: Creating the Learning Organization* (New York: The Free Press, 1988).

11. Also see Chapter 10 and D. Johnson, *An Empirical Investigation of Factors Influencing Reorganizations to Cellular Manufacturing* (Madison, WI: Unpublished Ph.D. dissertation, School of Business, University of Wisconsin-Madison, 1998).

12. See G. Rummler and A. Brache, *Improving Performance: How to Manage the White Space on the Organization Chart* (San Francisco: Jossey-Bass, 1995), p. 135.

13. See Johnson, *An Empirical Investigation of Factors Influencing Reorganizations to Cellular Manufacturing*.

14. C. Meyer, "How the Right Measures Help Teams Excel," *Harvard Business Review*, May-June 1994, pp. 95–103.

15. See S. A. Blenkinsop and N. Burns, "Performance Measurement Revisited," *Int. Journal of Operations and Production Management*, Vol. 12, No. 10, 1992, pp. 16–25.

16. See J. Dixon, A. Nanni, and T. Vollmann, *The New Performance Challenge: Measuring Operations for World-Class Performance* (Homewood, IL: Dow Jones-Irwin, 1990), p. 25.

17. Of course, there are situations where we may want to forget about the past. For example, we know of firms that have established cells after, in vain, trying to improve the performance of the existing plant. Creating a radically new organization based on cells, without performance links to the past or being locked into old ways of doing things, was a way to start afresh.

18. Note, however, that you should not necessarily react immediately to all information you collect. You must allow room for normal variations in the process before you take actions.

19. See K. Merkel, "Achieving Planned Performance Results Using Manufacturing Operations," *Industrial Engineering*, 1995, pp. 26–29 (see especially p. 28).

20. See M. Greif, *The Visual Factory* (Portland, OR: Productivity Press, 1991), pp. 189–190.

21. That is, the weighted average lead time for all parts = {[lead time for part 1]*[no. of orders per period of part 1] + [lead time for part 2]*[no. of orders per period of part 2] + ...]}/(total number of orders during the period).

22. See Greif, *The Visual Factory*. Also, in a recent study of 42 firms with cells, 79 percent displayed performance data publicly (see Marsh and Meredith, "Changes in Performance Measures on the Factory Floor"). This was a relatively new and growing trend among the cell users.

23. See K. Suzaki, *The New Shop Floor Management: Empowering People for Continuous Improvement* (New York: The Free Press, 1993).

24. See Greif, *The Visual Factory*. In a presentation we attended Greif discussed the use of "flash" information. For further reading see M. Greif, "Revolutionizing Internal Communication in Decentralized Organizations," *CEMS Business Review*, Vol. 1, 1996, pp. 27–35.

25. S. Desmukh, N. Burns, and C. Backhouse, "On Green Area Implementation Problems: A Case Study," *Int. Journal of Production Research*, Vol. 34, No. 11, 1996, 2981–2990.

26. In the end, of course, you have to decide what the most important measures are for your firm and its cells. You may, for example, make some metrics more explicit than we do in our performance matrix.

27. It should be noted that *all* performance measures, regardless of type, have a "per time unit" dimension that identifies the period over which data were recorded (e.g., customer complaints *during a month*, number of accidents *in the last three months*, average lead time over *the last 12 months*). This time dimension, which may not always be clearly stated in the metric, should not be confused with "timeliness."

28. Firms often reduce scrap by reworking, rather than wasting, defective units. This suggests that scrap and rework can be a joint measure. Ideally, though, separate measures for scrap and rework should be used. Also see D. Dhavale, *Management Accounting Issues in Cellular Manufacturing and Focused Factory Systems* (New Jersey: The IMA Foundation for Applied Research, 1996), p. 149.

29. T. Vollmann, "Performance Measures That Support World Class Manufacturing," in T. Wallace and S. Bennett (eds.), *World Class Manufacturing* (Essex Junction, VT: Omneo, 1994), p. 446.

30. See R. Kaplan and D. Norton, "The Balanced Scorecard—Measures That Drive Performance," *Harvard Business Review*, February 1992, pp. 71–79.

31. Disguised company name.

32. See Meyer, "How the Right Measures Help Teams Excel," p. 95.

Chapter 10

1. D. W. Swenson and J. Cassidy, "The Effect of JIT on Management Accounting," *Journal of Cost Management*, Spring 1993, p. 44. Also see Appendix D, last section.
2. See T. D. Fry, D. C. Steele, and B. A. Saladin, "The Role of Management Accounting in the Development of a Manufacturing Strategy," *Int. Journal of Operations and Production Management*, Vol. 15, No. 12, 1995, pp. 21–31.
3. These numbers come from a study by Price Waterhouse, as quoted in Fry et al., "The Role of Management Accounting …." A study by B. R. Gaumnitz and F. P. Kollaritsch (*Journal of Cost Management*, Spring 1991, pp. 58–64) claims that the percentage of standard cost system user is 87 percent. Studies quoted in Horngren et al., *Cost Accounting*, p. 225, put the usage rate at 86 percent in U.S. firms, 76 percent in UK firms, and 65 percent in Japanese companies.
4. Also see p. 697 in R. W. Hilton, M. W. Maher, and F. H. Selto, *Cost Management* (Boston: Irwin-McGraw-Hill, 2000).
5. This figure is inspired by A. A. Atkinson, R. D. Banker, R. S. Kaplan, and S. M. Young, *Management Accounting* (Upper Saddle River, NJ: Prentice-Hall, 1997), p. 249; and by C. T. Horngren, G. Foster, and S. M. Datar, *Cost Accounting: A Managerial Emphasis* (Upper Saddle River, NJ: Prentice-Hall, 1997), p. 485.
6. A cost pool is a collection of related costs.
7. See Atkinson et al., *Management Accounting*, p. 249.
8. The terms "allocation base" and "cost driver" are sometimes used interchangeably. We have here chosen to use allocation base for Stage 1 allocations and cost driver for Stage 2 allocations. Note that cost driver implies a cause-effect relation that is not always present. That is, an increased use of a cost driver, like direct labor hours, may not actually increase other costs in the manufacturing process.
9. Studies done on cost systems in the US, Australia, Ireland, Japan, and the UK indicate that direct labor hours or labor dollars are used to allocate overhead costs in between 52-62 percent of the firms, machine hours in 12-27 percent, direct materials dollars in 4-17 percent, units of production in 5-28 percent, and other in 9-17 percent of the firms (these figures vary across countries and exceed 100 percent since firms may use multiple allocation bases). See Horngren et al., *Cost Accounting*, p. 135.
10. "Brice" is a fictitious name. The plant only carried WIP inventory since finished goods were immediately shipped to customers or warehouses. For details about this plant and its experience, see W. M. Baker, T. D. Fry, and K. Karwan, "The Rise and Fall and Time-Based Manufacturing," *Management Accounting*, June 1994, pp. 56-59; and T. D. Fry, "Manufacturing Performance and Cost Accounting," *Production and Inventory Management*, Third Quarter 1992, pp. 30–35.
11. Although scrap here is measured in dollars, it is still an operational, non-financial metric.
12. See P. Åhlström and C. Karlsson, "Change Processes Towards Lean Manufacturing," *Int. Journal of Operations and Production Management*, Vol. 16, No. 11, 1996, pp. 42–56.
13. See Appendix A for an example of such comparisons. Although lowering product cost is a frequent goal, results achieved in this area are rarely reported in the literature on cellular manufacturing (the study by Wemmerlöv and Johnson reported in Chapter 3 is an exception; also see Chapter 8). We do not know whether this has something to do with the difficulty of establishing the "true" impact on product cost, whether few firms bother to make such pre/post comparisons, or whether firms are simply not willing to share this type of information. At any rate, although we have anecdotal evidence we know fairly little in a systematic way about cellular manufacturing's impact on product cost.
14. We say that while also noting that costs can be more or less accurate—but they can never be *absolutely* "true" or "accurate."
15. Note, however, that the sole use of cost per product data to justify cellular manufacturing is insufficient because it may ignore expenditures for implementation (see Chapter 8 and Appendix A).
16. For more on practical capacity, see Kaplan, *Measures for Manufacturing Excellence*, p. 33; Atkinson et al., Management Accounting, pp. 207-209; D. G. Dhavale, *Management Accounting Issues in Cellular Manufacturing and Focused Factory Systems* (Montvale, NJ: The IMA Foundation for Applied Research, 1996), pp. 179-182 and 221–226.
17. See Horngren et al., Cost Accounting, p. 316, and Dhavale, *Management Accounting Issues in Cellular Manufacturing and Focused Factory Systems*, p. 181.
18. You can also say that employees who do not assist each other, facilitate improvement, and show a willingness to learn demonstrate the "wrong behavior"; see Chapters 12 and 13.
19. Some experts are very blunt in this regard: "What is the place of variance reporting within world-class manufacturing? There is no place for variance reporting." See Maskell, *Performance Measurement for World-Class Manufacturing*, p. 360.

20. See Kaplan, *Measures for Manufacturing Excellence*, Chapter 1.
21. See R. S. Kaplan, "Yesterday's Accounting Undermines Production," *Harvard Business Review*, July-August 1984, p. 97.
22. See C. H. Durden, L. G. Hassell, and D. R. Upton, "Cost Accounting and Performance Measurement in a Just-In-Time Production Environment," *Asian Pacific Journal of Management*, Vol. 16, 1999, pp. 111–125.
23. For examples in Japanese firms, see T. Hiromoto, "Restoring the Relevance of Management Accounting," *Journal of Management Accounting Research*, Fall 1991, pp. 1–15, and M. Kawada and D. F. Johnson, "Strategic Management Accounting," *Management Accounting*, August 1993, pp. 32–38. For the Tektronix experience, see Harvard Business School case 9-188-143.
24. See, for example, Dhavale, *Management Accounting Issues in Cellular Manufacturing and Focused Factory Systems*, p. 121 and J. A. Heard, "JIT Accounting," *Readings in Zero Inventory* (Falls Church, VA: American Production and Inventory Control Society, 1984), pp. 20–23.
25. For a novel way of using time to allocate cost based on queuing theory, see S. Bhaskar, *A Two-Stage Cost Allocation Scheme to Support Quick Response Manufacturing* (Madison, WI: unpublished Ph.D. dissertation, University of Wisconsin-Madison, 2000).
26. This approach will, to some extent, account for the time spent in the cell, but since waiting time is not included it will likely not serve as an incentive to reduce lead time.
27. See K. A. Merchant and M. D. Shields, "When and Why to Measure Cost Less Accurately to Improve Decision Making," *Accounting Horizons*, Vol. 7, No. 2, June 1993, pp. 76–81.
28. See Chapter 1 in R. S. Kaplan (ed.), *Measures for Manufacturing Excellence* (Boston: Harvard Business School Press, 1990).
29. The problem with setting standards and tracking labor (as discussed later in the chapter) is another reason that piece rate compensation systems tied to individuals do not fit with cell-based manufacturing.
30. Computer simulation can be used to set standards in cells. See H. J. Steudel and P. Desruelle, *Manufacturing in the Nineties* (New York: Van Nostrand Reinhold, 1992), pp. 158–161.
31. This quote is from *Raychem Corporation Interconnection System Division* (Boston, MA: Harvard Business School Publishing, Case 9-694-063, 1997), p. 7.
32. See Atkinson et al., *Management Accounting*, p. 99. For more examples of cost drivers, see B. Maskell, *Performance Measurement for World-Class Manufacturing* (Portland, OR: Productivity Press, 1991), pp. 367–368 and p. 375.
33. See Horngren et al., *Cost Accounting*, page 514. Specifically, 19.4 percent of the firms used less than 25 activities, 28.1 percent used between 26 and 100 activities, and 52.5 percent relied on more than 100 activities. Of the same firms, 8.1 percent used less than 5 cost drivers, 26.1 percent used between 6 and 10 drivers, and 65.5 percent used more than 10 cost drivers
34. Note, of course, that even if you reduce setup cost per period from a product cost perspective, the actual cost incurred by the company does not necessarily decrease. This is because the personnel that perform the setups are still on the payroll. Also see Dhavale, *Management Accounting Issues in Cellular Manufacturing and Focused Factory Systems*, p. 176.
35. See Dhavale, *Management Accounting Issues in Cellular Manufacturing and Focused Factory Systems*, pp. 107, 119.
36. Of course, it can work the other way as well depending on the hourly cost of the new machine versus the overhead rate for the larger cost pool.
37. These types of waste are discussed in S. R. Hedin and G. R. Russell, "JIT Implementation: Interaction Between the Production and Cost Accounting Functions," *Production and Inventory Management*, Third Quarter 1992, pp. 68–73.
38. See Horngren et al., *Cost Accounting*, p. 41.
39. See Horngren et al., *Cost Accounting*, p. 719.
40. These results come from a 22-firm study by Swenson and Cassidy, "The Effect of JIT on Management Accounting."
41. For more information about backflush costing, see Horngren et al., *Cost Accounting*, pp. 726–734.
42. Note, thus, that backflushing requires accurate bills of materials to update inventory records correctly.
43. A combined raw materials and WIP inventory account, RIP, may also be used if WIP is to be recorded.
44. See Horngren et al., *Cost Accounting*, p. 731.

Chapter 11

1. See the following empirical studies: U. Wemmerlöv and N. L. Hyer, "Cellular Manufacturing in the U.S. Industry: A Survey of Users," *Int. Journal of Production Research*, Vol. 27, No. 9, 1989, pp. 1511-1530; and U. Wemmerlöv and D. J. Johnson, "Cellular Manufacturing at 46 User Plants: Implementation Experiences and Performance Improvements," *Int. Journal of Production Research*, Vol. 35, No. 1, 1997, pp. 29–49.

2. For a good overview of MPC techniques, see T. E. Vollmann, W. L. Berry, and D. C. Whybark, *Manufacturing Planning and Control Systems* (New York: Irwin/McGraw-Hill, 1997).

3. See F. Olorunniwo, "Changes in Production Planning and Control Systems with Implementation of Cellular Manufacturing," *Production and Inventory Management*, First Quarter 1996, pp. 65-69.

4. See our study "Cellular Manufacturing in the U.S. Industry."

5. For this type of MPC framework, see Vollmann et al., *Manufacturing Planning and Control Systems*, or A. Howard, A. Kochar, and J. Dilworth, "An Objective Approach for Generating the Functional Specification of Manufacturing Planning and Control Systems," *Int. Journal of Operations & Production Management*, Vol. 18, No. 8, 1998, pp. 710–726.

6. See U. Wemmerlöv, *Capacity Management Techniques for Manufacturing Companies with MRP Systems* (Falls Church, VA: American Production and Inventory Control Society, 1984).

7. See Vollmann et al., *Manufacturing Planning and Control Systems.*

8. See Wemmerlöv, *Capacity Management Techniques for Manufacturing Companies with MRP Systems.*

9. See Wemmerlöv, *Capacity Management Techniques for Manufacturing Companies with MRP Systems* for details.

10. For reports on load imbalances, see Wemmerlöv and Hyer, "Cellular Manufacturing in the U.S. Industry: A Survey of Users" and Wemmerlöv and Johnson, "Cellular Manufacturing at 46 User Plants: Implementation Experiences and Performance Improvements."

11. See Wemmerlöv and Hyer, "Cellular Manufacturing in the U.S. Industry: A Survey of Users."

12. See R. F. Conti, "Variable Manning JIT: An Innovative Answer to Team Absenteeism," *Production and Inventory Management*, First Quarter 1996, pp. 24–27.

13. See F. Olorunniwo, "Changes in Production Planning and Control Systems with Implementation of Cellular Manufacturing" and Wemmerlöv and Hyer, "Cellular Manufacturing in the U.S. Industry."

14. See S. A. Melnyk and P. L. Carter, *Production Activity Control* (Homewood, IL: Dow-Jones-Irwin, 1987).

15. The structure for the shop floor control system we use here is influenced by Chapter 5 in P. Higgins, P. Le Roy, and L. Tierney, *Manufacturing Planning and Control: Beyond MRPII* (London: Chapman & Hall, 1996), and by Chapter F1 by J. Riezebos, G. Shambu, and N. C. Suresh in N. C. Suresh and J. M. Kay (eds.), *Group Technology and Cellular Manufacturing* (Boston: Kluwer Academic Publishers, 1998). The activity that manages material transportation has been excluded.

16. It is possible to avoid MRP systems and their backwards scheduling-to-infinite capacity approach. Thus, you can forward schedule to finite capacity all forecasted and confirmed orders, and let the calculated delivery dates fall where they may.

17. O. Wight, "Input/Output Control—A Real Handle on Lead Time," *Production and Inventory Management*, Third Quarter 1970, pp. 9–31.

18. You may recognize these simple and intuitive calculations as illustrations of Little's Law (discussed in Chapter 7).

19. This quote is from Wemmerlöv and Hyer, "Cellular Manufacturing in the U.S. Industry."

20. In our study of cell users (Wemmerlöv and Hyer, "Cellular Manufacturing in the U.S. Industry," p. 1519), we found a clear relationship between number of machines in a cell and the cell's flow dominance. Larger cells tend to have more complex materials flows.

21. Information on Applicon can be found in Vollmann et al., *Manufacturing Planning and Control Systems*, and in *Applicon* (case prepared by E. A. F. Fakhoury and T. E. Vollmann, Boston University, 1987).

22. A planning bill is a bill of materials that is structured to order major modules and components rather than complete products. Planning bills are used in assemble-to-order manufacturing systems.

23. For good introductions to pull systems, see K. Suzaki, *The New Manufacturing Challenge* (New York: The Free Press, 1987), and Y. Monden, *Toyota Production System* (Norcross, GA: Industrial Engineering and Management Press, 1983). It can be noted that Hopp and Spearman use a definition of pull that does not specify removal of inventory. Their definition simply states that "a pull system authorizes the release of work based on system status." See W. J. Hopp and M. L. Spearman, *Factory Physics: The Foundations of Manufacturing Management* (Chicago: Irwin, 1996), p. 317.

24. MRP systems are often characterized as push systems; however, the discussion of push versus pull can be purely semantic and is not always of practical interest.

25. See Monden, *Toyota Production System*, p. 170, Vollmann et al., *Manufacturing Planning and Control Systems*, p. 94, or H. J. Steudel and P. Desruelle, *Manufacturing in the Nineties: How to Become a Mean, Lean, World-Class Competitor* (New York: Van Nostrand Reinhold, 1992), pp. 244–261. The last text contains several numerical examples for the determination of kanban cards.

26. This system is referred to as "FIFO lane" in M. Rother and J. Shook, *Learning to See: Value Stream Mapping to Create Value and Eliminate Muda* (Brookline, MA: The Lean Enterprise Institute, 1999), p. 48. For an interesting application of Kanban lanes at a Spanish mill work, see R. L. Harmon and L. D. Peterson, *Reinventing the Factory* (New York: The Free Press, 1990), pp. 213–214.

27. Long existing in industry and in Japanese literature without a special name, this system has been coined CONWIP (Constant Work In Process). See Hopp and Spearman, *Factory Physics*, p. 317.

28. Although Hopp and Spearman define CONWIP as a system where a new job enters the line as soon as one leaves, their graphical illustrations of CONWIP indicates that it works through removal of items from a buffer at the end of the line. Thus, there may be a difference in how the system boundaries are drawn. The result is a difference in the amount of inventory controlled by the pull system. See Hopp and Spearman, *Factory Physics*, p. 323.

29. See Hopp and Spearman, *Factory Physics*, pp. 444–447.

30. For details, see E. Goldratt and J. Cox, *The Goal* (Croton-on-Hudson: North River Press, 1984), E. Goldratt and R. Fox, *The Race* (Croton-on-Hudson: North River Press, 1986), or M. M. Umble and M. L. Srikanth, *Synchronous Manufacturing* (Cincinnati, OH: South-Western Publishing, 1990).

31. See S. S. Chakravorty, "Robert Bowden Inc.: A Case Study of Cellular Manufacturing and Drum-Buffer-Rope Implementation," *Production and Inventory Management*, Third Quarter 1996, pp. 15–19.

32. For a discussion on how to fit work boundaries to the underlying processes, see Hopp and Spearman, *Factory Physics*, pp. 432–444.

33. For details on the POLCA system, see R. Suri, *Quick Response Manufacturing* (Portland, OR: Productivity Press, 1998), pp. 243–265.

34. See X. Zhou, P. B. Luh, and R. N. Tomastik, "The Performance of a New Material Control and Replenishment System: A Simulation and Comparative Study," *Proceedings of the Quick Response Manufacturing 2000 Conference* (Dearborn: Society of Manufacturing Engineers, 2000, pp. 805–826), and A. Krishnamurthy, R. Suri, and M. Vernon, "Re-examining the Performance of Push, Pull and Hybrid Materials Control Strategies for Multi-Product Flexible Manufacturing Systems," Technical Report (Madison, WI: Center for Quick Response Manufacturing System, December 2000).

35. For details on Waterville TG, Inc., see S. Landry, C. R. Duguay, S. Chaussé, and J.-L. Themens, "Integrating MRP, Kanban and Barcoding Systems to Achieve JIT Procurement," *Production and Inventory Management*, First Quarter 1997, pp. 8–13. Figures 11-22 and 11-23 are from this article.

36. For a detailed treatment of transfer batching in flow shops, see S. Y. Hyun, *The Determination and Evaluation of Transfer Batches for Multi-Stage Flow Shops* (Madison, WI: University of Wisconsin-Madison, unpublished Ph.D. dissertation, 1996). Transfer batches are also discussed in Hopp and Spearman, *Factory Physics*, pp. 289–292.

37. Special kanban cards—signal cards—are used to control lot sizes and their timing. See Suzaki, *The New Manufacturing Challenge*, pp. 158–160.

38. We assume here that a full container is the same as the stipulated lot or batch size. Obviously, we can produce or move containers that are less than full.

39. For an overview of sequencing rules and their performance, see Vollmann et al., *Manufacturing Planning and Control Systems*, pp. 533–537.

40. For a discussion of the impact of setup time reduction through sequencing, see U. Wemmerlöv and A. J. Vakharia, "On the Impact of Family Scheduling Procedures," *IIE Transactions*, Vol. 25, No. 4, 1993, pp. 102–103.

41. For overviews of studies of family sequencing rules, see Chapter F3 in Suresh and Kay, *Group Technology and Cellular Manufacturing*, or Chapter 5 in S. A. Irani (ed.), *Handbook of Cellular Manufacturing Systems* (New York: John Wiley & Sons, 1999).

42. See U. Wemmerlöv, "Fundamental Insights into Part Family Scheduling: The Single Machine Case," *Decision Sciences*, Vol. 23, 1992, No. 3, pp. 565–595.

43. See F. R. Jacobs and D. J. Bragg, "Repetitive Lots: Flow-Time Reductions through Sequencing and Dynamic Batch Sizing," *Decision Sciences*, Vol. 19, 1988, pp. 281–294 and Wemmerlöv, "Fundamental Insights into Part Family Scheduling: The Single Machine Case."

44. For more information on the tractor plant, see M. S. Spencer, "Group Technology at John Deere: Production Planning and Control Issues," Chapter 15 in Suresh and Kay (eds.), *Group Technology and Cellular Manufacturing*.

45. For a similar leapfrogging mechanism in an automotive plant (although based on golf balls), see Suzaki, *The New Manufacturing Challenge*, p. 176. Also see the footnote on p. 316 in Hopp and Spearman, *Factory Physics*.

46. Note, of course, that if you operate a system with very small queues, FCFS may *by default* become the actual sequencing rule (since there are no jobs to choose among).

47. They also write down the date and time batches are started and completed so that lead times can be calculated.

48. See U. Wemmerlöv, "Assemble-to-Order Manufacturing: Implications for Materials Management," *Journal of Operations Management*, Vol. 4, No. 4, 1984, pp. 347–368, and Vollmann et al., *Manufacturing Planning and Control Systems*, Chapter 9. For a detailed discussion of a framework for MPC system and software specification, much more complex than the one we carry out here, see Howard et al., "An Objective Approach for Generating the Functional Specification of Manufacturing Planning and Control Systems."

49. Also see Chapter 5 for a discussion of outsourcing.

50. This quote is from C. Y. Baldwin and K. B. Clark, "Managing in an Age of Modularity," *Harvard Business Review*, September-October 1997, p. 87.

51. Table 11-4 has been influenced in part by U. Wemmerlöv, *Production Planning and Control Procedures for Cellular Manufacturing Systems: Concepts and Practices* (Falls Church, VA: American Production and Inventory Control Society, 1988), and D. C. Steele, W. L. Berry, and S. N. Chapman, "Planning and Control in Multi-Cell Manufacturing," *Decision Sciences*, Vol. 26, No.1, 1995, pp. 1–34.

52. In functional organizations, although machines are organized into departments, centralized planning and control goes down to the machine level. This is unlike cellular structures where the "authority" of the centralized MPC systems most often stops at the cell border. The choice between centralized and decentralized authority over tasks applies not just to MPC activities but also to quality assurance, maintenance, material handling, tooling, and so on. For similar perspectives, see *Production Islands*, published by the AWF Committee for Economical Manufacture (original in German, date and publisher unknown), and Steudel and Desruelle, *Manufacturing in the Nineties*, p. 307.

53. See *Industry Week*, June 8, 1998, p. 38.

54. See Suzaki, *The New Manufacturing Challenge*. Also see R. R. Inman, "Are You Implementing a Pull System by Putting the Cart Before the Horse?," *Production and Inventory Management*, Second Quarter 1999, pp. 67–71.

55. See D. J. Johnson and U. Wemmerlöv, "On the Relative Performance of Functional and Cellular Layouts—An Analysis of the Model-Based Comparative Studies Literature," *Production and Operations Management*, Vol. 5, No. 4, 1996, p. 316.

Chapter 12

1. J. Bratton, "Cellular Manufacturing: Some Human Resource Implications," *The Int. Journal of Human Factors in Manufacturing*, Vol. 3, No. 4, 1993, pp. 381–399. The quotes are from p. 388.

2. J. Dean and S. Snell, "Integrated Manufacturing and Job Design: Moderating Effects of Organizational Inertia," *Academy of Management Journal*, Vol. 34, No. 4, 1991, pp. 776–804. They consider various contextual factors and their relationship to job design in plants with integrated manufacturing. They conclude that "the relationship between integrated manufacturing and job design is anything but automatic" (see p. 795).

3. R. Noe, J. Hollenbeck, B. Gerhart, and P. Wright, *Human Resource Management: Gaining a Competitive Advantage* (Boston, MA: Irwin McGraw-Hill, 2000), p. 127.

4. R. Chase, N. Aquilano, and F. R. Jacobs, *Production and Operations Management: Manufacturing and Services* (Boston, MA: Irwin/McGraw-Hill, 1998), p. 414.

5. M. Beer, B. Spector, P. Lawrence, D. Mills, and R. Walton, *Managing Human Assets* (New York: The Free Press, 1984), p. 10.

6. Information included in Table 12-1 is drawn from M. Campion and G. Medsker, "Job Design," in G. Salvendy (ed.), *Handbook of Industrial Engineering* (New York: John Wiley & Sons, 1992), pp. 848–854.

7. In the research literature, tasks that require hand-offs are called "sequentially interdependent." Tasks that require interaction are called "reciprocally interdependent." See the discussion in G. Stewart,

C. Manz, and H. Sims, *Team Work and Group Dynamics* (New York: John Wiley & Sons, 1999), pp. 32–34.

8. For example, despite significant effort, most apparel assembly has remained stubbornly manual. Efforts to introduce labor-saving automation in many steps of apparel production, and especially in garment assembly, have been unsuccessful. For a great discussion see E. Appelbaum, T. Bailey, P. Berg, and A. Kalleberg, *Manufacturing Advantage: Why High-Performance Work Systems Pay Off* (Ithaca, NY: Cornell University Press, 2000). They note that "of the five stages of production—design and sample making, pattern preparation, cutting, preparation of the parts, and assembly—automation has been important only in pattern making, cutting, and parts preparation. Technological advances in the assembly of garments have been much more limited. The limits to labor-saving automation have proved to be too great to allow domestic producers to overcome wage differentials through the use of technology alone" (see pp. 68–69).

9. See Chase et al., *Production and Operations Management: Manufacturing and Services*, p. 416, and E. McCormick, *Job Analysis: Methods and Applications* (New York: AMACOM, 1979), p. 277.

10. Chase et al., *Production and Operations Management: Manufacturing and Services*, p. 416.

11. Stewart et al., *Team Work and Group Dynamics*, p. 3.

12. The only possible exception are multi-operator rabbit-chase cells where operators have no responsibility for indirect labor tasks. In these cells, individual operators build products start-to-finish and, therefore, the tasks do not require them to work closely with one another.

13. This list of guidelines is adapted from Campion and Medsker, "Job Design," p. 871. The categories are our own.

14. D. Woolson and M. Husar, "Transforming a Plant to Lean in a Large, Traditional Company: Delphi Saginaw Steering Systems, GM," in J. Liker (ed.), *Becoming Lean: Inside Stories of U.S. Manufacturers* (Portland, OR: Productivity Press, 1998), p. 131.

15. R. Magjuka and R. Schmenner, "Cellular Manufacturing and Plant Administration: Some Initial Evidence," *Labor Studies Journal*, Summer 1992, pp. 44–63; see especially p. 51. This finding is consistent with Huber and Brown's observation that with multi-functional operators, fewer job categories may be necessary. See V. Huber and K. Brown, "Human Resource Issues in Cellular Manufacturing: A Sociotechnical Analysis," *Journal of Operations Management*, Vol. 10, No. 1, 1991, pp. 138–159; see especially p. 144.

16. M. Hequet, "Ergomania," *Training*, May 1995, pp. 45–50.

17. Appelbaum et al., *Manufacturing Advantage: Why High-Performance Work Systems Pay Off*, pp. 78–79.

18. See Chapter 13 for a discussion of KSAOs and their role in selection and training of cell employees. Also see H. Heneman, T. Judge, and R. Heneman, *Staffing Organizations* (Boston, MA: Irwin McGraw-Hill, 2000), pp. 168–173, for an in-depth discussion of KSAOs, and pp. 155–209 for information on job analysis.

19. For an excellent discussion of socio-technical systems theory, see W. Pasmore, *Designing Effective Organizations: The Sociotechnical Systems Perspective* (New York: John Wiley and Sons, 1988).

20. Stewart et al., *Team Work and Group Dynamics*, p. 3.

21. As noted above (see endnote 12) multi-operator rabbit-chase cells where operators have no responsibility for indirect labor tasks do not fit the definition of a team.

22. Stewart et al., *Team Work and Group Dynamics*, pp. 34–36, categorize teams as externally led, self-managing, and self leading.

23. This definition of "self-managed" comes from J. Hackman, "Creating More Effective Work Groups in Organizations," in J. Hackman (ed.), *Groups That Work (and Those That Don't)* (San Francisco, CA: Jossey-Bass, 1990), p. 484.

24. The discussion of advantages in this section is drawn from Campion and Medsker, "Job Design," pp. 868–870.

25. Again, for more information see Campion and Medsker, "Job Design," p. 868. Citing ample research literature, they note that "Heterogeneity of abilities and personalities has been found to have a generally positive effect on group performance, especially when task requirements are diverse."

26. E. Lawler, *The Ultimate Advantage: Creating the High-Involvement Organization* (San Francisco, CA: Jossey-Bass, 1992), p. 98.

27. See the discussion of environmental contingencies in D. Yeatts and C. Hyten, *High-Performing Self-Managed Work Teams: A Comparison of Theory to Practice* (Thousand Oaks, CA: Sage, 1998), pp. 22–23.

28. This study is reported in Appelbaum et al., *Manufacturing Advantage: Why High-Performance Work Systems Pay Off*.

29. See Campion and Medsker, "Job Design," p. 872.

30. P. Yetton and P. Bottger, "The Relationship Among Group Size, Member Abilities, Social Decision Schemes and Performance," *Organization Behavior and Human Performance*, October 1983, pp. 145–159.

31. J. Katzenbach and D. Smith, *The Wisdom of Teams: Creating the High-Performance Organization* (New York: HarperCollins, 1993), pp. 45–47.

32. R. Moreland and J. Levine, "The Composition of Small Groups," in E. Lawler, B. Markovsky, C. Ridgeway, H. Walker (eds.), *Advances in Group Processes*, Vol. 9 (Greenwich, CT: JAI Press, 1992), pp. 237–280.

33. Campion and Medsker, "Job Design," p. 868 and pp. 870–871.

34. L. Nyman (ed.), *Making Manufacturing Cells Work* (Dearborn, MI: Society of Manufacturing Engineers, 1992), p. 44.

35. Magjuka and Schmenner, "Cellular Manufacturing and Plant Administration: Some Initial Evidence," pp. 51–52.

36. See the following for background reading on supervisors and changing roles: J. Klein, "The Human Costs of Manufacturing Reform," *Harvard Business Review*, Vol. 67, No. 2, 1989, pp. 60–66; and K. Suzaki, *The New Shop Floor Management: Empowering People for Continuous Improvement* (New York: The Free Press, 1993).

Chapter 13

1. W. Borman, N. Peterson, and T. Russell, "Selection, Training, and Development of Personnel," in G. Salvendy (ed.), *Handbook of Industrial Engineering* (New York: John Wiley & Sons, 1992), p. 882.

2. We have witnessed several implementations that were stymied by inattention to worker issues. For examples, see the opening pages of N. Hyer, K. Brown, and S. Zimmerman, "A Socio-Technical Systems Approach to Cell Design: Case Study and Analysis," *Journal of Operations Management*, Vol. 17, No. 2, 1999, pp. 179–203. For other examples see the opening pages of V. Huber and K. Brown, "Human Resource Issues in Cellular Manufacturing: A Sociotechnical Analysis," *Journal of Operations Management*, Vol. 10, No. 1, 1991, pp. 138–159.

3. Recent surveys reveal that most cells are created in existing facilities. See U. Wemmerlöv and D. Johnson, "Cellular Manufacturing at 46 User Plants: Implementation Experiences and Performance Improvements," *Int. Journal of Production Research*, Vol. 35, No. 1, 1997, pp. 29–49; and U. Wemmerlöv and N. Hyer, "Cellular Manufacturing in the U.S. Industry: A Survey of Users," *Int. Journal of Production Research*, Vol. 27, No. 9, 1989, pp. 1511–1530.

4. For a discussion of KSAOs see Borman et al., "Selection, Training, and Development of Personnel," pp. 883–884; H. Heneman, T. Judge and R. Heneman, *Staffing Organizations* (Boston, MA: Irwin McGraw-Hill, 2000), pp. 168–173; R. Noe, J. Hollenbeck, B. Gerhart, and P. Wright, *Human Resource Management: Gaining a Competitive Advantage* (Boston, MA: Irwin McGraw-Hill, 2000), p. 119; and R. Gatewood and H. Feild, *Human Resource Selection* (Fort Worth, TX: The Dryden Press, 1998), pp. 342–345.

5. See Borman et al., "Selection, Training, and Development of Personnel," p. 883. There is a well-developed body of literature on job analysis. The steps to follow, ways of identifying job tasks, and the appropriate process for translating job tasks into specific knowledge, skill, ability, and other characteristics are well articulated. Other good references include E. McCormick, *Job Analysis: Methods and Applications* (New York: AMACOM, 1979) and Heneman et al., *Staffing Organizations*, pp. 155–209.

6. Heneman et al., *Staffing Organizations*, p. 162 and pp. 174–176. Also see Noe et al., *Human Resource Management: Gaining a Competitive Advantage*, p. 119.

7. When individual jobs have been enriched or enlarged—terms we describe in detail in Chapter 12 and Appendix F—job responsibilities change, as do the skills and abilities required to perform them. Job enlargement requires workers to perform a wider array of production tasks. Job enrichment, on the other hand, will require operators to make decisions and solve problems. In the presence of teamwork, operators will also need interpersonal skills. Finally, in situations where the cell is self-managing, administrative and management skills will be important. There are a number of frameworks covering the skills and abilities needed in these production settings. Our framework is loosely based on ideas presented in D. Yeatts and C. Hyten, *High-Performing Self-Managed Work Teams: A Comparison of Theory and Practice* (Thousand Oaks, CA: Sage, 1998), pp. 173–174; and E. Lawler, *The Ultimate Advantage: Creating the High-Involvement Organization* (San Francisco: Jossey-Bass, 1992), pp. 93–94. These two sources focus on the types of training that will be required in team-based environments. G. Stewart, C. Manz, and H. Sims, *Team Work and Group Dynamics* (New York: John

Wiley & Sons, 1999), pp. 38–42, offers a third framework focusing on the "task and socioemotional roles" that team members play and the implications this has for selection. Technical skills, interpersonal skills, and self-management skills (e.g., self-goal setting) figure prominently in their framework.

8. R. Cardy and G. Stewart, "Quality and Teams: Implications for HRM Theory and Research," in *Advances in Management of Organizational Quality*, Vol. 3. (Greenwich, CT: JAI Press, 1998), pp. 89–120. The authors note that for team-based organizations, "Hiring someone because of his or her fit with a narrowly defined position can thus be counterproductive in that it fails to account for potential contributions across other tasks and over time" (p. 100).

9. This definition of interpersonal skills is from Yeatts and Hyten, *High-Performing Self-Managed Work Teams: A Comparison of Theory and Practice*, p. 174.

10. M. Stevens, and M. Campion, "The Knowledge, Skill, and Ability Requirements for Teamwork: Implications for Human Resource Management," *Journal of Management*, Vol. 20, 1994, pp. 503–530. These researchers identify 14 KSA's necessary for teamwork, which they group into five categories: conflict resolution, collaborative problem solving, communication, goal setting and performance management, and planning and task coordination. Interpersonal skills figure prominently in many of these KSA categories. Most of those who study teamwork acknowledge the importance of interpersonal skills in effectiveness.

11. For various methods for employee selection, see Borman et al., "Selection, Training, and Development of Personnel," pp. 884–889, and Noe et al., *Human Resource Management: Gaining a Competitive Advantage*, pp. 192–201.

12. There is a significant body of knowledge about selection test reliability, validity, generalizability, utility and legality, the most commonly noted criteria. We refer to specific studies in our discussion of individual methods. Two excellent resources, which are generally regarded as the leading texts, are Heneman et al., *Staffing Organizations*, and Gatewood and Feild, *Human Resource Selection*. The complexity of this entire area underscores the importance of partnering with your HR specialist in the design and administration of the selection process.

13. Noe et al., *Human Resource Management: Gaining a Competitive Advantage*, pp. 188–190.

14. It is important to make some estimates of how much the company can expect to gain by hiring employees that either perform better or are a better fit to the job. This estimate should be used as the upper bound for costs associated with the selection system. There are formulas available to aid in making these estimates. Your human resource representative should be able to provide you these formulas. In a very general sense, the lesser expensive selection methods (all else equal) are going to aid in creating a selection system that has a high rate of return—that is, greater utility—for your company.

15. Recent research suggests that interviews are "notoriously poor" as a selection method. For a good discussion, see Borman et al., "Selection, Training, and Development of Personnel," p. 888. See also Noe et al., *Human Resource Management: Gaining a Competitive Advantage*, pp. 192–193.

16. Based on recent research, Gatewood and Feild, *Human Resource Selection*, p. 479, conclude that "designed appropriately and used correctly, the interview is good!"

17. Noe et al., *Human Resource Management: Gaining a Competitive Advantage*, p. 193. Note that these authors suggest a "small number" of goals. We suggest 3 or 4.

18. Heneman et al., *Staffing Organizations*, p. 459. They also discuss the issue of fit. Also see Gatewood and Feild, *Human Resource Selection*, pp. 482–483.

19. Definition of values is from M. Harris and R. Eder, "The State of Employment Interview Practice: Commentary and Extension," in R. Eder and M. Harris (eds.), *The Employment Interview Handbook* (Thousand Oaks, CA: Sage, 1999), p. 372.

20. J. Hunter and R. Hunter, "Validity and Utility of Alternative Predictors of Job Performance," *Psychological Bulletin 96*, Vol. 96, No. 1, 1984, pp. 72–98.

21. Noe et al., *Human Resource Management: Gaining a Competitive Advantage*, p. 194

22. See J. Hogan, "Physical Abilities" in M. Dunnette and L. Hough (eds.), *Handbook of Industrial & Organizational Psychology*, Vol. 2 (Palo Alto, CA: Consulting Psychologists Press, 1991), pp. 753–831.

23. For a good review see Hogan, "Physical Abilities." For a short review, see Gatewood and Feild, *Human Resource Selection*, pp. 533–537.

24. See Noe et al., *Human Resource Management: Gaining a Competitive Advantage*, p. 196.

25. See Gatewood and Feild, *Human Resource Selection*, pp. 525–529 for a review. Also see Heneman et al., *Staffing Organizations*, pp. 432–439 for information on tests, their costs, and sources.

26. For a review see J. Hunter, "Cognitive Ability, Cognitive Aptitudes, Job Knowledge, and Job Performance," *Journal of Vocational Behavior*, Vol. 29, 1986, pp. 340–362.

27. Heneman et al., *Staffing Organizations*, p. 435. Their conclusion is based on research findings of M. Ree and J. Earles, "Predicting Training Success: Not Much More Than g," *Personnel Psychology*, Vol. 44, 1991, pp. 321–332.

28. See Noe et al., *Human Resource Management: Gaining a Competitive Advantage*, p. 196 for a discussion and further references.

29. Heneman et al., *Staffing Organizations*, p. 427. See p. 428 for information on common tests and their sources. Definitions in Table 13-4 are adapted from Heneman et al., *Staffing Organizations*, pp. 428–429; Gatewood and Feild, *Human Resource Selection*, p. 564; and Noe et al., *Human Resource Management: Gaining a Competitive Advantage*, p. 196.

30. You may be familiar with an additional personality inventory, the Myers-Briggs Type Indicator (MBTI), which is frequently used by organizations for leadership training and work group development. However, MBTI is not recommended as a selection test. The scoring system used by this inventory precludes the calculation of meaningful validity coefficients between MBTI scales and job performance measures. See Gatewood and Feild, *Human Resource Selection*, pp. 565–567 for an in-depth discussion.

31. Quote is from Heneman et al., *Staffing Organizations*, p. 429 based on research findings in M. Barrick and M. Mount, "The Big Five Personality Dimensions and Job Performance: A Meta Analysis," *Personnel Psychology*, Vol. 44, 1991, pp. 1–26. Noe et al., *Human Resource Management: Gaining a Competitive Advantage*, p. 196 also note that research has consistently shown that "Conscientiousness is one of the few factors that displays any validity across a number of different job categories, and many real world managers rate this as one of the most important characteristics they look for in employees."

32. M. Barrick, G. Stewart, M. Neubert, and M. Mount, "Relating Member Ability and Personality to Work Team Processes and Team Effectiveness," *Journal of Applied Psychology*, Vol. 83, 1998, pp. 377–391. Also see the discussion in Stewart et al., *Team Work and Group Dynamics*, pp. 40–42.

33. Stewart et al., *Team Work and Group Dynamics*, pp. 41–42.

34. See Noe at al., *Human Resource Management: Gaining a Competitive Advantage*, p. 197.

35. See Heneman et al., *Staffing Organizations*, p. 431 for a discussion of the limitations of personality inventories.

36. See Noe et al., *Human Resource Management: Gaining a Competitive Advantage*, p. 197.

37. J. Hunter and R. Hunter, "Validity and Utility of Alternative Predictors of Job Performance."

38. See Heneman et al., *Staffing Organizations*, pp. 445–446 for a discussion of the advantages and costs of work-sample testing. Also see Gatewood and Feild, *Human Resource Selection*, pp. 588–589.

39. See Heneman et al., *Staffing Organizations*, p. 508 for examples of peer assessment methods.

40. Heneman et al., *Staffing Organizations*, p. 517, observe that: "Between two-thirds and four-fifths of union contracts stipulate that seniority be considered in promotion decisions, and about 50% mandate that it be the determining factor. In policy, nonunion organizations claim to place less weight on seniority than other factors in making advancement decisions. In practice, however, at least one study showed that regardless of the wording in policy statements, heavy emphasis is still placed on seniority in nonunion settings."

41. See Heneman et al., *Staffing Organizations*, pp. 516–518 for a review of the literature on seniority and experience in selection decisions.

42. For an excellent discussion see Chapter 6 "Strategies for Selection Decision Making" in Gatewood and Feild, *Human Resource Selection*, pp. 215–241. Also, for a good review see B. Kleinmutz, "Why We Still Use Our Heads Instead of Formulas: Toward an Integrative Approach," *Psychological Bulletin*, Vol. 107, No. 3, 1990, pp. 296–310.

43. Again, see Gatewood and Feild, *Human Resource Selection*, pp. 220–232, for an excellent discussion of various mechanisms for combining results.

44. For a review of research on the superiority of statistical combinations versus pure judgement, see the discussion in Gatewood and Feild, *Human Resource Selection,* pp. 219–220.

45. Wemmerlöv and Hyer, "Cellular Manufacturing in the U.S. Industry: A Survey of Users," p. 1523.

46. J. Hassard and S. Proctor, "Manufacturing Change: Introducing Cellular Production in Two British Factories," *Personnel Review*, Vol. 20, No. 4, 1991, pp. 15–24.

47. Anonymous, "Organisational Change in Bonas Machine Company," *IRS Employment Review*, Vol. 610, June 1996, pp. 5–10. Quoted phrases are from page 9.

48. See Heneman et al., *Staffing Organizations*, pp. 523–528 for a good discussion of assessment centers. See also Noe et al., *Human Resource Management: Gaining a Competitive Advantage*, pp. 197–198.

49. Fitzgerald Battery, for example, uses assessment centers to select new employees who will subsequently join a cell. "An evaluation team, consisting of one manager, one coordinator, one team leader,

and two members of different teams, observed candidates during interpersonal exercises and provided ratings and final judgments." Stewart et al., *Team Work and Group Dynamics*, p. 51.

50. See Heneman et al., *Staffing Organizations*, p. 527.

51. D. Woolson and M. Husar, "Transforming a Plant to Lean in a Large, Traditional Company: Delphi Saginaw Steering Systems, GM," in J. Liker (ed.), *Becoming Lean* (Portland, OR: Productivity Press, 1998), pp. 120–159. The description of supervisory roles and selection appears on pp. 131–133.

52. Woolson and Husar, "Transforming a Plant to Lean in a Large, Traditional Company: Delphi Saginaw Steering Systems, GM," pp. 132–133.

53. Yeatts and Hyten, *High-Performing Self-Managed Work Teams: A Comparison of Theory and Practice*, p. 275.

54. Stewart et al., *Team Work and Group Dynamics*, p. 50.

55. Yeatts and Hyten, *High-Performing Self-Managed Work Teams: A Comparison of Theory and Practice*, pp. 304–305.

56. Noe et al., *Human Resource Management: Gaining a Competitive Advantage*, p. 208.

57. P. Blanchard and J. Thacker, *Effective Training: Systems, Strategies, and Practice* (Englewood Cliffs, NJ: Prentice Hall, 1999), p. 9.

58. Huber and Brown, "Human Resource Issues in Cellular Manufacturing: A Sociotechnical Analysis," p. 146. They note that "new responsibilities associated with the management of information, including the interpretation of statistical process control charts, review of documents, and report writing, are likely to make this training essential" for cell operators.

59. J. Bratton, "Cellular Manufacturing: Some Human Resource Implications," *The Int. Journal of Human Factors in Manufacturing*, Vol. 3, No. 4, 1993, pp. 381–399. Quote is from pp. 392–393.

60. See Borman et al., "Selection, Training, and Development of Personnel," p. 904, and K. Brown and T. Mitchell, "A Comparison of Just-in-Time and Batch Manufacturing: The Role of Performance Obstacles," *Academy of Management Journal*, Vol. 34, No. 4, 1991, pp. 907–917. See especially p. 914.

61. M. Campion and G. Medsker, "Job Design," in G. Salvendy (ed.), *Handbook of Industrial Engineering* (New York: John Wiley & Sons, 1992), pp. 868–870.

62. See, for example, E. Molleman and J. Slomp, "Functional Flexibility and Team Performance," *Int. Journal of Production Research*, Vol. 37, No. 8, 1999, pp. 1837–1858.

63. Borman et al., "Selection, Training, and Development of Personnel," p. 902. They reference and quote J. Hinrichs, "Personnel Training," in M. Dunnette (ed.), *Handbook of Industrial and Organizational Psychology, Third Edition* (Chicago, IL: Rand McNally, 1976), p. 842.

64. These guidelines are based, in part, on a list presented in Borman et al., "Selection, Training, and Development of Personnel," pp. 902 and 906.

65. Borman et al., "Selection, Training, and Development of Personnel," pp. 906–907.

66. For lots of ideas on methods to evaluate training see J. Phillips, *Handbook of Training Evaluation and Measurement Methods* (Houston, TX: Gulf Publishing, 1983). Also see Blanchard and Thacker, *Effective Training: Systems, Strategies, and Practices*, pp. 221–274, for a good overview.

67. Huber and Brown, "Human Resource Issues in Cellular Manufacturing: A Sociotechnical Analysis," p. 150.

68. See Wemmerlöv and Hyer, "Cellular Manufacturing in the U.S. Industry: A Survey of Users," pp. 1527–1529, for a discussion and some lessons learned about the importance of training for cell implementation.

69. Anonymous, "Organisational Change in Bonas Machine Company," p. 10.

Chapter 14

1. According to "Employer Spending for Benefits," *Employee Benefit News Benefits Sourcebook 8* (United States: Securities Data Publishing, 1999), total benefits represent about 20 percent of total compensation in the United States.

2. B. Gerhart and G. Milkovich, "Employee Compensation: Research and Practice," in M. Dunnette and L. Hough (eds.), *Handbook of Industrial & Organizational Psychology*, Second Edition, Vol. 3 (Palo Alto, CA: Consulting Psychologists Press, 1992), pp. 481–569; see especially p. 482.

3. R. Noe, J. Hollenbeck, B. Gerhart, and P. Wright, *Human Resource Management: Gaining a Competitive Advantage* (Boston, MA: Irwin McGraw-Hill, 2000), pp. 441–442

4. See, for example, S. Snell and J. Dean, "Strategic Compensation for Integrated Manufacturing: The Moderating Effects of Jobs and Organizational Inertia," *Academy of Management Journal*, Vol. 37, No. 5, 1994, pp. 1109–1140.

5. See E. Lawler, *Rewarding Excellence: Pay Strategies for the New Economy* (San Francisco, CA: Jossey-Bass, 2000) for a discussion of the need to move toward reward systems appropriate for interdependent work. See especially, pp. 28–33.

6. S. Rynes, "Compensation Strategies for Recruiting," *Topics in Total Compensation*, Vol. 2, 1987, pp. 185–196. This author notes that "compensation systems are capable of attracting (or repelling) the right kinds of people because they communicate so much about an organization's philosophy, values, and practices," p. 190. Further, G. Milkovich and J. Newman, *Compensation* (Chicago, IL: Irwin, 1996), present ample research evidence to support the notion that "level of pay and pay system characteristics influence a job candidate's decision to join a firm" (see pp. 310–312). They also note recent research suggesting that "job candidates look for organizations with reward systems that fit their personalities." From their review of the research literature, they also conclude, "pay can be a factor in decisions to stay or leave," underscoring the connection between pay and the ability to retain employees.

7. Lawler, *Rewarding Excellence: Pay Strategies for the New Economy*, pp. 134–135.

8. This set of characteristics is based on our own work with firms and a review of the literature on compensation. See in particular, D. Yeatts and C. Hyten, *High-Performing Self-Managed Work Teams: A Comparison of Theory to Practice* (Thousand Oaks, CA: Sage, 1998), pp. 142–156; Milkovich and Newman, *Compensation*, pp. 11–13; Lawler, *Rewarding Excellence: Pay Strategies for the New Economy*, pp. 40–57.

9. B. Gerhart, "Designing Rewards Systems: Balancing Results and Behavior," in C. Fay (ed.), *The Executive Handbook on Compensation* (New York: The Free Press, 2001), p. 214.

10. G. Milkovich and A. Wigdor, *Pay for Performance* (Washington, D.C.: National Academy Press, 1991), p. 54.

11. This type of measurement falls under the "resource" category in our Process Performance Measurement Matrix described in Chapter 9.

12. S. Mohrman, S. Cohen, and A. Mohrman, *Designing Team-Based Organizations: New Forms for Knowledge Work* (San Francisco, CA: Jossey-Bass, 1995), p. 230.

13. See E. Lawler, *The Ultimate Advantage: Creating the High-Involvement Organization* (San Francisco, CA: Jossey-Bass, 1992); B. Gerber, "The Bugaboo of Team Pay," *Training*, Vol. 32, No. 8, 1995, pp. 25–34, and the discussion in Yeatts and Hyten, *High-Performing Self-Managed Work Teams: A Comparison of Theory to Practice*, pp. 151–152. Finally, Snell and Dean, "Strategic Compensation for Integrated Manufacturing: The Moderating Effects of Jobs and Organizational Inertia," conclude that "as plants implement various aspects of integrated manufacturing, there may be a simultaneous need for individual and collective effort," p. 1132.

14. Gerhart and Milkovich, "Employee Compensation: Research and Practice," p. 521.

15. The term for this is "line of sight." See E. Lawler, *High-Involvement Management* (San Francisco, CA: Jossey-Bass, 1986); J. McAdams, *The Reward Plan Advantage: A Manager's Guide to Improving Business Performance Through People* (San Francisco, CA: Jossey-Bass, 1996); Yeatts and Hyten, *High-Performing Self-Managed Work Teams: A Comparison of Theory to Practice*, p. 152; R. Heneman, G. Ledford, M. Gresham, "The Changing Nature of Work and Its Effects on Compensation Design and Delivery," in S. Rynes and B. Gerhart (eds.), *Compensation in Organizations: Current Research and Practice* (San Francisco, CA: Jossey-Bass, 2000), p. 209.

16. See the discussion in Yeatts and Hyten, *High-Performing Self-Managed Work Teams: A Comparison of Theory to Practice*, p. 152.

17. T. Zenger and C. Marshall, "Group-Based Plans: An Empirical Test of the Relationships Among Size, Incentive, Intensity, and Performance," *Academy of Management Journal-Best Paper Proceedings* (New Brunswick, NJ: Academy of Management, 1995), pp. 161–165.

18. Noe et al., *Human Resource Management: Gaining a Competitive Advantage*, pp. 388–389. Also see Milkovich and Newman, *Compensation*, pp. 61–63.

19. Equity theory maintains that perceived inequity on the part of an employee may cause that employee to take action to restore equity. Some of these ways may be "counterproductive" (for example, not working as hard, leaving the organization, or stealing from the organization). See the discussion in Noe et al., *Human Resource Management: Gaining a Competitive Advantage*, pp. 389–390. Also see the discussion in Milkovich and Newman, *Compensation*, pp. 310–312.

20. Milkovich and Newman, *Compensation*, p. 62. A fourth characteristic related to employee perceptions of fairness in pay systems is the presence of an appeals procedure.

21. See Milkovich and Newman, *Compensation*, pp. 12 and 62 for a discussion of procedural justice and additional sources. Also see W. Kim and R. Mauborgne, "Fair Process: Managing in the Knowledge Economy," *Harvard Business Review*, Vol. 75, No. 4, July-August 1997, pp. 65–75.

22. See the excellent discussion of variable pay in Heneman et al., "The Changing Nature of Work and Its Effects on Compensation Design and Delivery," pp. 219–225.

23. "Broadbanding" and "delayering" are terms used to refer to the general practice of establishing fewer, broader job classes. For a discussion see R. Cardy and G. Stewart, "Quality and Teams: Implications for HRM Theory and Research," in *Advances in the Management of Organizational Quality*, Vol. 3 (Greenwich, CT: JAI Press, 1998), pp. 89–120. Broadbanding is discussed on p. 113. See also Noe et al., *Human Resource Management: Gaining a Competitive Advantage*, pp. 404–405.

24. D. Woolson and M. Husar, "Transforming a Plant to Lean in a Large, Traditional Company: Delphi Saginaw Steering Systems, GM," in J. Liker (ed.), *Becoming Lean: Inside Stories of U.S. Manufacturers* (Portland, OR: Productivity Press, 1998), p. 131.

25. N. Harvey, *The Socio-Technical Implementation of Cellular Manufacturing in American and German Metal Working Firms* (Madison, WI: Unpublished Ph.D. dissertation, University of Wisconsin-Madison, 1993), p. 283.

26. See Milkovich and Newman, *Compensation*, pp. 325–332 for a discussion and examples.

27. U. Wemmerlöv and N. Hyer, "Cellular Manufacturing in the U.S. Industry: A Survey of Users," *Int. Journal of Production Research*, Vol. 27, No. 9, 1989, p. 1524.

28. Wemmerlöv and Hyer, "Cellular Manufacturing in the U.S. Industry: A Survey of Users," p. 1524.

29. See R. Walton and G. Susman, "People Policies for New Machines," *Harvard Business Review*, Vol. 65, No. 2, 1987, pp. 98–106; B. Wilkinson, *The Shopfloor Politics of New Technology* (London: Heinemann, 1983); and S. Zuboff, *In the Age of the Smart Machine* (New York: Basic Books, 1988). Snell and Dean, "Strategic Compensation for Integrated Manufacturing: The Moderating Effects of Jobs and Organizational Inertia," p. 1116, conclude that "the differentiation between managers as thinkers and workers as doers is severely diminished, if not eliminated entirely, in the integrated manufacturing paradigm."

30. Snell and Dean, "Strategic Compensation for Integrated Manufacturing: The Moderating Effects of Jobs and Organizational Inertia," p. 1116, and A. Majchrzak, *The Human Side of Factory Automation* (San Francisco, CA: Jossey-Bass, 1988).

31. Wemmerlöv and Hyer, "Cellular Manufacturing in the U.S. Industry: A Survey of Users," p. 1524.

32. Gerhart, "Designing Rewards Systems: Balancing Results and Behavior," p. 219.

33. E. Lawler, *Pay and Organizational Effectiveness: A Psychological View* (New York: McGraw Hill, 1971). It can be noted, by the way, that in order to make clearer distinctions between employees, companies have increasingly started to rely on forced distributions ("grading on a scale") of their professional employees. However, this system has also been perceived as unfair and has led to several lawsuits of companies such as Ford, Microsoft, and Conoco. See R. Abelson, "Companies Turn to Grades, and Employees Go to Court," *The New York Times*, March 19, 2001, p. A1.

34. Gerhart and Milkovich, "Employee Compensation: Research and Practice," p. 505.

35. P. Gavejian, "Compensation: Today and Tomorrow," *HRFOCUS*, November 1998, pp. S5–S6. The study also reported that 2.7 percent of the 406 firms responding currently were implementing skill-based pay, while another 17.3 percent were "considering" it. Other studies report a higher percentage. For example, Heneman et al., "The Changing Nature of Work and Its Effects on Compensation Design and Delivery," p. 213, report that "almost two thirds" of Fortune 1000 companies use skill-based pay.

36. Heneman et al., "The Changing Nature of Work and Its Effects on Compensation Design and Delivery," p. 213. For more information on incidence of skill-based pay, see E. Lawler, S. Mohrman, and G. Ledford, *Strategies for High Performing Organizations* (San Francisco, CA: Jossey-Bass, 1998).

37. B. Murray and B. Gerhart, "An Empirical Analysis of a Skill-Based Pay Program and Plant Performance Outcomes," *Academy of Management Journal*, Vol. 41, No. 1, 1998, pp. 68–78.

38. For examples of case studies see K. Parent and C. Weber, "Case Study: Does Paying for Knowledge Pay Off?" *Compensation and Benefits Review*, Vol. 26, No. 5, 1994, pp. 44–50; and B. Johnson and H. Ray, "Employee Developed Pay System Increases Productivity," *Personnel Journal*, Vol. 72, No. 11, 1993, pp. 112–118. General descriptions of skill-based pay systems can be found in, for example, E. Lawler and G. Ledford, "Skill-Based Pay: A Concept That's Catching On," *Management Review*, Vol. 76, No. 2, 1987, pp. 46–51; R. Shenberger, "Still Paying for Hours on the Job? Think Again," *Journal for Quality and Participation*, Vol. 18, 1995, pp. 88–91; and H. Tosi and L. Tosi, "What Managers Need to Know about Knowledge-Based Pay," *Organizational Dynamics*, Vol. 14, No. 3, 1986, pp. 52–64. For examples of surveys of personnel managers see, for example, N. Gupta, G. Jenkins, and W. Curington, "Paying for Knowledge: Myths and Realities," *National Productivity Review*, Vol. 5, 1986, pp. 107–123; and G. Jenkins, G. Ledford, N. Gupta and D. Doty, *Skill-Based Pay: Practices, Payoffs, Pitfalls and Prescriptions* (Phoenix, AZ: American Compensation

Association, 1992). Murray and Gerhart, "An Empirical Analysis of a Skill-Based Pay Program and Plant Performance Outcomes," p. 68, note that prior research offers "some support" for the benefits of skill-based pay.

39. Murray and Gerhart, "An Empirical Analysis of a Skill-Based Pay Program and Plant Performance Outcomes."

40. Yeatts and Hyten, *High-Performing Self-Managed Work Teams: A Comparison of Theory to Practice*, p. 163.

41. K. Turley, "First Ask 'Why?' Then Ask 'How?'" *Target*, Vol. 11, No. 1, 1995, pp. 41–45. The article describes compensation policies used for XEL's 12 "self-directed" production work teams. While not called cells in the article, these production work teams fit our definitional criteria for cells.

42. E. Lawler, G. Ledford, and L. Chang, "Who Uses Skill-Based Pay and Why," *Compensation and Benefits Review*, Vol. 25, No. 2, 1993, pp. 22–26.

43. At XEL Communications one manager notes that skill-based pay created an "entitlement mentality. If you want me to do X, then you must pay me for it." See Turley, "First Ask 'Why?' Then Ask 'How?'" p. 43.

44. Heneman et al., "The Changing Nature of Work and Its Effects on Compensation Design and Delivery," p. 217.

45. Milkovich and Newman, *Compensation*, p. 679.

46. Gavejian, "Compensation: Today and Tomorrow," p. S6.

47. Snell and Dean, "Strategic Compensation for Integrated Manufacturing: The Moderating Effects of Jobs and Organizational Inertia," pp. 1131 and 1133.

48. B. Saven, "Motivation—The Single Most Important Factor for Improved Manufacturing Performance: A Case Study," (Linköping, Sweden: Linköping Institute of Technology, Working Paper, 1990).

49. Heneman et al., "The Changing Nature of Work and Its Effects on Compensation Design and Delivery," p. 219. These authors estimate that 45 percent of large U.S. companies have gainsharing programs in place. This number seems quite high and may overstate the incidence of such programs.

50. Gerhart and Milkovich, "Employee Compensation: Research and Practice," p. 528.

51. Noe et al., *Human Resource Management: Gaining a Competitive Advantage,* p. 435.

52. This list of features is adapted from Yeatts and Hyten, *High-Performing Self-Managed Work Teams: A Comparison of Theory to Practice*, pp. 166–170.

53. Yeatts and Hyten, *High-Performing Self-Managed Work Teams: A Comparison of Theory to Practice*, p. 168.

54. For some specific examples of gainsharing formulas see J. Belcher, *Gainsharing* (Houston, TX: Gulf, 1991).

55. See the excellent summary of research in Gerhart and Milkovich, "Employee Compensation: Research and Practice," pp. 528–530. See also Gerhart, "Designing Rewards Systems: Balancing Results and Behavior," pp. 220–221.

56. Milkovich and Newman, *Compensation*, p. 314.

57. According to Heneman et al., "The Changing Nature of Work and Its Effects on Compensation Design and Delivery," p. 219, approximately 69% of large U.S. companies have profit sharing programs in place. We consider this estimate to be on the high side and probably includes deferred profits going into retirement accounts. Further, this estimate does not indicate the spread of profit sharing inside firms: such programs may be limited to only a few employees.

58. See the discussion in Gerhart and Milkovich, "Employee Compensation: Research and Practice," pp. 525–528.

59. Turley, "First Ask 'Why?' Then Ask 'How?'" p. 42.

60. C. Karlsson and P. Åhlström, "Change Processes Toward Lean Production: The Role of the Remuneration System," *Int. Journal of Operations & Production Management*, Vol. 15, No. 11, 1995, pp. 80–99. Our Figure 14-5 is based on information contained in Figure 8 on p. 89 of this article.

61. Saven, "Motivation—The Single Most Important Factor for Improved Manufacturing Performance: A Case Study."

62. Again, see the discussion in Snell and Dean, "Strategic Compensation for Integrated Manufacturing: The Moderating Effects of Jobs and Organizational Inertia," pp. 1118–1120.

63. Yeatts and Hyten, *High-Performing Self-Managed Work Teams: A Comparison of Theory to Practice*, p. 144. They summarize recent research in this area and conclude that organizations "have been slow to change either their performance measurement systems or their reward systems to match the needs of their new team environment."

64. R. Pullen, "A Survey of Cellular Manufacturing Cells," *Production Engineer*, Vol. 55, 1976, pp. 451–454.

65. For a discussion and additional citations, see Noe et al., *Human Resource Management: Gaining a Competitive Advantage*, pp. 401–404 and 439–441.

66. See Kim and Mauborgne, "Fair Process: Managing in the Knowledge Economy," pp. 65–75.

67. For a nice discussion of recognition and reward systems for team-based systems, see Yeatts and Hyten, *High-Performing Self-Managed Work Teams: A Comparison of Theory to Practice*, pp. 157–160.

68. Yeatts and Hyten, *High-Performing Self-Managed Work Teams: A Comparison of Theory to Practice*, p. 158.

69. Again, see Yeatts and Hyten, *High-Performing Self-Managed Work Teams: A Comparison of Theory to Practice*, pp. 157–160.

70. Personal correspondence and plant tour notes from Karen Brown, University of Washington-Bothell, 1999.

Chapter 15

1. This case is described in detail in N. Hyer, K. Brown, and S. Zimmerman, "A Socio-Technical Systems Approach to Cell Design: Case Study and Analysis," *Journal of Operations Management*, Vol. 17, 1999, pp. 179–203. We also discuss the case in Chapter 4 of this book.

2. L. Nyman (ed.), *Making Manufacturing Cells Work* (Dearborn, MI: Society of Manufacturing Engineers, 1992), p. 285.

3. We have based this model on J. Kotter, "Leading Change: Why Transformation Efforts Fail," *Harvard Business Review On Change* (Boston, MA: Harvard Business School Press, 1998), pp. 1–20; and R. Kanter, B. Stein and T. Jick, *The Challenge of Organizational Change: How Companies Experience It and How Leaders Guide It* (New York: The Free Press, 1992). See, in particular, Chapter 10, "The Challenge of Execution: Roles and Tasks in the Change Process," pp. 369–394. The "Ten Commandments of Change" are described on pp. 382–386.

4. Kotter, "Leading Change: Why Transformation Efforts Fail," p. 9.

5. Kotter, "Leading Change: Why Transformation Efforts Fail," p. 10.

6. Kotter, "Leading Change: Why Transformation Efforts Fail," p. 5.

7. See Nyman, *Making Manufacturing Cells Work*, pp. 58–59, for a nice discussion of the communication process and its importance.

8. Adapted from Kanter et al., *The Challenge of Organizational Change: How Companies Experience It and How Leaders Guide It*, p. 380.

9. R. Eade, *Cellular Manufacturing in a Global Marketplace*, Video Reference Supplement (Dearborn, MI: Society of Manufacturing Engineers, 1995), pp. 41–42.

10. U. Wemmerlöv and D. Johnson, "Cellular Manufacturing at 46 User Plants: Implementation Experiences and Performance Improvements," *Int. Journal of Production Research*, Vol. 35, No. 1, 1997, pp. 29–49; see in particular pp. 40–41.

11. Wemmerlöv and Johnson, "Cellular Manufacturing at 46 User Plants: Implementation Experiences and Performance Improvements," p. 41.

12. For a discussion of "functional drift," see N. Hyer and K. Brown, "The Life Cell Dynamics of Manufacturing Cells: Evolution, Drift and Dissolution," working paper (Nashville, TN: Owen Graduate School of Management, 2000).

13. This list is based on prescriptions offered in A. Majchrzak and Q. Wang, "Breaking the Functional Mind-Set in Process Organizations," *Harvard Business Review*, September-October 1996, pp. 92–99.

14. U. Wemmerlöv and D. Johnson, "Empirical Findings on Manufacturing Cell Design," *Int. Journal of Production Research*, Vol. 38, No. 3, 2000, pp. 481–507. The data are from p. 486.

15. Wemmerlöv and Johnson, "Cellular Manufacturing at 46 User Plants: Implementation Experiences and Performance Improvements," p. 42.

16. W. Kim and R. Mauborgne, "Fair Process: Managing in the Knowledge Economy," *Harvard Business Review*, Vol. 75, No. 4, July-August 1997, pp. 65–75.

17. Kim and Mauborgne, "Fair Process: Managing in the Knowledge Economy," p. 67.

18. The article by Kim and Mauborgne provides an excellent discussion of fair process.

19. Kim and Mauborgne, "Fair Process: Managing in the Knowledge Economy," p. 69.

20. Wemmerlöv and Johnson, "Cellular Manufacturing at 46 User Plants: Implementation Experiences and Performance Improvements," p. 40.

21. Anonymous, "Organisational Change in Bonas Machine Company," *IRS Employment Review*, Vol. 610, June 1996, pp. 5–10; see p. 10.

22. Kotter, "Leading Change: Why Transformation Efforts Fail," p. 18.

23. For a good general reference on project management, see S. Baker and K. Baker, *The Complete Idiot's Guide to Project Management* (New York: Alpha Books, 1998). Chapter 1 describes why organizations need project management.

24. The overall structure and many of the project management tools we recommend are from IPS Associates, *Project Management Manual*, Harvard Business School Case #9–967–034 (Boston, MA: Harvard Business School Publishing, 1996).

25. See Nyman, *Making Manufacturing Cells Work*, p. 49: "... the most important element of a successful manufacturing cell program is a strong project team. The team oversees program activities and serves as the driving force, keeping efforts focused on the program goals."

26. One of our recent surveys gathered information regarding the organization of the cell project at a sample of U.S. manufacturing firms. These data are reported in Wemmerlöv and Johnson, "Empirical Findings on Manufacturing Cell Design," pp. 481–507; see especially pp. 484–485.

27. See the sample team membership matrix and explanation in Nyman, *Making Manufacturing Cells Work*, pp. 52–54.

28. See J. Katzenbach, and D. Smith, *The Wisdom of Teams: Creating the High-Performance Organization* (New York: HarperCollins, 1993), p. 45.

29. See Katzenbach and Smith, *The Wisdom of Teams: Creating the High-Performance Organization*, pp. 119–127 for a discussion of common approaches for building team performance. Point 7 is "spend lots of time together." The authors also note that teams "should invest just as much time and effort crafting their working approach as shaping their purpose," p. 56.

30. IPS Associates, *Project Management Manual*, p. 14.

31. For additional ideas on ground rules see T. Bacon, *High Impact Facilitation* (Durango, CO: International LearningWorks, 1996), pp. 140–141; and P. Scholtes, B. Joiner and B. Streibel, *The Team Handbook: Second Edition* (Madison, WI: Oriel Corporation, 1996), pp. 4–37 and 4–38. Ground rules regarding attitude are modeled after those used by teams at a large electronics organization.

32. IPS Associates, *Project Management Manual*, pp. 11–12.

33. Criteria for project objective statement adapted from IPS Associates, *Project Management Manual*, Harvard Business School Case #9-967-034 (Boston, MA: Harvard Business School Publishing, 1996), p. 12. They stipulate "25 words or less." We recommend as close to 25 words as possible.

34. IPS Associates, *Project Management Manual*, pp. 12–13.

35. IPS Associates, *Project Management Manual*, p. 13.

36. IPS Associates, *Project Management Manual*, pp. 15–16.

37. For background reading on stakeholders and project communication see Baker and Baker, *The Complete Idiot's Guide to Project Management*, pp. 21–28, 176–179, and 211–218. The particular method we present for stakeholder analysis was introduced to us by Scott Burton, an organization redesign consultant for several large Fortune 500 companies.

38. For a good discussion of the benefits of distilling lessons learned, see T. Ricks, "Army Devises System to Decide What Does, and Does Not, Work," *Wall Street Journal*, May 23, 1997, pp. A1 and A10.

Chapter 16

1. R. Eade, *Cellular Manufacturing in a Global Marketplace*, Video Reference Supplement (Dearborn, MI: Society of Manufacturing Engineers, 1995), p. 8.

2. U. Wemmerlöv and D. Johnson, "Cellular Manufacturing at 46 User Plants: Implementation Experiences and Performance Improvements," *Int. Journal of Production Research*, Vol. 35, No. 1, 1997, pp. 29–49. The quote is from p. 42.

3. See N. Hyer, K. Brown, and S. Zimmerman, "A Socio-Technical Systems Approach to Cell Design: Case Study and Analysis," *Journal of Operations Management*, Vol. 17, No. 2, 1999, pp. 179–203. The quote is from p. 192.

4. U. Wemmerlöv and D. Johnson, "Empirical Findings on Manufacturing Cell Design," *Int. Journal of Production Research*, Vol. 38, No. 3, 2000, pp. 481–507. The quote is from p. 489.

5. U. Wemmerlöv and N. Hyer, "Cellular Manufacturing in the U.S. Industry: A Survey of Users," *Int. Journal of Production Research*, Vol. 27, No. 9, 1989, pp. 1511–1530. The discussion of problems appears on pp. 1526–1527.

6. Wemmerlöv and Johnson, "Cellular Manufacturing at 46 User Plants: Implementation Experiences and Performance Improvements," pp. 41–43.

7. Wemmerlöv and Johnson, "Empirical Findings on Manufacturing Cell Design," p. 493.

8. N. Hyer and K. Brown, "The Life Cycle Dynamics of Manufacturing Cells: Evolution, Drift and Dissolution," working paper (Nashville, TN: Owen Graduate School of Management, 2000), p. 11.

9. This was mentioned by a number of firms in Wemmerlöv and Johnson, "Cellular Manufacturing at 46 User Plants: Implementation Experiences and Performance Improvements," p. 42.

10. Wemmerlöv and Johnson, "Cellular Manufacturing at 46 User Plants: Implementation Experiences and Performance Improvements," p. 41.

11. See *Connecticut Spring and Stamping Corporation (A)*, Harvard Business School Case #9-694-009 (Boston, MA: Harvard Business School Publishing, 1993), pp. 5–6.

12. Wemmerlöv and Johnson, "Cellular Manufacturing at 46 User Plants: Implementation Experiences and Performance Improvements," p. 42.

13. *Doré-Doré*, Harvard Business School Case 9-962-028 (Boston, MA: Harvard Business School Publishing, 1991), p. 7.

14. N. Hyer and K. Brown, "The Discipline of Real Cells," *Journal of Operations Management*, Vol. 17, No. 5, 1999, pp. 557–574. This case is described on p. 567.

15. Hyer and Brown, "The Discipline of Real Cells," p. 569.

16. See S. Collett and R. Spicer, "Improving Productivity through Cellular Manufacturing," *Production and Inventory Management*, First Quarter 1995, pp. 71–75.

17. Personal correspondence and plant tour notes from Karen Brown, University of Washington-Bothell, 2000.

18. See N. Hyer and K. Brown, "A Taxonomy of Cell Management Challenges and Outcomes: An Electronics Industry Field Study," working paper (Nashville, TN: Owen Graduate School of Management, 2000), p. 27.

19. See Hyer and Brown, "A Taxonomy of Cell Management Challenges and Outcomes: An Electronics Industry Field Study," p. 27.

20. Eade, *Cellular Manufacturing in a Global Marketplace*, p. 8.

21. Wemmerlöv and Johnson, "Empirical Findings on Manufacturing Cell Design," p. 494.

22. D. Johnson, *An Empirical Investigation of Factors Influencing Reorganizations to Cellular Manufacturing*, unpublished Ph.D. dissertation (Madison, WI: School of Business, University of Wisconsin-Madison, 1998).

23. Results of this survey are published in Wemmerlöv and Hyer, "Cellular Manufacturing in the U.S. Industry: A Survey of Users," pp. 1511–1530.

24. Wemmerlöv and Johnson, "Cellular Manufacturing at 46 User Plants: Implementation Experiences and Performance Improvements," p. 42.

25. This list of reasons was developed based on a discussion in K. Knauss and M. Matusak, "The Implications of Cell Manufacturing for U.S. Factory Workers and Their Unions," *Labor Studies Journal*, Spring 1989, pp. 19–29.

26. R. Noe, J. Hollenbeck, B. Gerhart, and P. Wright, *Human Resource Management: Gaining a Competitive Advantage* (Boston, MA: Irwin McGraw-Hill, 2000), p. 520.

27. The company experiences described here are taken from N. Harvey, "How Unions Should Respond to Cells," *Labor Studies Journal*, Vol. 18, No. 4, Winter 1994, pp. 21–38.

28. Wemmerlöv and Hyer, "Cellular Manufacturing in the U.S. Industry: A Survey of Users," p. 1524.

29. This list is based on discussions found in Knauss and Matusak, "The Implications of Cell Manufacturing for U.S. Factory Workers and Their Unions"; Noe et al., *Human Resource Management: Gaining a Competitive Advantage*, pp. 519–21; and Harvey, "How Unions Should Respond to Cells."

30. L. Nyman (ed.), *Making Manufacturing Cells Work* (Dearborn, MI: Society of Manufacturing Engineers, 1992), p. 290.

31. Wemmerlöv and Hyer, "Cellular Manufacturing in the U.S. Industry: A Survey of Users," p. 1523.

32. Wemmerlöv and Johnson, "Cellular Manufacturing at 46 User Plants: Implementation Experiences and Performance Improvements," p. 42.

33. Wemmerlöv and Johnson, "Cellular Manufacturing at 46 User Plants: Implementation Experiences and Performance Improvements," p. 42.

34. Personal correspondence and plant tour notes from Karen Brown, University of Washington-Bothell, 2000.

35. V. Huber and K. Brown, "Human Resource Issues in Cellular Manufacturing: A Sociotechnical Analysis," *Journal of Operations Management*, Vol. 10, No. 1, 1991, pp. 138–159. The quote is from p. 139.

36. Hyer and Brown, "A Taxonomy of Cell Management Challenges and Outcomes: An Electronics Industry Field Study," p. 25.

37. Hyer and Brown, "The Discipline of Real Cells," pp. 566–567.

38. Wemmerlöv and Johnson, "Cellular Manufacturing at 46 User Plants: Implementation Experiences and Performance Improvements," p. 42.

39. See R. Marsh, "How Well Do Manufacturing Cells Age?" *Production and Inventory Management,* Third Quarter 1995, pp. 1–4.
40. For a good discussion and summary of several research contributions on the topic of cell life cycle, see Wemmerlöv and Johnson, "Empirical Findings on Manufacturing Cell Design," pp. 500–502.
41. Hyer and Brown, "A Taxonomy of Cell Management Challenges and Outcomes: An Electronics Industry Field Study," p. 25.
42. Eade, *Cellular Manufacturing in a Global Marketplace,* p. 16.
43. Hyer and Brown, "The Life Cycle Dynamics of Manufacturing Cells: Evolution, Drift and Dissolution," pp. 17–18.
44. Nyman, *Making Manufacturing Cells Work,* p. iii (our italics).
45. The experience of this company is described in S. Datar, S. Kekre, T. Mukhopadyay, and E. Svaan, "Overloaded Overheads: Activity-Based Cost Analysis of Material Handling in Cell Manufacturing," *Journal of Operations Management,* Vol. 10, No. 1, 1991, pp. 119–137. The quote is from p. 127.
46. Hyer and Brown, "A Taxonomy of Cell Management Challenges and Outcomes: An Electronics Industry Field Study," p. 21.
47. Hyer and Brown, "A Taxonomy of Cell Management Challenges and Outcomes: An Electronics Industry Field Study," p. 23.
48. Wemmerlöv and Johnson, "Cellular Manufacturing at 46 User Plants: Implementation Experiences and Performance Improvements," p. 41.
49. Hyer and Brown, "The Life Cycle Dynamics of Manufacturing Cells: Evolution, Drift and Dissolution," p. 9.
50. Hyer and Brown, "The Life Cycle Dynamics of Manufacturing Cells: Evolution, Drift and Dissolution," p. 10.

Chapter 17

1. See the discussion in C. Fine, *Clockspeed: Winning Industry Control in the Age of Temporary Advantage* (Reading, MA: Perseus Books, 1998).
2. M. Imai, *Gemba Kaizen* (New York: McGraw-Hill, 1997), pp. 75–86.
3. K. Suzaki, *The New Manufacturing Challenge: Techniques for Continuous Improvement* (New York: The Free Press, 1987), pp. 12–18. See also Imai, *Gemba Kaizen,* pp. 75–86. Along with muda (waste) and its various forms, Imai discusses mura (irregularity) and muri (strenuous work). Any irregularity in the smooth flow of production is usually the source of waste. Likewise, strenuous work is likely to create waste. In your efforts to eliminate muda, mura and muri can help you identify likely targets of opportunity. Muda, mura, and muri are often referred to as the three MUs (or three M's) in Japan.
4. This definition of waste is attributed to Fujio Cho of Toyota Motor Company as quoted in Suzaki, *The New Manufacturing Challenge: Techniques for Continuous Improvement,* p. 8.
5. See the discussion of value in P. Scholtes, B. Joiner, and B. Streibel, *The Team Handbook: Second Edition* (Madison, WI: Oriel Corporation, 1996), p. 2–7. We have also based our definition of value-added on the work of Joseph Blackburn, James Speyer Professor of Production Management at Vanderbilt University.
6. For some excellent references on the improvement process and quality movement, see Scholtes et al., *The Team Handbook: Second Edition*; M. Brassard and D. Ritter, *The Memory Jogger II* (Methuen, MA: GOAL/QPC, 1994); and Chapter 1 of D. Wheeler and D. Chambers, *Understanding Statistical Process Control* (Knoxville, TN: SPC Press, 1992). See Imai, *Gemba Kaizen,* pp. 4–7 for a discussion of the role PDCA in kaizen efforts. For a discussion of the role of the improvement model in Six Sigma efforts, see P. Pande, R. Neuman, and R. Cavanaugh, *The Six Sigma Way: How GE, Motorola, and Other Top Companies Are Honing their Performance* (New York: McGraw-Hill, 2000). See especially pp. 19–40.
7. M. Harry and R. Schroeder, *Six Sigma: The Breakthrough Management Strategy Revolutionizing the World's Top Corporations* (New York: Currency Books, 2000), p. vii.
8. For a discussion of Define-Measure-Analyze-Improve-Control, see Pande et al., *The Six Sigma Way: How GE, Motorola, and Other Top Companies Are Honing their Performance,* pp. 37–40. Also see the excellent checklists for each phase that appear on pp. 386–390. See the references in endnote 6 for discussions of PDCA. In addition to these models, Imai, *Gemba Kaizen,* p. 5, uses the "Standardize–Do–Check–Act" cycle to refer to efforts to stabilize a new work process. Once a process is stable, the team can begin an unending series of PDCA cycles.

9. Scholtes et al., *The Team Handbook: Second Edition*, present an excellent discussion of various types of flowcharts along with examples of each. See pp. 2–16 through 2–19.

10. J. Day, "Learning about Lean Systems at Freudenberg-NOK: Where Continuous Improvement Is a Way of Life," in J. Liker (ed.), *Becoming Lean: Inside Stories of U.S. Manufacturers* (Portland, OR: Productivity Press, 1998), p. 195.

11. See Brassard and Ritter, *The Memory Jogger II*; M. Brassard, C. Field, F. Oddo, B. Page, D. Ritter, and L. Smith, *The Problem Solving Memory Jogger* (Salem, NH: GOAL/QPC, 2000); Chapter 2, "Getting Started: Learning the Tools" in Scholtes et al., *The Team Handbook: Second Edition*; and D. Ritter and M. Brassard, *The Creativity Tools Memory Jogger* (Lawrence, MA: GOAL/QPC, 1998).

12. J. Womack and D. Jones, *Lean Thinking: Banish Waste and Create Wealth in Your Corporation* (New York: Simon & Schuster, 1996). The other two elements of lean thinking are flow and pull.

13. This discussion of kaizen is from J. Shook, "Bringing the Toyota Production System to the United States: A Personal Perspective," in Liker, *Becoming Lean: Inside Stories of U.S. Manufacturers*, pp. 65–66.

14. Shook, "Bringing the Toyota Production System to the United States: A Personal Perspective," p. 66.

15. H. Hirano, *JIT Factory Revolution: A Pictorial Guide to Factory Design of the Future* (Cambridge, MA: Productivity Press, 1988), pp. 16–17.

16. This quote is from U. Wemmerlöv and D. Johnson, "Cellular Manufacturing at 46 User Plants: Implementation Experiences and Performance Improvements," *Int. Journal of Production Research*, Vol. 35, No. 1, 1997, p. 40. Respondents noted that continual improvement was among "the most frequent positive unexpected outcome." There was "a pervasive sentiment emerging from the survey responses, namely the discovery of the great potential for operator involvement in the workplace suddenly unleashed through the reorganization to cellular manufacturing."

17. For more on cells and learning see V. R. Kannan, "Incorporating the Impact of Learning in Assessing the Effectiveness of Cellular Manufacturing," *Int. Journal of Production Research*, Vol. 34, No. 12, December 1996, pp. 3327–3340.

18. M. Zayko, W. Hancock, and D. Broughman, "Implementing Lean Manufacturing at Gelman Sciences, Inc.," in Liker, *Becoming Lean: Inside Stories of U.S. Manufacturers*, p. 285. We discussed Gelman Sciences in Chapter 1 as well.

19. N. Hyer and K. Brown, "The Life Cycle Dynamics of Manufacturing Cells: Evolution, Drift and Dissolution," working paper (Nashville, TN: Owen Graduate School of Management, 2000), p. 9.

20. Hirano, *JIT Factory Revolution: A Pictorial Guide to Factory Design of the Future*, pp. 28–63. These pages provide examples and explanations of each "S." Imai, *Gemba Kaizen*, pp. 63–73, provides another excellent discussion. In Hirano's text the English translations of the Japanese words appear on p. 28 and are proper arrangement (Seiri), orderliness (Seiton), cleanliness (Seiso), cleanup (Seiketsu), and discipline (Shitsuke). Imai refers to them as sort, straighten, scrub, systematize, and standardize. Other translations refer to the 5 Ss as sort, straighten, sanitize, sweep, and sustain; sort, set in order, shine, standardize, and sustain. See J. Shook, "Introduction: Bringing Lean Back to the U.S.A.," in Liker, *Becoming Lean: Inside Stories of U.S. Manufacturers*, p. 21.

21. M. McGovern and B. Andrews, "Operational Excellence: A Manufacturing Metamorphosis at Western Geophysical Exploration Products," in Liker, *Becoming Lean: Inside Stories of U.S. Manufacturers*, p. 396.

22. Zayko et al., "Implementing Lean Manufacturing at Gelman Sciences, Inc.," pp. 289–290. Also for more examples, see Suzaki, *The New Manufacturing Challenge: Techniques for Continuous Improvement*, pp. 27–31.

23. D. Woolson and M. Husar, "Transforming a Plant to Lean in a Large Traditional Company: Delphi Saginaw Steering Systems, GM," in Liker, *Becoming Lean: Inside Stories of U. S. Manufacturers*, p. 150.

24. The contrast between asking WHY not WHO is discussed in Shook, "Bringing the Toyota Production System to the United States: A Personal Perspective," pp. 58–59. He observes that it is critically important to "call attention to the problem to solve it, or to the behavior to change it, but not to the individual for being somehow 'wrong' " (p. 59).

25. H. Steudel and P. Desruelle, *Manufacturing in the Nineties: How to Become a Mean, Lean, World-Class Competitor* (New York: Van Nostrand Reinhold, 1992), p. 165. Their chapter devoted to setup reduction is particularly good. Also for more information on setup reduction see S. Shingo, *A Revolution in Manufacturing: The SMED System* (Cambridge, MA: Productivity Press, 1985).

26. N. Hyer and K. Brown, "The Life Cycle Dynamics of Manufacturing Cells: Evolution, Drift and Dissolution," p. 6.

27. See case #9-694-009, *Connecticut Spring and Stamping Corporation (A)* (Boston, MA: Harvard Business School Publishing, 1993) for a good description of failed cells due to insufficient setup reduction.

28. See Chapter 6, "Setup-Time Reduction," in Steudel and Desruelle, *Manufacturing in the Nineties: How to Become a Mean, Lean, World-Class Competitor*, pp. 163–210. K. Sekine, *One-Piece Flow: Cell Design for Transforming the Production Process* (Portland, OR: Productivity Press, 1992) provides excellent coverage of tools for conducting time-and-motion studies for setup reduction. See especially Chapter 10, pp. 143–158.

29. Hirano, *JIT Factory Revolution: A Pictorial Guide to Factory Design of the Future*, p. 79.

30. For some great examples see Suzaki, *The New Manufacturing Challenge*, pp. 100–101.

31. This example comes from Sekine, *One-Piece Flow: Cell Design for Transforming the Production Process*, pp. 197–204. The entire book is full of examples illustrating how to create cells and improve them once in place. This is an excellent source for improvement ideas.

32. See Zayko et al., "Implementing Lean Manufacturing at Gelman Sciences, Inc.," p. 272, for a similar example.

33. McGovern and Andrews, "Operational Excellence: A Manufacturing Metamorphosis at Western Geophysical Exploration Products," p. 398.

34. Zayko et al., "Implementing Lean Manufacturing at Gelman Sciences, Inc.," p. 289.

35. J. Flaherty, "Management: Bosses Make Cost Consultants Out of Blue-Collar Workers," *New York Times*, April 18, 2001, pp. C1 and C7.

36. Flaherty, "Management: Bosses Make Cost Consultants Out of Blue-Collar Workers," pp. C1 and C7.

37. J. Liker, "Conclusions: What We Have Learned about Becoming Lean," in Liker, *Becoming Lean: Inside Stories of U.S. Manufacturers*, pp. 506–509.

38. U. Wemmerlöv and N. Hyer, "Cellular Manufacturing in the U.S. Industry: A Survey of Users," *Int. Journal of Production Research*, Vol. 27, No. 9, 1989, pp. 1511–1530. See in particular pp. 1519–1520.

39. See R. Marsh, "How Well Do Manufacturing Cells Age?," *Production and Inventory Management*, Third Quarter 1995, pp. 1–4. The quote is from p. 1.

40. These strategies were used by respondents to the previously cited study by Marsh, "How Well Do Manufacturing Cells Age?"

41. N. Hyer and K. Brown, "A Taxonomy of Cell Management Challenges and Outcomes: An Electronics Industry Field Study," working paper (Nashville, TN: Owen Graduate School of Management, 2000), p. 23.

42. Hyer and Brown, "The Life Cycle Dynamics of Manufacturing Cells: Evolution, Drift and Dissolution," p. 16.

43. See the discussion in U. Wemmerlöv and D. Johnson, "Empirical Findings on Manufacturing Cell Design," *Int. Journal of Production Research*, Vol. 38, No. 3, 2000, pp. 481–507. See especially the discussion on pp. 500–502.

44. Wemmerlöv and Johnson, "Empirical Findings on Manufacturing Cell Design," pp. 485 and 499.

45. Hyer and Brown, "The Life Cycle Dynamics of Manufacturing Cells: Evolution, Drift and Dissolution," p. 16.

46. Marsh, "How Well Do Manufacturing Cells Age?," pp. 1–4.

47. Hyer and Brown, "The Life Cycle Dynamics of Manufacturing Cells: Evolution, Drift and Dissolution," p. 11.

48. Hyer and Brown, "The Life Cycle Dynamics of Manufacturing Cells: Evolution, Drift and Dissolution," p. 21.

49. J. Slomp, "Design of Manufacturing Cells: PFA Applications in Dutch Industry," in N. Suresh and J. Kay (eds.), *Group Technology and Cellular Manufacturing: State-of-the-Art Synthesis of Research and Practice* (Boston, MA: Kluwer Academic Publishers, 1998), pp. 153–168. This case, in which CNC machining reduced manufacturing steps, is discussed on p. 166.

50. Committee on Visionary Manufacturing Challenges, Board on Manufacturing and Engineering Design, Commission on Engineering and Technical Systems, National Research Council, *Visionary Manufacturing Challenges for 2020* (Washington, D.C.: National Academy Press, 1998). See also J. Jordan and F. Michel, *Next Generation Manufacturing* (Dearborn, MI: Society of Manufacturing Engineers, 1999).

51. Hyer and Brown, "A Taxonomy of Cell Management Challenges and Outcomes: An Electronics Industry Field Study," p. 22.

52. Hyer and Brown, "The Life Cycle Dynamics of Manufacturing Cells: Evolution, Drift and Dissolution," p. 17.

53. Slomp, "Design of Manufacturing Cells: PFA Applications in Dutch Industry," pp. 166–167.
54. Slomp, "Design of Manufacturing Cells: PFA Applications in Dutch Industry," p. 166.
55. Slomp, "Design of Manufacturing Cells: PFA Applications in Dutch Industry," p. 165.
56. Hyer and Brown, "A Taxonomy of Cell Management Challenges and Outcomes: An Electronics Industry Field Study," p. 23.
57. Hyer and Brown, "The Life Cycle Dynamics of Manufacturing Cells: Evolution, Drift and Dissolution," p. 17.
58. See Wemmerlöv and Hyer, "Cellular Manufacturing in the U.S. Industry: A Survey of Users," pp. 1511–1530. On p. 1529 we report that "close to 70% also stated that more cells will be built at their plants in the future."
59. Zayko et al. "Implementing Lean Manufacturing at Gelman Sciences, Inc.," pp. 275–276.
60. See Zayko et al., "Implementing Lean Manufacturing at Gelman Sciences, Inc.," p. 278, for an excellent example.
61. Hyer and Brown, "A Taxonomy of Cell Management Challenges and Outcomes: An Electronics Industry Field Study," p. 22.

Chapter 18

1. Based on findings reported in R. Suri, U. Wemmerlöv, F. Rath, R. Gadh, and R. Veeramani, "Practical Issues in Implementing Quick Response Manufacturing: Insights from Fourteen Projects with Industry," *Proceedings of the Manufacturing and Service Operations (MSOM) Conference*, Dartmouth College, Hanover, NH, June 24–25, 1996. Also reported in R. Suri, *Quick Response Manufacturing* (Portland, OR: Productivity Press, 1998), p. 304.
2. T. Koulopoulos, *The Workflow Imperative* (New York: Van Nostrand Reinhold, 1995), p. 9.
3. J. Blackburn, "Time-Based Competition: White-Collar Activities," *Business Horizons*, July–August 1992, pp. 96–100. See p. 99.
4. Blackburn, "Time-Based Competition: White-Collar Activities," p. 96.
5. Our discussion of routine and non-routine knowledge work draws heavily from S. Mohrman, S. Cohen and A. Mohrman, *Designing Team-Based Organizations: New Forms for Knowledge Work* (San Francisco, CA: Jossey-Bass, 1995), pp. 15–19.
6. M. Wayman, "Order Processing Lead Time Reduction: A Case Study," *International Industrial Engineering Conference and Societies' Manufacturing and Productivity Symposium Proceedings* (Norcross, GA: Institute of Industrial Engineers, 1995), pp. 400–409. See p. 403.
7. Blackburn, "Time-Based Competition: White-Collar Activities," p. 99.
8. Blackburn, "Time-Based Competition: White-Collar Activities," p. 96.
9. This example comes from work at IBM Credit reported in M. Hammer and J. Champy, *Reengineering the Corporation* (New York: HarperCollins, 1993), pp. 36–39.
10. Koulopoulos, *The Workflow Imperative*, p. 138. The author states that "99.75% of the business cycle was dedicated to transfer time and not task time." Clearly, however, much of what the author calls "transfer time" was actually queue or wait time.
11. Blackburn, "Time-Based Competition: White-Collar Activities," p. 100.
12. For a fabulous description of complexity see T. Fuller, "Eliminating Complexity from Work: Improving Productivity by Enhancing Quality," *National Productivity Review*, Autumn 1985, pp. 327–344.
13. Fuller, "Eliminating Complexity from Work: Improving Productivity by Enhancing Quality," pp. 339–343.
14. B. Shapiro, V. Rangan and J. Sviokla, "Staple Yourself to an Order," *Harvard Business Review*, July–August 1992, pp. 113–122. See discussion on p. 115. Also, M. Hammer, "Reengineering Work: Don't Automate, Obliterate," *Harvard Business Review*, July–August 1990, pp. 104–112. See p. 108.
15. For a good discussion, see Hammer and Champy, *Reengineering the Corporation*, pp. 26–30.
16. Blackburn, "Time-Based Competition: White-Collar Activities," p. 97.
17. For a good discussion of this see G. Rummler and A. Brache, *Improving Performance: How to Manage the White Space on the Organization Chart* (San Francisco, CA: Jossey-Bass, 1990).
18. Blackburn, "Time-Based Competition: White-Collar Activities," pp. 97–98.
19. See Chapter 2 and Hammer and Champy, *Reengineering the Corporation*, pp. 50–64.
20. M. Hammer, *Beyond Reengineering* (New York: HarperCollins, 1996), pp. 28–30. Aetna's work reconfiguration satisfies our four perspectives on cells although the organization did not label them as such.

21. R. Schonberger, *Building a Chain of Customers: Linking Business Functions to Create the World Class Company* (New York: The Free Press, 1990), pp. 47–48.

22. In Hammer and Champy, *Reengineering the Corporation*, p. 62, they refer to a single person office cell as a "case manager." Schonberger, writing earlier, in his book *Building a Chain of Customers: Linking Business Functions to Create the World Class Company*, p. 56, refers to this type of one-person cell as a "unitary processor." We will use the term case worker.

23. This case is described in Hammer and Champy, *Reengineering the Corporation*, pp. 36–38. Again, this reconfiguration satisfies our four perspectives on cells although the organization did not label them as such.

24. Hammer and Champy in *Reengineering the Corporation*, pp. 65–68, refer to "process teams."

25. This case is described in Suri, *Quick Response Manufacturing*, pp. 352–361 and Wayman, "Order Processing Lead Time Reduction: A Case Study."

26. These criteria are adapted from M. Campion and G. Medsker, "Job Design," in G. Salvendy (ed.), *Handbook of Industrial Engineering* (New York: John Wiley & Sons, 1992), pp. 845–881. The criteria are presented on p. 871.

27. Hammer, *Beyond Reengineering*, p. 25. Again, this reconfiguration satisfies our four perspectives on cells although the organization did not label them as such.

28. Wayman, "Order Processing Lead Time Reduction: A Case Study," p. 404.

29. Mohrman et al., *Designing Team-Based Organizations*, pp. 83–84.

30. Mohrman et al., *Designing Team-Based Organizations*, pp. 84–87.

31. Hammer and Champy, *Reengineering the Corporation*, p. 38.

32. Hammer and Champy, *Reengineering the Corporation*, p. 55.

33. Schonberger, *Building a Chain of Customers: Linking Business Functions to Create the World Class Company*, pp. 47–48.

34. Hammer, *Beyond Reengineering*, pp. 28–29.

35. A. Majchrzak and Q. Wang, "Breaking the Functional Mind-Set in Process Organizations," *Harvard Business Review*, September–October 1996, pp. 92–99. See pp. 94 and 96.

36. Hammer and Champy, *Reengineering the Corporation*, p. 53 and pp. 58–59.

37. J. Owen, "From Suits to Cells," *Manufacturing Engineering*, Vol. 122, No. 6, June 1999, pp. 62–67.

38. M. Hammer and S. Stanton, "How Process Enterprises Really Work," *Harvard Business Review*, November–December 1999, pp. 108–118. See p. 116.

39. Majchrzak and Wang, "Breaking the Functional Mind-Set in Process Organizations," p. 95.

40. Wayman, "Order Processing Lead Time Reduction: A Case Study," p. 406.

41. See Mohrman et al., *Designing Team-Based Organizations*, p. 310.

42. Suri, *Quick Response Manufacturing*, pp. 350–351.

43. Hammer, *Beyond Reengineering*, p. 22.

44. Owen, "From Suits to Cells," p. 64.

45. See the discussion in W. Kim and R. Mauborgne, "Fair Process: Managing in the Knowledge Economy," *Harvard Business Review*, Vol. 75, No. 4, July–August 1997, pp. 65–75.

46. Majchrzak and Wang, "Breaking the Functional Mind-Set in Process Organizations," pp. 96–99. The quote is also from p. 99.

Chapter 19

1. These particular characteristics come from the Committee on Visionary Manufacturing Challenges, Board on Manufacturing and Engineering Design, Commission on Engineering and Technical Systems, National Research Council, *Visionary Manufacturing Challenges for 2020* (Washington, D.C.: National Academy Press, 1998). For another perspective on future manufacturing see J. Jordan and F. Michel, *Next Generation Manufacturing* (Dearborn, MI: Society of Manufacturing Engineers, 1999).

2. National Research Council, *Visionary Manufacturing Challenges for 2020*. See, in particular Chapter 2, "Grand Challenges for Manufacturing."

3. J. Katzenbach and D. Smith, *The Wisdom of Teams: Creating the High-Performance Organization* (New York: HarperCollins, 1993), p. 15.

4. See Katzenbach and Smith, *The Wisdom of Teams: Creating the High-Performance Organization*, p. 19.

Appendix A

1. See R. Suri, *Quick Response Manufacturing* (Portland, OR: Productivity Press, 1998), pp. 130–131.
2. Based on the setup and run times in Table A-1c, the average time per piece for the shear should be 0.10/10 + 0.135 = 0.145. However, under the assumption that labor is reduced by 15 percent due to less scrap and rework, the effective time per piece is estimated to be 0.145*0.85 = 0.123 hours. Same for the other two machines.

Appendix B

1. Adapted from L. R. Nyman, (ed.), *Making Manufacturing Cells Work* (Dearborn, MI: Society of Manufacturing Engineers, 1992), pp. 133–134.

Appendix D

1. This table is from A. A. Atkinson, R. D. Banker, R. S. Kaplan, and S. M. Young, *Management Accounting* (Upper Saddle River, NJ: Prentice-Hall, 1997), p. 56. Note that although we here refer to financial and management accounting as two separate systems, they are actually different parts of a single accounting system.
2. In fact, the requirement to value inventory and goods sold for external reporting often dictates or constrains the design of the cost accounting system. Also see R. S. Kaplan, "One Cost System Isn't Enough," *Harvard Business Review*, January–February 1988, pp. 61–66.
3. This is an abbreviated version of the Institute of Management Accountants' definition. For a full definition, see, for example, Atkinson et al., *Management Accounting*, p. 34.
4. Also see Atkinson et al., *Management Accounting*, pp. 11–12.
5. "Operational control" includes the use of cost data to make long- and short-term decisions. For instance: Should you hire more people or create a third shift?, What machine should you use for a job?, Should you make or buy a component?, How much overtime should you schedule to meet an order due date?, How large should lot sizes be?, and so on.
6. Manufacturing overhead is also referred to as "burden," manufacturing support costs," or "indirect manufacturing costs."
7. This list is from p. 148 in J. G. Miller and T. E. Vollmann, "The Hidden Factory," *Harvard Business Review*, September–October 1985, pp. 142–150.
8. These data apply to U.S. firms and come from T. D. Fry, D. C. Steele, and B. A. Saladin, "The Role of Management Accounting in the Development of a Manufacturing Strategy," *Int. Journal of Operations and Production Management*, Vol. 15, No. 12, 1995, pp. 21–31; R. D. Banker, G. Potter, and R. G. Schroeder, "An Empirical Study of Manufacturing Overhead Drivers," *Journal of Accounting and Economics*, January 1995, pp. 115–138; and S. R. Hedin and G. R. Russell, "JIT Implementation: Interaction Between the Production and Cost-Accounting Functions," *Production and Inventory Management*, Third Quarter 1992, pp. 68–73.
9. Essentially, a "period cost" is an expense that never shows up on the balance sheet in the form of inventory.
10. This figure is adapted from Exhibit 2-10 in C. T. Horngren, G. Foster, and S. M. Datar, *Cost Accounting: A Managerial Emphasis* (Upper Saddle River, NJ: Prentice-Hall, 1997).
11. In reality, very few costs are truly variable. For example, the labor cost does not necessarily vary with shifts in volume. Thus, the classification is used for cost allocation purposes rather than reflecting actual cost behavior.
12. See C. T. Horngren, *Introduction to Management Accounting* (Englewood Cliffs, NJ: Prentice-Hall, 1984), p. 454. In general, for the influence of volume on (flexible) budgets, see Atkinson et al., *Management Accounting*, pp. 556–561, or Horngren et al., *Cost Accounting: A Managerial Emphasis*, pp. 254–267.
13. See, for example, W. M. Baker, T. D. Fry, and K. Karwan, "The Rise and Fall and Time-Based Manufacturing," *Management Accounting*, June 1994, pp. 56–59.
14. "Absorption costing" means that all fixed and variable manufacturing costs are inventoriable. This is in contrast to "variable costing" systems, where only variable manufacturing costs are included in inventory costs and fixed costs are treated as expenses for the period. See Horngren et al., *Cost Accounting*, p. 298.

15. This underabsorbed overhead was also mentioned in the quote provided in the opening section of Chapter 10.
16. See Horngren et al., *Cost Accounting*, p. 306. For similar examples, see J. P. Womack and D. T. Jones, *Lean Thinking* (New York: Simon & Schuster, 1996, p. 138), and D. Dugdale and C. Jones, "Accounting for Throughput: Techniques for Performance Measurement, Decisions, and Control," *Management Accounting*, December 1997, pp. 52–56.

Appendix E

1. See J. Nolen, *Computer-Automated Process Planning for World-Class Manufacturing* (New York: Marcel Dekker, Inc., 1989), Appendix 2.

Appendix F

1. F. W. Taylor, *The Principles of Scientific Management* (New York: Norton, 1911).
2. This list of advantages and disadvantages is adapted from R. Chase, N. Aquilano, and F. R. Jacobs, *Production and Operations Management: Manufacturing and Services* (Boston, MA: Irwin/McGraw-Hill, 1998), p. 416.
3. J. Hackman and G. Oldham, *Work Redesign* (Reading, MA: Addison-Wesley, 1980). For more information on job characteristics see, for example, M. Campion and G. Medsker, "Job Design," in G. Salvendy (ed.), *Handbook of Industrial Engineering* (New York: John Wiley & Sons, 1992), pp. 845–881. Job characteristics are described in detail on p. 850. Also see J. Dean and S. Snell, "Integrated Manufacturing and Job Design: Moderating Effects of Organizational Inertia," *Academy of Management Journal*, Vol. 34, No. 4, 1991, pp. 776–804 (see especially, pp. 781–783); R. Noe, J. Hollenbeck, B. Gerhart, and P. Wright, *Human Resource Management: Gaining a Competitive Advantage* (Boston, MA: Irwin McGraw-Hill, 2000), pp. 127–130. V. Huber and K. Brown, "Human Resource Issues in Cellular Manufacturing: A Sociotechnical Analysis," *Journal of Operations Management*, Vol. 10, No. 1, 1991, pp. 138–159, considers job characteristics specifically with respect to cell jobs.
4. See V. Huber and N. Hyer, "The Human Factor in Cellular Manufacturing," *Journal of Operations Management*, Vol. 5, No. 2, 1985, p. 216 for a nice summary and further references.
5. R. Magjuka and R. Schmenner, "Cellular Manufacturing and Plant Administration: Some Initial Evidence," *Labor Studies Journal*, Summer 1992, p. 44–63.
6. See the discussion in Huber and Brown, "Human Resource Issues in Cellular Manufacturing: A Sociotechnical Analysis," p. 144, pp. 149–150, and p. 153.
7. Chase et al., *Production and Operations Management: Manufacturing and Services*, p. 416.
8. Chase et al., *Production and Operations Management: Manufacturing and Services*, p. 416.
9. Chase et al., *Production and Operations Management: Manufacturing and Services*, p. 416. Also see E. Lawler, *The Ultimate Advantage: Creating the High-Involvement Organization* (San Francisco, CA: Jossey-Bass, 1992), pp. 80–82. Although not shown here, the current practice is to combine job enrichment and job enlargement and refer to them together as job enrichment; this acknowledges that the motivating potential of a job is most likely to increase in the presence of both vertical and horizontal loading.
10. For reviews of the research literature on the effects of job enrichment and job enlargement see, for example, D. Yeatts and C. Hyten, *High-Performing Self-Managed Work Teams: A Comparison of Theory to Practice* (Thousand Oaks, CA: Sage, 1998), pp. 249–252; T. Kochan and P. Osterman, *The Mutual Gains Enterprise: Forging a Winning Partnership Among Labor, Management, and Government* (Boston, MA: Harvard Business School Press, 1994), pp. 66–71; Lawler, *The Ultimate Advantage: Creating the High-Involvement Organization*, pp. 85–88; and E. McCormick, *Job Analysis: Methods and Applications* (New York: AMACOM, 1979), pp. 280–283.
11. McCormick, *Job Analysis: Methods and Applications*, p. 288.
12. Kochan and Osterman, *The Mutual Gains Enterprise: Forging a Winning Partnership Among Labor, Management, and Government*, pp. 70–71.
13. For a discussion of several studies reviewing the research in this area, see Yeatts and Hyten, *High-Performing Self-Managed Work Teams: A Comparison of Theory to Practice*, pp. 249–252.
14. Noe et al., *Human Resource Management: Gaining a Competitive Advantage*, p. 130.
15. Chase et al., *Production and Operations Management: Manufacturing and Services*, p. 417.
16. Yeatts and Hyten, *High-Performing Self-Managed Work Teams: A Comparison of Theory to Practice*, pp. 249–250.

17. Campion and Medsker, "Job Design," p. 865–866.
18. Kochan and Osterman, *The Mutual Gains Enterprise: Forging a Winning Partnership Among Labor, Management, and Government*, p. 71.
19. E. Rosen, *Bitter Choices: Blue Collar Women In and Out of Work* (Chicago, IL: University of Chicago Press, 1987).
20. Kochan and Osterman, *The Mutual Gains Enterprise: Forging a Winning Partnership Among Labor, Management, and Government*, p. 71.

Appendix G

1. Adapted from W. Borman, N. Peterson, and T. Russell, "Selection, Training, and Development of Personnel," in G. Salvendy (ed.), *Handbook of Industrial Engineering* (New York: John Wiley & Sons, 1992), p. 888; R. Noe, J. Hollenbeck, B. Gerhart, and P. Wright, *Human Resource Management: Gaining a Competitive Advantage* (Boston, MA: Irwin McGraw-Hill, 2000), pp. 192–194; and H. Heneman, T. Judge, and R. Heneman, *Staffing Organizations* (Boston, MA: Irwin McGraw-Hill, 2000), pp. 452–464.

Appendix H

1. Excellent references to help you develop a course on interpersonal skills include: P. Scholtes, B. Joiner and B. Streibel, *The Team Handbook: Second Edition* (Madison, WI: Oriel Corporation 1996); L. Bendaly, *Games Teams Play: Dynamic Activities for Tapping Work Team Potential* (Toronto, Canada: McGraw-Hill Ryerson Limited, 1996); and S. Schoonover, *Managing to Relate: Interpersonal Skills at Work* (Reading, MA: Addison-Wesley, 1988).
2. Excellent references for developing a course on decision-making and problem-solving, include: Scholtes et al., *The Team Handbook: Second Edition*; D. Galloway, *Mapping Work Processes* (Milwaukee, WI: ASQC Quality Press, 1994); and R. Chang and P. Kelly, *Step-by-Step Problem Solving* (Irvine, CA: Richard Chang Associates, 1993).
3. Excellent references for developing a coaching and facilitation course for cell supervisors and leaders include: Scholtes et al., *The Team Handbook: Second Edition*; T. Kayser, *Mining Group Gold: How to Cash In On The Collaborative Brain Power of a Group* (El Segundo, CA: Serif Publishing, 1990); and F. Rees, *How to Lead Work Teams: Facilitation Skills* (Amsterdam: Pfeiffer, 1991); I. Bens, *Facilitation at a Glance!* (Methuen, MA: AQP/Participative Dynamics/Goal/QPC, 1999); and T. Bacon, *High Impact Facilitation* (Durango, CO: International LearningWorks, 1996).

Appendix K

1. The complete case history of Metalsa is found in L. Nyman (ed.), *Making Manufacturing Cells Work* (Dearborn, MI: Society of Manufacturing Engineers, 1992), pp. 361–368. The list of similarities between an auto race pit stop and machine setup is on p. 366.

Appendix L

1. For some good readings on mapping your processes, see M. Brassard and D. Ritter, *The Memory Jogger II* (Methuen, MA: GOAL/QPC, 1994); M. Rother and J. Shook, *Learning to See: Value Stream Mapping to Create Value and Eliminate Muda* (Brookline, MA: The Lean Enterprise Institute, 1999); and P. Scholtes, B. Joiner, and B. Streibel, *The Team Handbook: Second Edition* (Madison, WI: Oriel Corporation, 1996). Scholtes et al. use the term "deployment flow chart."
2. B. Shapiro, V. Rangan, and J. Sviokla, "Staple Yourself to an Order," *Harvard Business Review*, July–August 1992, pp. 113–122. See the discussion on p. 120.
3. Our tips for creating functional flow charts are based on our own experience working with organizations and on suggestions offered in Brassard and Ritter, *The Memory Jogger II*, Rother and Shook, *Learning to See: Value Stream Mapping to Create Value and Eliminate Muda*, and Scholtes et al., *The Team Handbook: Second Edition*.
4. R. Hall, "Value-Added Mapping: A Time-Based Technique for Reducing Lead Time," *American National Can*, January 1991, pp. 1–11.

References

Abelson, R., "Companies Turn to Grades, and Employees Go to Court," *New York Times*, March 19, 2001, p. A1.

Ackoff, R. L., "On the Use of Models in Corporate Planning," *Strategic Management Journal*, Vol. 2, No. 4, 1981, pp. 353–359.

Advances in Management of Organizational Quality, Vol. 3 (Greenwich, CT: JAI Press, 1998).

Åhlström, P. and Karlsson, C., "Change Processes Towards Lean Manufacturing," *Int. Journal of Operations and Production Management*, Vol. 16, No. 11, 1996, pp. 42–56.

Anonymous, "Organisational Change in Bonas Machine Company," *IRS Employment Review*, Vol. 610, June 1996, pp. 5–10.

Anonymous, *Survey of Cellular Manufacture: Cellular Manufacturing's Impact on Australian Industry* (Sydney, Australia: Report issued by the University of New South Wales, the University of Wollongong, and IE Management Consultants, 1995).

Appelbaum, E., Bailey, T., Berg, P., and Kalleberg, A., *Manufacturing Advantage: Why High Performance Work Systems Pay Off* (Ithaca, NY: Cornell University Press, 2000).

Askin, R. G. and Estrada, S., "Investigation of Cellular Manufacturing Practices," Chapter 1 in Irani, S. (ed.), *Handbook of Cellular Manufacturing Systems* (New York: John Wiley & Sons, Inc., 1999).

Askin, R. G. and Standridge, C. R., *Modeling and Analysis of Manufacturing Systems* (New York: John Wiley & Sons, 1993).

Atkinson, A. A., Banker, R. D., Kaplan, R. S., and Young, S. M., *Management Accounting* (Upper Saddle River, NJ: Prentice-Hall, 1997).

Bacon, T., *High Impact Facilitation* (Durango, CO: International LearningWorks, 1996).

Baker, S. and Baker, K., *The Complete Idiot's Guide to Project Management* (New York: Alpha Books, 1998).

Baker, W. M., Fry, T. D., and Karwan, K., "The Rise and Fall of Time-Based Manufacturing," *Management Accounting*, June 1994, pp. 56–59.

Baldwin, C. Y. and Clark, K. B., "Managing in an Age of Modularity," *Harvard Business Review*, September–October 1997, p. 87.

Banker, R. D., Potter, G., and Schroeder, R. G., "An Empirical Study of Manufacturing Overhead Drivers," *Journal of Accounting and Economics*, January 1995, pp. 115–138.

Barrick, M. and Mount, M., "The Big Five Personality Dimensions and Job Performance: A Meta Analysis," *Personnel Psychology*, Vol. 44, 1991, pp. 1–26.

Barrick, M., Stewart, G., Neubert, M., and Mount, M., "Relating Member Ability and Personality to Work Team Processes and Team Effectiveness," *Journal of Applied Psychology*, Vol. 83, 1998, pp. 377–391.

Beatty, C., "Implementing Advanced Manufacturing Technologies: Rules of the Road," *Sloan Management Review*, Summer 1992, pp. 49–60.

Beer, M., Spector, B., Lawrence, P., Mills, D., and Walton, R., *Managing Human Assets* (New York: The Free Press, 1984).

Belcher, J., *Gainsharing* (Houston, TX: Gulf, 1991).

Bendaly, L., *Games Teams Play: Dynamic Activities for Tapping Work Team Potential* (Toronto, Canada: McGraw-Hill Ryerson Limited, 1996).

Benders, J. and Badham, R., "A History of Cell-Based Manufacturing," in Beyerlein, M. (ed.), *Work Teams: Past, Present and Future* (Boston, MA: Kluwer Academic Publishers, 2000), pp. 45–47.

Bens, I., *Facilitation at a Glance!* (Methuen, MA: AQP/Participative Dynamics/Goal/ QPC, 1999).

Beyerlein, M. (ed.), *Work Teams: Past, Present and Future* (Boston, MA: Kluwer Academic Publishers, 2000).

Bhaskar, S., *A Two-Stage Cost Allocation Scheme to Support Quick Response Manufacturing*, unpublished Ph.D. dissertation (Madison, WI: University of Wisconsin-Madison, 2000).

Black, J. T., *The Design of the Factory with a Future* (New York: McGraw-Hill, 1991).

Blackburn, J., "Time-Based Competition: White-Collar Activities," *Business Horizons*, July–August 1992, pp. 96–100.

Blanchard, P. and Thacker, J., *Effective Training: Systems, Strategies, and Practice* (Englewood Cliffs, NJ: Prentice Hall, 1999).

Blenkinsop, S. A. and Burns, N., "Performance Measurement Revisited," *International Journal of Operations and Production Management*, Vol. 12, No. 10, 1992, pp. 16–25.

Borman, W., Peterson, N., and Russell, T., "Selection, Training, and Development of Personnel," in Salvendy, G. (ed.), *Handbook of Industrial Engineering* (New York: Wiley, 1992), pp. 882–915.

Boucher, T. O. and Muckstadt, J. A., "Cost Estimating Methods for Evaluating the Conversion from a Functional Manufacturing Layout to Group Technology," *IIE Transactions*, Vol. 17, No. 3, 1985, pp. 268–276.

Brassard, M. and Ritter, D., *The Memory Jogger II* (Methuen, MA: GOAL/QPC, 1994).

Brassard, M., Field, C., Oddo, F., Page, B., Ritter, D., and Smith, L., *The Problem Solving Memory Jogger* (Salem, NH: GOAL/QPC, 2000).

Bratton, J., "Cellular Manufacturing: Some Human Resource Implications," *The Int. Journal of Human Factors in Manufacturing*, Vol. 3, No. 4, 1993, pp. 381–399.

Brown, K. and Mitchell, T., "A Comparison of Just-In-Time and Batch Manufacturing: The Role of Performance Obstacles," *Academy of Management Journal*, Vol. 34, No. 4, 1991, pp. 907–917.

Burbidge, J. L., *The Introduction to Group Technology* (New York: John Wiley, 1975).

Burbidge, J. L., *Production Flow Analysis* (Oxford: Clarendon Press, 1989).

Burbidge, J. L. and Halsell, J., "Group Technology and Growth at Shalibane," *Int. Journal of Production Planning & Control*, Vol. 5, No. 2, 1994, pp. 213–218.

Burgess, A. G., Morgan, I., and Vollmann, T. E., "Cellular Manufacturing: Its Impact on the Total Factory," *Int. Journal of Production Research*, Vol. 31, No. 9, 1993, pp. 2059–2077.

Camp, R. C., *Benchmarking* (Milwaukee, WI: ASQC Quality Press, 1989).

Campion, M. and Medsker, G., "Job Design," in Salvendy, G. (ed.), *Handbook of Industrial Engineering* (New York: Wiley & Sons, 1992), pp. 845–881.

Cardy, R. and Stewart, G., "Quality and Teams: Implications for HRM Theory and Research," in *Advances in the Management of Organizational Quality*, Vol. 3, (Greenwich, CT: JAI Press, 1998), pp. 89–120.

Carrie, A., "The Layout of Multi-Product Lines," *Int. Journal of Production Research*, Vol. 13, No. 6, 1975, pp. 541–557.

Cesani, V. I., *An Investigation of Labor Flexibility in Cellular Manufacturing Systems*, unpublished Ph.D. dissertation (Madison, WI: University of Wisconsin-Madison, 1998).

Chakravorty, S. S., "Robert Bowden Inc.: A Case Study of Cellular Manufacturing and Drum-Buffer-Rope Implementation," *Production and Inventory Management*, Third Quarter 1996, pp. 15–19.

Chang, R. and Kelly, P., *Step-By-Step Problem Solving* (Irvine, CA: Richard Chang Associates, 1993).

Chase, R., Aquilano, N., and Jacobs, F. R., *Production and Operations Management: Manufacturing and Services* (Boston, MA: Irwin/McGraw-Hill, 1998).

Collett, S. and Spicer, R. J., "Improving Productivity through Cellular Manufacturing," *Production and Inventory Management*, First Quarter 1995, pp. 71–75.

Committee on Visionary Manufacturing Challenges, Board on Manufacturing and Engineering Design, Commission on Engineering and Technical Systems, National Research Council, *Visionary Manufacturing Challenges for 2020* (Washington, D.C.: National Academy Press, 1998).

Connecticut Spring and Stamping Corporation (A), Harvard Business School Case 9–694–009 (Boston, MA: Harvard Business School Publishing, 1993).

Conti, R. F., "Variable Manning JIT: An Innovative Answer to Team Absenteeism," *Production and Inventory Management*, First Quarter 1996, pp. 24–27.

Datar, S., Kekre, S., Mukhopadyay, T., and Svaan, E., "Overloaded Overheads: Activity-Based Cost Analysis of Material Handling in Cell Manufacturing," *Journal of Operations Management*, Vol. 10, No. 1, 1991, pp. 119–137.

Day, J., "Learning About Lean Systems at Freudenberg-NOK: Where Continuous Improvement Is a Way of Life," in Liker, J. (ed.), *Becoming Lean: Inside Stories of U.S. Manufacturers* (Portland, OR: Productivity Press, 1998), pp. 178–198.

Dean, J., "Measuring the Productivity of Capital," *Harvard Business Review*, January–February 1954, pp. 120–130.

Dean, J. and Snell, S., "Integrated Manufacturing and Job Design: Moderating Effects of Organizational Inertia," *Academy of Management Journal*, Vol. 34, No. 4, 1991, pp. 776–804.

Desmukh, S., Burns, N., and Backhouse, C., "On Green Area Implementation Problems: A Case Study," *Int. Journal of Production Research*, Vol. 34, No. 11, 1996, pp. 2981–2990.

Dhavale, D. G., *Management Accounting Issues in Cellular Manufacturing and Focused Factory Systems* (Montvale, NJ: The IMA Foundation for Applied Research, 1996).

Dixon, J., Nanni, A., and Vollmann, T., *The New Performance Challenge: Measuring Operations for World-Class Performance* (Homewood, IL: Dow Jones-Irwin, 1990).

Doré-Doré, Harvard Business School Case #9-962-028 (Boston, MA: Harvard Business School Publishing, 1991).

Dugdale, D. and Jones, C., "Accounting for Throughput: Techniques for Performance Measurement, Decisions, and Control," *Management Accounting*, December 1997, pp. 52–56.

Dunnette, M. (ed.), *Handbook of Industrial and Organizational Psychology*, Third Edition, (Chicago, IL: Rand McNally, 1976).

Dunnette, M. and Hough, L. (eds.), *Handbook of Industrial & Organizational Psychology*, Vol. 2 (Palo Alto, CA: Consulting Psychologists Press, 1991).

Dunnette, M. and Hough, L. (eds.), *Handbook of Industrial & Organizational Psychology*, Second Edition, Vol. 3 (Palo Alto, CA: Consulting Psychologists Press, 1992).

Durden, C. H., Hassell, L. G., and Upton, D. R., "Cost Accounting and Performance Measurement in a Just-In-Time Production Environment," *Asian Pacific Journal of Management*, Vol. 16, 1999, pp. 111–125.

Eade, R., *Cellular Manufacturing in a Global Marketplace*, Video Reference Supplement (Dearborn, MI: Society of Manufacturing Engineers, 1995).

Eder, R. and Harris, M. (eds.), *The Employment Interview Handbook* (Thousand Oaks, CA: Sage, 1999).

El-Jawhari, B., *Lead Time Reduction for General Purpose Relays at Deltrol Controls* (Madison, WI: Center for Quick Response Manufacturing, April 1995).

"Employer Spending for Benefits," *Employee Benefit News Benefits Sourcebook 8* (United States: Securities Data Publishing, 1999).

Fakhoury, E. A. F. and Vollmann, T. E., *Applicon* (Boston, MA: case study, Boston University, 1987).

Fay, C. H. (ed.), *The Executive Handbook on Compensation* (New York: The Free Press, 2001).

Fazakerley, M., "Social and Human Factors in Industrial Systems," *Int. Journal of Production Research*, Vol. 12, No. 1, 1974, pp. 139–147.

Fine, C. H., *Clockspeed: Winning Industry Control in the Age of Temporary Advantage* (Reading, MA: Perseus Books, 1998).

Flaherty, J., "Management: Bosses Make Cost Consultants Out of Blue-Collar Workers," *New York Times*, April 18, 2001, pp. C1 and C7.

Fox, J., Edwards, A., Watt, J., and Taylor, B., "Successful Techniques to Realize the Benefits of Cellular Manufacturing," (Wichita, KS: undated conference presentation by personnel from Boeing Commercial Airplane Group).

Fry, T. D., "Manufacturing Performance and Cost Accounting," *Production and Inventory Management*, Third Quarter 1992, pp. 30–35.

Fry, T. D., Steele, D. C., and Saladin, B. A., "The Role of Management Accounting in the Development of a Manufacturing Strategy," *Int. Journal of Operations and Production Management*, Vol. 15, No. 12, 1995, pp. 21–31.

Fuller, T., "Eliminating Complexity from Work: Improving Productivity by Enhancing Quality," *National Productivity Review*, Autumn 1985, pp. 327–344.

Galloway, D., *Mapping Work Processes* (Milwaukee, WI: ASQC Quality Press, 1994).

Garrett, S. E., "Strategy First: A Case in FMS Justification," in Stecke, K. and Suri, R. (eds.), *Proceedings of the Second ORSA/TIMS Conference on Flexible Manufacturing Systems: Operations Research Models and Applications* (Amsterdam, The Netherlands: Elsevier Science BV, 1986), pp. 17–29.

Gatewood, R. and Feild, H., *Human Resource Selection* (Fort Worth, TX: The Dryden Press, 1998).

Gaumnitz, B. R. and Kollaritsch, F. P., "Manufacturing Variances: Current Practices and Trends," *Journal of Cost Management*, Spring 1991, pp. 58–64.

Gavejian, P., "Compensation: Today and Tomorrow," *HRFOCUS*, November 1998, pp. S5–S6.

Gerber, B., "The Bugaboo of Team Pay," *Training*, Vol. 32, No. 8, 1995, pp. 25–34.

Gerhart, B., "Designing Rewards Systems: Balancing Results and Behavior," in Fay, C.H. (ed.), *The Executive Handbook on Compensation* (New York: The Free Press, 2001), pp. 214–237.

Gerhart, B. and Milkovich, G., "Employee Compensation: Research and Practice," in Dunnette, M. and Hough, L. (eds.), *Handbook of Industrial & Organizational Psychology*, Second Edition, Vol. 3 (Palo Alto, CA: Consulting Psychologists Press, 1992), pp. 481–569.

Gerwin, D., "A Theory of Innovation Processes for Computer-Aided Manufacturing Technology," *IEEE Transactions on Engineering Management*, Vol. 35, No. 2, May 1988, pp. 90–100.

Gettelman, K. M., "Organize Production For Parts—Not Processes," *Modern Machine Shop*, Vol. 44, No. 6, November 1971, pp. 50–60.

Goldratt, E. and Cox, J., *The Goal* (Croton-on-Hudson, NY: North River Press, 1984).

Goldratt, E. and Fox, R., *The Race* (Croton-on-Hudson, NY: North River Press, 1986).

Grant, R. M., "The Resource-Based Theory of Competitive Advantage: Implications for Strategy Formulation," *California Management Review*, Spring 1991, pp. 114–135.

Greif, M., *The Visual Factory: Building Participation Through Shared Information* (Portland, OR: Productivity Press, 1991).

Greif, M., "Revolutionizing Internal Communication in Decentralized Organizations," *CEMS Business Review*, Vol. 1, 1996, pp. 27–35.

Gupta, N., Jenkins, G., and Curington, W., "Paying for Knowledge: Myths and Realities," *National Productivity Review*, Vol. 5, 1986, pp. 107–123.

Hackman, J., "Creating More Effective Work Groups in Organizations," in Hackman, J. (ed.), *Groups That Work (and Those That Don't)* (San Francisco, CA: Jossey-Bass, 1990), pp. 479–504.

Hackman, J. (ed.), *Groups That Work (and Those That Don't)* (San Francisco, CA: Jossey-Bass, 1990).

Hackman, J. R. and Oldham, G. R., *Work Redesign* (Readings, MA: Addison-Wesley, 1980).

Hall, R., "Value-Added Mapping: A Time-Based Technique for Reducing Lead Time," *American National Can*, January 1991, pp. 1–11.

Hall, R. W., Johnson, H. T., and Turney, P. B. B., *Measuring Up: Charting Pathways to Manufacturing Excellence* (Homewood, IL: Business One Irwin, 1991).

Hammer, M., "Reengineering Work: Don't Automate, Obliterate," *Harvard Business Review*, July-August 1990, pp. 104–112.

Hammer, M., *Beyond Reengineering* (New York: HarperCollins, 1996).

Hammer, M. and Champy, J., *Reengineering the Corporation* (New York: HarperCollins, 1993).

Hammer, M. and Stanton, S., "How Process Enterprises Really Work," *Harvard Business Review*, November-December 1999, pp. 108–118.

Harmon, R. L. and Peterson, L. D., *Reinventing the Factory* (New York: The Free Press, 1990).

Harrington, H. J., *Business Process Improvement* (New York: McGraw Hill, 1991).

Harris, M. and Eder, R., "The State of Employment Interview Practice: Commentary and Extension," in Eder, R. and Harris, M. (eds.), 1999, *The Employment Interview Handbook*, (Thousand Oaks, CA: Sage), pp. 369–398.

Harry, M. and Schroeder, R., *Six Sigma: The Breakthrough Management Strategy Revolutionizing the World's Top Corporations* (New York: Currency Books, 2000).

Harvey, N., *The Socio-Technical Implementation of Cellular Manufacturing in American and German Metal Working Firms* (Madison, WI: unpublished Ph.D. dissertation, University of Wisconsin-Madison, 1993).

Harvey, N., "How Unions Should Respond to Cells," *Labor Studies Journal*, Vol. 18, No. 4, Winter 1994, pp. 21–38.

Hassard, J. and Proctor, S., "Manufacturing Change: Introducing Cellular Production in Two British Factories," *Personnel Review*, Vol. 20, No. 4, 1991, pp. 15–24.

Hayes, R., Wheelwright, S., and Clark, K., *Dynamic Manufacturing: Creating the Learning Organization* (New York: The Free Press, 1988).

Heard, J. A., "JIT Accounting," in *Readings in Zero Inventory* (Falls Church, VA: American Production and Inventory Control Society), 1984, pp. 20–23.

Hedin, S. R. and Russell, G. R., "JIT Implementation: Interaction Between the Production and Cost-Accounting Functions," *Production and Inventory Management*, Third Quarter 1992, pp. 68–73.

Hendricks, J., "Performance Measures for a JIT Manufacturer: The Role of the IE," *Industrial Engineering*, Vol. 25, No. 1, January 1994, pp. 26–29.

Heneman, H., Judge, T., and Heneman, R., *Staffing Organizations* (Boston, MA: Irwin McGraw-Hill, 2000).

Heneman, R., Ledford, G., Gresham, M., "The Changing Nature of Work and Its Effects on Compensation Design and Delivery," in Rynes, S. and Gerhart, B. (eds.), *Compensation in Organizations: Current Research and Practice* (San Francisco, CA: Jossey-Bass, 2000), pp. 195–240.

Hequet, M., "Ergomania," *Training*, May 1995, pp. 45–50.

Heragu, S., "Group Technology and Cellular Manufacturing," *IEEE Transactions on Systems, Man, and Cybernetics*, Vol. 24, No. 2, 1994, pp. 203–215.

Heragu, S., *Facilities Design* (Boston, MA: PWS Publishing Company, 1997).

Higgins, P., Le Roy, P., and Tierney, L., *Manufacturing Planning and Control: Beyond MRPII* (London: Chapman & Hall, 1996).

Hill, T., *Manufacturing Strategy* (Burr Ridge, IL: Irwin, 1994).

Hilton, R. W, Maher, M. W., and Selto, F. H., *Cost Management* (Boston, MA: Irwin McGraw-Hill, 2000).

Hinrichs, J., "Personnel Training," in Dunnette, M. (ed.), *Handbook of Industrial and Organizational Psychology*, Third Edition, (Chicago, IL: Rand McNally, 1976).

Hiromoto, T., "Restoring the Relevance of Management Accounting," *Journal of Management Accounting Research*, Fall 1991, pp. 1–15.

Hirano, H., *JIT Factory Revolution: A Pictorial Guide to Factory Design of the Future* (Cambridge, MA: Productivity Press, 1988).

Hobbs, O. K., "Application of JIT Techniques in a Discrete Batch Job Shop," *Production and Inventory Management*, First Quarter 1994, pp. 43–47.

Hogan, J., "Physical Abilities," in Dunnette, M. and Hough, L. (eds.), *Handbook of Industrial & Organizational Psychology*, Vol. 2 (Palo Alto, CA: Consulting Psychologists Press, 1991), pp. 753–831.

Hollier, R., "The Layout of Multi-Product Lines," *Int. Journal of Production Research*, Vol. 2, 1963, pp. 47–57.

Hopp, W. J. and Spearman, M. L., *Factory Physics: The Foundations of Manufacturing Management* (Chicago, IL: Irwin, 1996).

Horngren, C. T., *Introduction to Management Accounting* (Englewood Cliffs, NJ: Prentice-Hall, 1984).

Horngren, C. T., Foster, G., and Datar, S. M., *Cost Accounting: A Managerial Emphasis* (Upper Saddle River, NJ: Prentice-Hall, 1997).

Howard, A., Kochar, A., and Dilworth, J., "An Objective Approach for Generating the Functional Specification of Manufacturing Planning and Control Systems," *Int. Journal of Operations & Production Management*, Vol. 18, No. 8, 1998, pp. 710–726.

Huber, V. and Brown, K., "Human Resource Issues in Cellular Manufacturing: A Sociotechnical Analysis," *Journal of Operations Management*, Vol. 10, No. 1, 1991, pp. 138–159.

Huber, V. L. and Hyer, N. L., "The Human Factor in Cellular Manufacturing," *Journal of Operations Management*, Vol. 5, No. 2, 1985, pp. 213–228.

Hunter, J., "Cognitive Ability, Cognitive Aptitudes, Job Knowledge and Job Performance," *Journal of Vocational Behavior*, Vol. 29, 1986, pp. 340–362.

Hunter, J. and Hunter, R., "Validity and Utility of Alternative Predictors of Job Performance," *Psychological Bulletin*, Vol. 96, No. 1, 1984, pp. 72–98.

Hyde, W. F., *Improving Productivity by Classification, Coding, and Database Standardization* (New York: Marcel Dekker, 1981).

Hyer, N. L. and Brown, K., "The Discipline of Real Cells," *Journal of Operations Management*, Vol. 17, No. 5, 1999, pp. 557–574.

Hyer, N. L. and Brown, K., "A Taxonomy of Cell Management Challenges and Outcomes: An Electronics Industry Field Study," Working Paper (Nashville, TN: Owen Graduate School of Management, 2000).

Hyer, N. L. and Brown, K., "The Life Cycle Dynamics of Manufacturing Cells: Evolution, Drift and Dissolution," Working Paper (Nashville, TN: Owen Graduate School of Management, 2000).

Hyer, N. L., Brown, K., and Zimmerman, S., "A Socio-Technical Systems Approach to Cell Design: Case Study and Analysis," *Journal of Operations Management*, Vol. 17, No. 2, 1999, pp. 179–203.

Hyer, N. L. and Wemmerlöv, U., "Procedures for the Part Family/Machine Group Identification Problem in Cellular Manufacturing," *Journal of Operations Management*, Vol. 6, No. 2, 1986, pp. 125–147.

Hyer, N. L. and Wemmerlöv, U., "Group Technology in the US Manufacturing Industry: A Survey of Users," *Int. Journal of Production Research*, Vol. 27, No. 8, 1989, pp. 1287–1304.

Hyun, S. Y., *The Determination and Evaluation of Transfer Batches for Multi-Stage Flow Shops*, unpublished Ph.D. dissertation (Madison, WI: University of Wisconsin-Madison, School of Business, 1996).

Imai, M., *Gemba Kaizen* (New York: McGraw-Hill, 1997).

Industry Week, "The Real Problem: It's Negative Variety," June 8, 1998, p. 38.

Inman, R. R., "Are You Implementing a Pull System by Putting the Cart Before the Horse?" *Production and Inventory Management*, Second Quarter 1999, pp. 67–71.

IPS Associates, *Project Management Manual*, Harvard Business School Note #9-967-034 (Boston, MA: Harvard Business School Publishing, 1996).

Irani, S. A. (ed.), *Handbook of Cellular Manufacturing Systems* (New York: John Wiley & Sons, 1999).

Jacobs, F. R. and Bragg, D. J., "Repetitive Lots: Flow-Time Reductions through Sequencing and Dynamic Batch Sizing," *Decision Sciences*, Vol. 19, 1988, pp. 281–294.

Jenkins, G., Ledford, G., Gupta, N., and Doty, D., *Skill-Based Pay: Practices, Payoffs, Pitfalls and Prescriptions* (Phoenix, AZ: American Compensation Association, 1992).

Johnson, B. and Ray, H., "Employee Developed Pay System Increases Productivity," *Personnel Journal*, Vol. 72, No. 11, 1993, pp. 112–118.

Johnson, D. J., *An Empirical Investigation of Factors Influencing Reorganizations to Cellular Manufacturing*, unpublished Ph.D. dissertation (Madison, WI: School of Business, University of Wisconsin-Madison, 1998).

Johnson, D. J. and Wemmerlöv, U., "On the Relative Performance of Functional and Cellular Layouts—An Analysis of the Model-Based Comparative Studies Literature," *Production and Operations Management*, Vol. 5, No. 4, 1996, pp. 309–334.

Johnson, D. J. and Wemmerlöv, U., "Cellular Manufacturing Feasibility at Ingersoll Cutting Tool Co.," in Suresh, N. C. and Kay, J. M. (eds.), *Group Technology and Cellular Manufacturing: State-of-the-Art Synthesis of Research and Practice* (Boston, MA: Kluwer Academic Publishers, 1998), pp. 239–254.

Johnson, D. J. and Wemmerlöv, U., "Factors Influencing the Degree of Cell Penetration in Manufacturing Plants," Working Paper (Ames, IA and Madison, WI: Iowa State University and University of Wisconsin-Madison, June 1999).

Jordan, J. and Michel, F., *Next Generation Manufacturing* (Dearborn, MI: Society of Manufacturing Engineers, 1999).

Kannan, V. R., "Incorporating the Impact of Learning in Assessing the Effectiveness of Cellular Manufacturing," *Int. Journal of Production Research*, Vol. 34, No. 12, December 1996, pp. 3327–3340.

Kannan, V. R. and Ghosh, S., "A Virtual Cellular Manufacturing Approach to Batch Production," *Decision Sciences*, Vol. 27, No. 3, 1996, pp. 519–539.

Kanter, R. M., Stein, B. A., and Jick, T. D., *The Challenge of Organizational Change: How Companies Experience It and How Leaders Guide It* (New York: The Free Press, 1992).

Kaplan, R. S., "Yesterday's Accounting Undermines Production," *Harvard Business Review*, July–August 1984, pp. 95–101.

Kaplan, R. S., "Must CIM Be Justified By Faith Alone?," *Harvard Business Review*, March–April 1986, pp. 87–96.

Kaplan, R. S., "One Cost System Isn't Enough," *Harvard Business Review*, January–February 1988, pp. 61–66.

Kaplan, R. S. (ed.), *Measures for Manufacturing Excellence* (Boston, MA: Harvard Business School Press, 1990).

Kaplan, R. and Norton, D., "The Balanced Scorecard—Measures that Drive Performance," *Harvard Business Review*, February 1992, pp. 71–79.

Karanzalis, T. C., "Family Parts Line Production—A New Manufacturing Concept," text of presentation given at Industrial Management Seminar #35, Milwaukee, WI, October 1970.

Karle, M. P., "Group Technology Paves the Way for a Just-In-Time Manufacturing Philosophy," *Proceedings of the IXth ICPR Conference*, Cincinnati, OH, August 1987, pp. 910–917.

Karlsson, C. and Åhlström, P., "Change Processes Toward Lean Production: The Role of the Remuneration System," *Int. Journal of Operations and Production Management*, Vol. 15, No. 11, 1995, pp. 80–99.

Karmarker, U. S., "Lot Sizes, Lead-Times, and In-Process Inventories," *Management Science*, Vol. 33, No.3, 1987, pp. 409–418.

Katzenbach, J. and Smith, D., *The Wisdom of Teams: Creating the High-Performance Organization* (New York: HarperCollins, 1993).

Kawada, M. and Johnson, D. F., "Strategic Management Accounting," *Management Accounting*, August 1993, pp. 32–38.

Kayser, T., *Mining Group Gold: How to Cash In On The Collaborative Brain Power of a Group* (El Segundo, CA: Serif Publishing, 1990).

Kim, W. and Mauborgne, R., "Fair Process: Managing in the Knowledge Economy," *Harvard Business Review*, Vol. 75, No. 4, July–August 1997, pp. 65–75.

Klein, J., "The Human Costs of Manufacturing Reform," *Harvard Business Review*, Vol. 67, No. 2, 1989, pp. 60–66.

Kleinmutz, B., "Why We Still Use Our Heads Instead of Formulas: Toward an Integrative Approach," *Psychological Bulletin*, Vol. 107, No. 3, 1990, pp. 296–310.

Knauss, K. and Matusak, M., "The Implications of Cell Manufacturing for U.S. Factory Workers and Their Unions," *Labor Studies Journal*, Spring 1989, pp. 19–29.

Kochan, T. and Osterman, P., *The Mutual Gains Enterprise: Forging a Winning Partnership Among Labor, Management, and Government* (Boston, MA: Harvard Business School Press, 1994).

Kotter, J., "Leading Change: Why Transformation Efforts Fail," *Harvard Business Review On Change* (Boston, MA: Harvard Business School Press, 1998), pp. 1–20.

Koulopoulos, T., *The Workflow Imperative* (New York: Van Nostrand Reinhold, 1995).

Krishnamurthy, A., Suri, R., and Vernon, M., "Re-examining the Performance of Push, Pull and Hybrid Materials Control Strategies for Multi-Product Flexible Manufacturing

Systems," December 2000, Technical Report (Madison, WI: Center for Quick Response Manufacturing).

Landry, S., Duguay, C. R., Chaussé, S., and Themens, J.-L., "Integrating MRP, Kanban and Barcoding Systems to Achieve JIT Procurement," *Production and Inventory Management*, First Quarter 1997, pp. 8–13.

Lang, R. and Hellpach, W., *Gruppenfabrikation* (Berlin: Julius Springer, 1922).

Law, A. M. and Kelton, W. D., *Simulation Modeling and Analysis* (New York: McGraw-Hill, 1991).

Lawler, E., *Pay and Organizational Effectiveness: A Psychological View* (New York: McGraw-Hill, 1971).

Lawler, E., *High-Involvement Management* (San Francisco, CA: Jossey-Bass, 1986).

Lawler, E., *The Ultimate Advantage: Creating the High-Involvement Organization* (San Francisco, CA: Jossey-Bass, 1992).

Lawler, E., *Rewarding Excellence: Pay Strategies for the New Economy* (San Francisco, CA: Jossey-Bass, 2000).

Lawler, E. and Ledford, G., "Skill-Based Pay: A Concept That's Catching On," *Management Review*, Vol. 76, No. 2, 1987, pp. 46–51.

Lawler, E., Ledford, G., and Chang, L., "Who Uses Skill-Based Pay and Why," *Compensation and Benefits Review*, Vol. 25, No. 2, 1993, pp. 22–26.

Lawler, E., Markovsky, B., Ridgeway, C., Walker, H. (eds.), *Advances in Group Processes*, Vol. 9 (Greenwich, CT: JAI Press, 1992).

Lawler, E., Mohrman, S., and Ledford, G., *Strategies for High Performing Organizations* (San Francisco, CA: Jossey-Bass, 1998).

Lee, Q., *Facilities and Workplace Design: An Illustrated Guide* (Norcross, GA: Engineering and Management Press, 1996).

Levasseur, G. A., Helms, M. M., and Zink, A. A., "A Conversion from a Functional to a Cellular Manufacturing Layout at Steward, Inc.," *Production and Inventory Management*, Vol. 36, No. 3, 1995, pp. 37–42.

Liker, J., "Introduction: Bringing Lean Back to the U.S.A.," in Liker, J. (ed.), *Becoming Lean: Inside Stories of U.S. Manufacturers* (Portland, OR: Productivity Press, 1998), pp. 2–38.

Liker, J., "Conclusions: What We Have Learned About Becoming Lean," in Liker, J. (ed.), *Becoming Lean: Inside Stories of U.S. Manufacturers* (Portland, OR: Productivity Press, 1998), pp. 497–517.

Liker, J. (ed.), *Becoming Lean: Inside Stories of U.S. Manufacturers* (Portland, OR: Productivity Press, 1998).

Little, J. D. C., "A Proof of the Queuing Formula $L=\lambda W$," *Operations Research*, Vol. 9, 1961, pp. 383–387.

Magjuka, R. and Schmenner, R., "Cellular Manufacturing and Plant Administration: Some Initial Evidence," *Labor Studies Journal*, Summer 1992, pp. 44–63.

Majchrzak, A., *The Human Side of Factory Automation* (San Francisco, CA: Jossey-Bass, 1988).

Majchrzak, A. and Wang, Q., "Breaking the Functional Mind-Set in Process Organizations," *Harvard Business Review*, September–October 1996, pp. 92–99.

Marsh, R., "How Well Do Manufacturing Cells Age," *Production and Inventory Management*, Third Quarter 1995, pp. 1–4.

Marsh, R. F. and Meredith, J. R., "Changes in Performance Measures on the Factory Floor," *Production and Inventory Management*, First Quarter 1998, pp. 36–40.

Marsh, R. F., Meredith, J. R., and McCutcheon, D. M., "The Life Cycle of Manufacturing Cells," *Int. Journal of Operations and Production Management*, Vol. 17, No. 12, 1998, pp. 1167–1182.

Maskell, B., *Performance Measurement for World-Class Manufacturing* (Portland, OR: Productivity Press, 1991).

Mazany, P., "A Case Study: Lessons From the Progressive Implementation of Just-In-Time in a Small Knitwear Manufacturer," *Int. Journal of Operations and Production Management*, Vol. 15, No. 9, 1995, pp. 271–288.

McAdams, J., *The Reward Plan Advantage: A Manager's Guide to Improving Business Performance Through People* (San Francisco, CA: Jossey-Bass, 1996).

McCormick, E., *Job Analysis: Methods and Applications* (New York: AMACOM, 1979).

McGovern, M. and Andrews, B., "Operational Excellence: A Manufacturing Metamorphosis at Western Geophysical Exploration Products," in Liker, J. (ed.), *Becoming Lean: Inside Stories of U.S. Manufacturers* (Portland, OR: Productivity Press, 1998), pp. 389–406.

McLean, C. R., Bloom, H. M., and Hopp, T. H., "The Virtual Manufacturing Cell," *Proceedings of the Fourth IFAC/IFIP Conference on Information Control Problems in Manufacturing Technology*, Gaithersburg, MD, October 1982.

Melnyk, S. A. and Carter, P. L., *Production Activity Control* (Homewood, IL: Dow-Jones-Irwin, 1987).

Merchant, K. A. and Shields, M. D., "When and Why to Measure Cost Less Accurately to Improve Decision Making," *Accounting Horizons*, Vol. 7, No. 2, June 1993, pp. 76–81.

Merkel, K., "Achieving Planned Performance Results Using Manufacturing Operations," *Industrial Engineering*, April 1995, pp. 26–29.

Meyer, C., "How the Right Measures Help Teams Excel," *Harvard Business Review*, May–June 1994, pp. 95–103.

Milkovich, G. and Newman, J., *Compensation* (Chicago, IL: Irwin, 1996).

Milkovich, G. and Wigdor, A., *Pay for Performance* (Washington, D.C.: National Academy Press, 1991).

Miller, J. G. and Vollmann, T. E., "The Hidden Factory," *Harvard Business Review*, September–October 1985, pp. 142–150.

Mitrofanov, S. P., *The Scientific Principles of Group Technology* (Yorkshire: National Lending Library for Science and Technology, 1966).

Mohrman, S., Cohen, S., and Mohrman, A., *Designing Team-Based Organizations: New Forms for Knowledge Work* (San Francisco, CA: Jossey-Bass, 1995).

Molleman, E. and Slomp, J., "Functional Flexibility and Team Performance," *Int. Journal of Production Research*, Vol. 37, No. 8, 1999, pp. 1837–1858.

Monden, Y., *Toyota Production System* (Norcross, GA: Industrial Engineering and Management Press, 1983).

Montagno, R., Ahmed, N., and Firenze, R., "Perceptions of Operations Strategies and Technologies in U.S. Manufacturing Firms," *Production and Inventory Management*, Second Quarter 1995, pp. 22–27.

Moreland, R. and Levine, J., "The Composition of Small Groups," in Lawler, E., Markovsky, B., Ridgeway, C., Walker, H. (eds.), *Advances in Group Processes*, Vol. 9 (Greenwich, CT: JAI Press, 1992), pp. 237–280.

Murray, B. and Gerhart, B., "An Empirical Analysis of a Skill-Based Pay Program and Plant Performance Outcomes," *Academy of Management Journal*, Vol. 41, No. 1, 1998, pp. 68–78.

Muther, R., *Systematic Layout Planning* (Boston, MA: Cahners Books, 1973).

Nadler, D. A. and Tushman, M. L., "A Model for Diagnosing Organizational Behavior," *Organizational Dynamics*, Autumn 1980, pp. 35–51.

Neely, A., Mills, J., Platts, K., Gregory, M., and Richards, H., "Realizing Strategy Through Measurement," *Int. Journal of Operations and Production Management*, Vol. 14, No. 3, 1994, pp. 140–152.

New York Times, October 29, 1993, p. C5.

New York Times, March 9, 1999, p. C9.

New York Times, May 15, 1999, pp. B1 and B3.

Nimmons, T. A. K., *Improving the Process of Designing Cellular Manufacturing Systems* (Cranfield University, England: unpublished Ph.D. dissertation, 1996).

Noe, R., Hollenbeck, J., Gerhart, B., and Wright, P., *Human Resource Management: Gaining a Competitive Advantage* (Boston, MA: Irwin McGraw-Hill, 2000).

Nolen, J., *Computer-Automated Process Planning for World-Class Manufacturing* (New York: Marcel Dekker, Inc., 1989).

Nyman, L. R. (ed.), *Making Manufacturing Cells Work* (Dearborn, MI: Society of Manufacturing Engineers, 1992).

Olorunniwo, F., "Changes in Production Planning and Control Systems with Implementation of Cellular Manufacturing," *Production and Inventory Management*, First Quarter 1996, pp. 65–69.

Olorunniwo, F. O. and Udo, G. J., "Cell Design Practices in U.S. Manufacturing Firms," *Production and Inventory Management*, Third Quarter, 1996, pp. 27–33.

Owen, J., "From Suits to Cells," *Manufacturing Engineering*, Vol. 122, No. 6, June 1999, pp. 62–67.

Pande, P., Neuman, R. and Cavanaugh, R., *The Six Sigma Way: How GE, Motorola, and Other Top Companies are Honing Their Performance* (New York: McGraw-Hill, 2000).

Panizzolo, R., "Cellular Manufacturing at Zanussi-Electrolux Plant, Susegana, Italy," Chapter 13 in Suresh, N. C. and Kay, J. M. (eds.), *Group Technology and Cellular Manufacturing: State-of-the-Art Synthesis of Research and Practice* (Boston, MA: Kluwer Academic Publishers, 1998), pp. 475–490.

Parent, K. and Weber, C., "Case Study: Does Paying for Knowledge Pay Off?" *Compensation and Benefits Review*, Vol. 26, No. 5, 1994, pp. 44–50.

Pasmore, W., *Designing Effective Organizations: The Sociotechnical Systems Perspective* (New York: John Wiley and Sons, 1988).

Perona, M., "Cell Formation in a Coil Forging Shop: An Implementation Case," in Irani, S. (ed.), *Handbook of Cellular Manufacturing Systems* (New York: Wiley & Sons, 1999), pp. 555–587.

Phillips, J., *Handbook of Training Evaluation and Measurement Methods* (Houston, TX: Gulf Publishing, 1983).

Primrose, P. L. and Leonard, R., "Evaluating the 'Intangible' Benefits of Flexible Manufacturing Systems by Use of Discounted Cash Flow Algorithms Within a Comprehensive Computer Program," Proceedings, Part B (Management and Engineering Manufacture), *The Institution of Manufacturing Engineers*, 1985, pp. 289–294.

Production Islands, published by the AWF Committee for Economical Manufacture (original in German, date and publisher unknown).

Pullen, R., "A Survey of Cellular Manufacturing Cells," *Production Engineer*, Vol. 55, 1976, pp. 451–454.

Raychem Corporation Interconnection System Division, Harvard Business School Case 9–694–063 (Boston, MA: Harvard Business School Publishing, 1997).

Ree, M. and Earles, J., "Predicting Training Success: Not Much More Than *g*," *Personnel Psychology*, Vol. 44, 1991, pp. 321–332.

Rees, F., *How to Lead Work Teams: Facilitation Skills* (Amsterdam, The Netherlands: Pfeiffer, 1991).

Reisman, A., Kumar, A., Motwani, J., and Cheng, C. H., "Cellular Manufacturing: A Statistical Review of the Literature (1965–1995)," *Operations Research*, Vol. 45, No. 4, 1997, pp. 508–520.

Ricks, T., "Army Devises System to Decide What Does, and Does Not, Work," *Wall Street Journal*, May 23, 1997, pp. A1 and A10.

Riezebos, J., Shambu, G., and Suresh, N. C., Chapter F1, in Suresh, N. C. and Kay, J. M. (eds.), *Group Technology and Cellular Manufacturing* (Boston, MA: Kluwer Academic Publishers, 1998).

Ritter, D. and Brassard, M., *The Creativity Tools Memory Jogger* (Lawrence, MA: GOAL/QPC, 1998).

Rosen, E., *Bitter Choices: Blue Collar Women In and Out of Work* (Chicago, IL: University of Chicago Press, 1987).

Rosenthal, S. R., "Progress Toward the Factory of the Future," *Journal of Operations Management*, Vol. 4, 1984, pp. 203–230.

Rössle, R. and Züst, R., "Cellular Manufacturing in Highly Specialized Supply Industries," *Annals of the CIRP*, Vol. 43, No. 1, 1994, pp. 397–400.

Rother, M. and Shook, J., *Learning to See: Value Stream Mapping to Create Value and Eliminate Muda* (Brookline, MA: The Lean Enterprise Institute, 1999).

Rummler, G. and Brache, A., *Improving Performance: How to Manage the White Space on the Organization Chart* (San Francisco, CA: Jossey-Bass, 1995).

Rynes, S., "Compensation Strategies for Recruiting," *Topics in Total Compensation*, Vol. 2, 1987, pp. 185–196.

Rynes, S. and Gerhart, B. (eds.), *Compensation in Organizations: Current Research and Practice* (San Francisco, CA: Jossey-Bass, 2000).

Sakakibara, S., Flynn, B. B., and Schroeder, R. G., "A Framework and Measurement Instrument for Just-In-Time Manufacturing," *Production and Operations Management*, Vol. 2, No. 3, 1993, pp. 177–194.

Salvendy, G. (ed.), *Handbook of Industrial Engineering* (New York: Wiley & Sons, 1992).

Saven, B., "Motivation—The Single Most Important Factor for Improved Manufacturing Performance: A Case Study," Working Paper (Linköping, Sweden: Linköping Institute of Technology, 1990).

Schneier, C., Shaw, D., and Beatty, R., "Performance Measurement and Management: A Tool for Strategy Execution," *Human Resource Management*, Vol. 30, No. 3, Fall 1991, pp. 279–301.

Scholtes, P., Joiner, B., and Streibel, B., *The Team Handbook: Second Edition* (Madison, WI: Oriel Corporation, 1996).

Schonberger, R., *Building a Chain of Customers: Linking Business Functions to Create the World Class Company* (New York: The Free Press, 1990).

Schonberger, R., *World-Class Manufacturing: The Next Decade* (New York: The Free Press, 1996).

Schoonover, S., *Managing to Relate: Interpersonal Skills at Work* (Reading, MA: Addison-Wesley, 1988).

Sekine, K., *One-Piece Flow: Cell Design for Transforming the Production Process* (Portland, OR: Productivity Press, 1992).

Shapiro, B., Rangan, V., and Sviokla, J., "Staple Yourself to an Order," *Harvard Business Review*, July–August 1992, pp. 113–122.

Shenberger, R., "Still Paying for Hours on the Job? Think Again," *Journal for Quality and Participation*, Vol. 18, 1995, pp. 88–91.

Shingo, S., *A Revolution in Manufacturing: The SMED System* (Cambridge, MA: Productivity Press, 1985).

Shook, J., "Bringing the Toyota Production System to the United States: A Personal Perspective," in Liker, J. (ed.), *Becoming Lean: Inside Stories of U.S. Manufacturers* (Portland, OR: Productivity Press, 1998), pp. 40–69.

Sink, S. and Tuttle, T., *Planning and Measurement in Your Organization of the Future* (Norcross, GA: Industrial Engineering and Management Press, 1989).

Skinner, W., "Production Under Pressure," *Harvard Business Review*, November–December 1966, pp. 139–146.

Skinner, W., "The Focused Factory," *Harvard Business Review*, May–June 1974, pp. 113–121.

Slomp, J., "Design of Manufacturing Cells: PFA Applications in Dutch Industry," in Suresh, N. and Kay, J. (eds.), *Group Technology and Cellular Manufacturing: State-of-the-Art Synthesis of Research and Practice* (Boston, MA: Kluwer Academic Publishers, 1998), pp. 153–168.

Snell, S. and Dean, J., "Strategic Compensation for Integrated Manufacturing: The Moderating Effects of Jobs and Organizational Inertia," *Academy of Management Journal*, Vol. 37, No. 5, 1994, pp. 1109–1140.

Spencer, M. S., "Group Technology at John Deere: Production Planning and Control Issues," Chapter 15, in Suresh, N. C. and Kay, J. M. (eds.), *Group Technology and Cellular Manufacturing: State-of-the-Art Synthesis of Research and Practice* (Boston, MA: Kluwer Academic Publishers, 1998), pp. 501–516.

Stalk, G., Jr., "Time–The Next Source of Competitive Advantage," *Harvard Business Review*, July–August 1988, pp. 41–51.

Stalk, G., Jr., and Hout, T. M., *Competing Against Time* (New York: The Free Press, 1992).

Stecke, K. and Suri, R. (eds.), 1986, *Proceedings of the Second ORSA/TIMS Conference on Flexible Manufacturing Systems: Operations Research Models and Applications* (Amsterdam, The Netherlands: Elsevier Science BV).

Steele, D. C., Berry, W. L., and Chapman, S. N., "Planning and Control in Multi-Cell Manufacturing," *Decision Sciences*, Vol. 26, No. 1, 1995, pp. 1–34.

Steudel, H. J. and Desruelle, P., *Manufacturing in the Nineties: How to Become a Mean, Lean, World-Class Competitor* (New York: Van Nostrand Reinhold, 1992).

Stevens, M. and Campion, M., "The Knowledge, Skill, and Ability Requirements for Teamwork: Implications for Human Resource Management," *Journal of Management*, Vol. 20, 1994, pp. 503–550.

Stewart, G., Manz, C., and Sims, H., *Team Work and Group Dynamics* (New York: John Wiley & Sons, 1999).

Sugimori, Y., Kusunoki, K., Cho, F., and Uchikawa, S., "Toyota Production System and Kanban System: Materialization of Just-In-Time and Respect-For-Human System," *Int. Journal of Production Research*, Vol. 15, No. 6, 1977, pp. 553–564.

Sull, D. N., "Why Good Companies Go Bad," *Harvard Business Review*, July–August 1999, pp. 42–52.

Suresh, N. C. and Kay, J. M. (eds.), *Group Technology and Cellular Manufacturing: State-of-the-Art Synthesis of Research and Practice* (Boston, MA: Kluwer Academic Publishers, 1998).

Suresh, N. C. and Meredith, J. R., "Coping with the Loss of Pooling Synergy," *Management Science*, Vol. 40, No. 4, 1994, pp. 466–483.

Suri, R., *Quick Response Manufacturing* (Portland, OR: Productivity Press, 1998).

Suri, R., Wemmerlöv, U., Rath, F., Gadh, R., and Veeramani, R., "Practical Issues in Implementing Quick Response Manufacturing: Insights from Fourteen Projects with Industry," *Proceedings of the Manufacturing and Service Operations Management (MSOM) Conference*, Dartmouth College, Hanover, NH, June 24–25, 1996.

Suzaki, K., *The New Manufacturing Challenge: Techniques for Continuous Improvement* (New York: The Free Press, 1987).

Suzaki, K., *The New Shop Floor Management: Empowering People for Continuous Improvement* (New York: The Free Press, 1993).

Swamidass, P., *Technology on the Factory Floor III: Technology Use and Training in U.S. Manufacturing Firms* (Washington, D.C.: The Manufacturing Institute/National Association of Manufacturers, 1998).

Swenson, D. W. and Cassidy, J., "The Effect of JIT on Management Accounting," *Journal of Cost Management*, Spring 1993, pp. 39–47.

Tatikonda, M. and Wemmerlöv, U., "Adoption and Implementation of Group Technology Classification and Coding Systems—Insights from Seven Case Studies," *Int. Journal of Production Research*, Vol. 30, No. 9, 1992, pp. 2087–2110.

Taylor, F. W., *The Principles of Scientific Management* (New York: Norton, 1911).

Taylor, J. C. and Felten, D. F., *Performance by Design: Sociotechnical Systems in North America* (Englewood Cliffs, NJ: Prentice Hall, 1993).

Tektronix: Portable Instruments Division (B), Harvard Business School Case 9-188-143 (Boston, MA: Harvard Business School Publishing, 1991).

Tompkins, J. A., White, J. A., Bozer, Y. A., Frazelle, E. H., Tanchoco, J. M. A., and Trevino, J., *Facilities Planning* (New York: John Wiley & Sons, Inc., 1996).

Tosi, H. and Tosi, L., "What Managers Need to Know about Knowledge-Based Pay," *Organizational Dynamics*, Vol. 14, No. 3, 1986, pp. 52–64.

TRADE (Training Resources and Data Exchange) Performance-Based Management Special Interest Group, *How to Measure Performance—A Handbook of Techniques and Tools* (Oak Ridge, TN: Oak Ridge Associated Universities, 1995).

Turley, K., "First Ask 'Why?' Then Ask 'How?'," *Target*, Vol. 11, No. 1, 1995, pp. 41–45.

Tushman, M. L. and Moore, W. L. (eds.), *Readings in the Management of Innovation* (Cambridge, MA: Ballinger, 1980).

Umble, M. M. and Srikanth, M. L., *Synchronous Manufacturing* (Cincinnati, OH: South-Western Publishing, 1990).

Van der Veen, D. J. and Jordan, W. C., "Analyzing Trade-Offs between Machine Investment and Utilization," *Management Science*, Vol. 35, No. 10, 1989, pp. 1215–1226.

Vollmann, T., "Performance Measurements That Support World Class Manufacturing," in Wallace, T. and Bennett, S. (eds.), *World Class Manufacturing* (Essex Junction, VT: Omneo/Oliver Wight Publications, 1994), pp. 435–447.

Vollmann, T. E., Berry, W. L., and Whybark, D. C., *Manufacturing Planning and Control Systems* (New York: Irwin/McGraw-Hill, 1997).

Wallace, T. and Bennett, S. (eds.), *World Class Manufacturing* (Essex Junction, VT: Omneo, 1994).

Walton, R. and Susman, G., "People Policies for New Machines," *Harvard Business Review*, Vol. 65, No. 2, 1987, pp. 98–106.

Waterson, P. E., et al., "The Use and Effectiveness of Modern Manufacturing Practices: A Survey of UK Industry," *Int. Journal of Production Research*, Vol. 37, No. 10, 1999, pp. 2271–2292.

Wayman, M., "Order Processing Lead Time Reduction: A Case Study," *International Industrial Engineering Conference and Societies' Manufacturing and Productivity Symposium Proceedings* (Norcross, GA: Institute of Industrial Engineers, 1995), pp. 400–409.

Wemmerlöv, U., "Assemble-to-Order Manufacturing: Implications for Materials Management," *Journal of Operations Management*, Vol. 4, No. 4, 1984, pp. 347–368.

Wemmerlöv, U., *Capacity Management Techniques for Manufacturing Companies with MRP Systems* (Falls Church, VA: American Production and Inventory Control Society, 1984).

Wemmerlöv, U., *Production Planning and Control Procedures for Cellular Manufacturing Systems: Concepts and Practices* (Falls Church, VA: American Production and Inventory Control Society, 1988).

Wemmerlöv, U., "Economic Justification of Group Technology Software," *Journal of Operations Management*, Vol. 9, No. 4, 1990, pp. 500–525.

Wemmerlöv, U., "Fundamental Insights into Part Family Scheduling: The Single Machine Case," *Decision Sciences*, Vol. 23, No. 3, 1992, pp. 565–595.

Wemmerlöv, U. and Hyer, N. L., "Cellular Manufacturing in the U.S. Industry: A Survey of Users," *Int. Journal of Production Research*, Vol. 27, No. 9, 1989, pp. 1511–1530.

Wemmerlöv, U. and Johnson, D. J., "Cellular Manufacturing at 46 User Plants: Implementation Experiences and Performance Improvements," *Int. Journal of Production Research*, Vol. 35, No. 1, 1997, pp. 29–49.

Wemmerlöv, U. and Johnson, D. J., "Empirical Findings on Manufacturing Cell Design," *Int. Journal of Production Research*, Vol. 38, No. 3, 2000, pp. 481–507.

Wemmerlöv, U. and Vakharia, A. J., "On the Impact of Family Scheduling Procedures," *IIE Transactions*, Vol. 25, No. 4, 1993, pp. 102–103.

Wheeler, D. and Chambers, D., *Understanding Statistical Process Control* (Knoxville, TN: SPC Press, 1992).

Wight, O., "Input/Output Control–A Real Handle on Lead Time," *Production and Inventory Management*, Third Quarter 1970, pp. 9–31.

Wilkinson, B., *The Shopfloor Politics of New Technology* (London: Heinemann, 1983).

Womack, J. P. and Jones, D. T., *Lean Thinking: Banish Waste and Create Wealth in Your Corporation* (New York: Simon & Schuster, 1996).

Woolson, D. and Husar, M., "Transforming a Plant to Lean in a Large, Traditional Company: Delphi Saginaw Steering Systems, GM," in Liker, J. (ed.), *Becoming Lean: Inside Stories of U.S. Manufacturers* (Portland, OR: Productivity Press, 1998), pp. 120–159.

Wrennall, W. and Lee, Q. (eds.), *Handbook of Commercial and Industrial Facilities Management* (New York: McGraw-Hill, 1994).

Yeatts, D. and Hyten, C., *High-Performing Self-Managed Work Teams: A Comparison of Theory to Practice* (Thousand Oaks, CA: Sage, 1998).

Yetton, P. and Bottger, P., "The Relationship Among Group Size, Member Abilities and Social Decision Schemes and Performance," *Organization Behavior and Human Performance*, October 1983, pp. 145–159.

Zayko, M. J., Broughman, D. J., and Hancock, W. M., "Lean Manufacturing Yields World-Class Improvements for Small Manufacturer," *IIE Solutions*, April 1997, pp. 36–40.

Zayko, M., Hancock, W., and Broughman, D., "Implementing Lean Manufacturing at Gelman Sciences, Inc.," in Liker, J. (ed.), *Becoming Lean: Inside Stories of U.S. Manufacturers* (Portland, OR: Productivity Press, 1998).

Zenger, T. and Marshall, C., "Group-Based Plans: An Empirical Test of the Relationships Among Size, Incentive, Intensity, and Performance," *Academy of Management Journal— Best Paper Proceedings* (New Brunswick, NJ: Academy of Management, 1995), pp. 161–165.

Zhou, X., Luh, P. B., and Tomastik, R. N., "The Performance of a New Material Control and Replenishment System: A Simulation and Comparative Study," *Proceedings of the Quick Response Manufacturing 2000 Conference* (Dearborn, MI: Society of Manufacturing Engineers, 2000), pp. 805–826.

Zuboff, S., *In the Age of the Smart Machine* (New York: Basic Books, 1988).

Index